"I sat on my couch and started reading the graphic novel of *Window Horses* and couldn't get up until I finished the last page, because tears were in my eyes and my heart was so moved. The simplicity of Rosie and the richness of her environment, particularly as it changes and she goes deeper into her Persian and Chinese cultures, is lovingly affecting. It's amazing how much you can convey with a circle and a few lines. My nieces are mixed race and it's very important to me that they see themselves represented in this society. *Window Horses* includes many things that are important to me. Its hero is a girl, yay! And it champions art as a change agent for peace, diversity and understanding."

Sandra Oh, voice of Rosie Ming

"When I first was offered a role in the project *Window Horses*, I jumped at the opportunity. There are plenty of negative news stories that are associated with Iran. One simply has to Google the word "Iran." All this negative information is readily available on the internet. What's not so easy to find, and it requires some deep digging, is how absolutely beautiful its people and its culture are. *Window Horses* opens the "window," so to speak, and allows a peek into a culture that is often misunderstood. So an opportunity for me to get out there and promote the beautiful aspects of our culture was a no-brainer to me. I think we did just that."

Omid Abt

D1416613

Front cover art by Kevin Langdale
Interior and cover layout by Ryan Ferrier
Additional interior layout by Samantha Beiko

Library and Archives Canada Cataloguing in Publication

Fleming, Ann Marie, author
Window Horses : The Poetic Persian Epiphany of Rosie
Ming / Ann Marie Fleming; art by Kevin Langdale.

Based on the animated film Window Horses.
Issued in print and electronic formats.
ISBN 978-1-988715-02-5 (softcover).--ISBN 978-1-988715-01-8 (PDF)

1. Comics adaptations. I. Langdale, Kevin, illustrator. II. Title.

PN6733.F556W56 2017   741.5'971   C2017-900566-9
                                                C2017-900567-7

Printed and bound in Canada
19 18 17 16 15 1 2 3 4 5

Published by Bedside Press
248 Princess Street
Winnipeg, MB
R3B 1M2 Canada

bedsidepress.com

WINDOW HORSES
THE POETIC PERSIAN EPIPHANY OF ROSIE MING

ILLUSTRATED BY
KEVIN LANGDALE

YOUNGER GE
JANET PERLMAN
SADAF AMINI
DOMINIQUE DOKTOR
BAHRAM JAVAHERI
ELISA CHEE
JODY KRAMER
LILLIAN CHAN
KUNAL SEN
LOUISE JOHNSON
NATHANIEL AKIN
IAN GODFREY
BRAD GIBSON

STORY, CONCEPT & LAYOUT
ANN MARIE FLEMING

EDITED BY
NYALA ALI
& HOPE NICHOLSON

This is dedicated to all the poets in all cultures, who continue to connect us, throughout the millennia, by expressing so deeply what it is to be human.

WINDOW HORSES
The Poetic Persian Epiphany of Rosie Ming

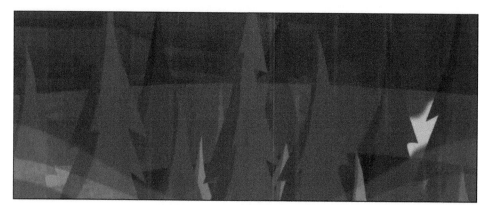

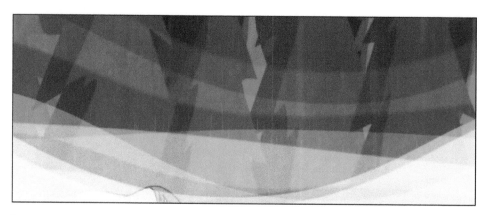

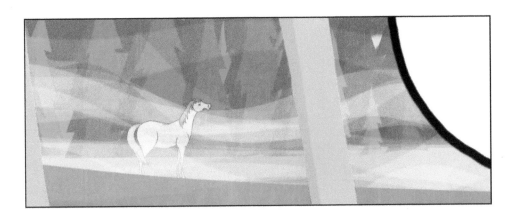

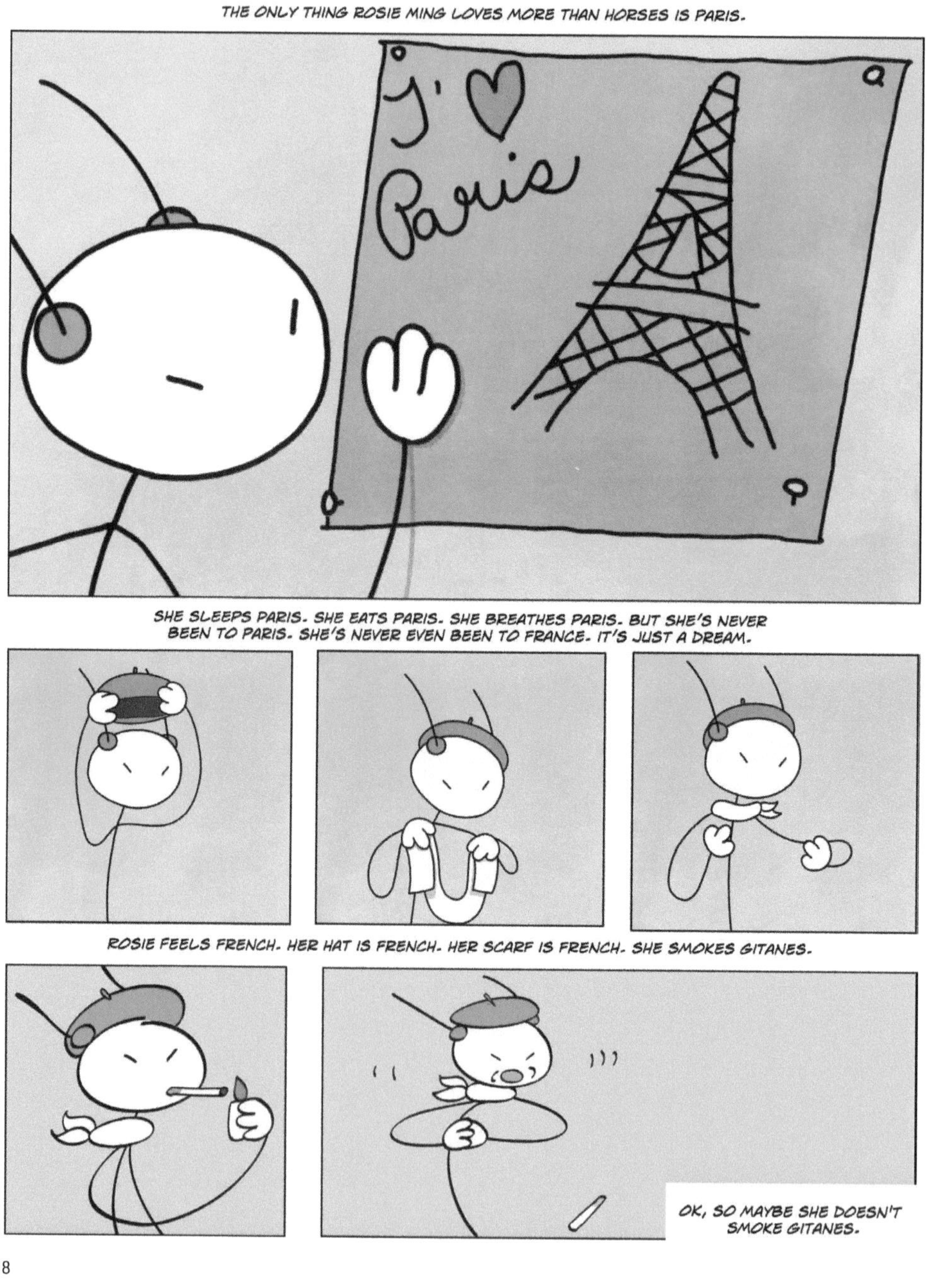
THE ONLY THING ROSIE MING LOVES MORE THAN HORSES IS PARIS.
J'♥ Paris
SHE SLEEPS PARIS. SHE EATS PARIS. SHE BREATHES PARIS. BUT SHE'S NEVER BEEN TO PARIS. SHE'S NEVER EVEN BEEN TO FRANCE. IT'S JUST A DREAM.
ROSIE FEELS FRENCH. HER HAT IS FRENCH. HER SCARF IS FRENCH. SHE SMOKES GITANES.
OK, SO MAYBE SHE DOESN'T SMOKE GITANES.

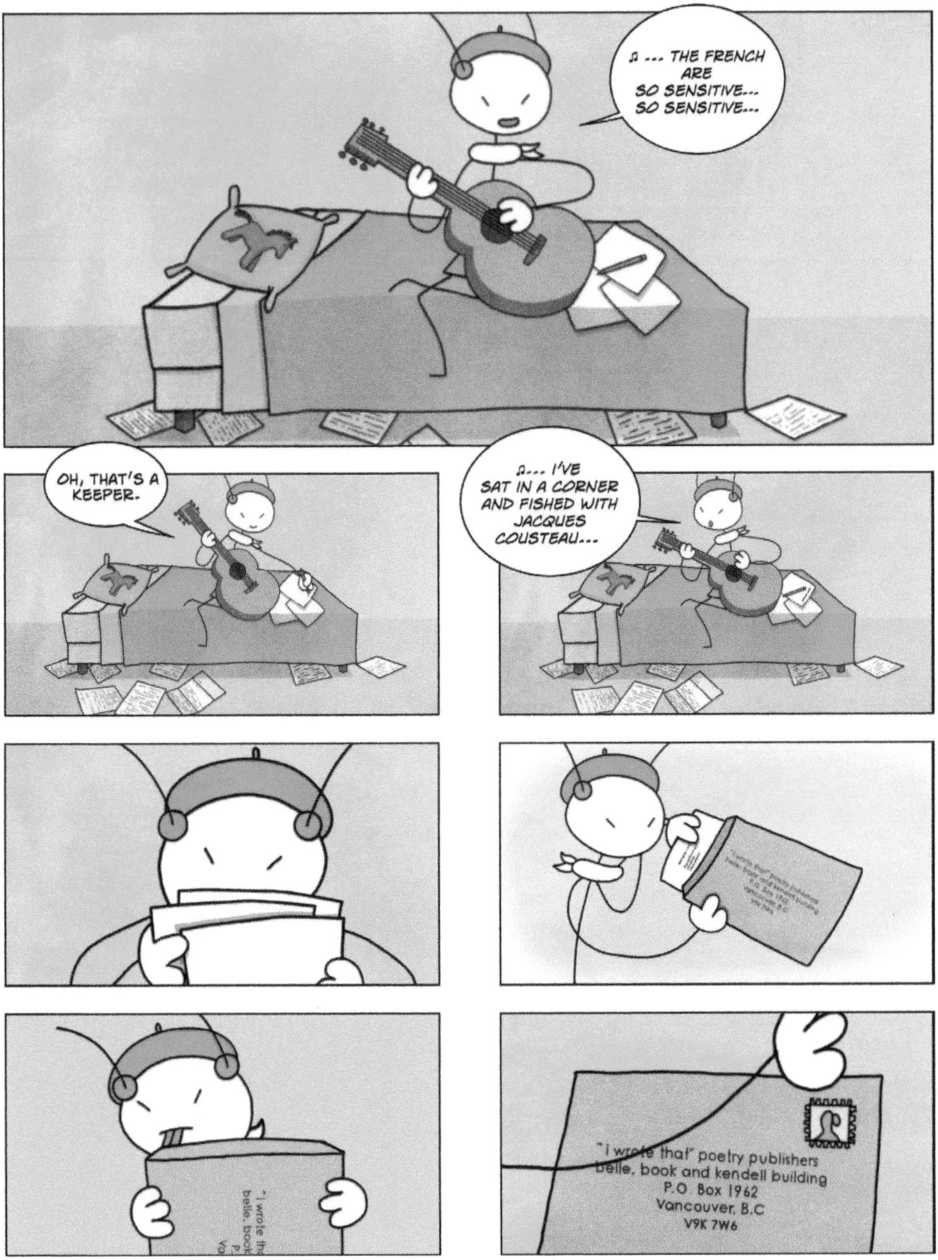
♫ ... THE FRENCH ARE SO SENSITIVE... SO SENSITIVE...
OH, THAT'S A KEEPER.
♫... I'VE SAT IN A CORNER AND FISHED WITH JACQUES COUSTEAU...
"i wrote that" poetry publishers
belle, book and kendell building
P.O. Box 1962
Vancouver, B.C
V9K 7W6

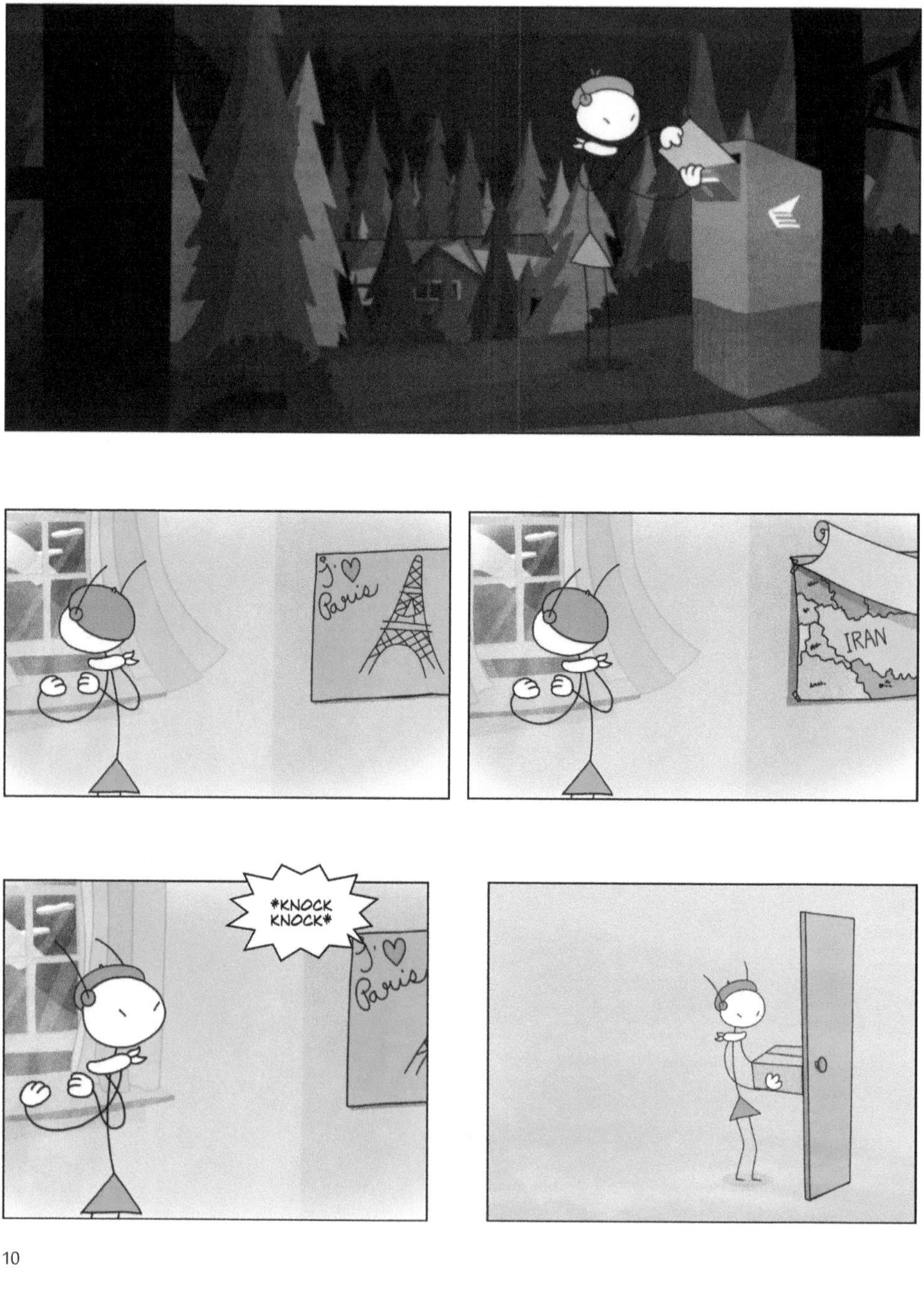
J'♥ Paris
IRAN
KNOCK KNOCK
J'♥ Paris

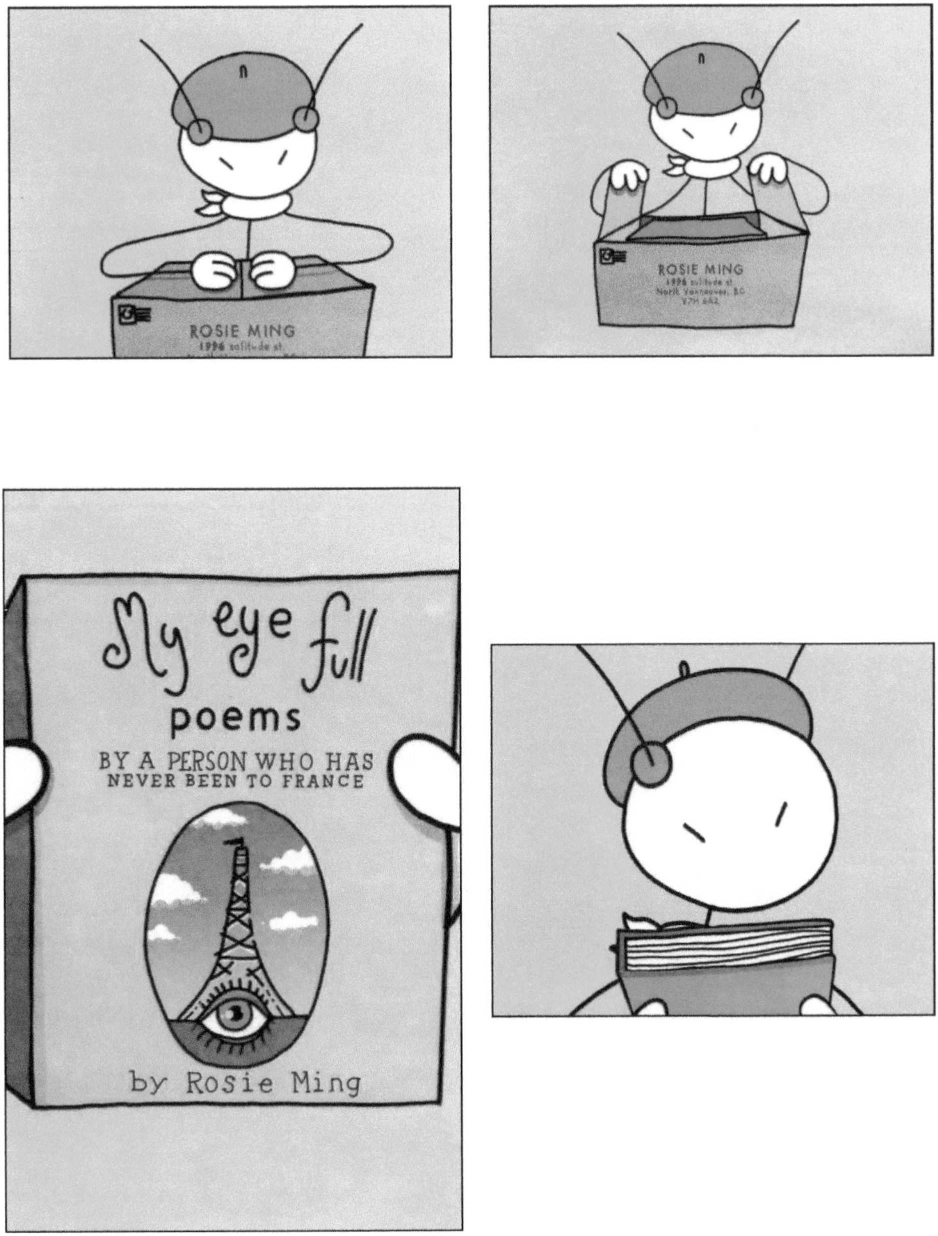

ROSIE MING
1996 solitude st.
ROSIE MING
1996 solitude st
North Vancouver, BC
My eye full
poems
BY A PERSON WHO HAS NEVER BEEN TO FRANCE
by Rosie Ming

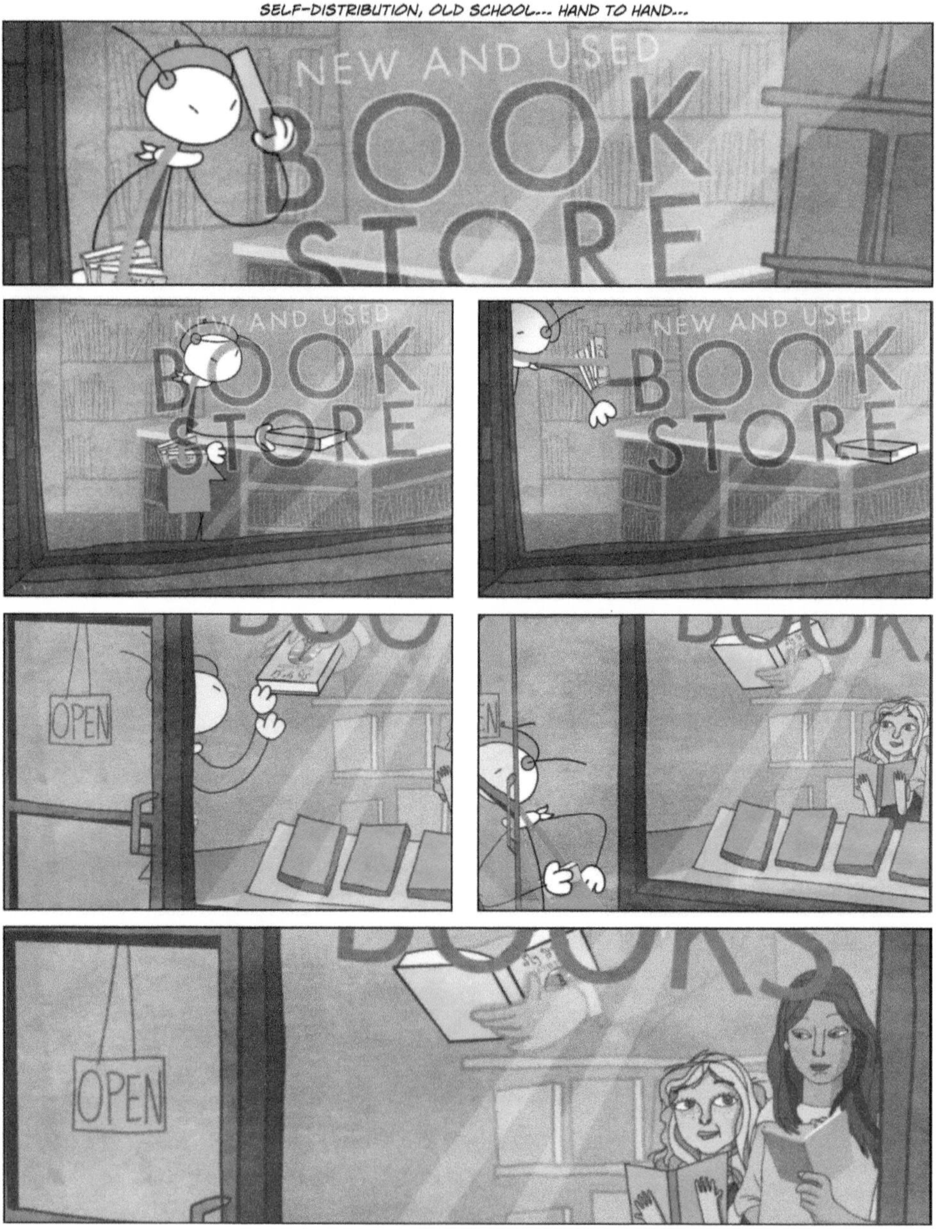
SELF-DISTRIBUTION, OLD SCHOOL... HAND TO HAND...
NEW AND USED
BOOK
STORE
OPEN

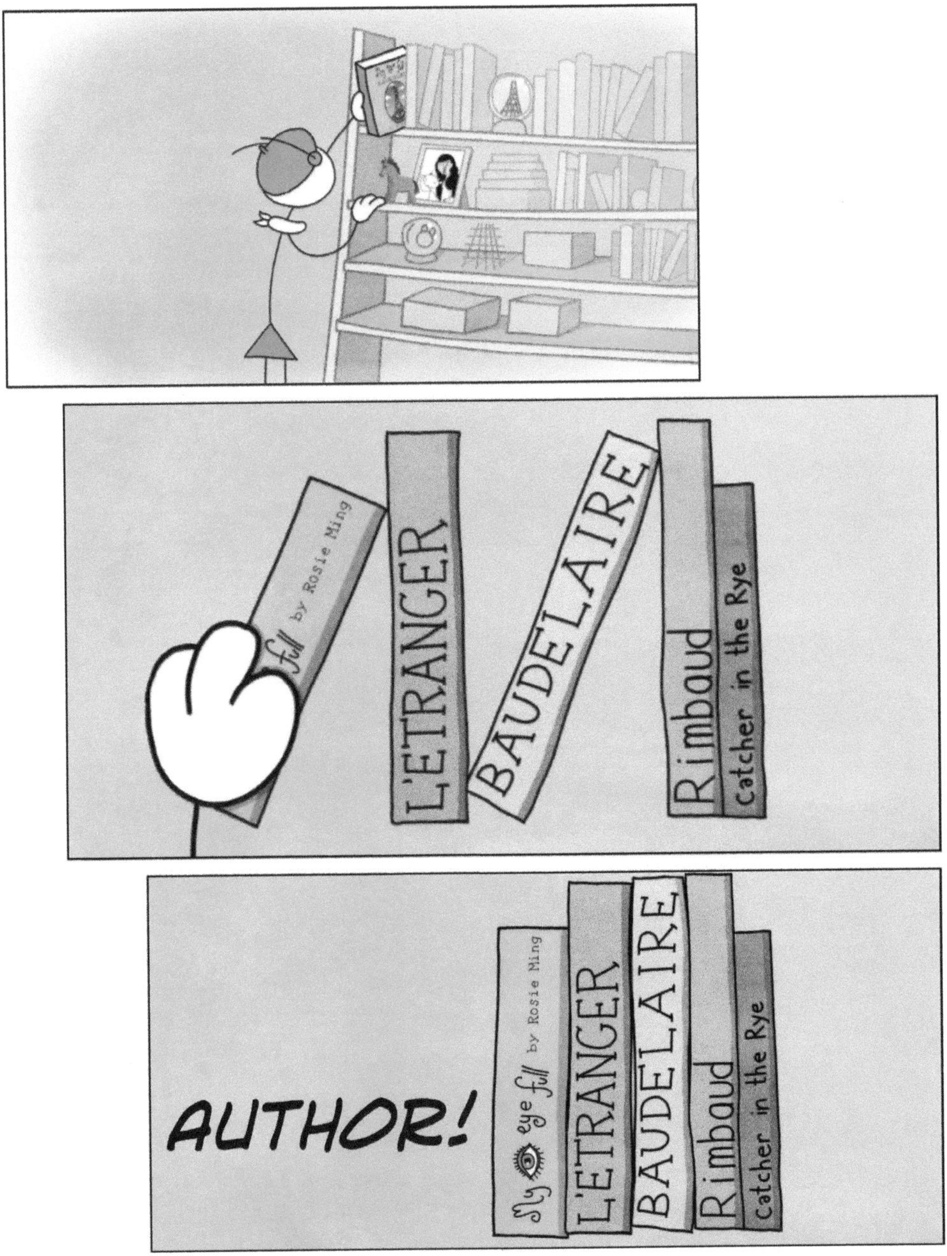
full by Rosie Ming
L'ETRANGER
BAUDELAIRE
Rimbaud
Catcher in the Rye
AUTHOR!
My eye full by Rosie Ming
L'ETRANGER
BAUDELAIRE
Rimbaud
Catcher in the Rye

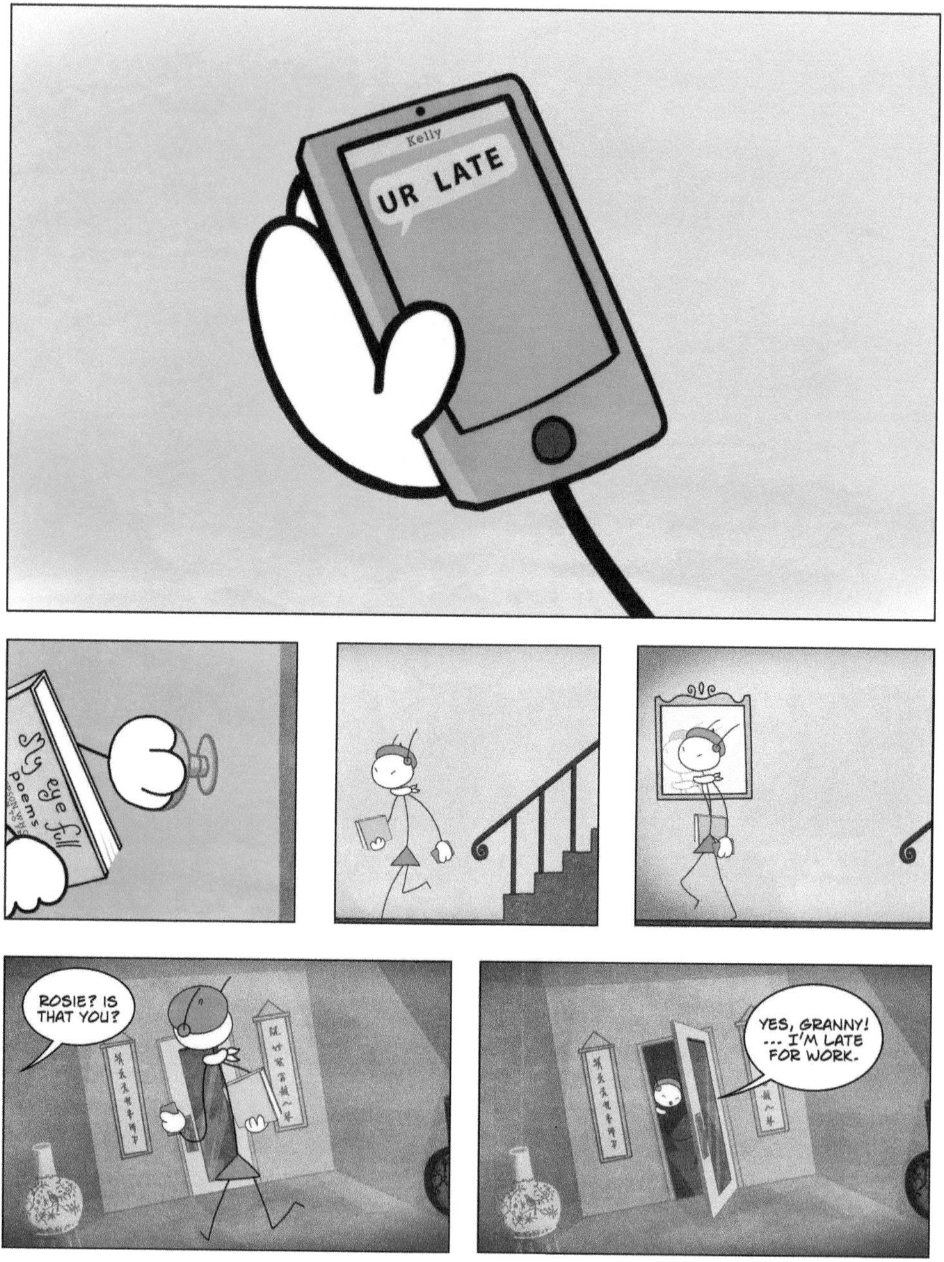
Kelly
UR LATE
My eye full
poems
ROSIE? IS THAT YOU?
YES, GRANNY! ... I'M LATE FOR WORK.

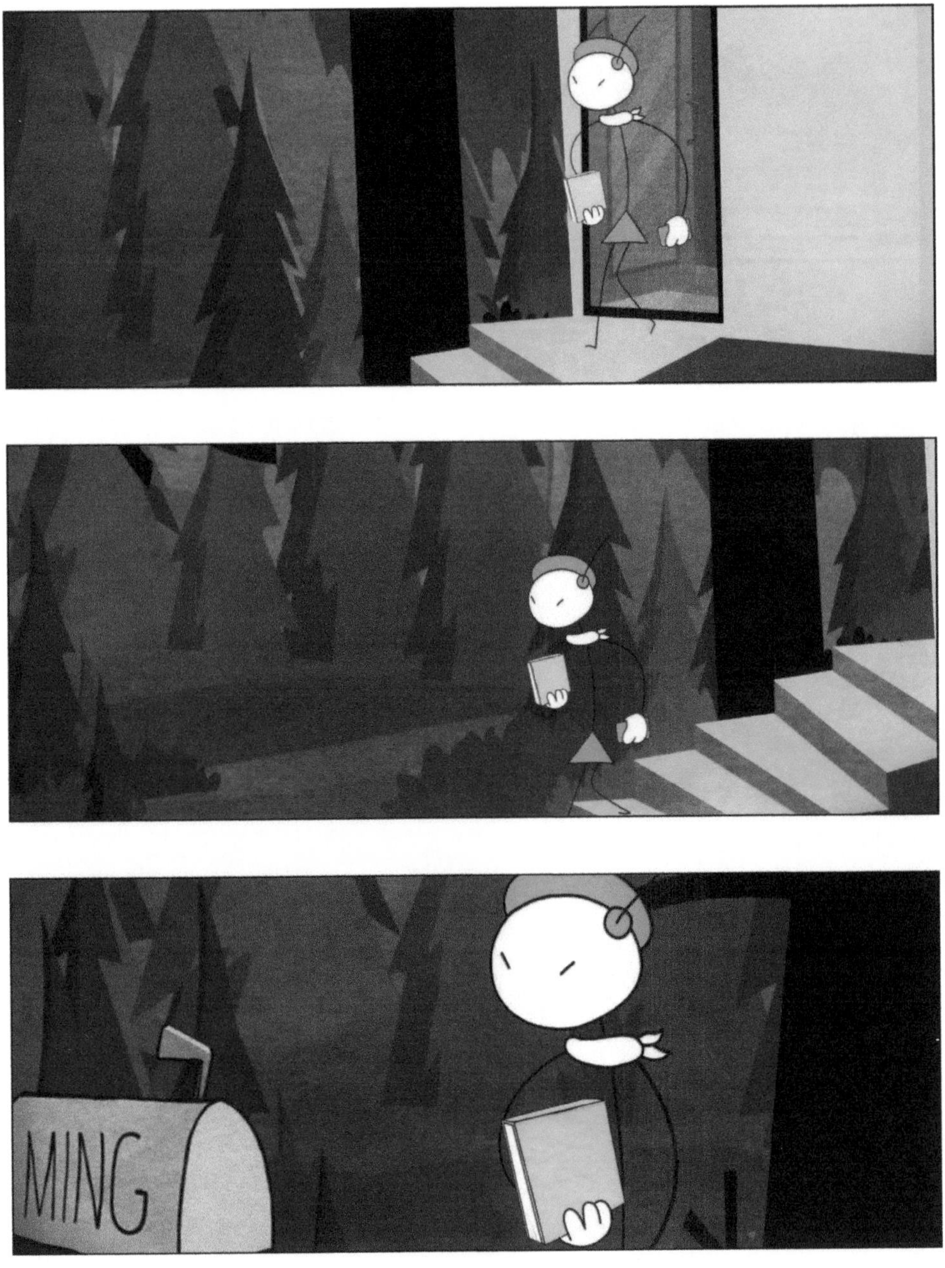
MING

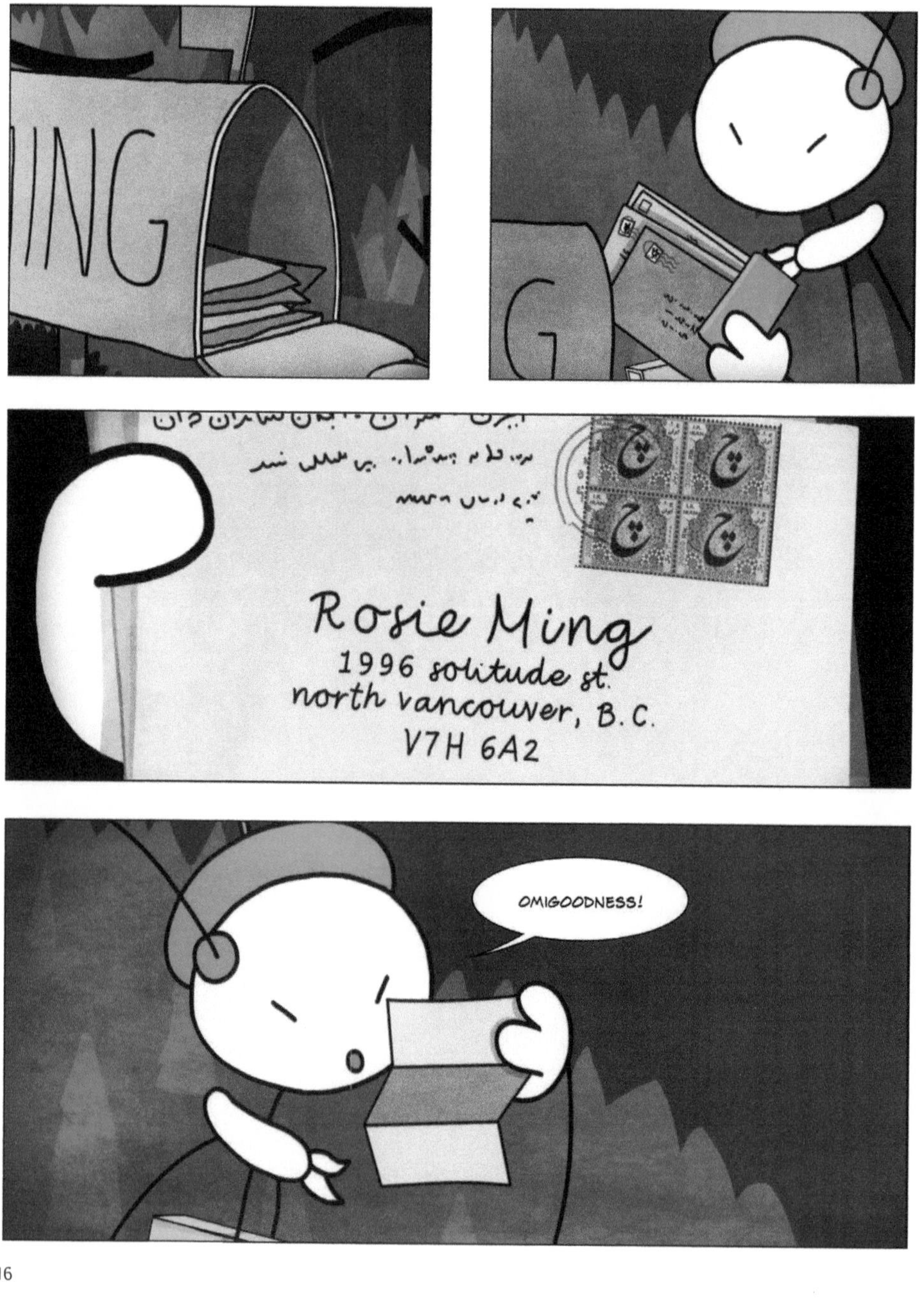
ING
Rosie Ming
1996 solitude st.
north vancouver, B.C.
V7H 6A2
OMIGOODNESS!

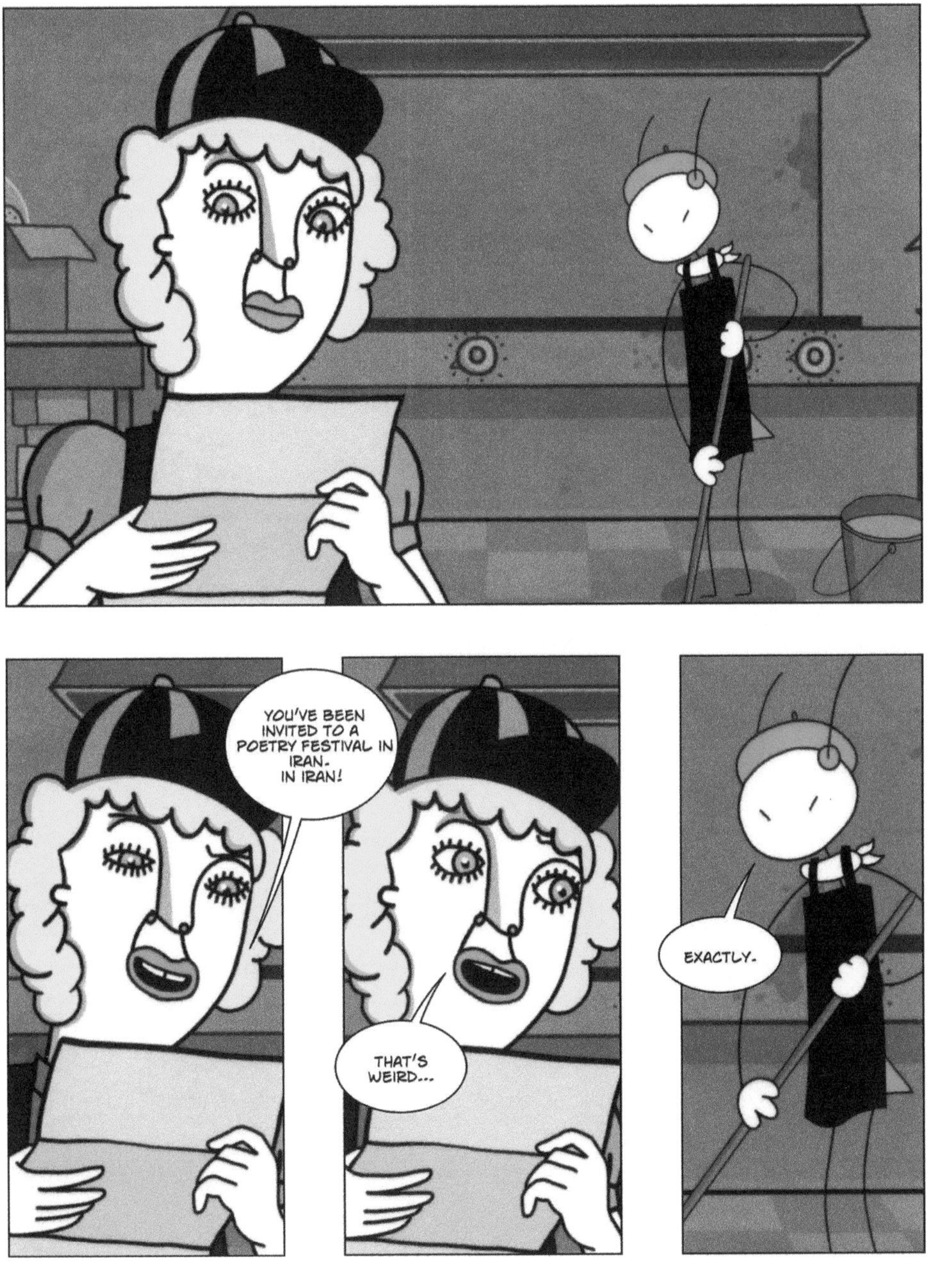
YOU'VE BEEN INVITED TO A POETRY FESTIVAL IN IRAN. IN IRAN!
THAT'S WEIRD...
EXACTLY.

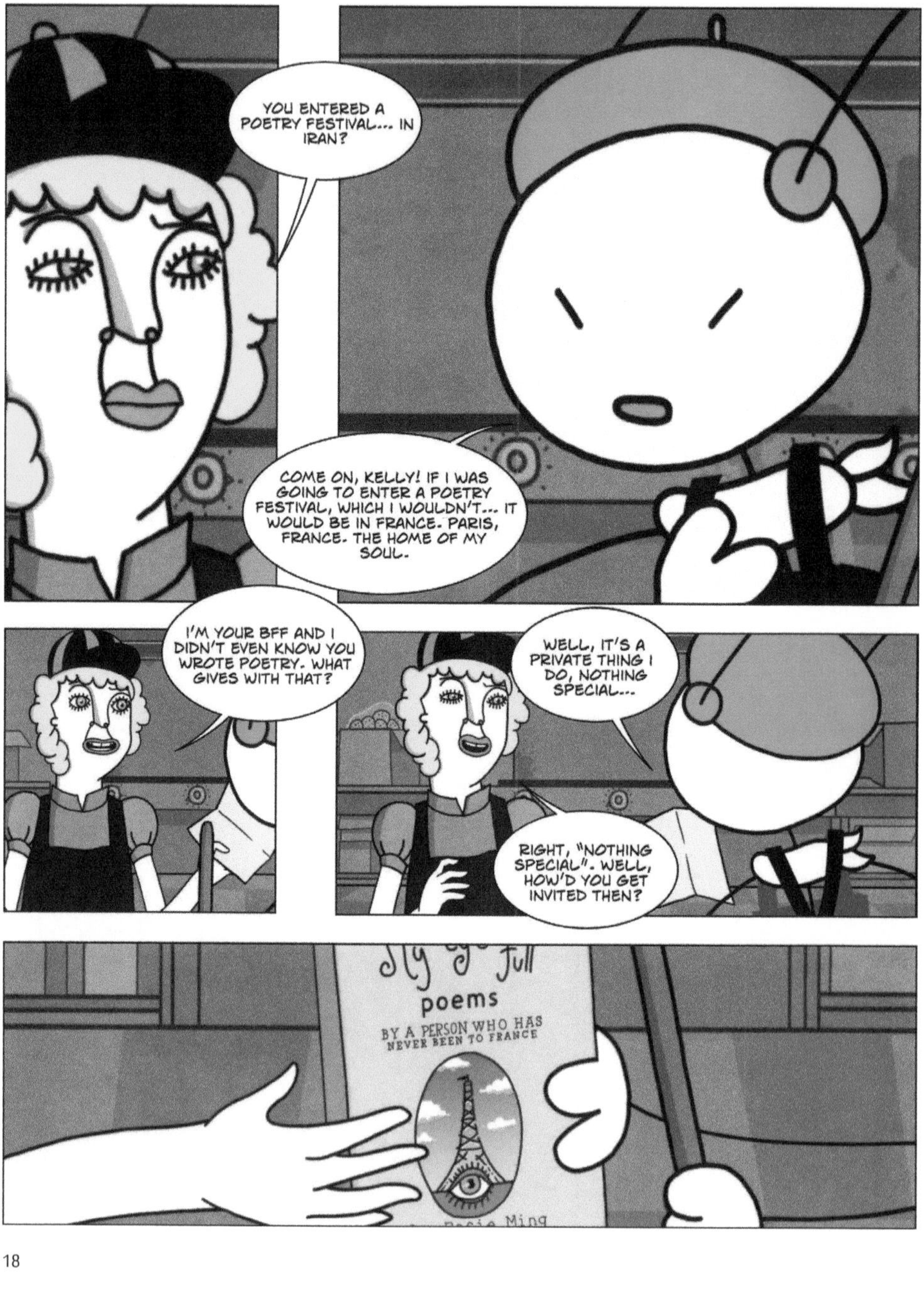
YOU ENTERED A POETRY FESTIVAL... IN IRAN?
COME ON, KELLY! IF I WAS GOING TO ENTER A POETRY FESTIVAL, WHICH I WOULDN'T... IT WOULD BE IN FRANCE. PARIS, FRANCE. THE HOME OF MY SOUL.
I'M YOUR BFF AND I DIDN'T EVEN KNOW YOU WROTE POETRY. WHAT GIVES WITH THAT?
WELL, IT'S A PRIVATE THING I DO, NOTHING SPECIAL...
RIGHT, "NOTHING SPECIAL". WELL, HOW'D YOU GET INVITED THEN?
poems
BY A PERSON WHO HAS
NEVER BEEN TO FRANCE

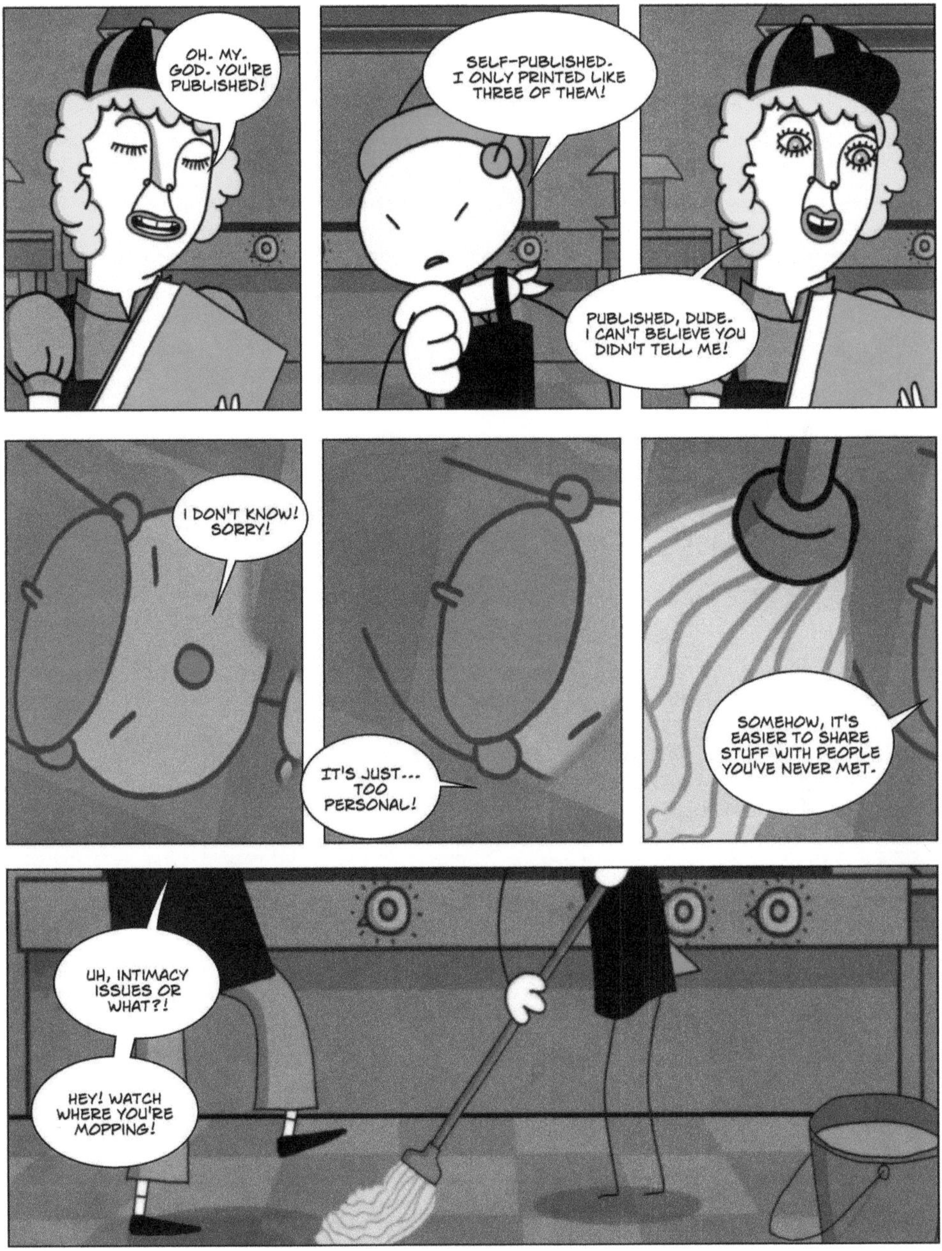
OH. MY. GOD. YOU'RE PUBLISHED!
SELF-PUBLISHED. I ONLY PRINTED LIKE THREE OF THEM!
PUBLISHED, DUDE. I CAN'T BELIEVE YOU DIDN'T TELL ME!
I DON'T KNOW! SORRY!
IT'S JUST... TOO PERSONAL!
SOMEHOW, IT'S EASIER TO SHARE STUFF WITH PEOPLE YOU'VE NEVER MET.
UH, INTIMACY ISSUES OR WHAT?!
HEY! WATCH WHERE YOU'RE MOPPING!

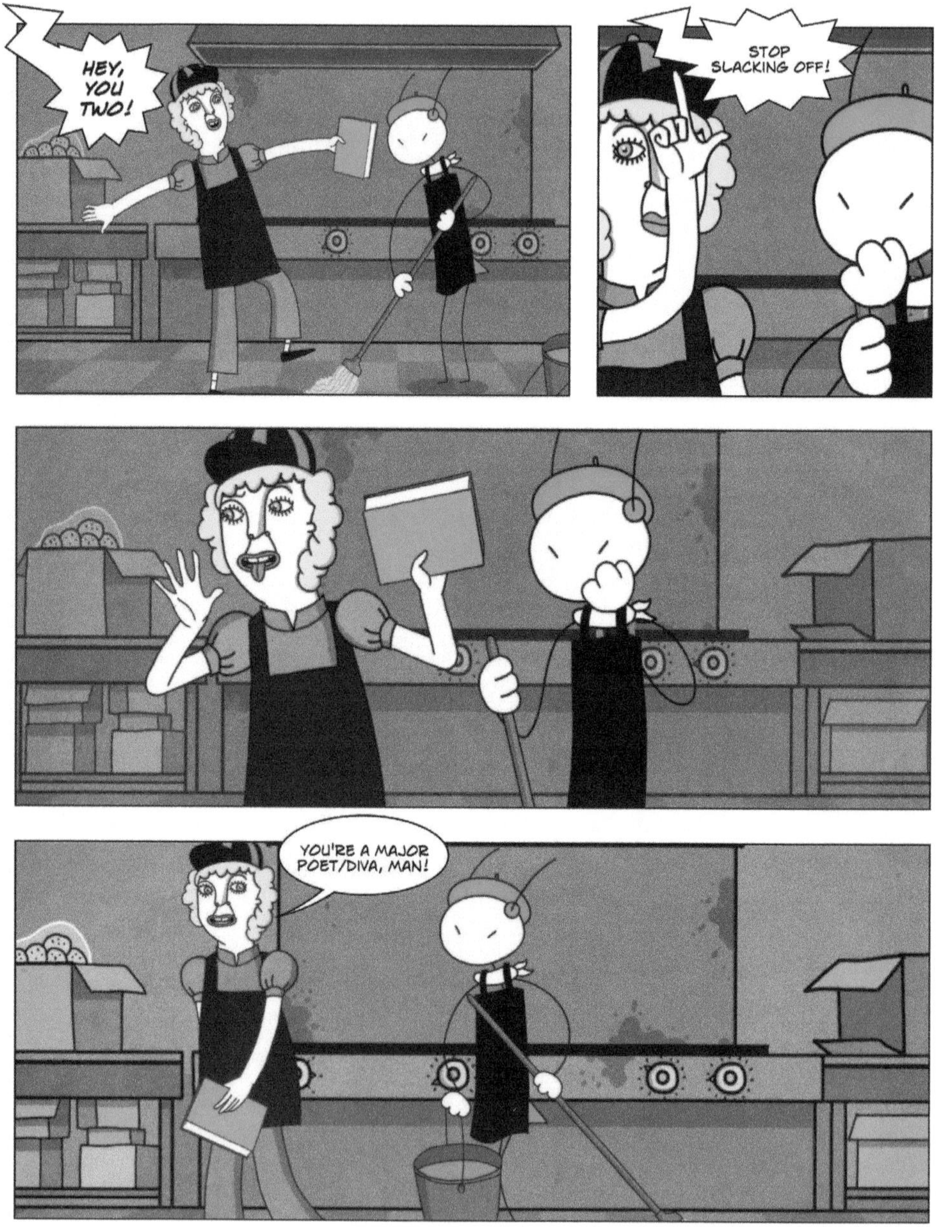
HEY, YOU TWO!
STOP SLACKING OFF!
YOU'RE A MAJOR POET/DIVA, MAN!

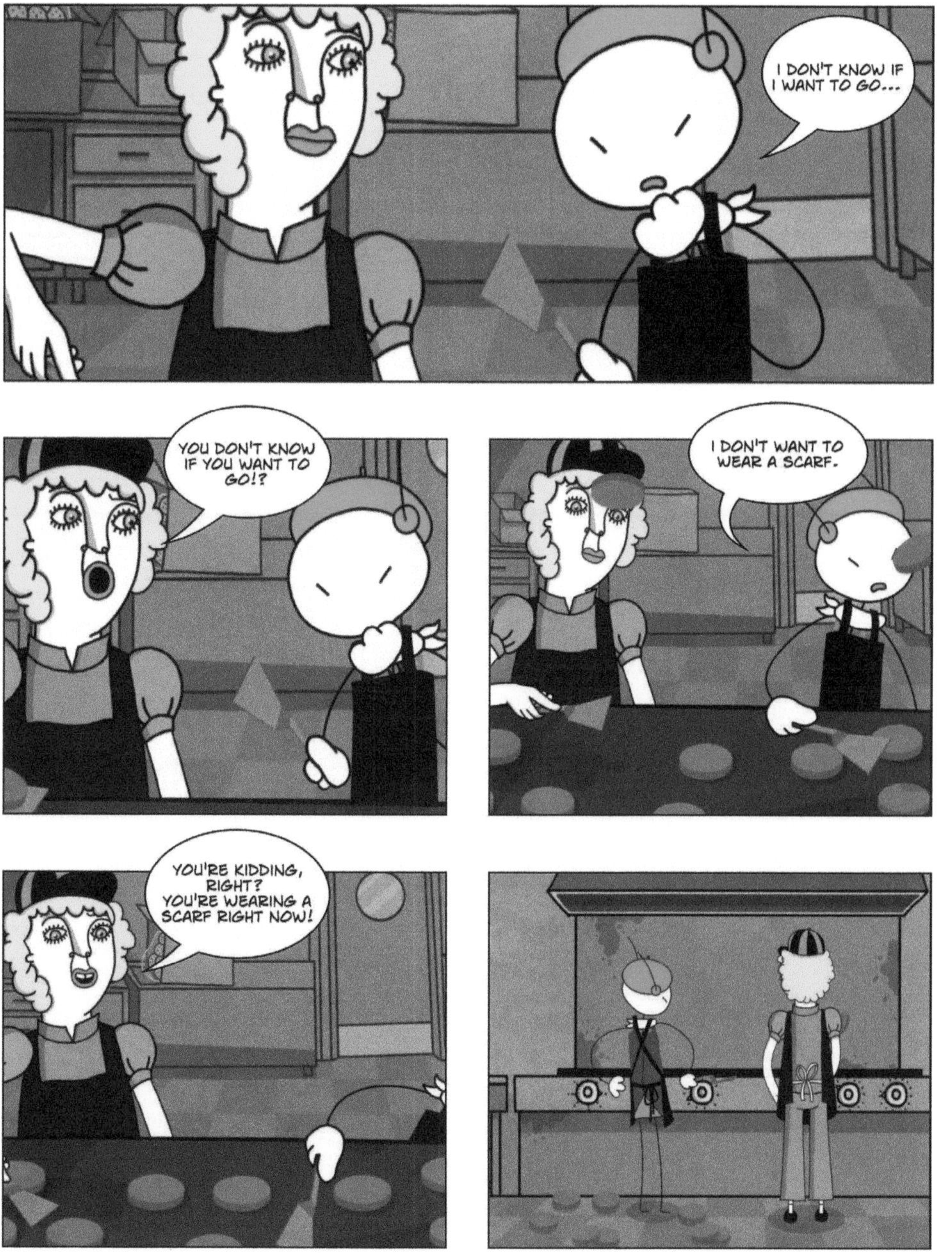
I DON'T KNOW IF I WANT TO GO...
YOU DON'T KNOW IF YOU WANT TO GO!?
I DON'T WANT TO WEAR A SCARF.
YOU'RE KIDDING, RIGHT? YOU'RE WEARING A SCARF RIGHT NOW!

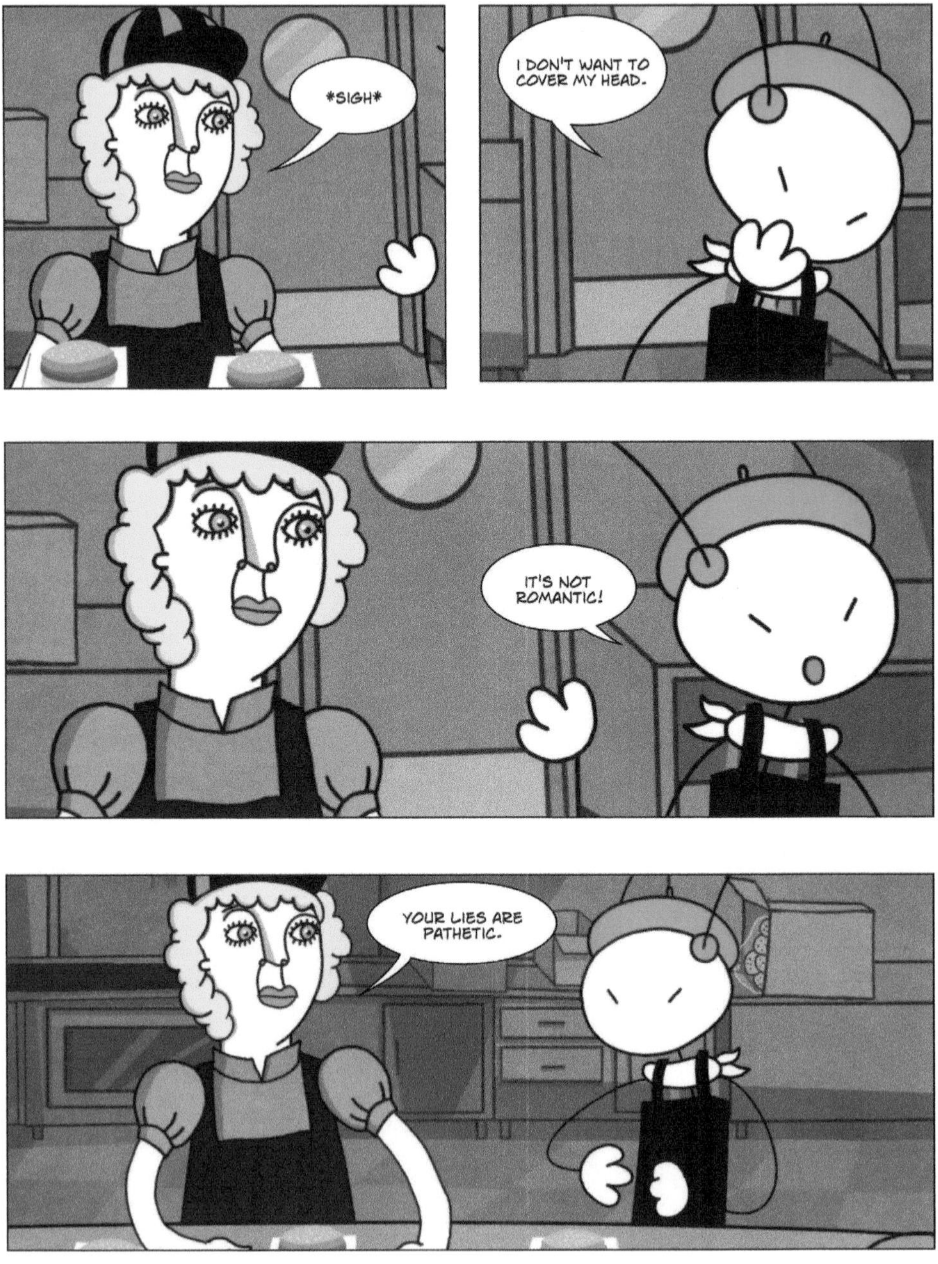
SIGH
I DON'T WANT TO COVER MY HEAD.
IT'S NOT ROMANTIC!
YOUR LIES ARE PATHETIC.

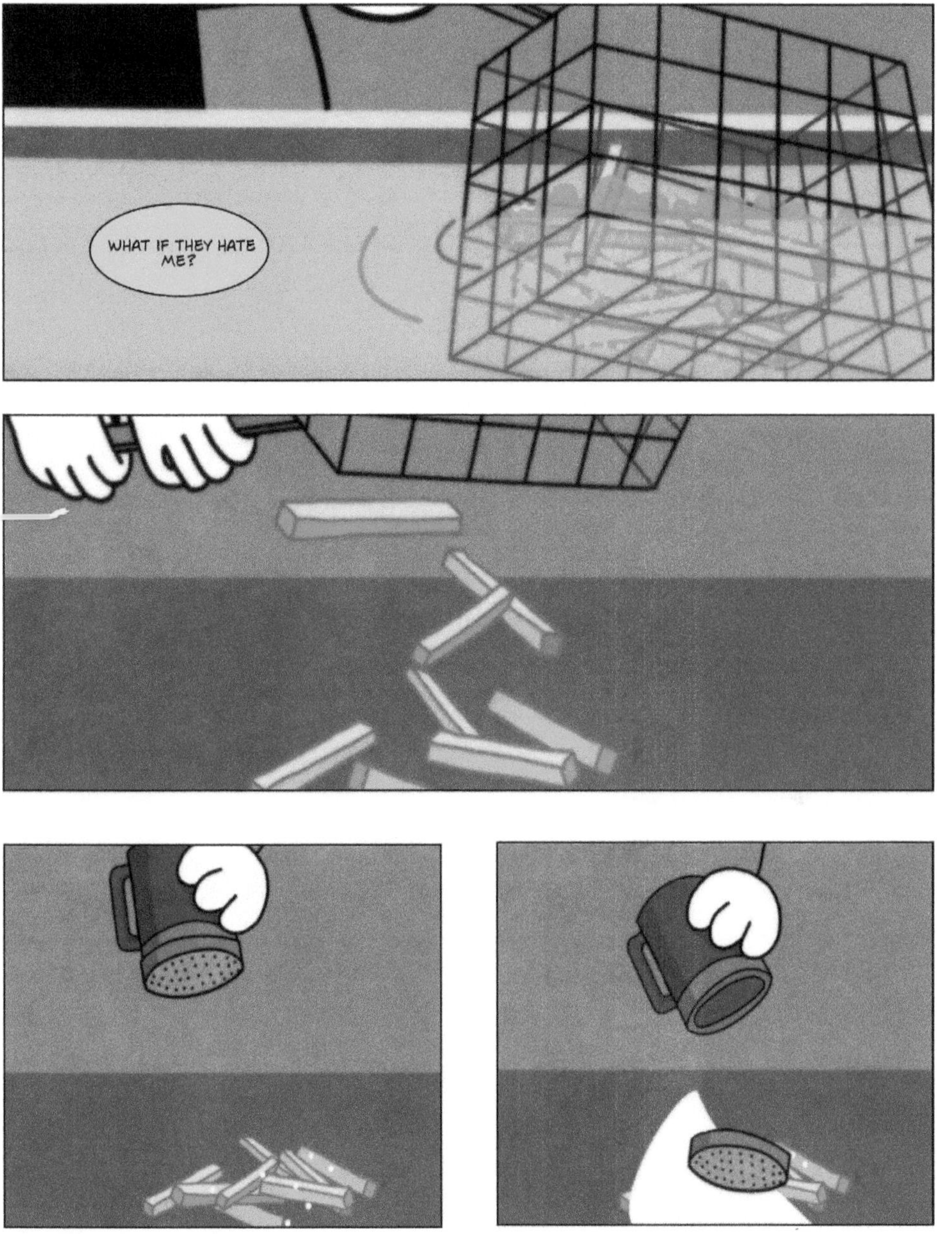
WHAT IF THEY HATE ME?

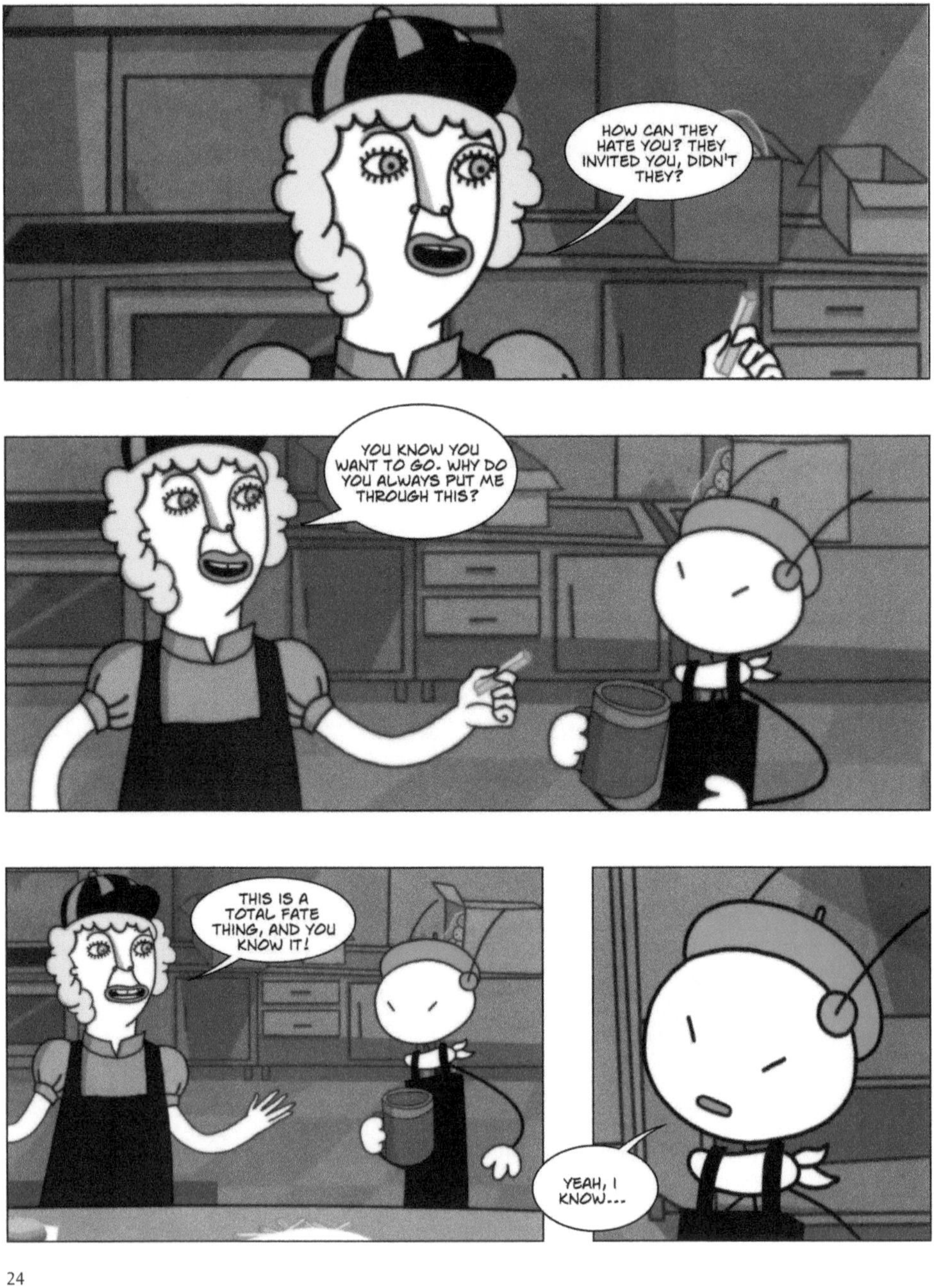
HOW CAN THEY HATE YOU? THEY INVITED YOU, DIDN'T THEY?
YOU KNOW YOU WANT TO GO. WHY DO YOU ALWAYS PUT ME THROUGH THIS?
THIS IS A TOTAL FATE THING, AND YOU KNOW IT!
YEAH, I KNOW...

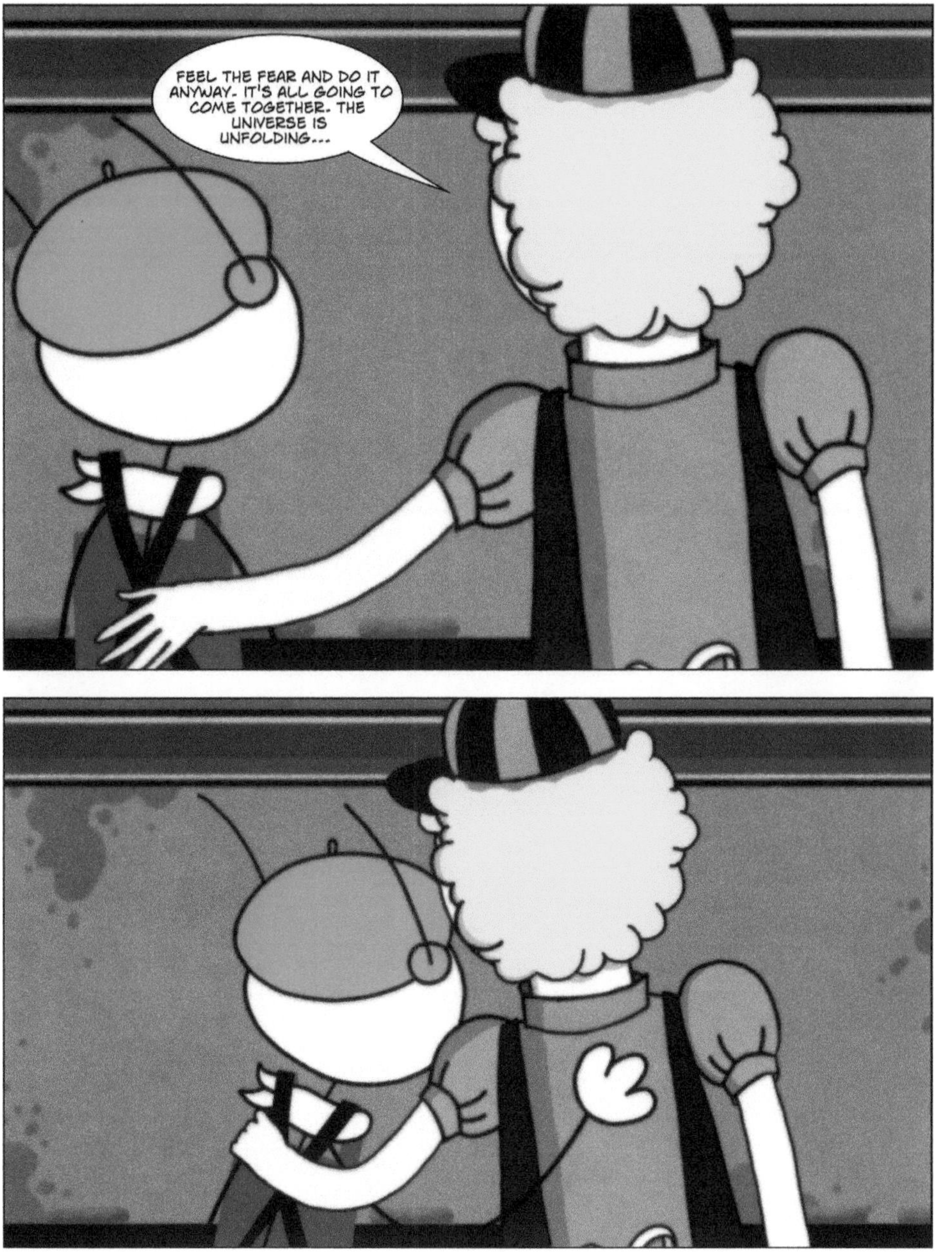
FEEL THE FEAR AND DO IT ANYWAY. IT'S ALL GOING TO COME TOGETHER. THE UNIVERSE IS UNFOLDING...

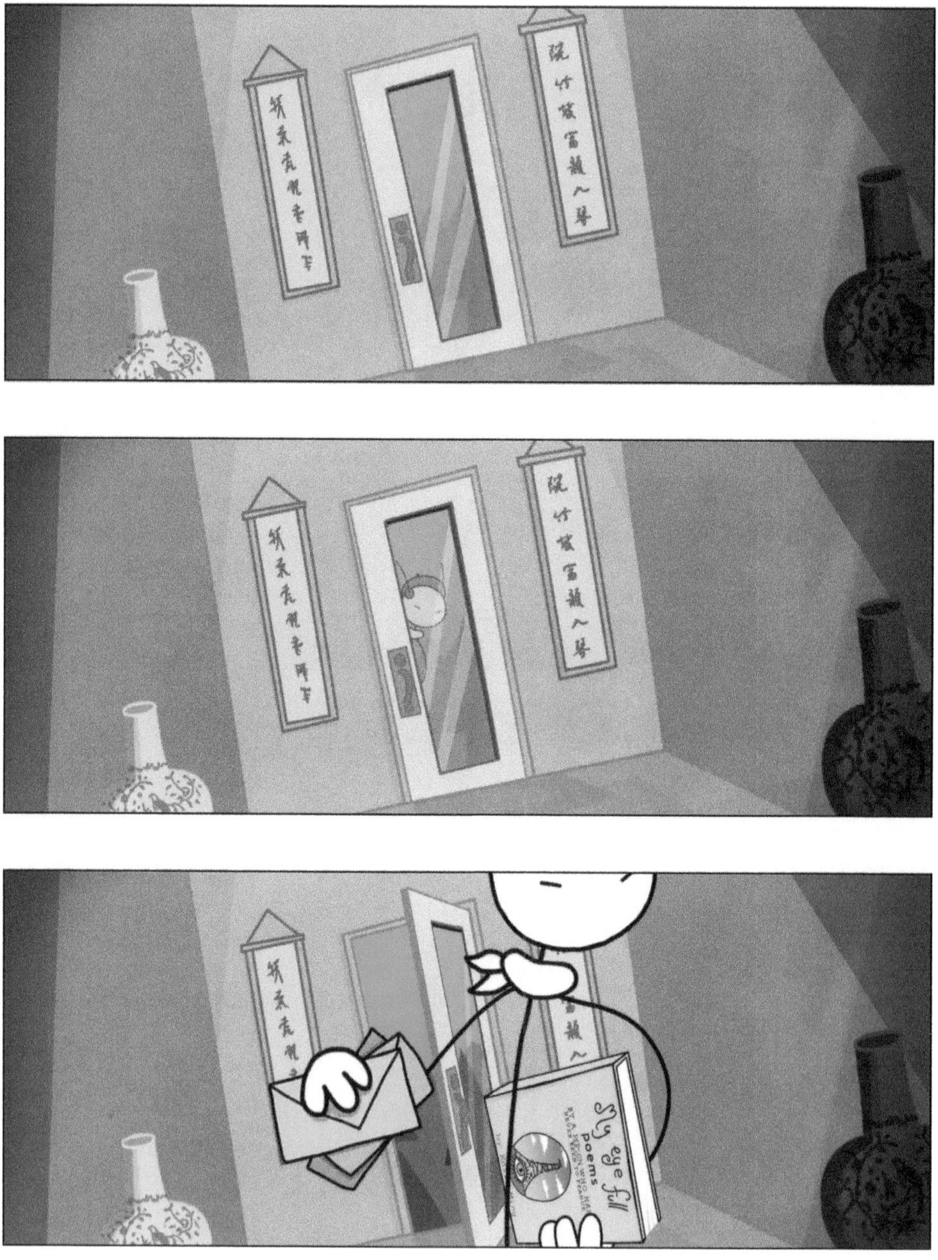
My eye full
Poems

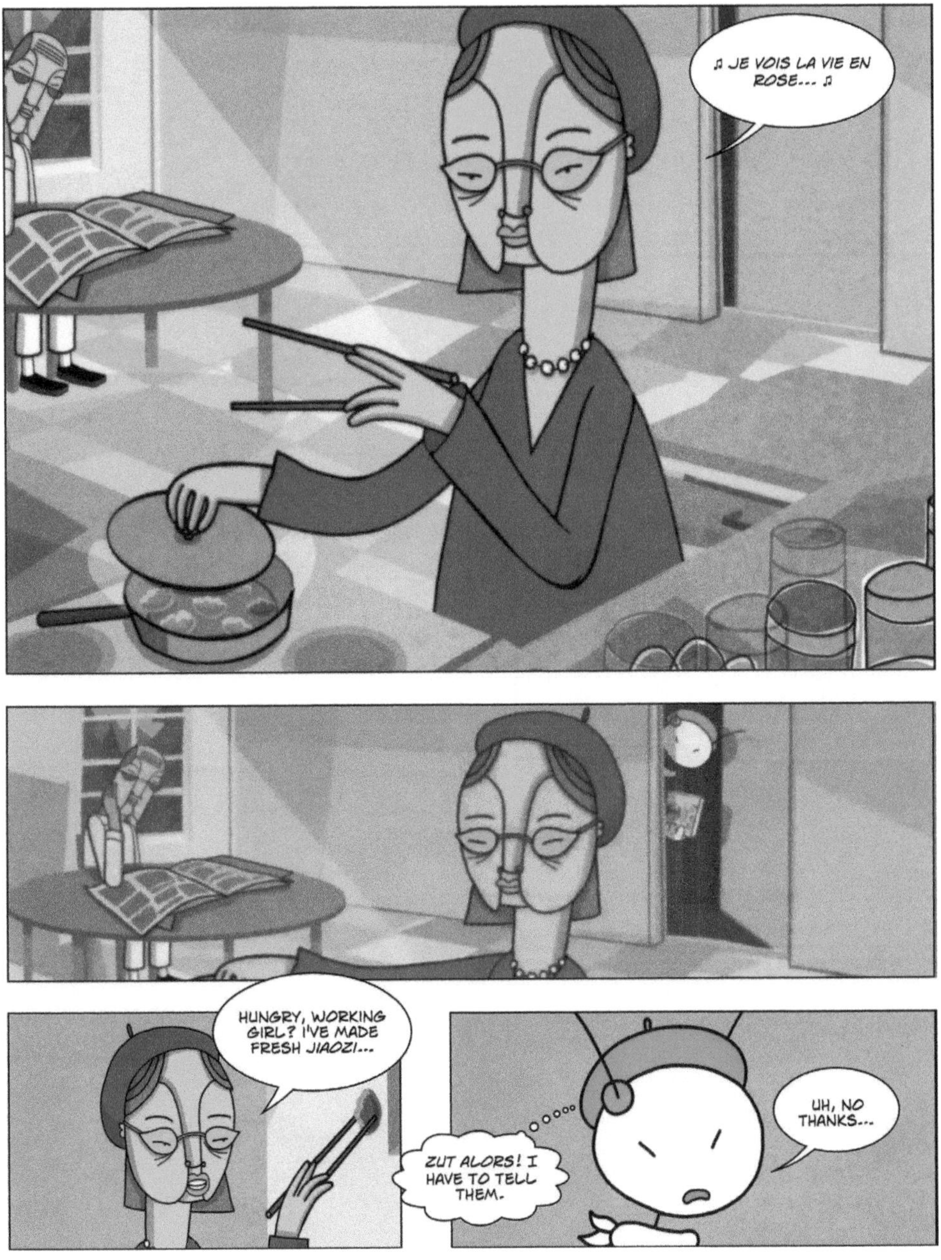
♫ JE VOIS LA VIE EN ROSE... ♫
HUNGRY, WORKING GIRL? I'VE MADE FRESH JIAOZI...
ZUT ALORS! I HAVE TO TELL THEM.
UH, NO THANKS...

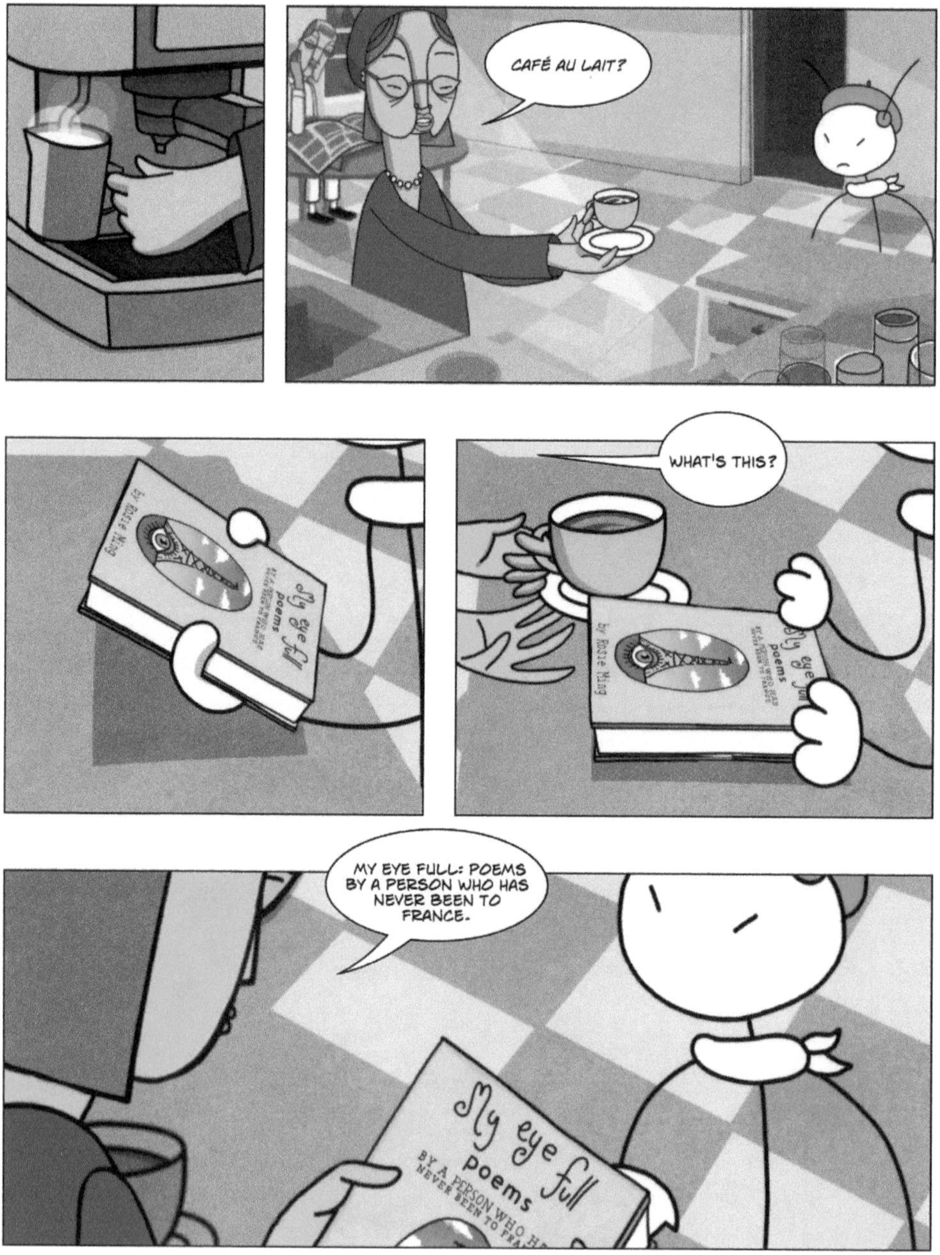
CAFÉ AU LAIT?
My eye full
poems
by Rosie Ming
WHAT'S THIS?
MY EYE FULL: POEMS BY A PERSON WHO HAS NEVER BEEN TO FRANCE.
My eye full
poems

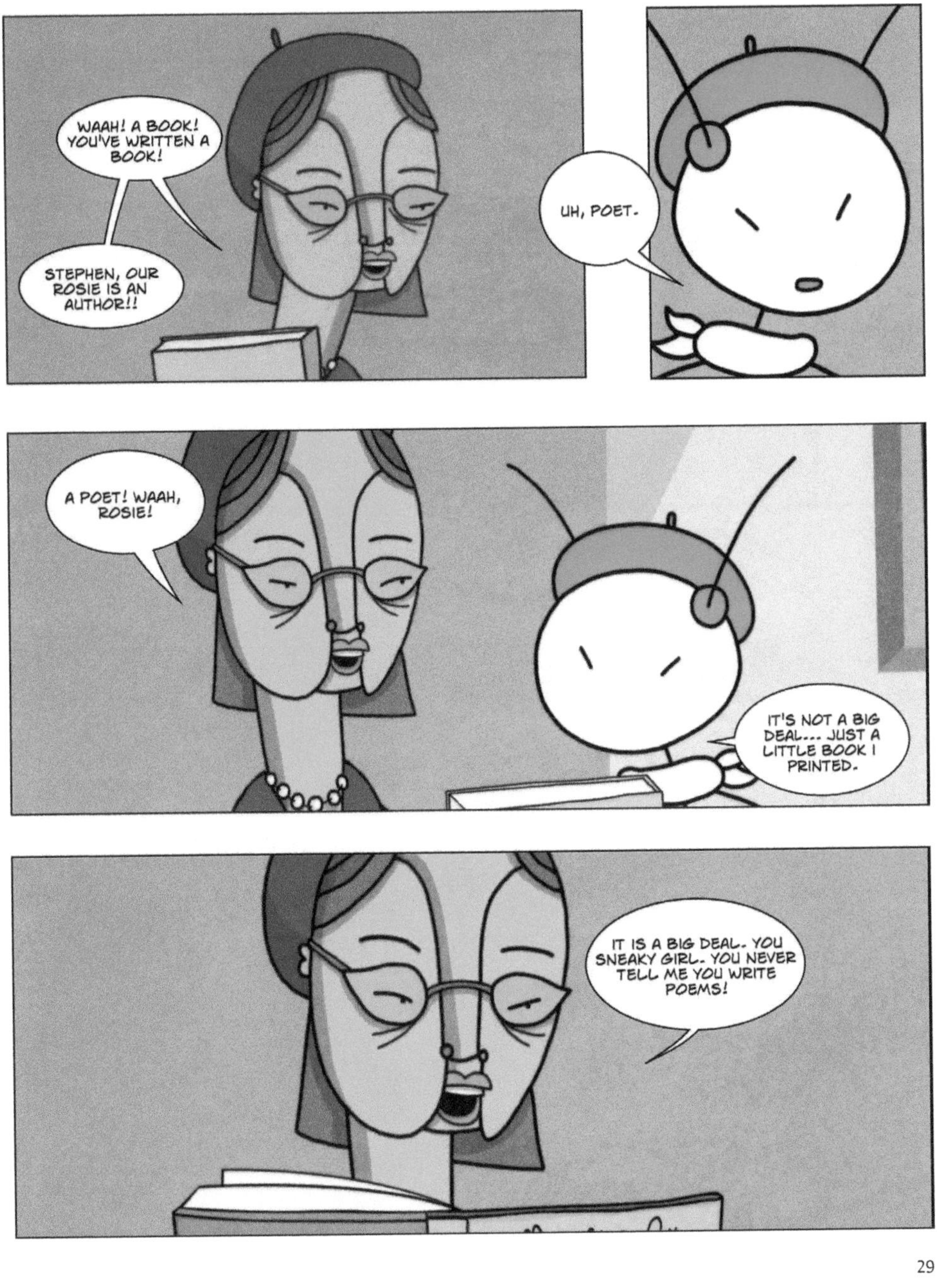

WAAH! A BOOK! YOU'VE WRITTEN A BOOK!
STEPHEN, OUR ROSIE IS AN AUTHOR!!
UH, POET.
A POET! WAAH, ROSIE!
IT'S NOT A BIG DEAL... JUST A LITTLE BOOK I PRINTED.
IT IS A BIG DEAL. YOU SNEAKY GIRL. YOU NEVER TELL ME YOU WRITE POEMS!

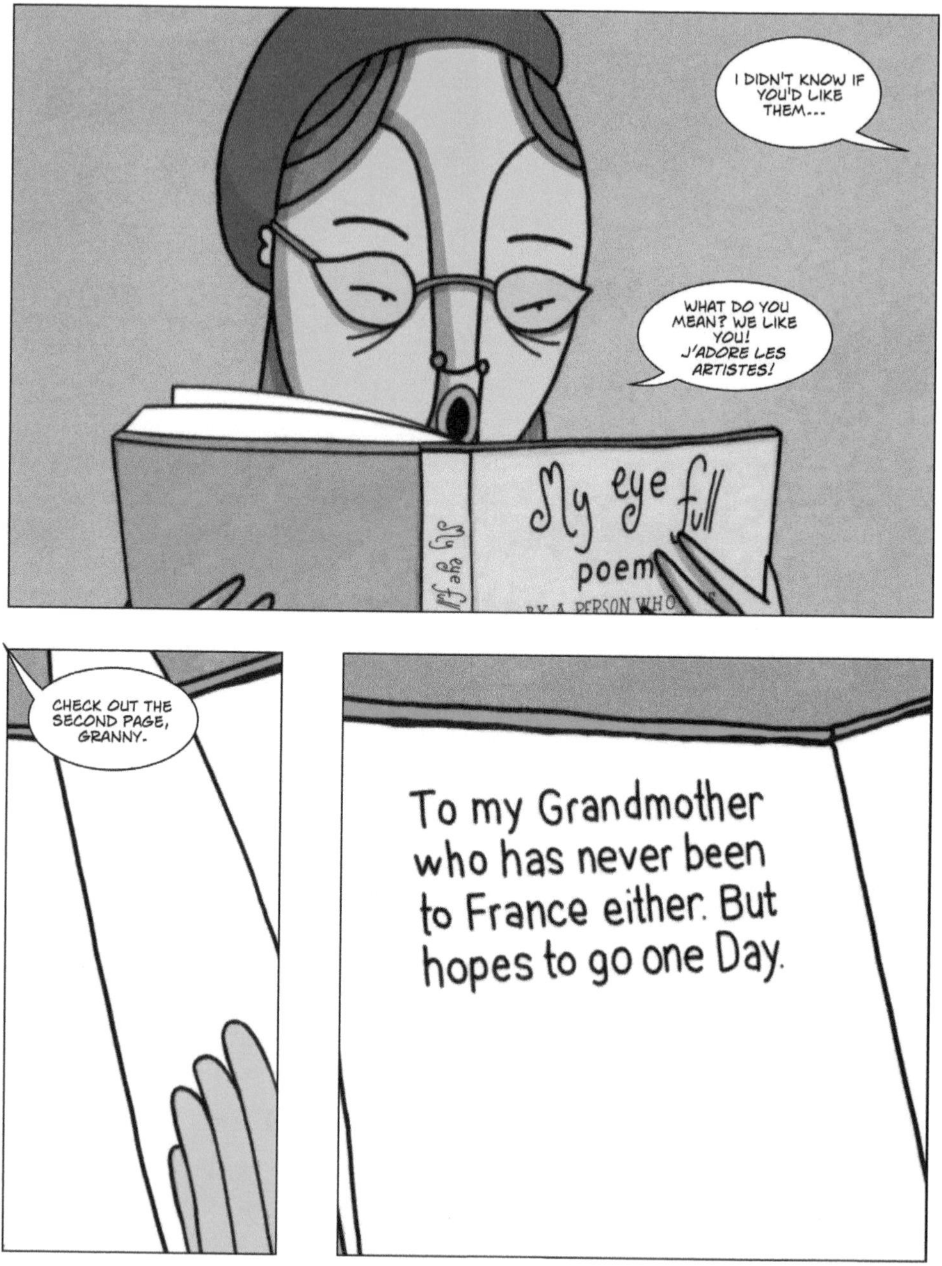
I DIDN'T KNOW IF YOU'D LIKE THEM...
WHAT DO YOU MEAN? WE LIKE YOU! J'ADORE LES ARTISTES!
My eye full
CHECK OUT THE SECOND PAGE, GRANNY.
To my Grandmother who has never been to France either. But hopes to go one Day.

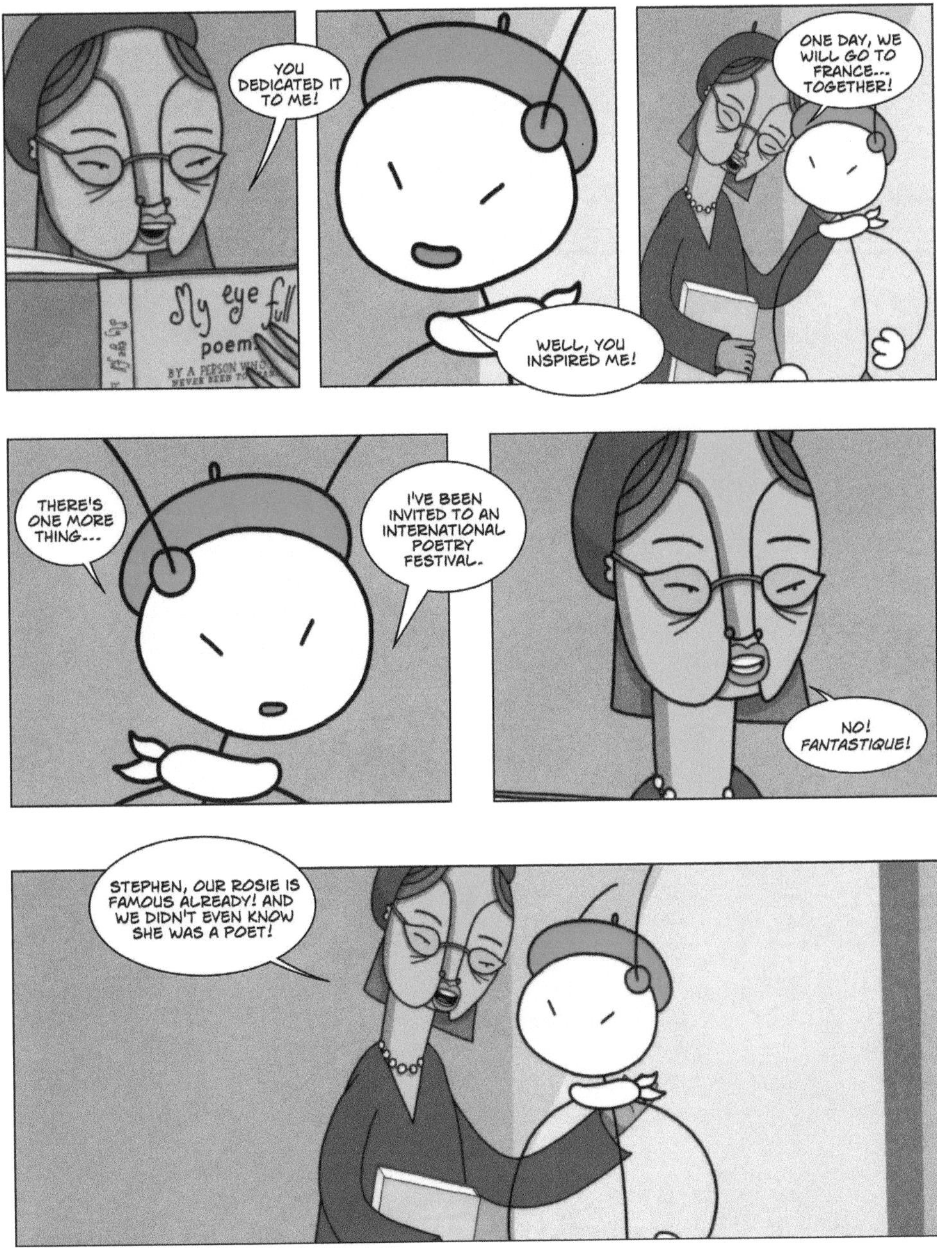
YOU DEDICATED IT TO ME!
My eye full
poems
WELL, YOU INSPIRED ME!
ONE DAY, WE WILL GO TO FRANCE... TOGETHER!
THERE'S ONE MORE THING...
I'VE BEEN INVITED TO AN INTERNATIONAL POETRY FESTIVAL.
NO! FANTASTIQUE!
STEPHEN, OUR ROSIE IS FAMOUS ALREADY! AND WE DIDN'T EVEN KNOW SHE WAS A POET!

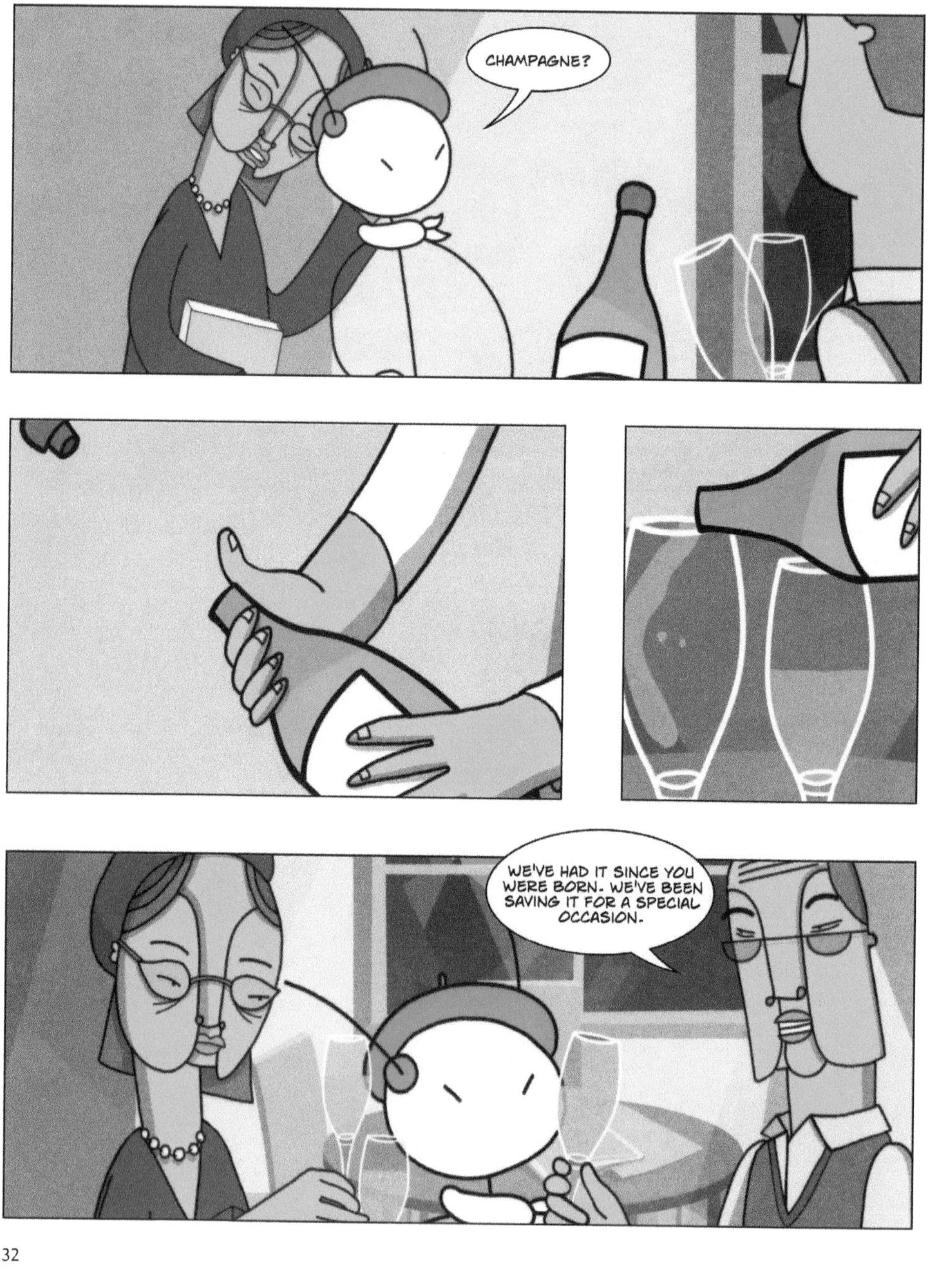
CHAMPAGNE?
WE'VE HAD IT SINCE YOU WERE BORN. WE'VE BEEN SAVING IT FOR A SPECIAL OCCASION.

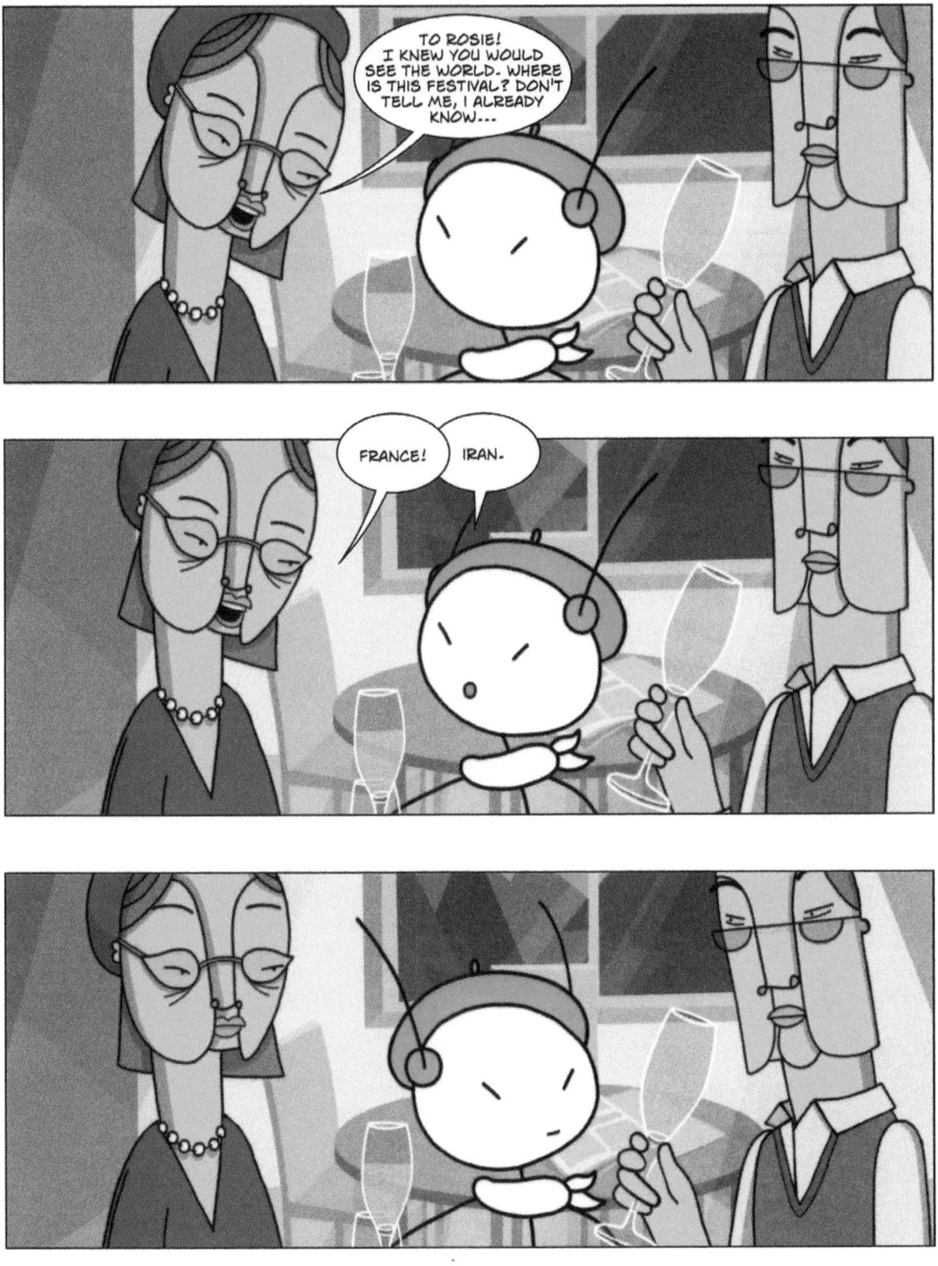
TO ROSIE! I KNEW YOU WOULD SEE THE WORLD. WHERE IS THIS FESTIVAL? DON'T TELL ME, I ALREADY KNOW...
FRANCE!
IRAN.

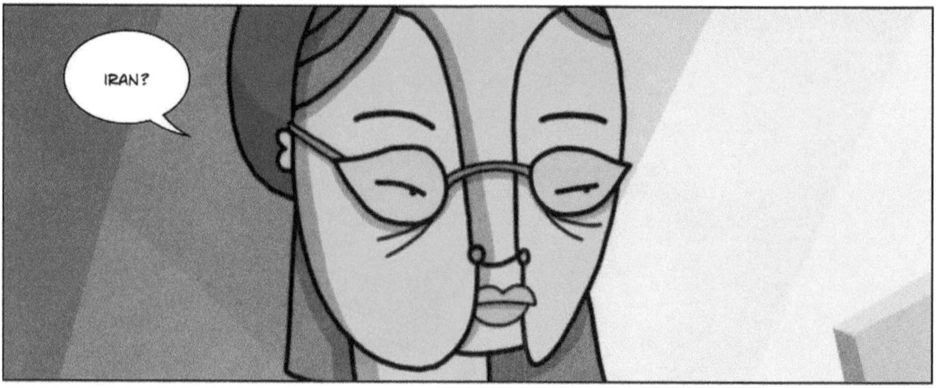
IRAN?

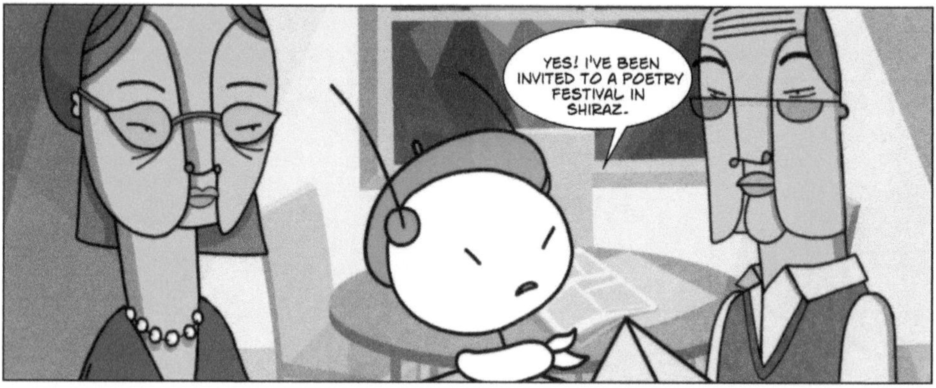
YES! I'VE BEEN INVITED TO A POETRY FESTIVAL IN SHIRAZ.

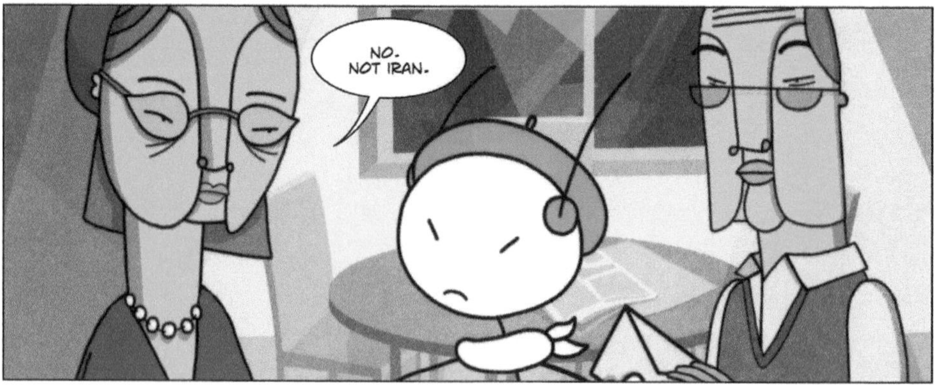
NO. NOT IRAN.

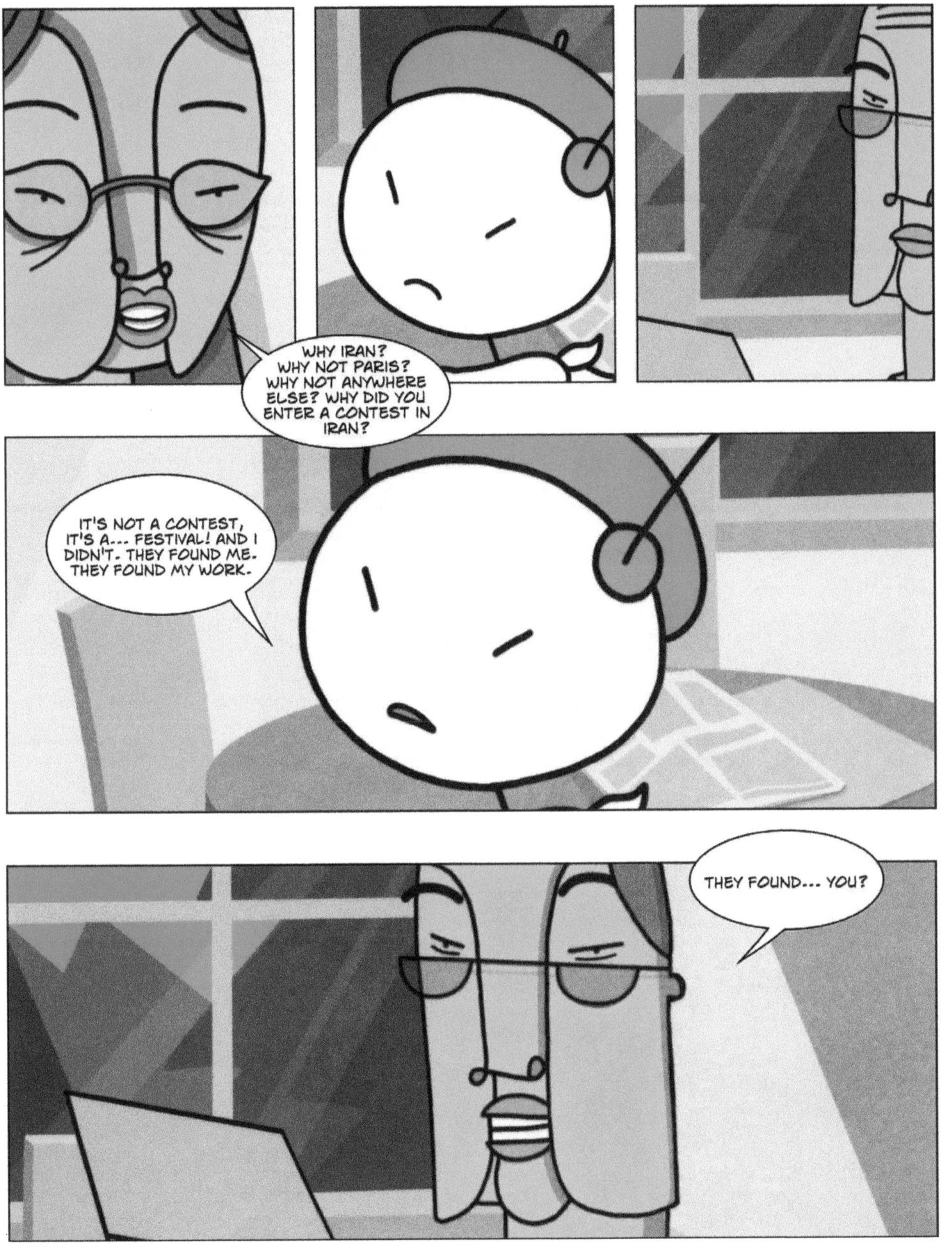

WHY IRAN? WHY NOT PARIS? WHY NOT ANYWHERE ELSE? WHY DID YOU ENTER A CONTEST IN IRAN?
IT'S NOT A CONTEST, IT'S A... FESTIVAL! AND I DIDN'T. THEY FOUND ME. THEY FOUND MY WORK.
THEY FOUND... YOU?

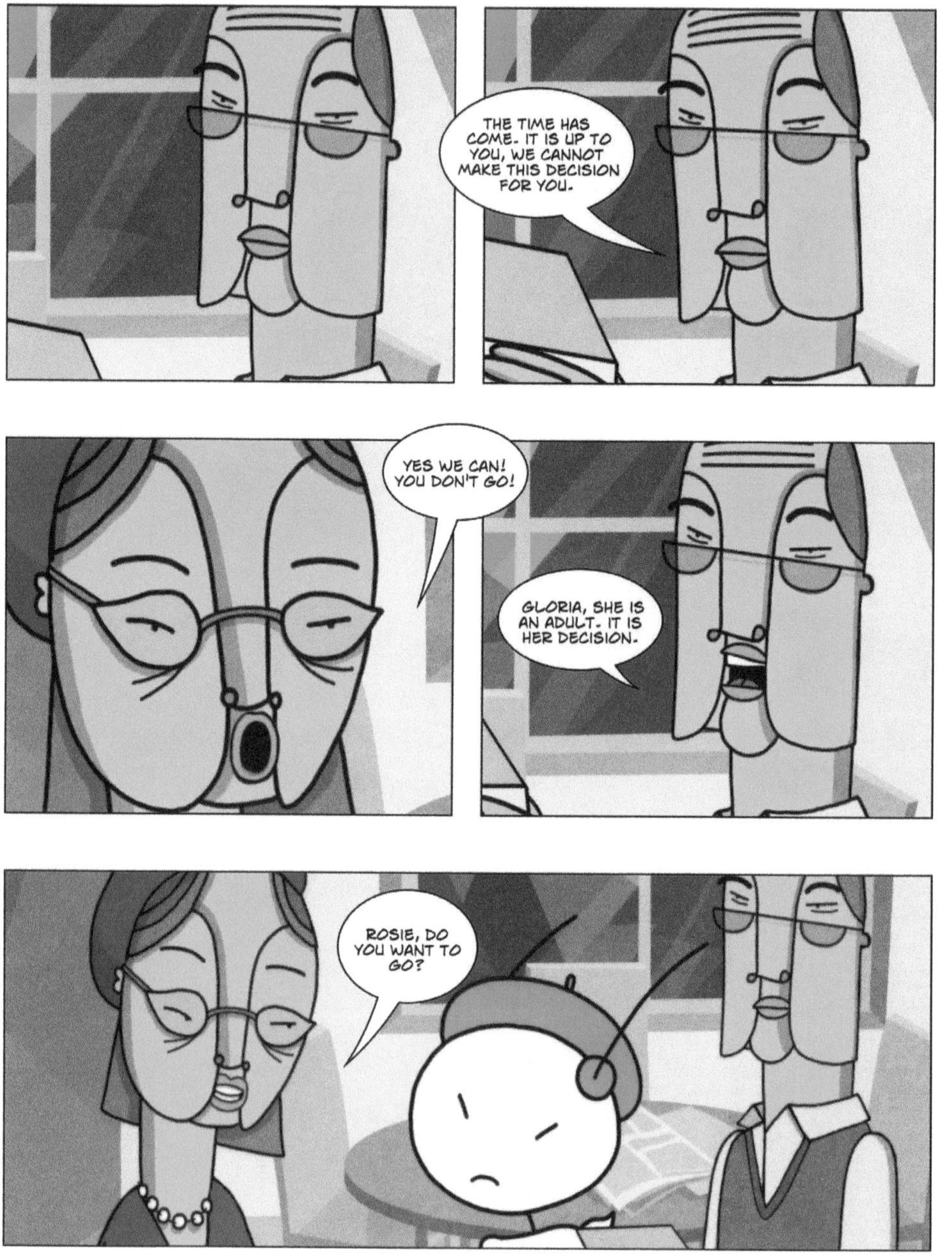
THE TIME HAS COME. IT IS UP TO YOU, WE CANNOT MAKE THIS DECISION FOR YOU.
YES WE CAN! YOU DON'T GO!
GLORIA, SHE IS AN ADULT. IT IS HER DECISION.
ROSIE, DO YOU WANT TO GO?

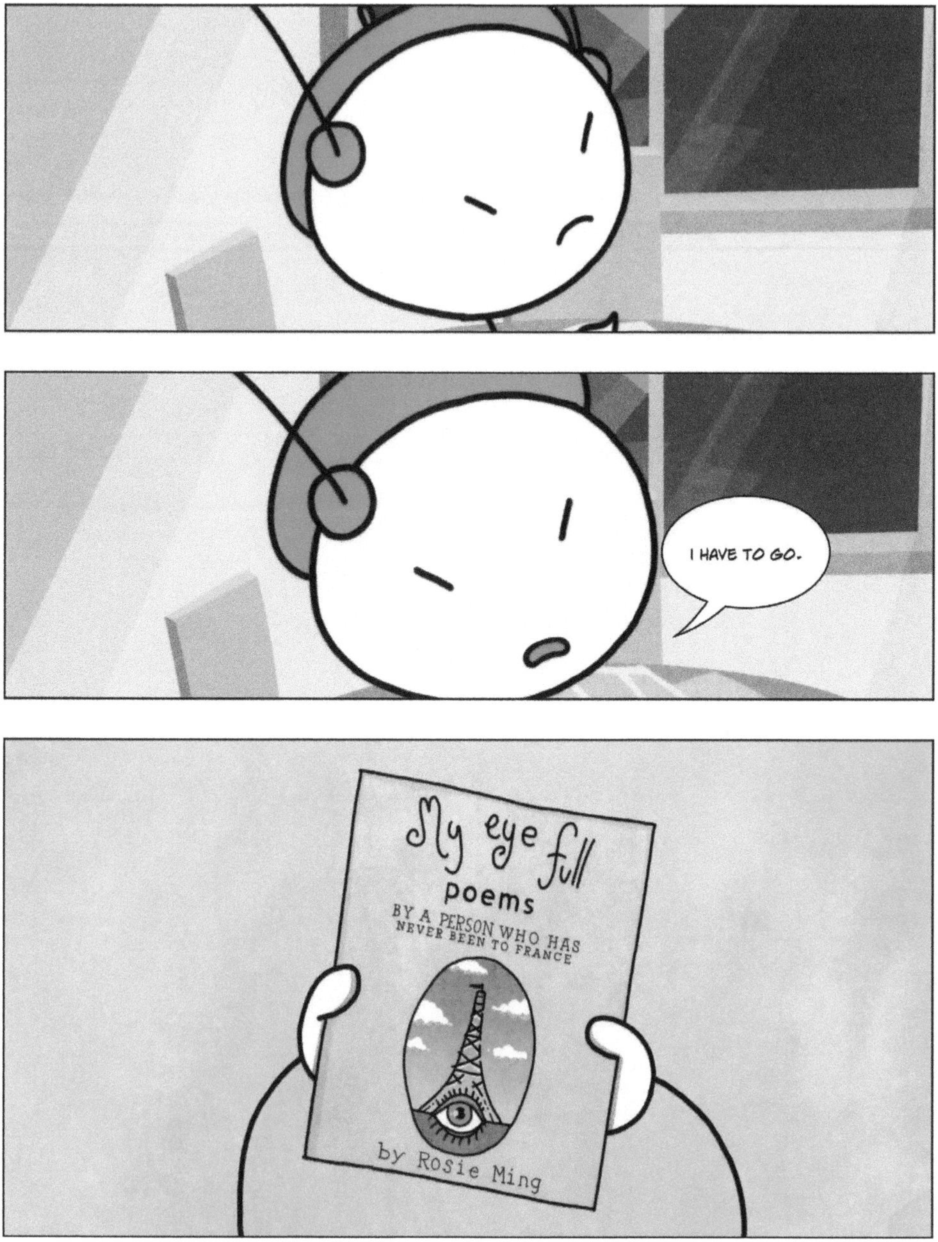
I HAVE TO GO.
My eye full
poems
BY A PERSON WHO HAS NEVER BEEN TO FRANCE
by Rosie Ming

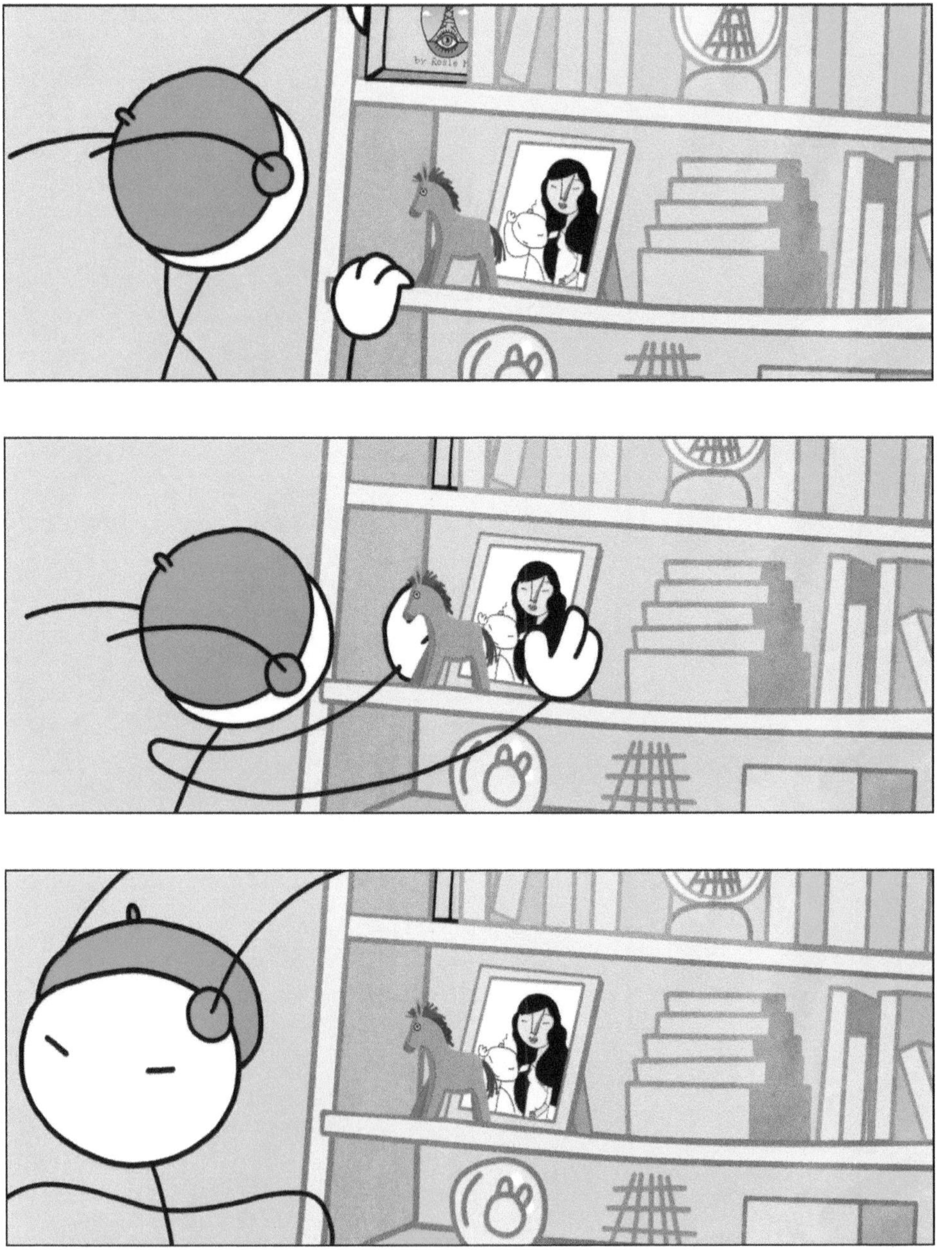
by Rosie M

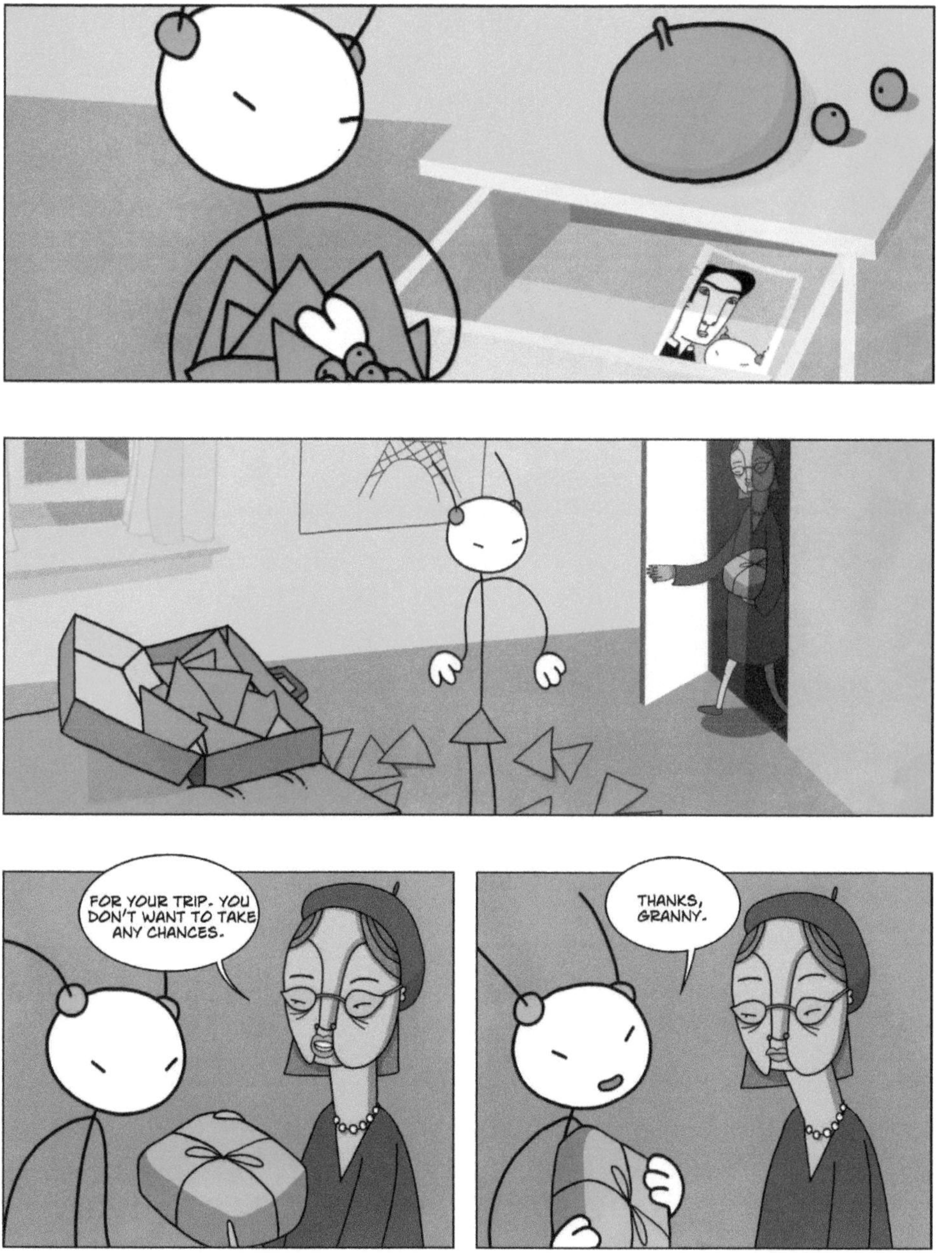
FOR YOUR TRIP. YOU DON'T WANT TO TAKE ANY CHANCES.
THANKS, GRANNY.

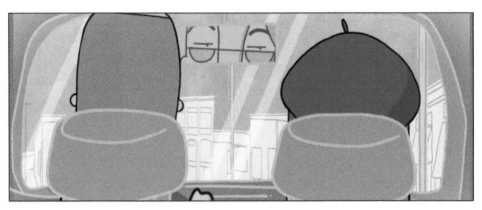

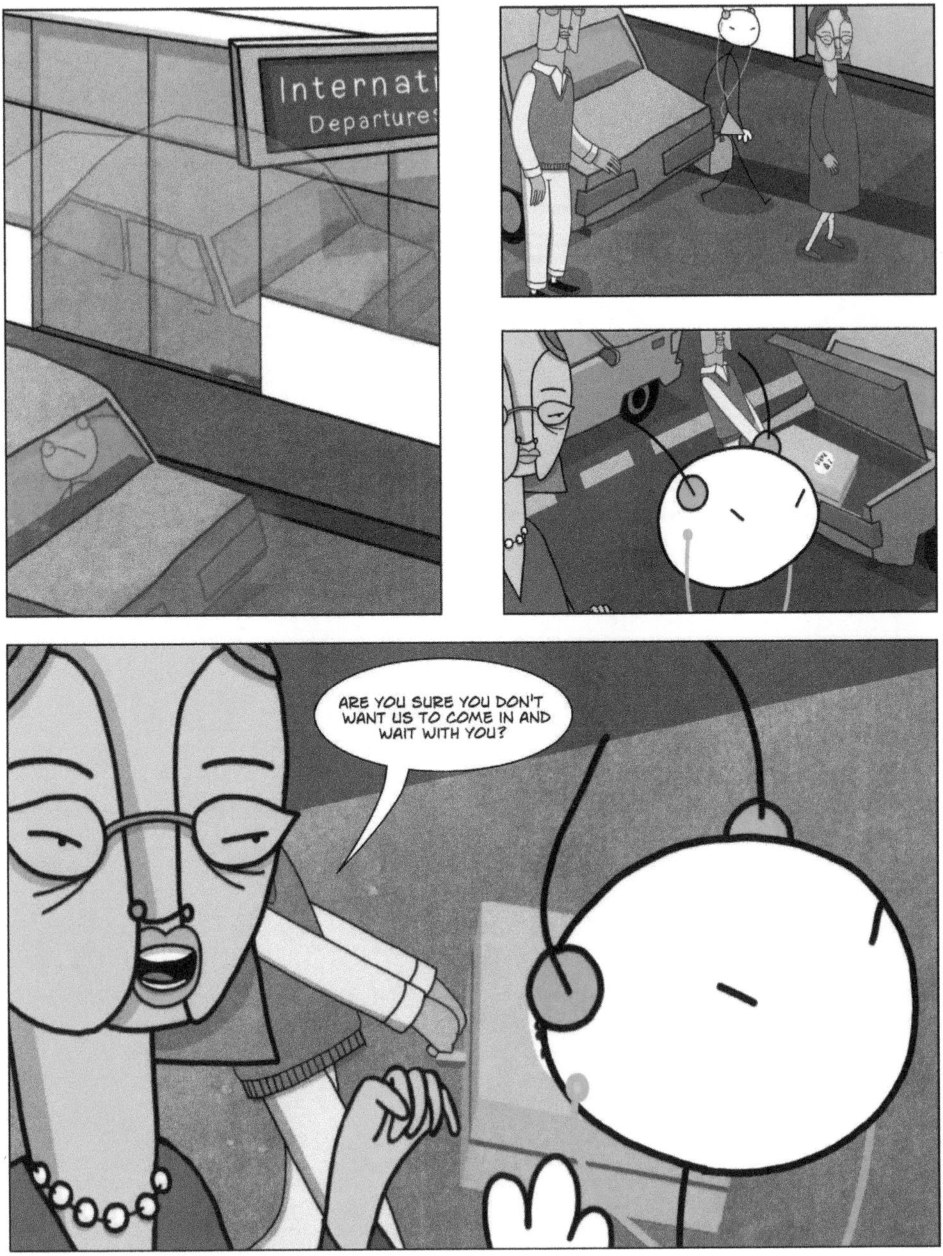
Internati
Departures
ARE YOU SURE YOU DON'T WANT US TO COME IN AND WAIT WITH YOU?

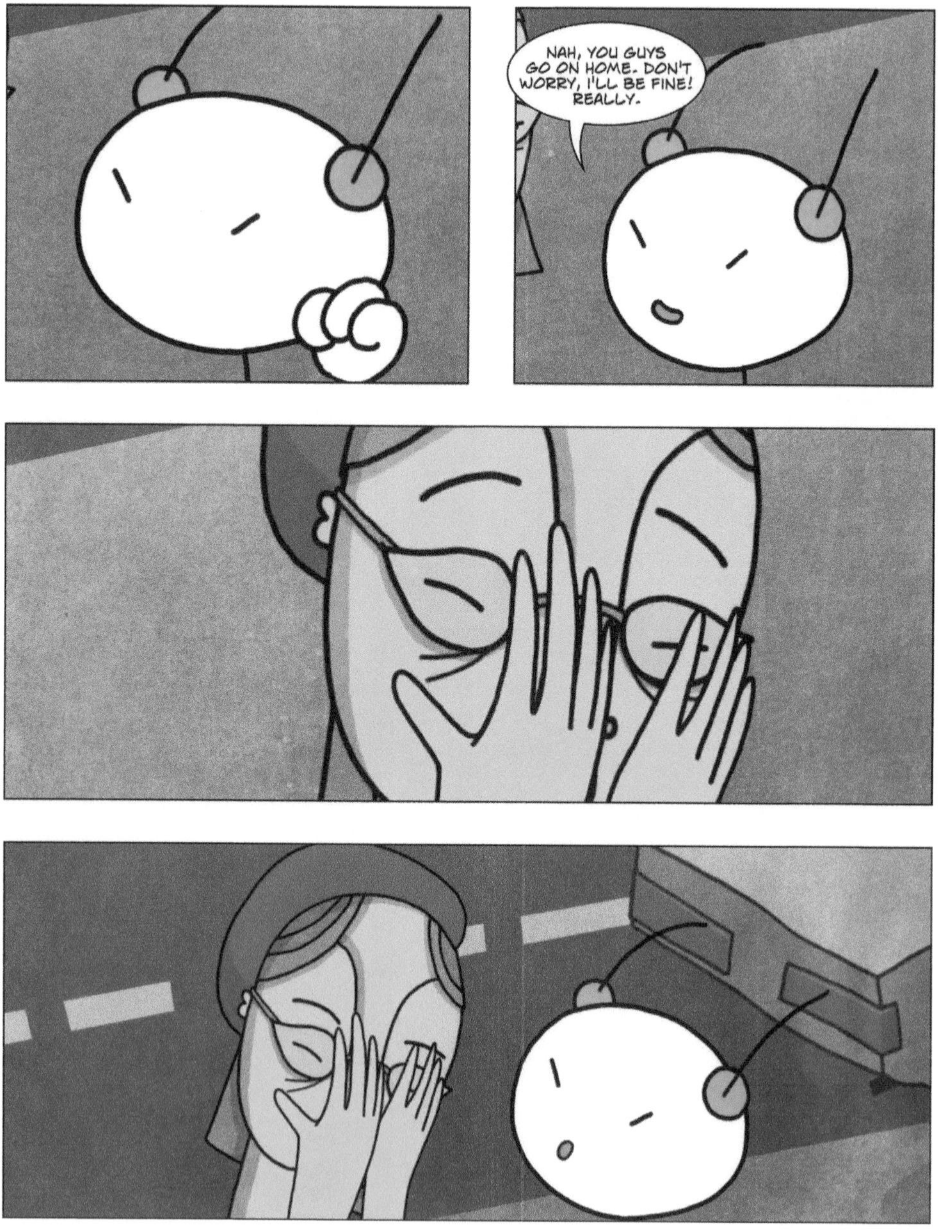
NAH, YOU GUYS GO ON HOME. DON'T WORRY, I'LL BE FINE! REALLY.

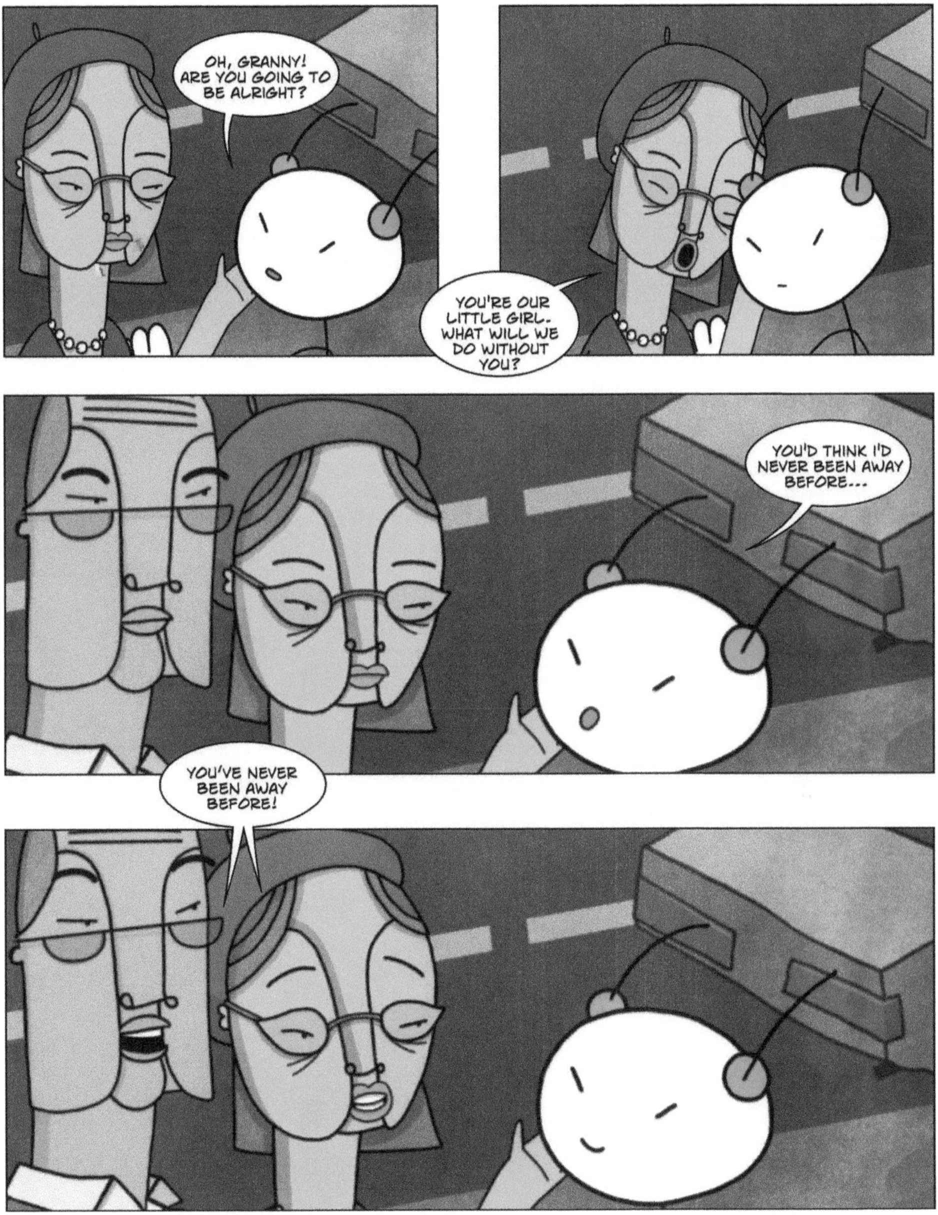
OH, GRANNY! ARE YOU GOING TO BE ALRIGHT?
YOU'RE OUR LITTLE GIRL. WHAT WILL WE DO WITHOUT YOU?
YOU'D THINK I'D NEVER BEEN AWAY BEFORE...
YOU'VE NEVER BEEN AWAY BEFORE!

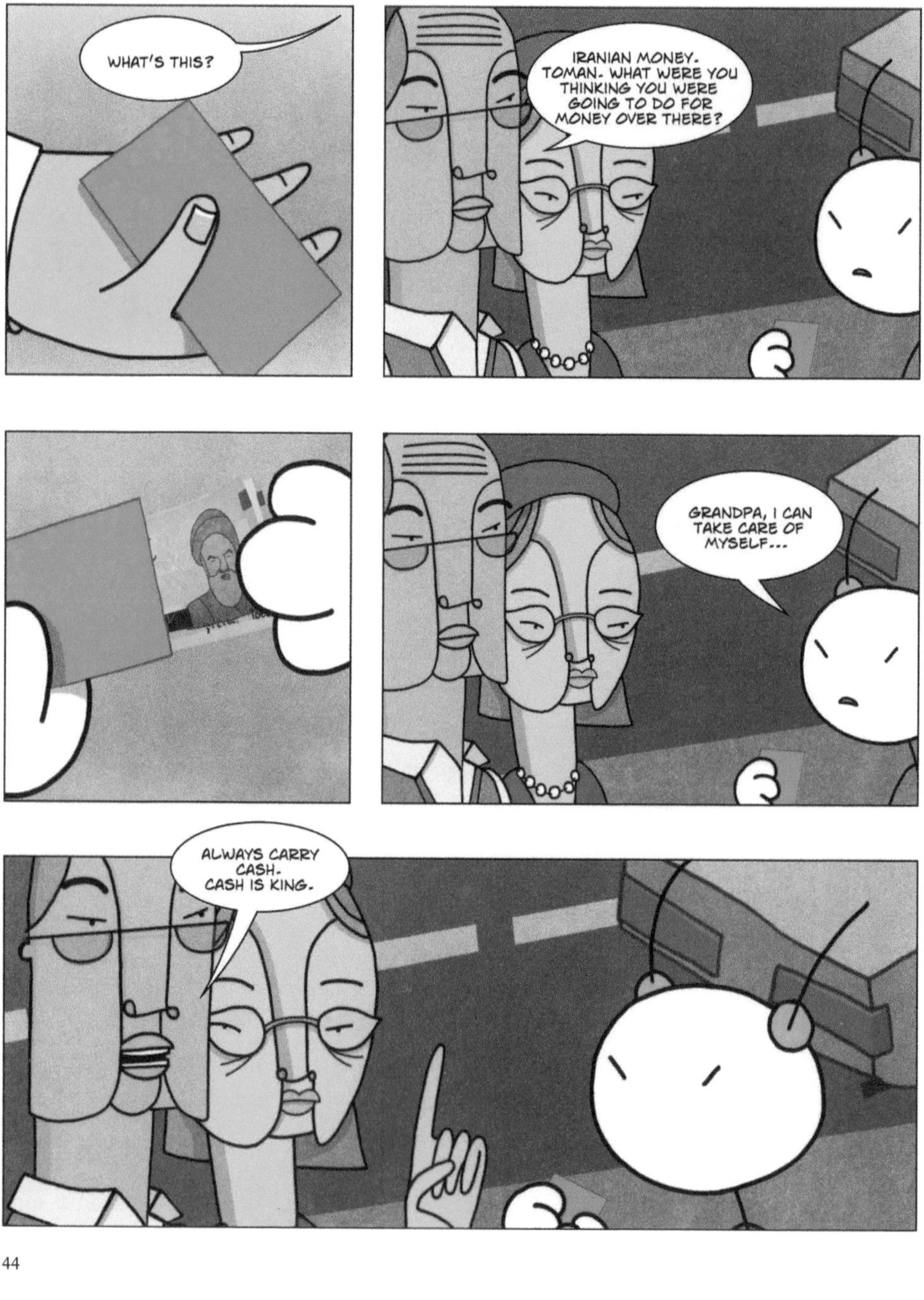
WHAT'S THIS?
IRANIAN MONEY. TOMAN. WHAT WERE YOU THINKING YOU WERE GOING TO DO FOR MONEY OVER THERE?
GRANDPA, I CAN TAKE CARE OF MYSELF...
ALWAYS CARRY CASH. CASH IS KING.

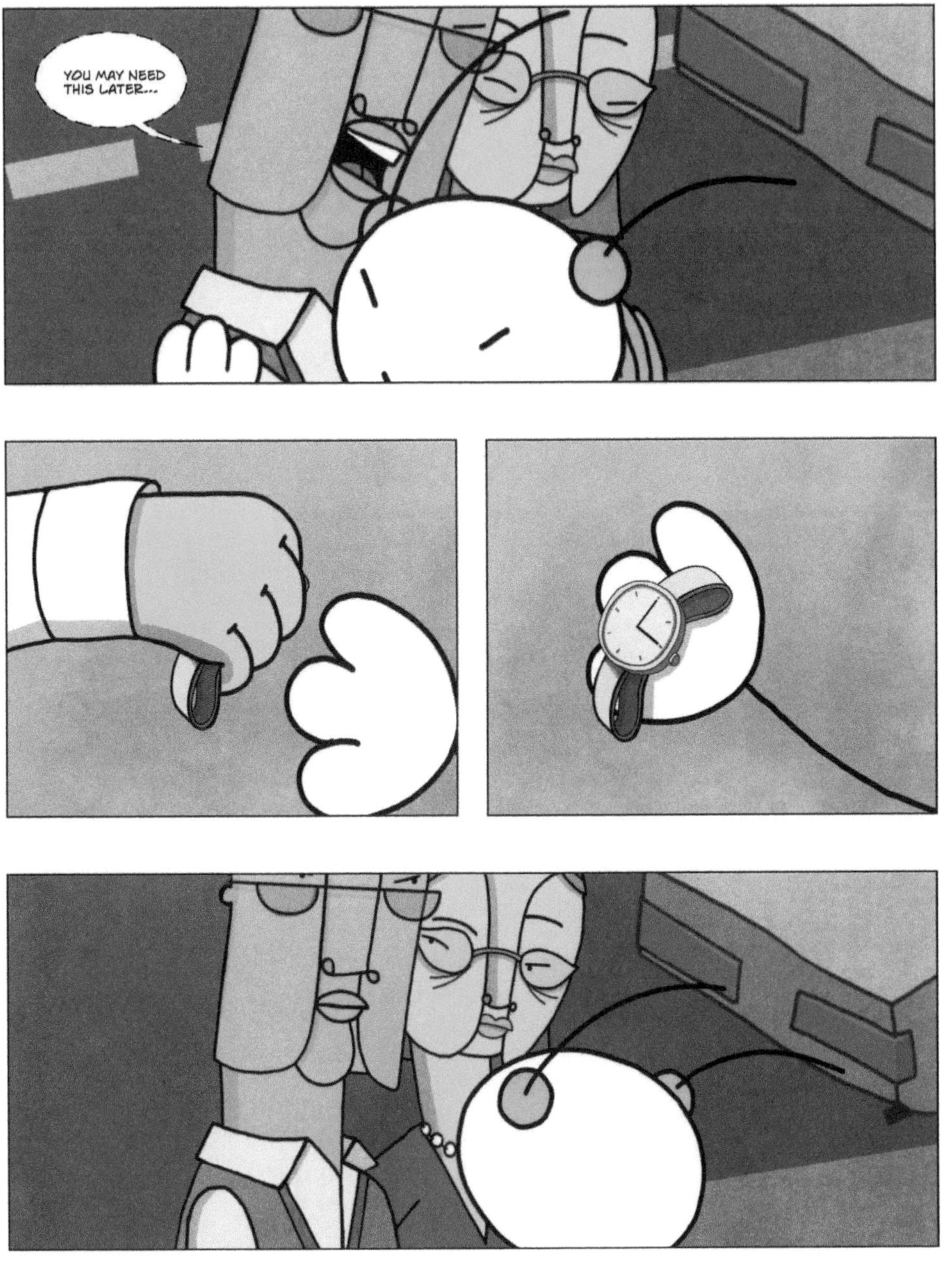
YOU MAY NEED THIS LATER...

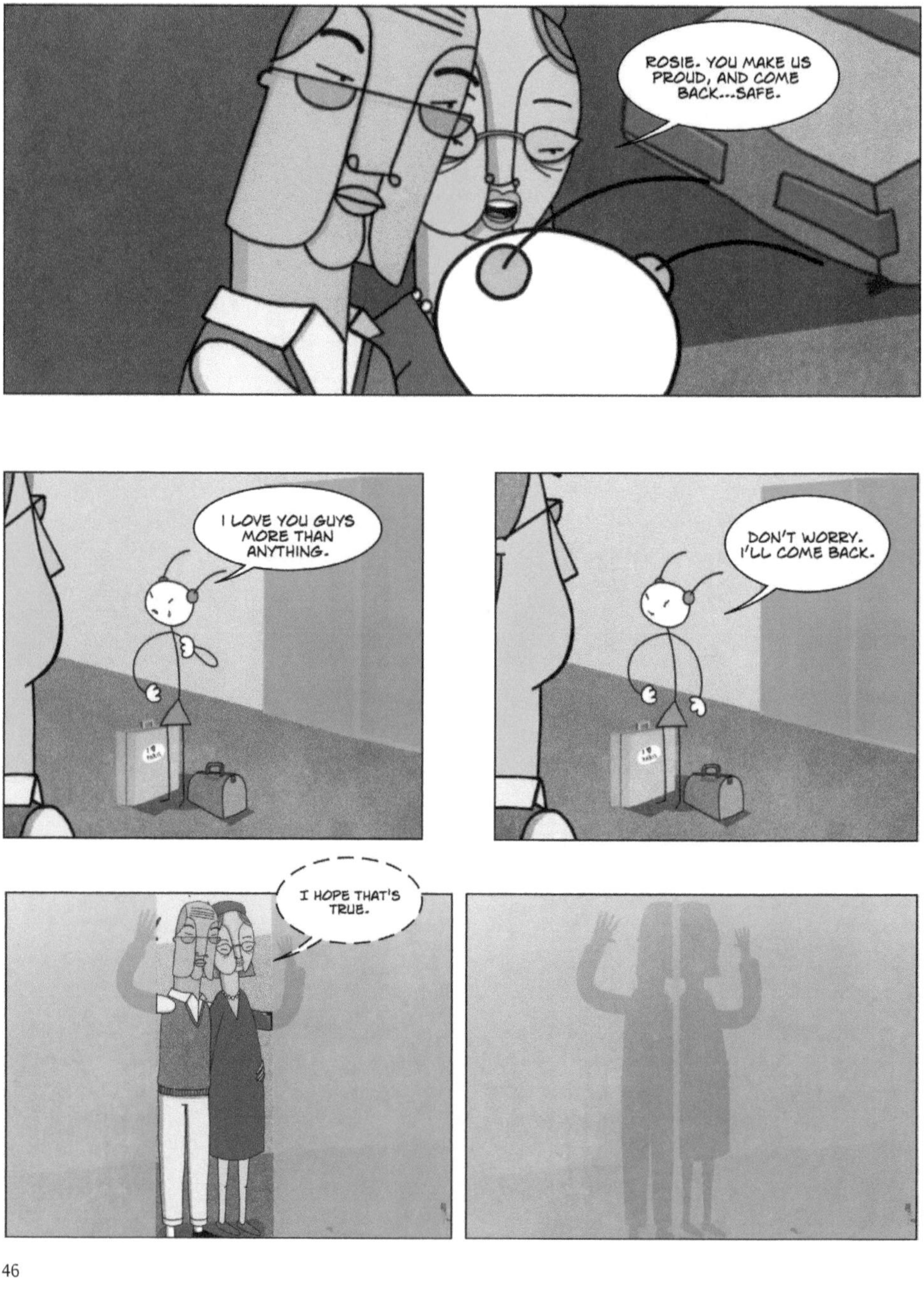
ROSIE. YOU MAKE US PROUD, AND COME BACK...SAFE.
I LOVE YOU GUYS MORE THAN ANYTHING.
DON'T WORRY. I'LL COME BACK.
I HOPE THAT'S TRUE.

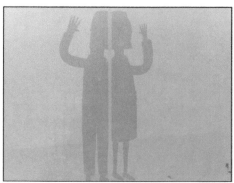

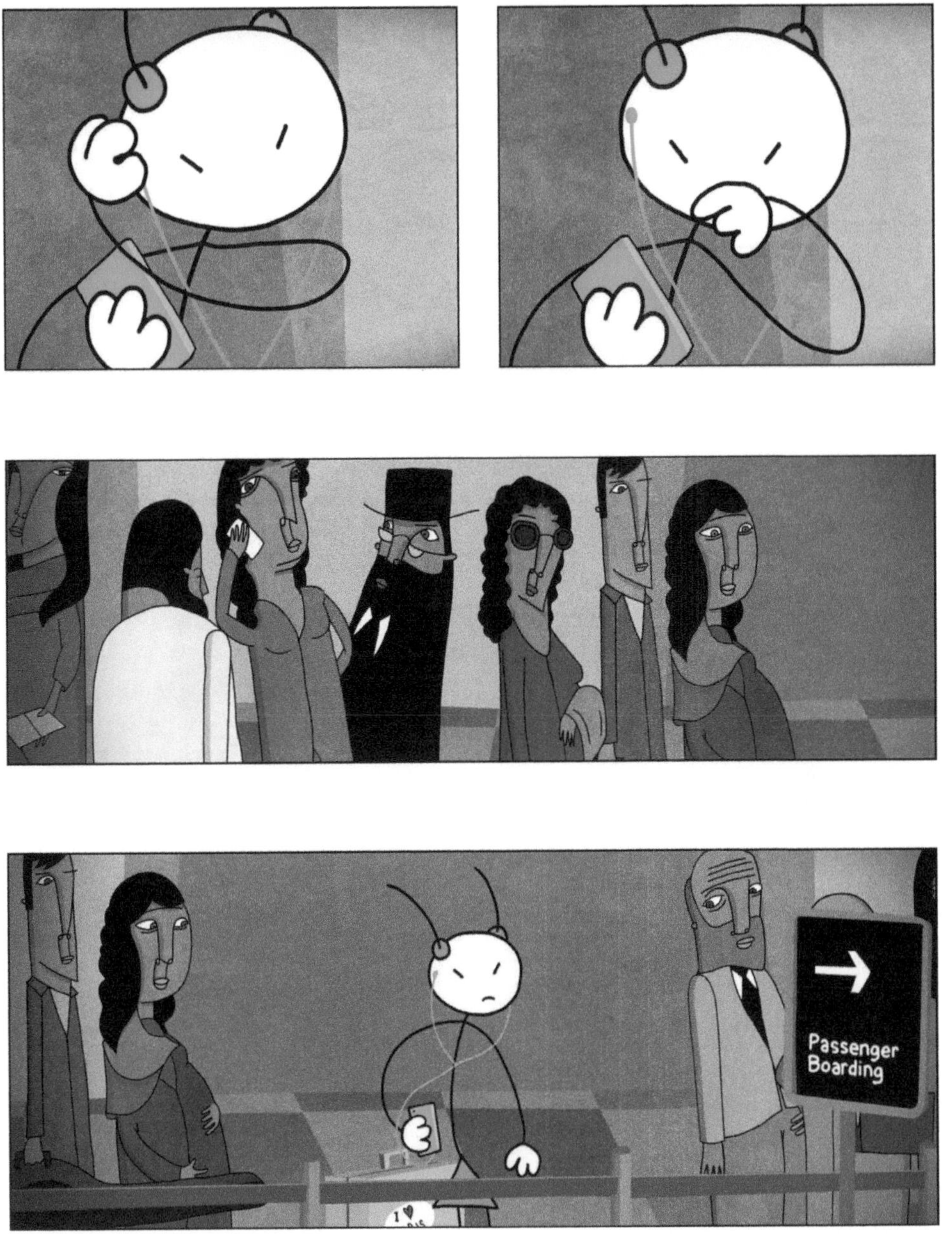
Passenger
Boarding

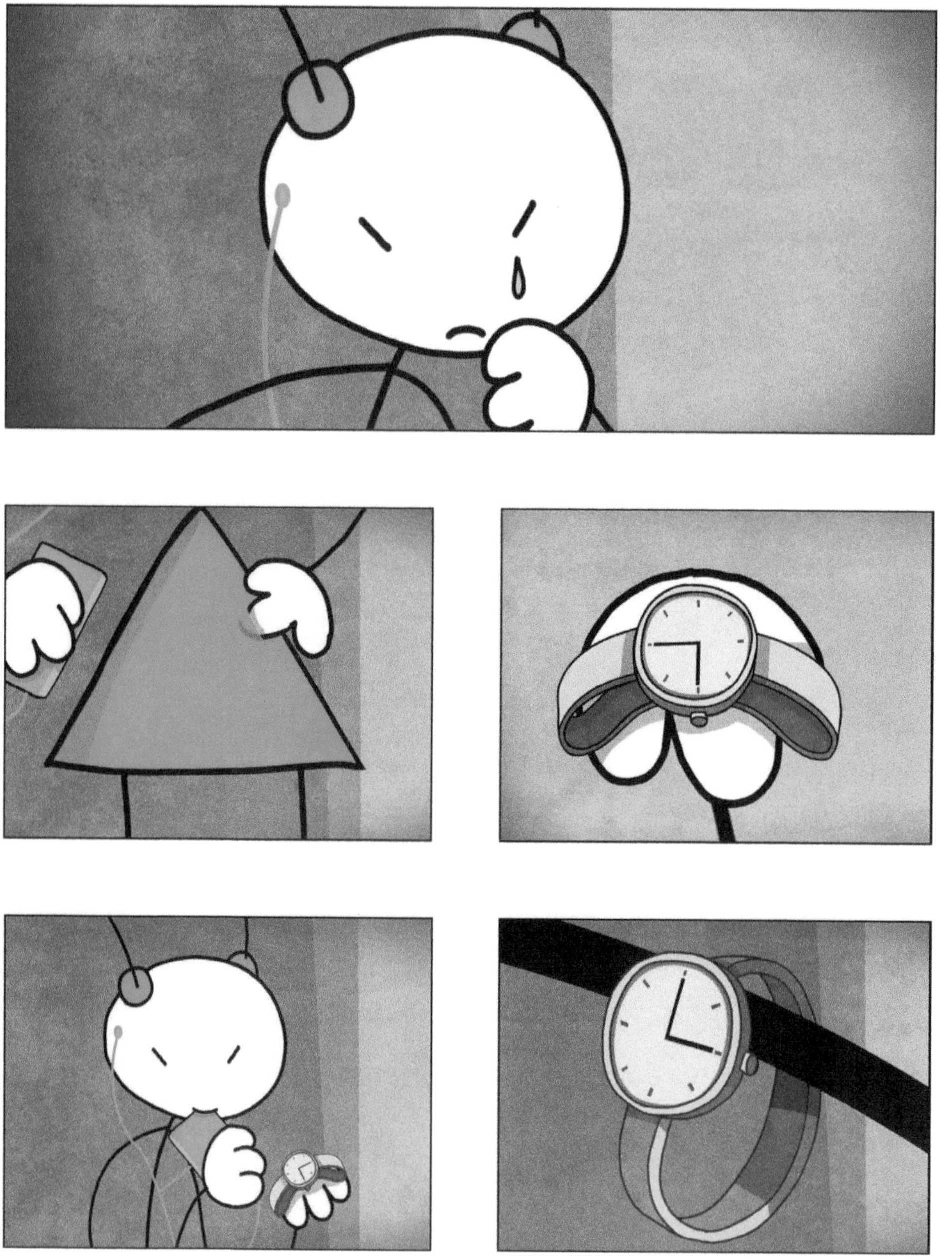

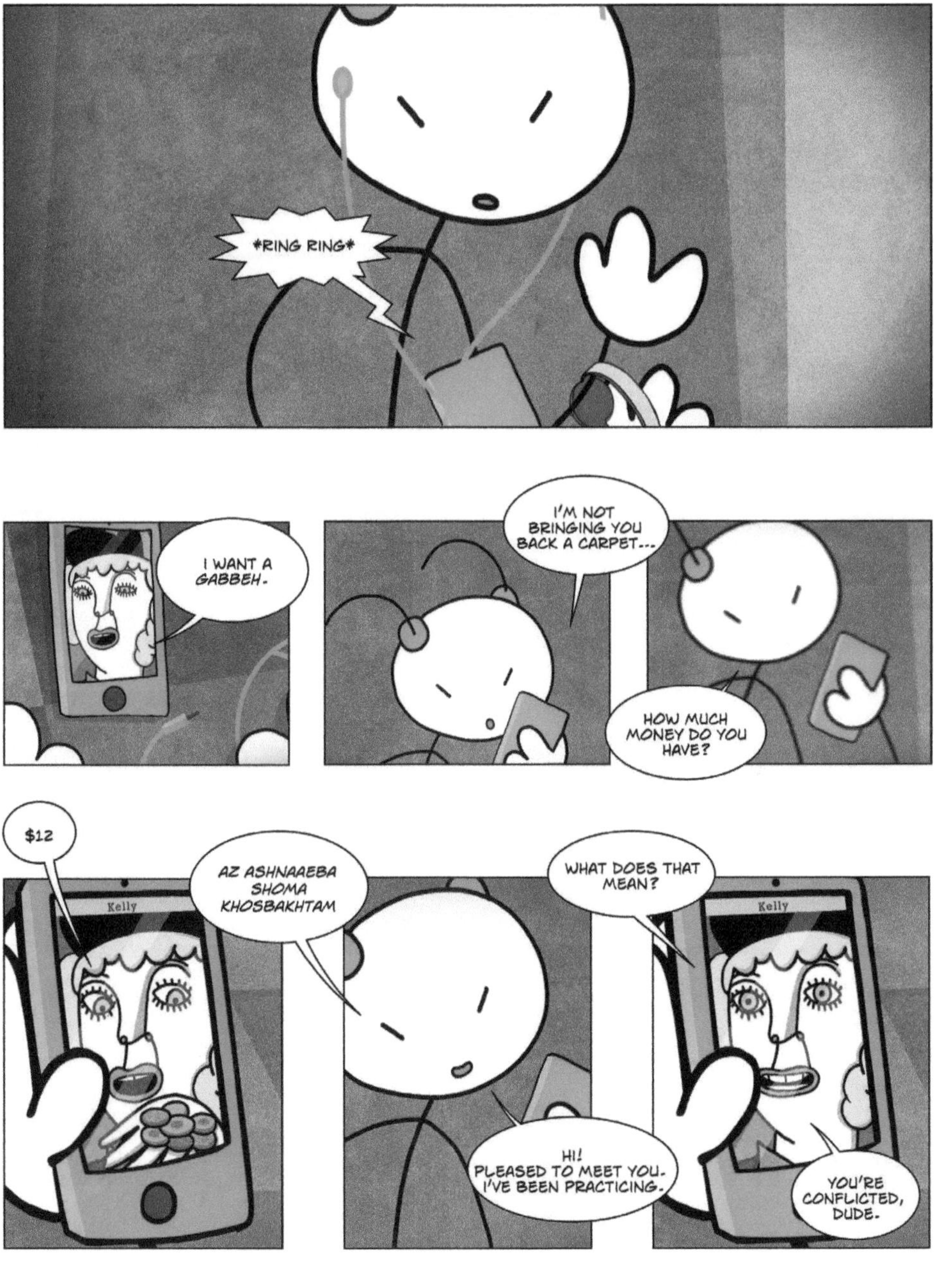
RING RING
I WANT A GABBEH.
I'M NOT BRINGING YOU BACK A CARPET...
HOW MUCH MONEY DO YOU HAVE?
$12
AZ ASHNAAEBA SHOMA KHOSBAKHTAM
HI! PLEASED TO MEET YOU. I'VE BEEN PRACTICING.
WHAT DOES THAT MEAN?
Kelly
YOU'RE CONFLICTED, DUDE.

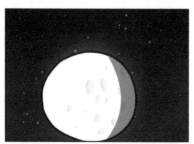

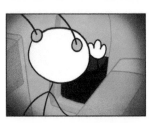

WE'RE
LANDING!

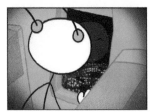

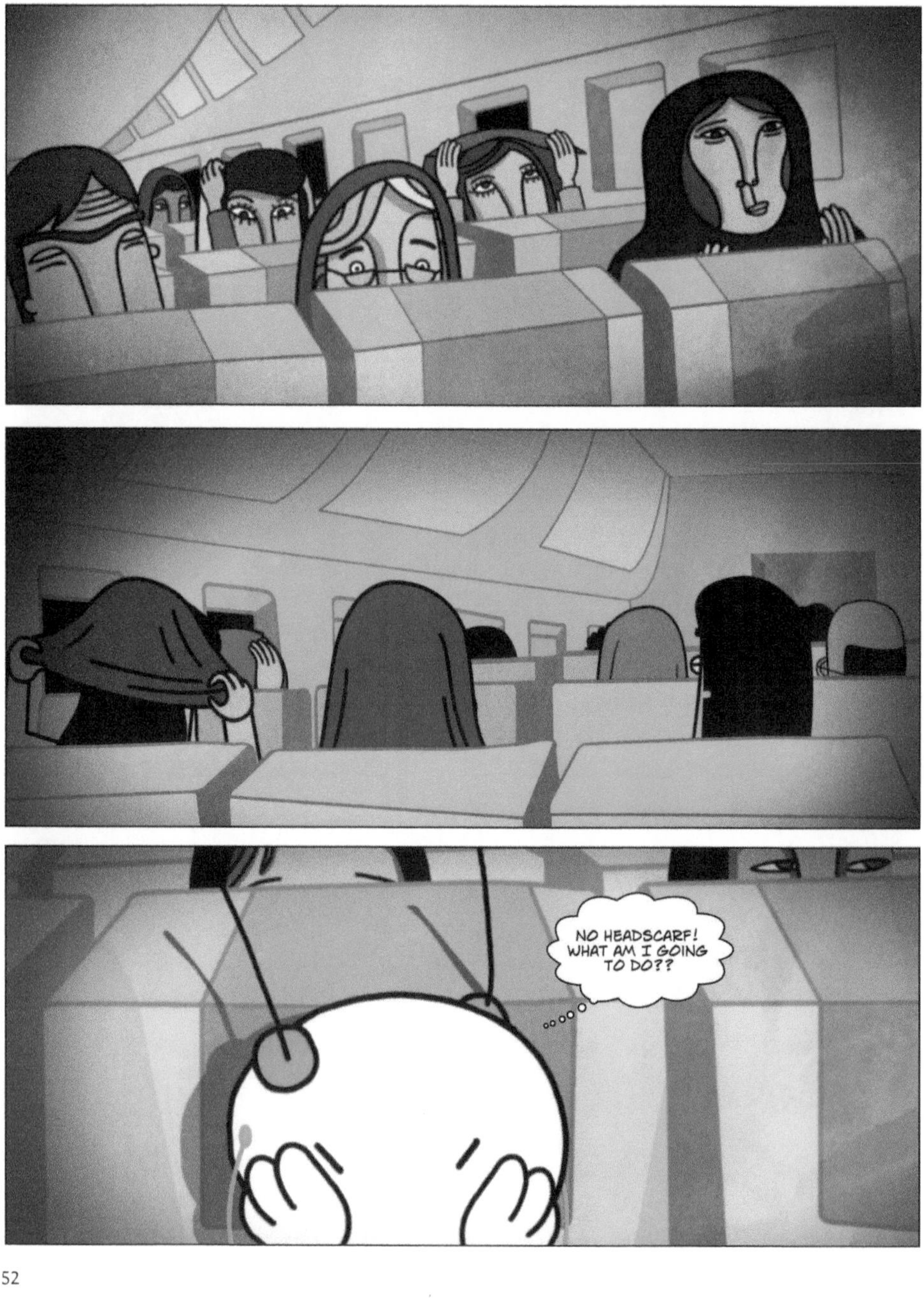
NO HEADSCARF! WHAT AM I GOING TO DO??

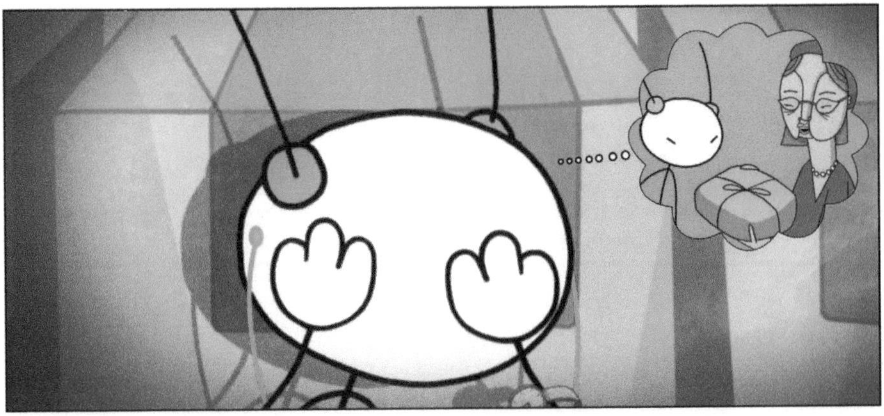

LUCKILY, GRANNY THINKS OF EVERYTHING!

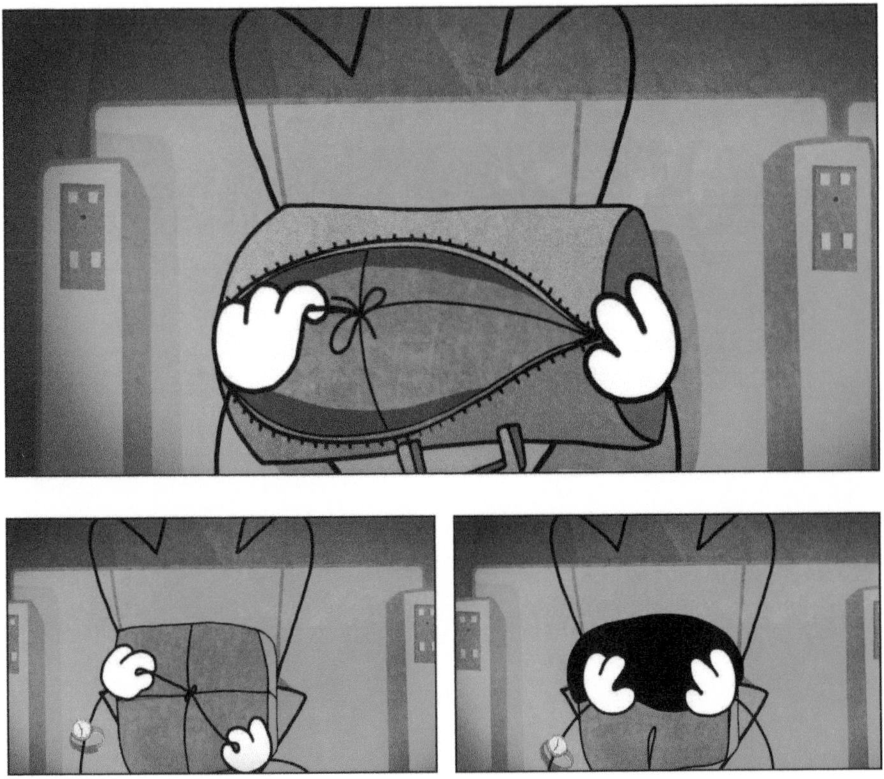

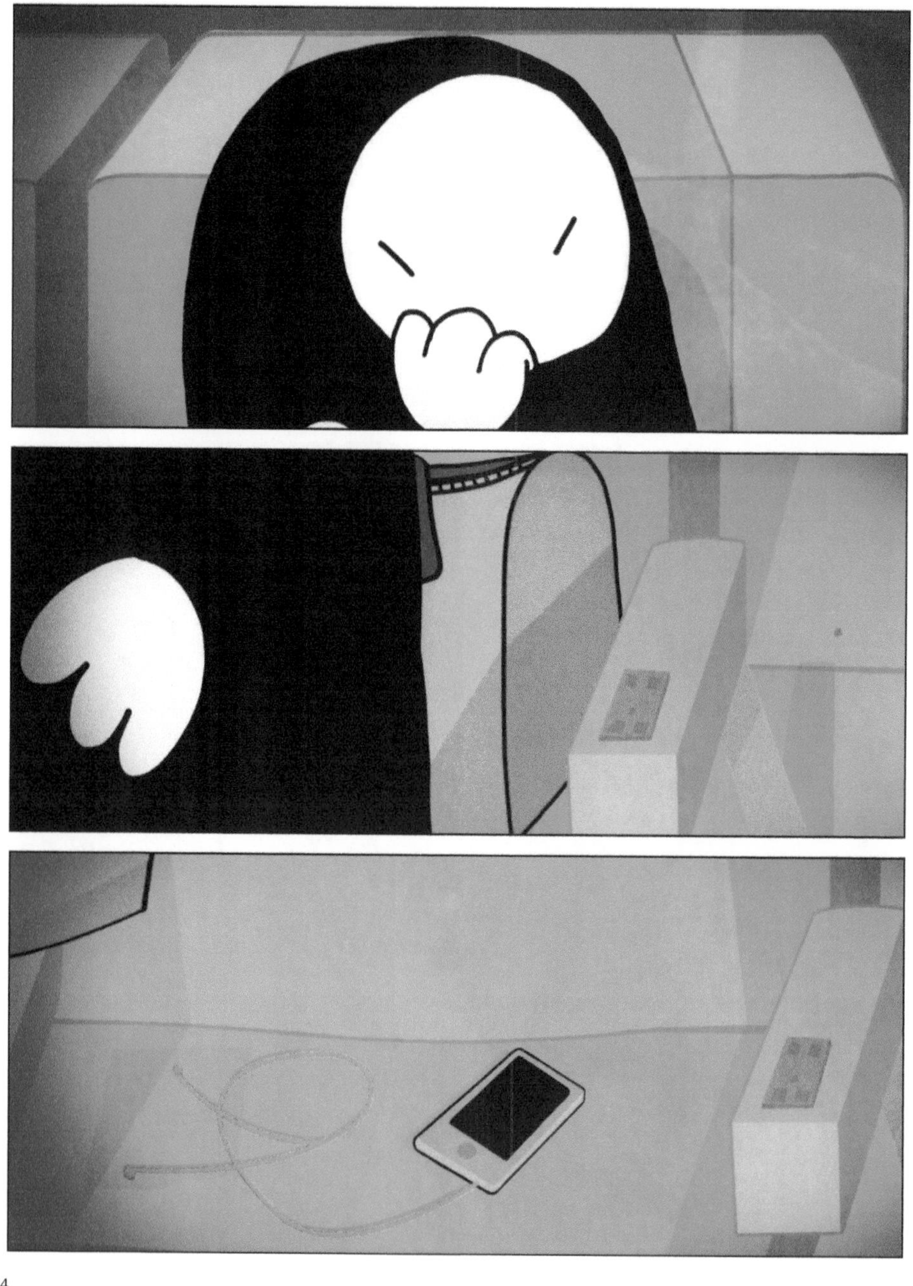

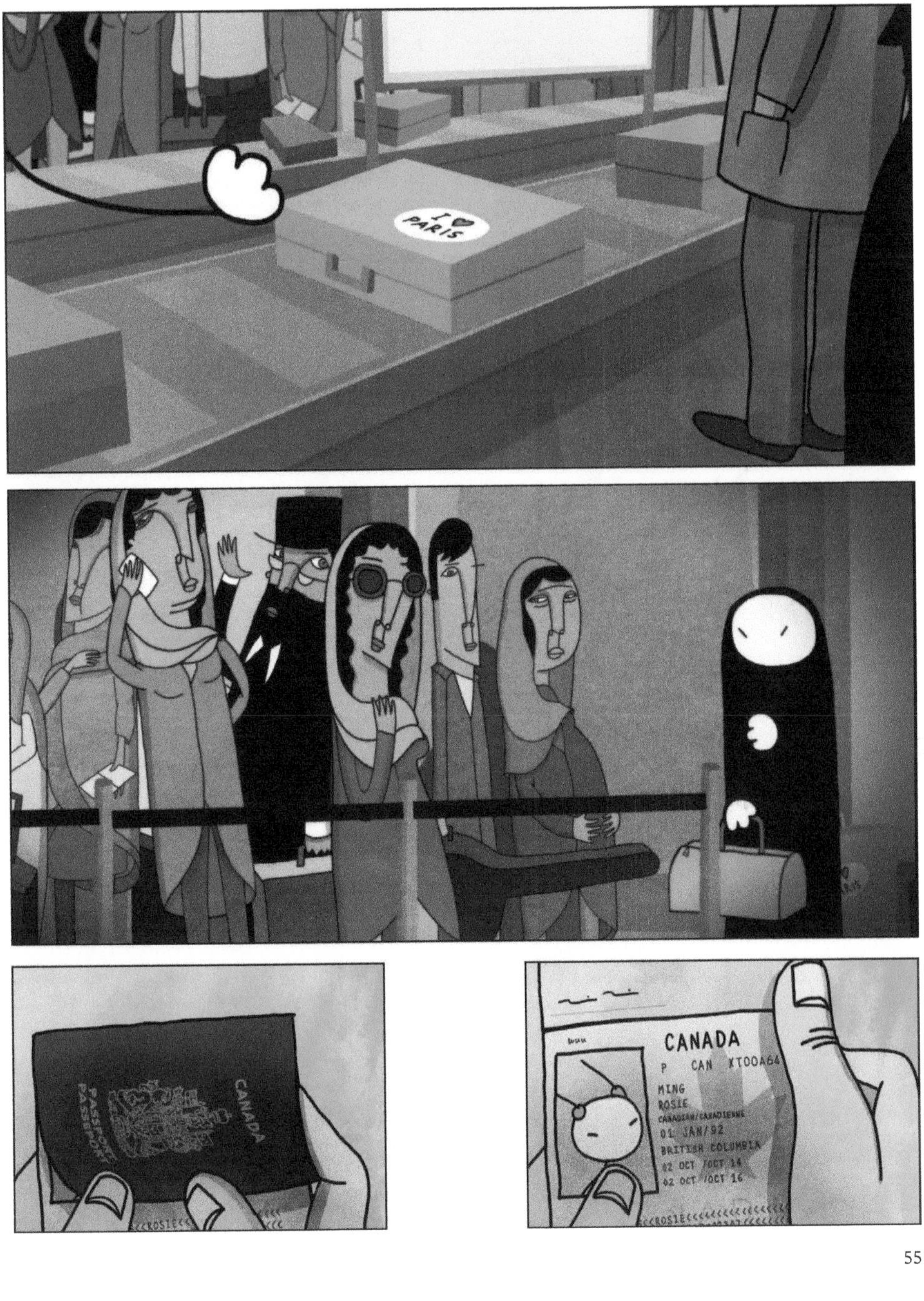
I ♥ PARIS
PASSPORT PASSEPORT CANADA
CANADA
P CAN XT00A64
MING
ROSIE
CANADIAN/CANADIENNE
01 JAN/92
BRITISH COLUMBIA
02 OCT /OCT 14
02 OCT /OCT 16

UH, SALAAM!
REASON FOR VISIT?
I'VE BEEN INVITED TO A POETRY FESTIVAL IN SHIRAZ.
I'M A POET.
AHHH. A POET! I AM A POET, TOO. IRAN IS THE LAND OF POETS. HOW LONG?

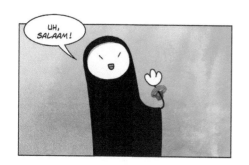

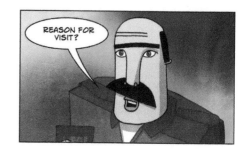

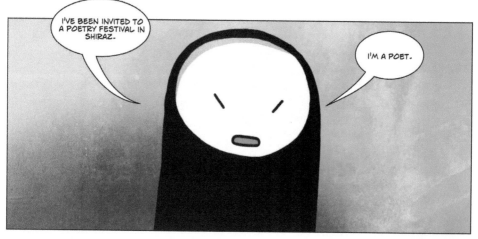

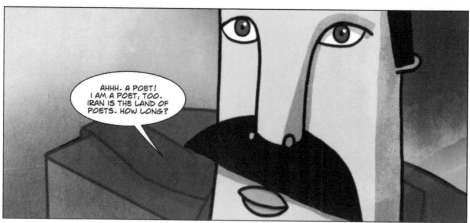

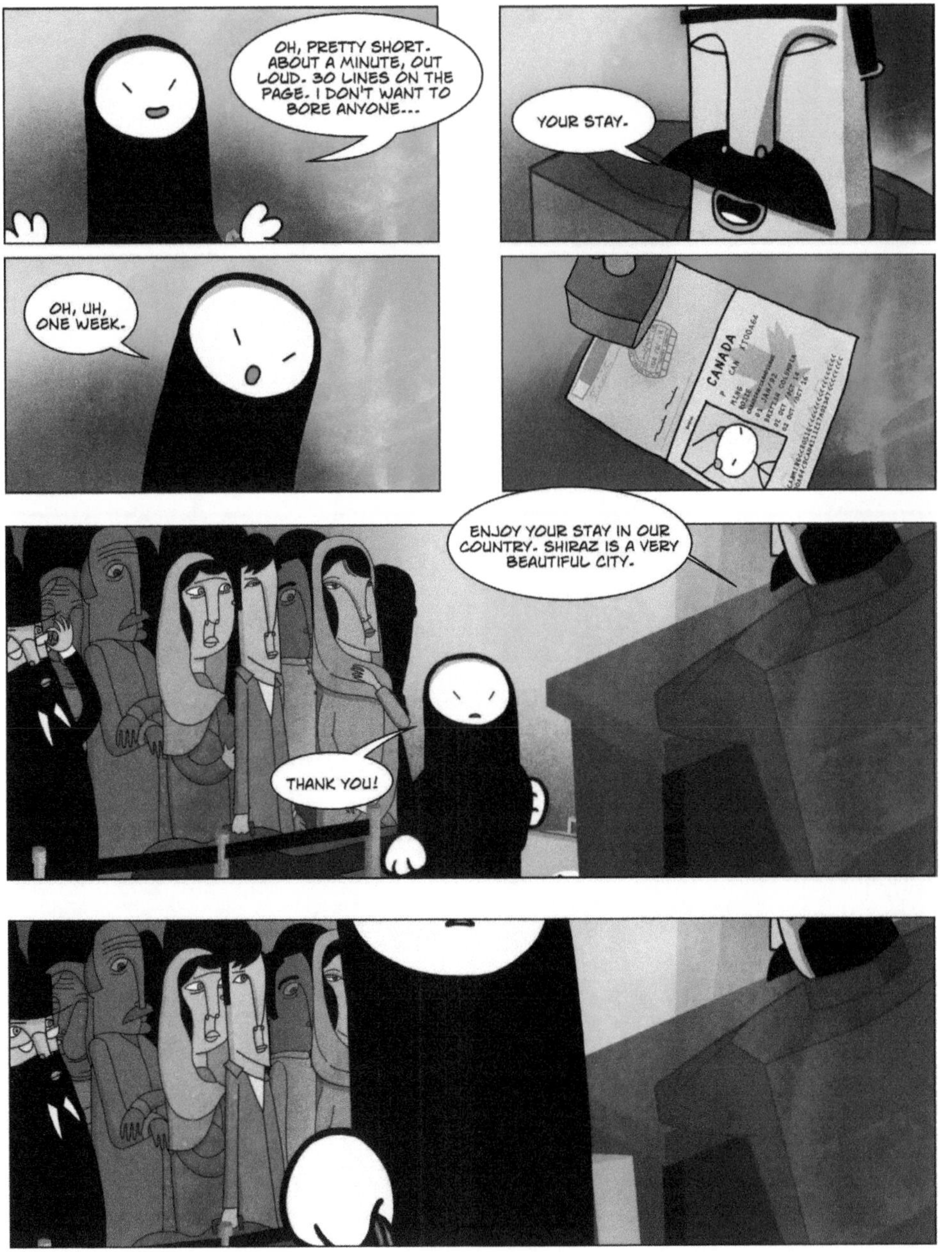
OH, PRETTY SHORT. ABOUT A MINUTE, OUT LOUD. 30 LINES ON THE PAGE. I DON'T WANT TO BORE ANYONE...
YOUR STAY.
OH, UH, ONE WEEK.
CANADA
ENJOY YOUR STAY IN OUR COUNTRY. SHIRAZ IS A VERY BEAUTIFUL CITY.
THANK YOU!

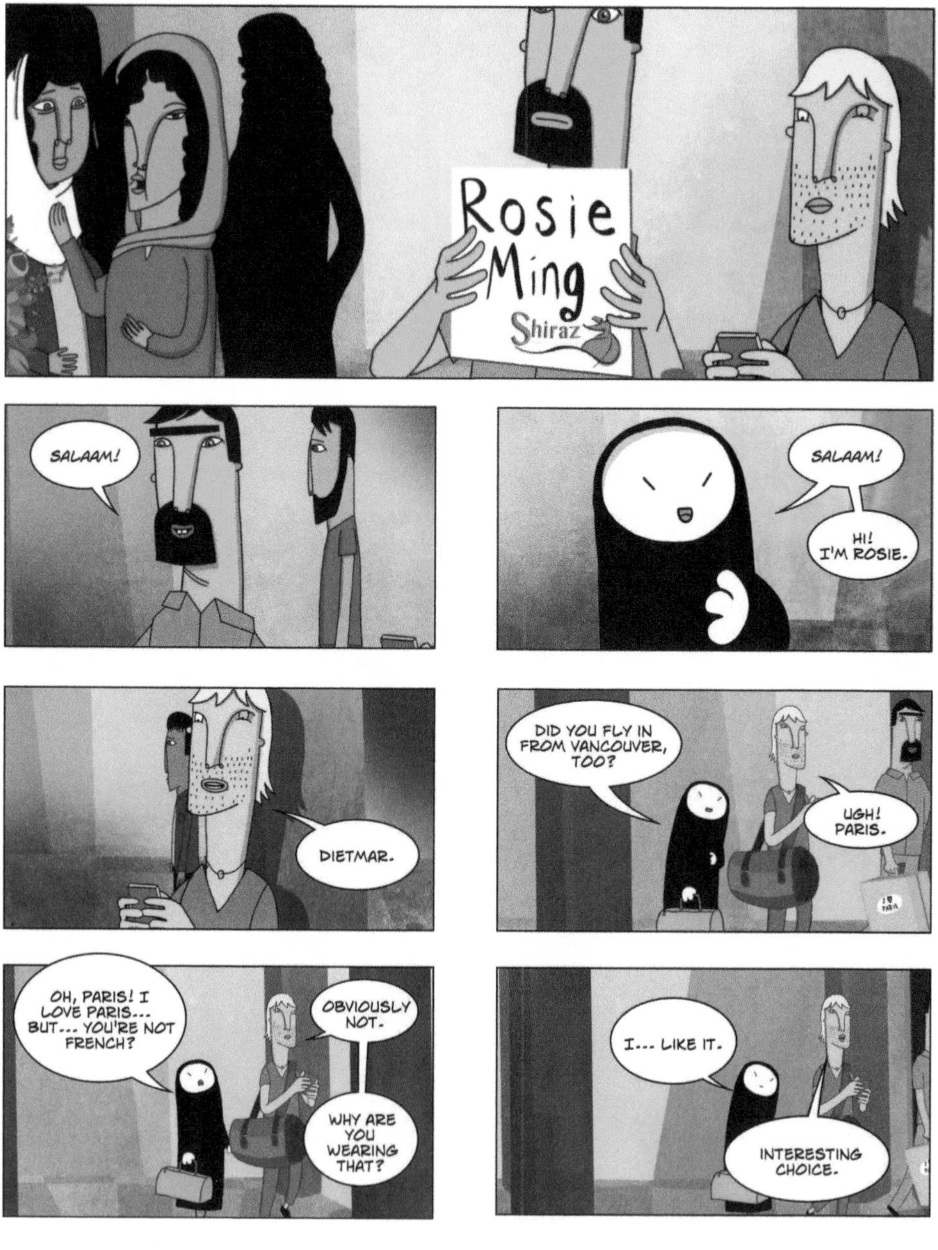
Rosie Ming
Shiraz
SALAAM!
SALAAM!
HI! I'M ROSIE.
DIETMAR.
DID YOU FLY IN FROM VANCOUVER, TOO?
UGH! PARIS.
OH, PARIS! I LOVE PARIS... BUT... YOU'RE NOT FRENCH?
OBVIOUSLY NOT.
WHY ARE YOU WEARING THAT?
I... LIKE IT.
INTERESTING CHOICE.

SO... HOW FAR IS SHIRAZ?

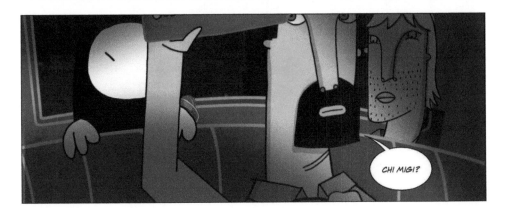

CHI MIGI?

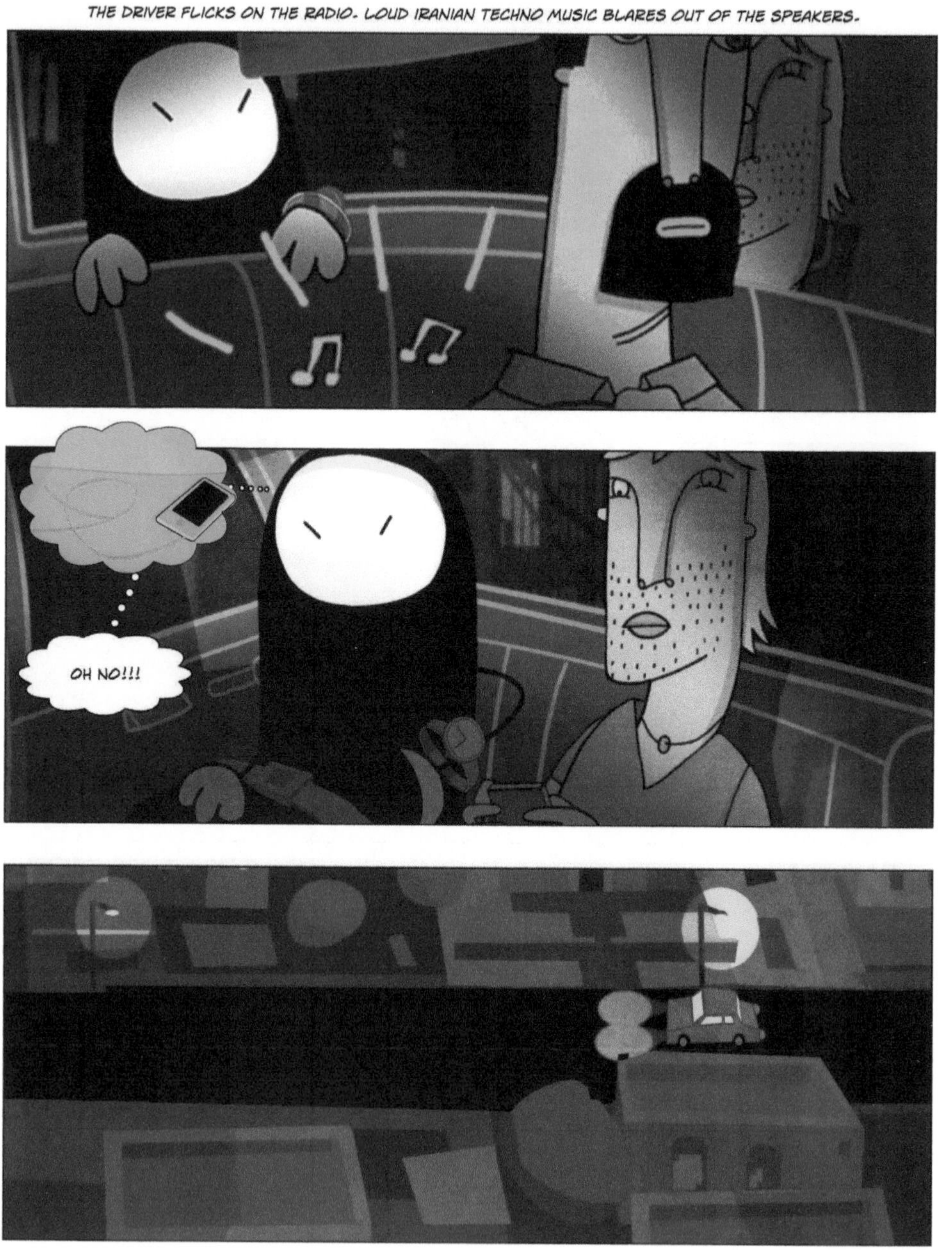
THE DRIVER FLICKS ON THE RADIO. LOUD IRANIAN TECHNO MUSIC BLARES OUT OF THE SPEAKERS.
OH NO!!!

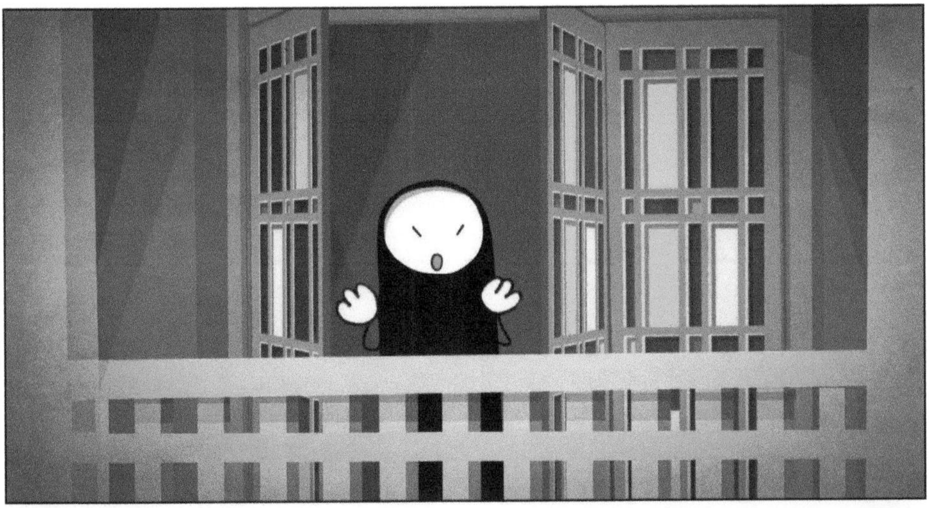

THE LOUDSPEAKERS IN THE MINARET REPLACE THE VOICE OF THE MUEZZIN, BLASTING OUT THE CALL TO PRAYER.

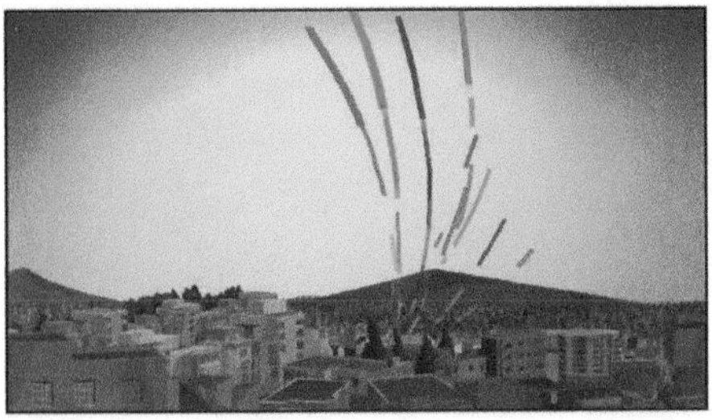

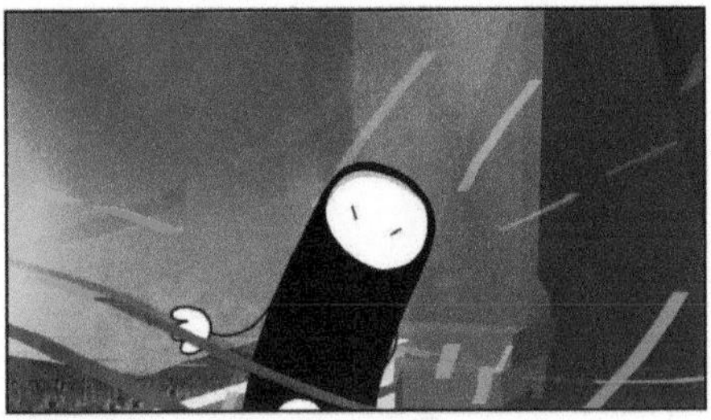

THE SOUND IS MAGICAL.

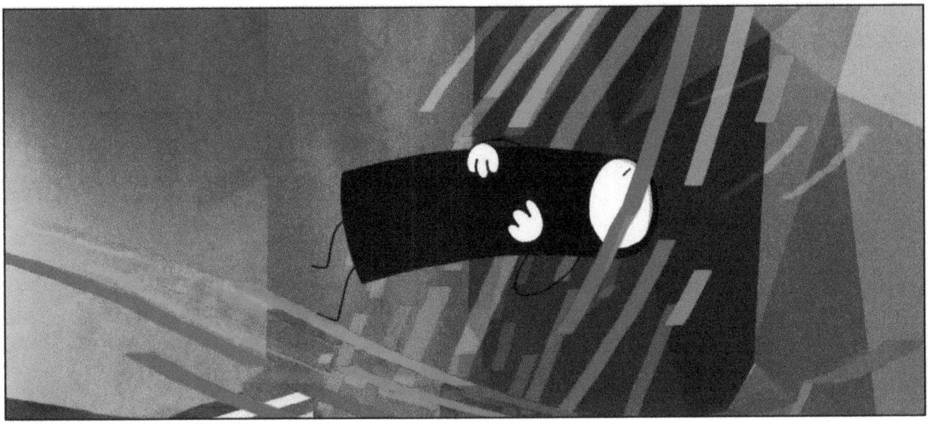

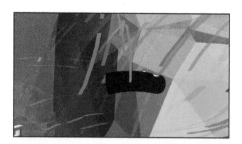

I REALLY
SHOULD HAVE
PACKED BETTER!

ACK!

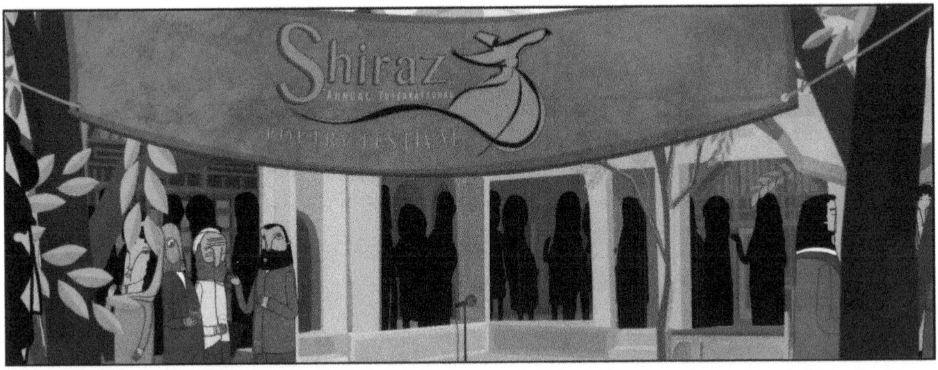
Shiraz

THE FIRST MORNING OF POETRY IS HELD IN THE COURTYARD OF AN IRANIAN FAMILY HOME. PEOPLE ARE GETTING ACQUAINTED AND TAKING THEIR SEATS...

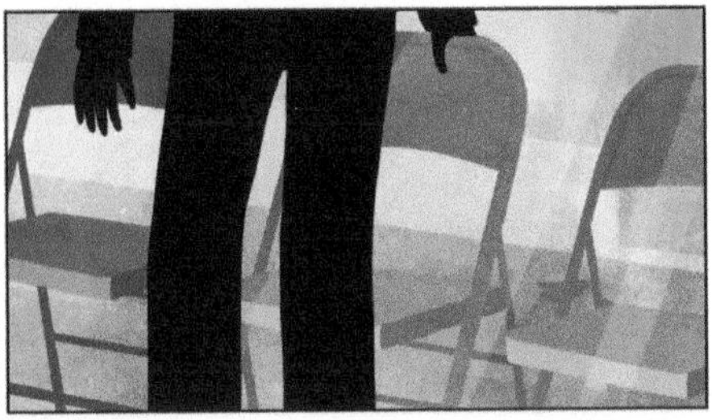

BUT ROSIE KNOWS NO ONE... EXCEPT...

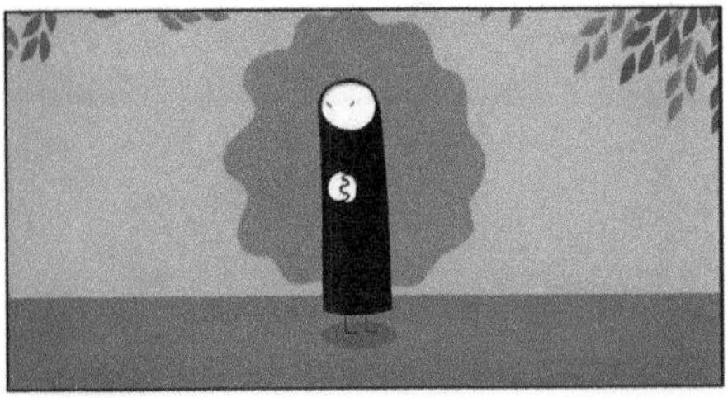

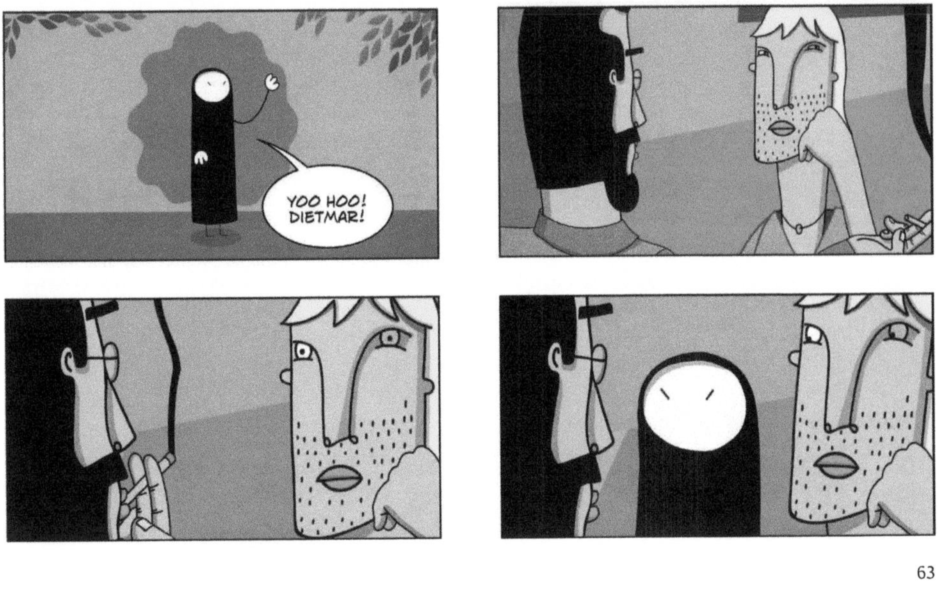
YOO HOO! DIETMAR!

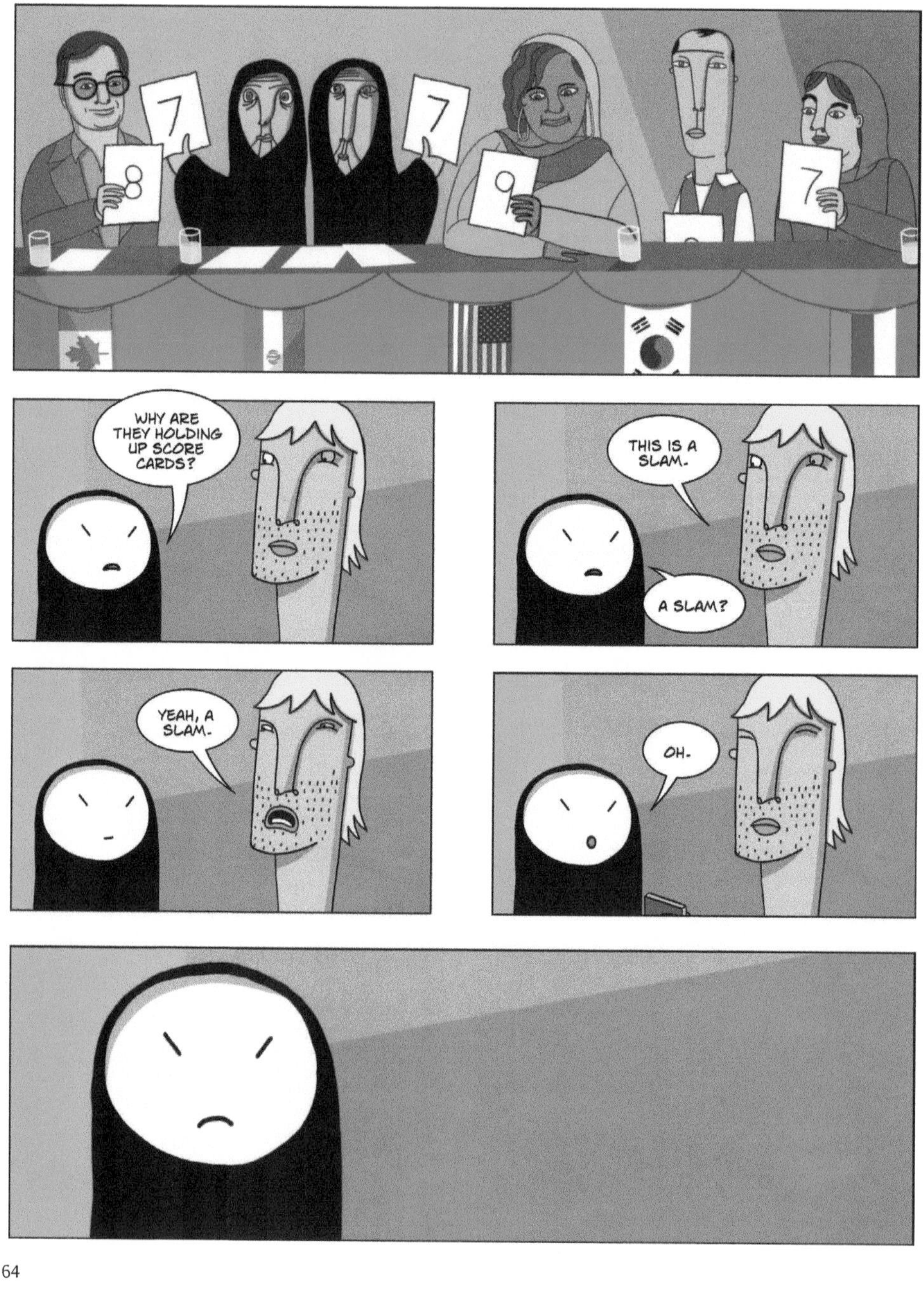

7
7
8
9
7
WHY ARE THEY HOLDING UP SCORE CARDS?
THIS IS A SLAM.
A SLAM?
YEAH, A SLAM.
OH.

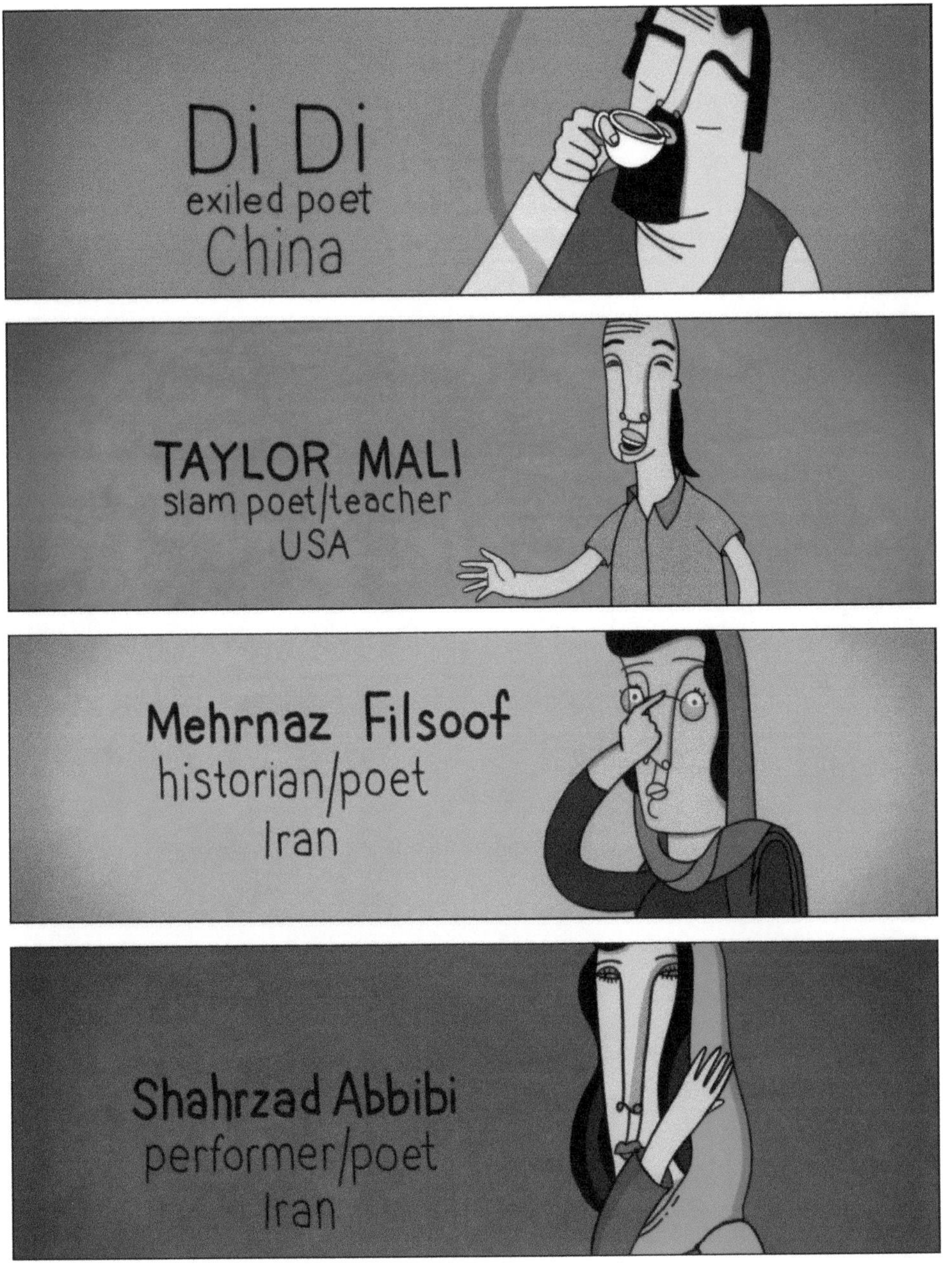

Di Di
exiled poet
China
TAYLOR MALI
slam poet/teacher
USA
Mehrnaz Filsoof
historian/poet
Iran
Shahrzad Abbibi
performer/poet
Iran

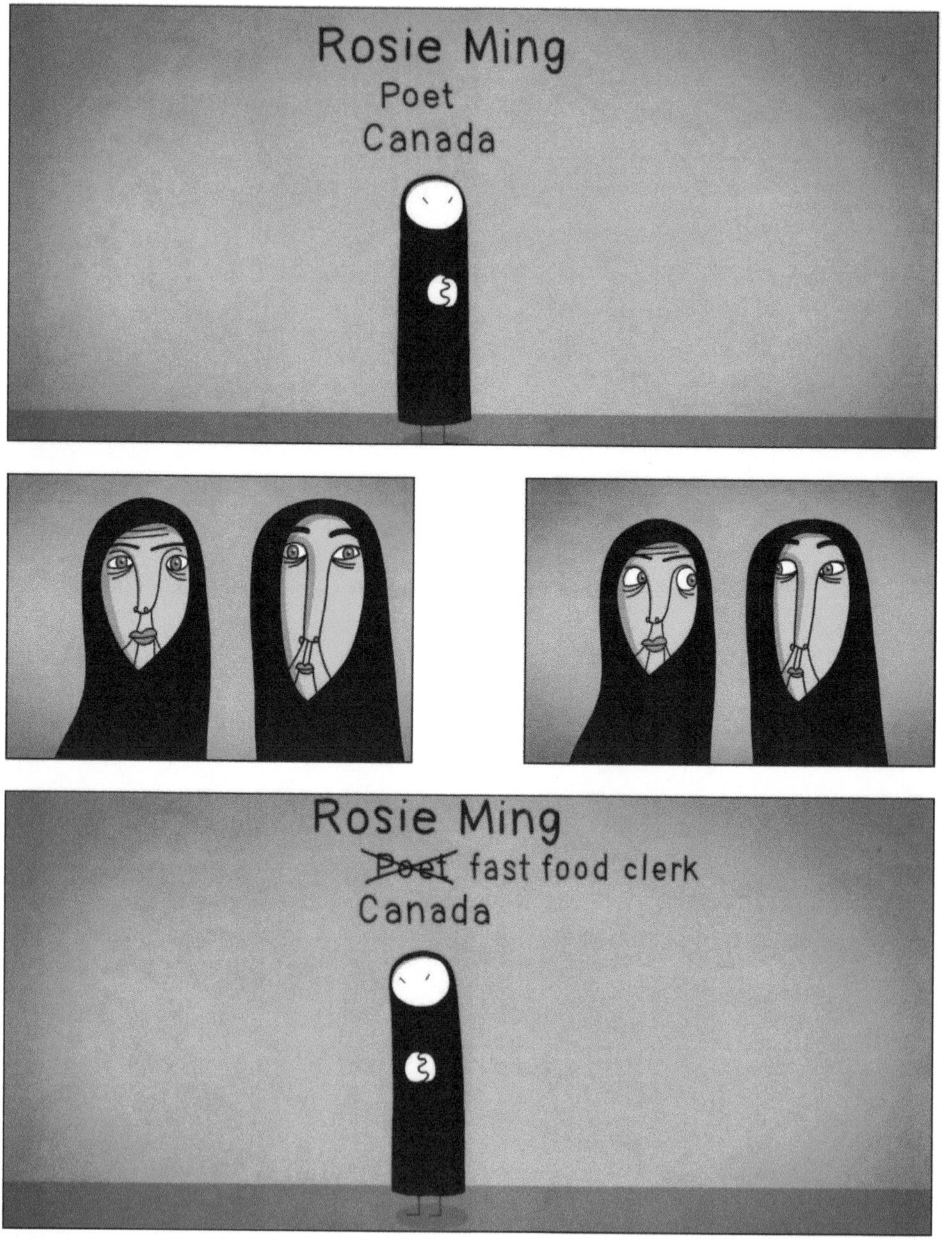
Rosie Ming
Poet
Canada
Rosie Ming
~~Poet~~ fast food clerk
Canada

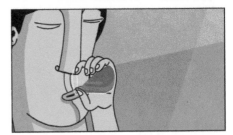

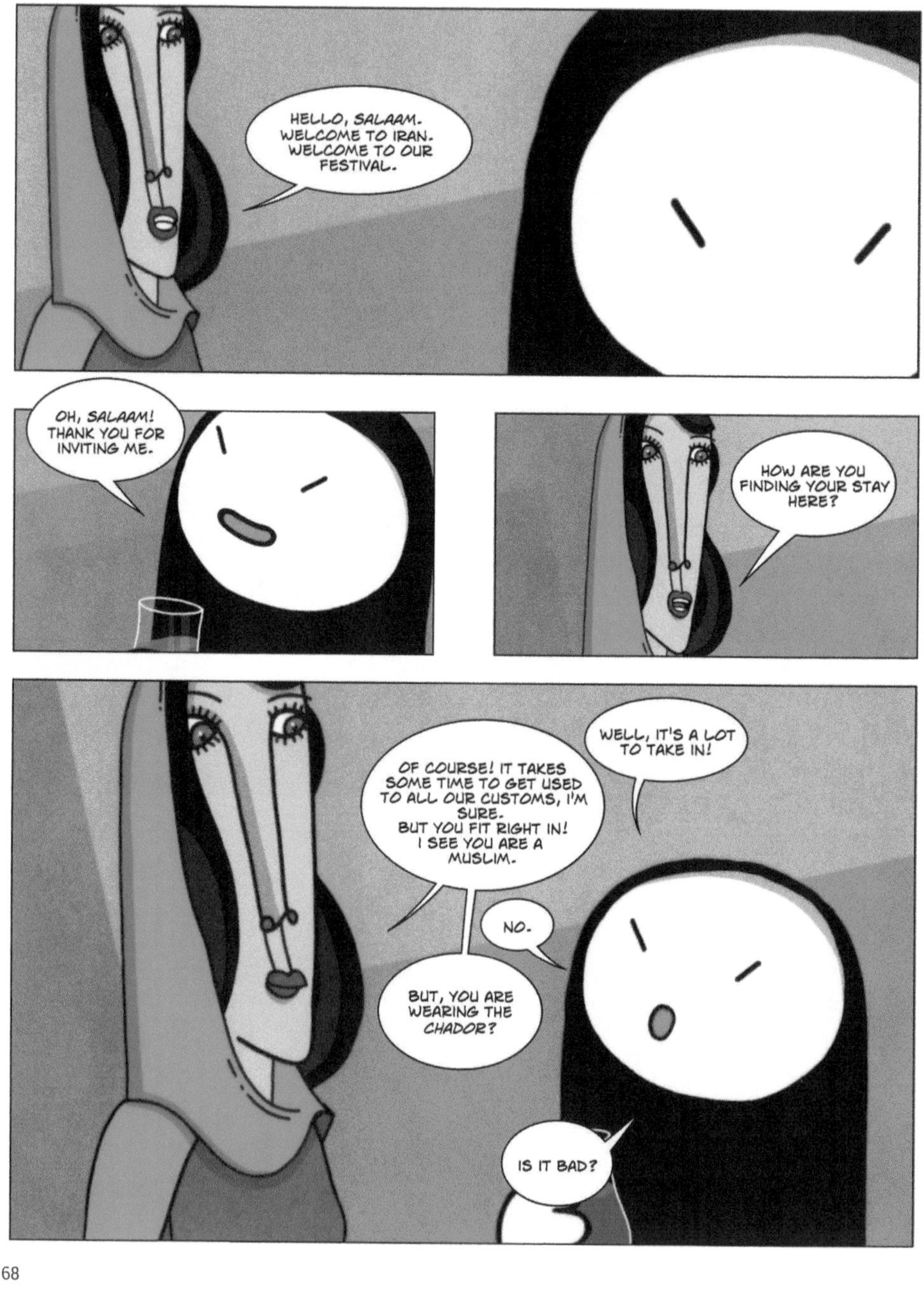
HELLO, SALAAM. WELCOME TO IRAN. WELCOME TO OUR FESTIVAL.
OH, SALAAM! THANK YOU FOR INVITING ME.
HOW ARE YOU FINDING YOUR STAY HERE?
WELL, IT'S A LOT TO TAKE IN!
OF COURSE! IT TAKES SOME TIME TO GET USED TO ALL OUR CUSTOMS, I'M SURE. BUT YOU FIT RIGHT IN! I SEE YOU ARE A MUSLIM.
NO.
BUT, YOU ARE WEARING THE CHADOR?
IS IT BAD?

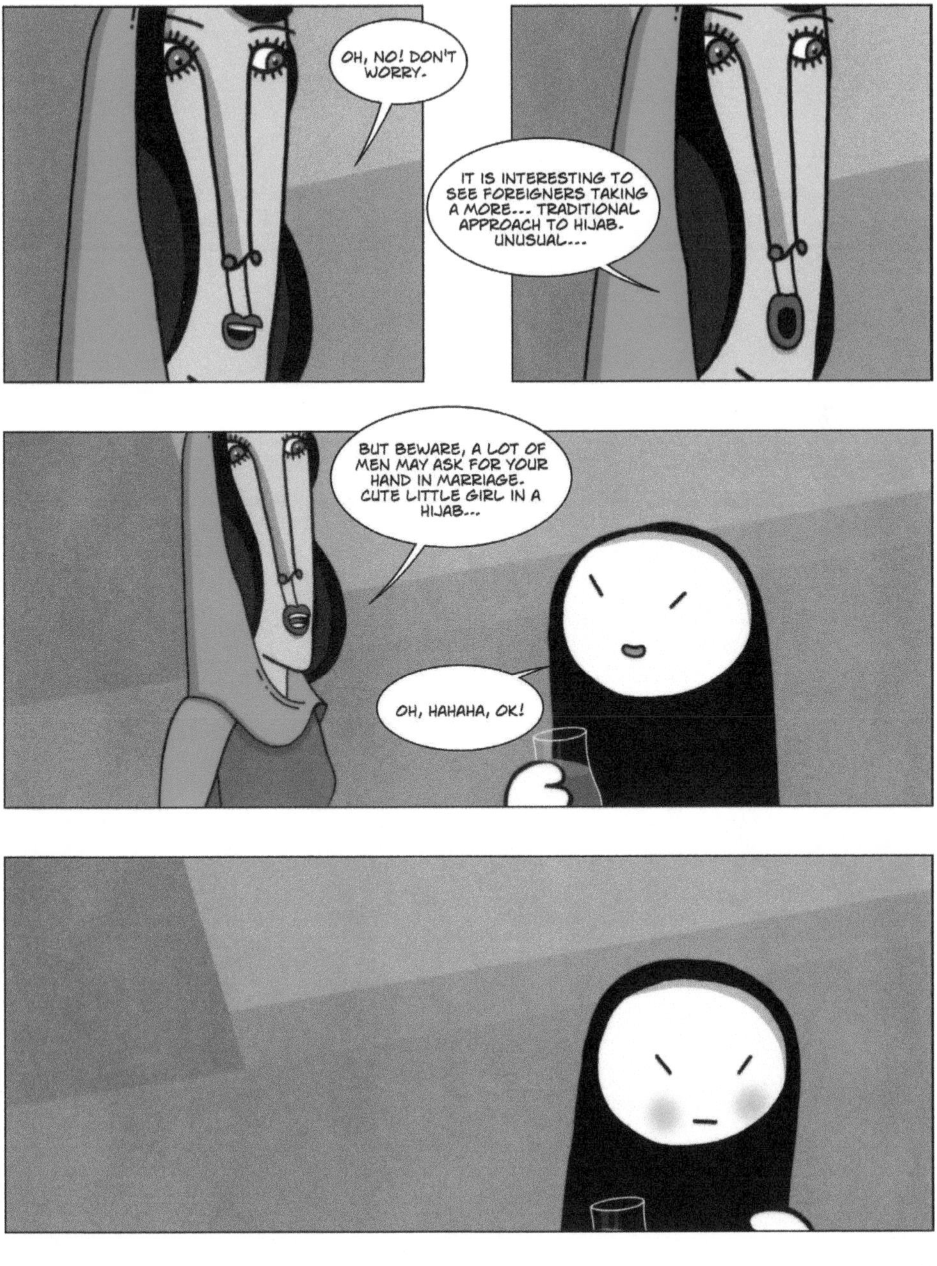
OH, NO! DON'T WORRY.
IT IS INTERESTING TO SEE FOREIGNERS TAKING A MORE... TRADITIONAL APPROACH TO HIJAB. UNUSUAL...
BUT BEWARE, A LOT OF MEN MAY ASK FOR YOUR HAND IN MARRIAGE. CUTE LITTLE GIRL IN A HIJAB...
OH, HAHAHA, OK!

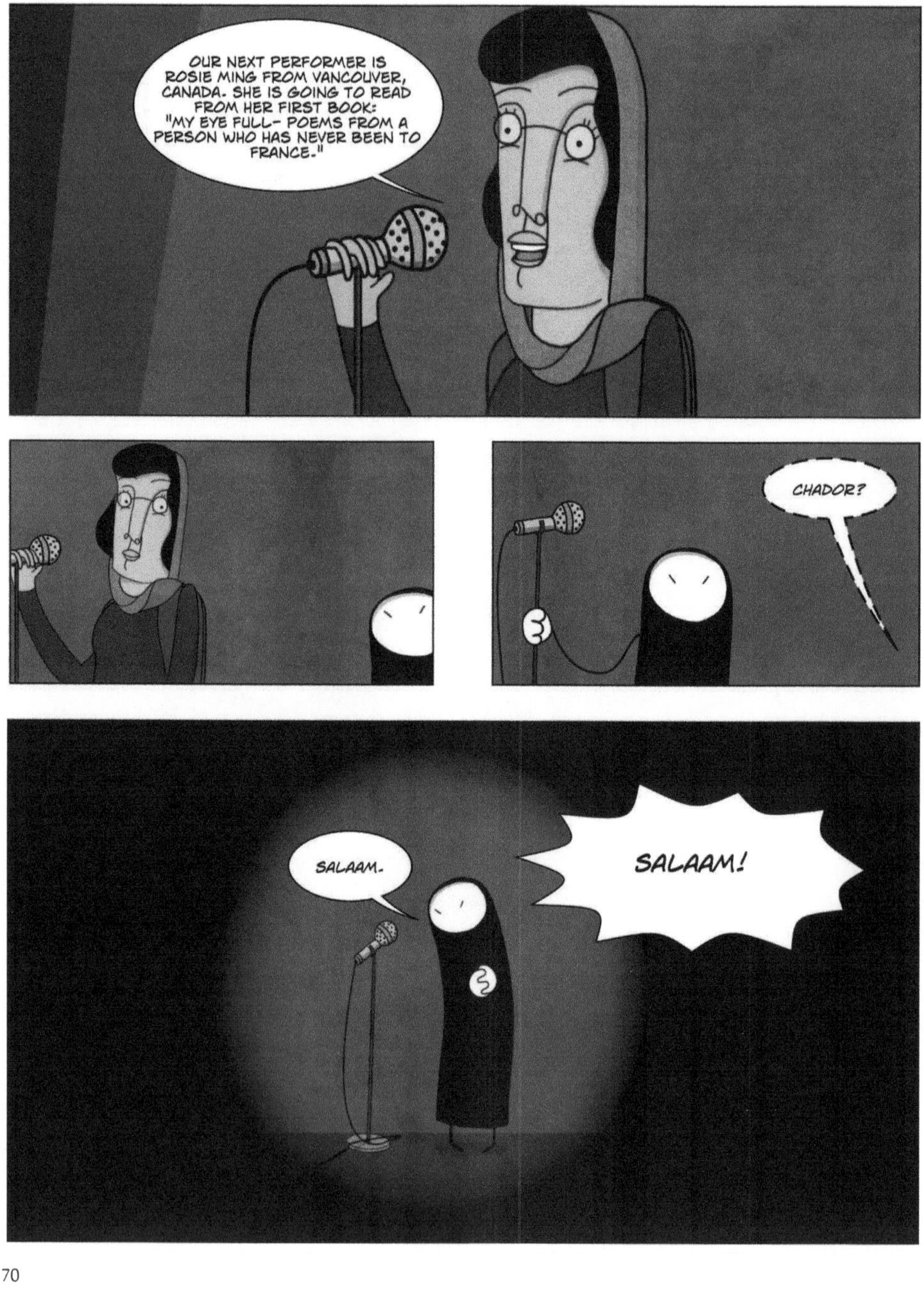
OUR NEXT PERFORMER IS ROSIE MING FROM VANCOUVER, CANADA. SHE IS GOING TO READ FROM HER FIRST BOOK: "MY EYE FULL- POEMS FROM A PERSON WHO HAS NEVER BEEN TO FRANCE."
CHADOR?
SALAAM.
SALAAM!

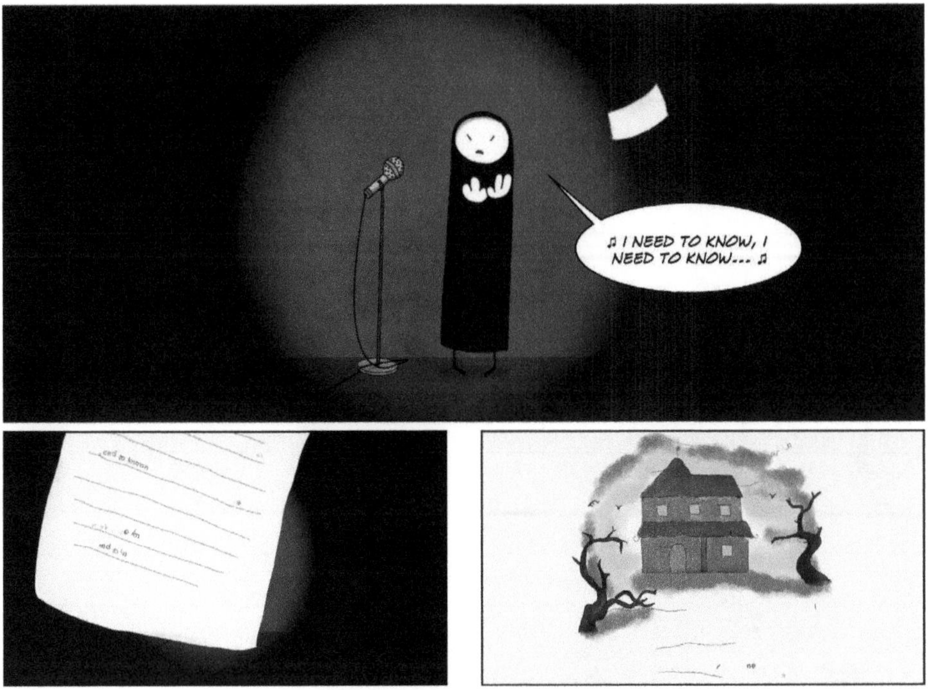
♫ I NEED TO KNOW, I NEED TO KNOW... ♫

♫... IF YOU NEED A HOUSE LIKE EDGAR ALLAN POE... ♫

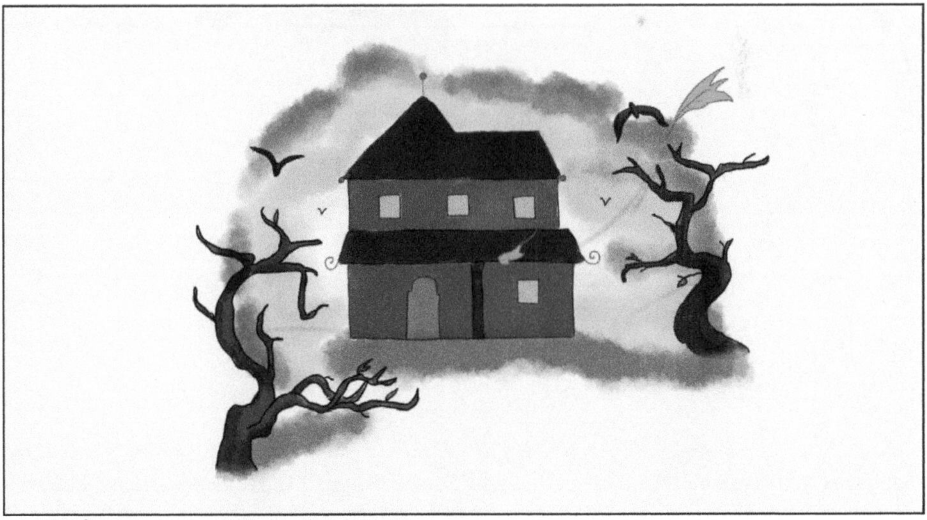

* ROSIE'S POEM ILLUSTRATED BY JANET PERLMAN

... THERE'S A WHITE PICKET FENCE LIKE THE ONE YOU SWORE YOU'D NEVER HAVE. ♫

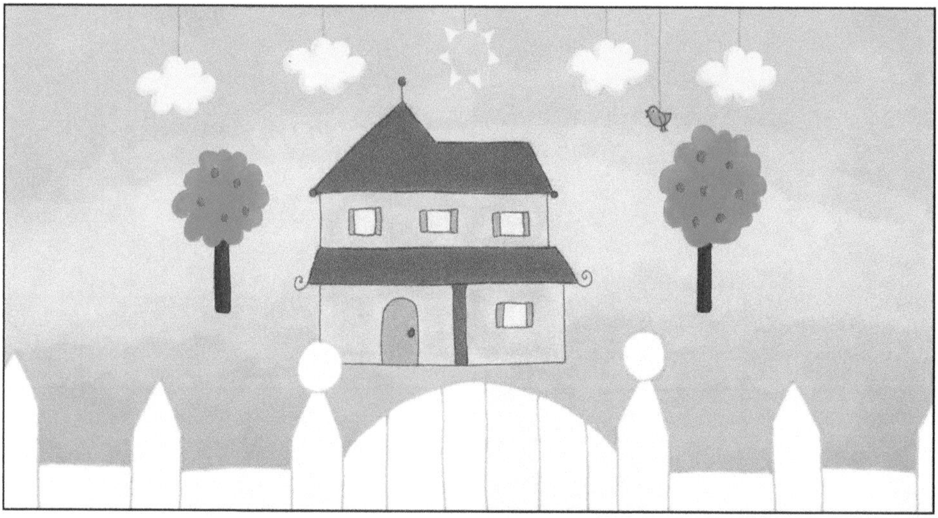

♫ A GARDEN THAT NEEDS TENDING...

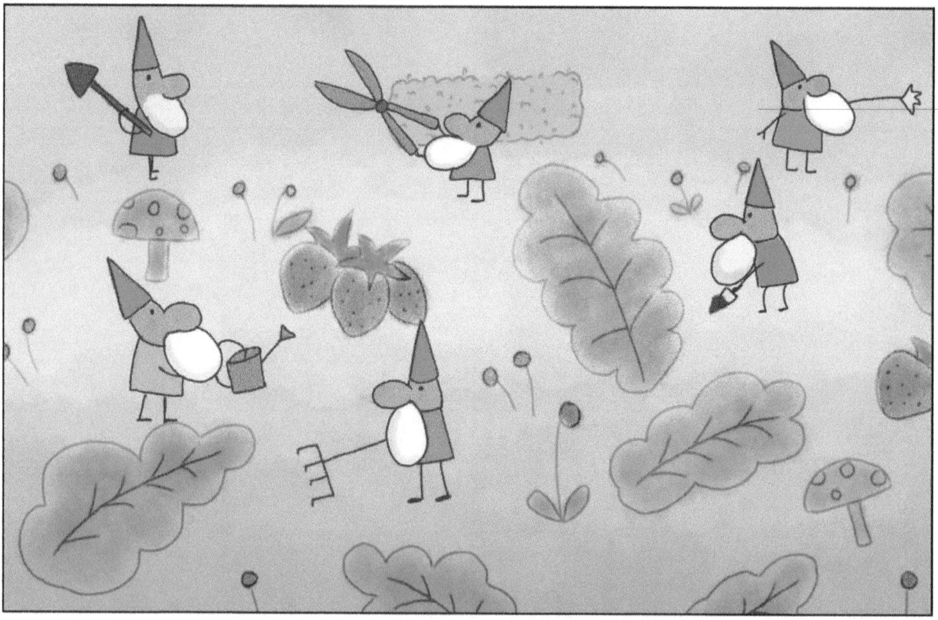

... AND A TRIMMED HEDGE, WAIST HIGH... ♫

♫ A FARMHOUSE WITH A ROCKING CHAIR...

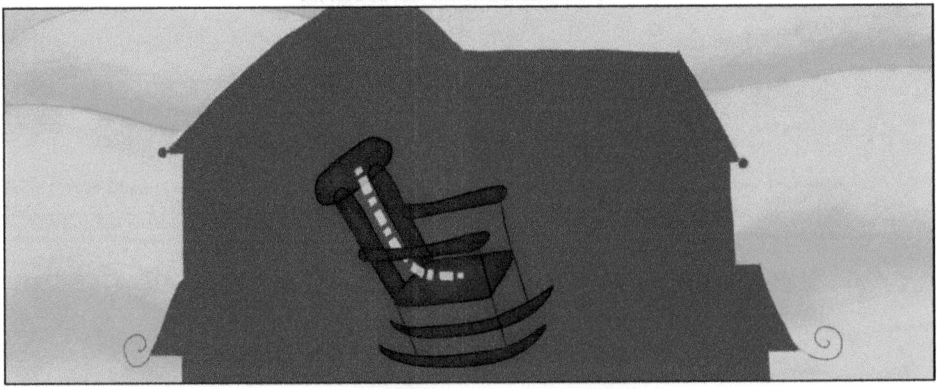

... THAT SENDS CHILLS UP MAGRITTE'S SPINE ♫

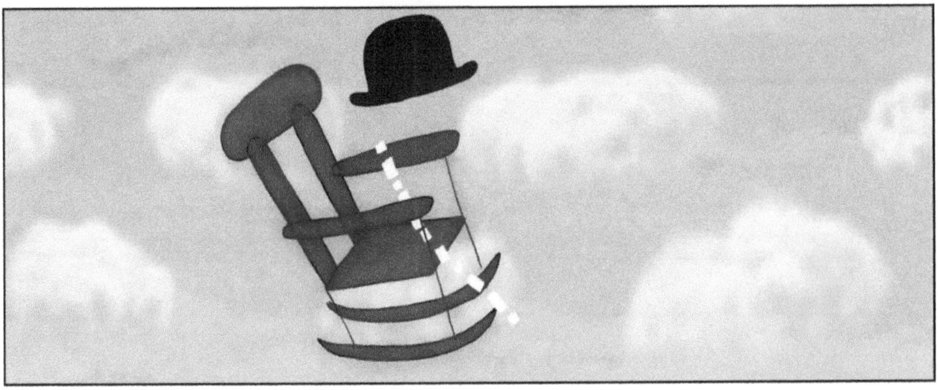

... WHEN HE TOUCHED THE RIGHT ARM
THE FRENCH... ARE SO SENSITIVE! ♫

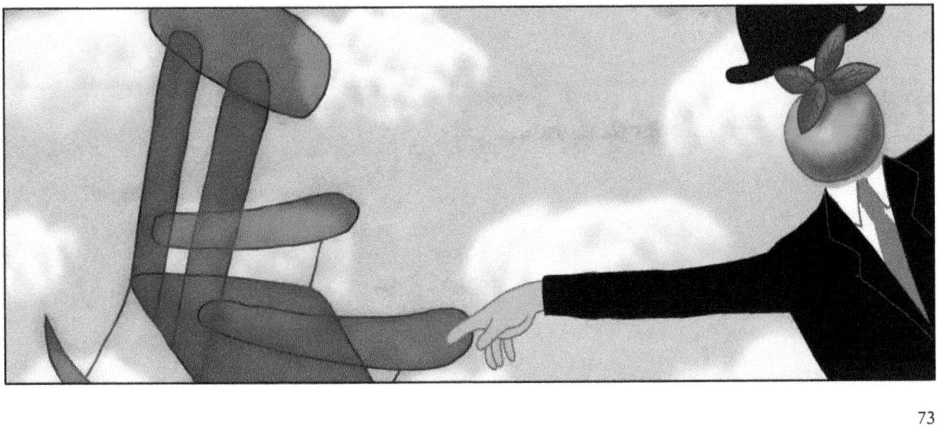

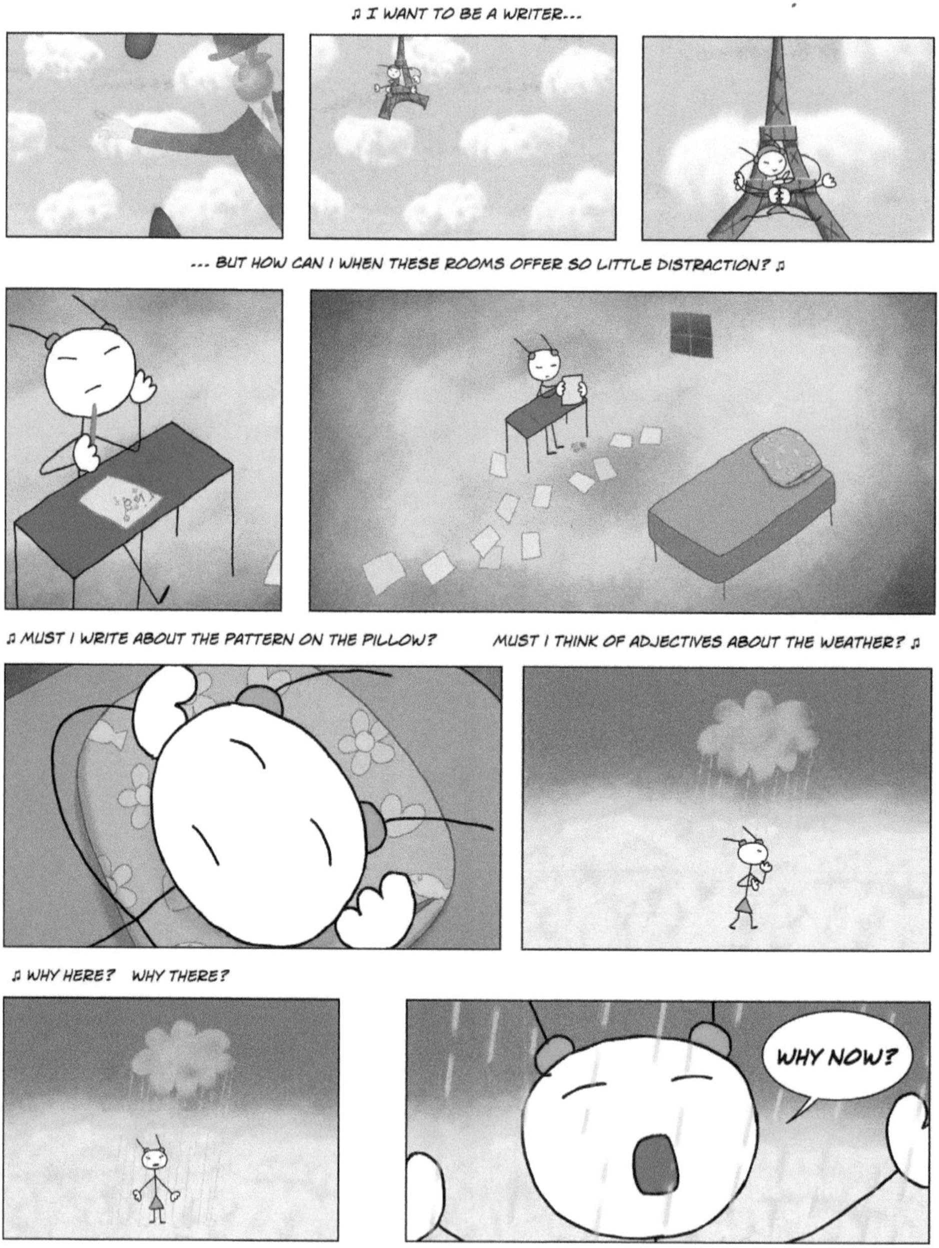
♫ I WANT TO BE A WRITER...
... BUT HOW CAN I WHEN THESE ROOMS OFFER SO LITTLE DISTRACTION? ♫
♫ MUST I WRITE ABOUT THE PATTERN ON THE PILLOW?
MUST I THINK OF ADJECTIVES ABOUT THE WEATHER? ♫
♫ WHY HERE? WHY THERE?
WHY NOW?

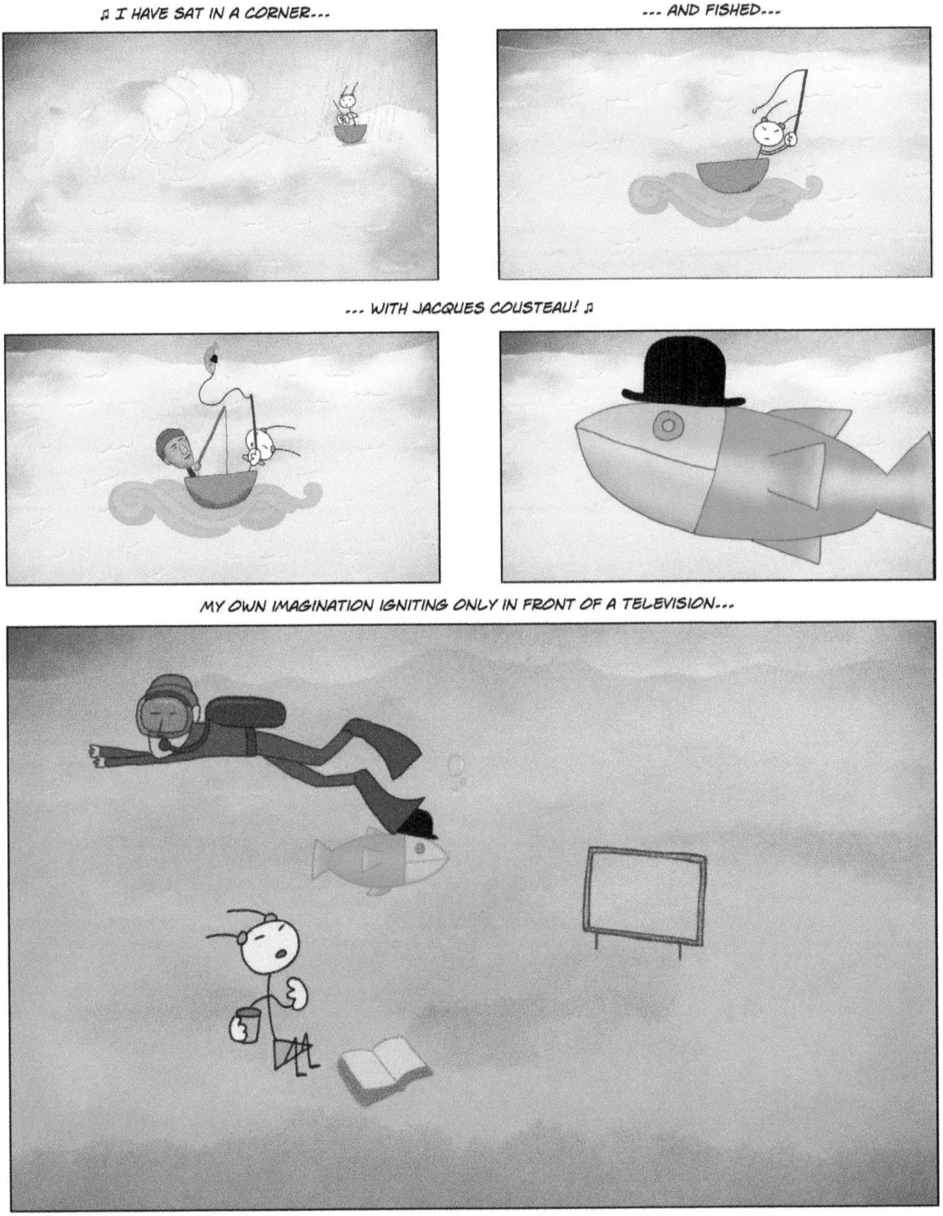
♫ I HAVE SAT IN A CORNER...
... AND FISHED...
... WITH JACQUES COUSTEAU! ♫
MY OWN IMAGINATION IGNITING ONLY IN FRONT OF A TELEVISION...
... OR HOVERING ABOVE A BOOK. ♫

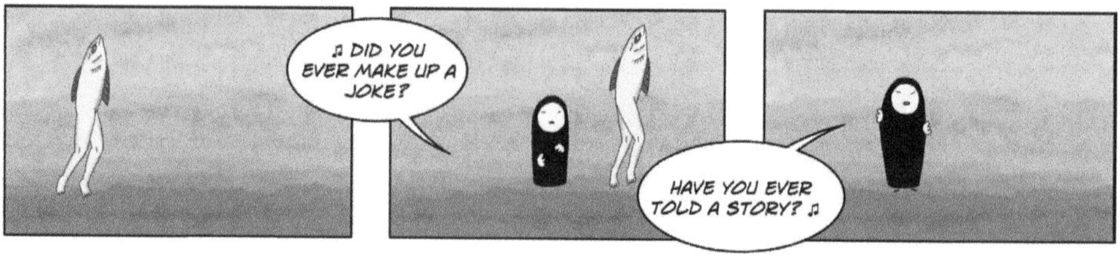
♫ DID YOU EVER MAKE UP A JOKE?
HAVE YOU EVER TOLD A STORY? ♫

I SAW A PICTURE.
IT SPOKE TO ME OF A THOUSAND WORDS.

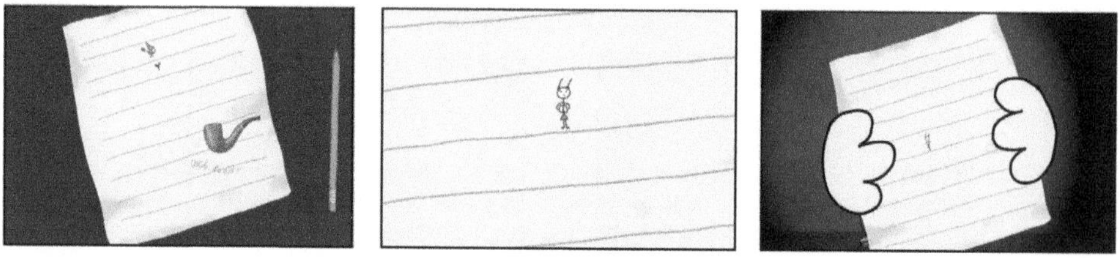

THEY WERE NOT MINE.

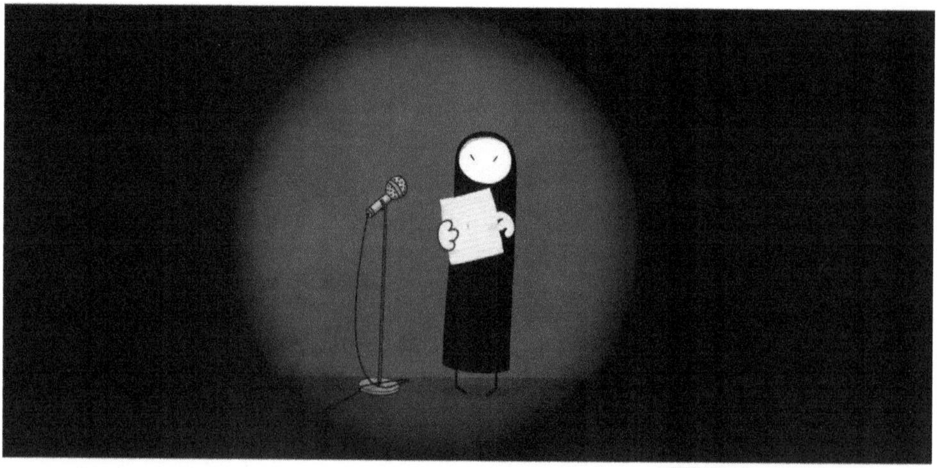

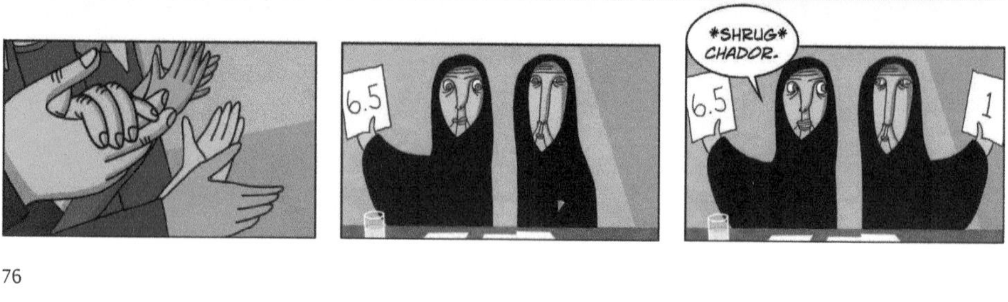
6.5
6.5
SHRUG CHADOR.
1

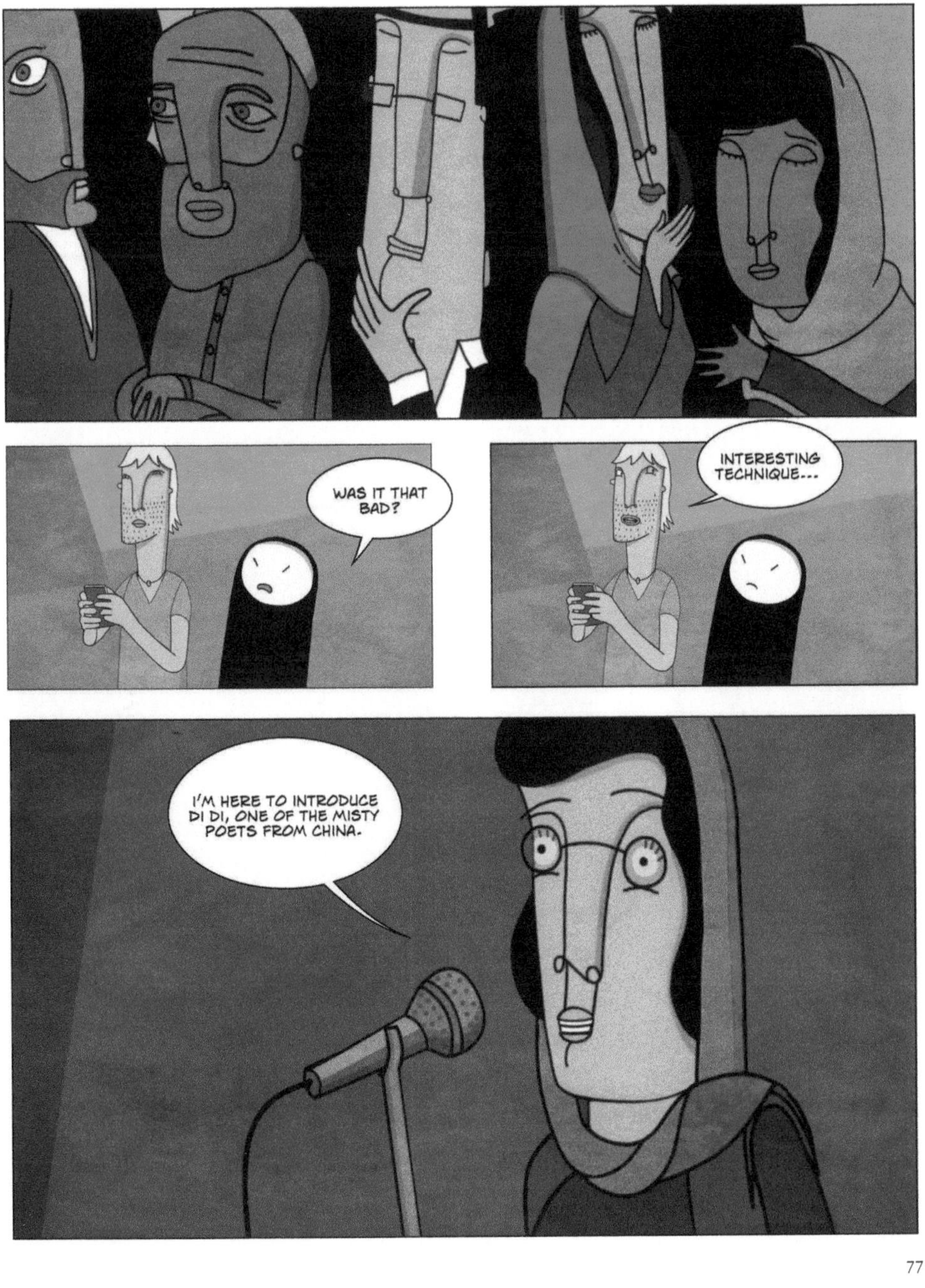
WAS IT THAT BAD?
INTERESTING TECHNIQUE...
I'M HERE TO INTRODUCE DI DI, ONE OF THE MISTY POETS FROM CHINA.

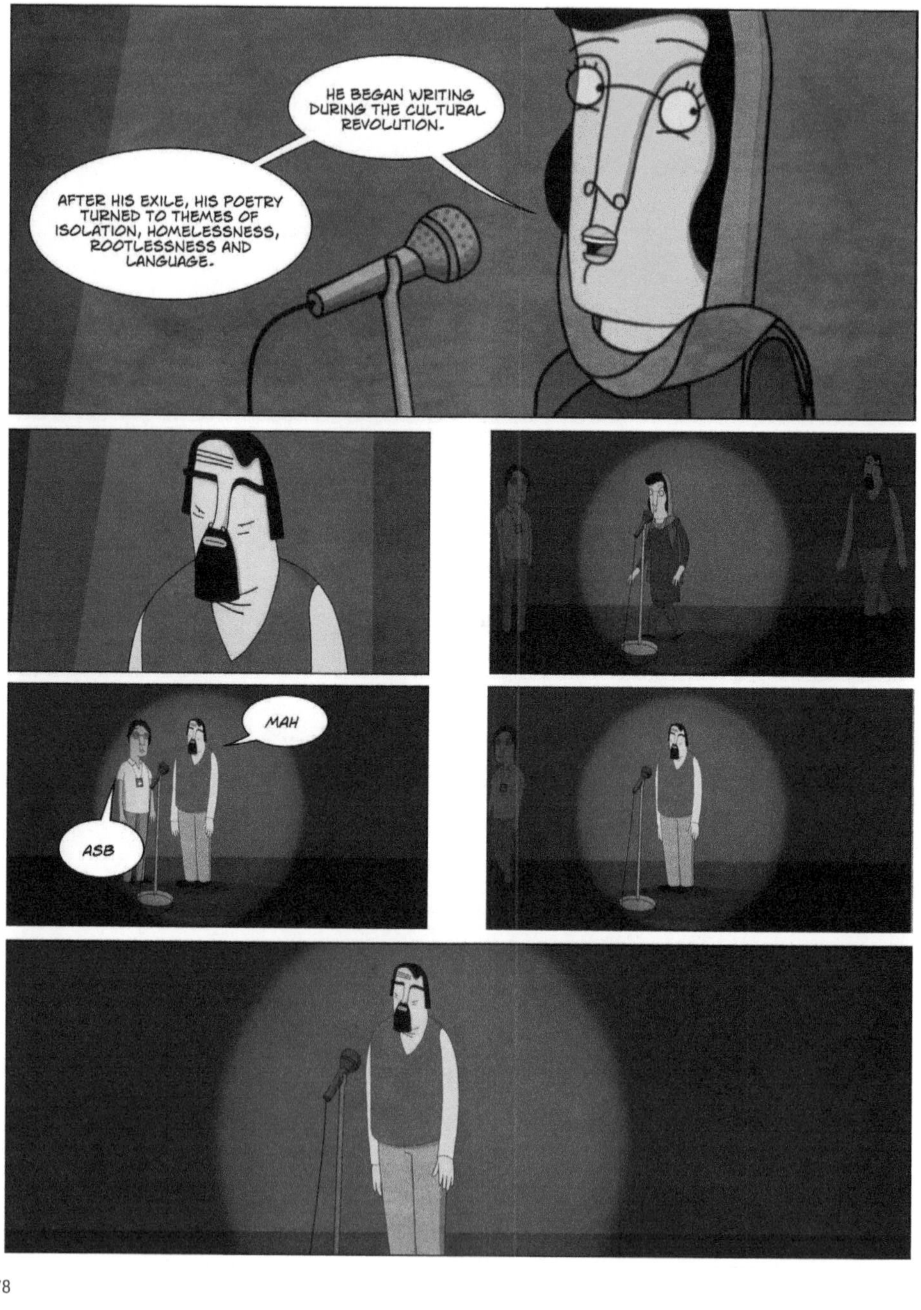
HE BEGAN WRITING DURING THE CULTURAL REVOLUTION.
AFTER HIS EXILE, HIS POETRY TURNED TO THEMES OF ISOLATION, HOMELESSNESS, ROOTLESSNESS AND LANGUAGE.
MAH
ASB

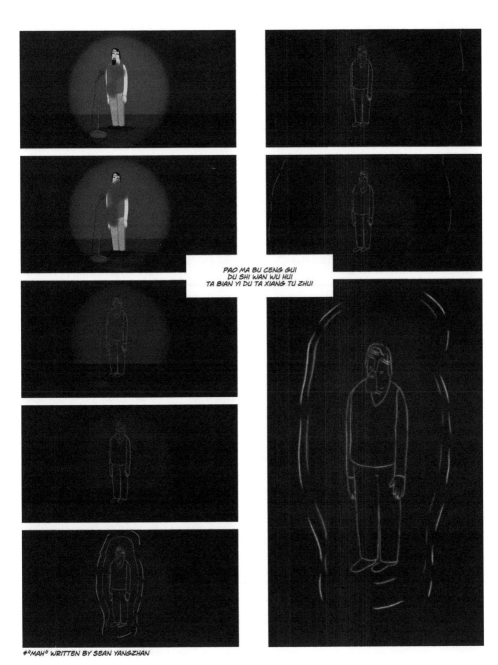

PAO MA BU CENG GUI
DU SHI WAN WU HUI
TA BIAN YI DU TA XIANG TU ZHUI

#"MAH" WRITTEN BY SEAN YANGZHAN

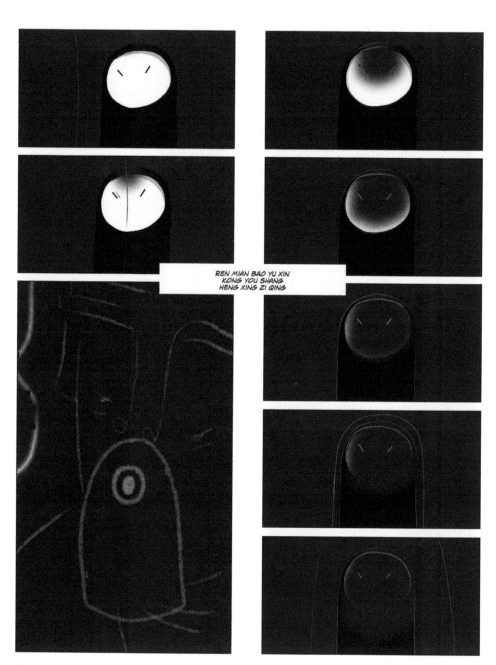

REN MIAN BAO YU XIN
KONG YOU SHANG
HENG XING ZI QING

JIN TIAN, WO KEN JIN LEF QIN DE YA
TAZI DALING YEG NU HI
TAZI YEN DOY FEN CIDAN.

ASB, BAR POSHTE ASB, BEDONE BARGASHT...
9
10

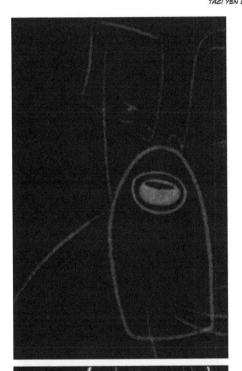

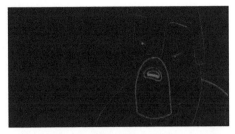

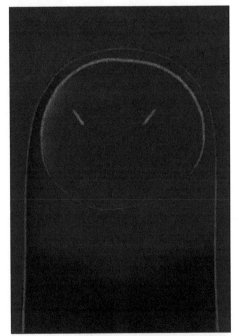

* THE FARSI TRANSLATION

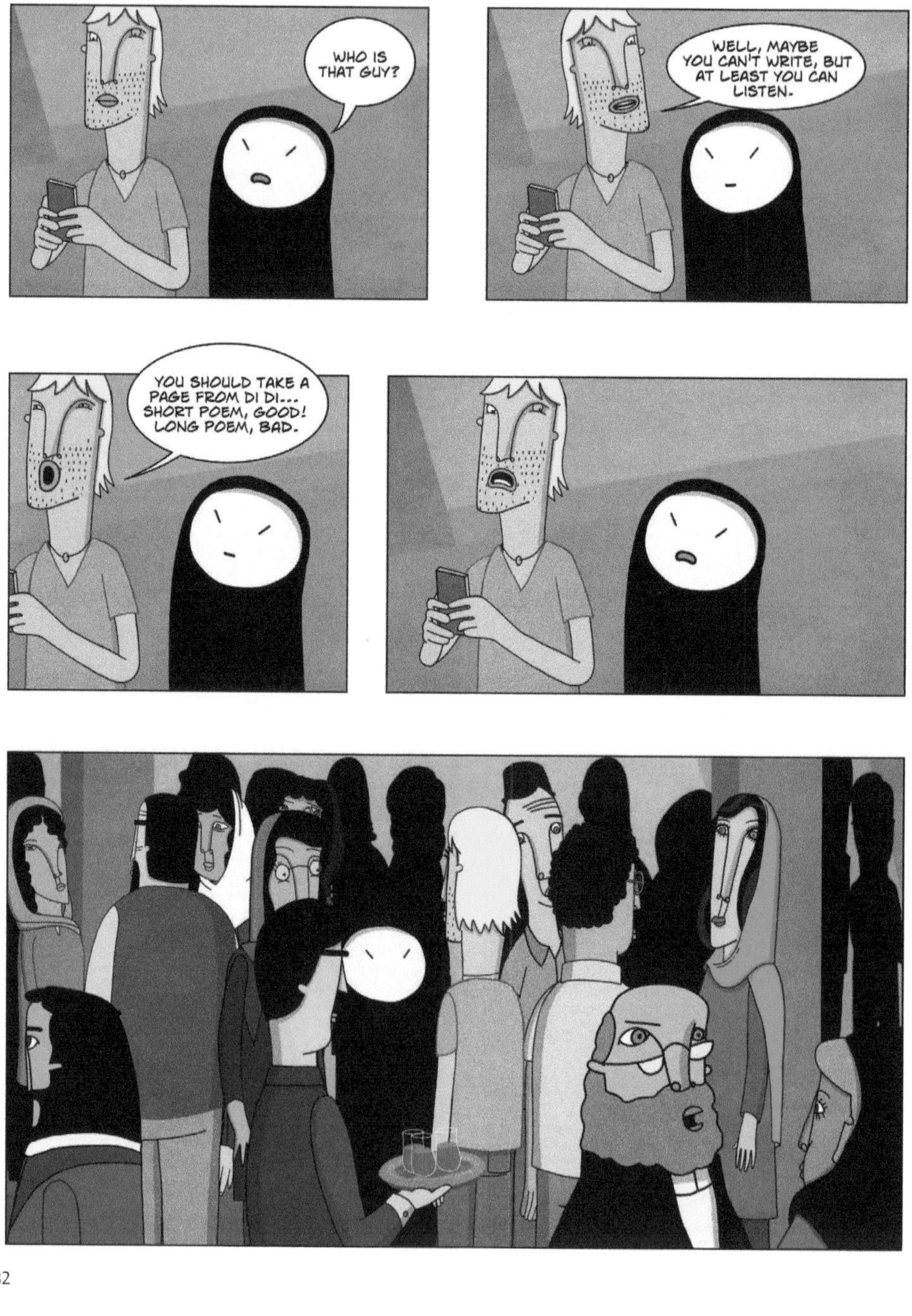

WHO IS THAT GUY?
WELL, MAYBE YOU CAN'T WRITE, BUT AT LEAST YOU CAN LISTEN.
YOU SHOULD TAKE A PAGE FROM DI DI... SHORT POEM, GOOD! LONG POEM, BAD.

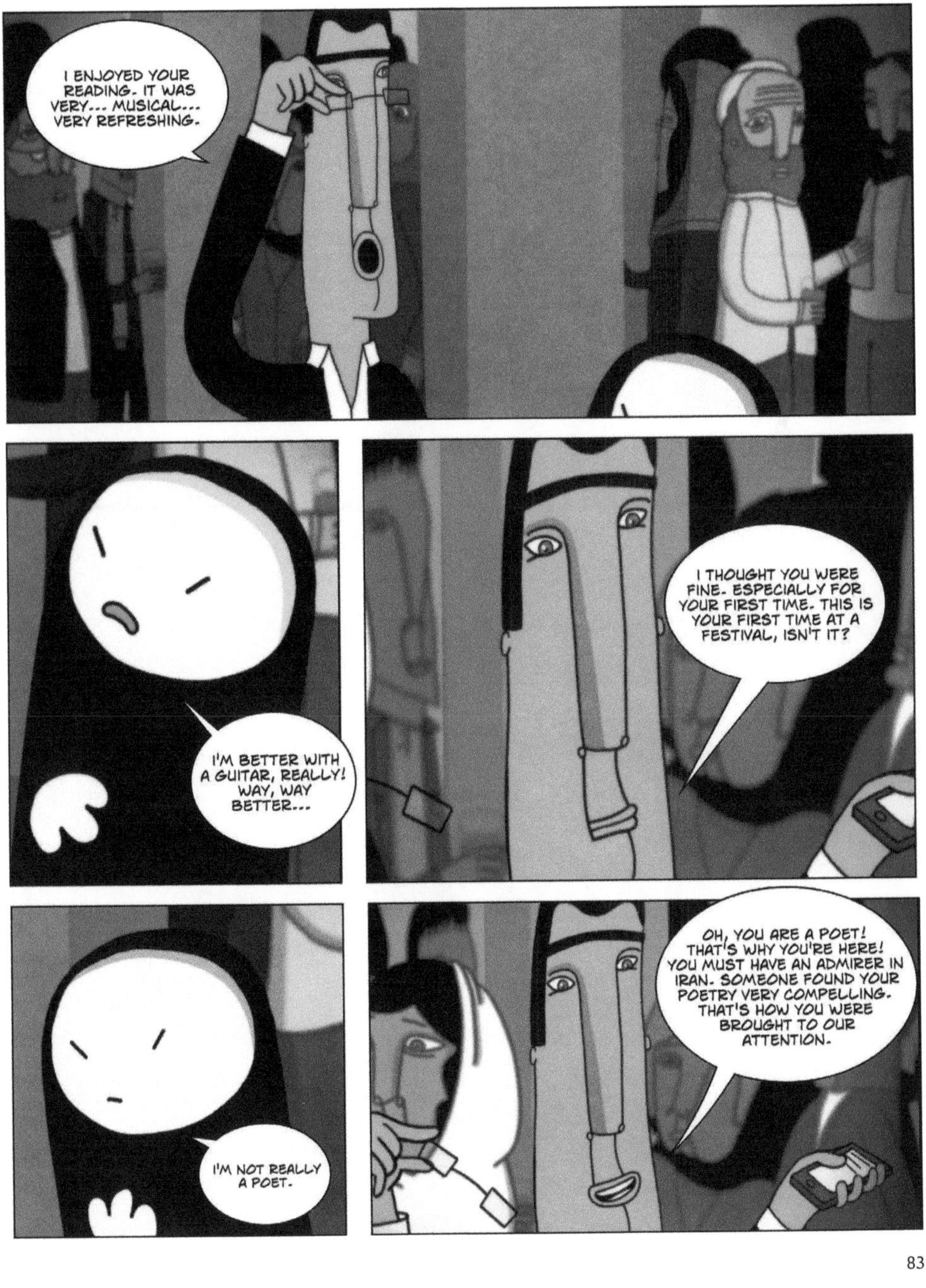
I ENJOYED YOUR READING. IT WAS VERY... MUSICAL... VERY REFRESHING.
I'M BETTER WITH A GUITAR, REALLY! WAY, WAY BETTER...
I THOUGHT YOU WERE FINE. ESPECIALLY FOR YOUR FIRST TIME. THIS IS YOUR FIRST TIME AT A FESTIVAL, ISN'T IT?
I'M NOT REALLY A POET.
OH, YOU ARE A POET! THAT'S WHY YOU'RE HERE! YOU MUST HAVE AN ADMIRER IN IRAN. SOMEONE FOUND YOUR POETRY VERY COMPELLING. THAT'S HOW YOU WERE BROUGHT TO OUR ATTENTION.

I ONLY GOT A 1.

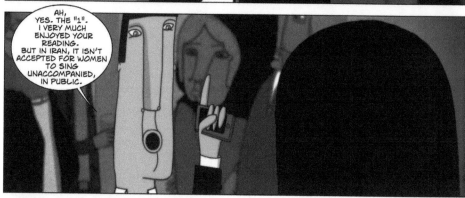

AH, YES. THE "1". I VERY MUCH ENJOYED YOUR READING. BUT IN IRAN, IT ISN'T ACCEPTED FOR WOMEN TO SING UNACCOMPANIED, IN PUBLIC.

IT'S TOO... PROVOCATVE...

NO, NO! DON'T BE EMBARRASSED. HOW COULD YOU KNOW?

I THINK THEY GET CARRIED AWAY BECAUSE THIS IS ONE PLACE IN IRAN WHERE THEIR FULL VOTE COUNTS...

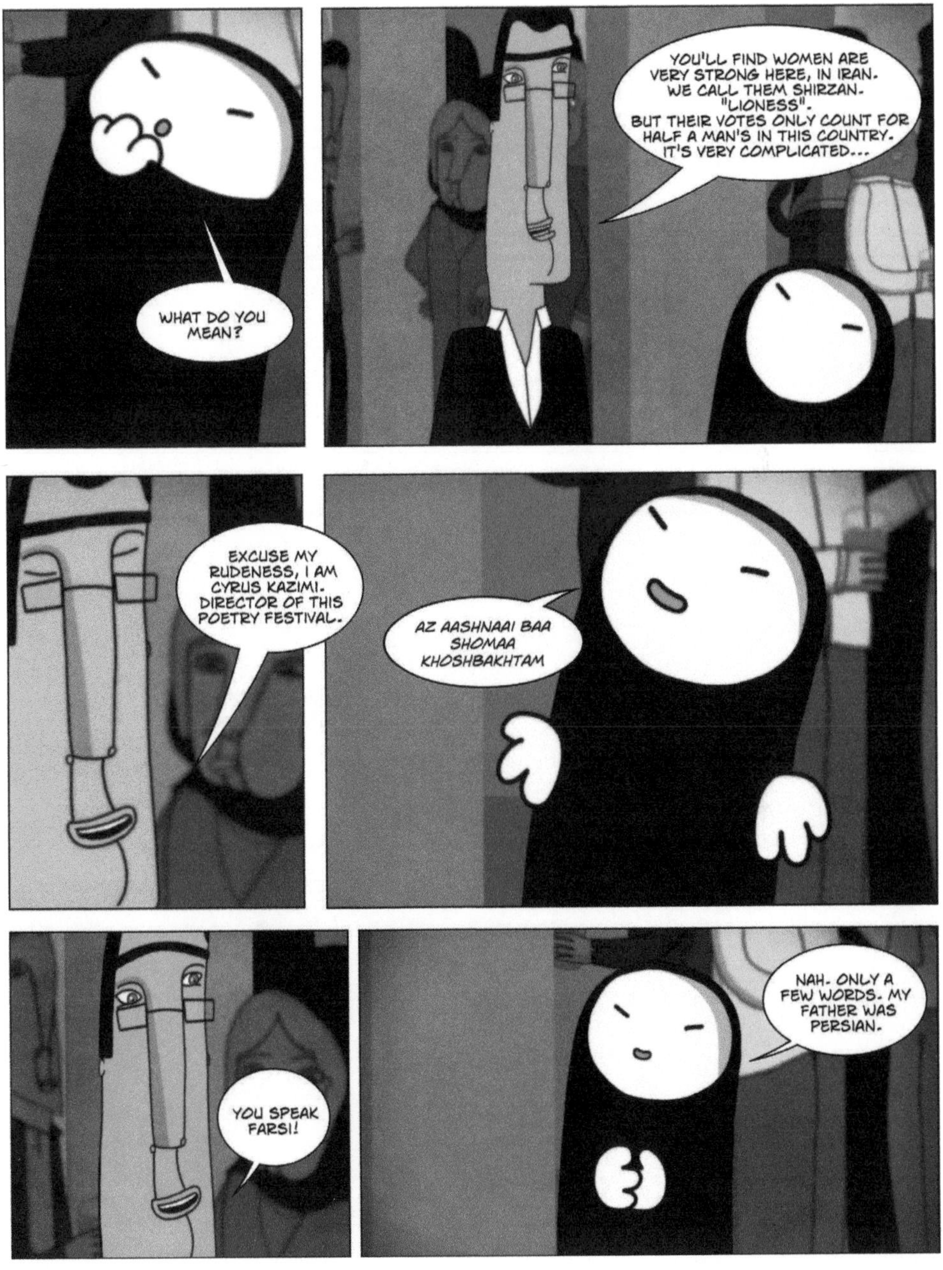
WHAT DO YOU MEAN?
YOU'LL FIND WOMEN ARE VERY STRONG HERE, IN IRAN. WE CALL THEM SHIRZAN- "LIONESS". BUT THEIR VOTES ONLY COUNT FOR HALF A MAN'S IN THIS COUNTRY. IT'S VERY COMPLICATED...
EXCUSE MY RUDENESS, I AM CYRUS KAZIMI. DIRECTOR OF THIS POETRY FESTIVAL.
AZ AASHNAAI BAA SHOMAA KHOSHBAKHTAM
YOU SPEAK FARSI!
NAH. ONLY A FEW WORDS. MY FATHER WAS PERSIAN.

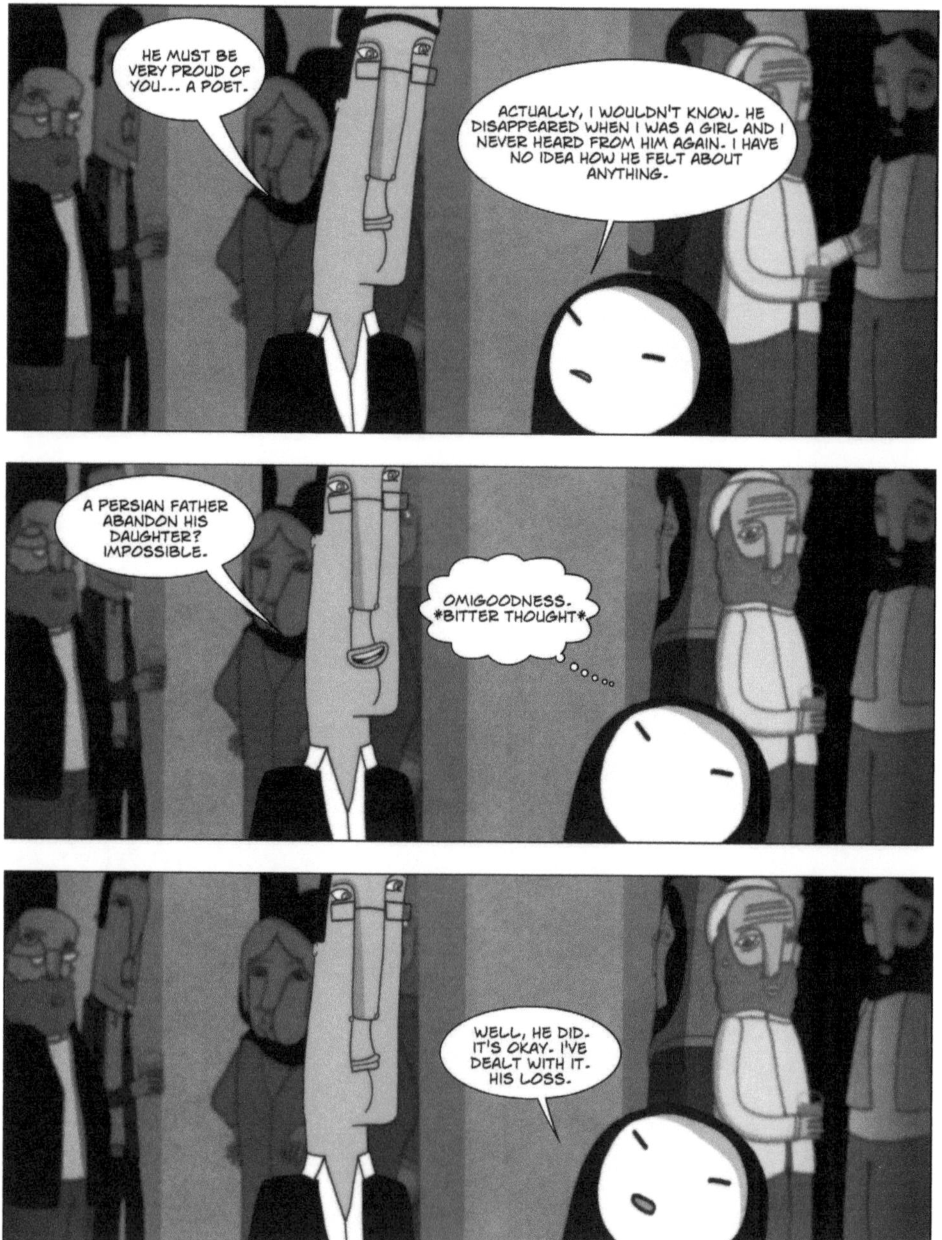
HE MUST BE VERY PROUD OF YOU... A POET.
ACTUALLY, I WOULDN'T KNOW. HE DISAPPEARED WHEN I WAS A GIRL AND I NEVER HEARD FROM HIM AGAIN. I HAVE NO IDEA HOW HE FELT ABOUT ANYTHING.
A PERSIAN FATHER ABANDON HIS DAUGHTER? IMPOSSIBLE.
OMIGOODNESS. *BITTER THOUGHT*
WELL, HE DID. IT'S OKAY. I'VE DEALT WITH IT. HIS LOSS.

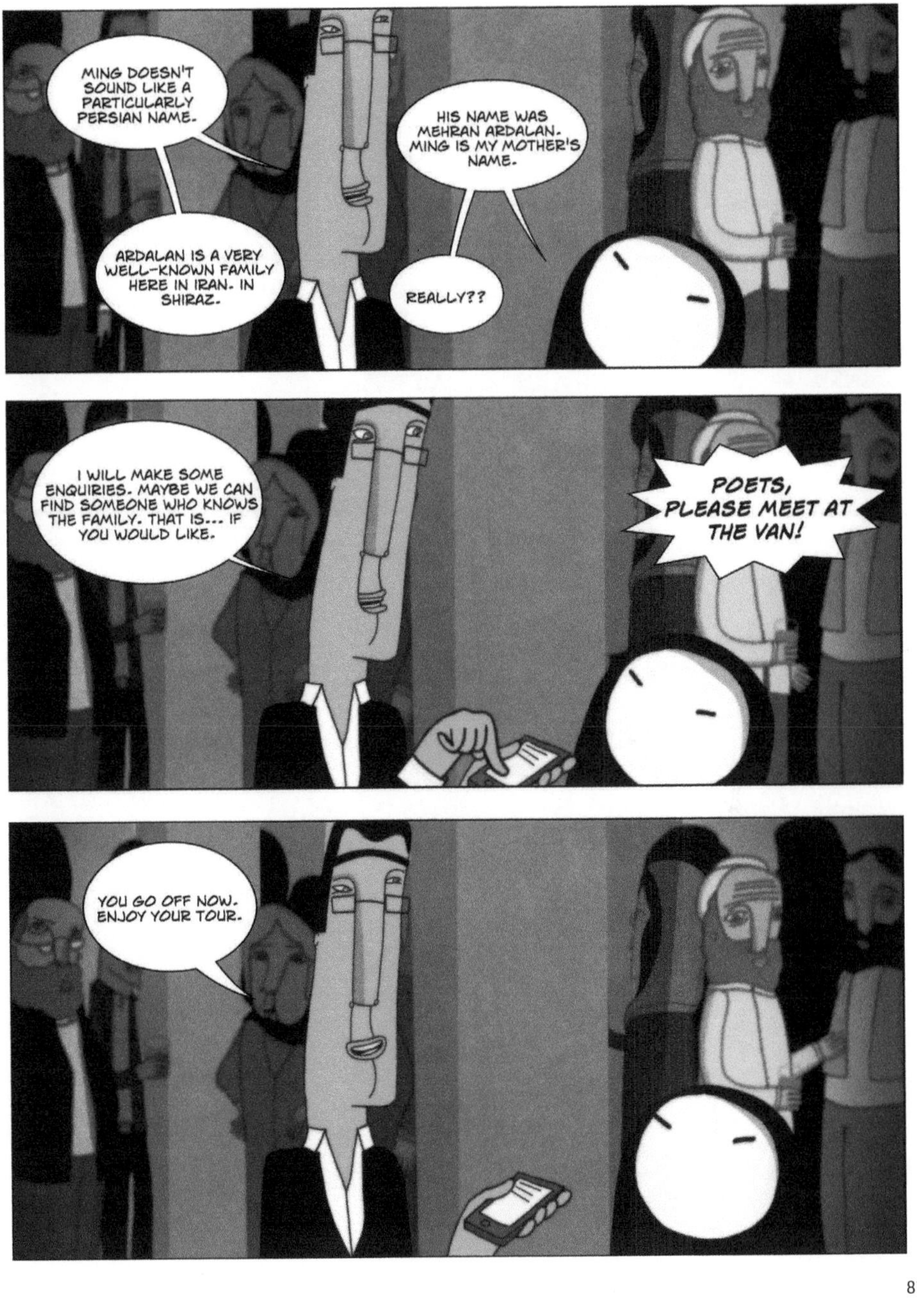

MING DOESN'T SOUND LIKE A PARTICULARLY PERSIAN NAME.
HIS NAME WAS MEHRAN ARDALAN. MING IS MY MOTHER'S NAME.
ARDALAN IS A VERY WELL-KNOWN FAMILY HERE IN IRAN. IN SHIRAZ.
REALLY??
I WILL MAKE SOME ENQUIRIES. MAYBE WE CAN FIND SOMEONE WHO KNOWS THE FAMILY. THAT IS... IF YOU WOULD LIKE.
POETS, PLEASE MEET AT THE VAN!
YOU GO OFF NOW. ENJOY YOUR TOUR.

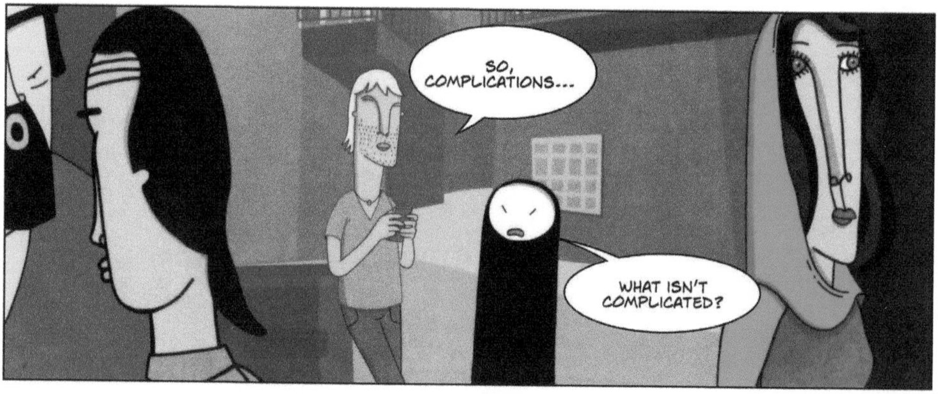
SO, COMPLICATIONS...
WHAT ISN'T COMPLICATED?

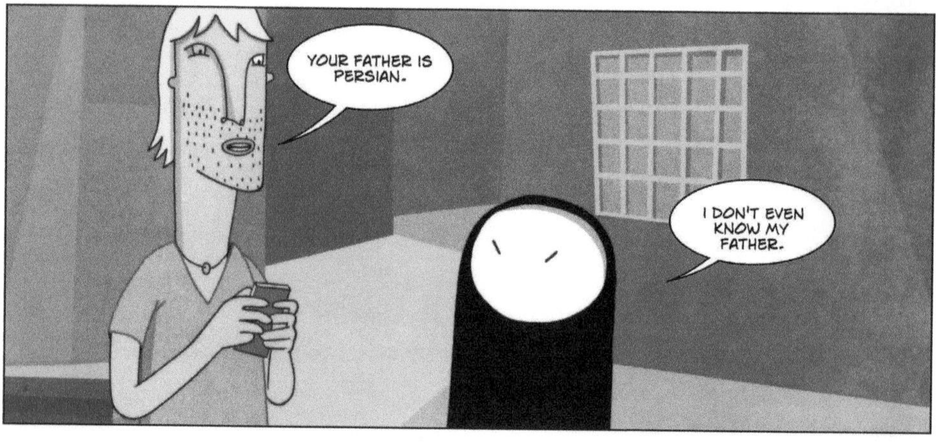
YOUR FATHER IS PERSIAN.
I DON'T EVEN KNOW MY FATHER.

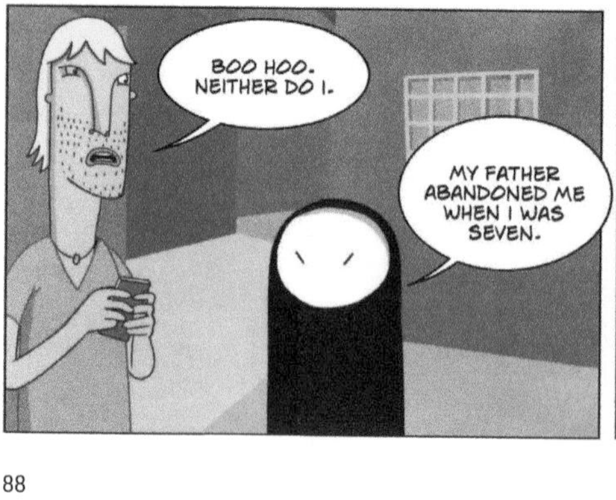
BOO HOO. NEITHER DO I.
MY FATHER ABANDONED ME WHEN I WAS SEVEN.

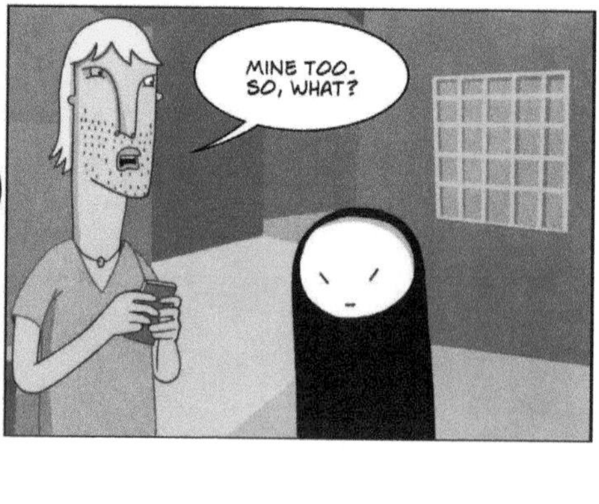
MINE TOO. SO, WHAT?

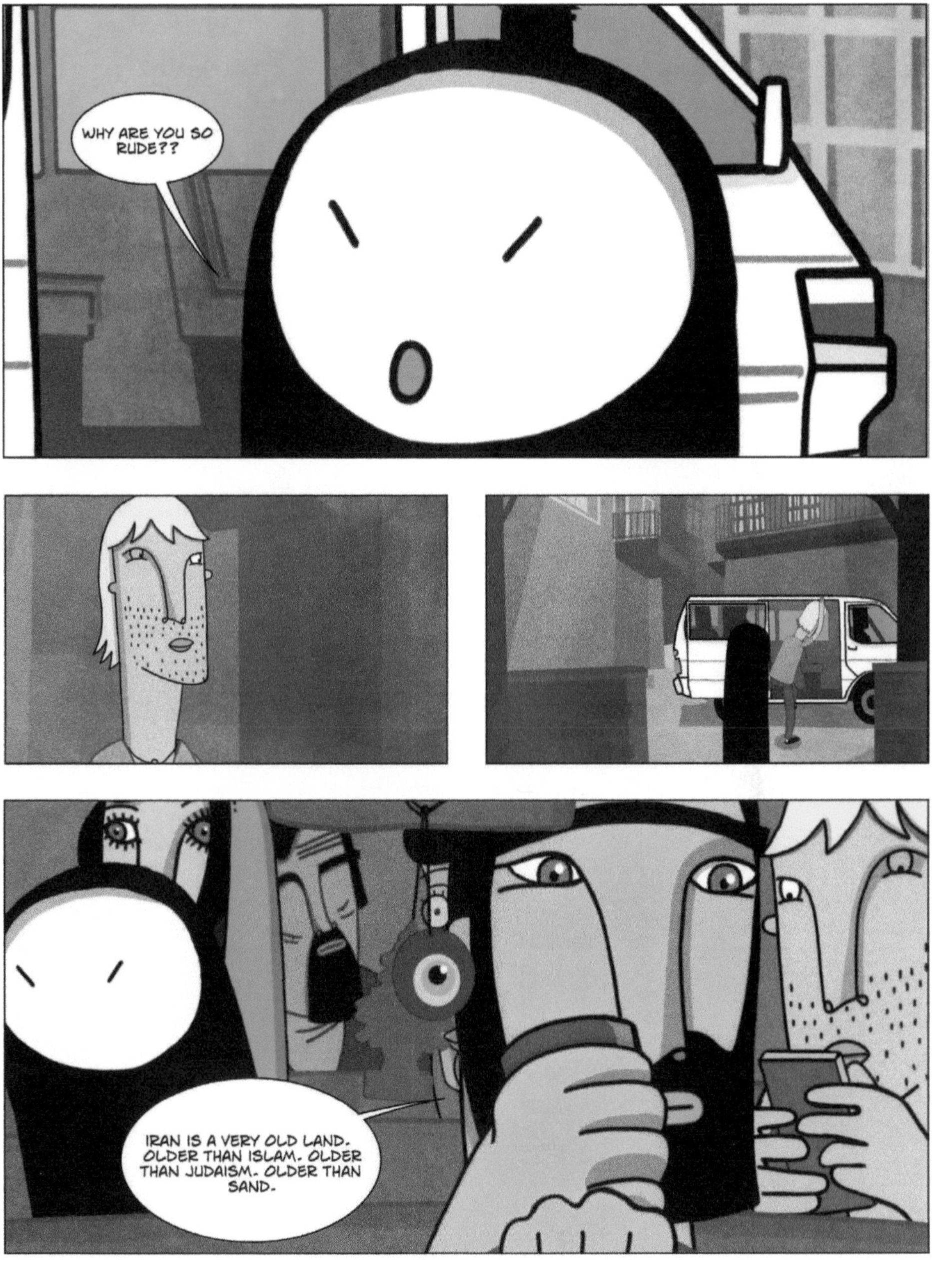
WHY ARE YOU SO RUDE??
IRAN IS A VERY OLD LAND. OLDER THAN ISLAM. OLDER THAN JUDAISM. OLDER THAN SAND.

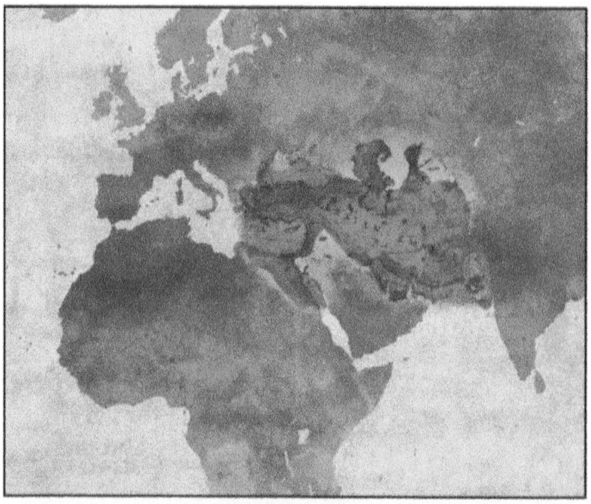

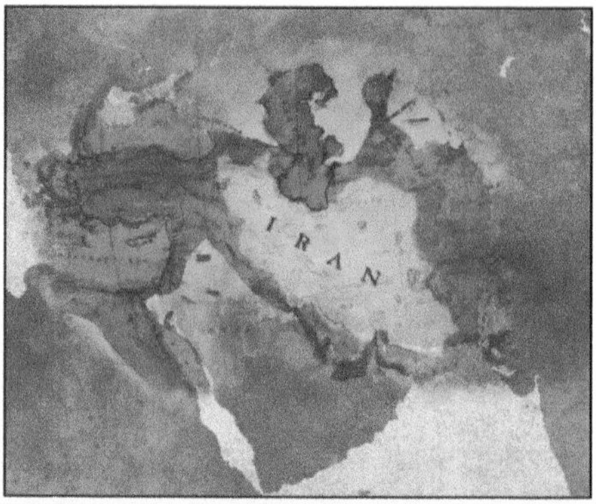
IRAN

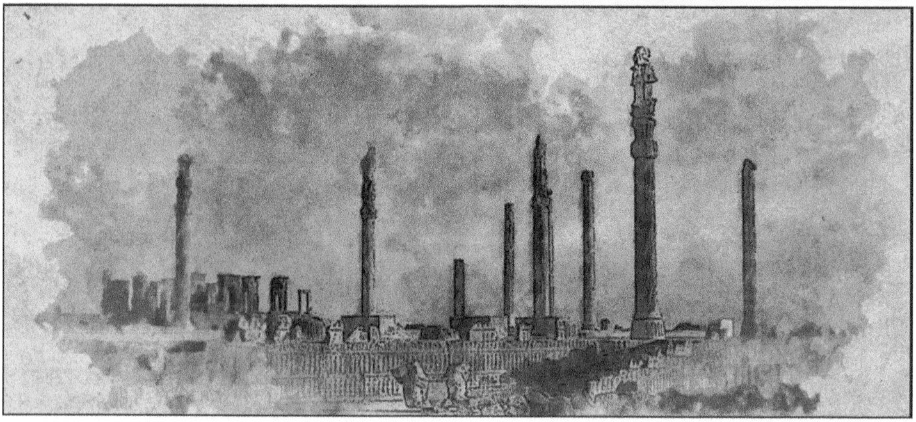

SHIRAZ IS IRAN'S FIFTH LARGEST CITY, WITH A POPULATION OF OVER 850 THOUSAND...

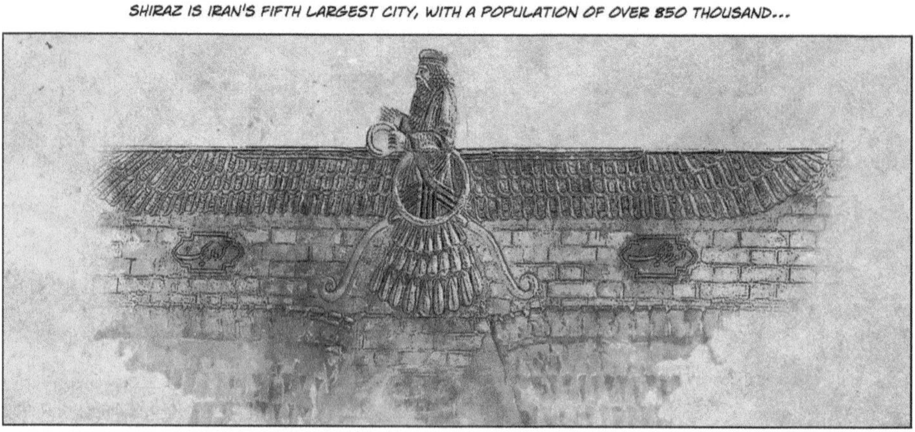

* ILLUSTRATIONS OF IRANIAN HISTORY BY SADAF AMINI

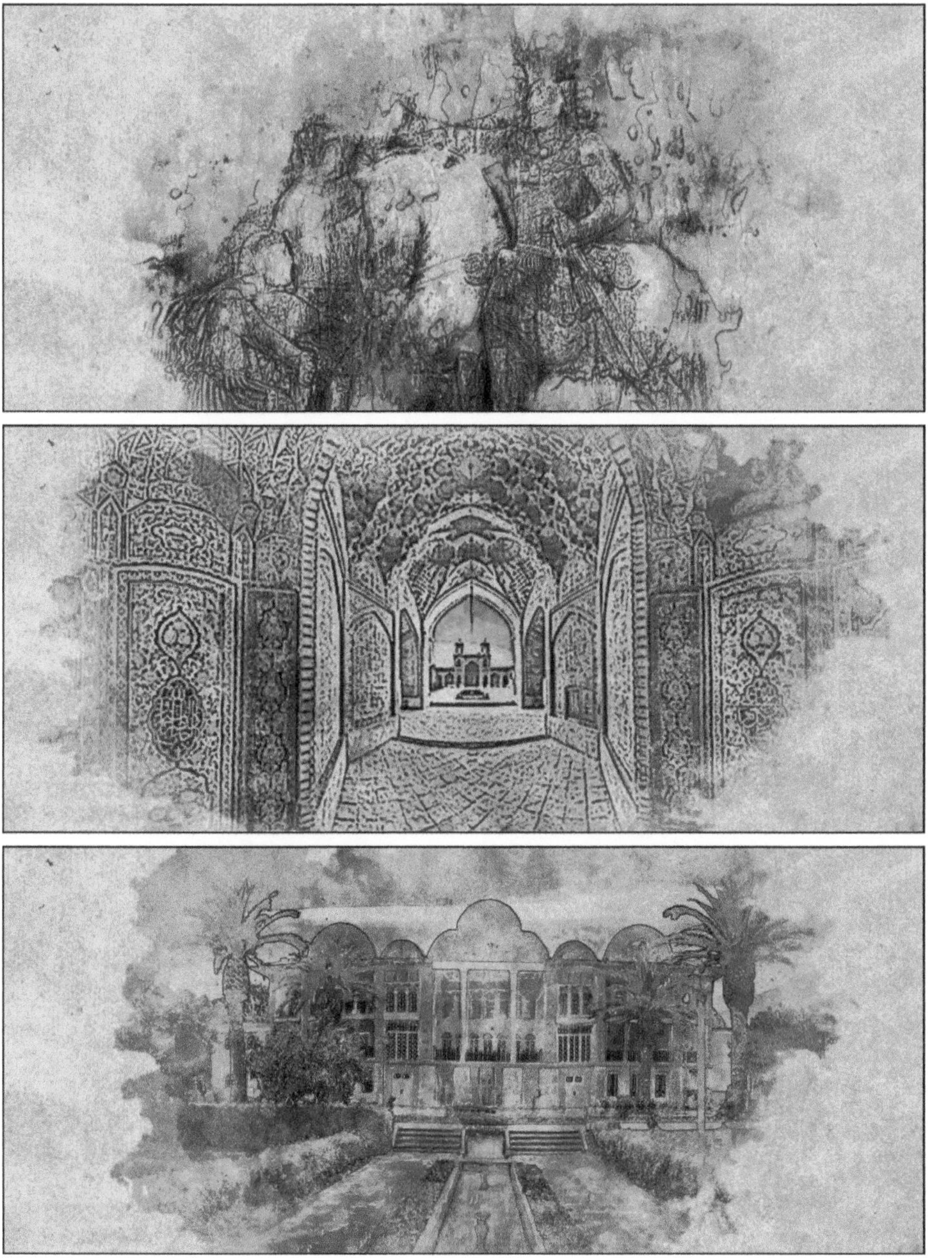

IT IS THE CAPITAL OF FARS, WHERE THE LANGUAGE OF FARSI COMES FROM.

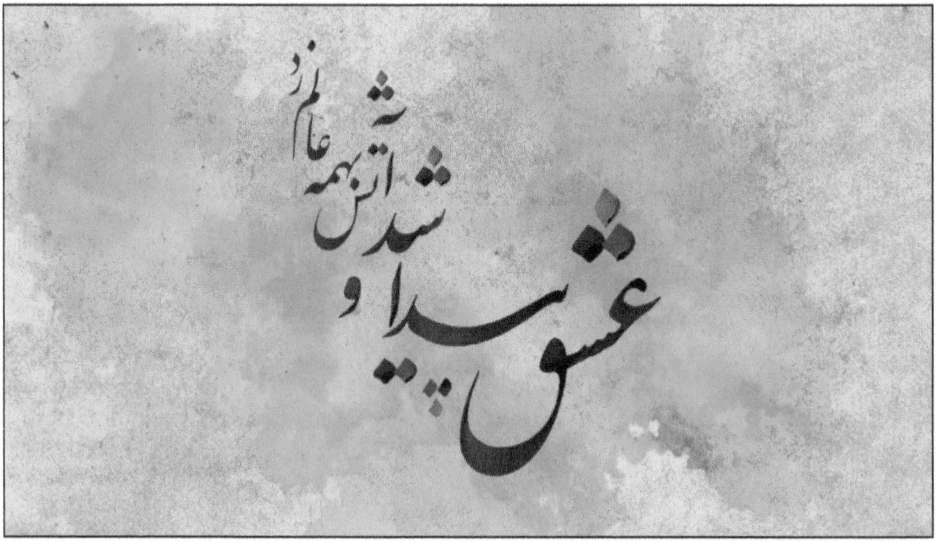
عشق پیدا شد و آتش به همه عالم زد

IT IS THE POETRY CAPITAL OF PERSIA BECAUSE TWO OF OUR VERY GREATEST POWTS ARE FROM HERE.
HAFIZ AND SA'DI.

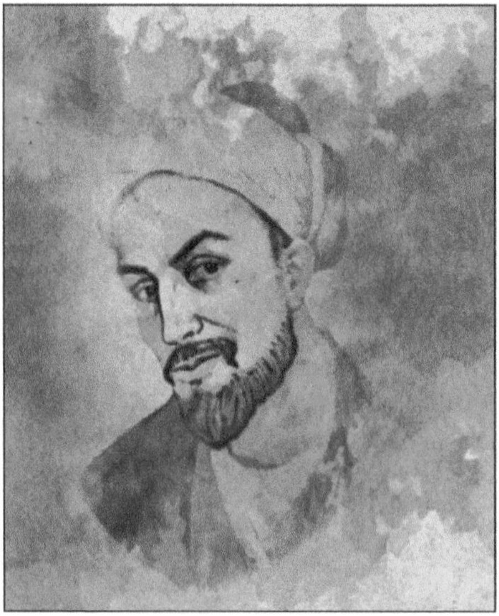

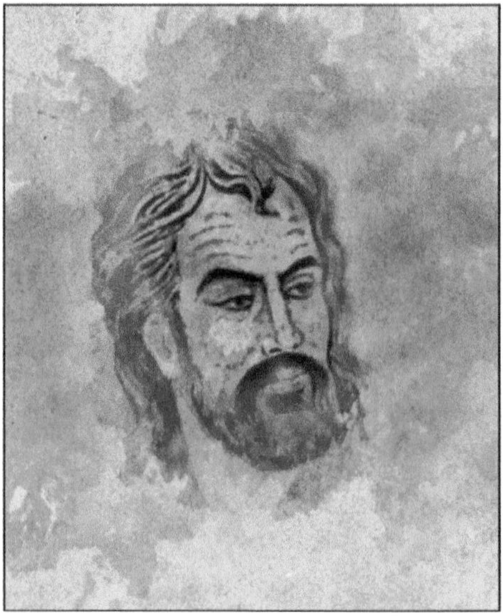

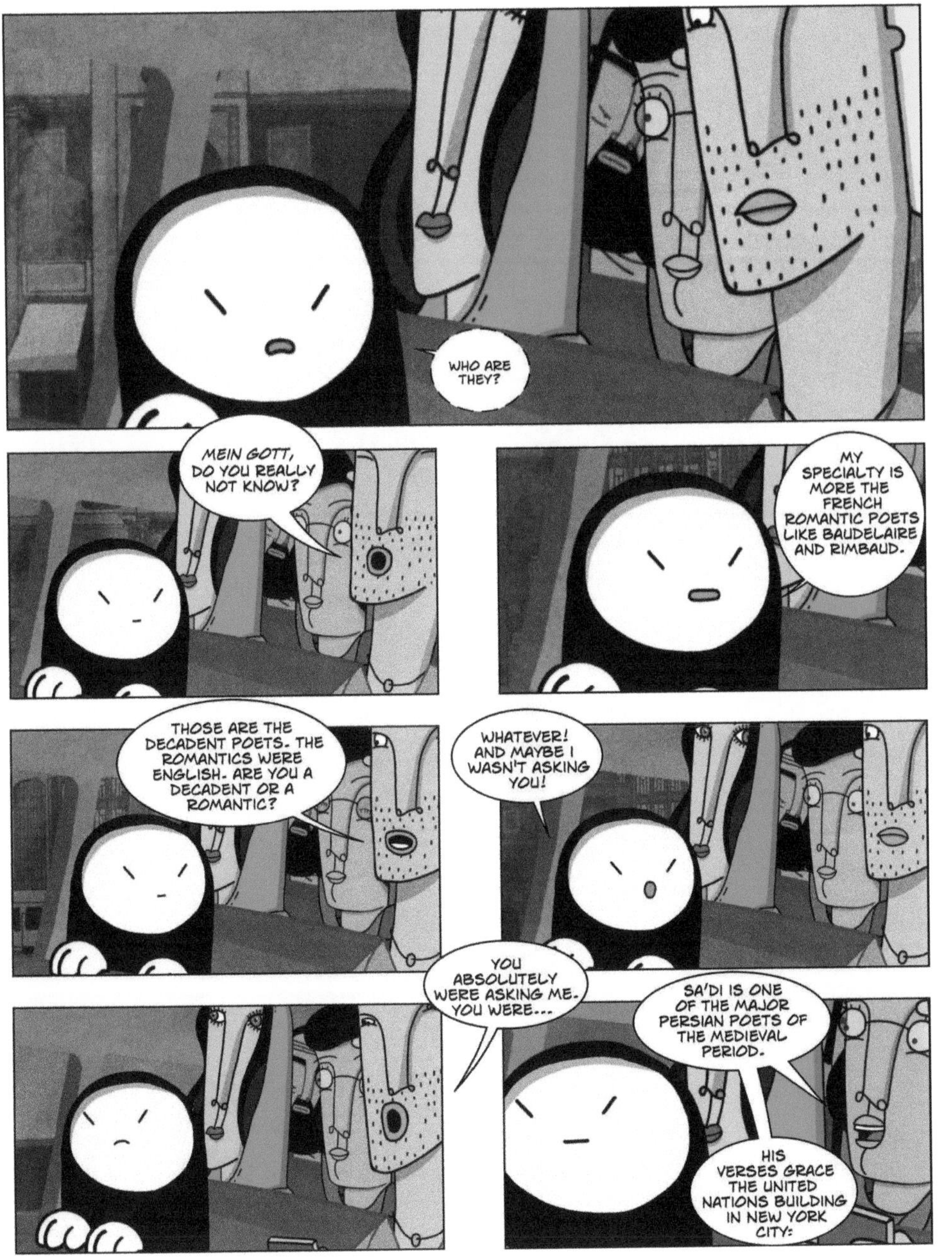
WHO ARE THEY?
MEIN GOTT, DO YOU REALLY NOT KNOW?
MY SPECIALTY IS MORE THE FRENCH ROMANTIC POETS LIKE BAUDELAIRE AND RIMBAUD.
THOSE ARE THE DECADENT POETS. THE ROMANTICS WERE ENGLISH. ARE YOU A DECADENT OR A ROMANTIC?
WHATEVER! AND MAYBE I WASN'T ASKING YOU!
YOU ABSOLUTELY WERE ASKING ME. YOU WERE...
SA'DI IS ONE OF THE MAJOR PERSIAN POETS OF THE MEDIEVAL PERIOD.
HIS VERSES GRACE THE UNITED NATIONS BUILDING IN NEW YORK CITY:

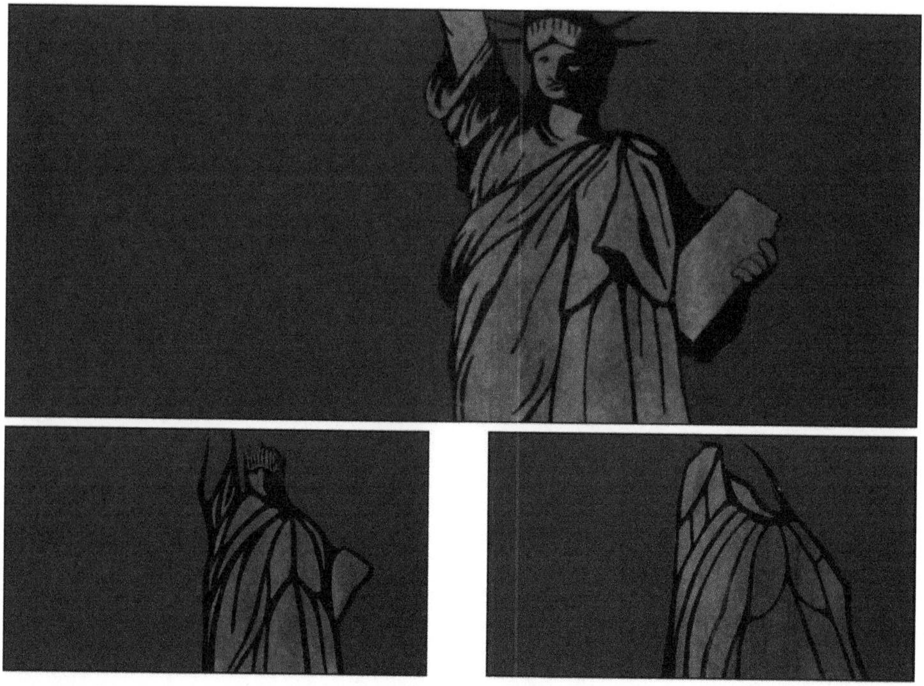

BANI AADAM AAZAYE YEK DIGARAND
KE DAR AAFARINESH ZE YEK GOOHARAND

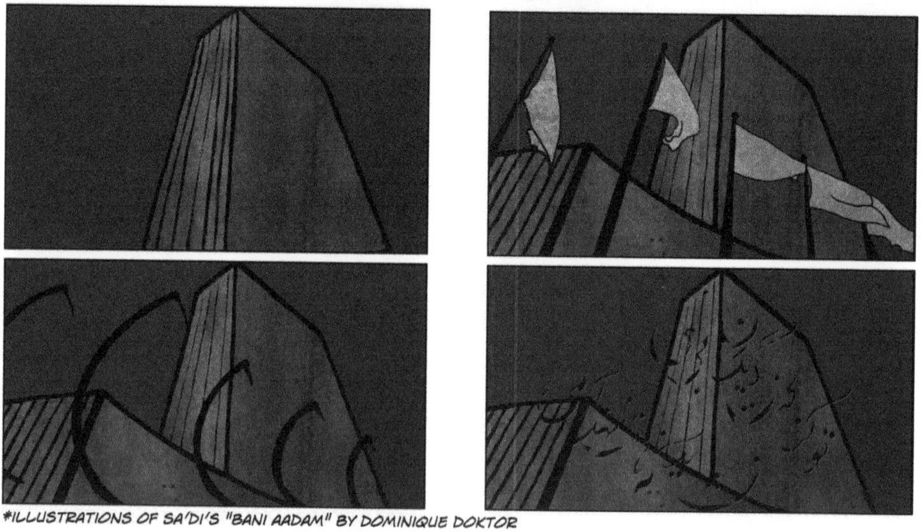

*ILLUSTRATIONS OF SA'DI'S "BANI AADAM" BY DOMINIQUE DOKTOR

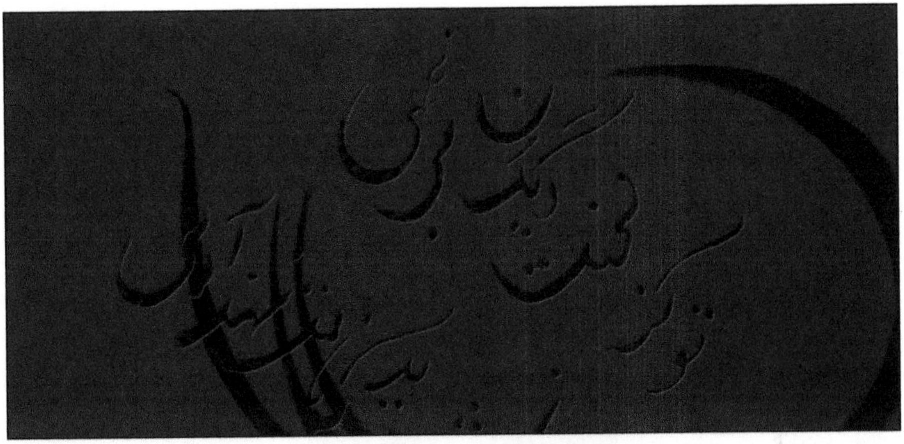

CHO OZVI BE DARD AAVARAD ROOZEGAAR
DEGAR OZVHAA RAA NAMAANAD GHARAAR

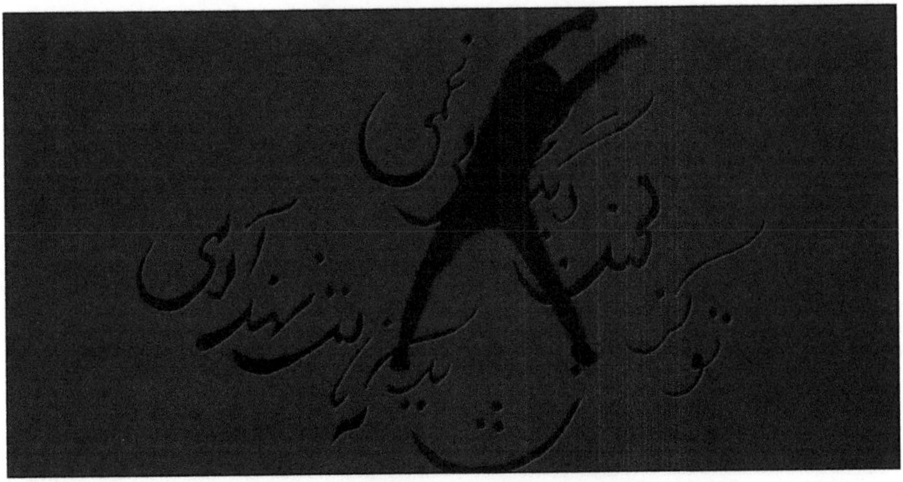

TO KAZ MEHNATE DIGARAAN BI GHAMI
NASHAAYAD KE NAAMAT NAHAND AADAMI

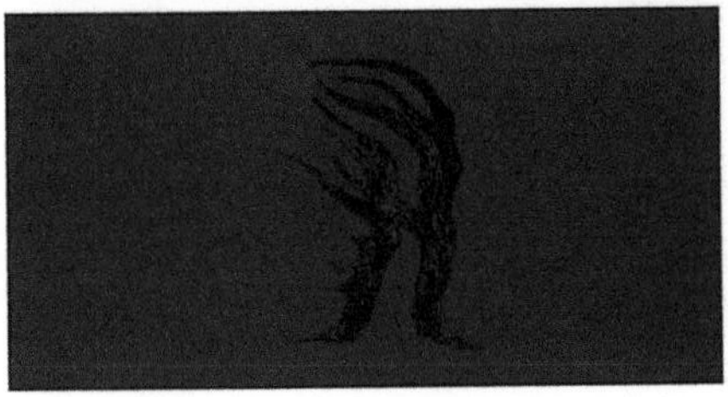

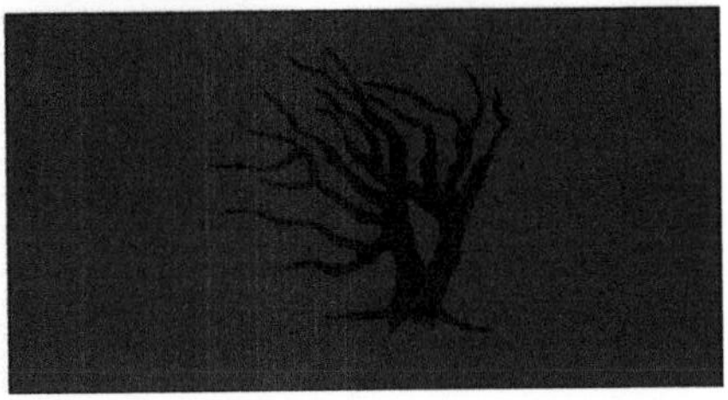

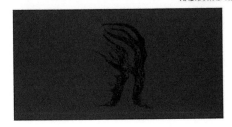

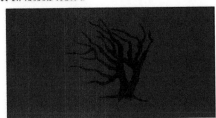

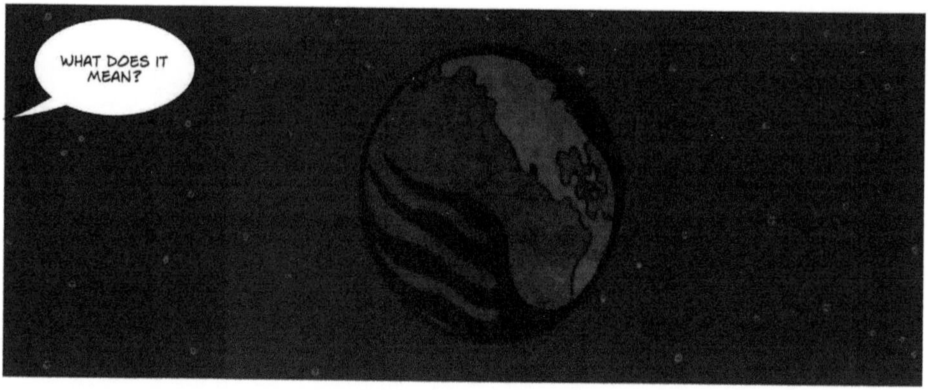
WHAT DOES IT MEAN?

WE ARE ALL CREATED FROM ONE ESSENCE AND WHEN THE CALAMITY OF TIME AFFECTS ONE LIMB, THE OTHERS CANNOT REST. IF WE CANNOT FEEL SYMPATHY FOR THE TROUBLES OF OTHERS, WE CANNOT BE CALLED HUMAN.

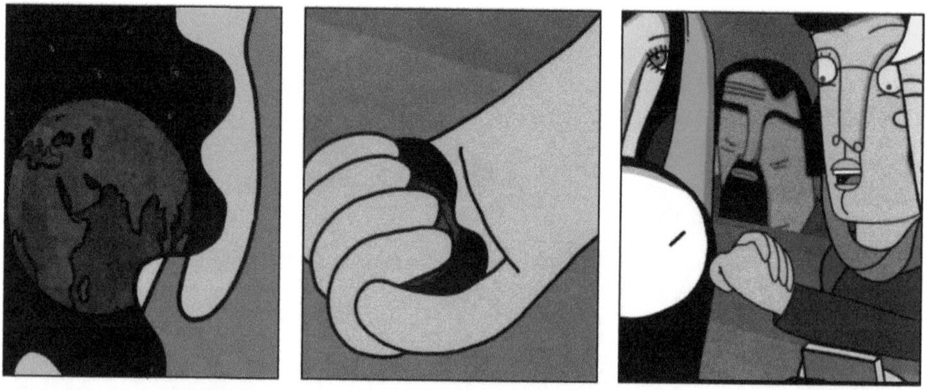

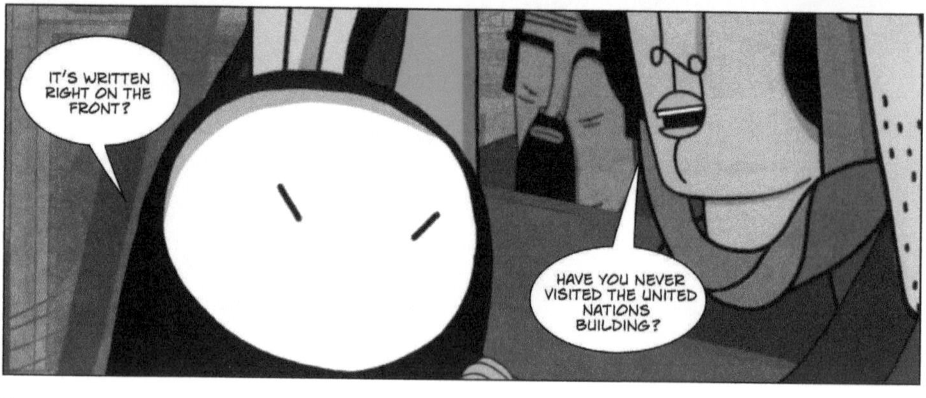
IT'S WRITTEN RIGHT ON THE FRONT?
HAVE YOU NEVER VISITED THE UNITED NATIONS BUILDING?

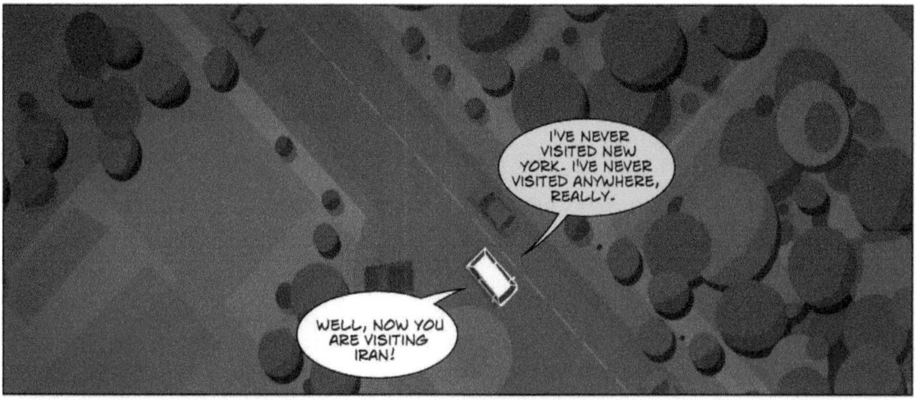
I'VE NEVER VISITED NEW YORK. I'VE NEVER VISITED ANYWHERE, REALLY.
WELL, NOW YOU ARE VISITING IRAN!

THIS IS THE TOMB OF THE GREAT IRANIAN POET, HAFIZ.

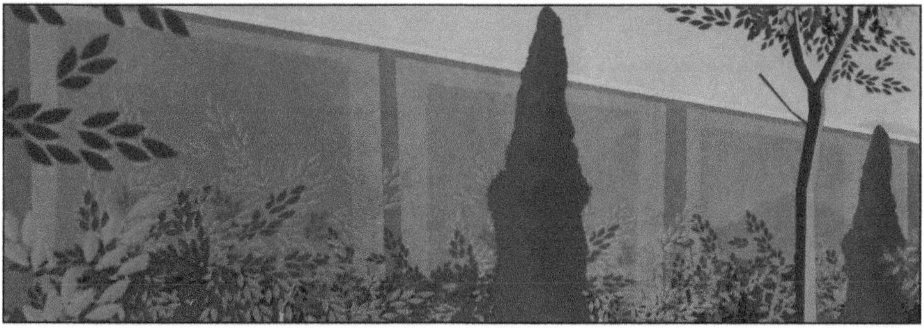

HE WAS BORN AROUND 1310 A.D. IN SHIRAZ.

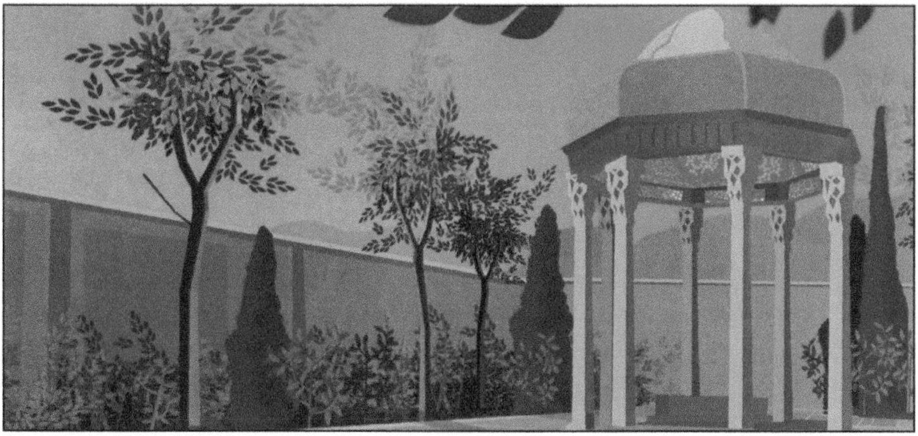

AS A CHILD, HE MEMORIZES THE Q'RAN BY LISTENING TO HIS FATHER'S RECITATIONS, AS WELL AS LEARNING THE WORKS OF ALL THE GREAT POETS: RUMI, MAZAMI, SA'DI, ATTAR...

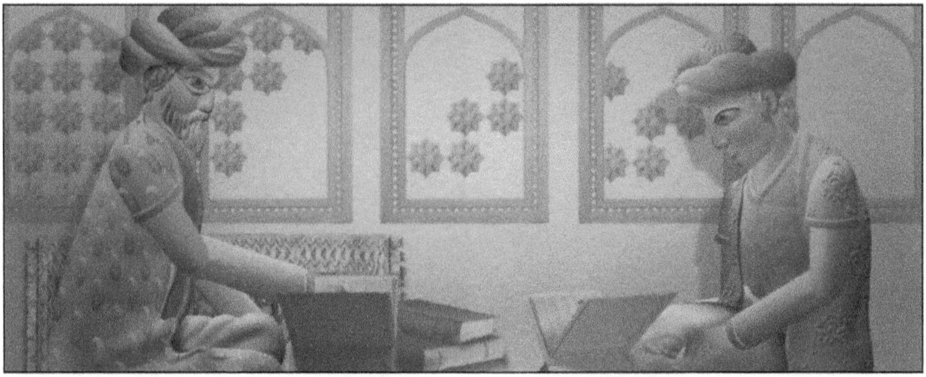

HIS FATHER DIES, LEAVING THE FAMILY IMPOVERISHED.

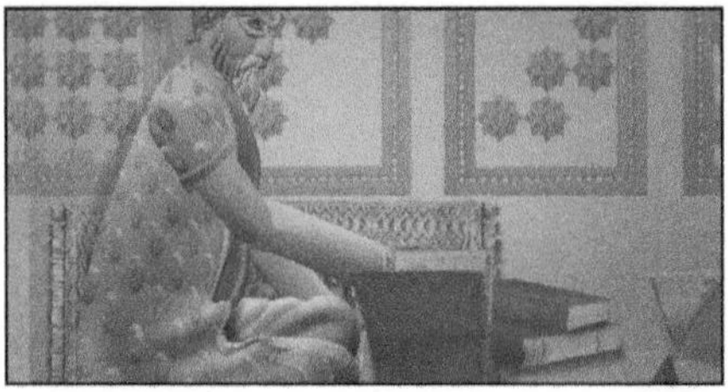

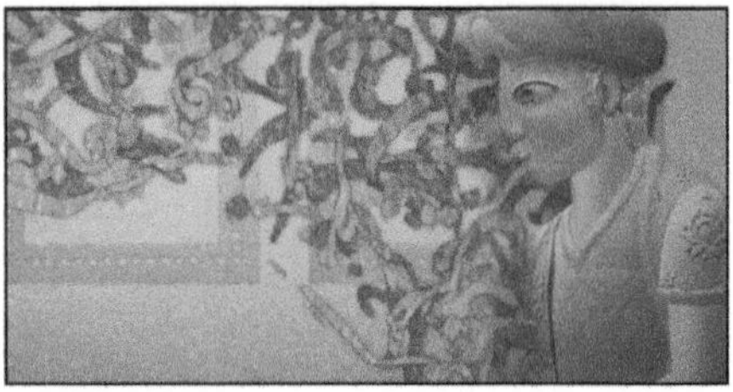

HAFIZ MUST LEAVE SCHOOL...

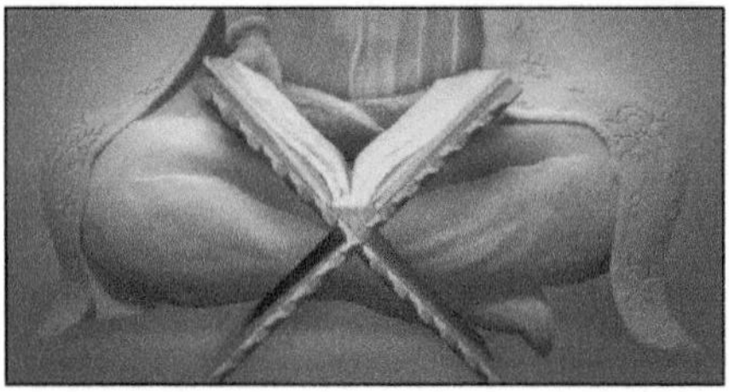

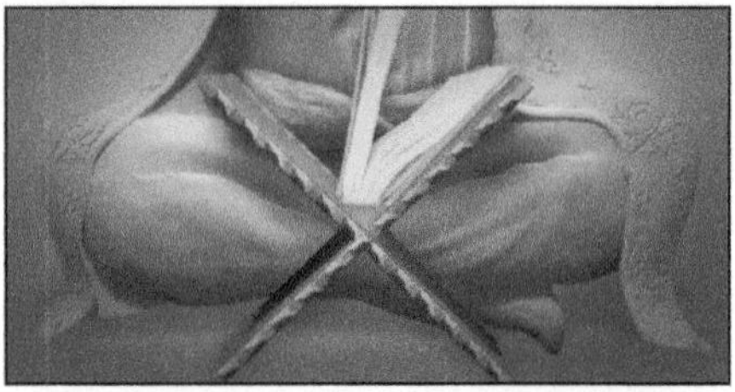

... AND FIND WORK IN A BAKERY.

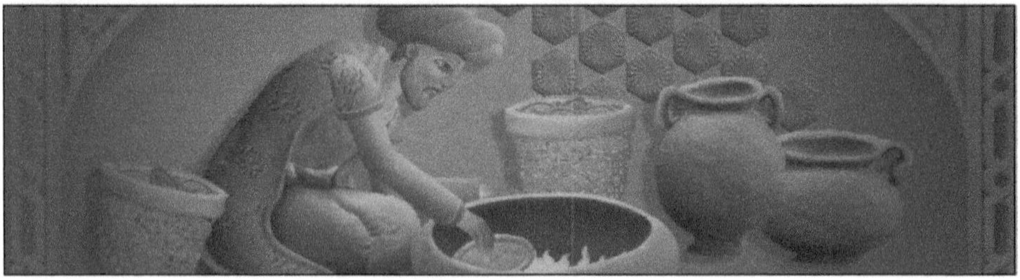

* STORY OF HAFIZ ILLUSTRATED BY BAHRAM JAVAHERI

AT AGE 21, HE DELIVERS BREAD TO THE WEALTHY PART OF TOWN... AND FALLS IN LOVE WITH SHAKH-E NABAT...

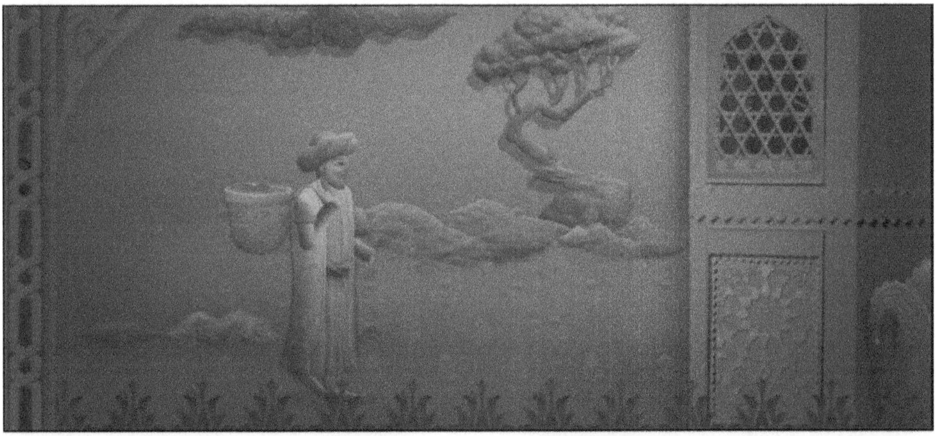

A YOUNG WOMAN OF INCREDIBLE BEAUTY.

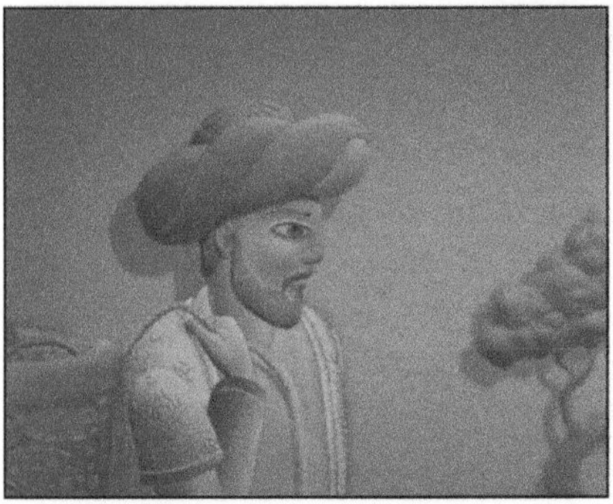

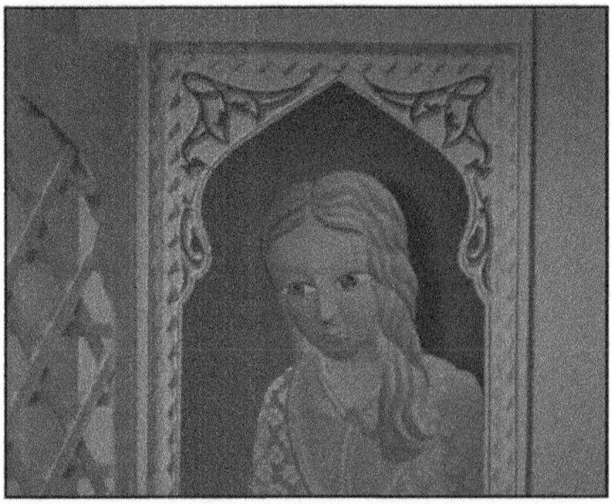

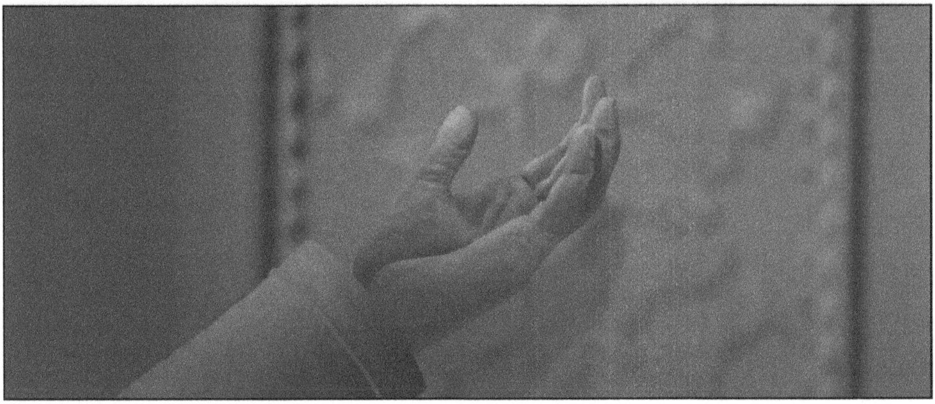

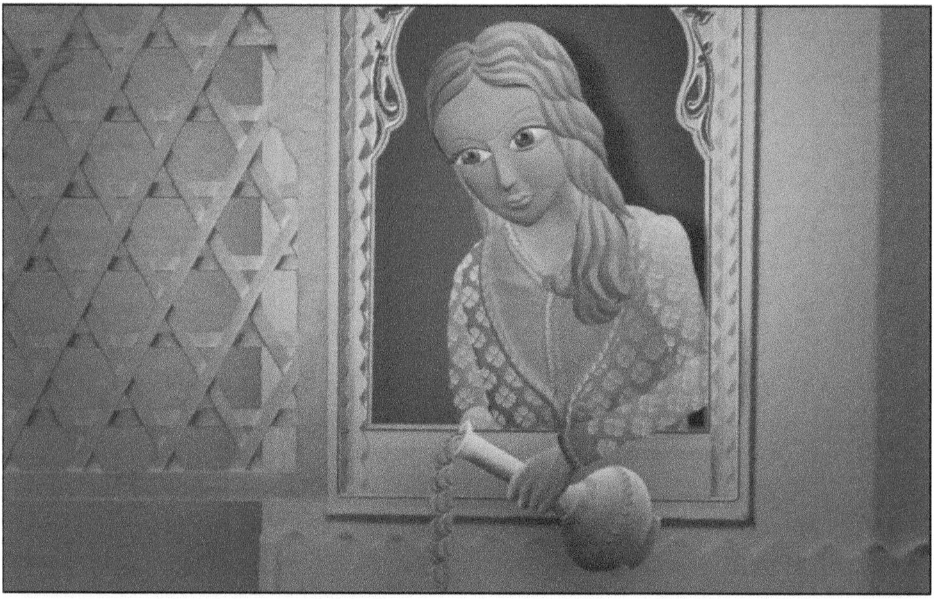

MANY OF HIS POEMS ARE ADDRESSED TO HER.

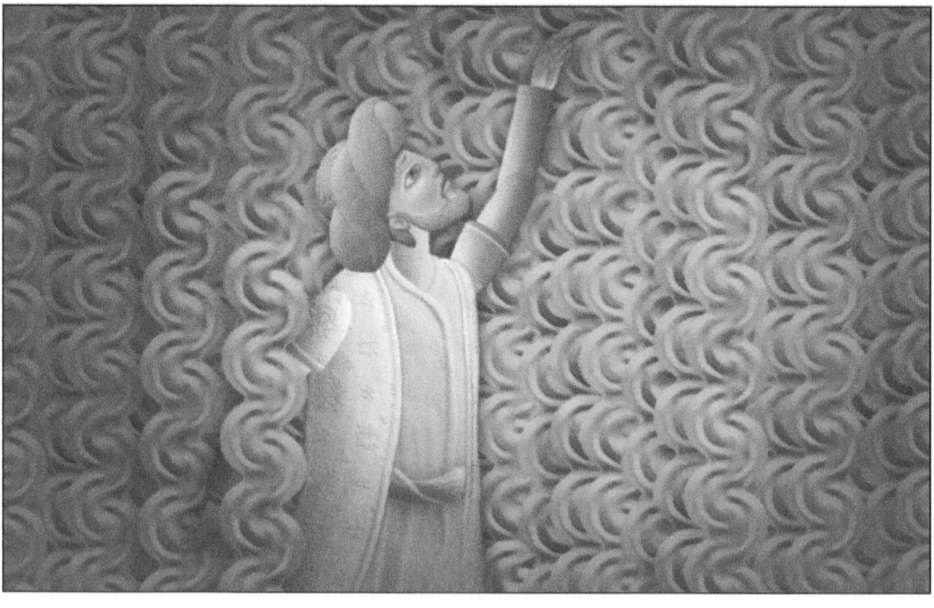

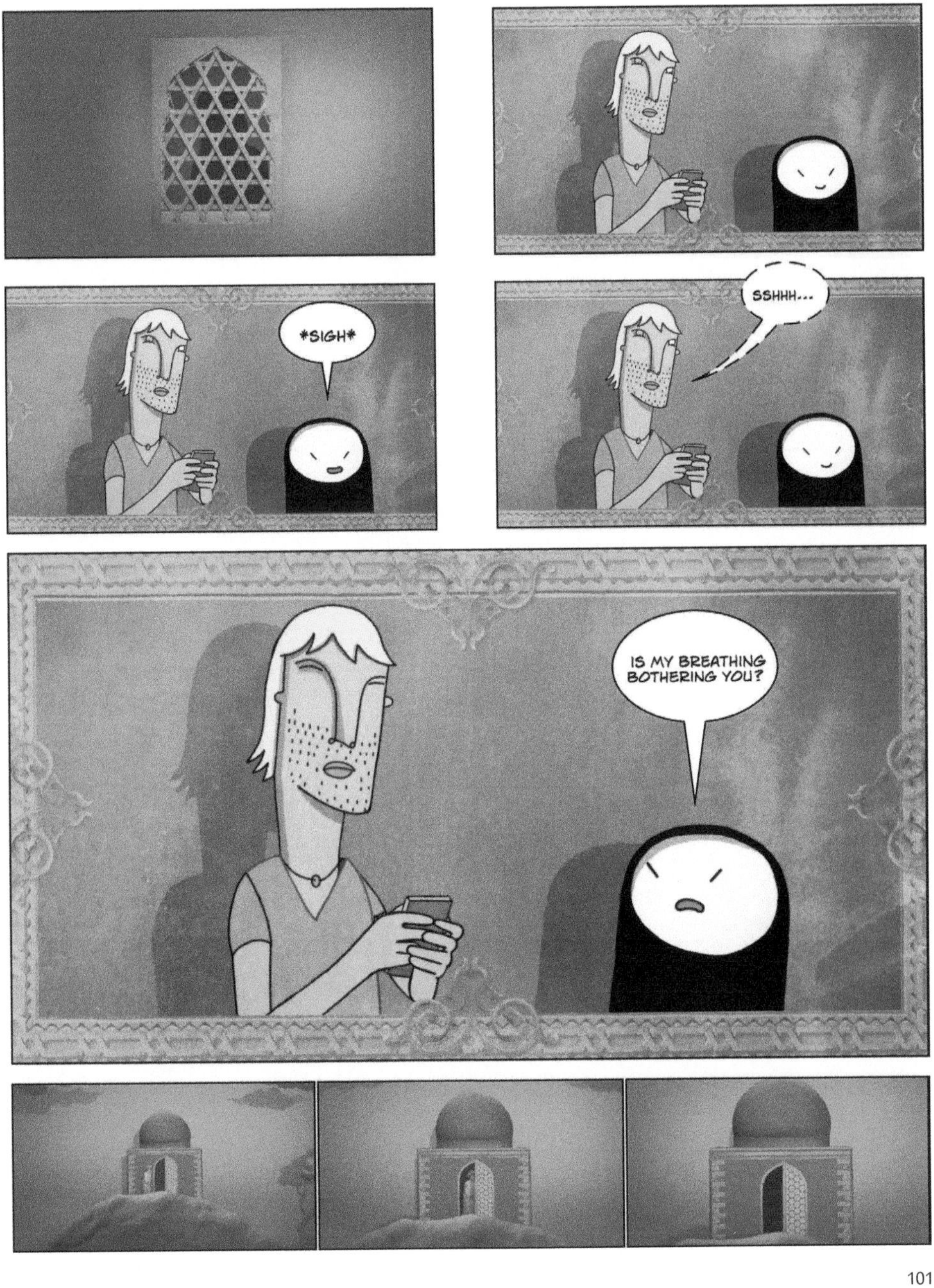
SIGH
SSHHH...
IS MY BREATHING BOTHERING YOU?

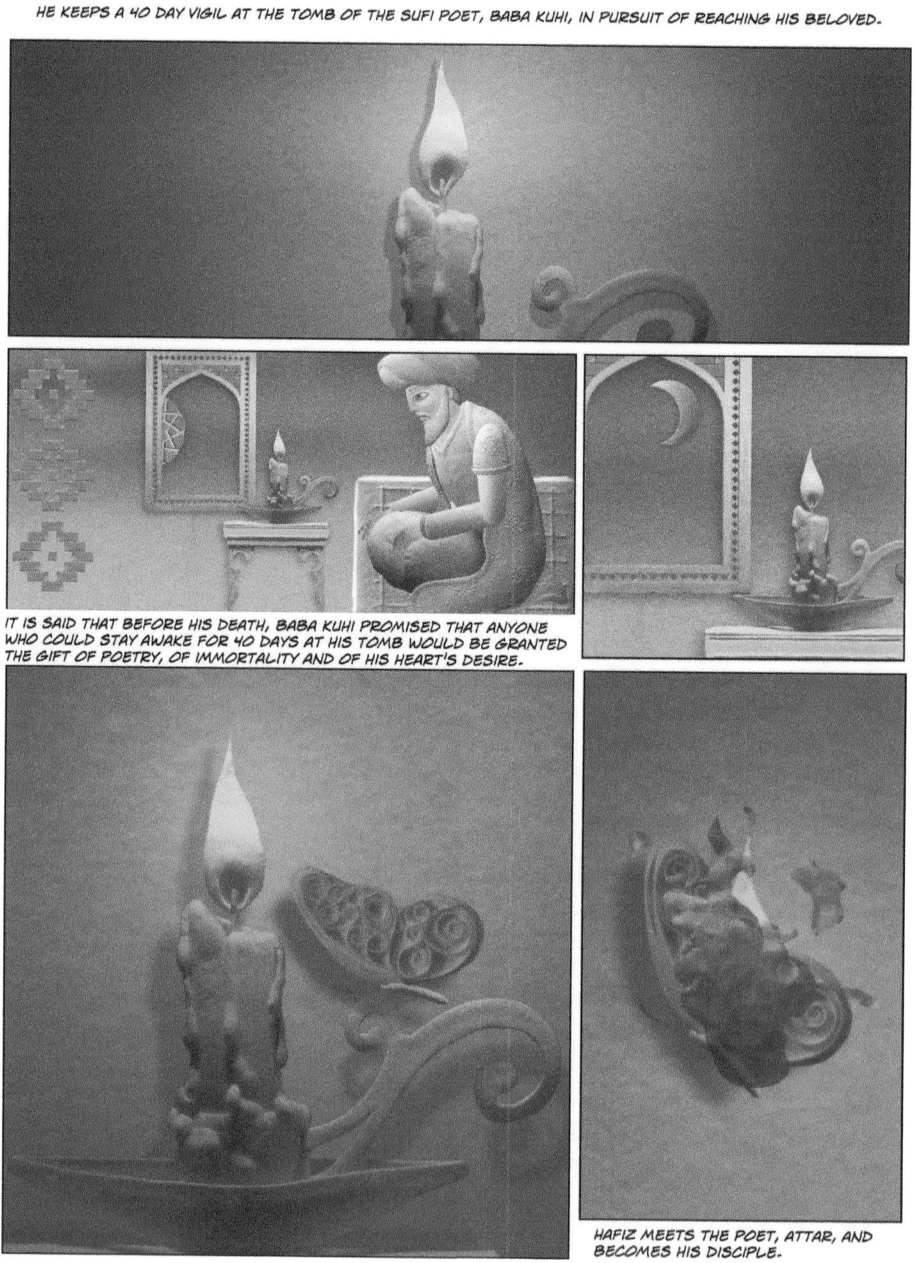
HE KEEPS A 40 DAY VIGIL AT THE TOMB OF THE SUFI POET, BABA KUHI, IN PURSUIT OF REACHING HIS BELOVED.
IT IS SAID THAT BEFORE HIS DEATH, BABA KUHI PROMISED THAT ANYONE WHO COULD STAY AWAKE FOR 40 DAYS AT HIS TOMB WOULD BE GRANTED THE GIFT OF POETRY, OF IMMORTALITY AND OF HIS HEART'S DESIRE.
HAFIZ MEETS THE POET, ATTAR, AND BECOMES HIS DISCIPLE.

HE BECOMES A POET OF THE COURT OF ABU ISHAK, AND BECOMES VERY FAMOUS AS A "SPIRITUAL ROMANTIC."

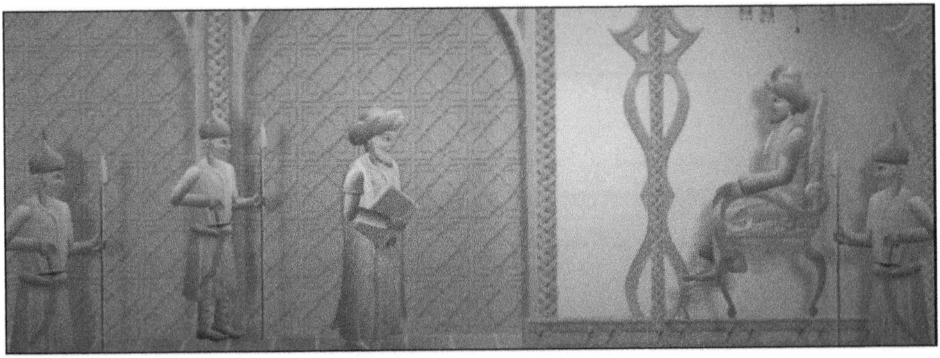

HAFIZ MARRIES AND HAS A SON...

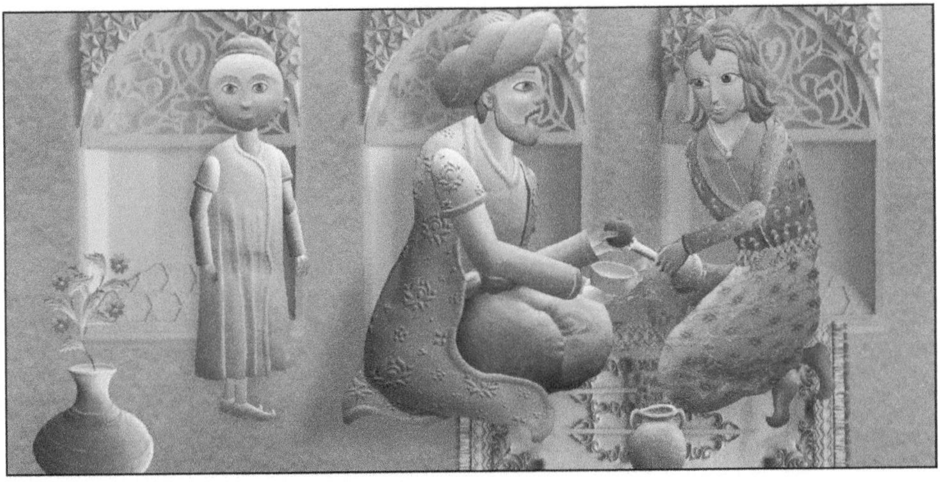

BUT KEEPS SHAKH-E NABAT AS HIS POETIC MUSE.

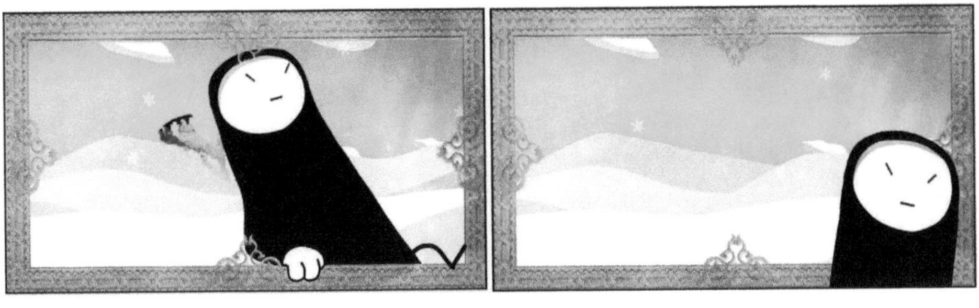

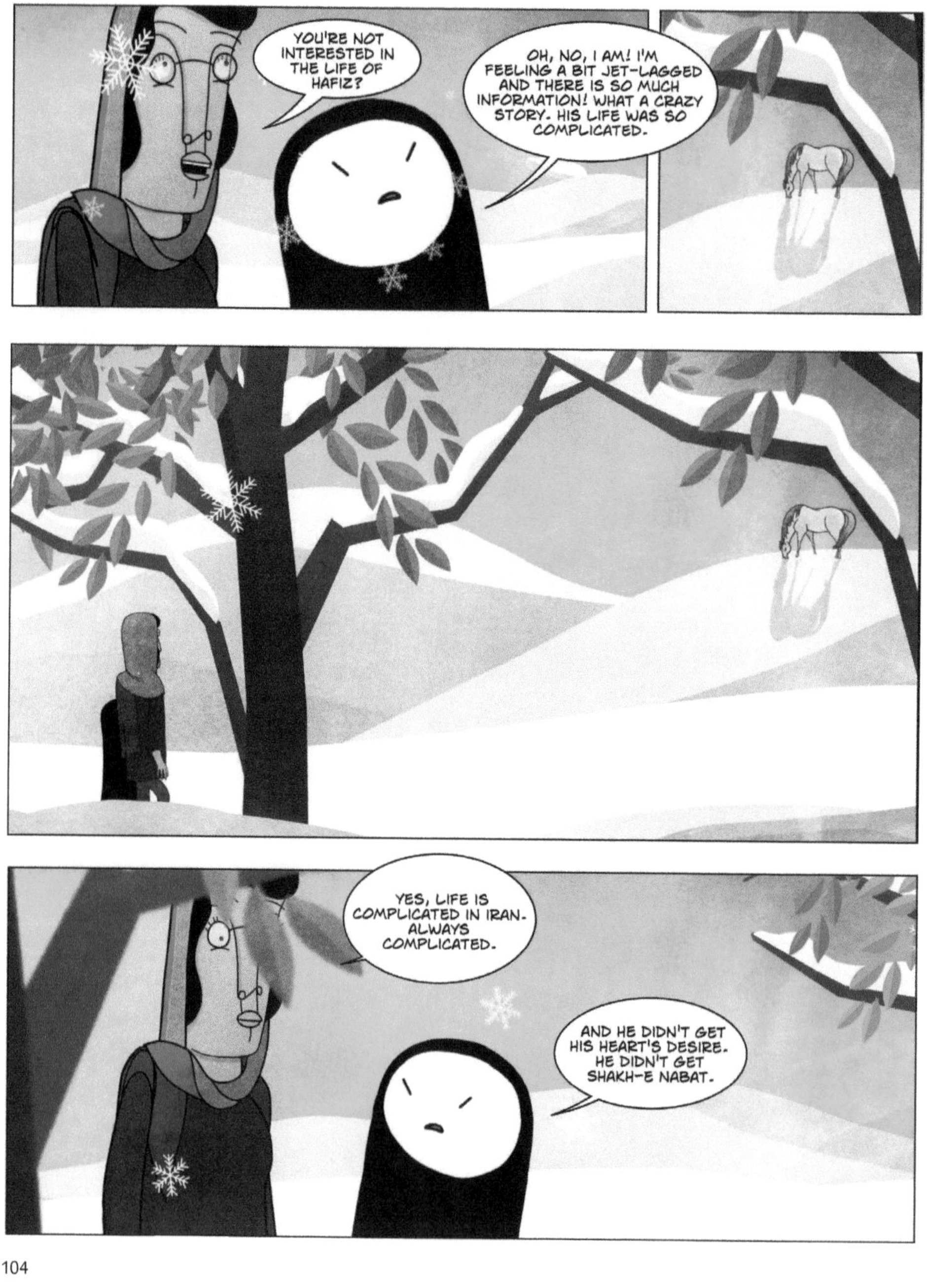
YOU'RE NOT INTERESTED IN THE LIFE OF HAFIZ?
OH, NO, I AM! I'M FEELING A BIT JET-LAGGED AND THERE IS SO MUCH INFORMATION! WHAT A CRAZY STORY. HIS LIFE WAS SO COMPLICATED.
YES, LIFE IS COMPLICATED IN IRAN. ALWAYS COMPLICATED.
AND HE DIDN'T GET HIS HEART'S DESIRE. HE DIDN'T GET SHAKH-E NABAT.

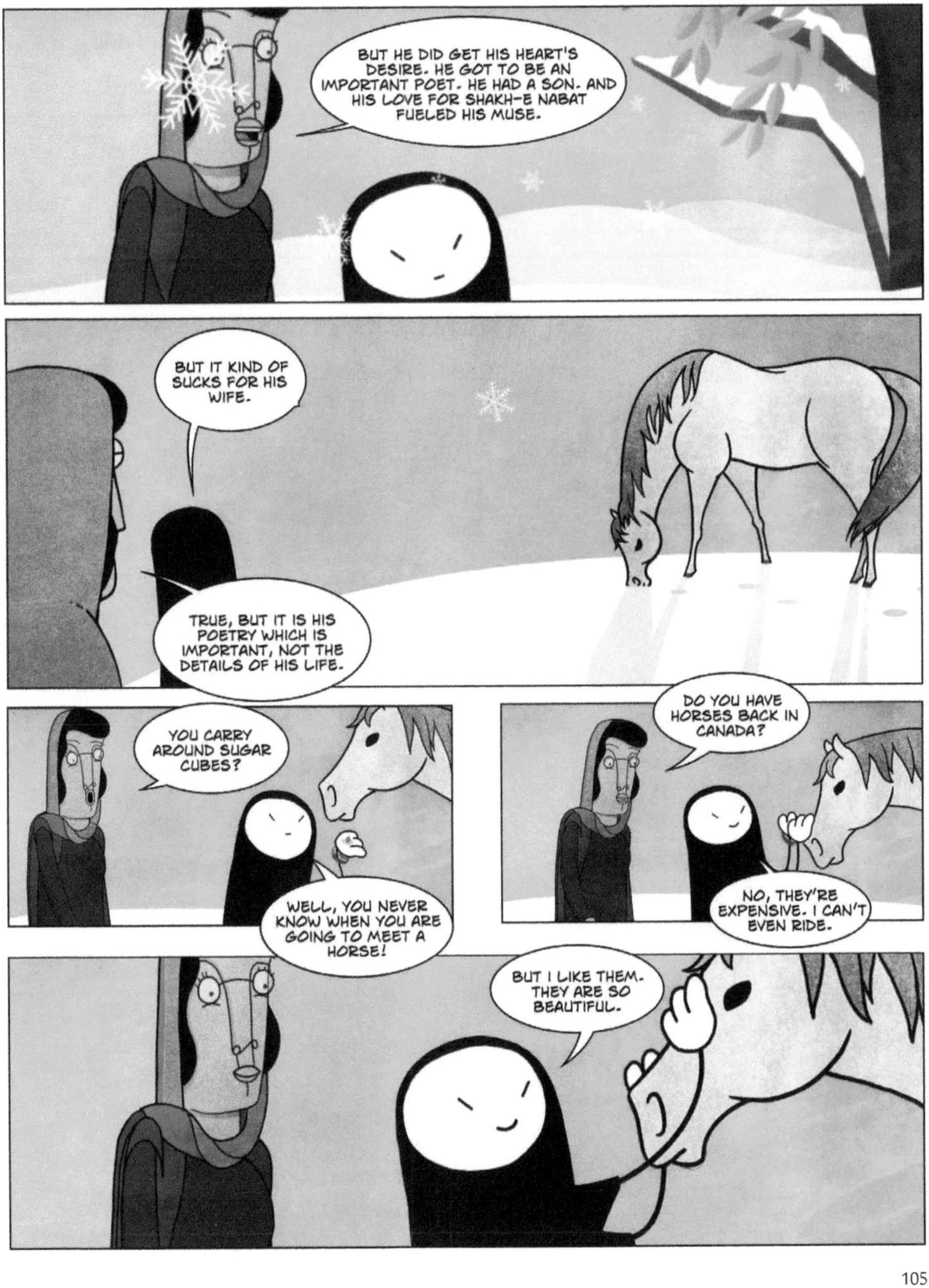
BUT HE DID GET HIS HEART'S DESIRE. HE GOT TO BE AN IMPORTANT POET. HE HAD A SON. AND HIS LOVE FOR SHAKH-E NABAT FUELED HIS MUSE.
BUT IT KIND OF SUCKS FOR HIS WIFE.
TRUE, BUT IT IS HIS POETRY WHICH IS IMPORTANT, NOT THE DETAILS OF HIS LIFE.
YOU CARRY AROUND SUGAR CUBES?
WELL, YOU NEVER KNOW WHEN YOU ARE GOING TO MEET A HORSE!
DO YOU HAVE HORSES BACK IN CANADA?
NO, THEY'RE EXPENSIVE. I CAN'T EVEN RIDE.
BUT I LIKE THEM. THEY ARE SO BEAUTIFUL.

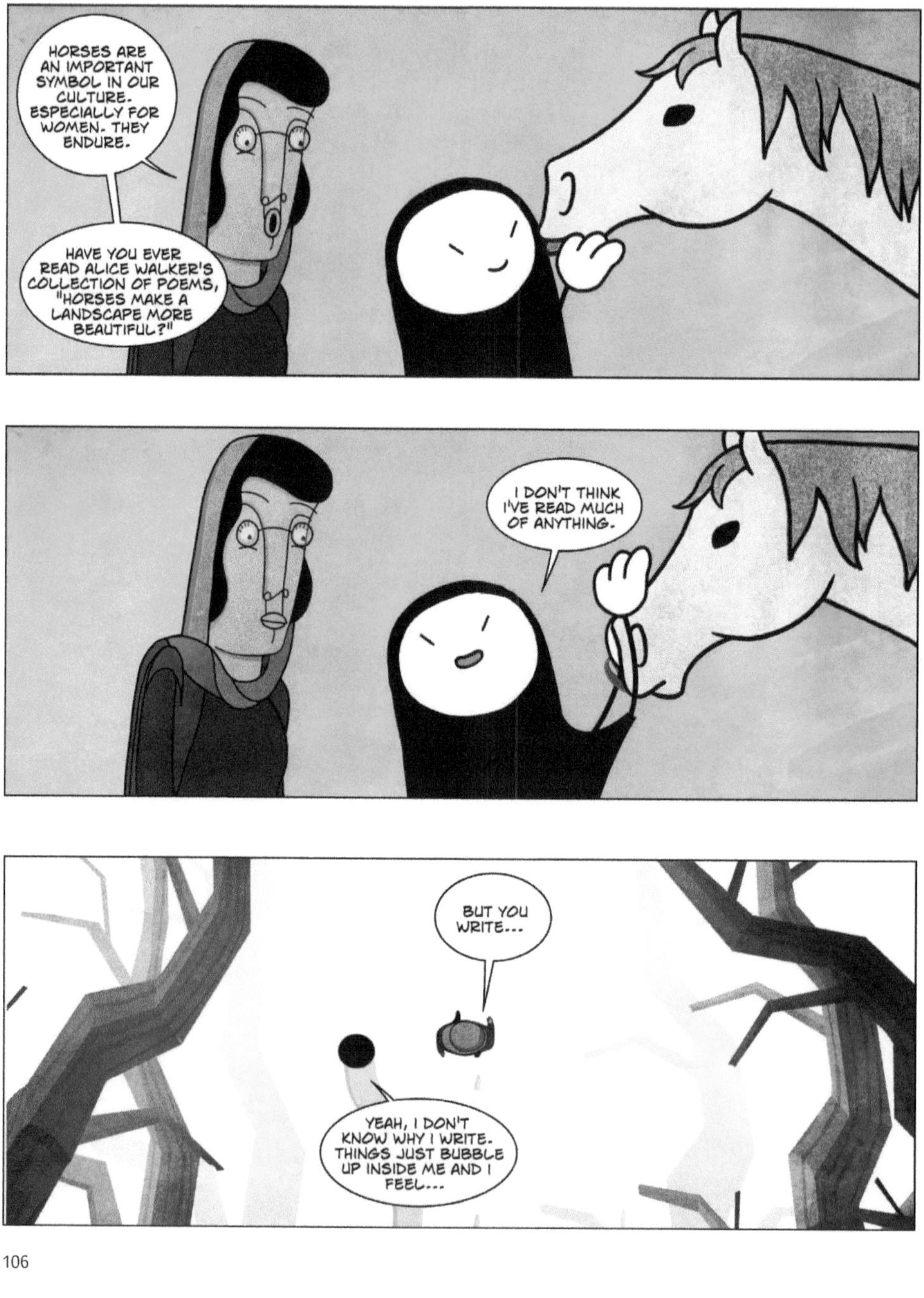
HORSES ARE AN IMPORTANT SYMBOL IN OUR CULTURE. ESPECIALLY FOR WOMEN. THEY ENDURE.
HAVE YOU EVER READ ALICE WALKER'S COLLECTION OF POEMS, "HORSES MAKE A LANDSCAPE MORE BEAUTIFUL?"
I DON'T THINK I'VE READ MUCH OF ANYTHING.
BUT YOU WRITE...
YEAH, I DON'T KNOW WHY I WRITE. THINGS JUST BUBBLE UP INSIDE ME AND I FEEL...

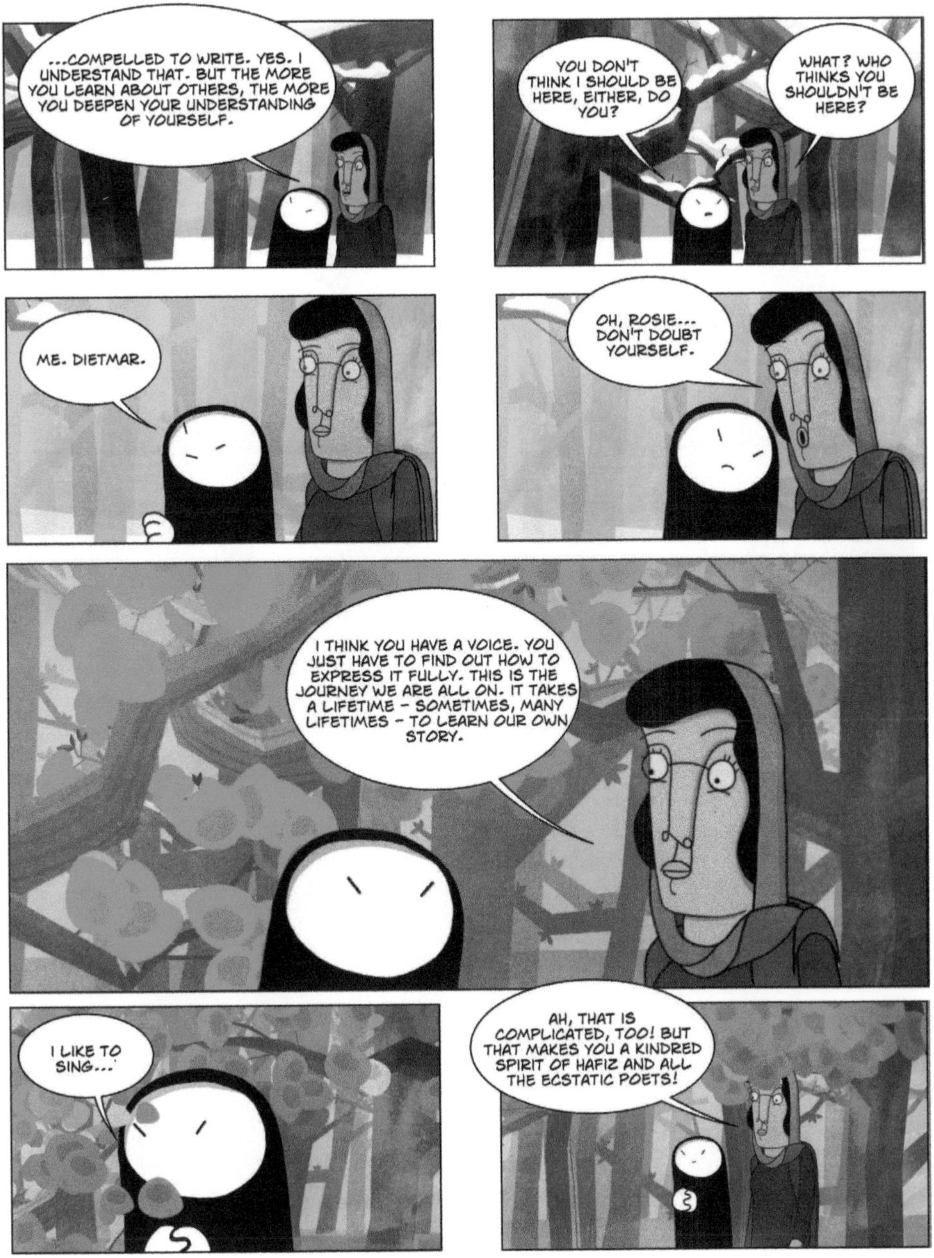
...COMPELLED TO WRITE. YES. I UNDERSTAND THAT. BUT THE MORE YOU LEARN ABOUT OTHERS, THE MORE YOU DEEPEN YOUR UNDERSTANDING OF YOURSELF.
YOU DON'T THINK I SHOULD BE HERE, EITHER, DO YOU?
WHAT? WHO THINKS YOU SHOULDN'T BE HERE?
ME. DIETMAR.
OH, ROSIE... DON'T DOUBT YOURSELF.
I THINK YOU HAVE A VOICE. YOU JUST HAVE TO FIND OUT HOW TO EXPRESS IT FULLY. THIS IS THE JOURNEY WE ARE ALL ON. IT TAKES A LIFETIME - SOMETIMES, MANY LIFETIMES - TO LEARN OUR OWN STORY.
I LIKE TO SING...
AH, THAT IS COMPLICATED, TOO! BUT THAT MAKES YOU A KINDRED SPIRIT OF HAFIZ AND ALL THE ECSTATIC POETS!

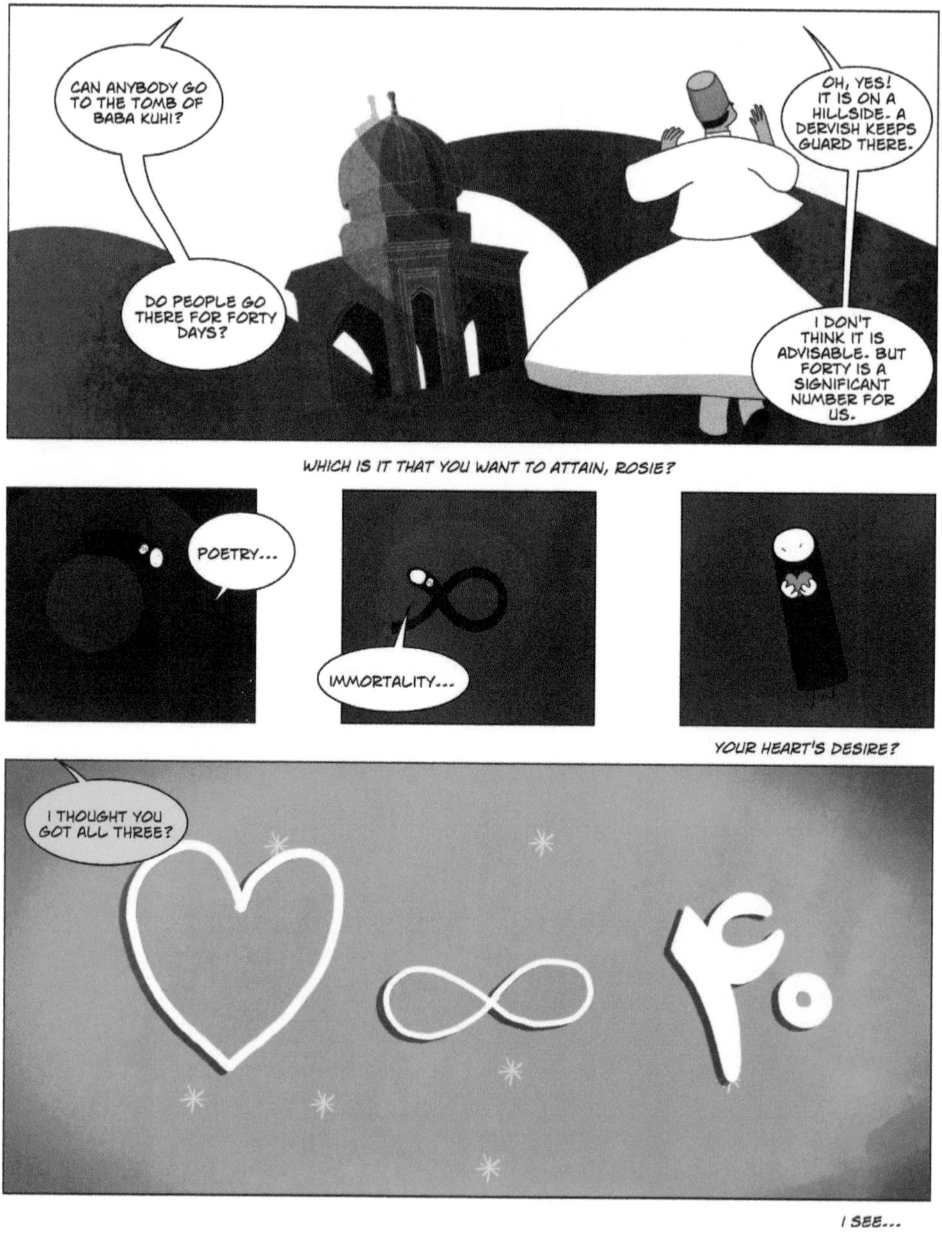
CAN ANYBODY GO TO THE TOMB OF BABA KUHI?
OH, YES! IT IS ON A HILLSIDE. A DERVISH KEEPS GUARD THERE.
DO PEOPLE GO THERE FOR FORTY DAYS?
I DON'T THINK IT IS ADVISABLE. BUT FORTY IS A SIGNIFICANT NUMBER FOR US.
WHICH IS IT THAT YOU WANT TO ATTAIN, ROSIE?
POETRY...
IMMORTALITY...
YOUR HEART'S DESIRE?
I THOUGHT YOU GOT ALL THREE?
۴۰
I SEE...

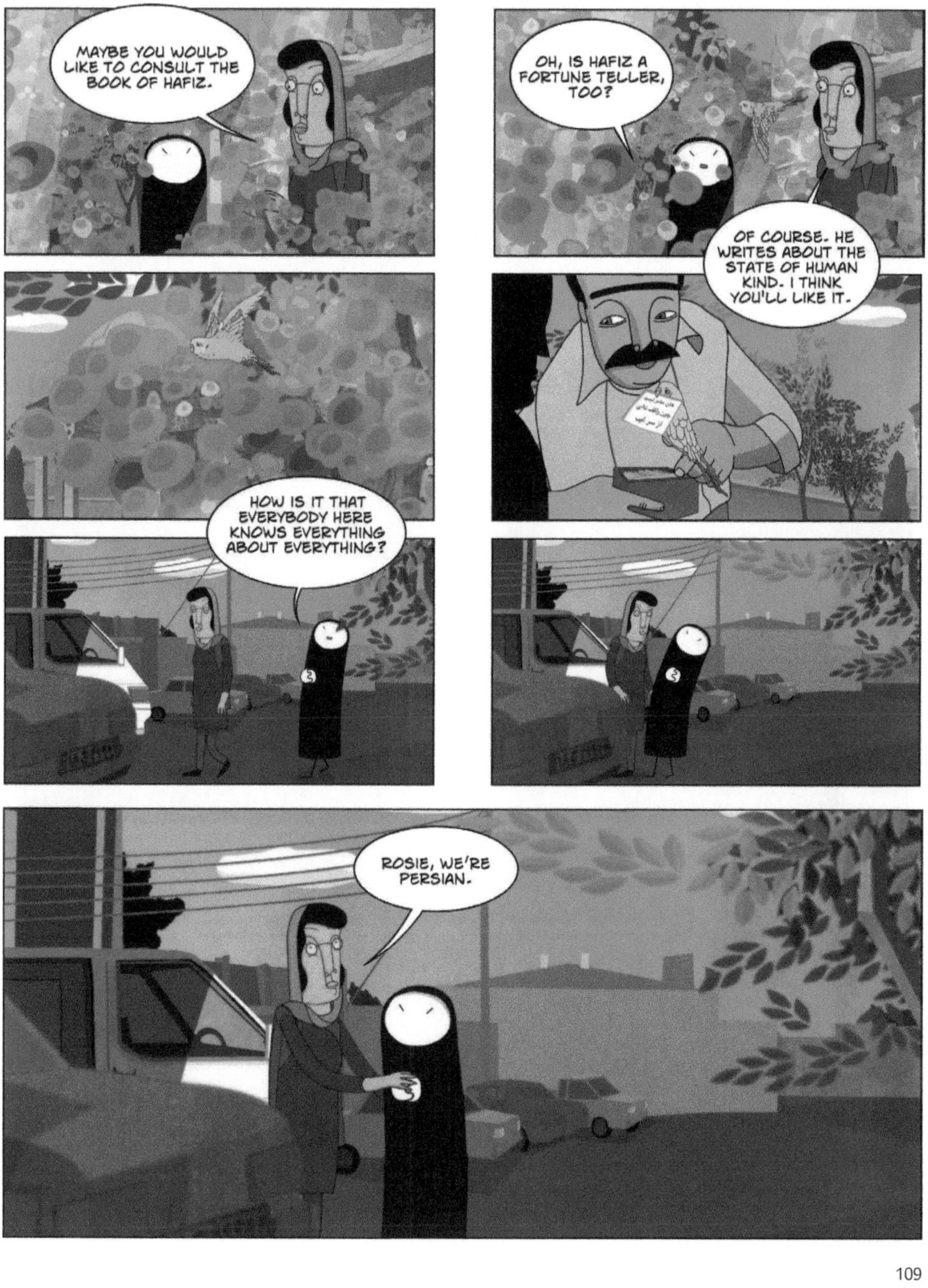
MAYBE YOU WOULD LIKE TO CONSULT THE BOOK OF HAFIZ.
OH, IS HAFIZ A FORTUNE TELLER, TOO?
OF COURSE. HE WRITES ABOUT THE STATE OF HUMAN KIND. I THINK YOU'LL LIKE IT.
HOW IS IT THAT EVERYBODY HERE KNOWS EVERYTHING ABOUT EVERYTHING?
ROSIE, WE'RE PERSIAN.

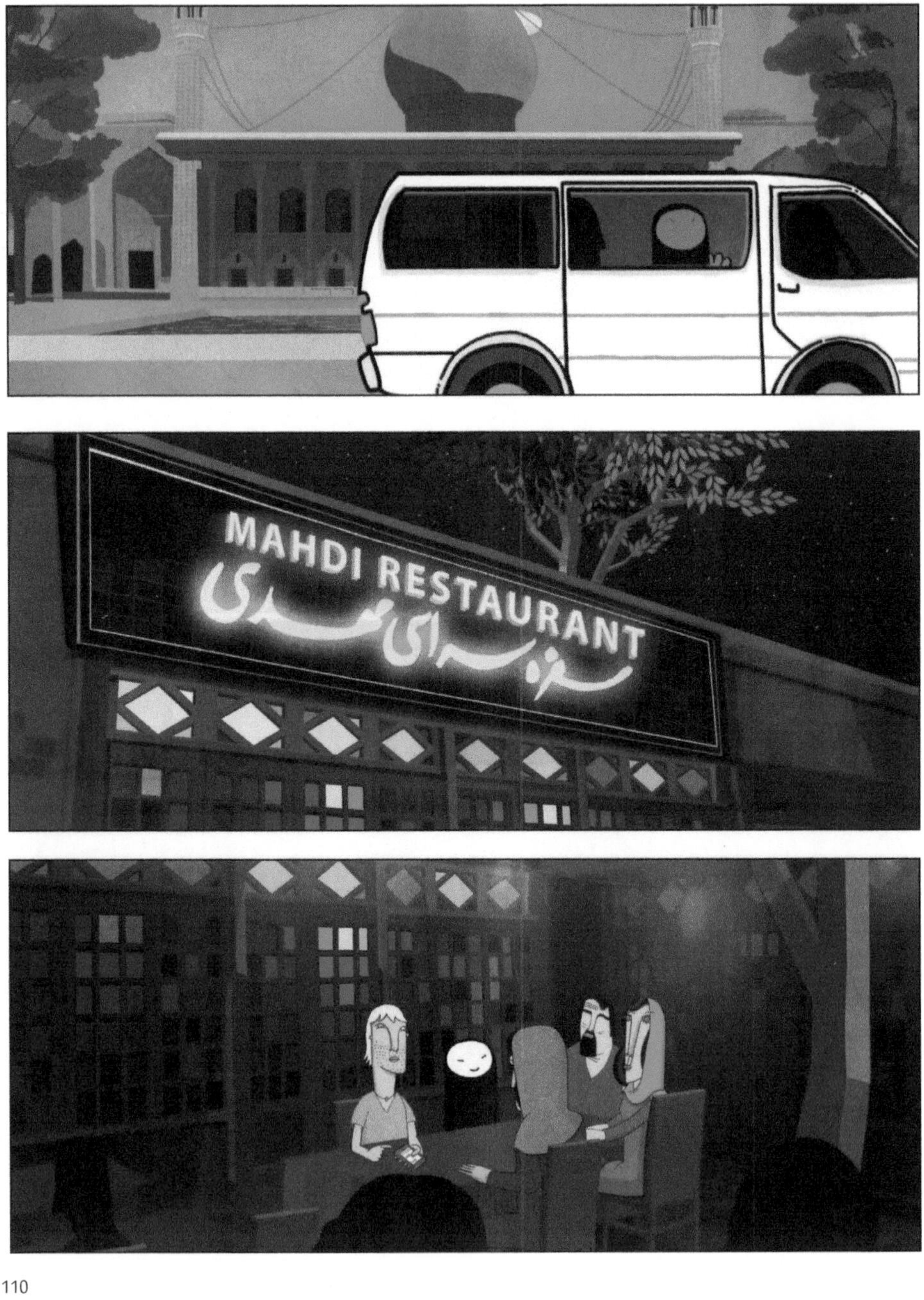
MAHDI RESTAURANT
سفره سرای مهدی

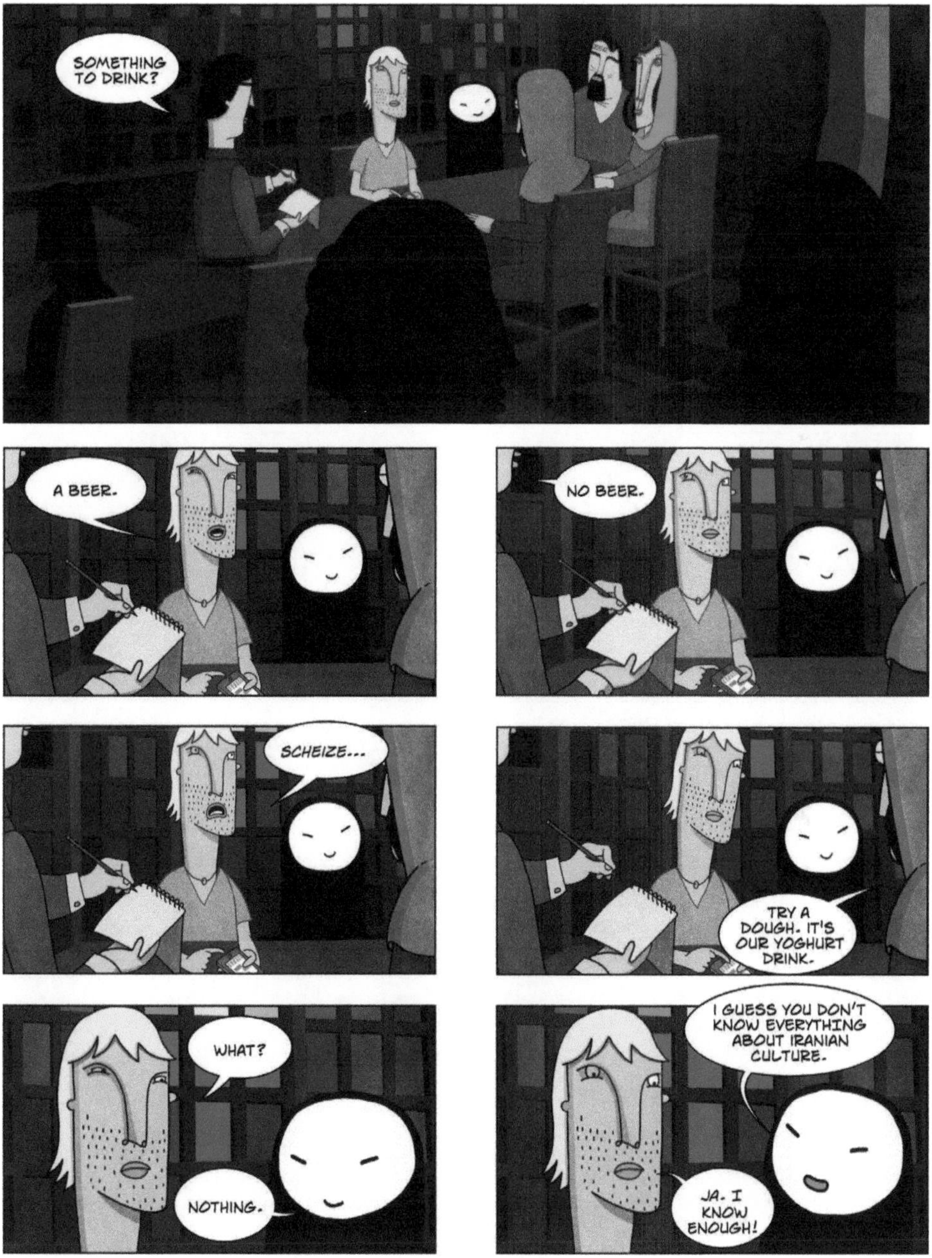
SOMETHING TO DRINK?
A BEER.
NO BEER.
SCHEIZE...
TRY A DOUGH. IT'S OUR YOGHURT DRINK.
WHAT?
NOTHING.
I GUESS YOU DON'T KNOW EVERYTHING ABOUT IRANIAN CULTURE.
JA. I KNOW ENOUGH!

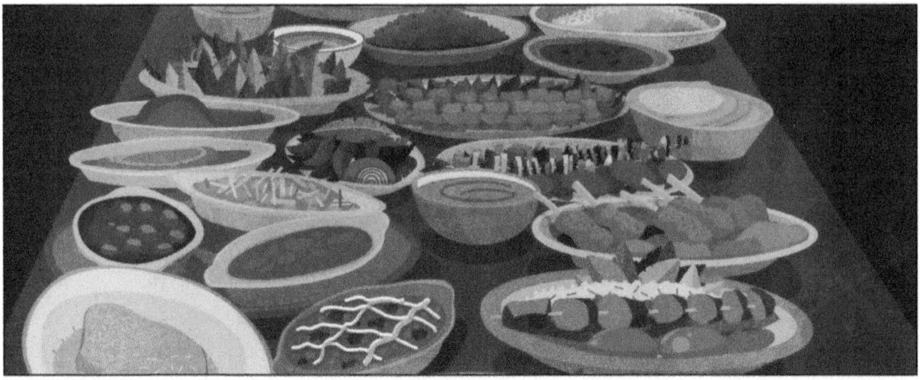

LAMB KABOB, CHERRY RICE, CHICKEN DISHES...

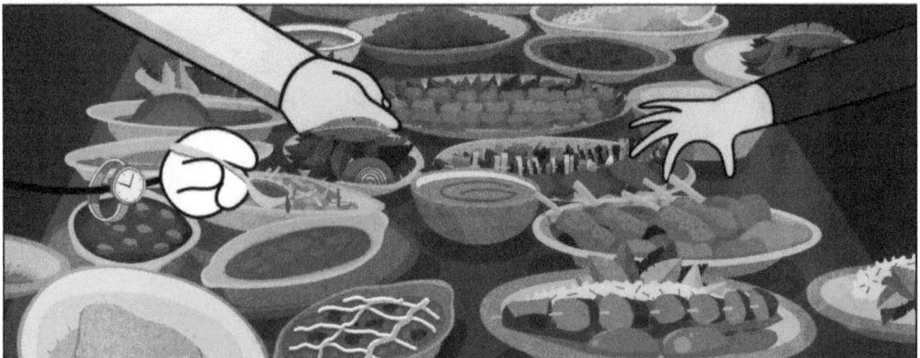

... A DELICIOUS MEAL!

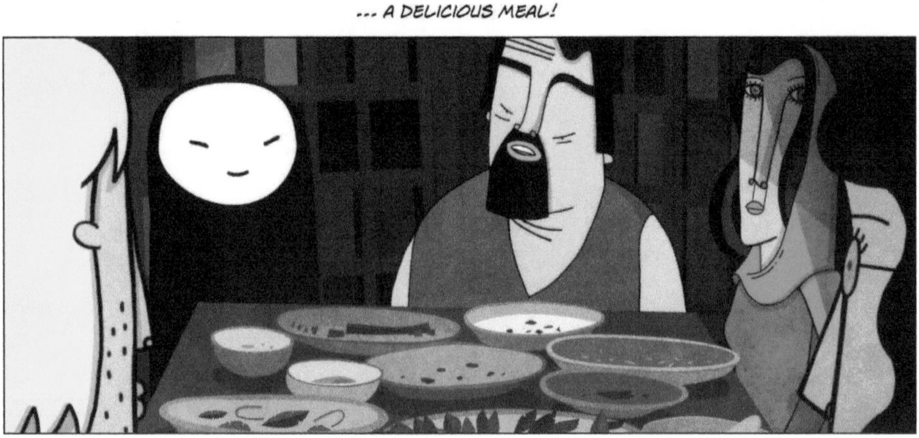

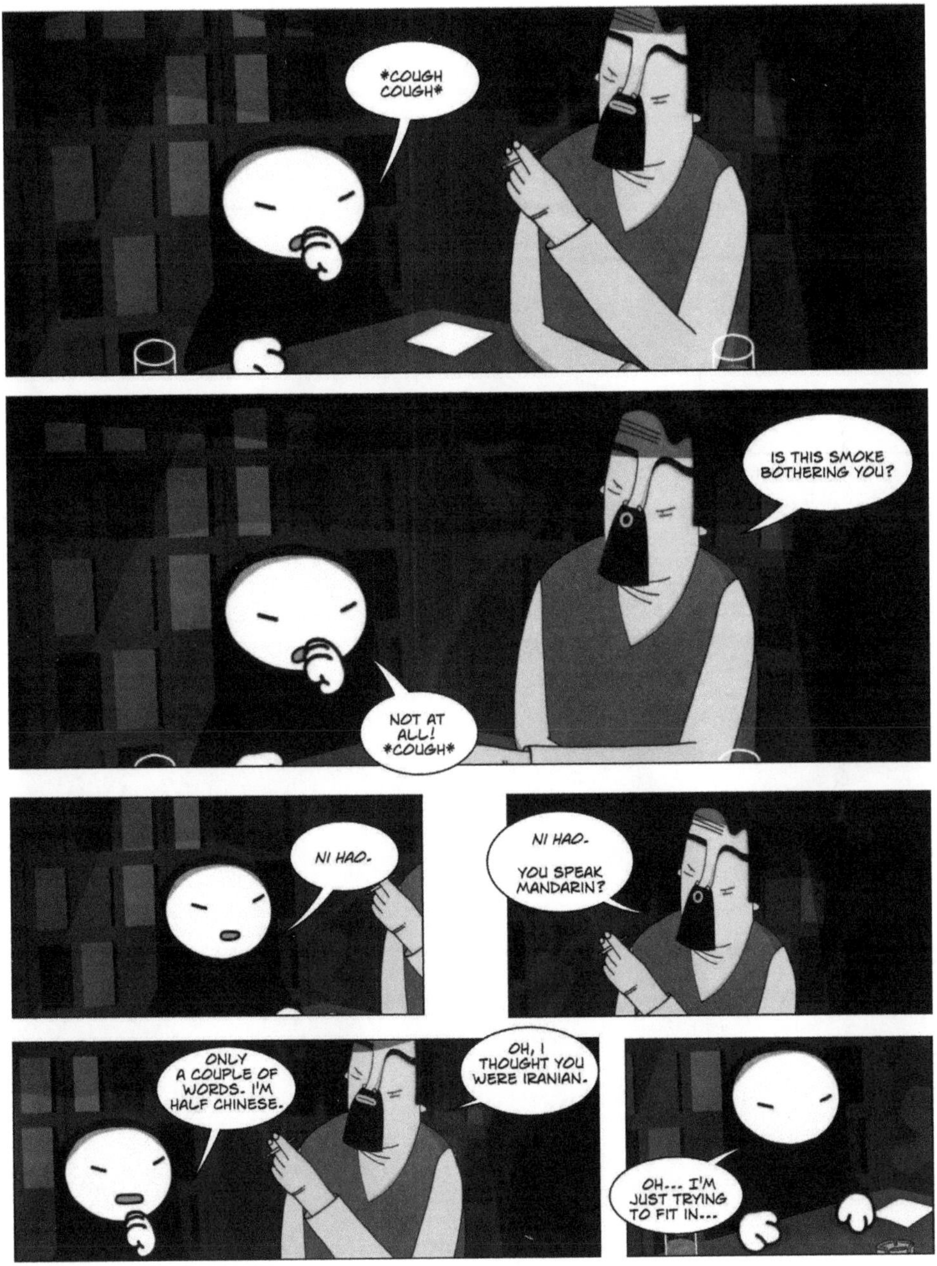
COUGH COUGH
IS THIS SMOKE BOTHERING YOU?
NOT AT ALL! *COUGH*
NI HAO.
NI HAO.
YOU SPEAK MANDARIN?
ONLY A COUPLE OF WORDS. I'M HALF CHINESE.
OH, I THOUGHT YOU WERE IRANIAN.
OH... I'M JUST TRYING TO FIT IN...

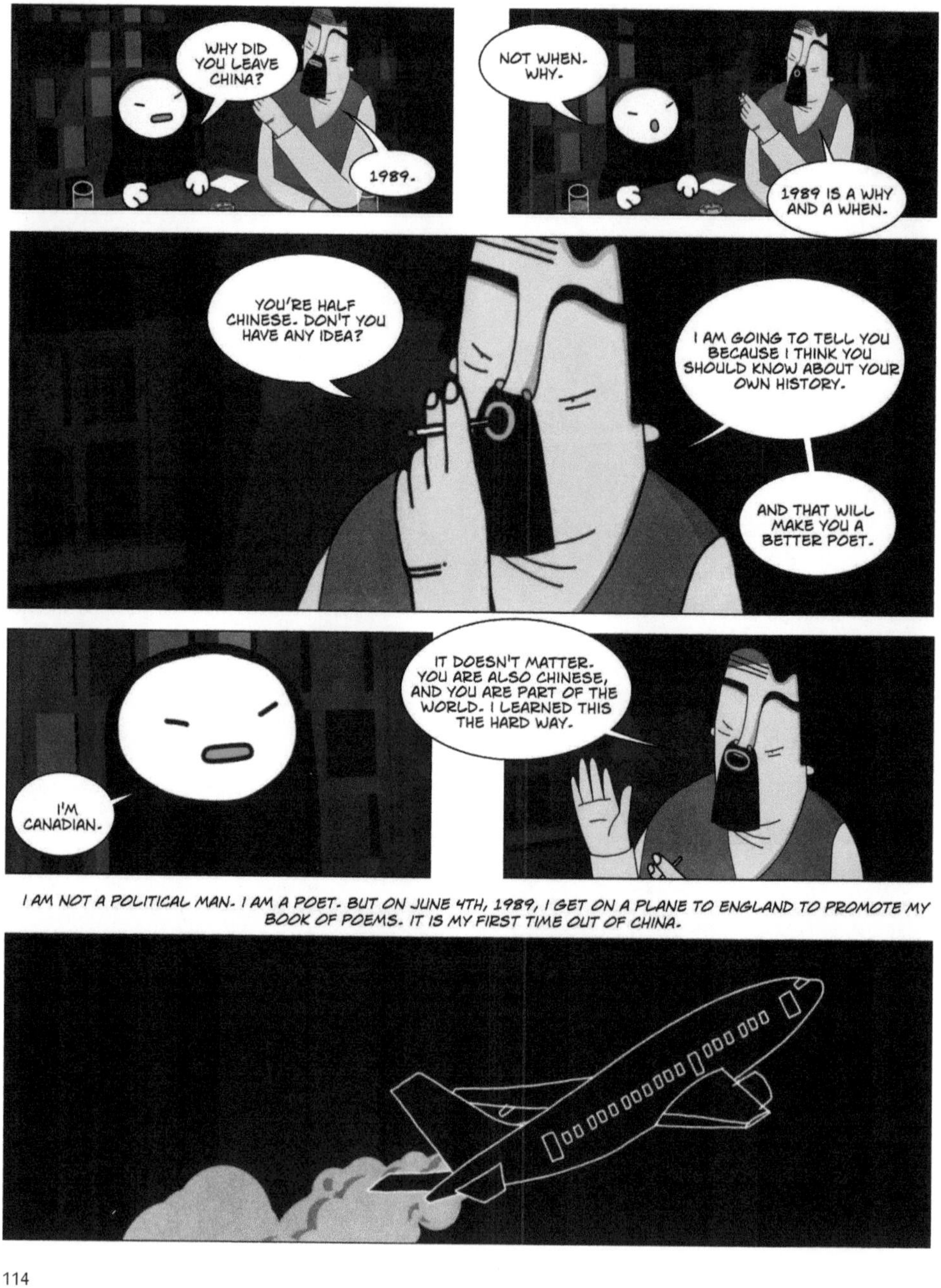
WHY DID YOU LEAVE CHINA?
1989.
NOT WHEN. WHY.
1989 IS A WHY AND A WHEN.
YOU'RE HALF CHINESE. DON'T YOU HAVE ANY IDEA?
I AM GOING TO TELL YOU BECAUSE I THINK YOU SHOULD KNOW ABOUT YOUR OWN HISTORY.
AND THAT WILL MAKE YOU A BETTER POET.
I'M CANADIAN.
IT DOESN'T MATTER. YOU ARE ALSO CHINESE, AND YOU ARE PART OF THE WORLD. I LEARNED THIS THE HARD WAY.
I AM NOT A POLITICAL MAN. I AM A POET. BUT ON JUNE 4TH, 1989, I GET ON A PLANE TO ENGLAND TO PROMOTE MY BOOK OF POEMS. IT IS MY FIRST TIME OUT OF CHINA.

WHEN I ARRIVE, THERE ARE MANY REPORTERS AT THE AIRPORT, ALL WITH MICROPHONES AND CAMERAS ASKING ME WHAT MY OPINION OF THE EVENTS IN CHINA IS.
"WHAT EVENTS IN CHINA?", I ASK.

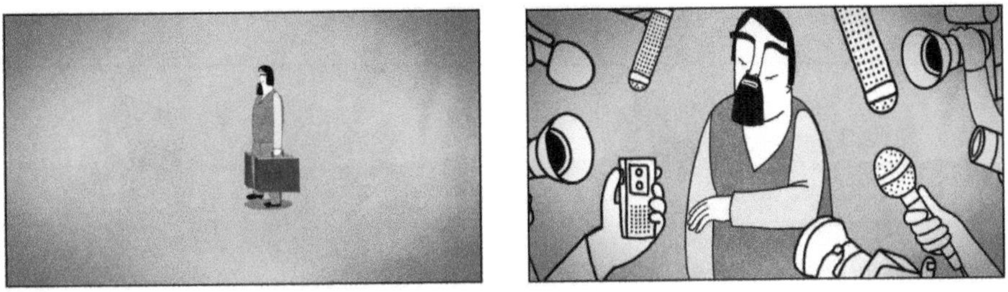

THEY TELL ME ABOUT WHAT HAPPENED IN TIANANMEN SQUARE.
I HAD SEEN THE PROTESTS BEFORE. SOME OF MY FRIENDS WERE TAKING PART.

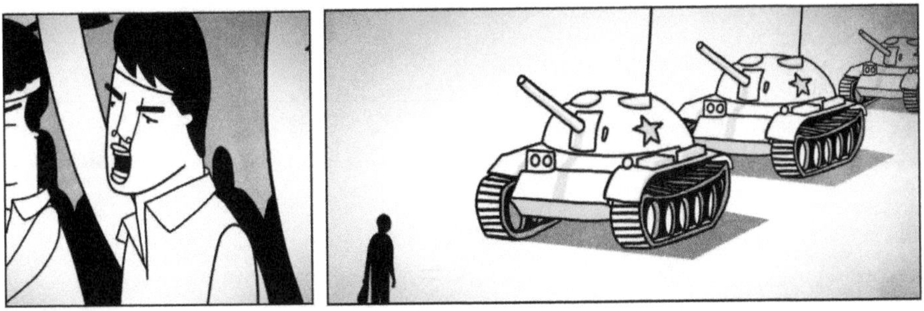

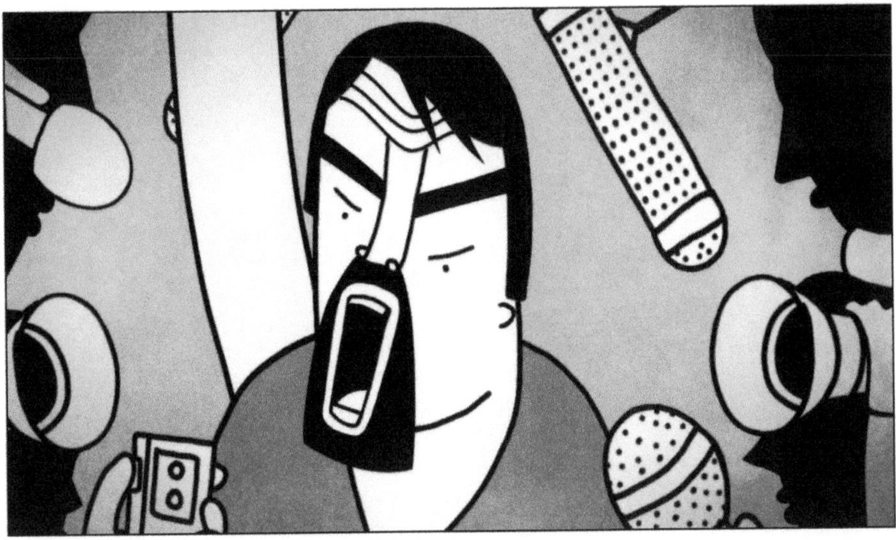

RIGHT THERE, I KNOW I HAVE TO MAKE A CHOICE, AND I DENOUNCE THE VIOLENCE AGAINST THE STUDENTS AND I CAN NEVER GO HOME AGAIN. AND I BECOME A POLITICAL MAN. LIKE THAT.

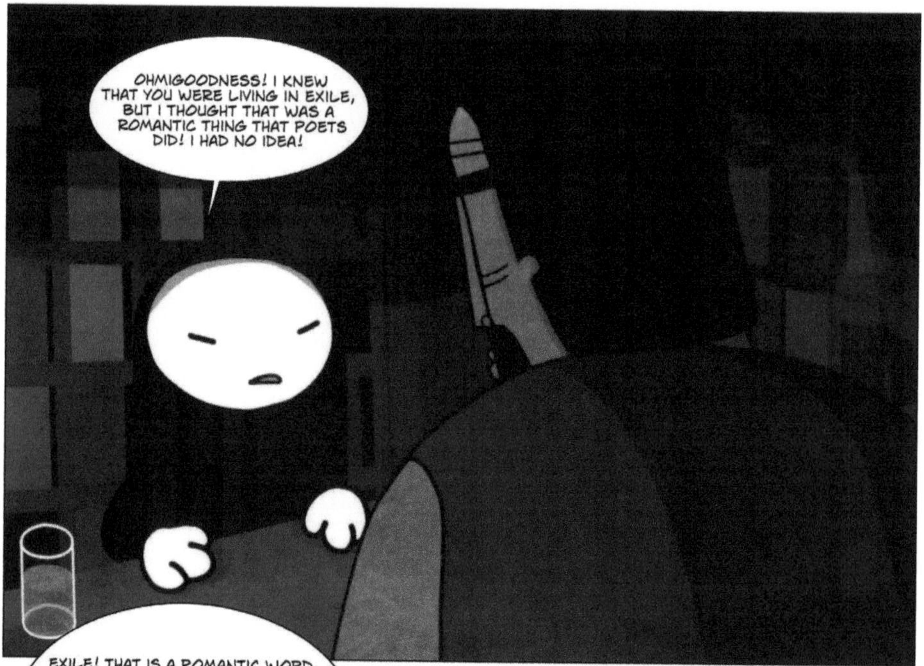
OHMIGOODNESS! I KNEW THAT YOU WERE LIVING IN EXILE, BUT I THOUGHT THAT WAS A ROMANTIC THING THAT POETS DID! I HAD NO IDEA!

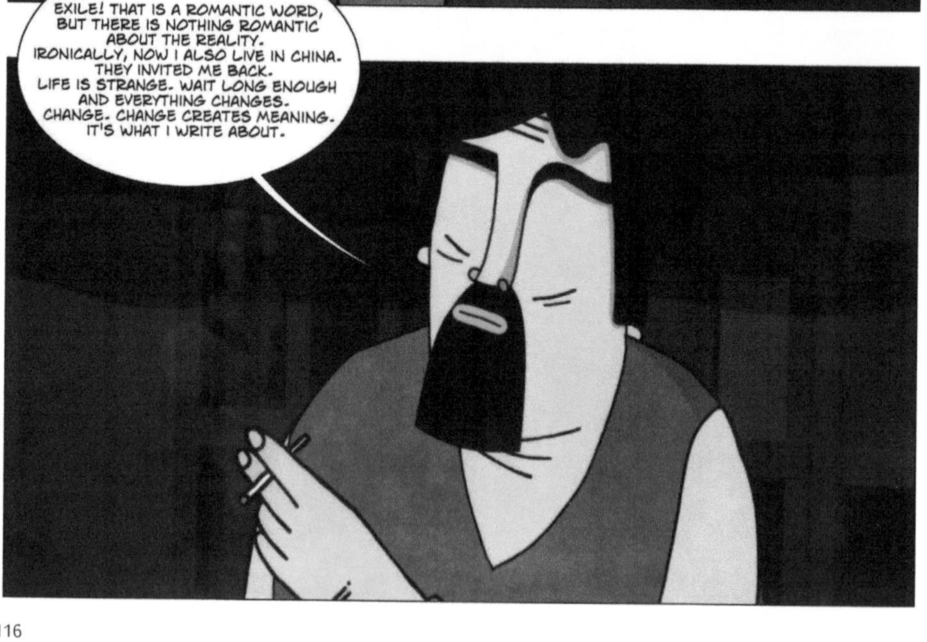
EXILE! THAT IS A ROMANTIC WORD, BUT THERE IS NOTHING ROMANTIC ABOUT THE REALITY. IRONICALLY, NOW I ALSO LIVE IN CHINA. THEY INVITED ME BACK. LIFE IS STRANGE. WAIT LONG ENOUGH AND EVERYTHING CHANGES. CHANGE. CHANGE CREATES MEANING. IT'S WHAT I WRITE ABOUT.

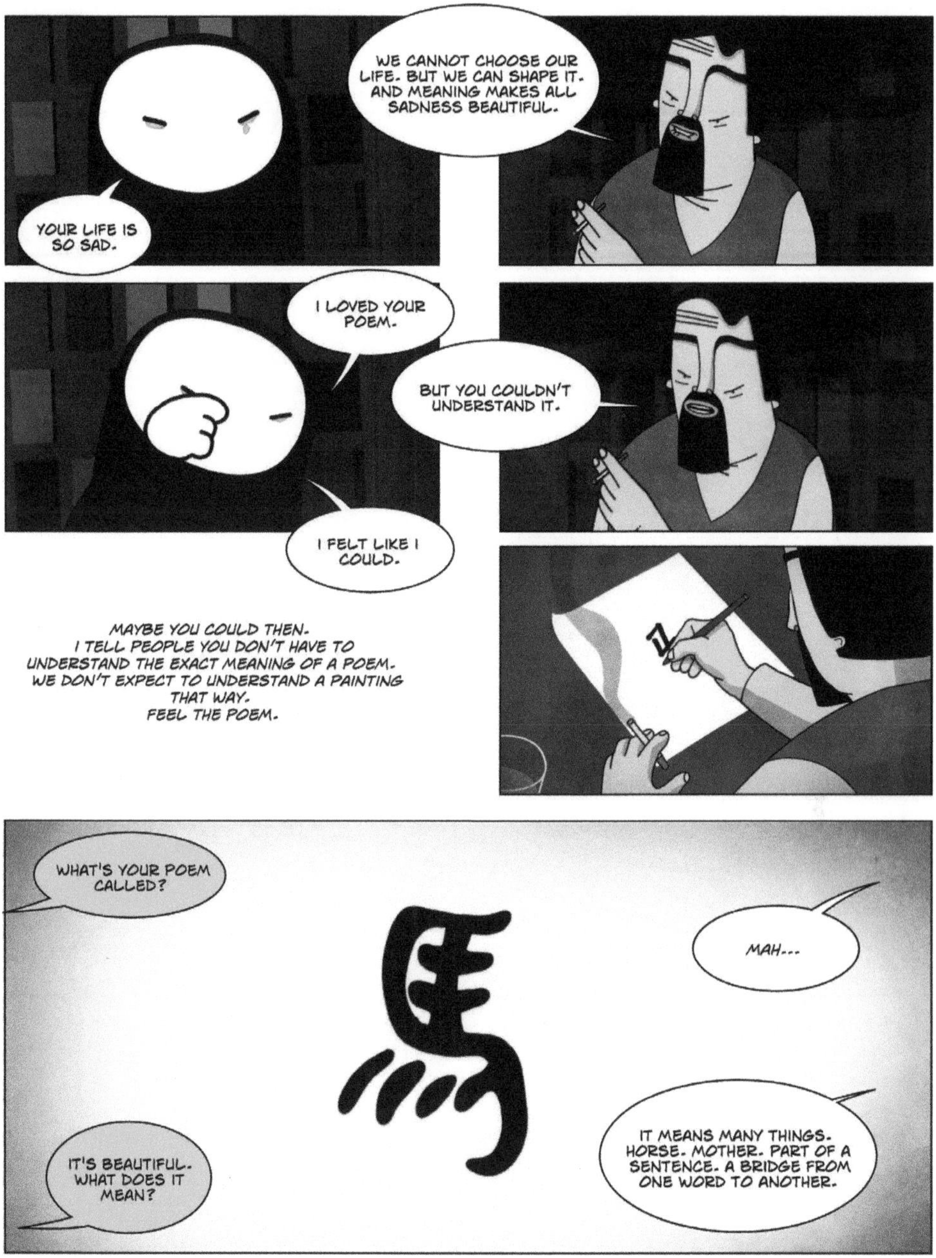
YOUR LIFE IS SO SAD.
WE CANNOT CHOOSE OUR LIFE. BUT WE CAN SHAPE IT. AND MEANING MAKES ALL SADNESS BEAUTIFUL.
I LOVED YOUR POEM.
BUT YOU COULDN'T UNDERSTAND IT.
I FELT LIKE I COULD.
MAYBE YOU COULD THEN.
I TELL PEOPLE YOU DON'T HAVE TO UNDERSTAND THE EXACT MEANING OF A POEM.
WE DON'T EXPECT TO UNDERSTAND A PAINTING THAT WAY.
FEEL THE POEM.
WHAT'S YOUR POEM CALLED?
馬
MAH...
IT'S BEAUTIFUL. WHAT DOES IT MEAN?
IT MEANS MANY THINGS. HORSE. MOTHER. PART OF A SENTENCE. A BRIDGE FROM ONE WORD TO ANOTHER.

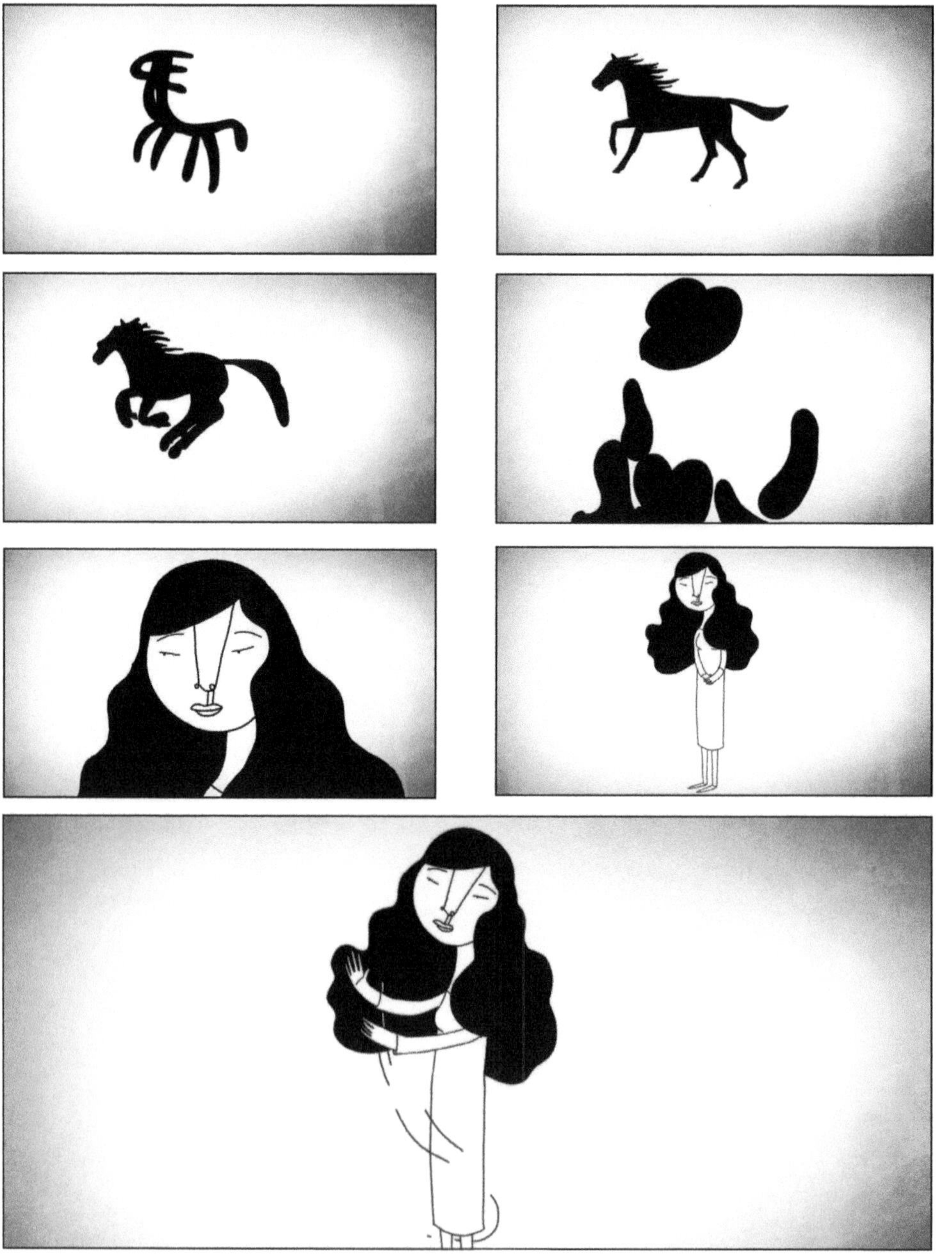

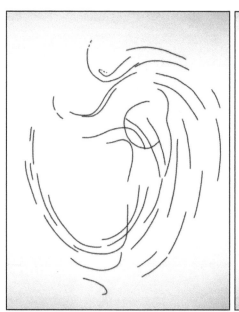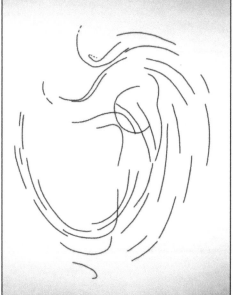

晚年不常乐
独驰骋无端
路逢异都他乡土
追
人面荡於心
空忧伤恨形自清

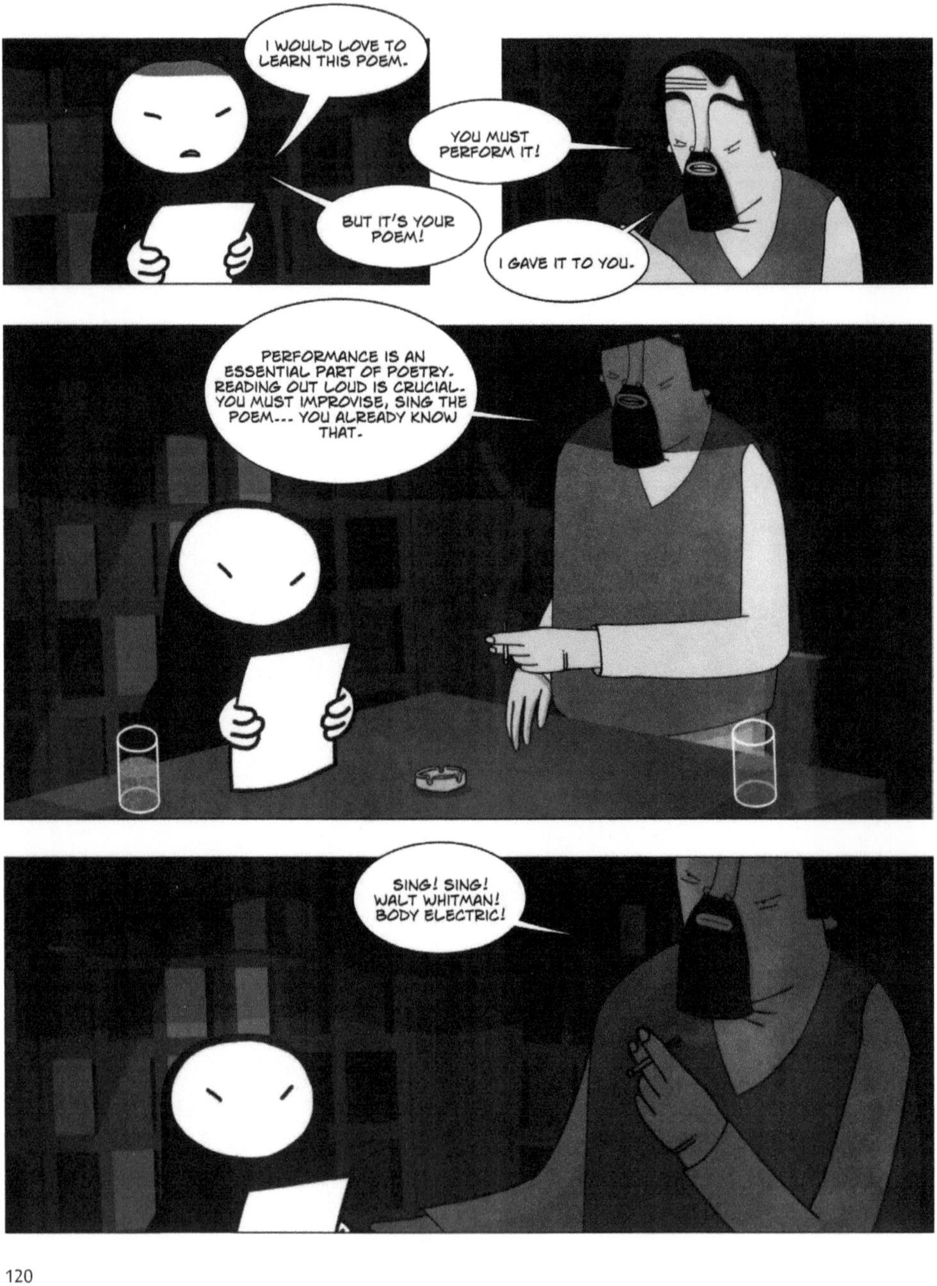
I WOULD LOVE TO LEARN THIS POEM.
YOU MUST PERFORM IT!
BUT IT'S YOUR POEM!
I GAVE IT TO YOU.
PERFORMANCE IS AN ESSENTIAL PART OF POETRY. READING OUT LOUD IS CRUCIAL. YOU MUST IMPROVISE, SING THE POEM... YOU ALREADY KNOW THAT.
SING! SING! WALT WHITMAN! BODY ELECTRIC!

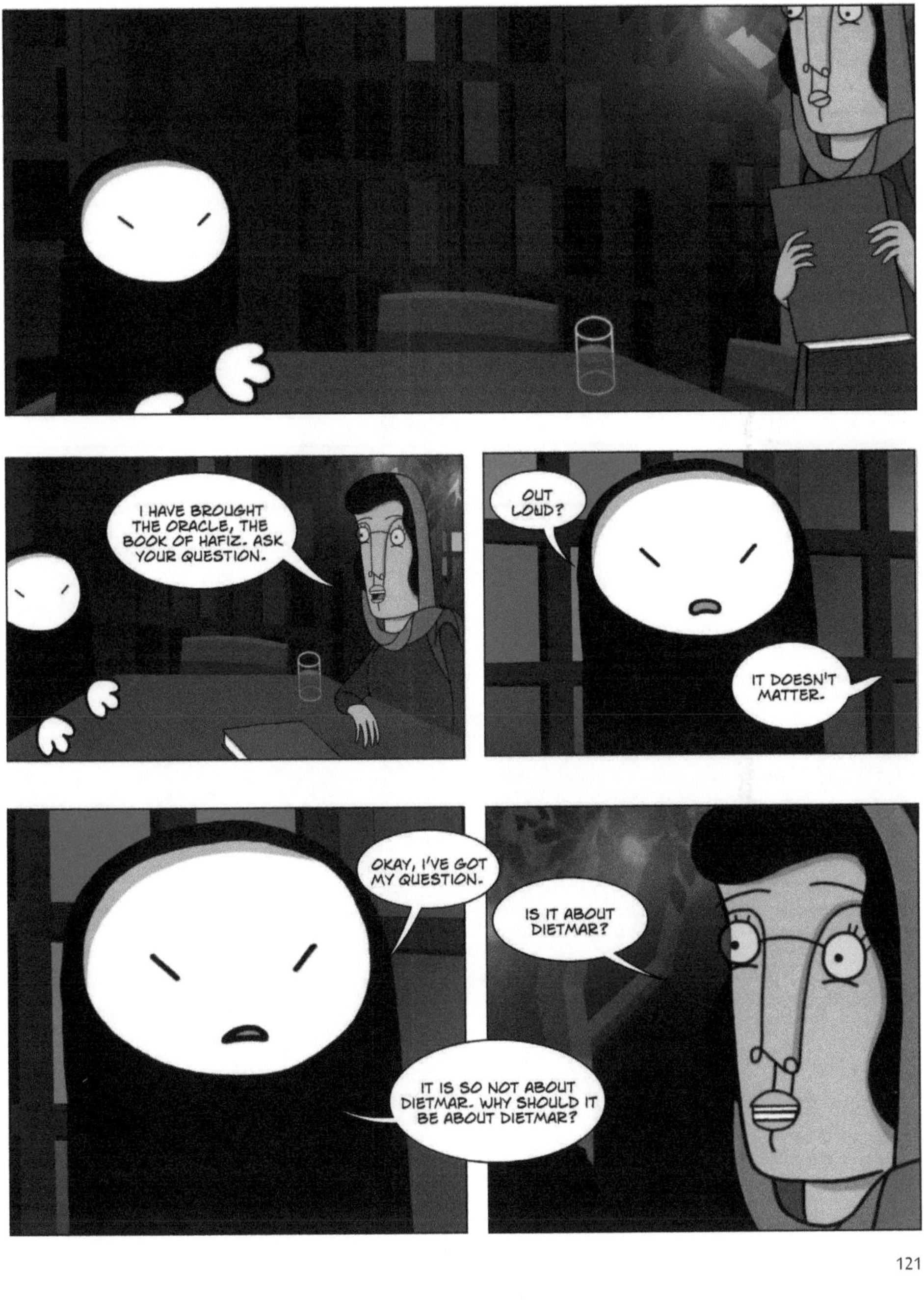
I HAVE BROUGHT THE ORACLE, THE BOOK OF HAFIZ. ASK YOUR QUESTION.
OUT LOUD?
IT DOESN'T MATTER.
OKAY, I'VE GOT MY QUESTION.
IS IT ABOUT DIETMAR?
IT IS SO NOT ABOUT DIETMAR. WHY SHOULD IT BE ABOUT DIETMAR?

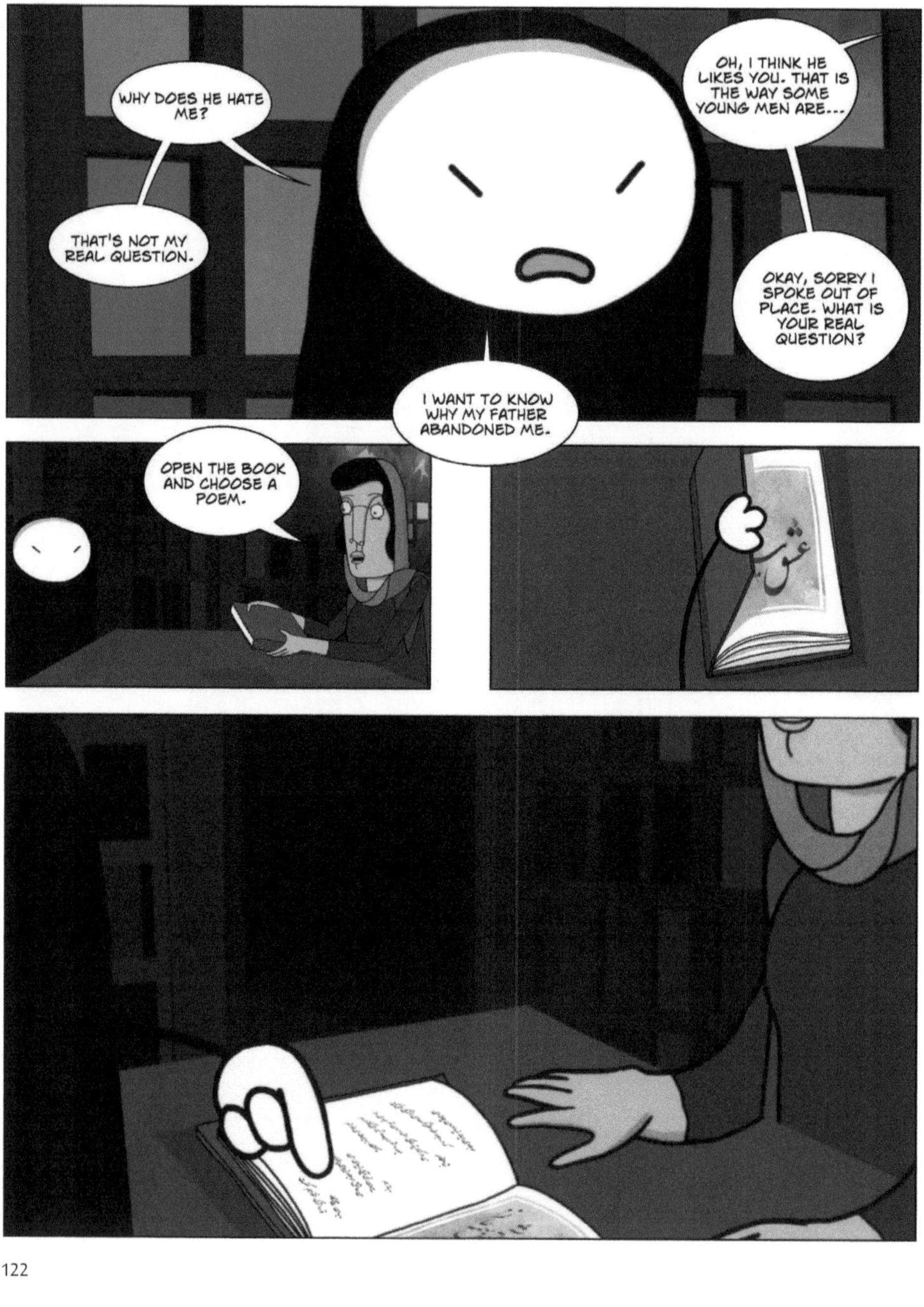
WHY DOES HE HATE ME?
OH, I THINK HE LIKES YOU. THAT IS THE WAY SOME YOUNG MEN ARE...
THAT'S NOT MY REAL QUESTION.
OKAY, SORRY I SPOKE OUT OF PLACE. WHAT IS YOUR REAL QUESTION?
I WANT TO KNOW WHY MY FATHER ABANDONED ME.
OPEN THE BOOK AND CHOOSE A POEM.

THERE IS A BEAUTIFUL CREATURE LIVING IN A HOLE YOU HAVE DUG.

*FROM "I HEARD GOD LAUGHING" BY HAFIZ
TRANSLATED BY DANIEL LADINSKY
COPYRIGHT 1996, 2006, AND USED WITH PERMISSION.

*ILLUSTRATIONS BY JODY KRAMER

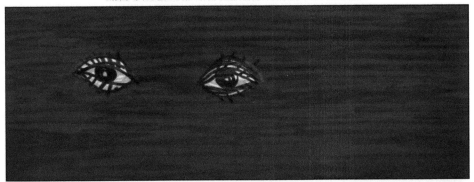

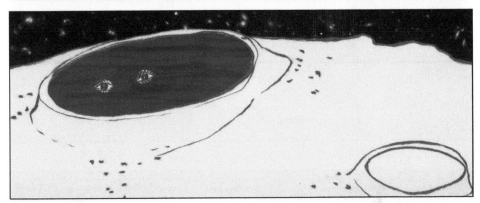

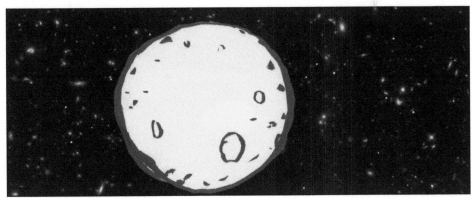

SO AT NIGHT I SET FRUITS AND GRAINS
AND LITTLE POTS OF WINE AND MILK
BESIDE YOUR SOFT EARTHEN MOUNDS

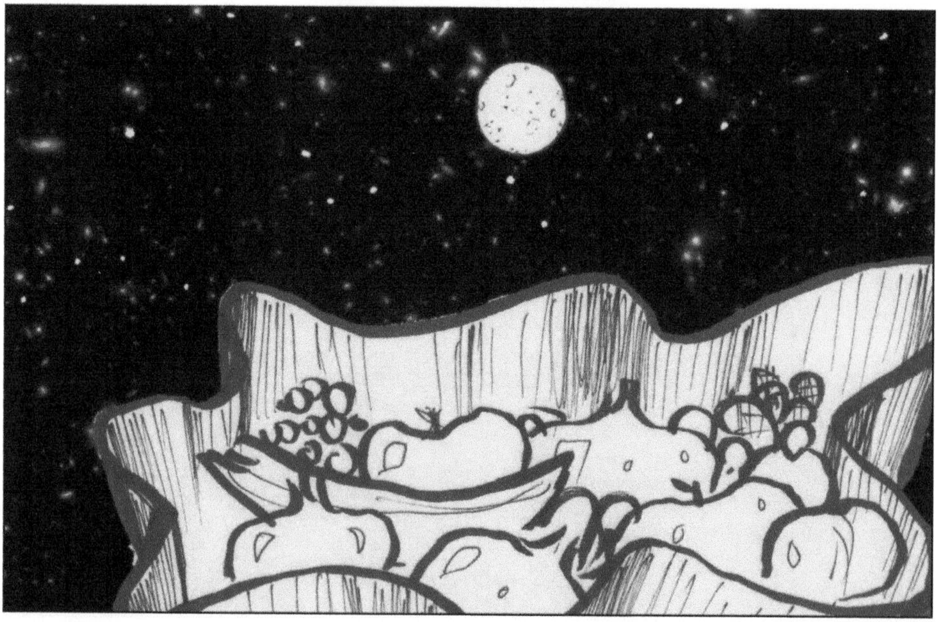

AND I OFTEN SING...

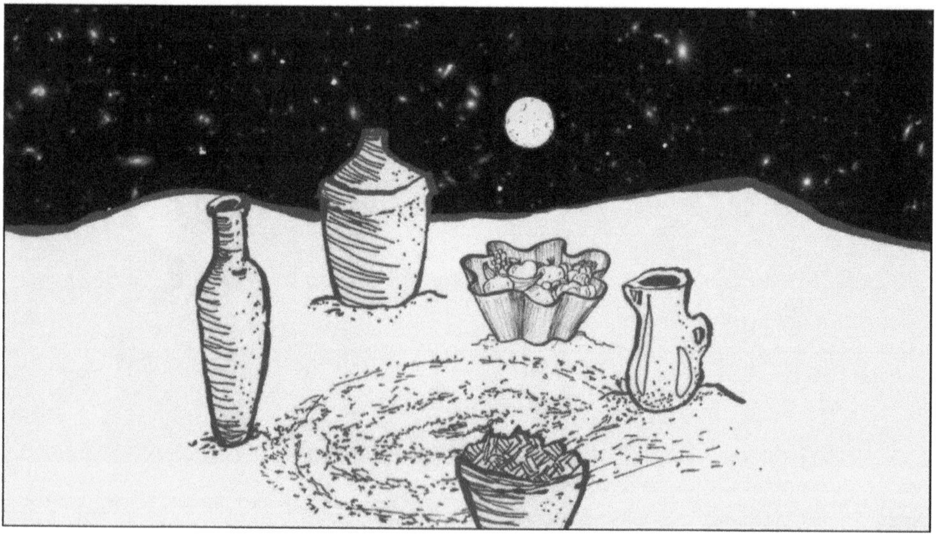

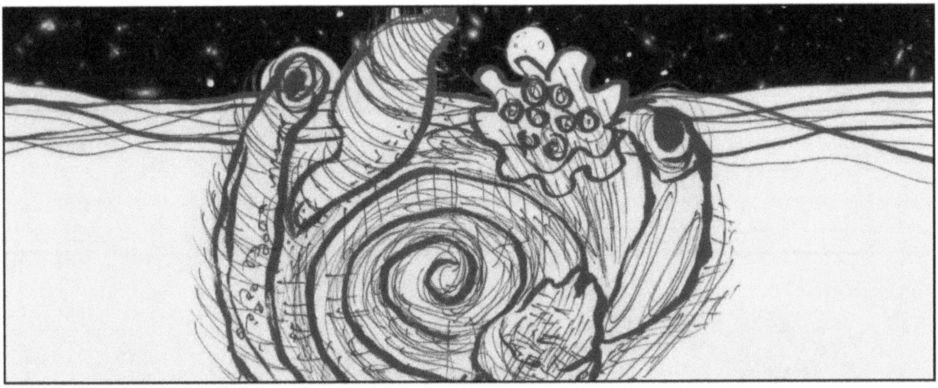

BUT STILL, MY DEAR
YOU DON'T COME OUT

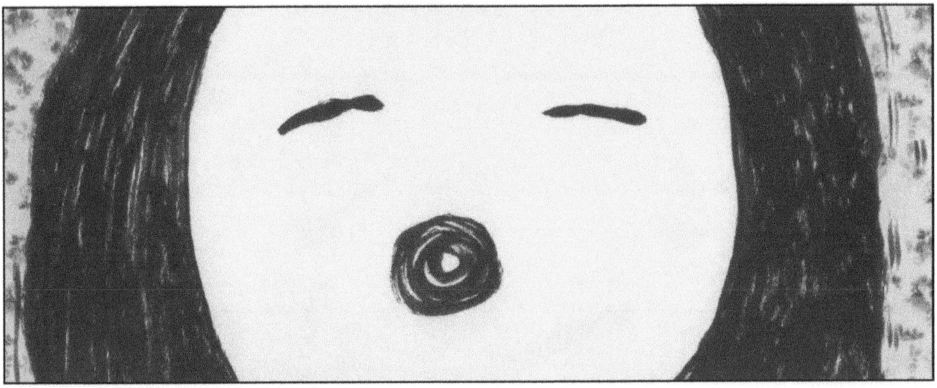

I HAVE FALLEN IN LOVE WITH SOMEONE INSIDE YOU.

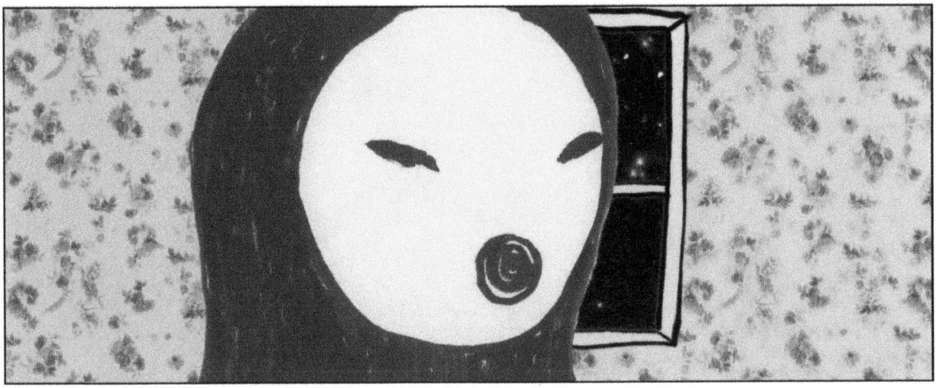

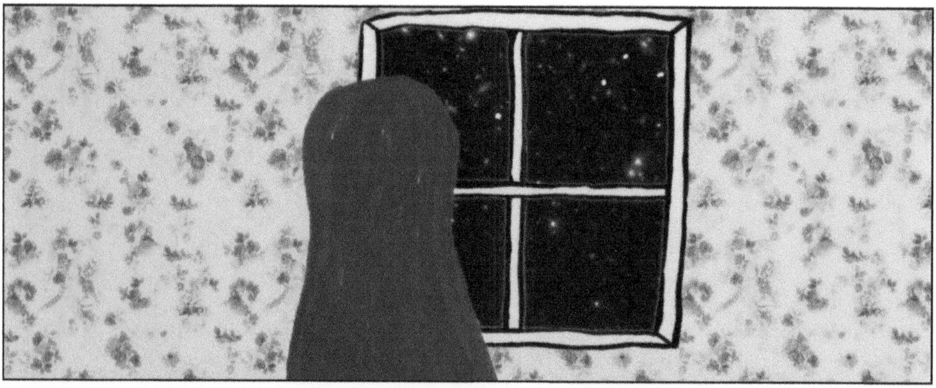

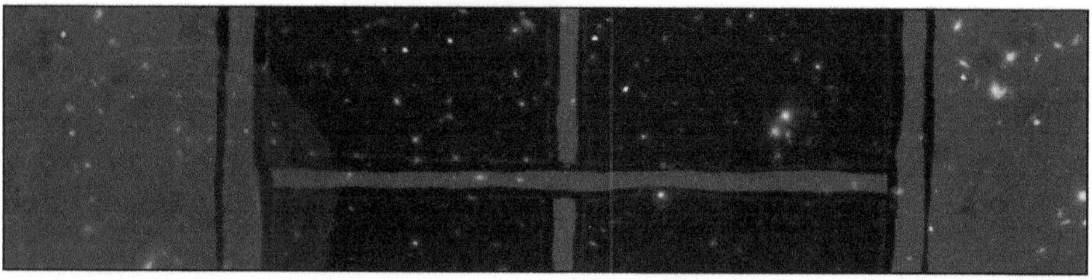

WE SHOULD TALK ABOUT THIS PROBLEM...
OTHERWISE, I WILL NEVER LEAVE YOU ALONE.

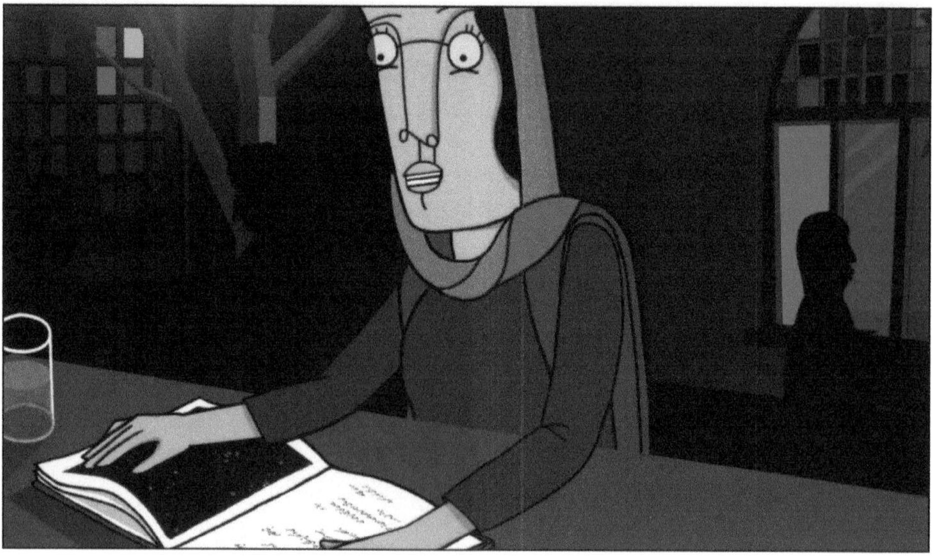

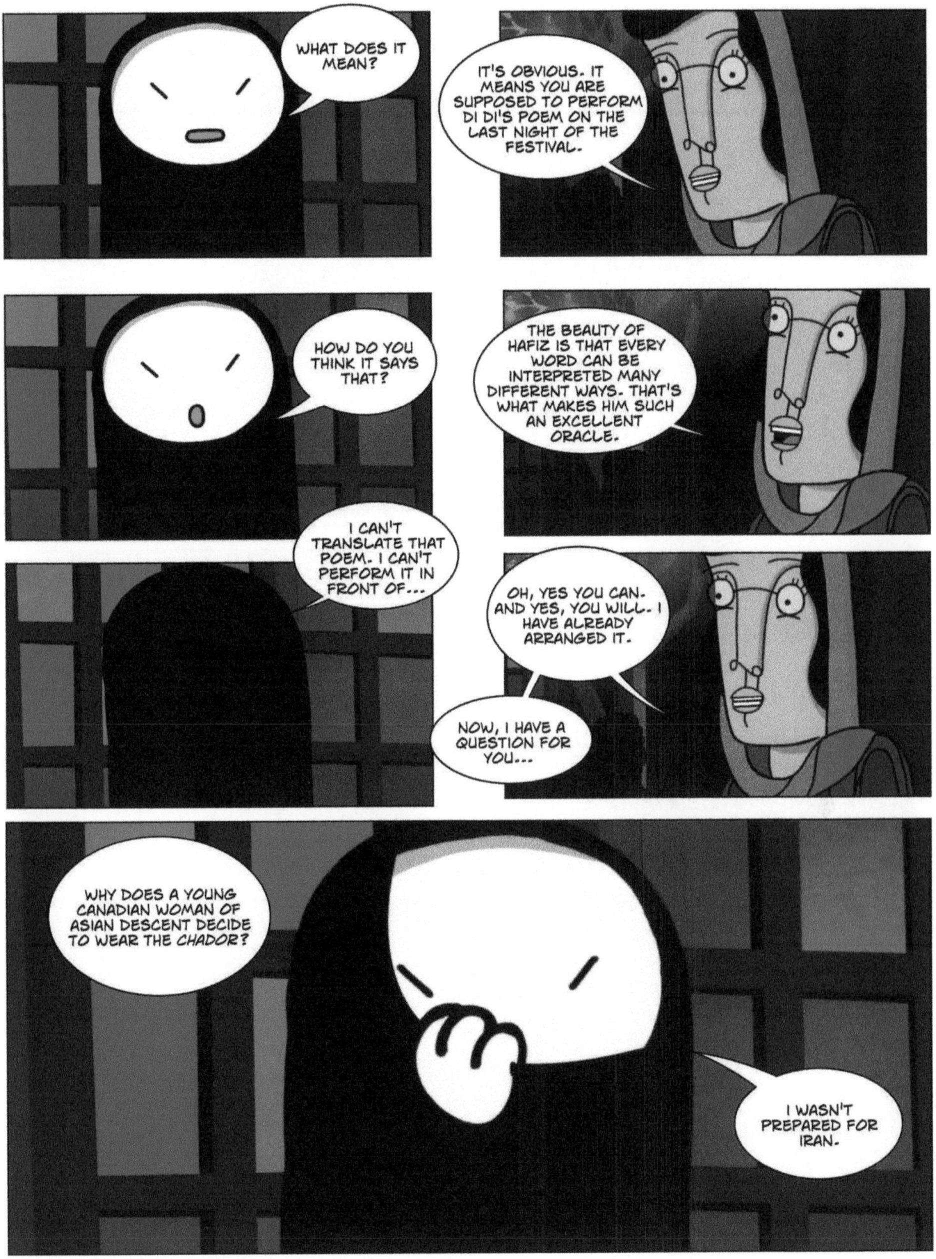
WHAT DOES IT MEAN?
IT'S OBVIOUS. IT MEANS YOU ARE SUPPOSED TO PERFORM DI DI'S POEM ON THE LAST NIGHT OF THE FESTIVAL.
HOW DO YOU THINK IT SAYS THAT?
THE BEAUTY OF HAFIZ IS THAT EVERY WORD CAN BE INTERPRETED MANY DIFFERENT WAYS. THAT'S WHAT MAKES HIM SUCH AN EXCELLENT ORACLE.
I CAN'T TRANSLATE THAT POEM. I CAN'T PERFORM IT IN FRONT OF...
OH, YES YOU CAN. AND YES, YOU WILL. I HAVE ALREADY ARRANGED IT.
NOW, I HAVE A QUESTION FOR YOU...
WHY DOES A YOUNG CANADIAN WOMAN OF ASIAN DESCENT DECIDE TO WEAR THE CHADOR?
I WASN'T PREPARED FOR IRAN.

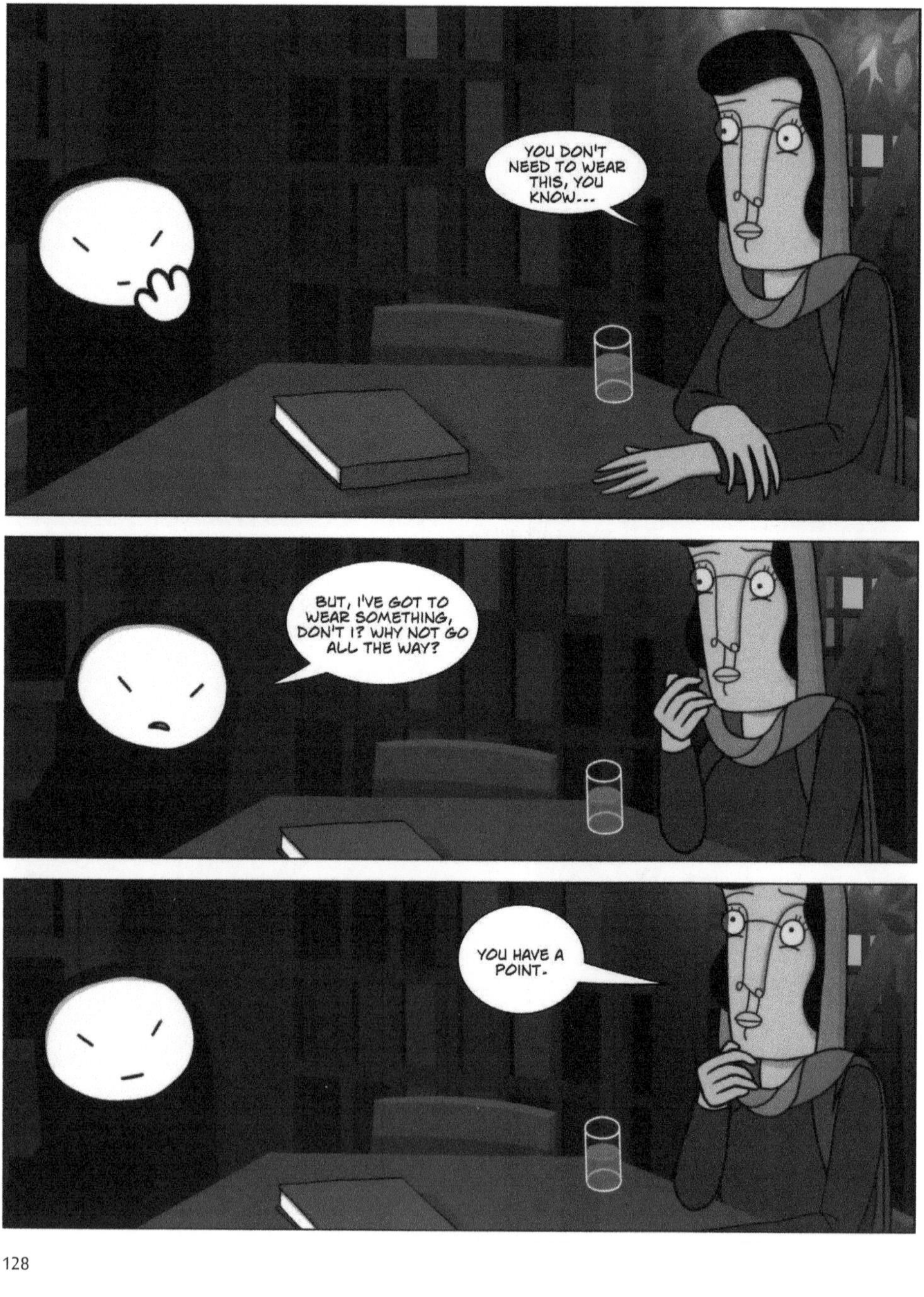
YOU DON'T NEED TO WEAR THIS, YOU KNOW...
BUT, I'VE GOT TO WEAR SOMETHING, DON'T I? WHY NOT GO ALL THE WAY?
YOU HAVE A POINT.

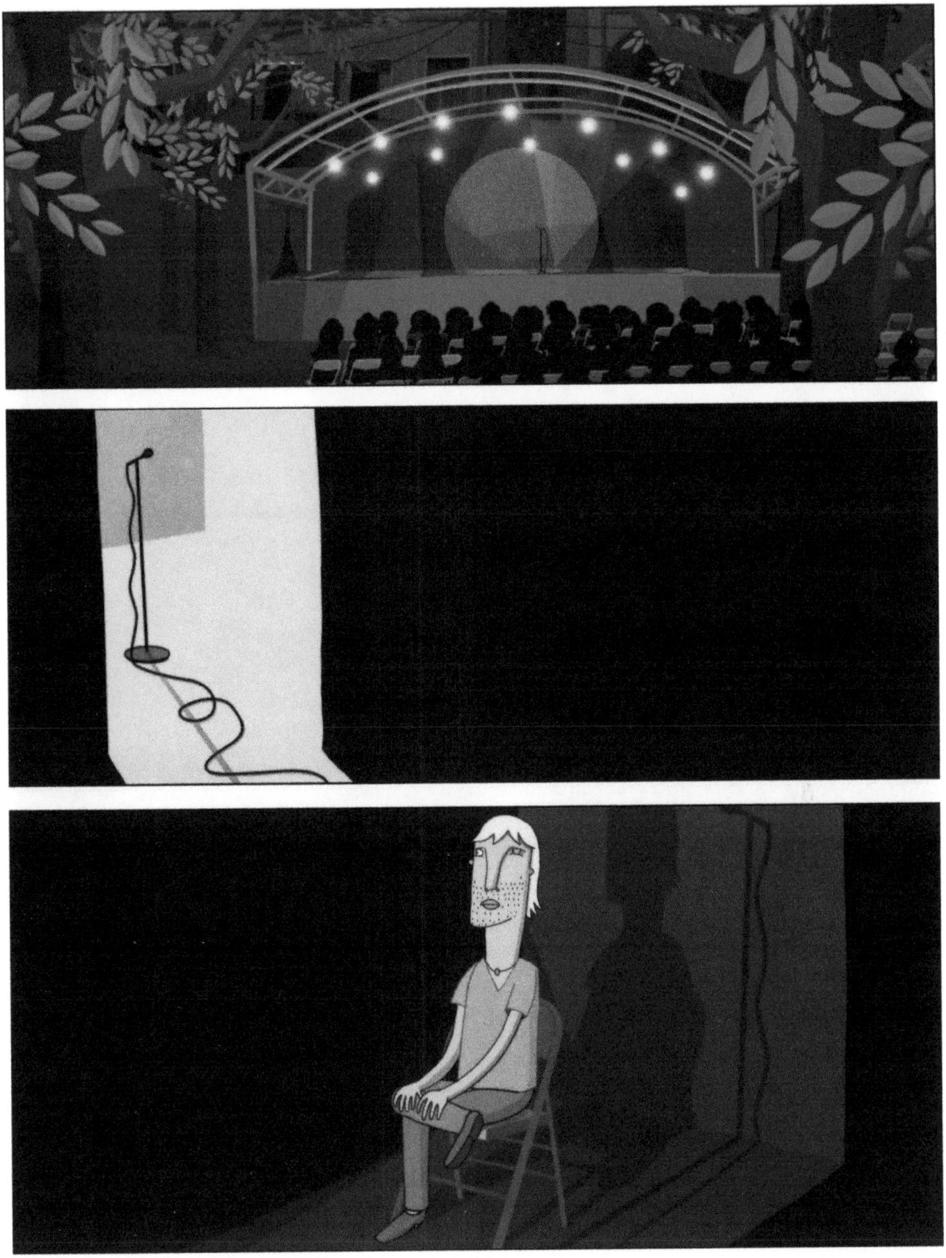

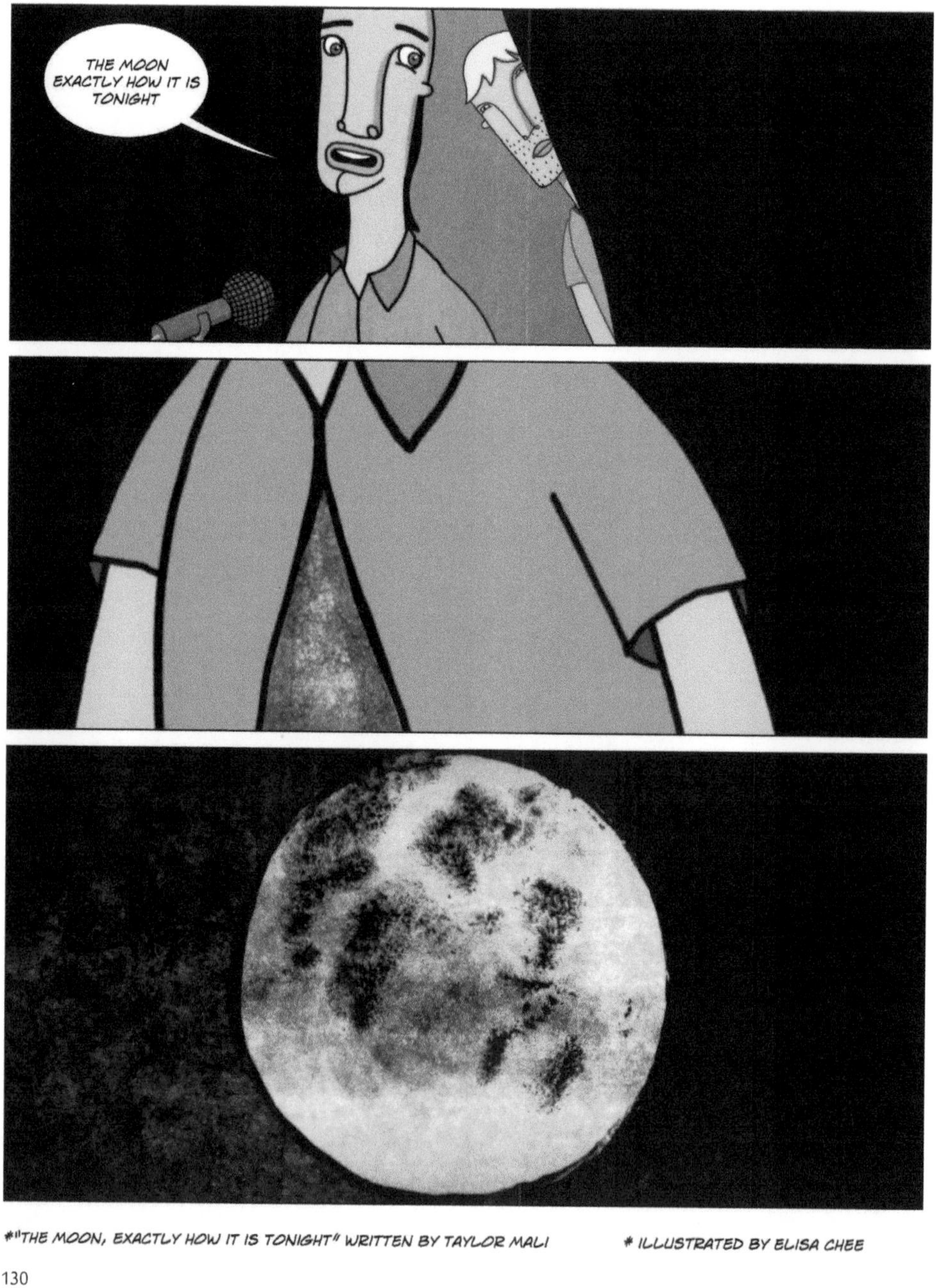
THE MOON EXACTLY HOW IT IS TONIGHT

*"THE MOON, EXACTLY HOW IT IS TONIGHT" WRITTEN BY TAYLOR MALI * ILLUSTRATED BY ELISA CHEE

WHEN MOUNT EVEREST WAS MEASURED IN 1856,
IT WAS DISCOVERED TO BE 29,000 FEET EXACTLY.
BUT SINCE NO ONE WOULD HAVE BELIEVED THE FIGURE,

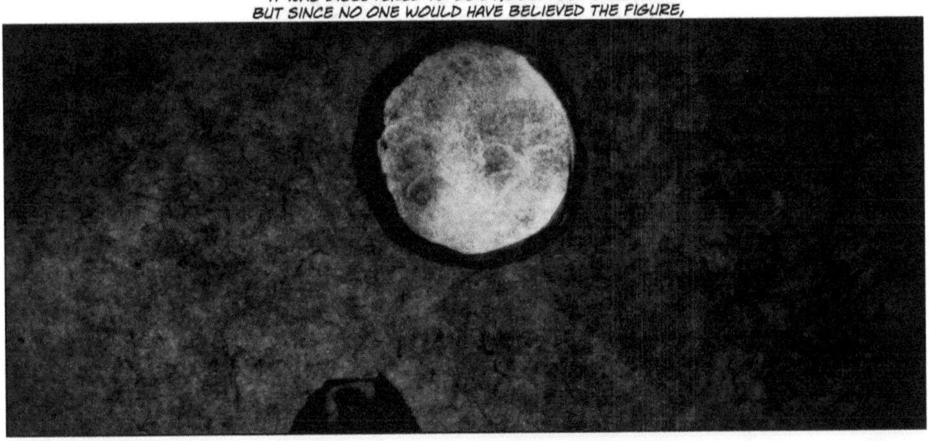

SOUNDING AS IT DOES TOO CLOSE TO SOMETHING
ROUNDED OFF, TWO EXTRA FEET WERE FOUND,
INVENTED OUT OF THIN AIR, THE THINNEST ON EARTH,

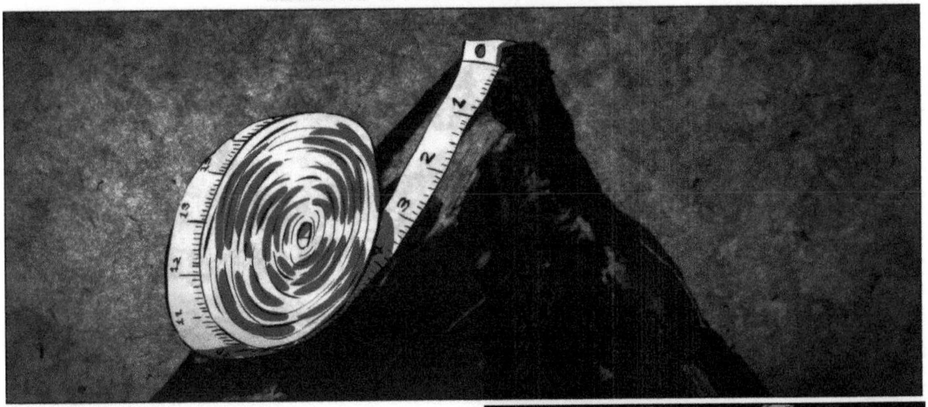

AND ADDED TO THE MOUNTAIN'S TOP
TO PROVIDE THE APPEARANCE OF PRECISION.
TWENTY-NINE THOUSAND AND TWO.

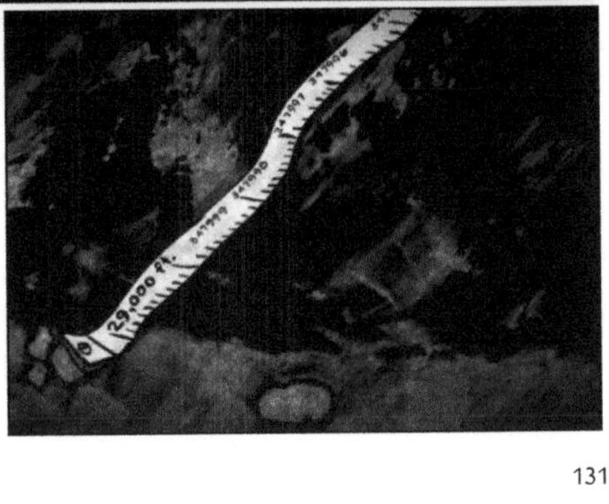
29,000 ft.

SO, TOO, TONIGHT, A CLOUD HAS PASSED
BEFORE THE MOON IN SUCH A WAY
THAT WERE I ABLE TO DESCRIBE IT

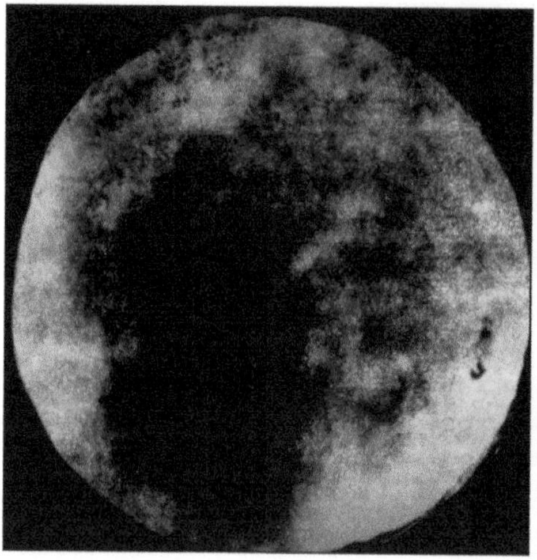

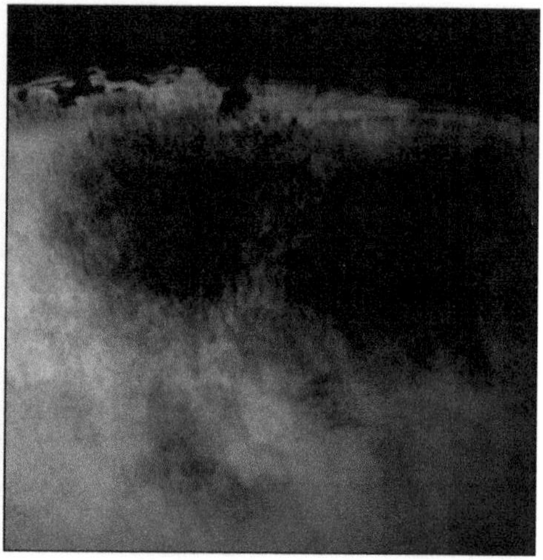

EXACTLY HOW IT IS, NO ONE WOULD BELIEVE ME.
WHICH IS WHY I NEED TWO EXTRA FEET OF MOONLIGHT,
OR DARK CLOUD, OR TO BE FAIR, ONE FOOT OF EACH.

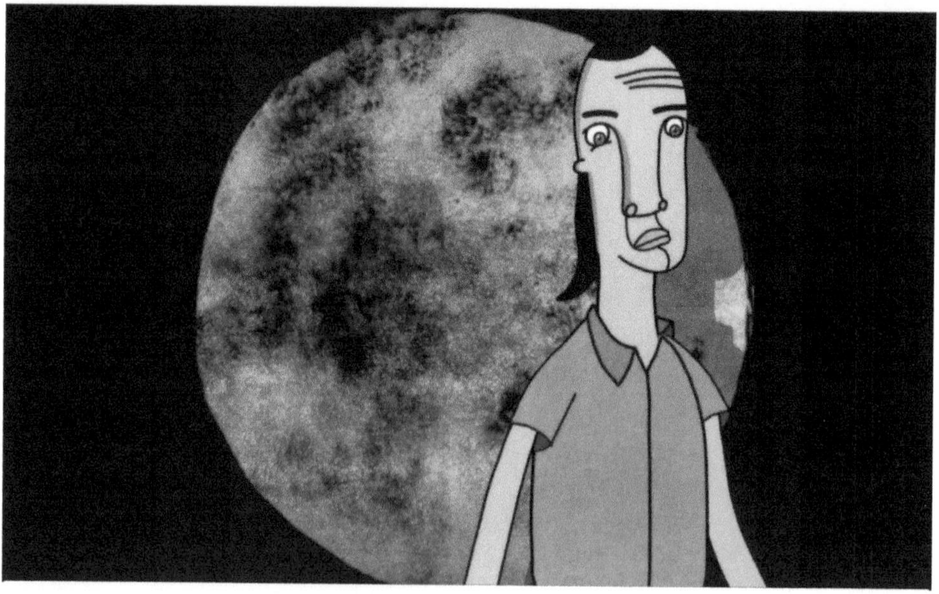

TAYLOR LEAVES THE STAGE TO THUNDEROUS APPLAUSE.

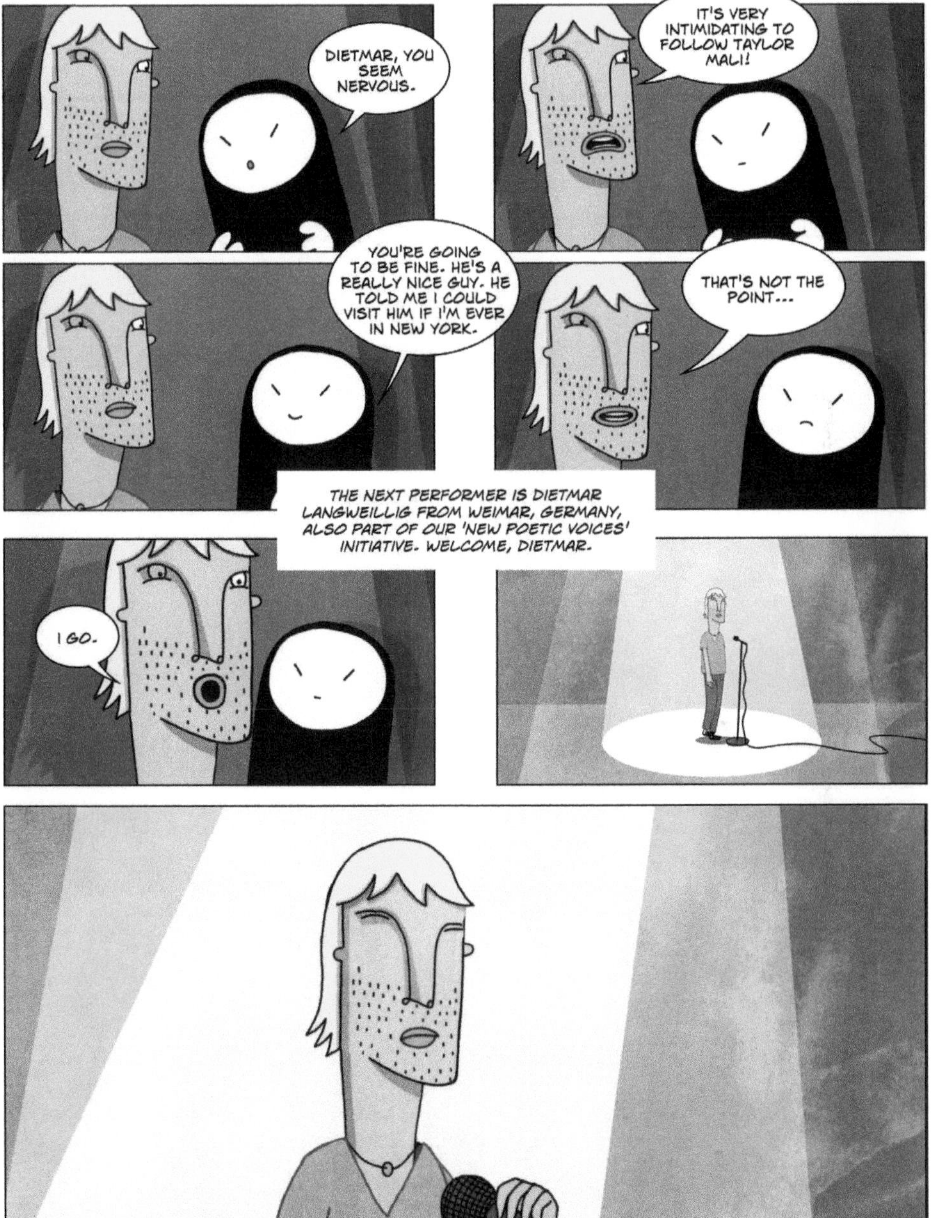
DIETMAR, YOU SEEM NERVOUS.
IT'S VERY INTIMIDATING TO FOLLOW TAYLOR MALI!
YOU'RE GOING TO BE FINE. HE'S A REALLY NICE GUY. HE TOLD ME I COULD VISIT HIM IF I'M EVER IN NEW YORK.
THAT'S NOT THE POINT...
I GO.
THE NEXT PERFORMER IS DIETMAR LANGWEILLIG FROM WEIMAR, GERMANY, ALSO PART OF OUR 'NEW POETIC VOICES' INITIATIVE. WELCOME, DIETMAR.

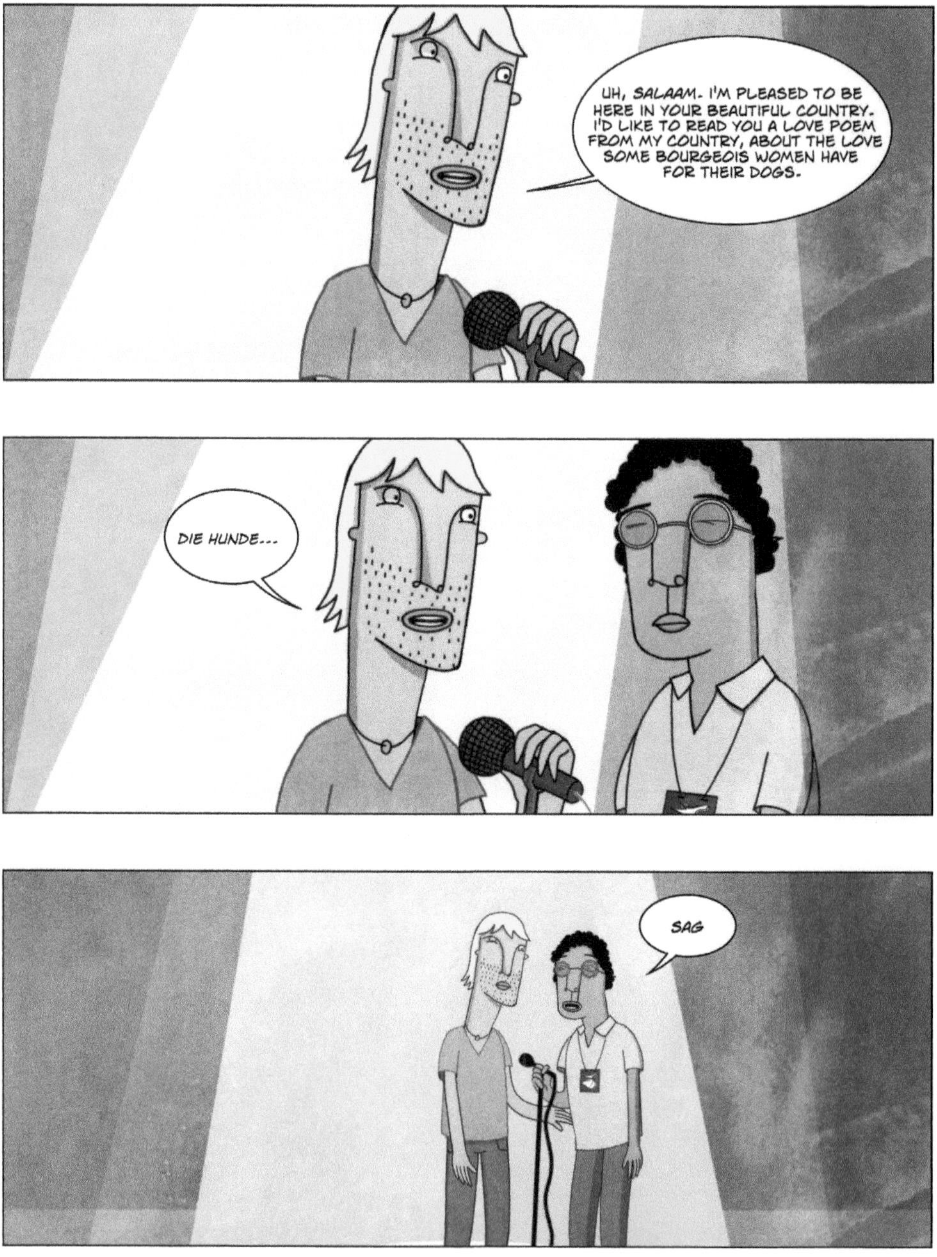
UH, SALAAM. I'M PLEASED TO BE HERE IN YOUR BEAUTIFUL COUNTRY. I'D LIKE TO READ YOU A LOVE POEM FROM MY COUNTRY, ABOUT THE LOVE SOME BOURGEOIS WOMEN HAVE FOR THEIR DOGS.
DIE HUNDE...
SAG

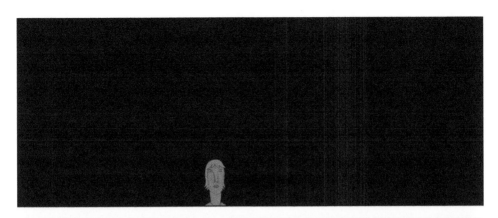

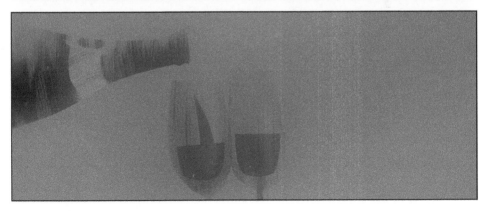

*"DIE HUNDE" ILLUSTRATED BY MICHAEL MANN

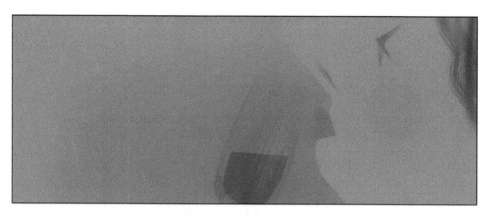

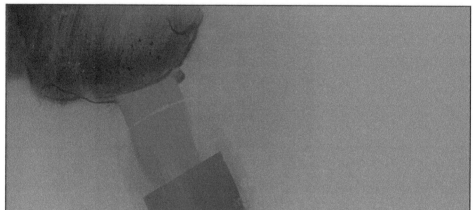

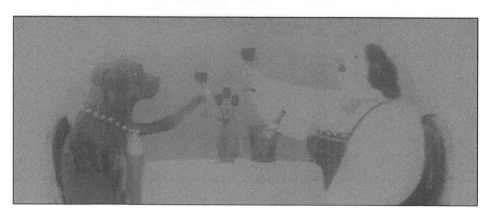

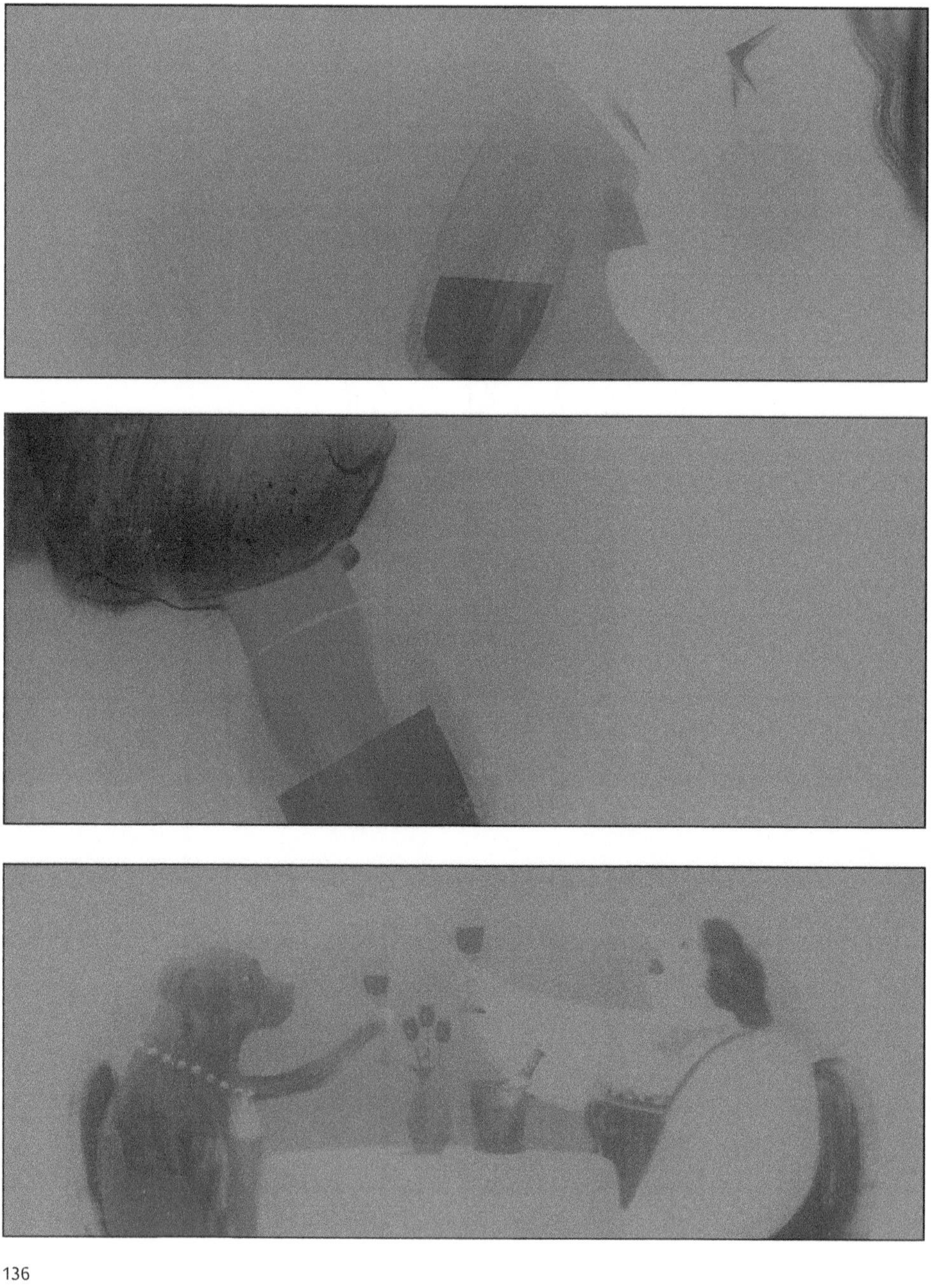

IT IS NOT GOING WELL.

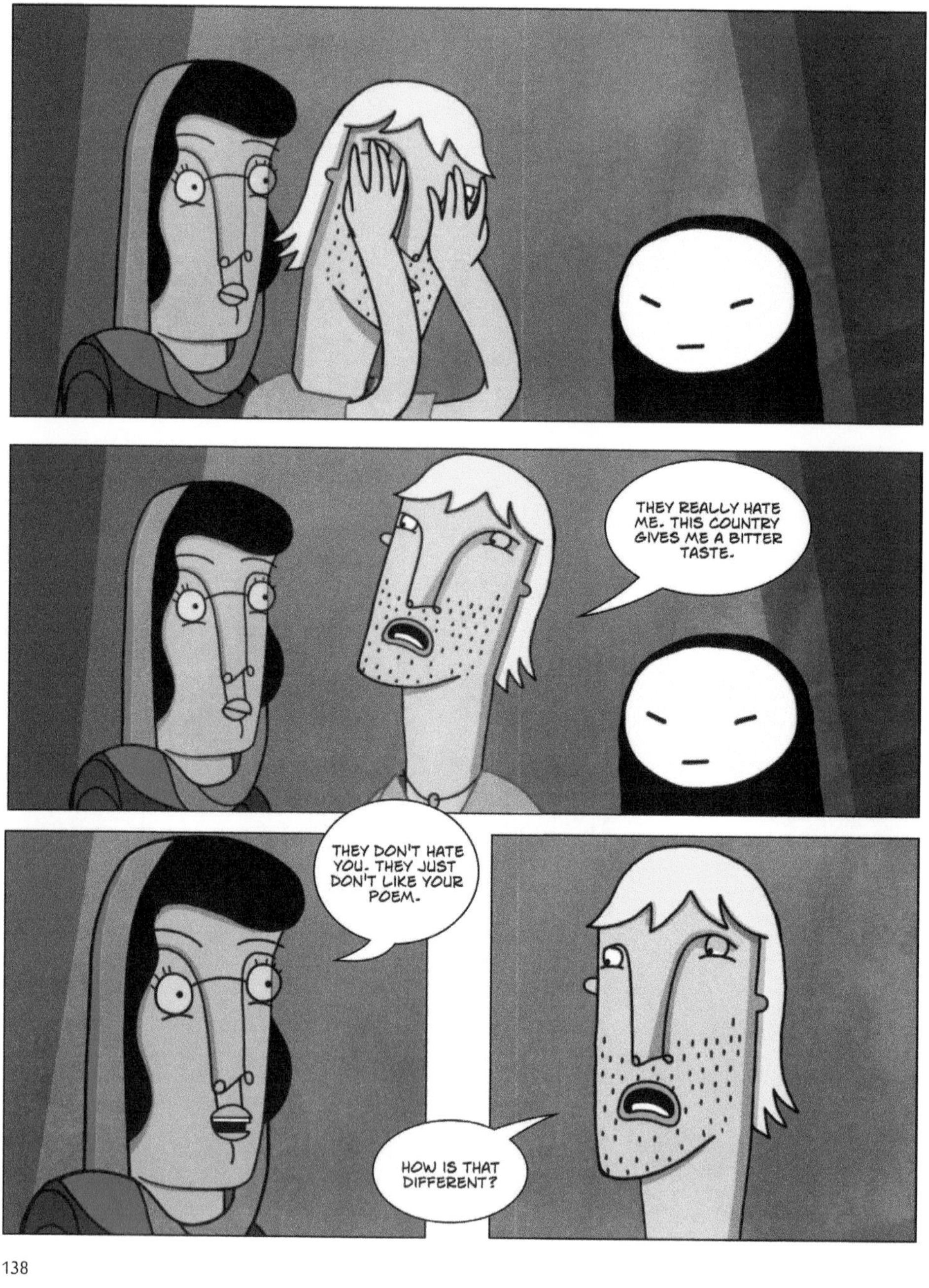
THEY REALLY HATE ME. THIS COUNTRY GIVES ME A BITTER TASTE.
THEY DON'T HATE YOU. THEY JUST DON'T LIKE YOUR POEM.
HOW IS THAT DIFFERENT?

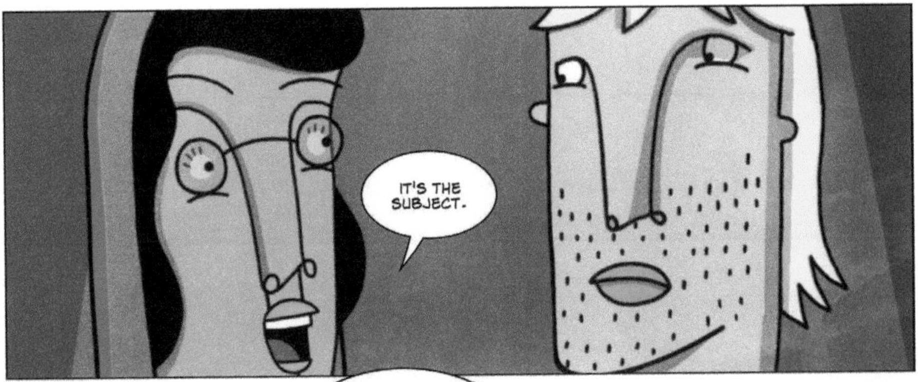
IT'S THE SUBJECT.
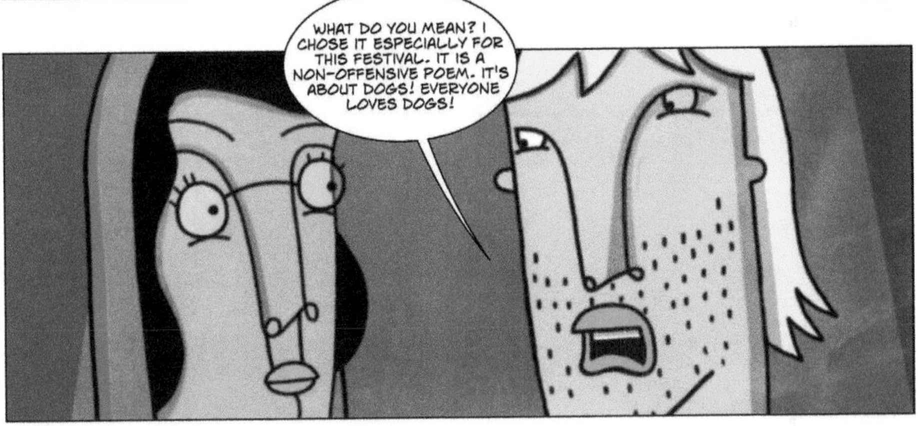
WHAT DO YOU MEAN? I CHOSE IT ESPECIALLY FOR THIS FESTIVAL. IT IS A NON-OFFENSIVE POEM. IT'S ABOUT DOGS! EVERYONE LOVES DOGS!
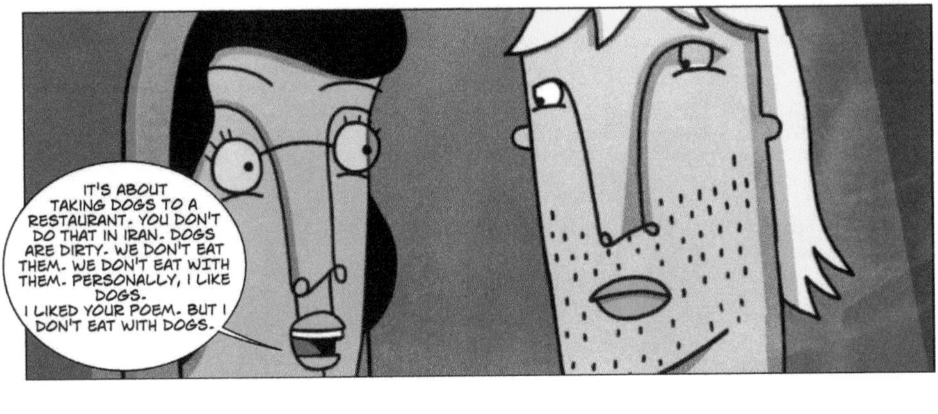
IT'S ABOUT TAKING DOGS TO A RESTAURANT. YOU DON'T DO THAT IN IRAN. DOGS ARE DIRTY. WE DON'T EAT THEM. WE DON'T EAT WITH THEM. PERSONALLY, I LIKE DOGS. I LIKED YOUR POEM. BUT I DON'T EAT WITH DOGS.

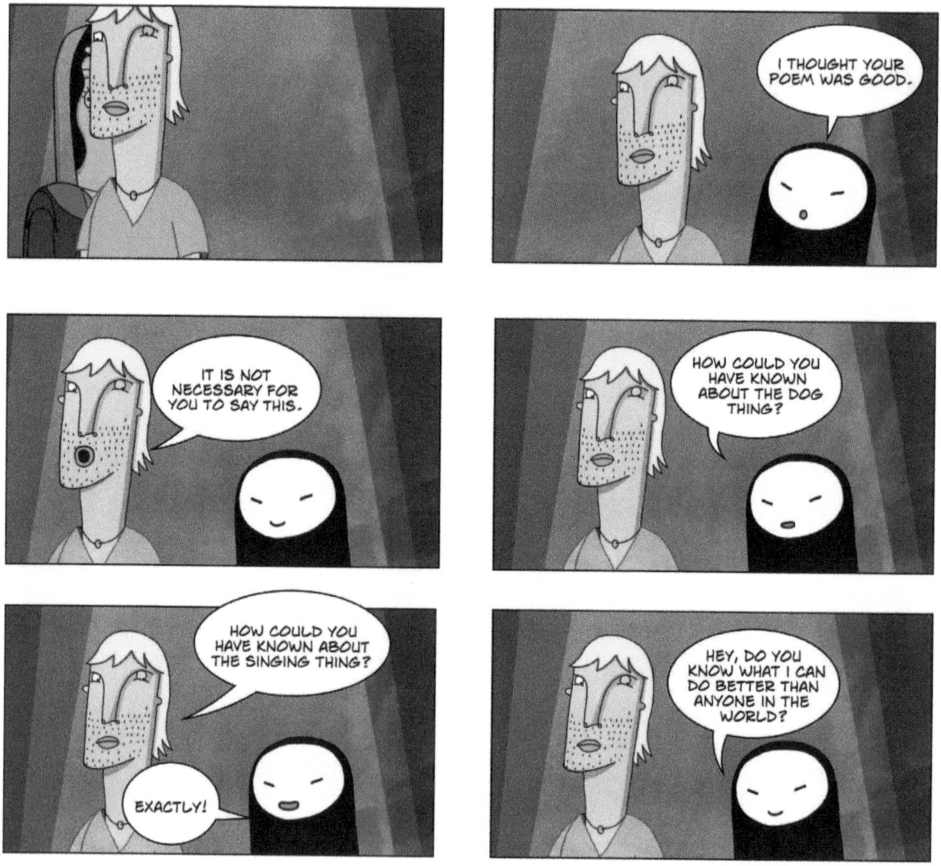
I THOUGHT YOUR POEM WAS GOOD.
IT IS NOT NECESSARY FOR YOU TO SAY THIS.
HOW COULD YOU HAVE KNOWN ABOUT THE DOG THING?
HOW COULD YOU HAVE KNOWN ABOUT THE SINGING THING?
EXACTLY!
HEY, DO YOU KNOW WHAT I CAN DO BETTER THAN ANYONE IN THE WORLD?

ROSIE MOVES HER FINGERS BACK AND FORTH QUICKLY IN A COMPLICATED PATTERN.

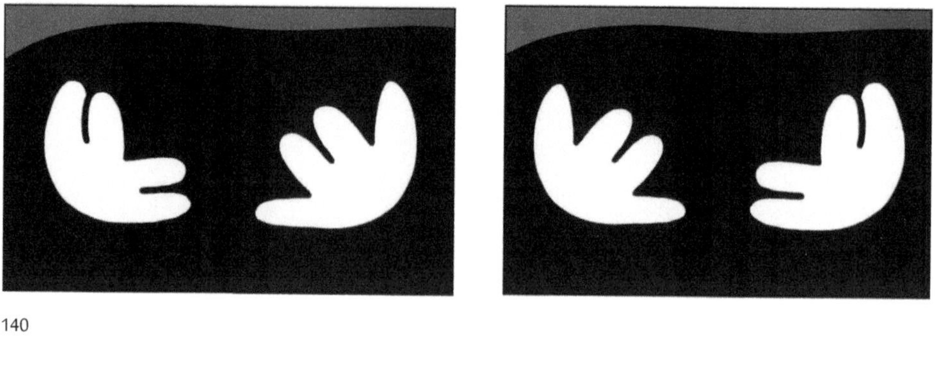

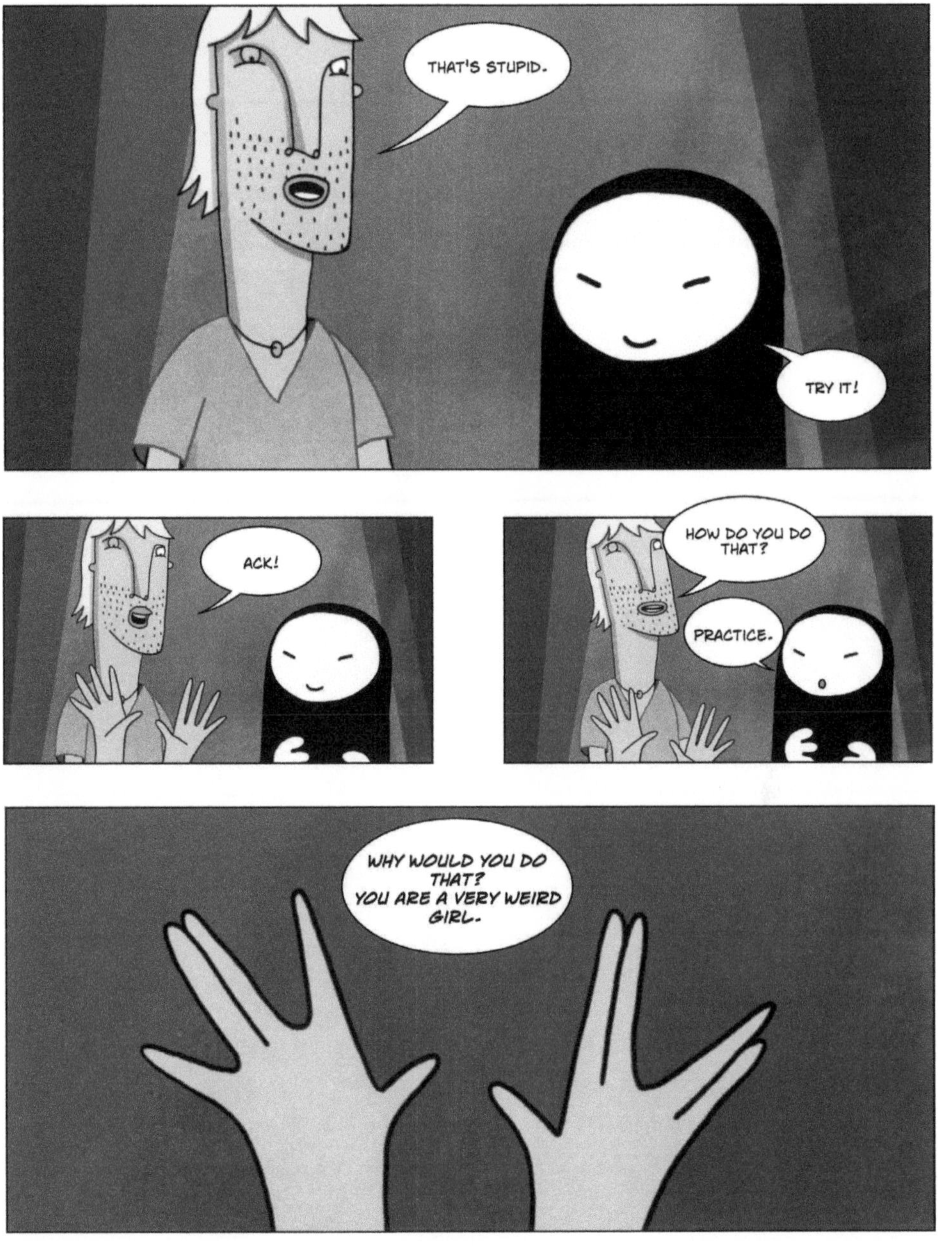
THAT'S STUPID.
TRY IT!
ACK!
HOW DO YOU DO THAT?
PRACTICE.
WHY WOULD YOU DO THAT? YOU ARE A VERY WEIRD GIRL.

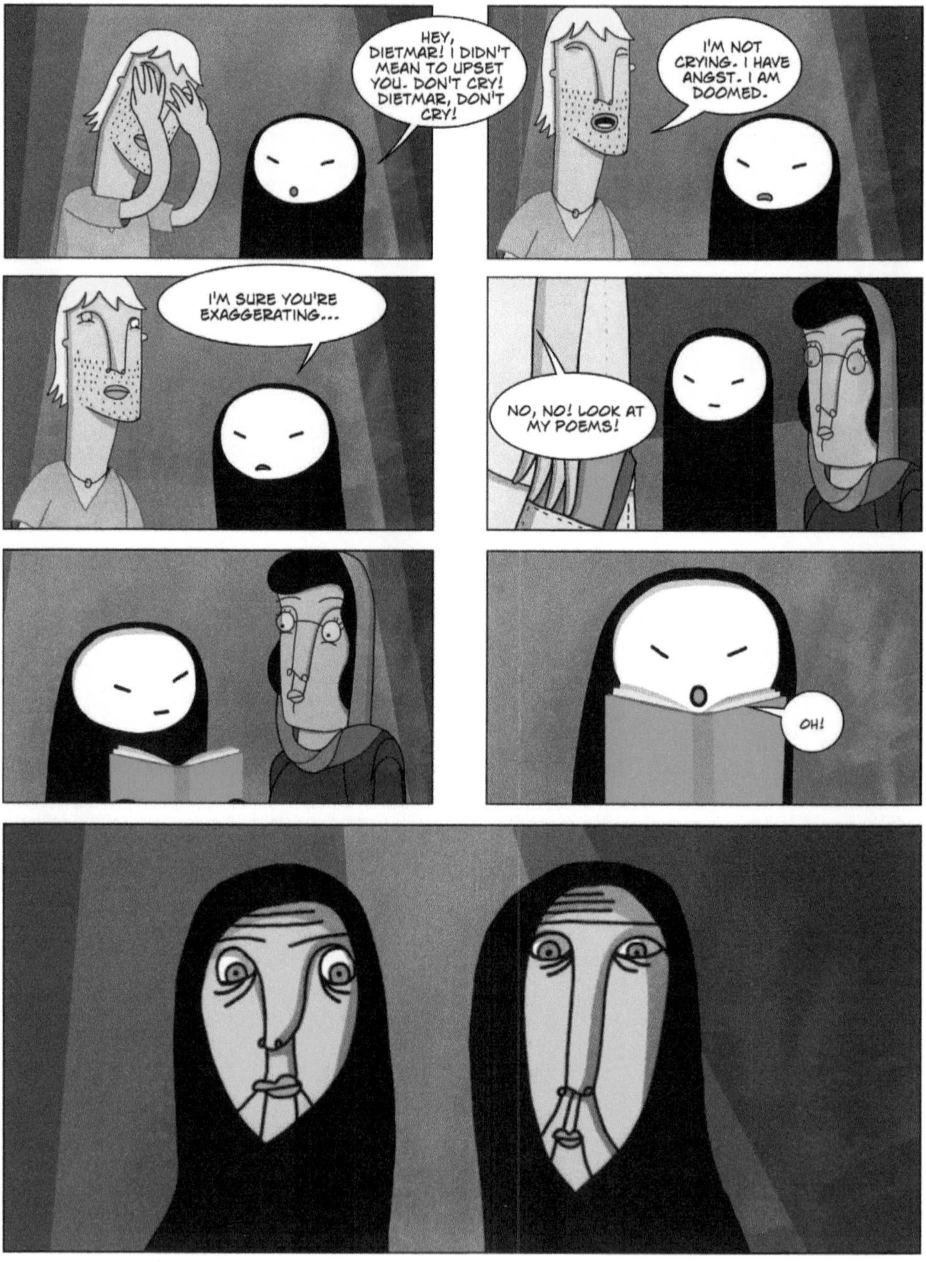
HEY, DIETMAR! I DIDN'T MEAN TO UPSET YOU. DON'T CRY! DIETMAR, DON'T CRY!
I'M NOT CRYING. I HAVE ANGST. I AM DOOMED.
I'M SURE YOU'RE EXAGGERATING...
NO, NO! LOOK AT MY POEMS!
OH!

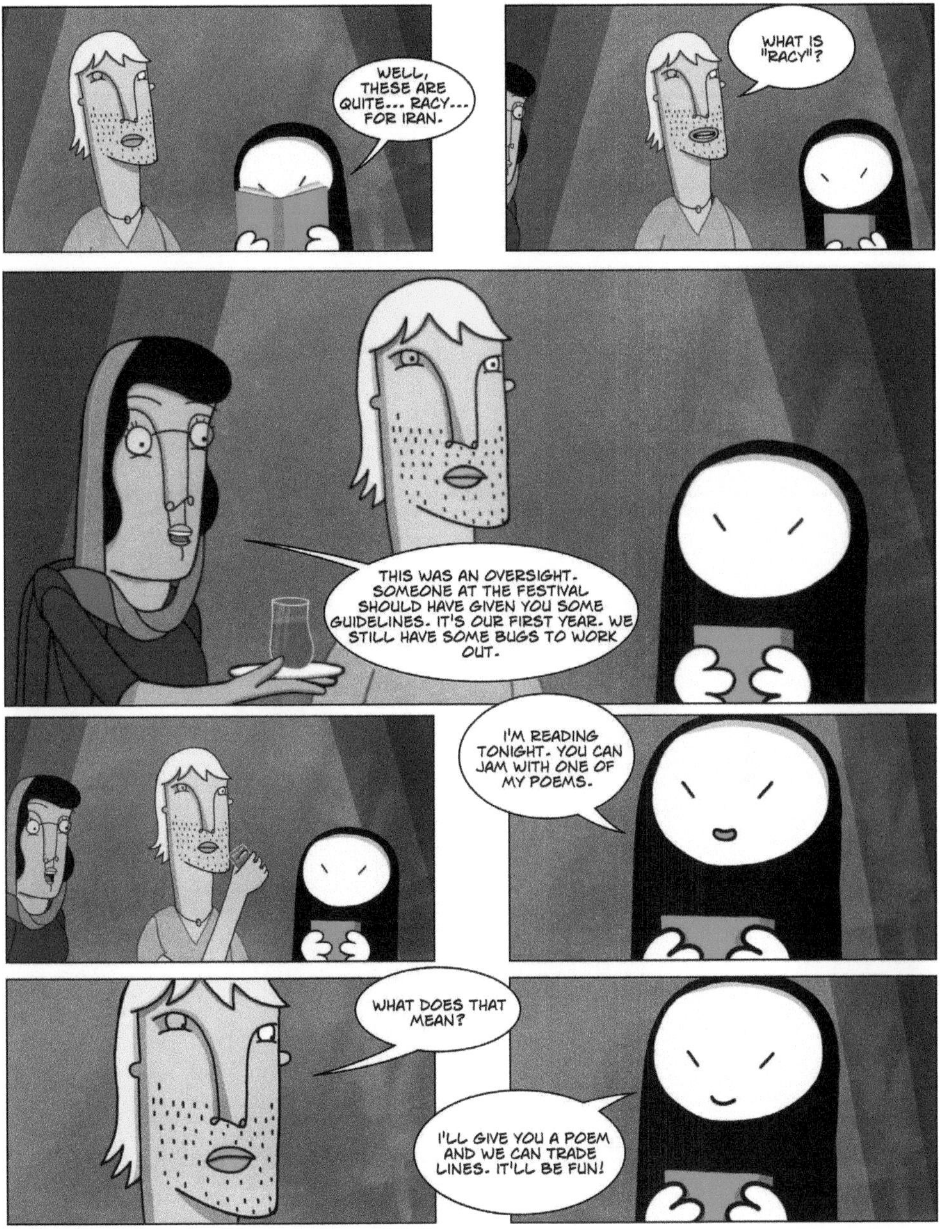
WELL, THESE ARE QUITE... RACY... FOR IRAN.
WHAT IS "RACY"?
THIS WAS AN OVERSIGHT. SOMEONE AT THE FESTIVAL SHOULD HAVE GIVEN YOU SOME GUIDELINES. IT'S OUR FIRST YEAR. WE STILL HAVE SOME BUGS TO WORK OUT.
I'M READING TONIGHT. YOU CAN JAM WITH ONE OF MY POEMS.
WHAT DOES THAT MEAN?
I'LL GIVE YOU A POEM AND WE CAN TRADE LINES. IT'LL BE FUN!

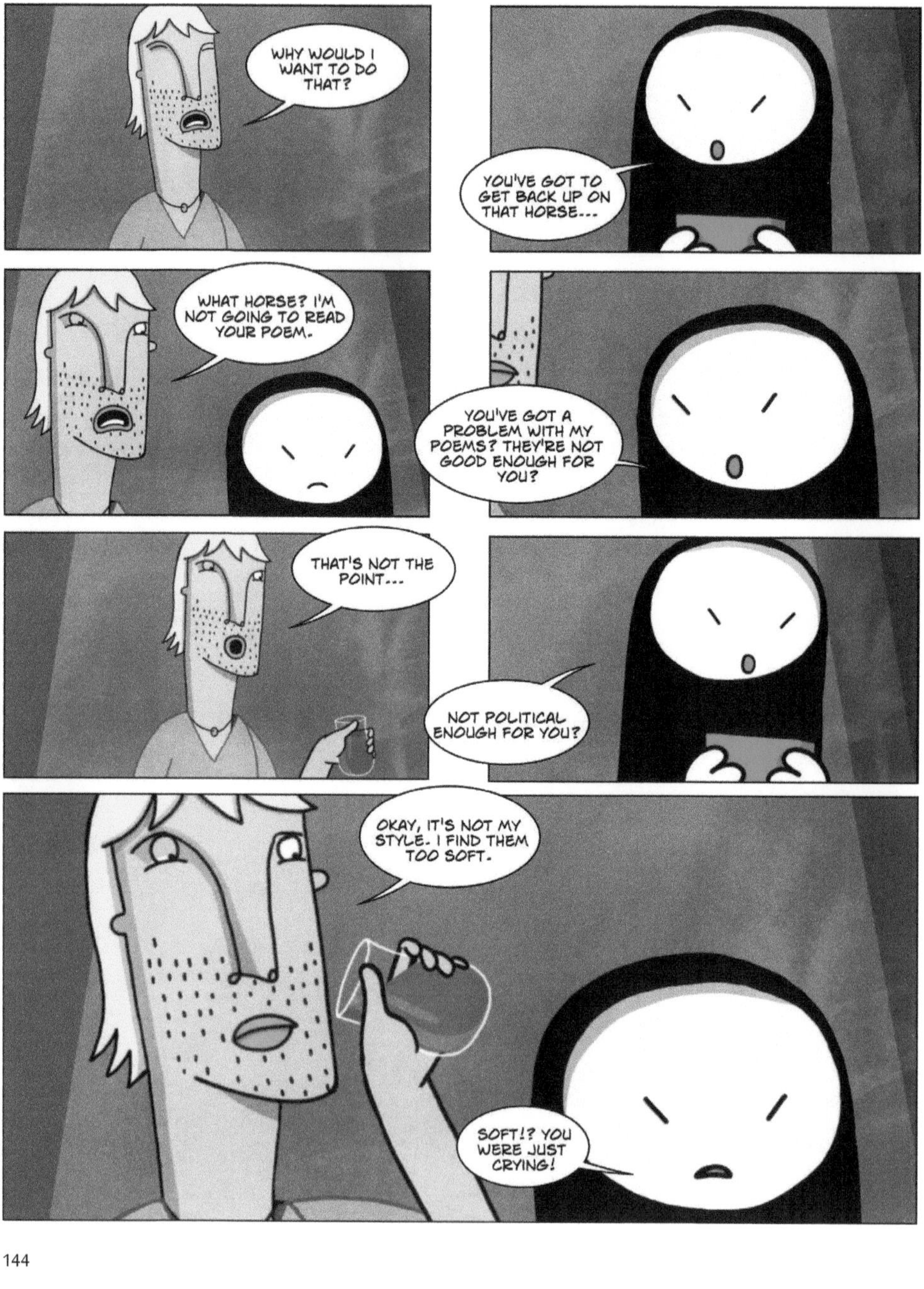
WHY WOULD I WANT TO DO THAT?
YOU'VE GOT TO GET BACK UP ON THAT HORSE...
WHAT HORSE? I'M NOT GOING TO READ YOUR POEM.
YOU'VE GOT A PROBLEM WITH MY POEMS? THEY'RE NOT GOOD ENOUGH FOR YOU?
THAT'S NOT THE POINT...
NOT POLITICAL ENOUGH FOR YOU?
OKAY, IT'S NOT MY STYLE. I FIND THEM TOO SOFT.
SOFT!? YOU WERE JUST CRYING!

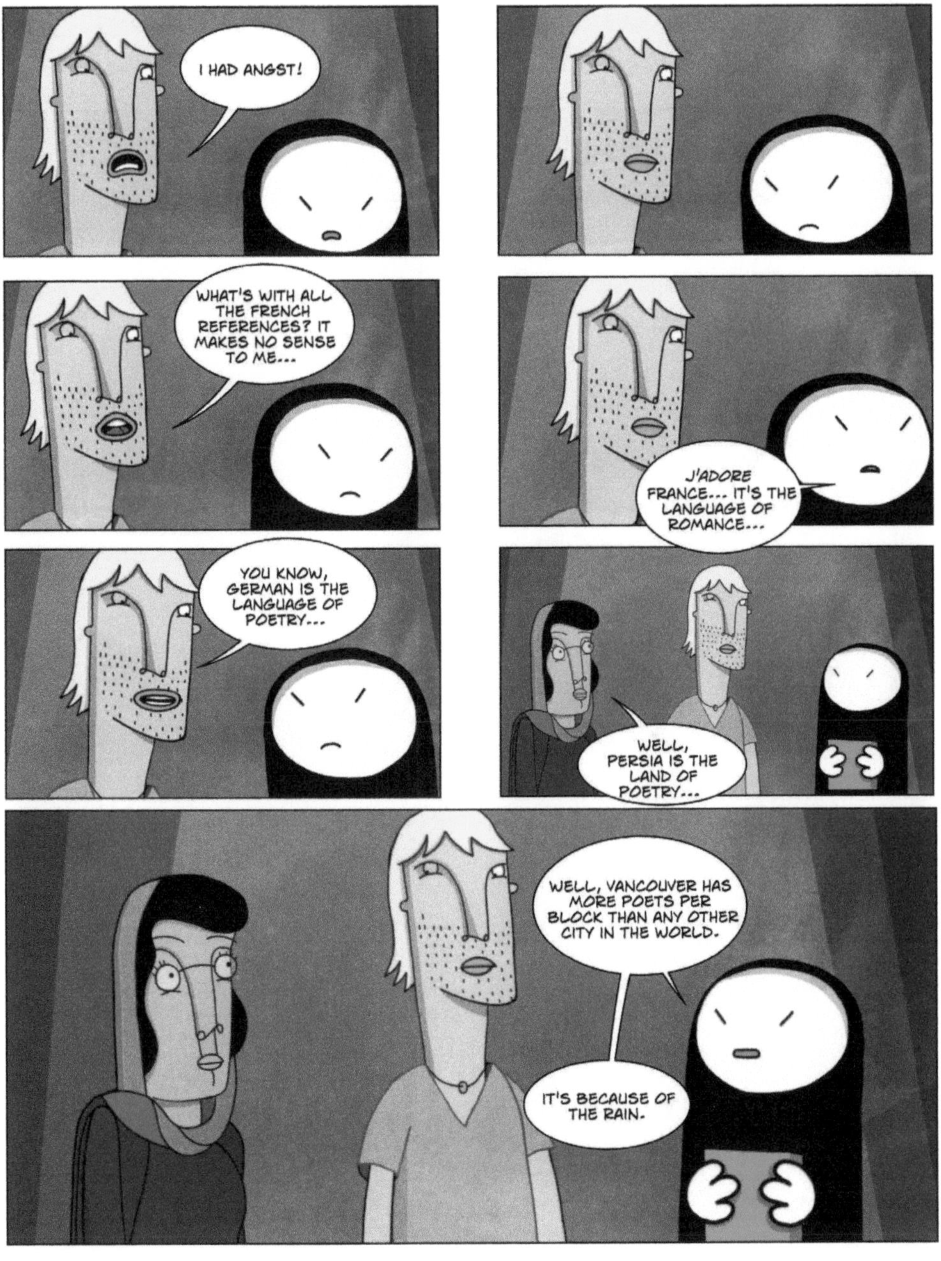
I HAD ANGST!
WHAT'S WITH ALL THE FRENCH REFERENCES? IT MAKES NO SENSE TO ME...
J'ADORE FRANCE... IT'S THE LANGUAGE OF ROMANCE...
YOU KNOW, GERMAN IS THE LANGUAGE OF POETRY...
WELL, PERSIA IS THE LAND OF POETRY...
WELL, VANCOUVER HAS MORE POETS PER BLOCK THAN ANY OTHER CITY IN THE WORLD.
IT'S BECAUSE OF THE RAIN.

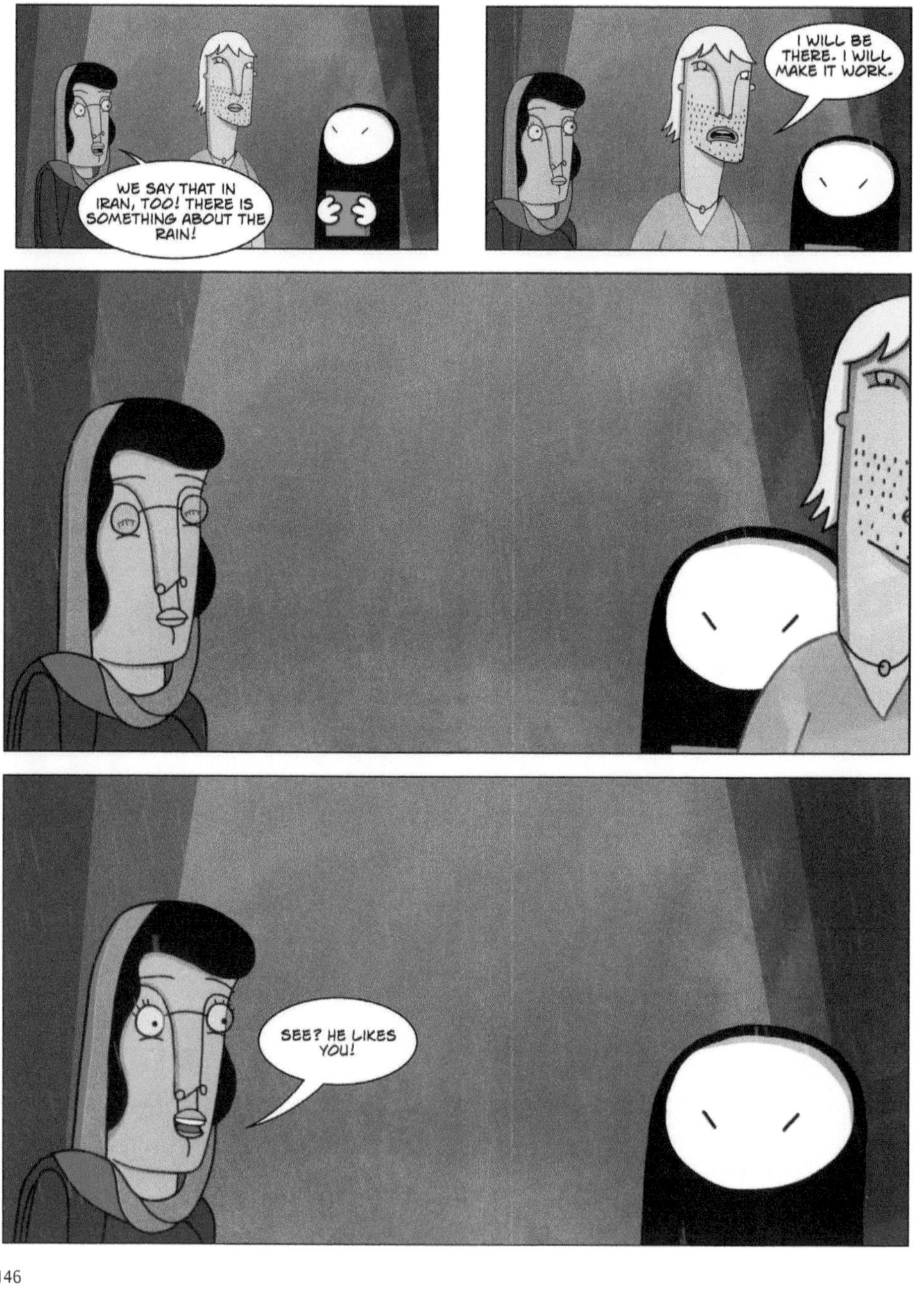
WE SAY THAT IN IRAN, TOO! THERE IS SOMETHING ABOUT THE RAIN!
I WILL BE THERE. I WILL MAKE IT WORK.
SEE? HE LIKES YOU!

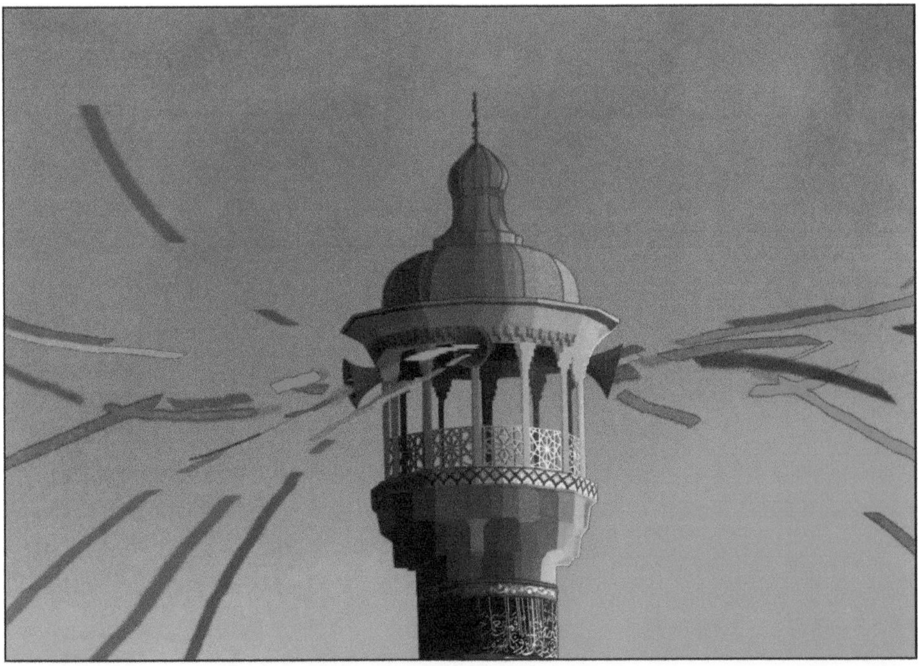

IT'S DAY TWO OF THE FIRST ANNUAL SHIRAZ INTERNATIONAL POETRY FESTIVAL. STILL JET-LAGGED, ROSIE MING IS ONE OF THE FIRST TO ARRIVE.

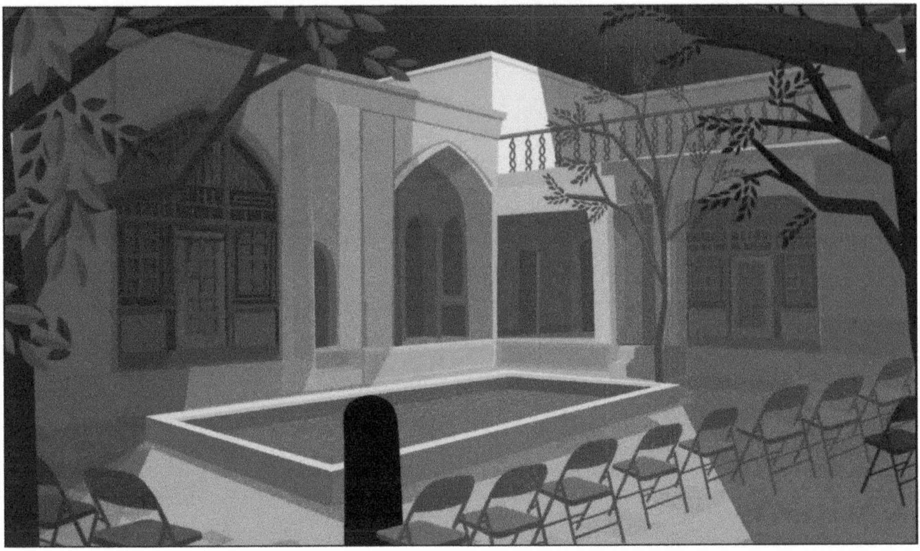

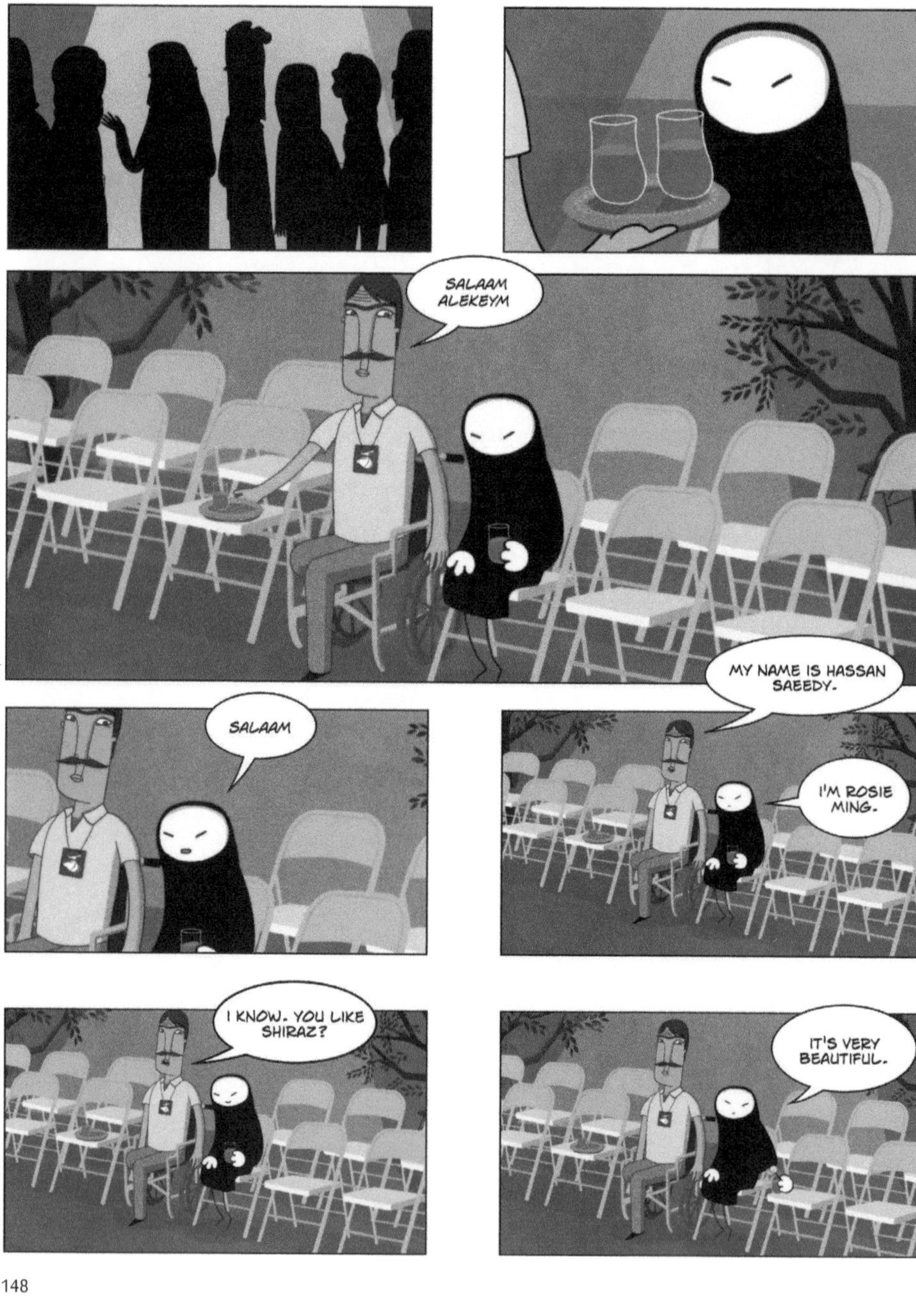
SALAAM ALEKEYM
SALAAM
MY NAME IS HASSAN SAEEDY.
I'M ROSIE MING.
I KNOW. YOU LIKE SHIRAZ?
IT'S VERY BEAUTIFUL.

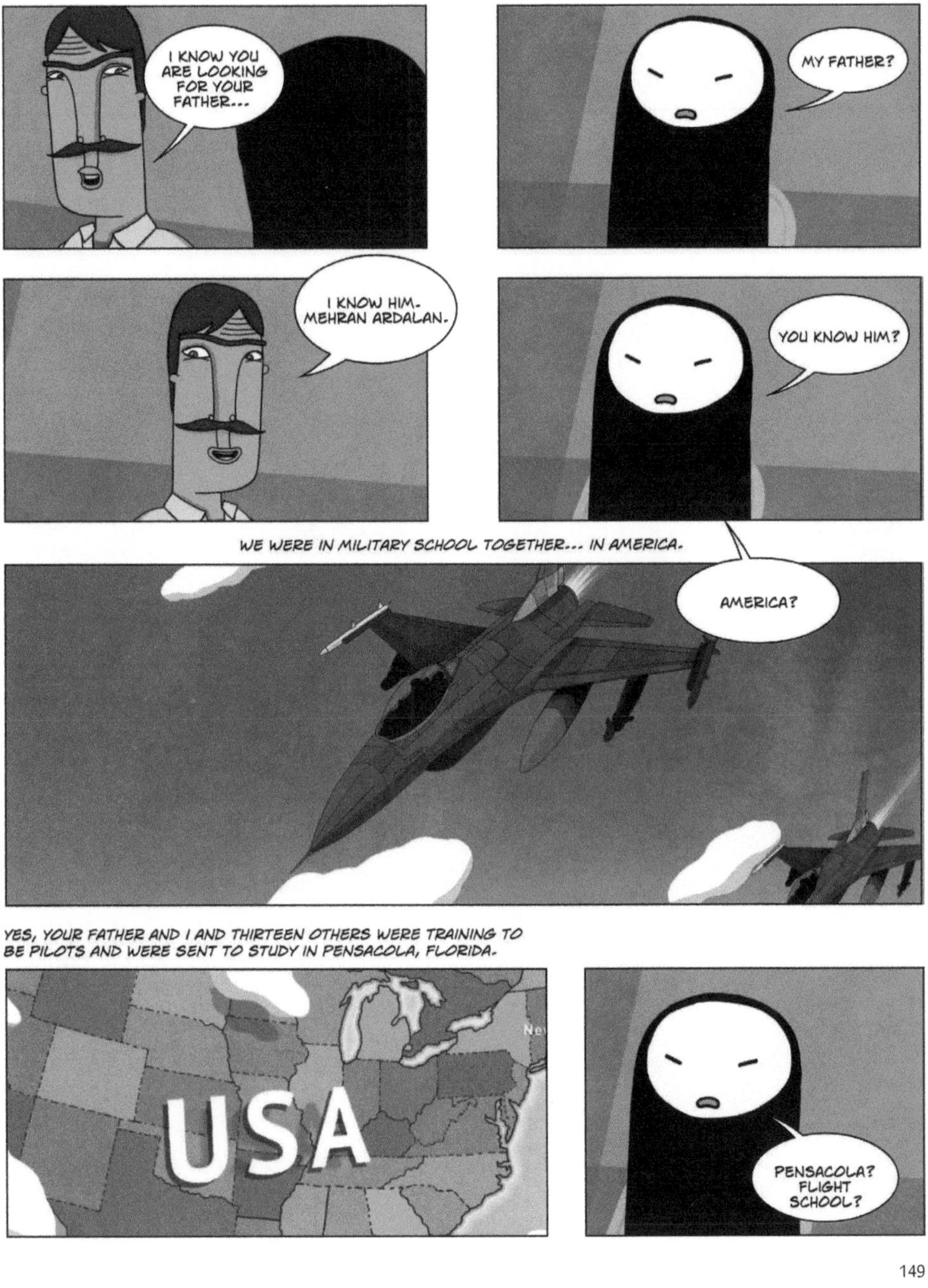
I KNOW YOU ARE LOOKING FOR YOUR FATHER...
MY FATHER?
I KNOW HIM. MEHRAN ARDALAN.
YOU KNOW HIM?
WE WERE IN MILITARY SCHOOL TOGETHER... IN AMERICA.
AMERICA?
YES, YOUR FATHER AND I AND THIRTEEN OTHERS WERE TRAINING TO BE PILOTS AND WERE SENT TO STUDY IN PENSACOLA, FLORIDA.
USA
PENSACOLA? FLIGHT SCHOOL?

YES, PENSACOLA, FLORIDA. WE ALSO TRAINED AT THE NAVAL ACADEMY IN NEWPORT, RHODE ISLAND.

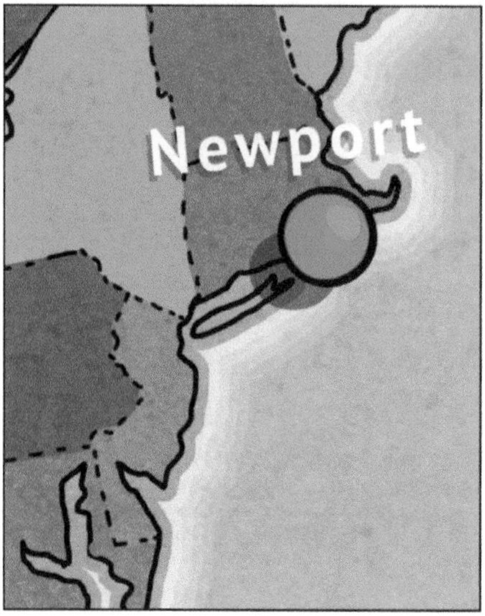
Newport

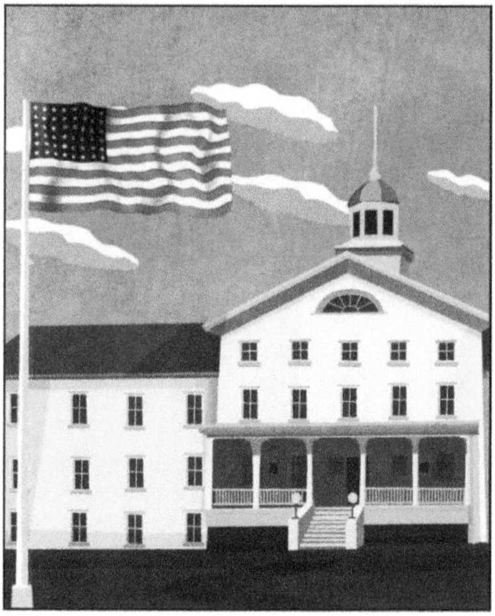

BEAUTIFUL COUNTRY! BEAUTIFUL HOUSES...

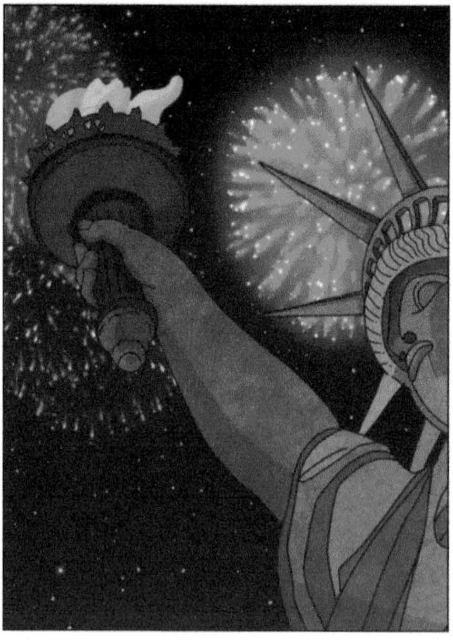

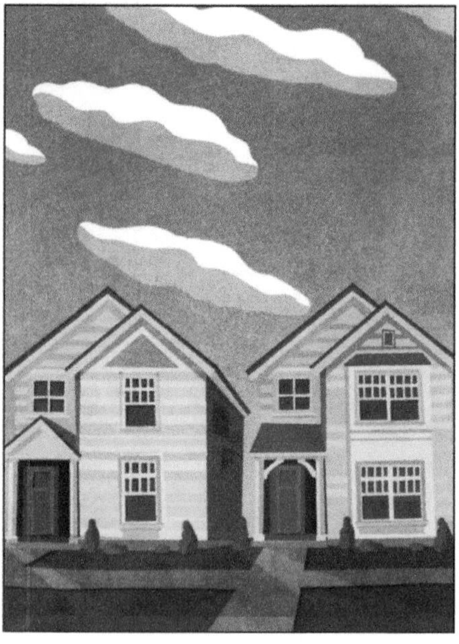

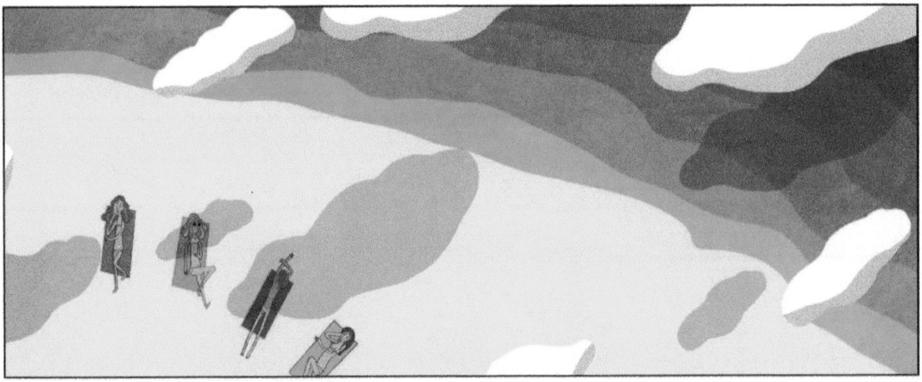

BEAUTIFUL SCENERY, BEAUTIFUL WOMEN... SUCH BEAUTIFUL WOMEN!

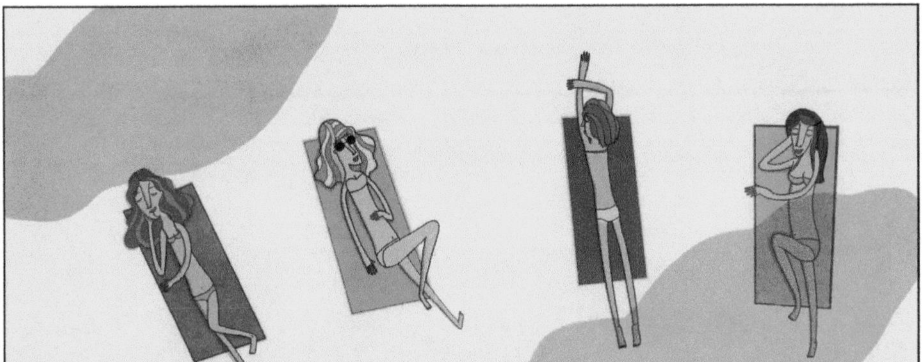

THE SHAH SENT US OVER TO AMERICA. HE WAS GOOD FRIENDS WITH AMERICA.

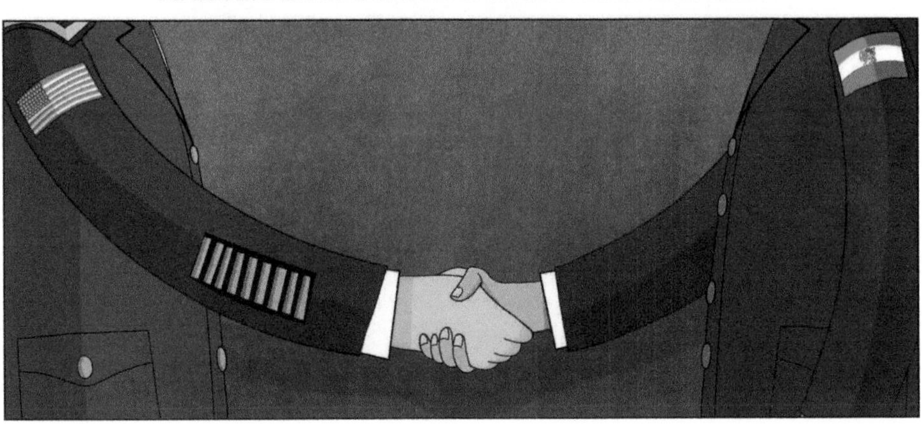

WE WERE ALL NEW, YOUNG OFFICERS. VERY VERY YOUNG.

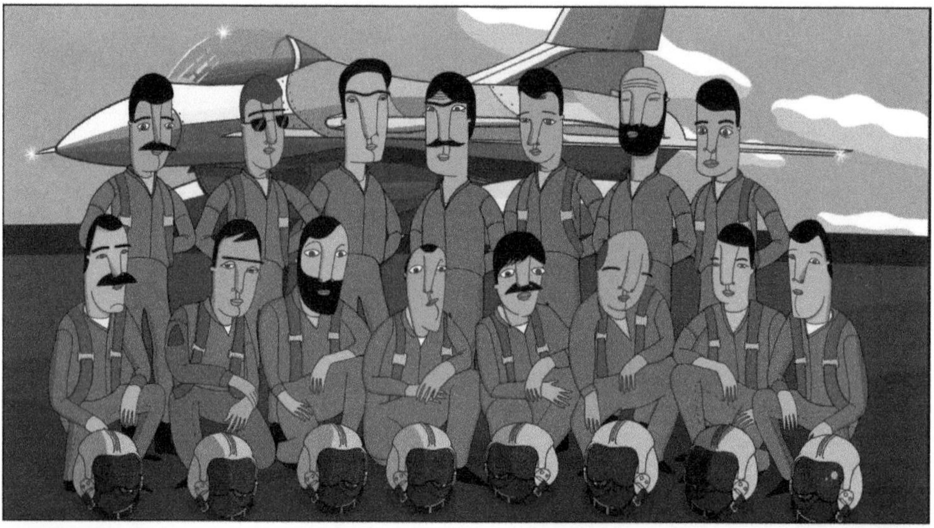

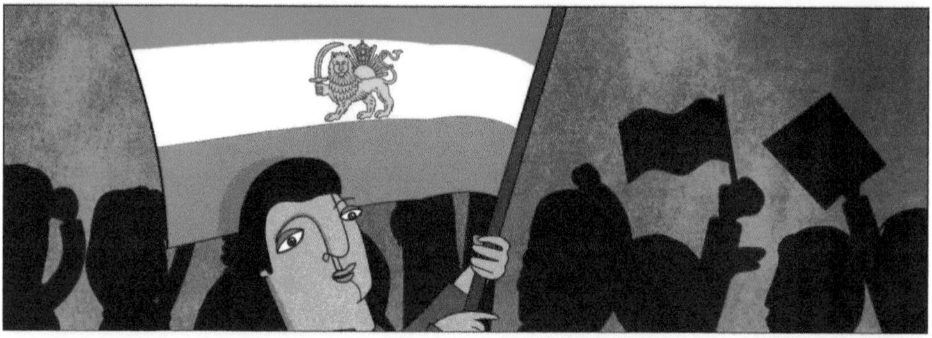

BUT THEN THE ISLAMIC REVOLUTION HAPPENED AND WE WERE ALL OFFERED ASYLUM IN THE UNITED STATES.

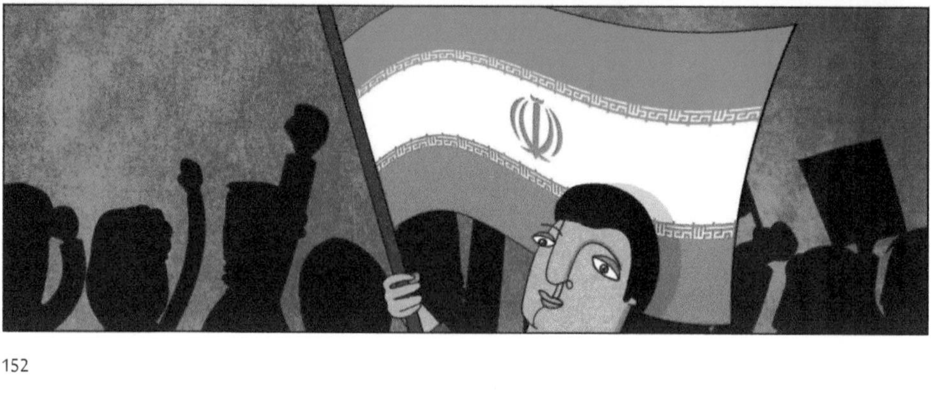

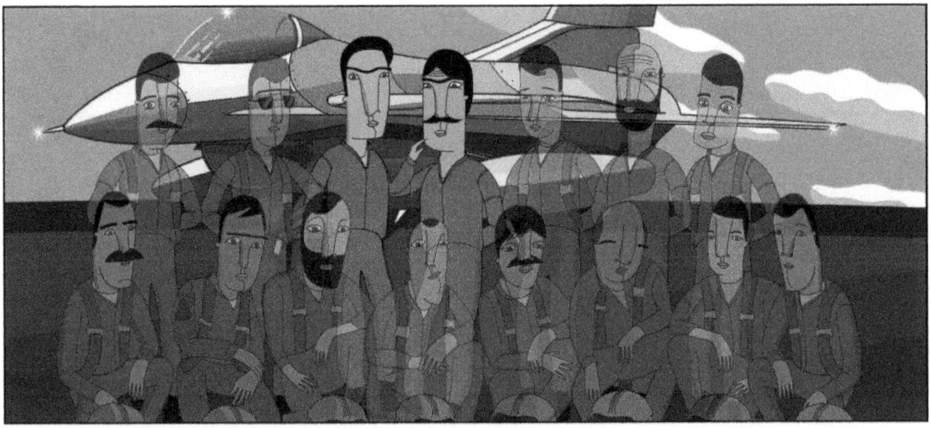

THIRTEEN OF US STAYED. BUT YOUR FATHER, MEHRAN, AND ME, WE WERE DIFFERENT.

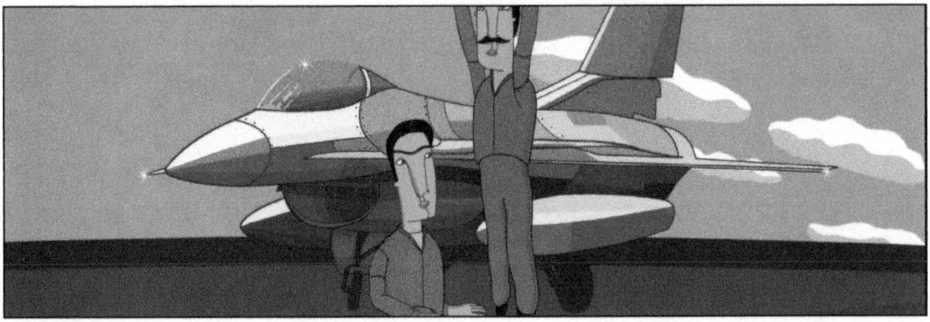

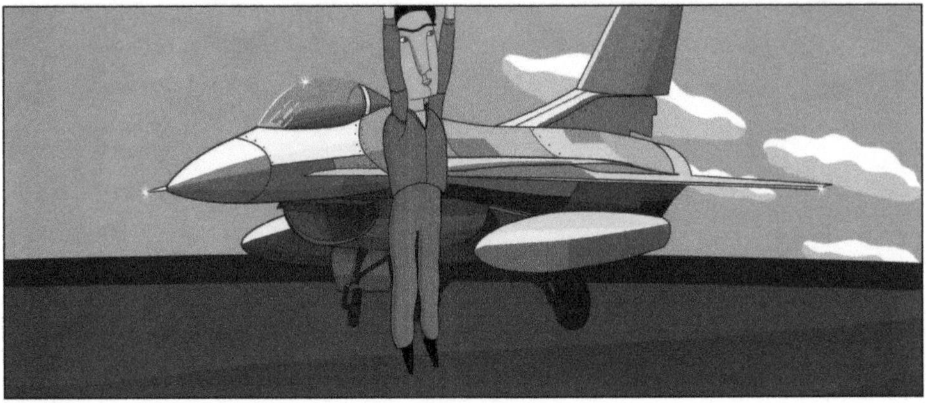

WE DIDN'T WANT TO LEAVE OUR FAMILIES. WE DIDN'T WANT TO LEAVE OUR COUNTRY. WE THOUGHT THE REVOLUTION WOULD BE A GOOD THING.

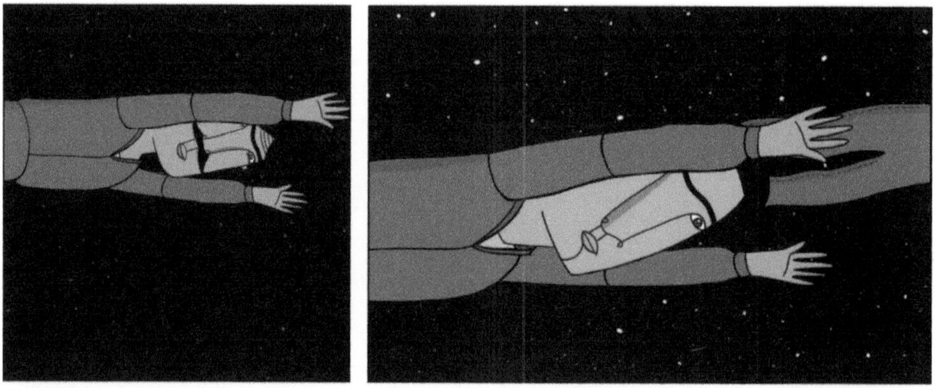

WHEN WE CAME BACK, YOUR FATHER WAS REJECTED BY THE MILITARY BECAUSE OF HIS FAMILY'S TIES TO THE SHAH.

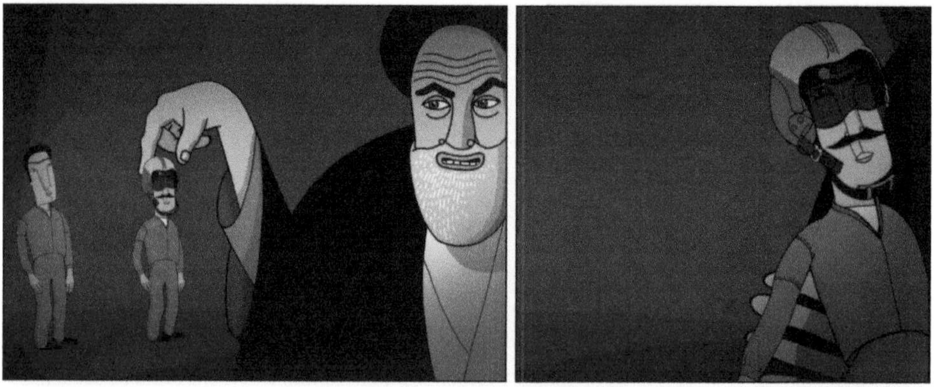

HE HAD NO WORK. THEN, HIS FATHER DIED.

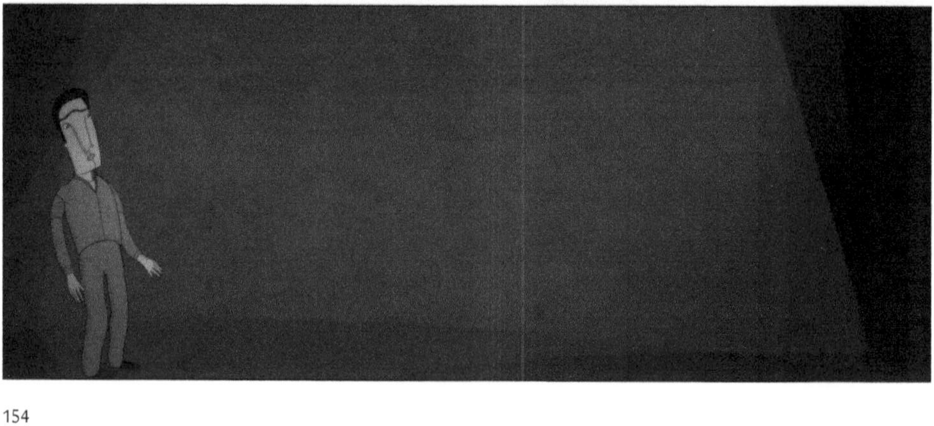

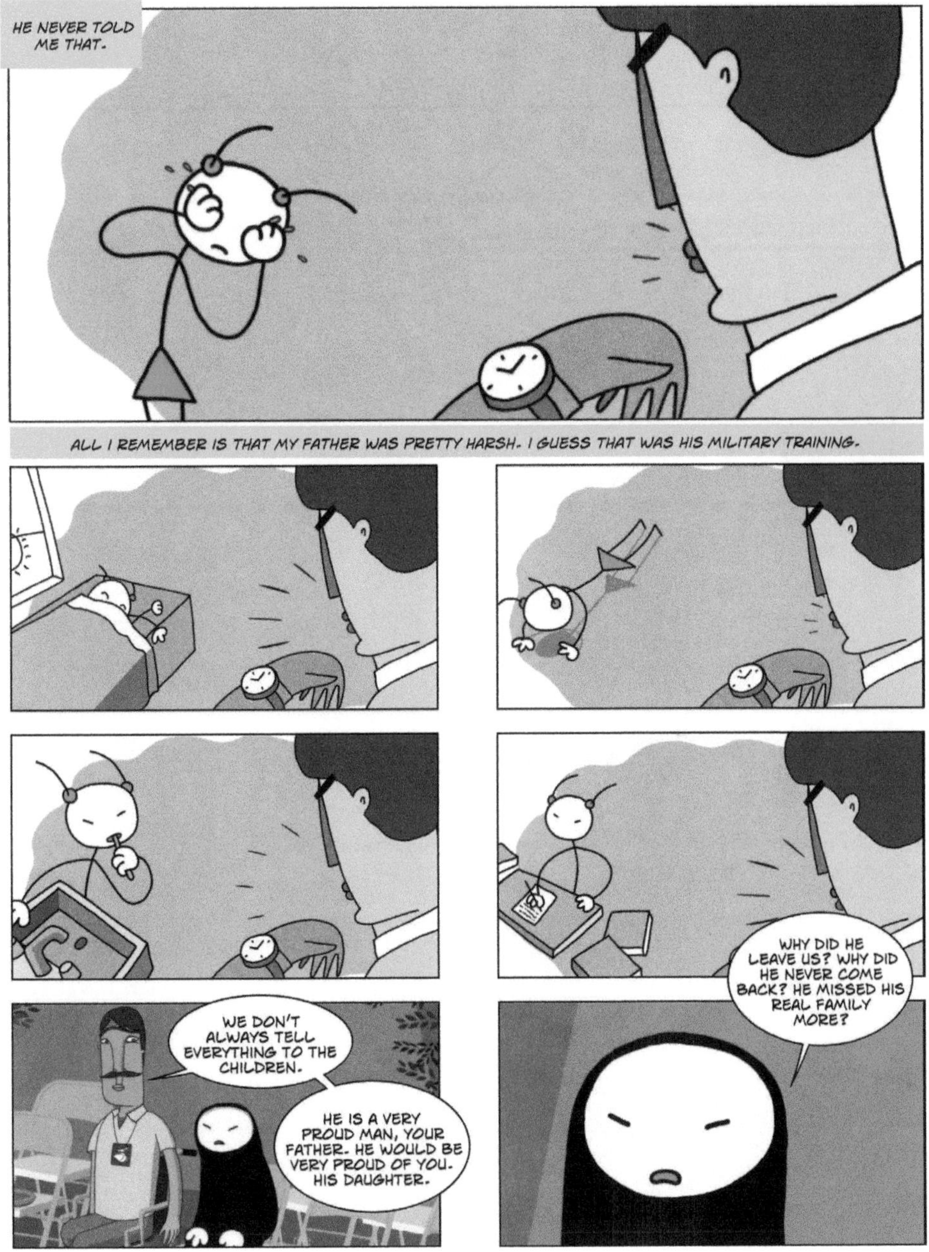
HE NEVER TOLD ME THAT.
ALL I REMEMBER IS THAT MY FATHER WAS PRETTY HARSH. I GUESS THAT WAS HIS MILITARY TRAINING.
WE DON'T ALWAYS TELL EVERYTHING TO THE CHILDREN.
HE IS A VERY PROUD MAN, YOUR FATHER. HE WOULD BE VERY PROUD OF YOU. HIS DAUGHTER.
WHY DID HE LEAVE US? WHY DID HE NEVER COME BACK? HE MISSED HIS REAL FAMILY MORE?

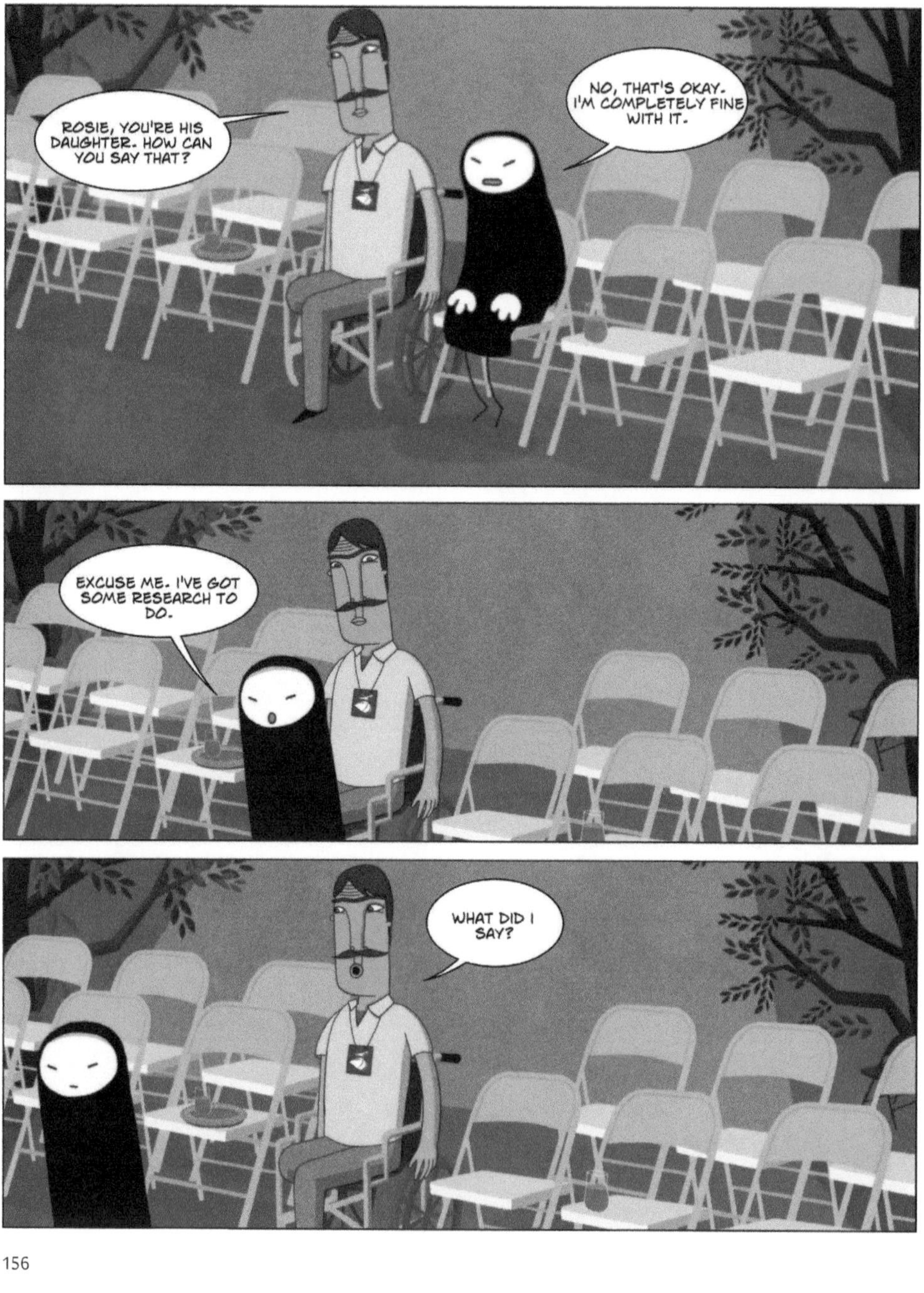
ROSIE, YOU'RE HIS DAUGHTER. HOW CAN YOU SAY THAT?
NO, THAT'S OKAY. I'M COMPLETELY FINE WITH IT.
EXCUSE ME. I'VE GOT SOME RESEARCH TO DO.
WHAT DID I SAY?

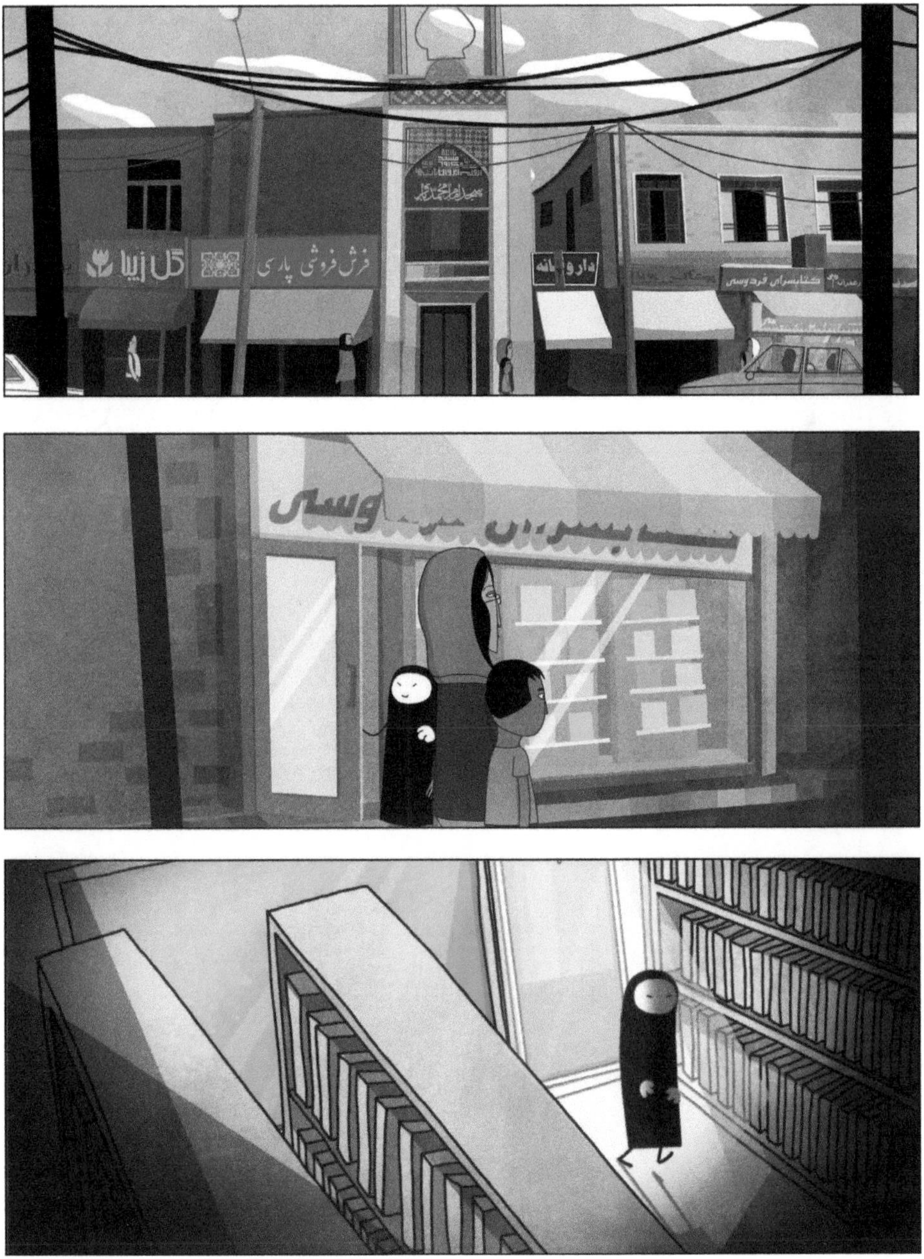
گل زیبا
فرش فروشی پارسی

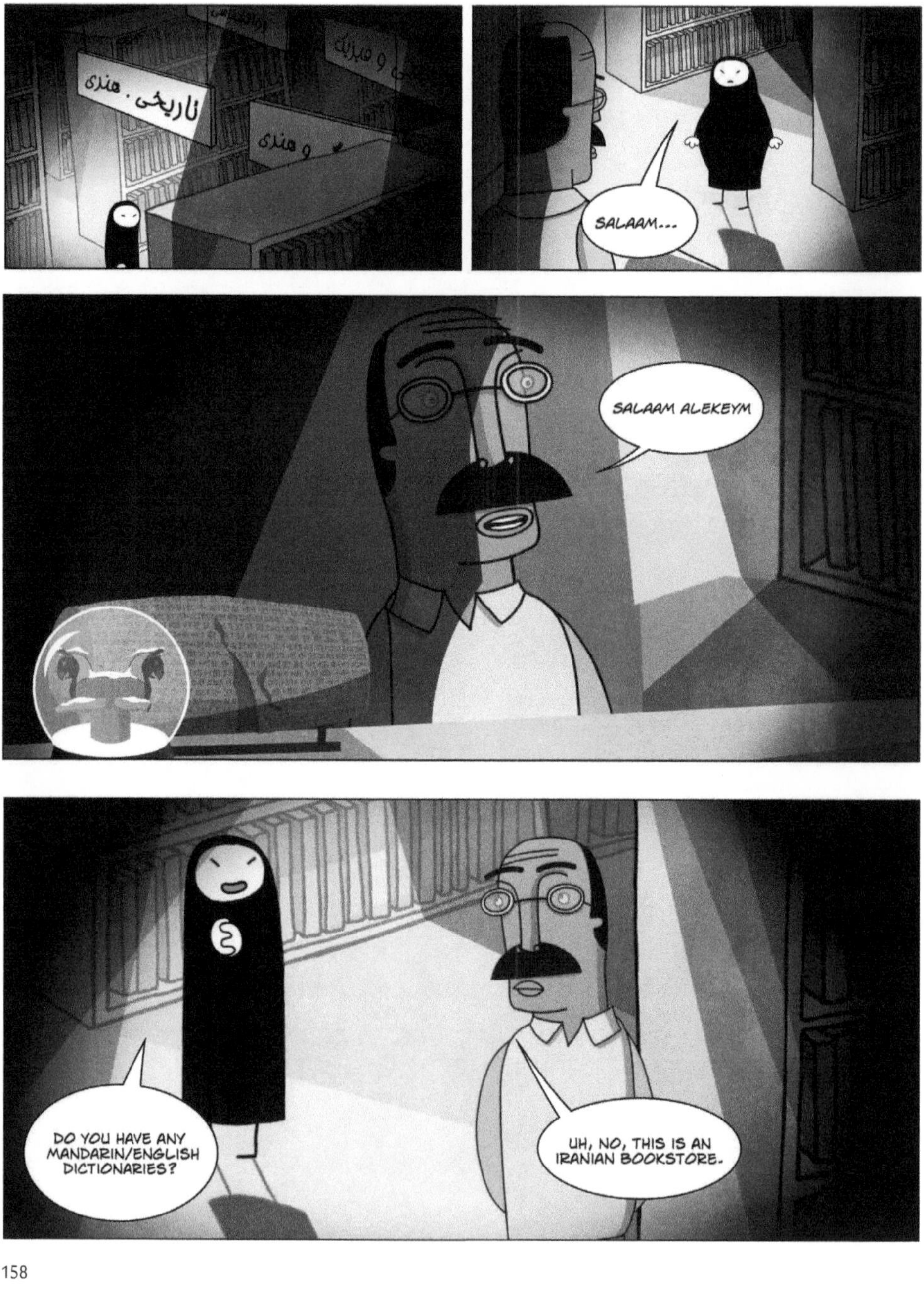
SALAAM...
SALAAM ALEKEYM
DO YOU HAVE ANY MANDARIN/ENGLISH DICTIONARIES?
UH, NO, THIS IS AN IRANIAN BOOKSTORE.

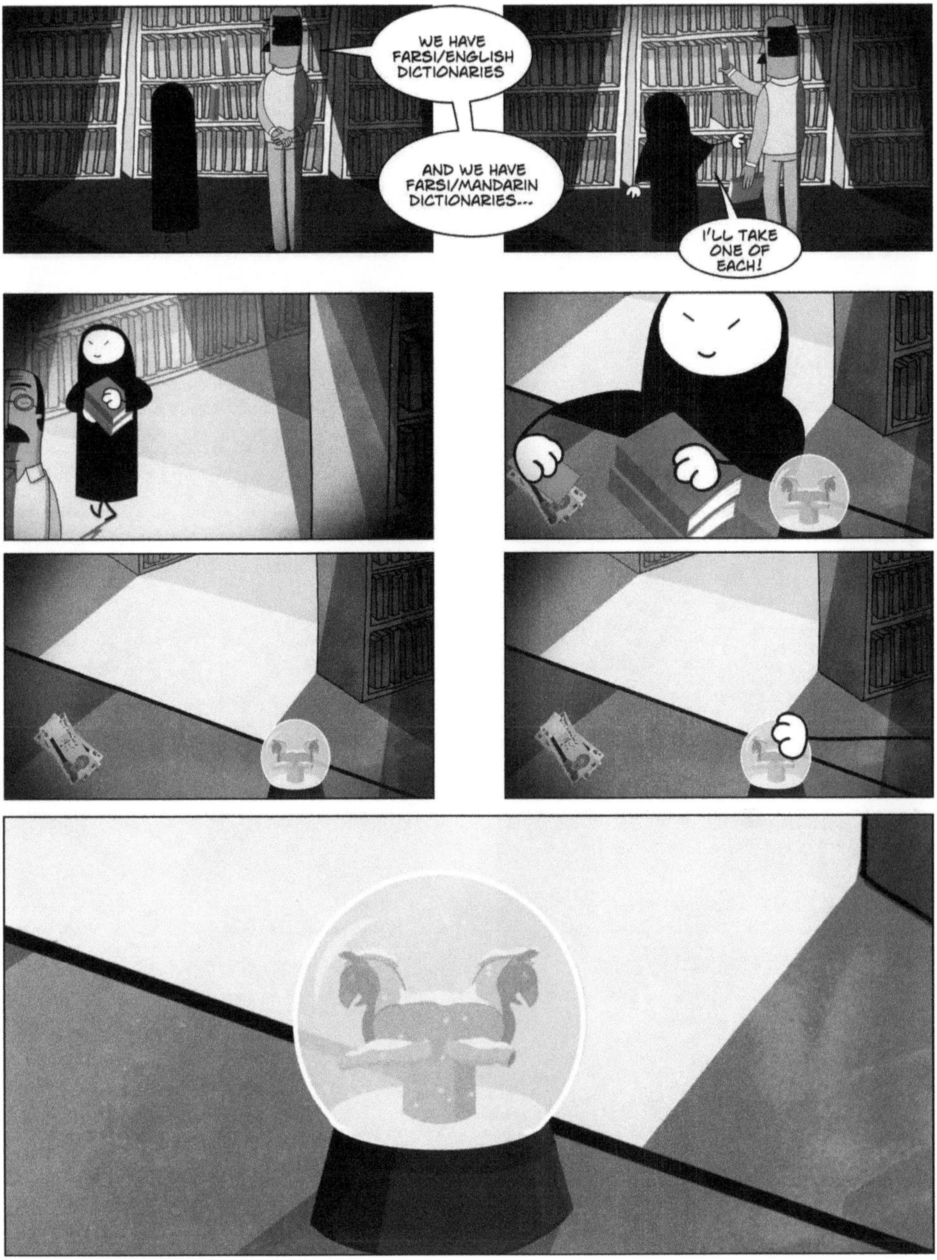
WE HAVE FARSI/ENGLISH DICTIONARIES
AND WE HAVE FARSI/MANDARIN DICTIONARIES...
I'LL TAKE ONE OF EACH!

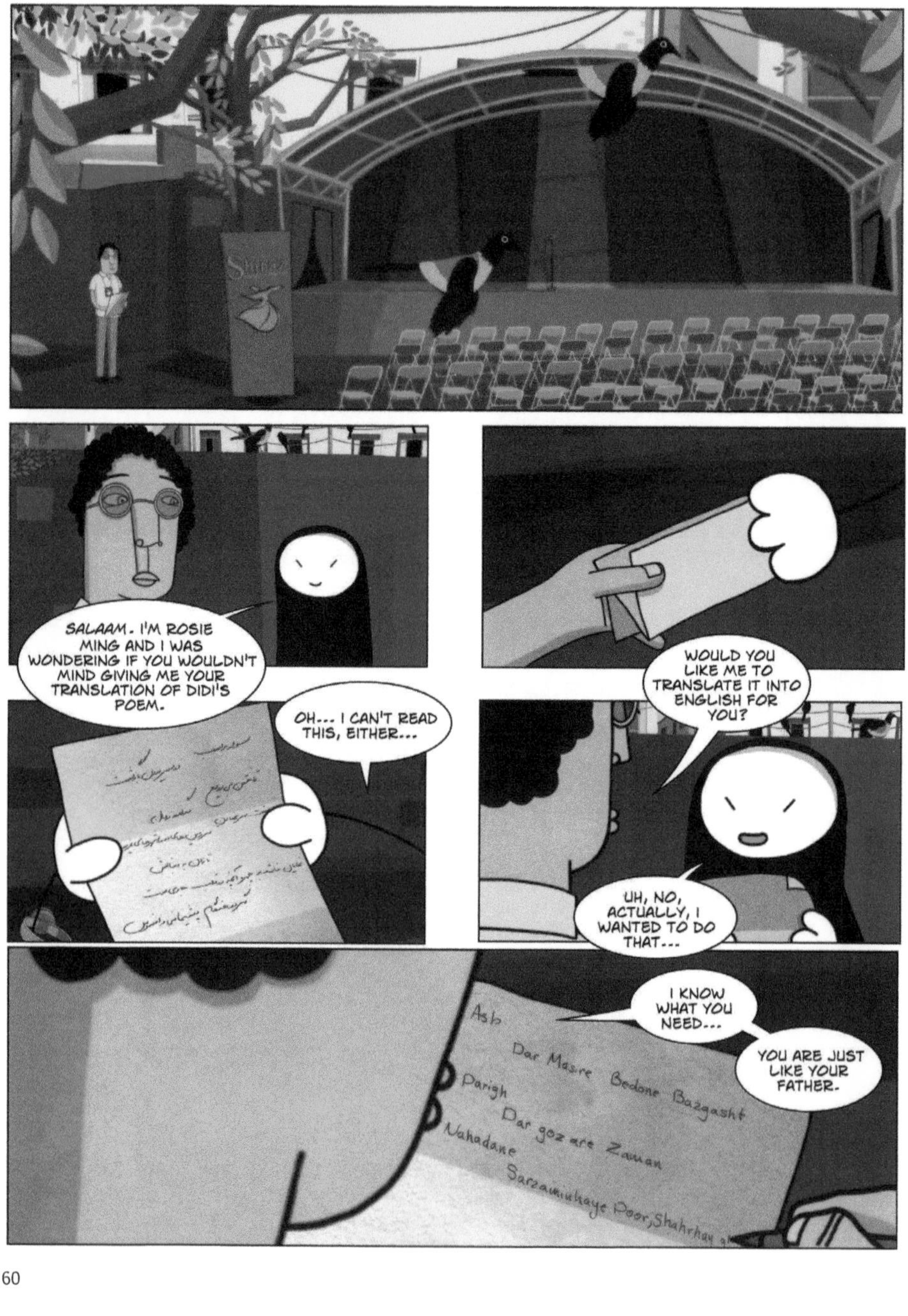
SALAAM. I'M ROSIE MING AND I WAS WONDERING IF YOU WOULDN'T MIND GIVING ME YOUR TRANSLATION OF DIDI'S POEM.
WOULD YOU LIKE ME TO TRANSLATE IT INTO ENGLISH FOR YOU?
OH... I CAN'T READ THIS, EITHER...
UH, NO, ACTUALLY, I WANTED TO DO THAT...
I KNOW WHAT YOU NEED...
YOU ARE JUST LIKE YOUR FATHER.
Asb
Dar Masre Bedone Bazgasht
Parigh
Dar gozare Zaman
Nahadane
Sarzaminhaye Poor, Shahrhay

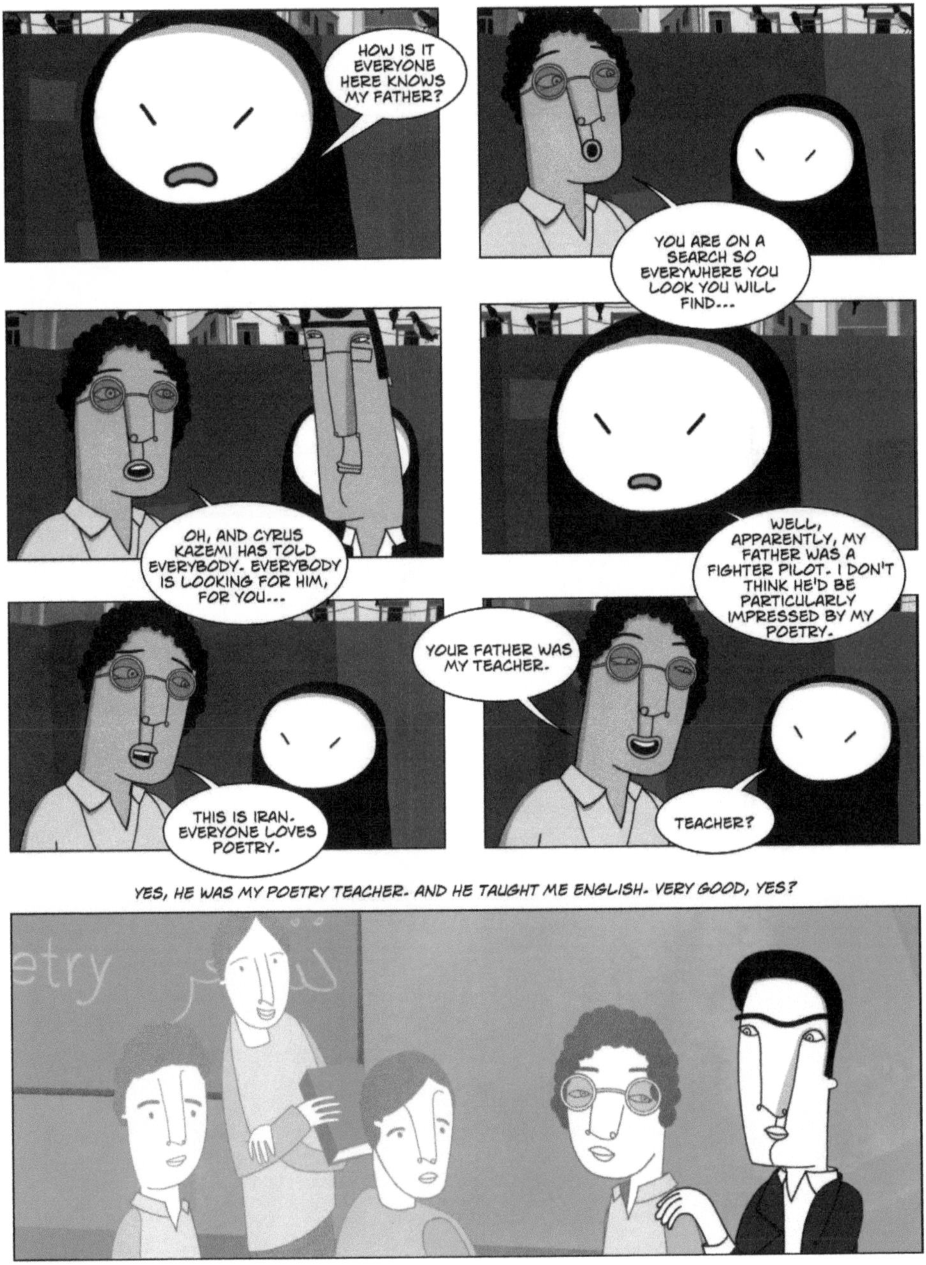
HOW IS IT EVERYONE HERE KNOWS MY FATHER?
YOU ARE ON A SEARCH SO EVERYWHERE YOU LOOK YOU WILL FIND...
OH, AND CYRUS KAZEMI HAS TOLD EVERYBODY. EVERYBODY IS LOOKING FOR HIM, FOR YOU...
WELL, APPARENTLY, MY FATHER WAS A FIGHTER PILOT. I DON'T THINK HE'D BE PARTICULARLY IMPRESSED BY MY POETRY.
THIS IS IRAN. EVERYONE LOVES POETRY.
YOUR FATHER WAS MY TEACHER.
TEACHER?
YES, HE WAS MY POETRY TEACHER. AND HE TAUGHT ME ENGLISH. VERY GOOD, YES?
etry

HE WAS A YOUNG MAN, THE REVOLUTION WAS NEW. A LOT OF PEOPLE TOOK ON NEW JOBS.

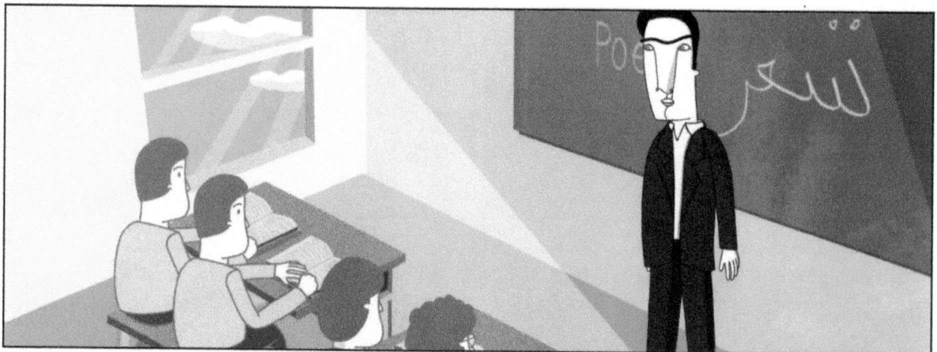
Poe
شعر

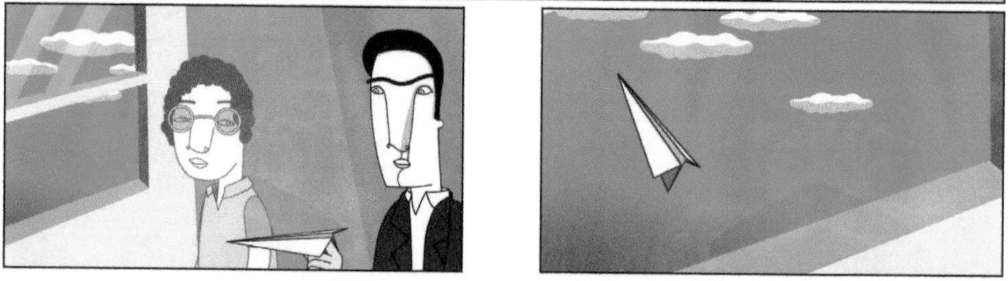

YOUR FATHER TOLD ME WHEN I WAS A BOY... I WAS VERY BAD IN ENGLISH... HE SAID I MUST NOT GIVE UP. THAT IT IS A WINDOW INTO A BIGGER WORLD OUT THERE. AND THAT IT WOULD CHANGE MY LIFE. I JUST COULDN'T SEE HOW YET.

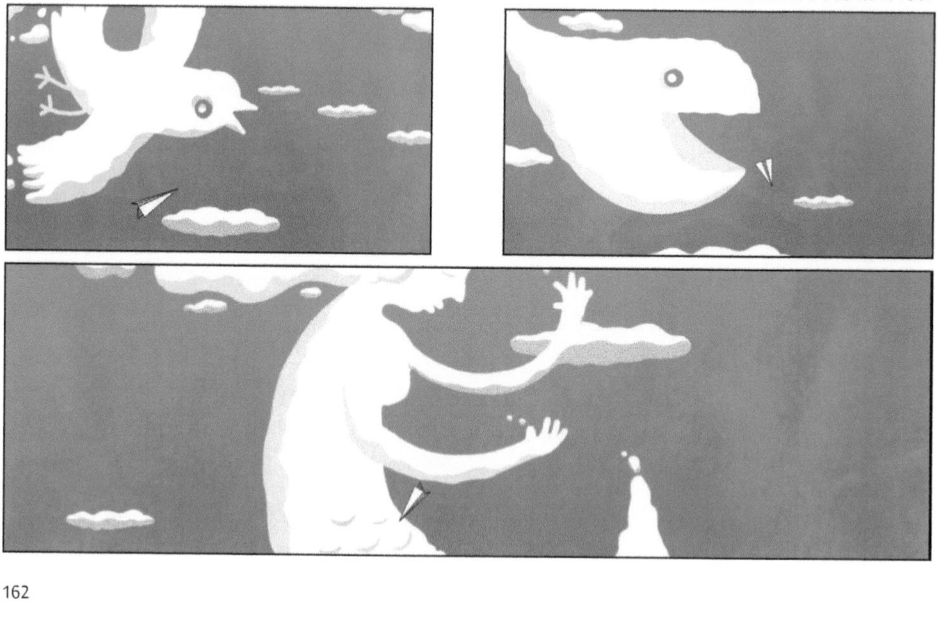

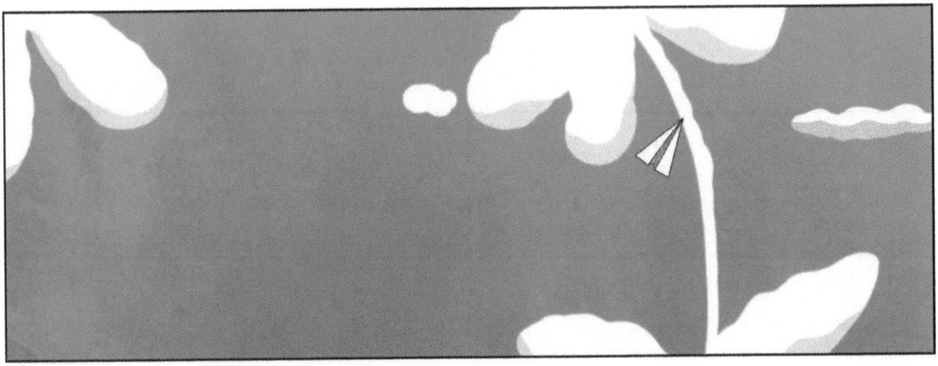

HE TOLD STORIES ABOUT FLYING JETS. WE LIKED THOSE STORIES. HE WROTE A POEM ABOUT A JET, ONCE...

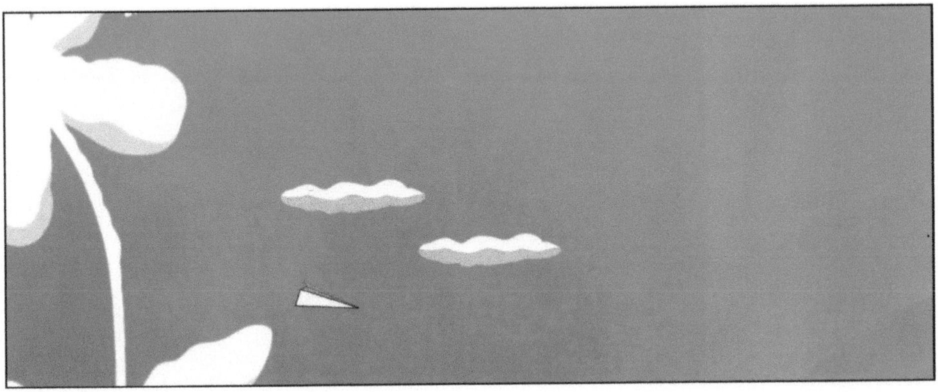

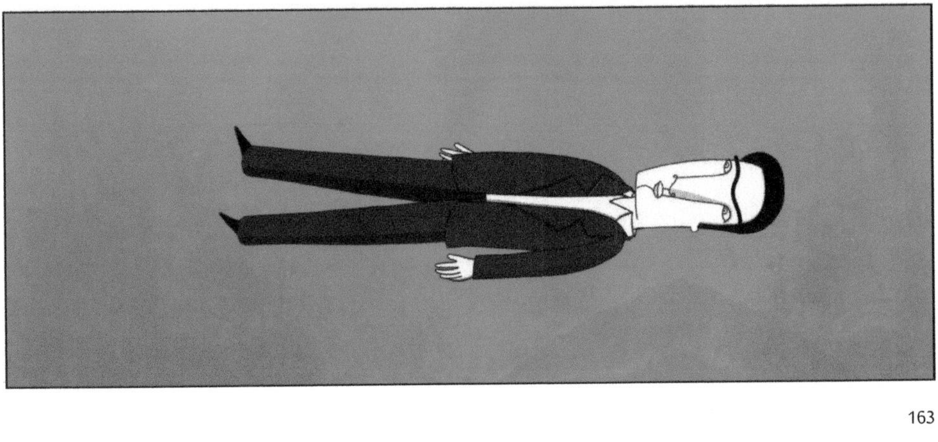

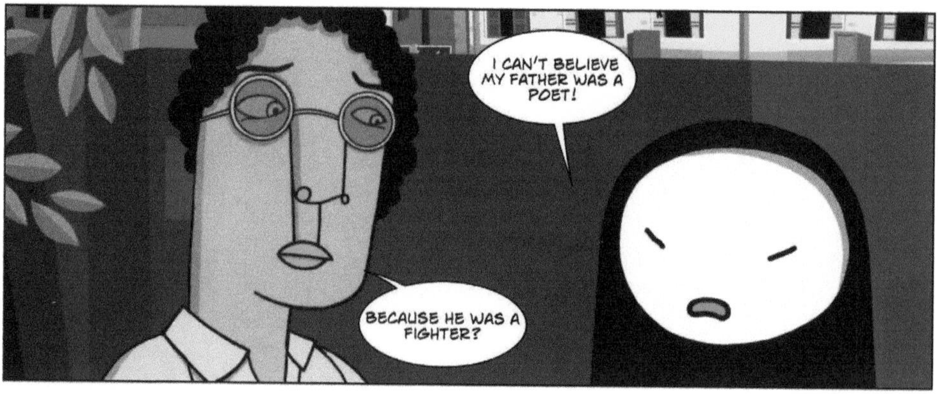
I CAN'T BELIEVE MY FATHER WAS A POET!
BECAUSE HE WAS A FIGHTER?

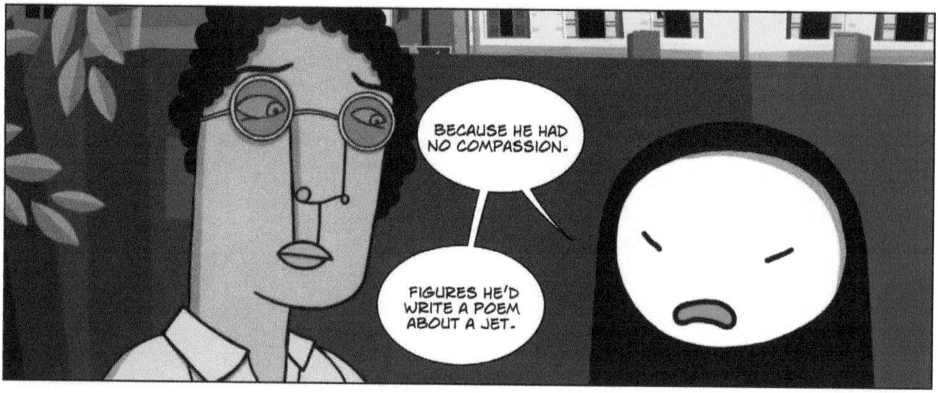
BECAUSE HE HAD NO COMPASSION.
FIGURES HE'D WRITE A POEM ABOUT A JET.

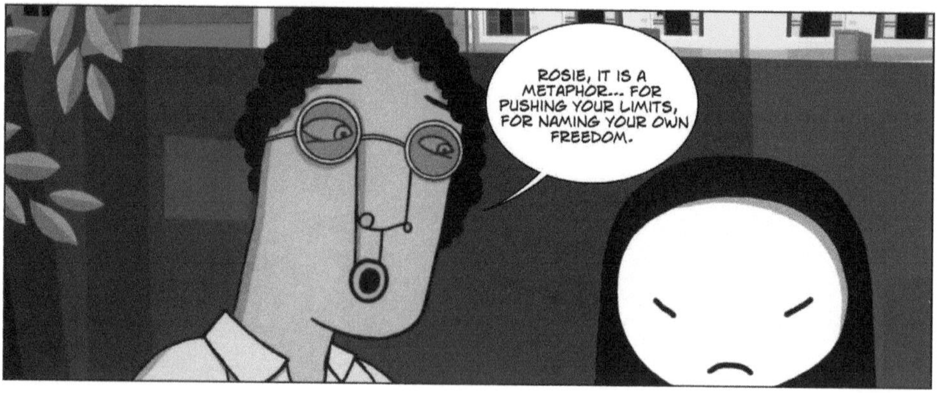
ROSIE, IT IS A METAPHOR... FOR PUSHING YOUR LIMITS, FOR NAMING YOUR OWN FREEDOM.

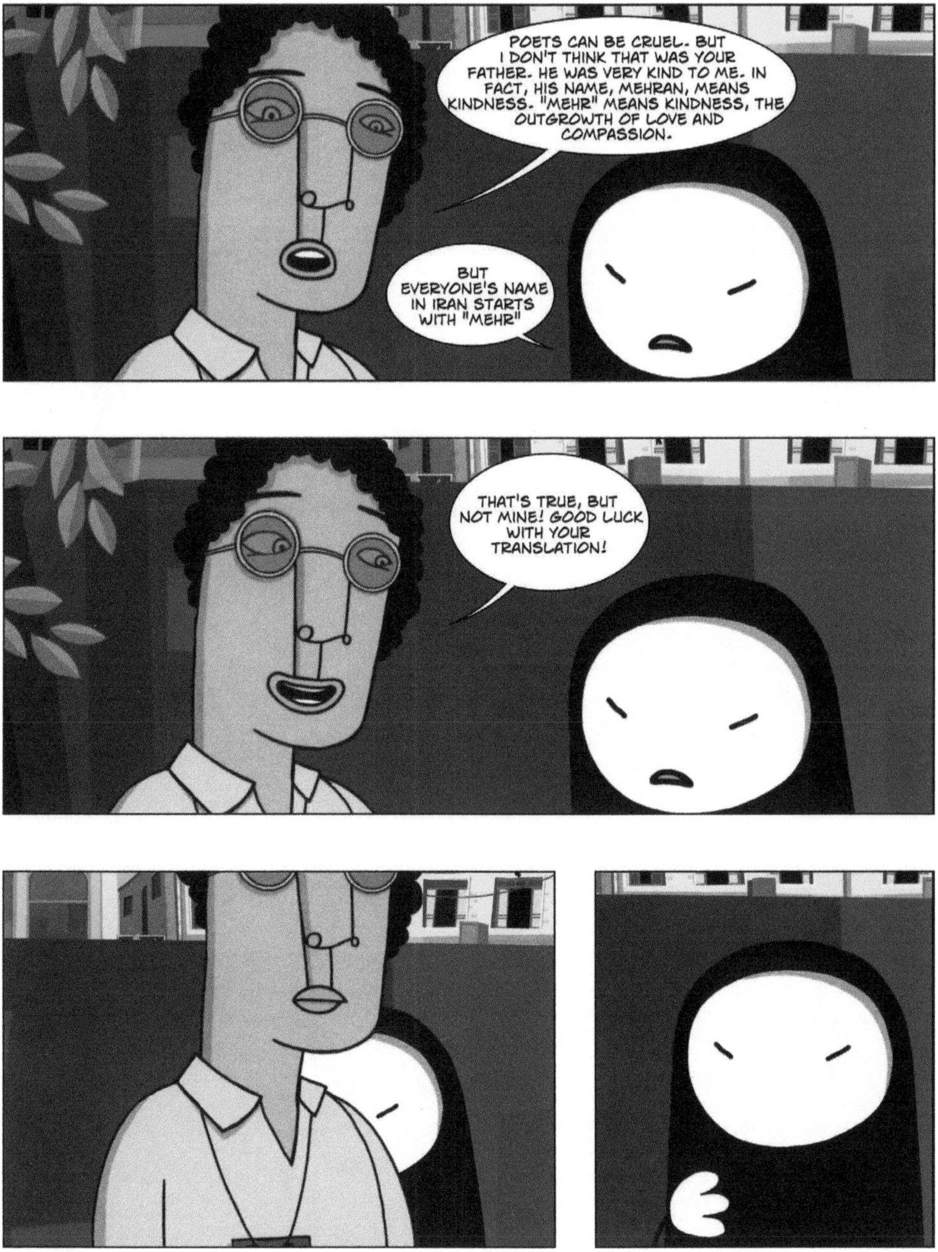
POETS CAN BE CRUEL. BUT I DON'T THINK THAT WAS YOUR FATHER. HE WAS VERY KIND TO ME. IN FACT, HIS NAME, MEHRAN, MEANS KINDNESS. "MEHR" MEANS KINDNESS, THE OUTGROWTH OF LOVE AND COMPASSION.
BUT EVERYONE'S NAME IN IRAN STARTS WITH "MEHR"
THAT'S TRUE, BUT NOT MINE! GOOD LUCK WITH YOUR TRANSLATION!

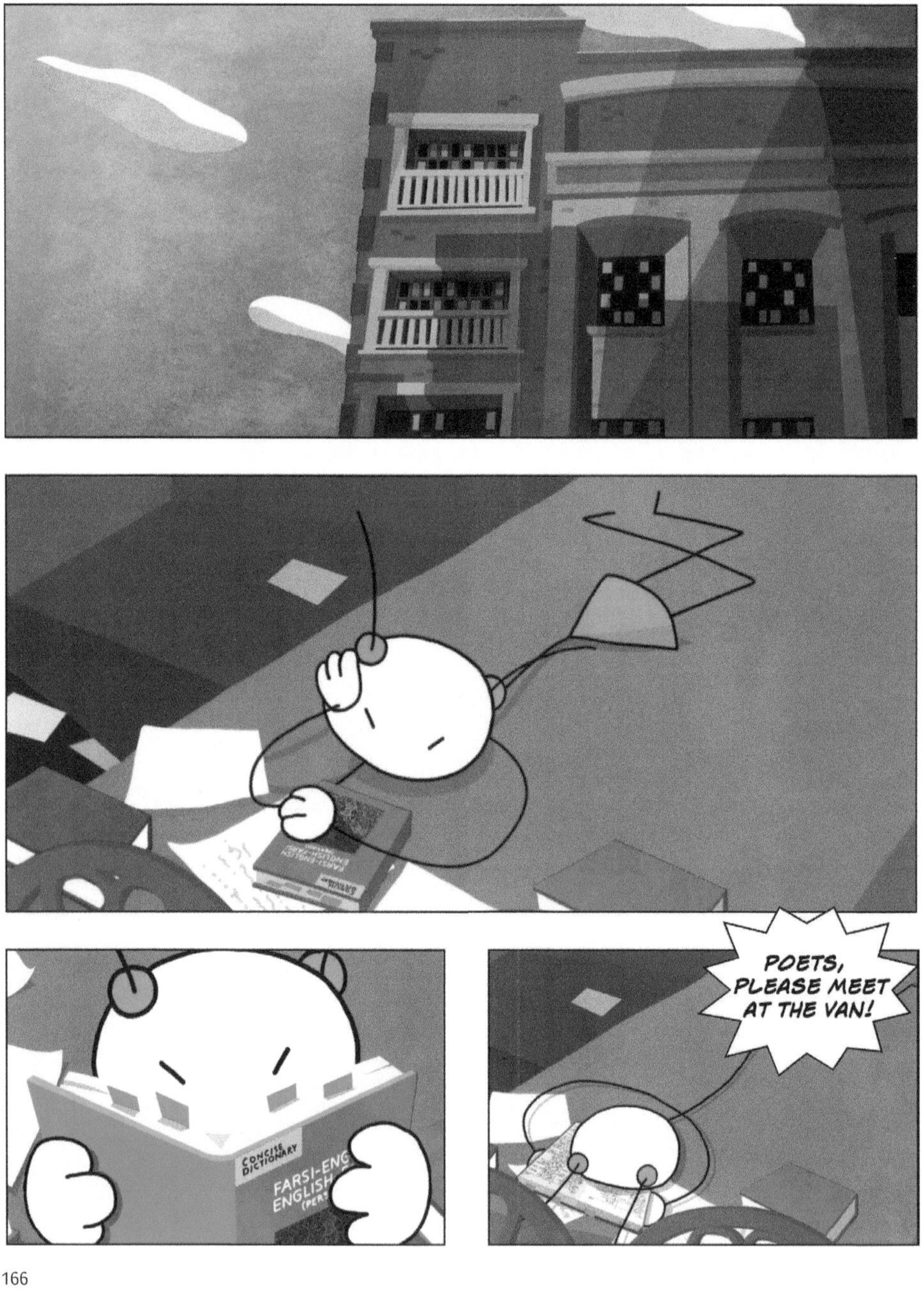
CONCISE DICTIONARY
POETS, PLEASE MEET AT THE VAN!

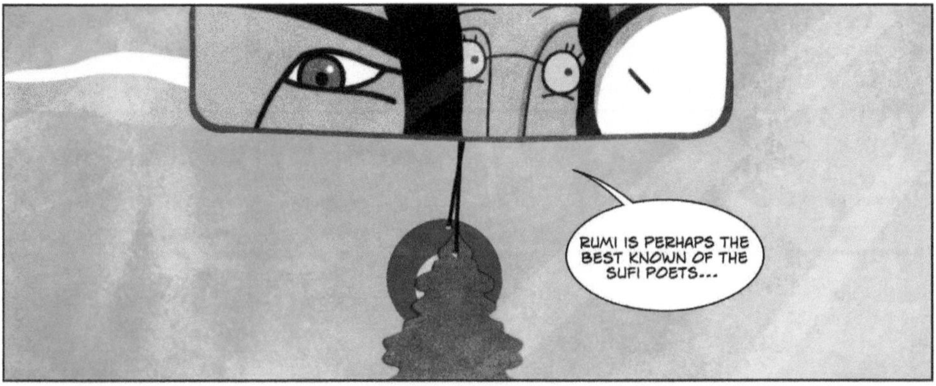
RUMI IS PERHAPS THE BEST KNOWN OF THE SUFI POETS...

...WHOSE BELIEFS INCLUDE THE IDEA THAT HUMAN BEINGS ARE LIKE THE REED THAT BECOMES A FLUTE.

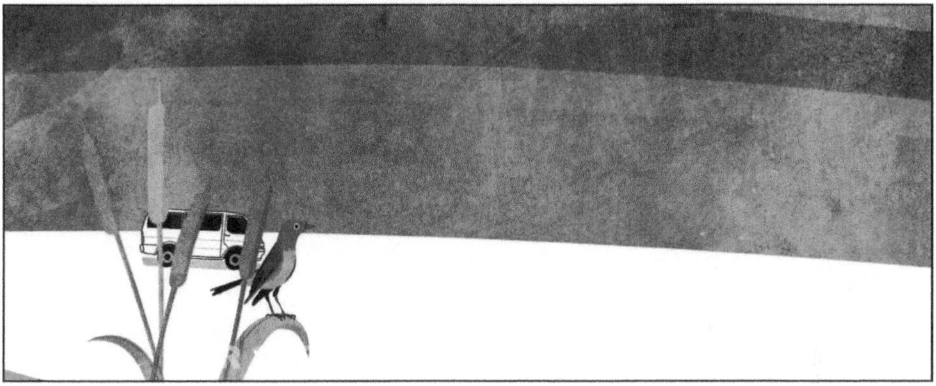

THE PLAINTIVE SOUND OF THE NEY THAT CRIES FOR ITS HOME IN THE RIVER. WE ARE LIKE THAT REED THAT LONGS TO BE REUNITED WITH OUR CREATOR.

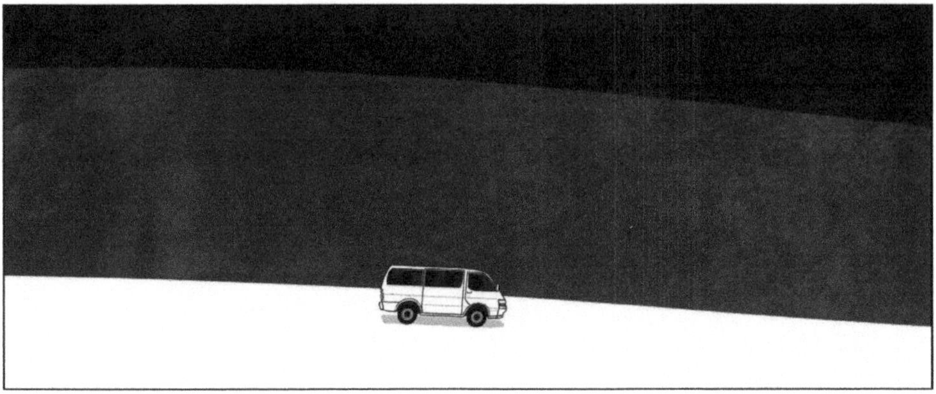

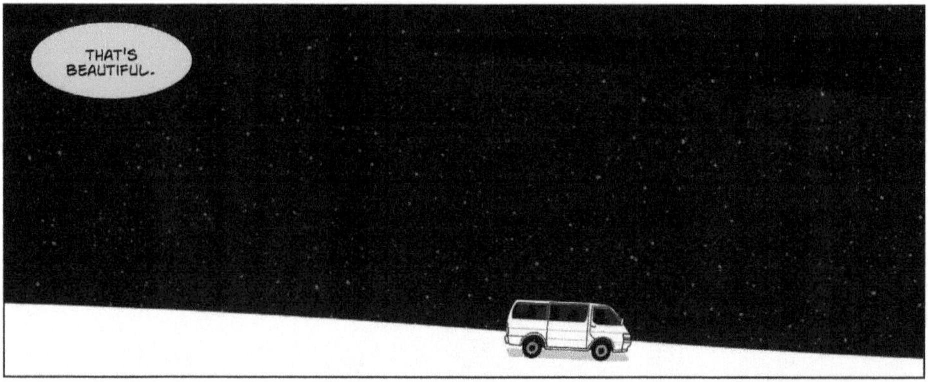
THAT'S BEAUTIFUL.

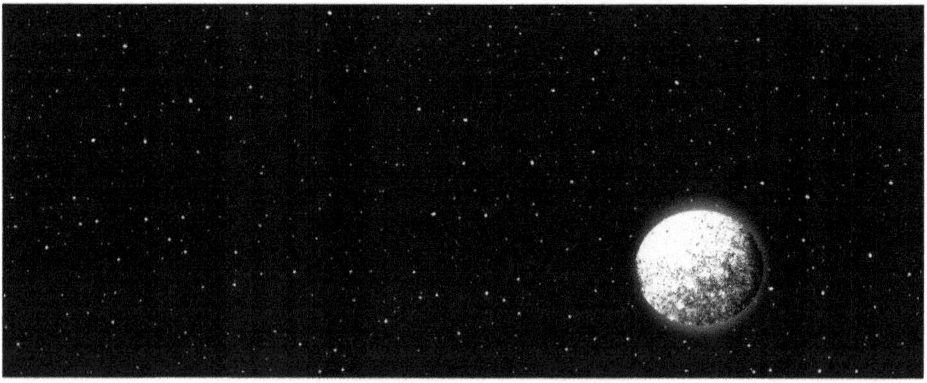

BESHNO AZ NEY CHON HEKAAYAT MIKONAD
AZ JODAAYEEHAA SHEKAAYAT MIKONAD

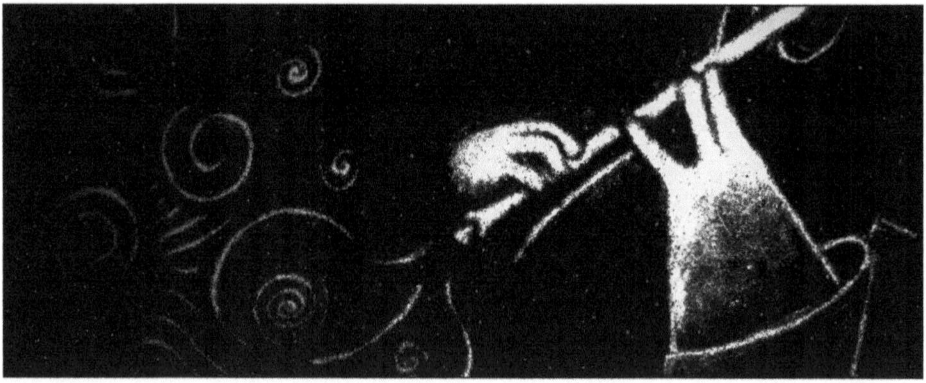

*ILLUSTRATION OF MASNEVI BY LOUISE JOHNSON

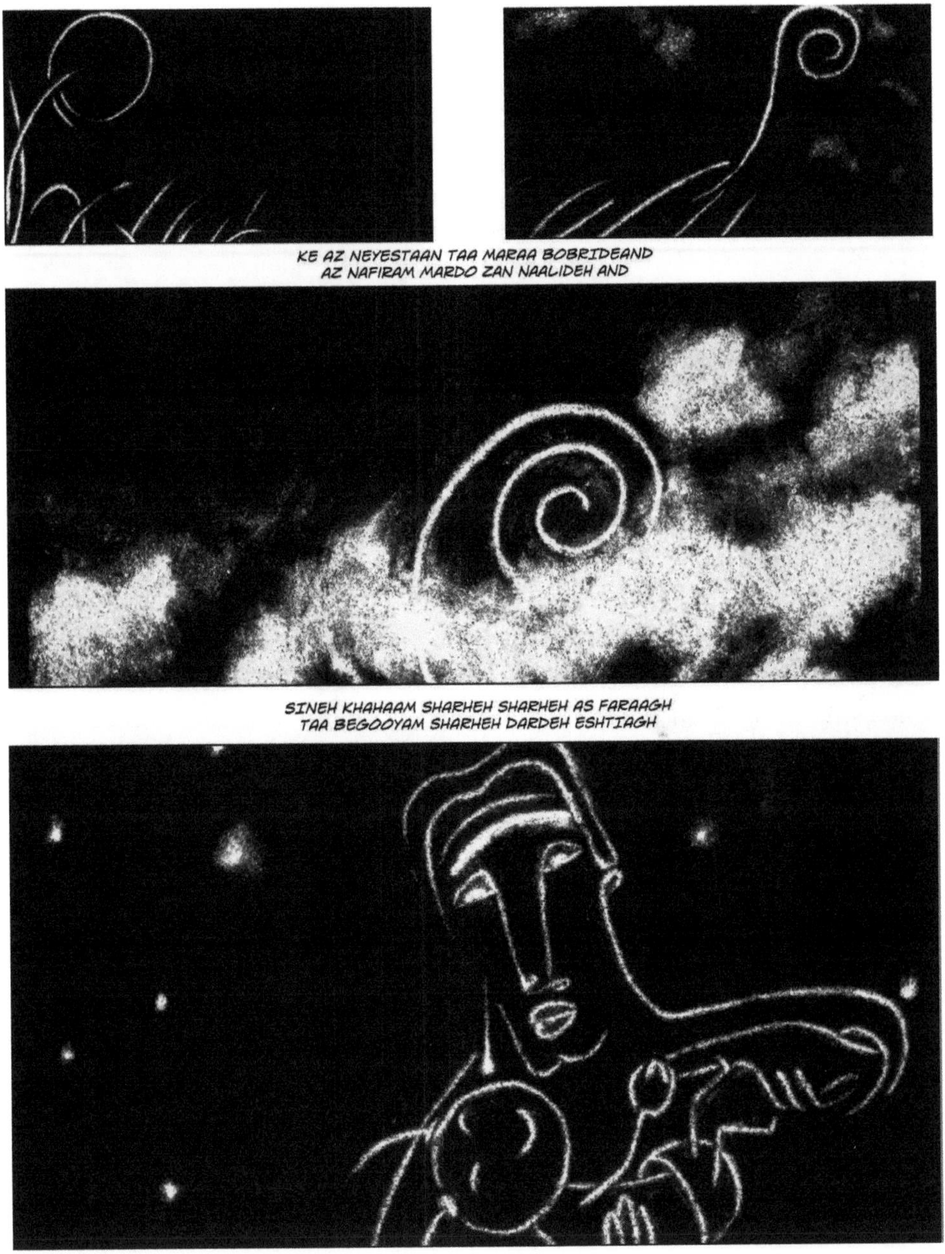
KE AZ NEYESTAAN TAA MARAA BOBRIDEAND
AZ NAFIRAM MARDO ZAN NAALIDEH AND
SINEH KHAHAAM SHARHEH SHARHEH AS FARAAGH
TAA BEGOOYAM SHARHEH DARDEH ESHTIAGH

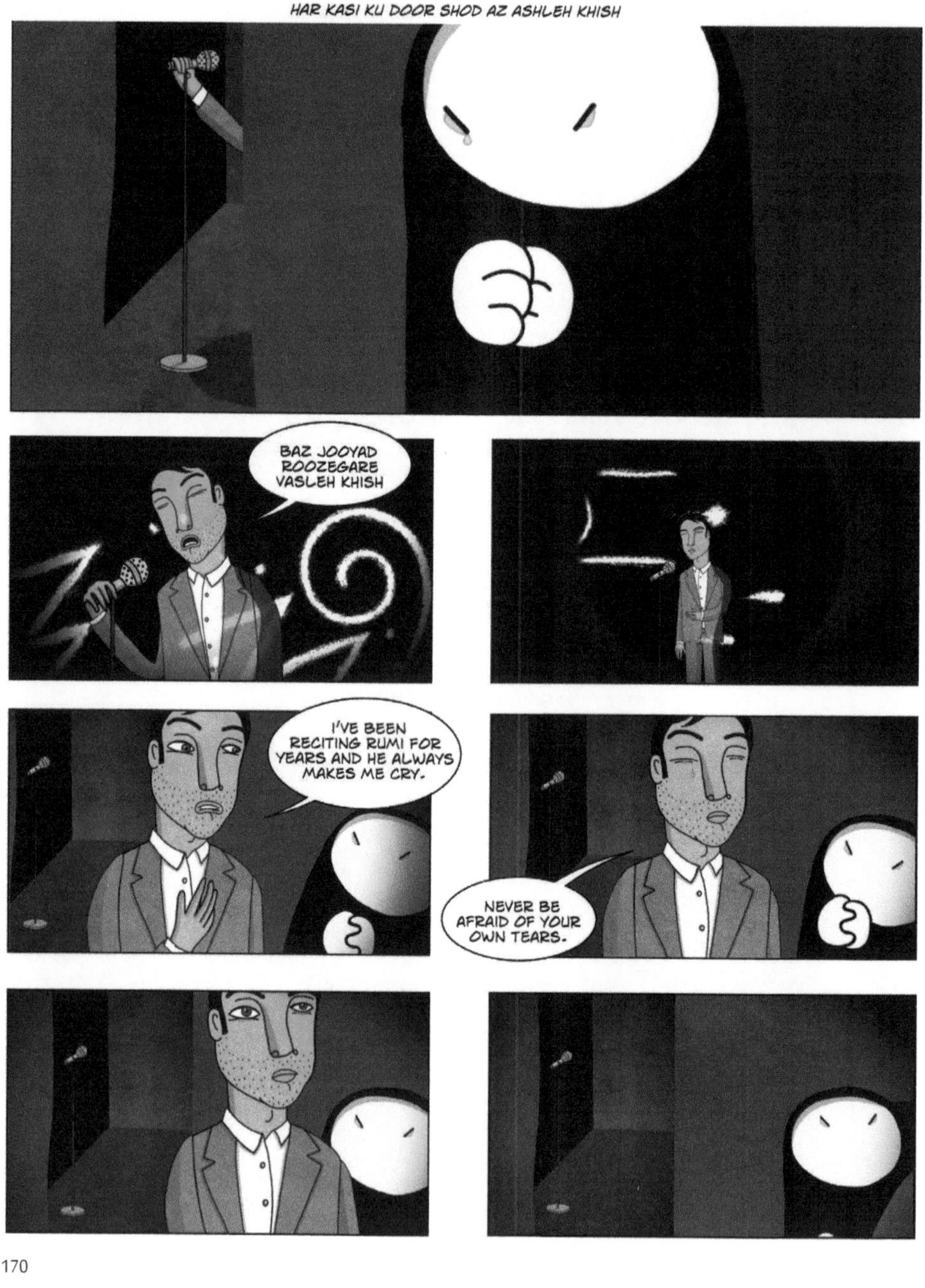
HAR KASI KU DOOR SHOD AZ ASHLEH KHISH
BAZ JOOYAD ROOZEGARE VASLEH KHISH
I'VE BEEN RECITING RUMI FOR YEARS AND HE ALWAYS MAKES ME CRY.
NEVER BE AFRAID OF YOUR OWN TEARS.

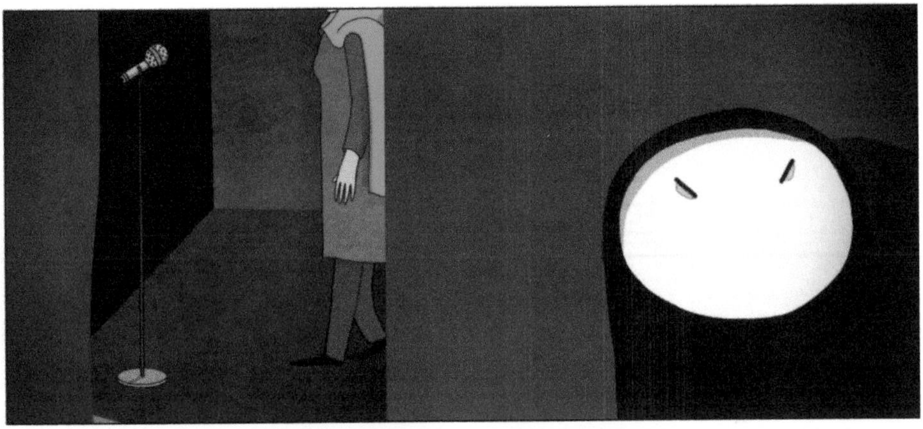
DAANI KE CHE MIGOOYAD IN BAANGE ROBAAB.
ANDAR PEYE MAN BIA O RAH RA DARYAAB

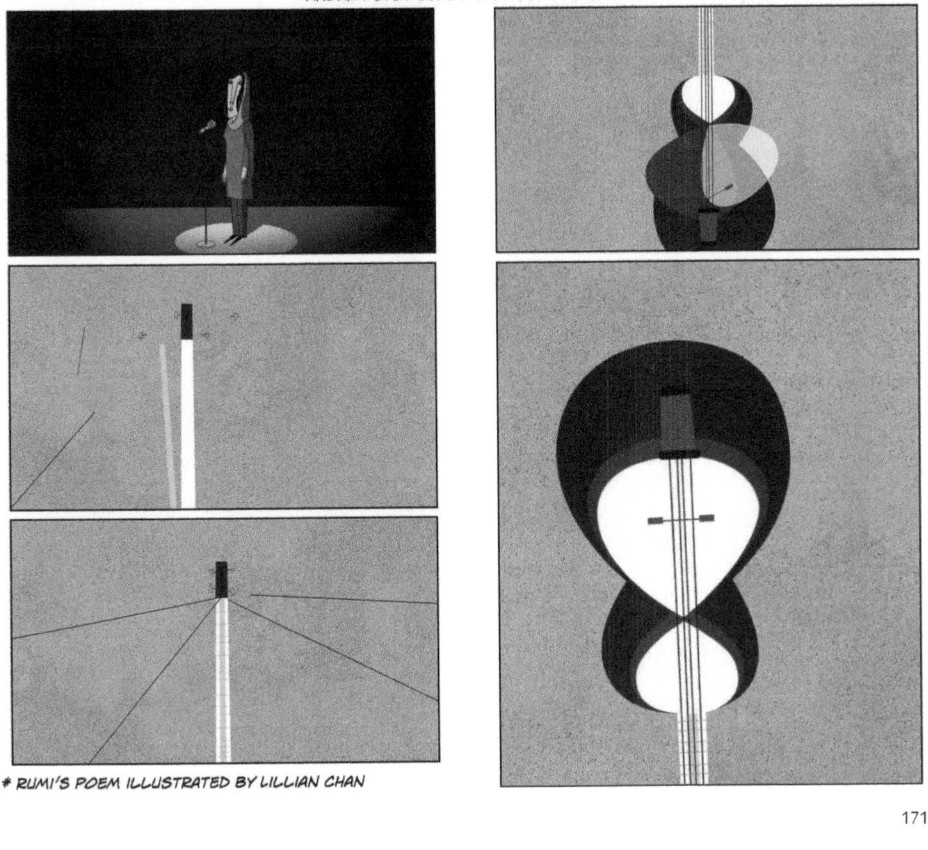

* RUMI'S POEM ILLUSTRATED BY LILLIAN CHAN

ZIRAA BE KHATAA RAH BARI SOOYE SAVAAB
ZIRAA BE SOAAL RAH BARI SOOYE JAVAAB

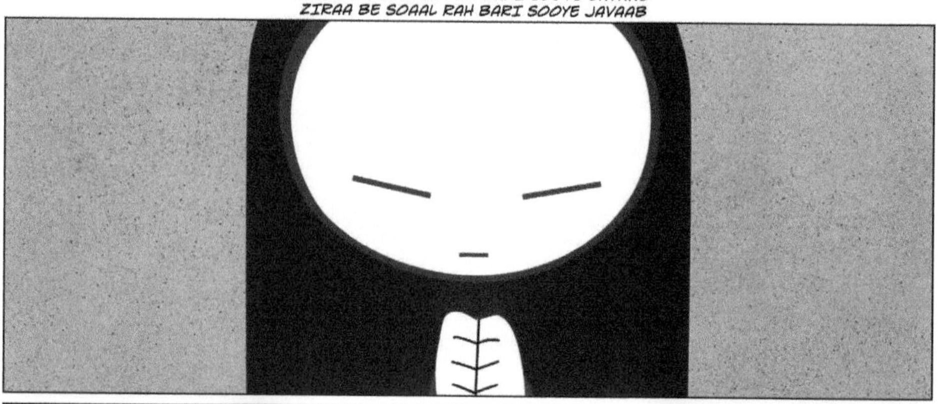

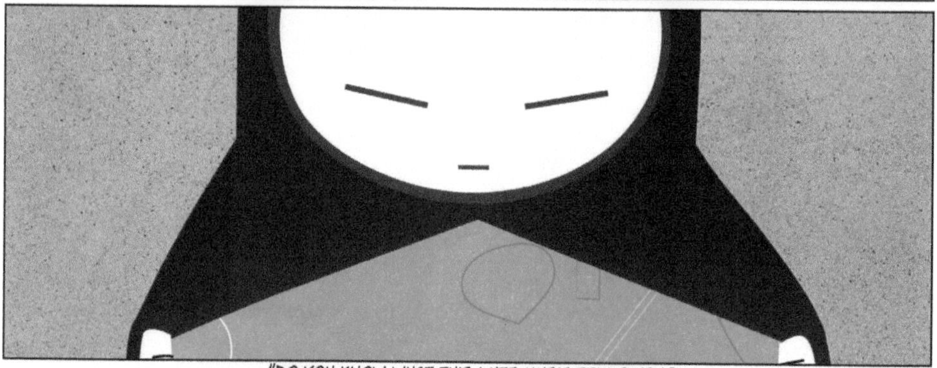

"DO YOU KNOW WHAT THIS LUTE MUSIC TELLS YOU?
IT SAYS: FOLLOW ME AND YOU'LL FIND THE WAY.
MISTAKES WILL MAKE YOU STUMBLE TOWARDS GOODNESS.
QUESTIONS WILL PUT YOU ON THE ANSWER PATHWAY."

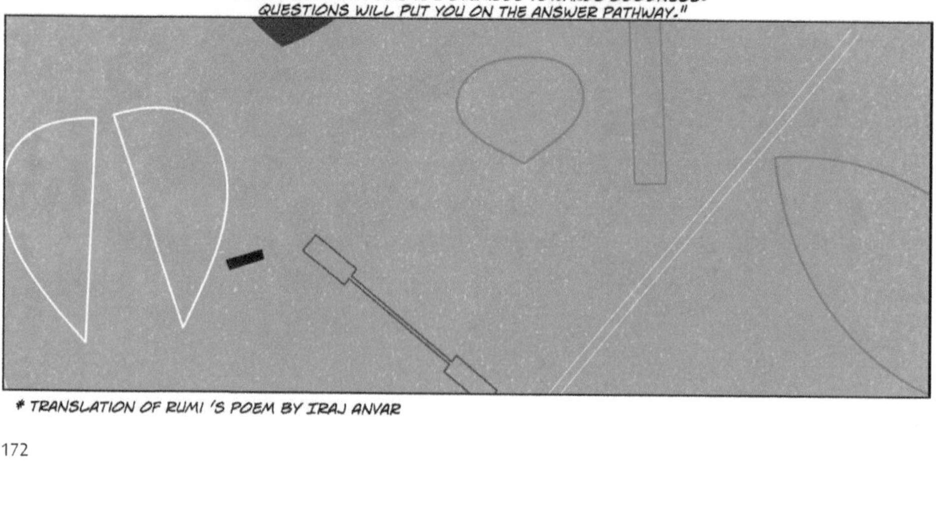

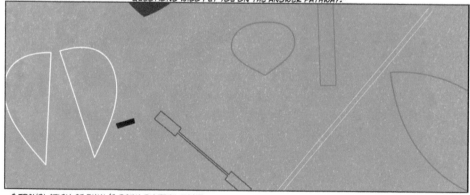

* TRANSLATION OF RUMI 'S POEM BY IRAJ ANVAR

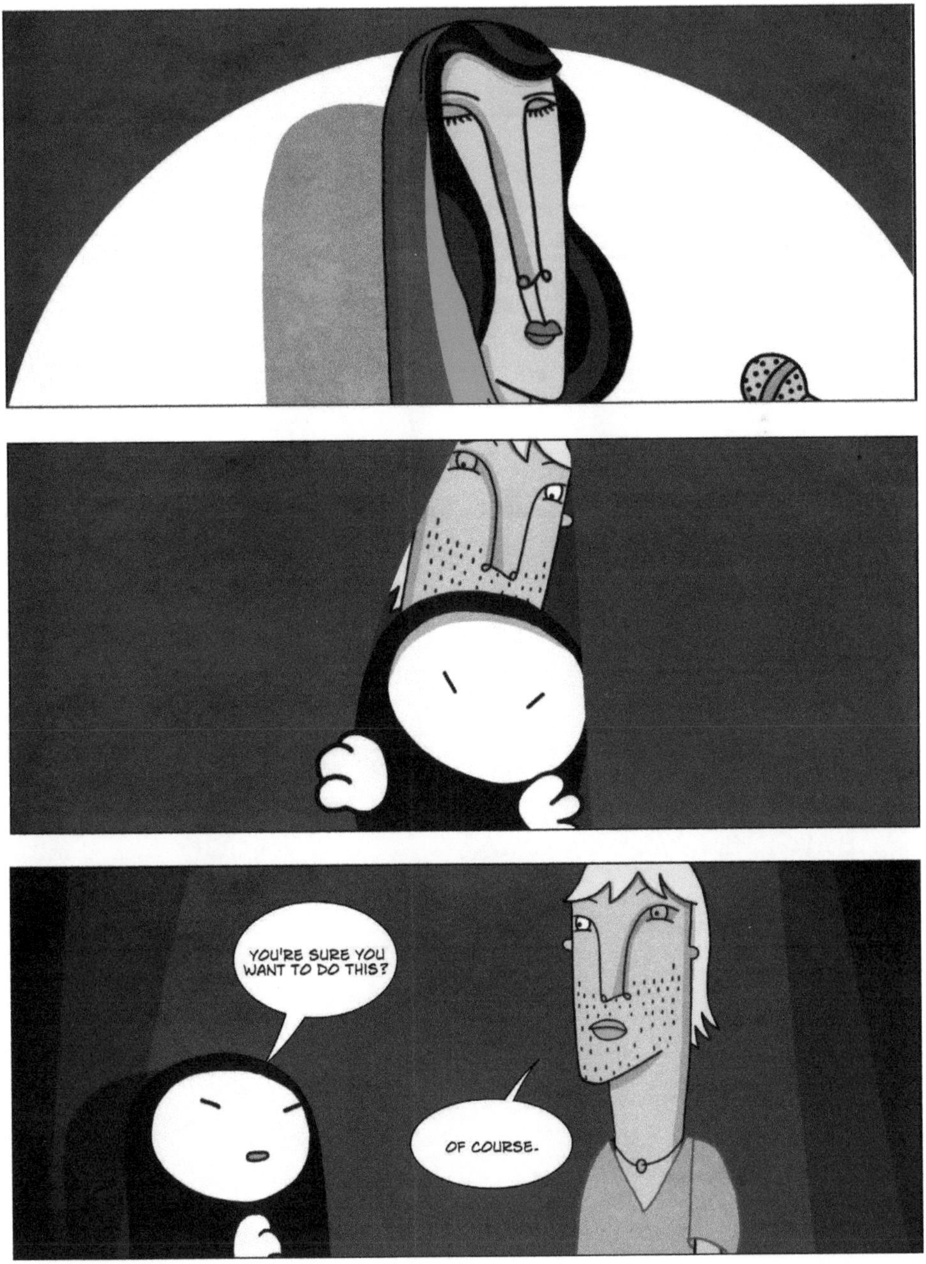
YOU'RE SURE YOU WANT TO DO THIS?
OF COURSE.

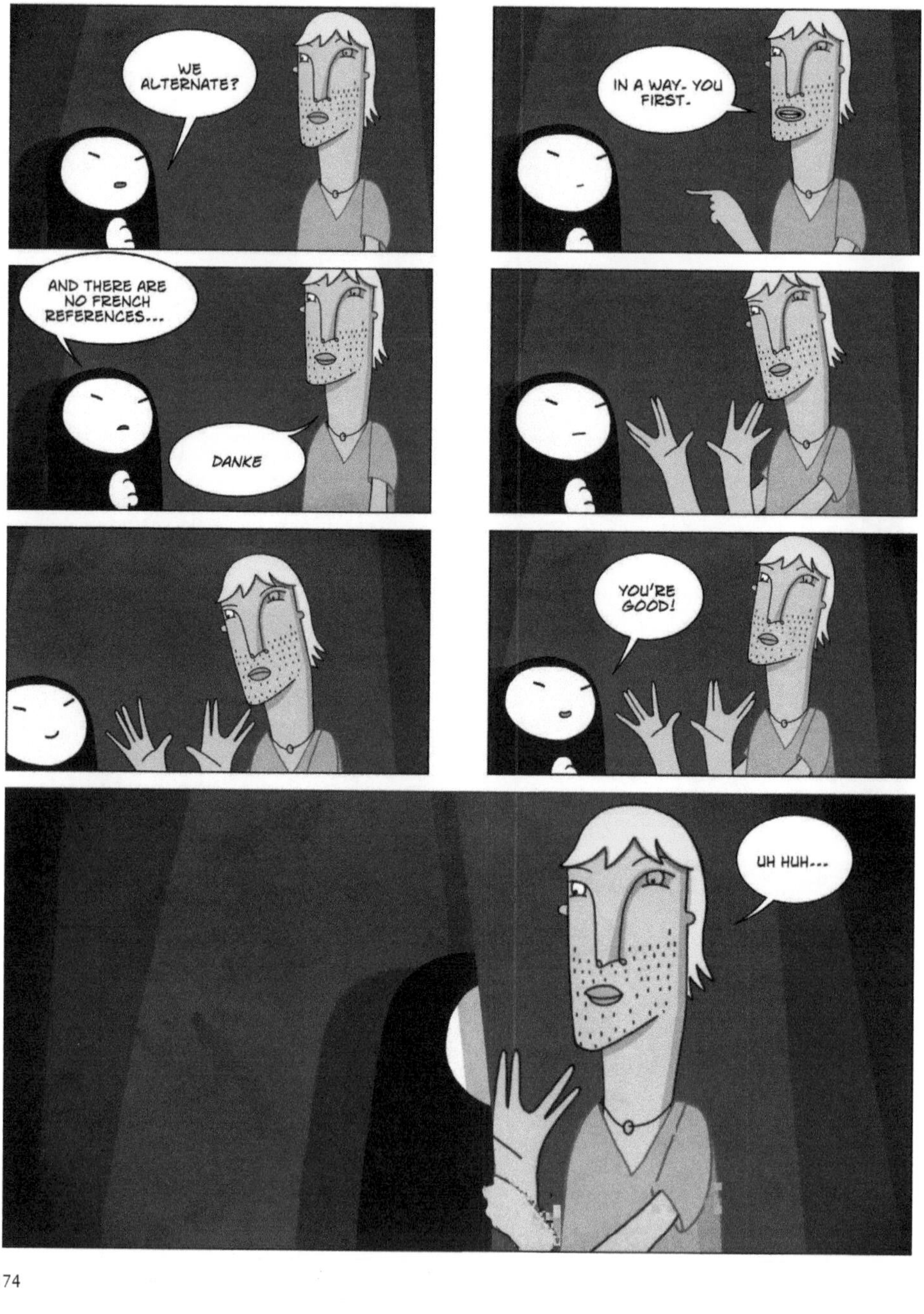
WE ALTERNATE?
IN A WAY. YOU FIRST.
AND THERE ARE NO FRENCH REFERENCES...
DANKE
YOU'RE GOOD!
UH HUH...

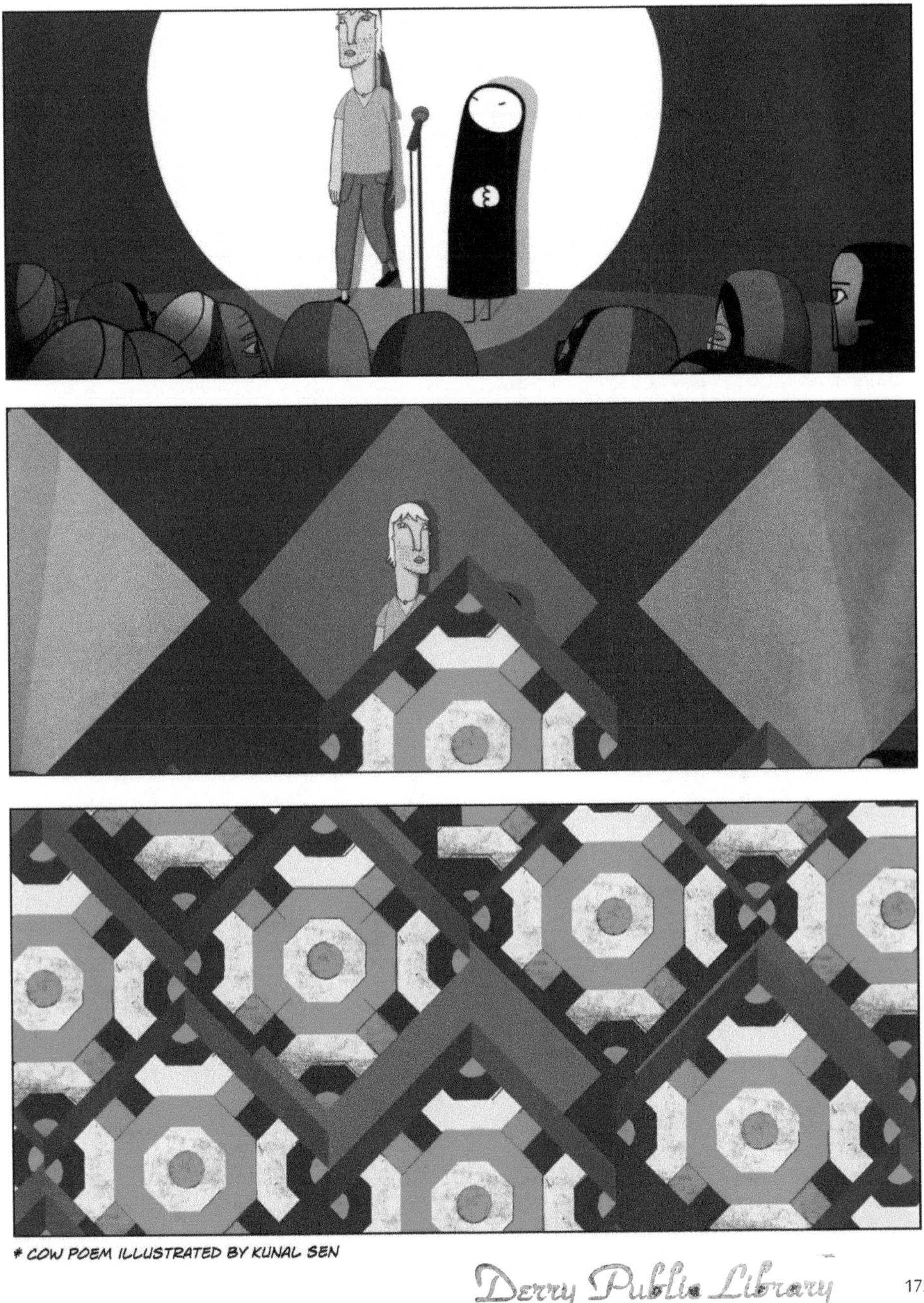

* COW POEM ILLUSTRATED BY KUNAL SEN

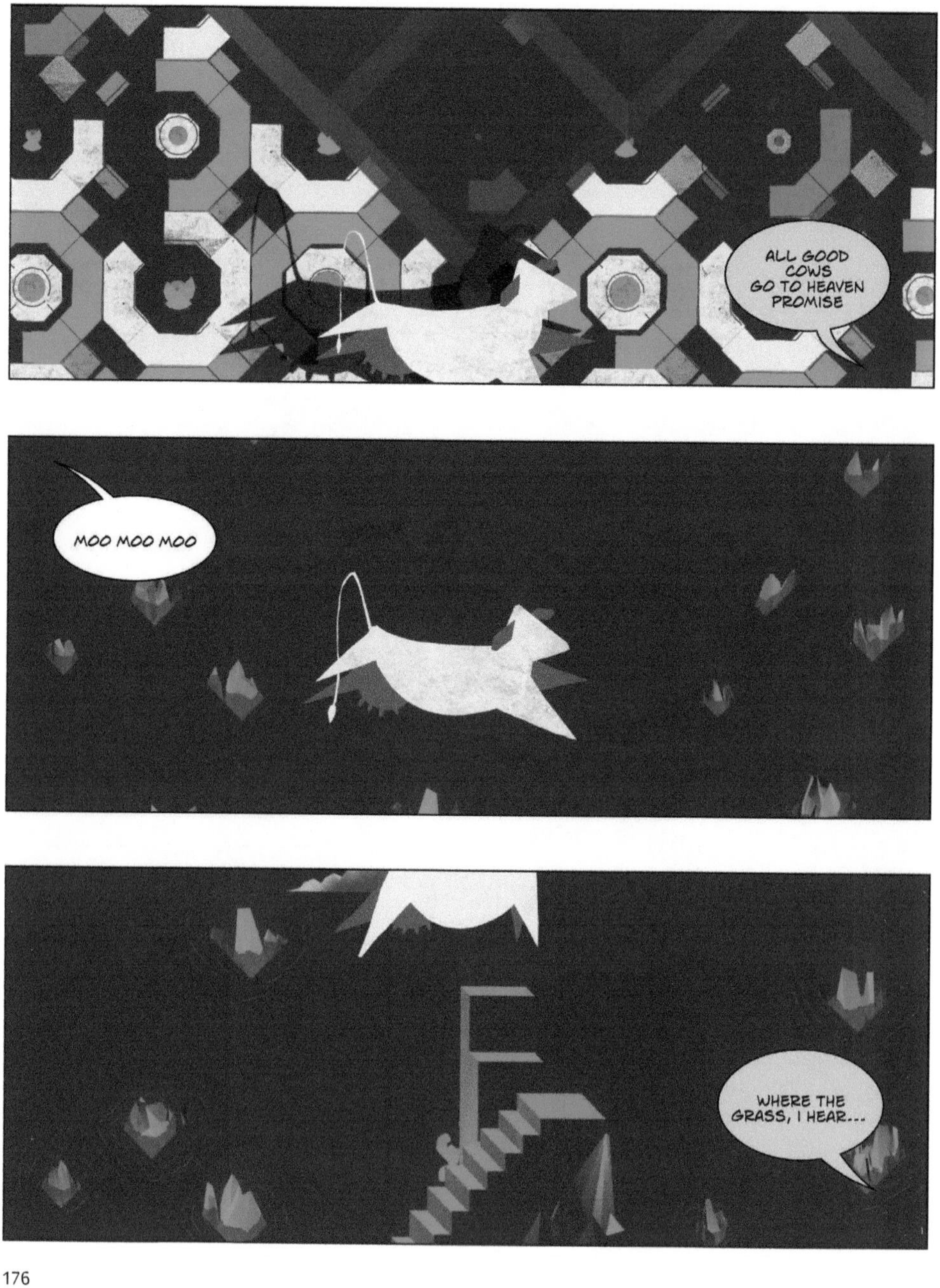
ALL GOOD COWS GO TO HEAVEN PROMISE
MOO MOO MOO
WHERE THE GRASS, I HEAR...

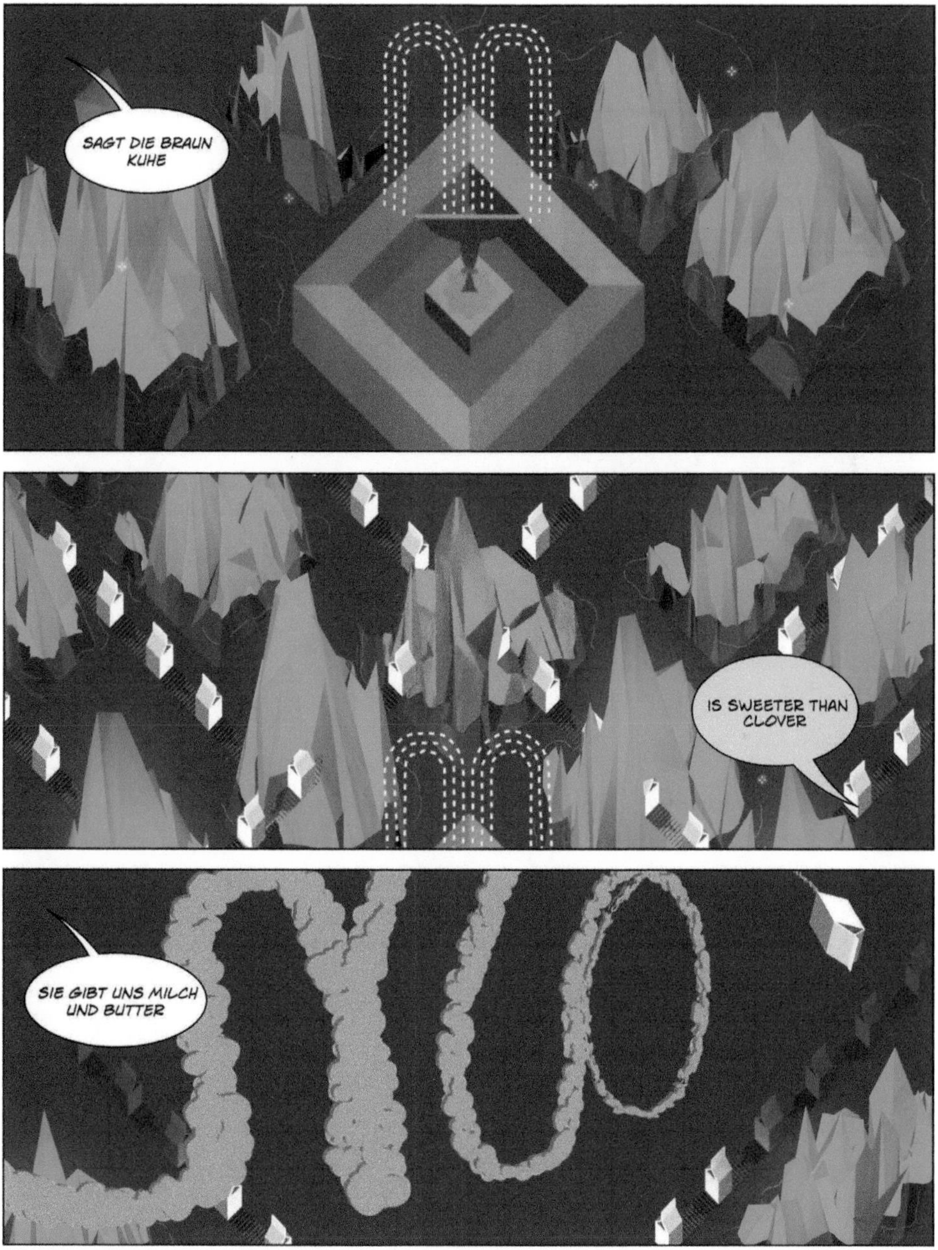
SAGT DIE BRAUN KUHE
IS SWEETER THAN CLOVER
SIE GIBT UNS MILCH UND BUTTER

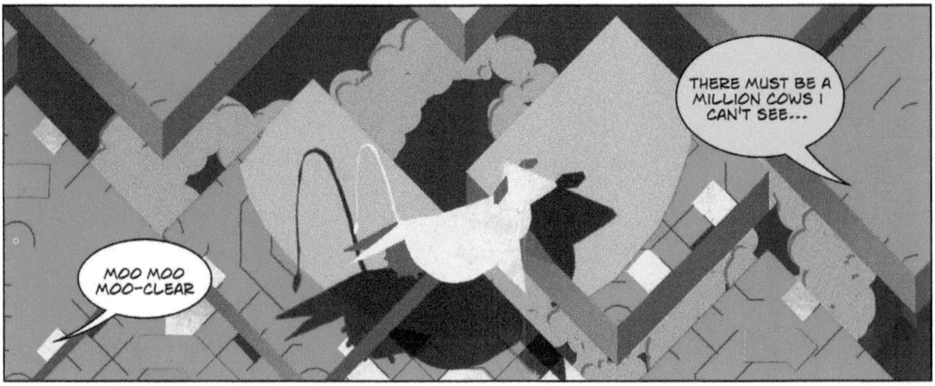
THERE MUST BE A MILLION COWS I CAN'T SEE...
MOO MOO MOO-CLEAR

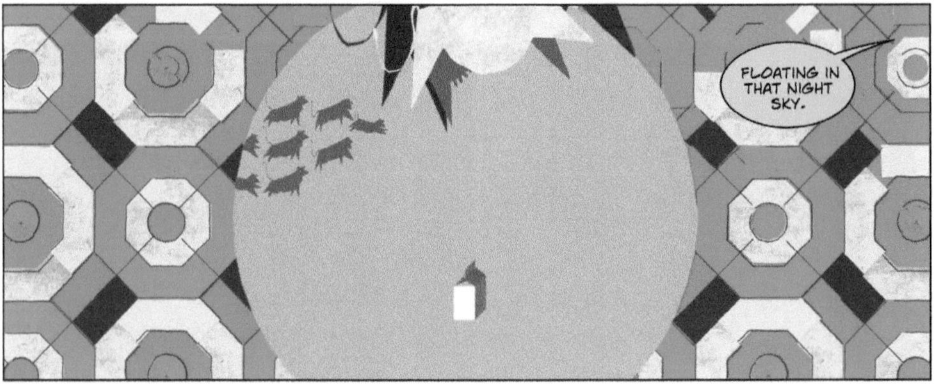
FLOATING IN THAT NIGHT SKY.

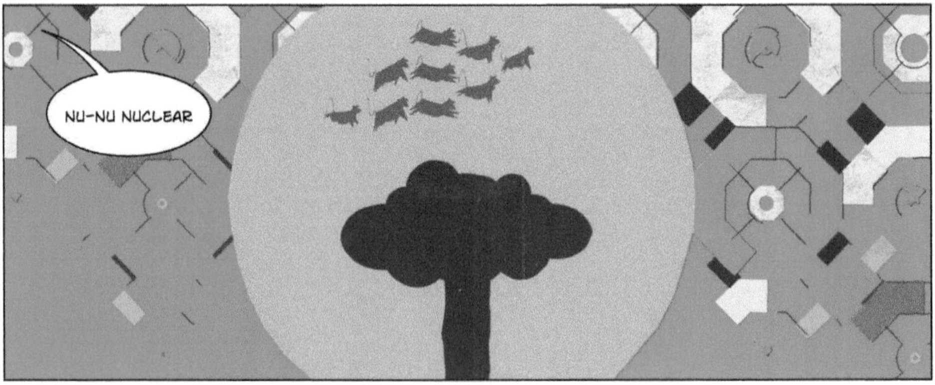
NU-NU NUCLEAR

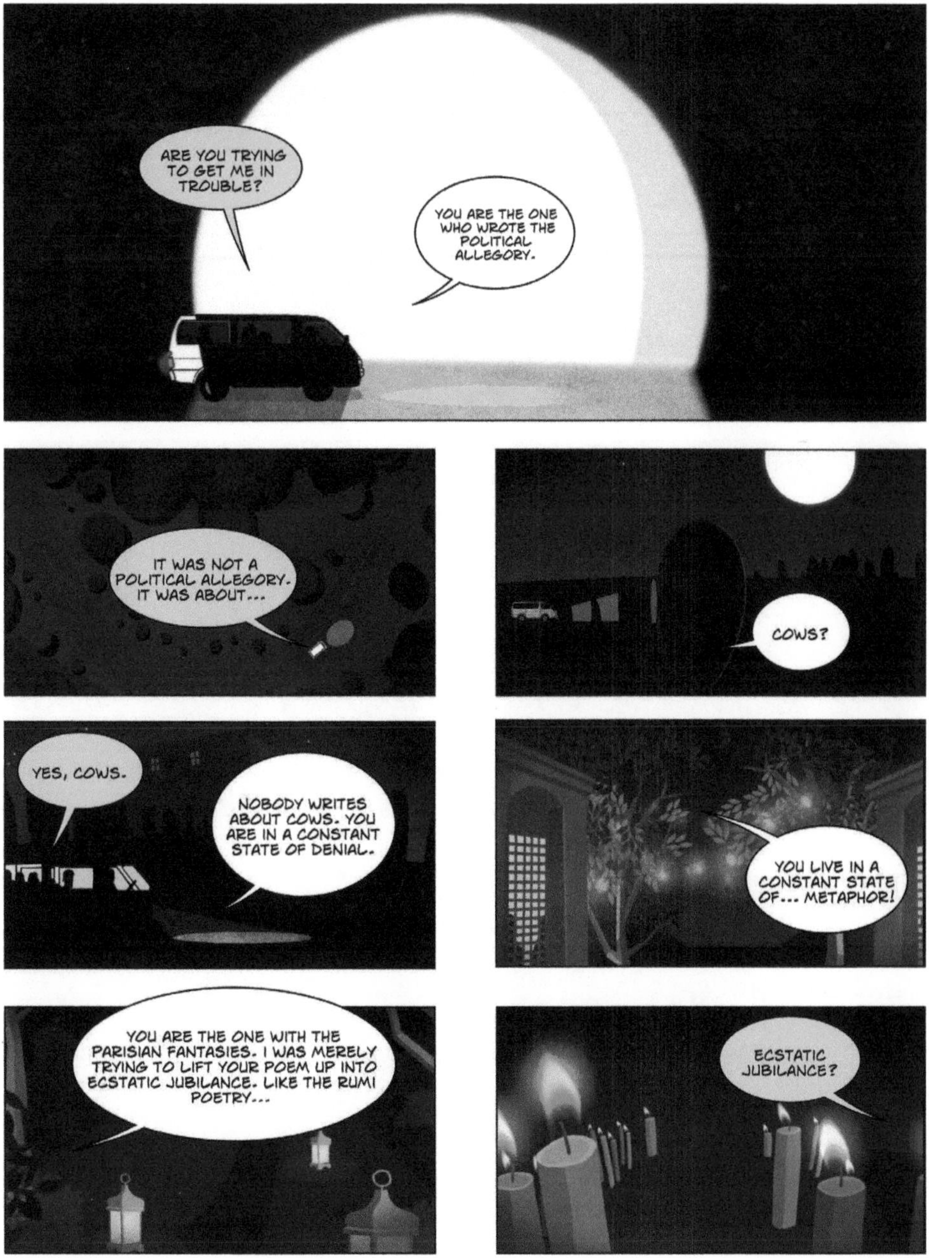
ARE YOU TRYING TO GET ME IN TROUBLE?
YOU ARE THE ONE WHO WROTE THE POLITICAL ALLEGORY.
IT WAS NOT A POLITICAL ALLEGORY. IT WAS ABOUT...
COWS?
YES, COWS.
NOBODY WRITES ABOUT COWS. YOU ARE IN A CONSTANT STATE OF DENIAL.
YOU LIVE IN A CONSTANT STATE OF... METAPHOR!
YOU ARE THE ONE WITH THE PARISIAN FANTASIES. I WAS MERELY TRYING TO LIFT YOUR POEM UP INTO ECSTATIC JUBILANCE. LIKE THE RUMI POETRY...
ECSTATIC JUBILANCE?

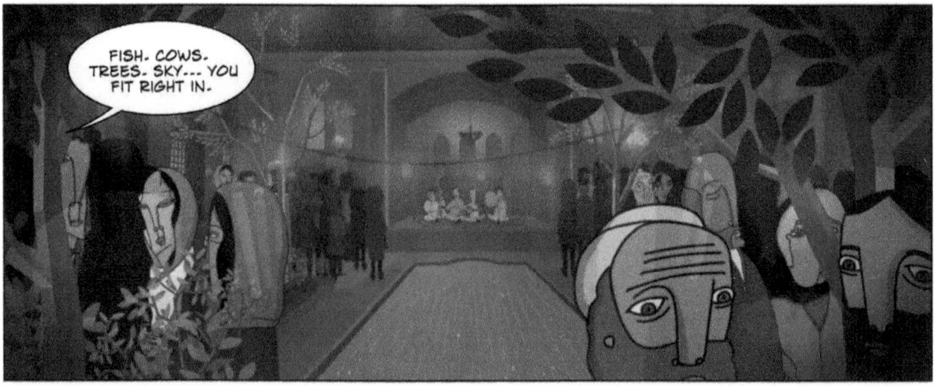
FISH. COWS. TREES. SKY... YOU FIT RIGHT IN.

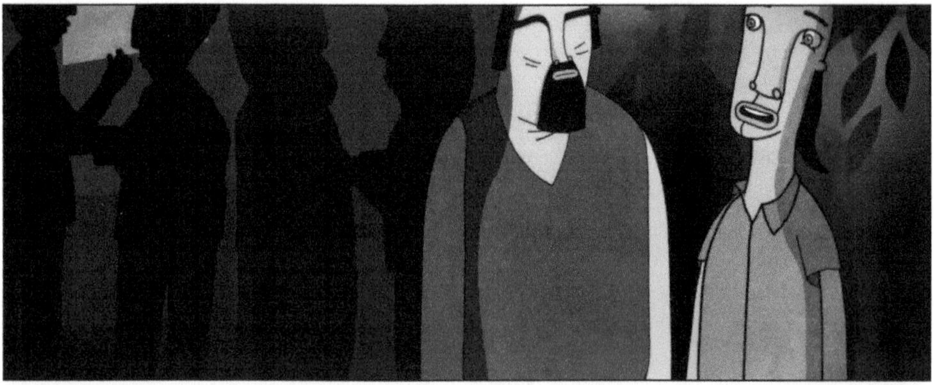

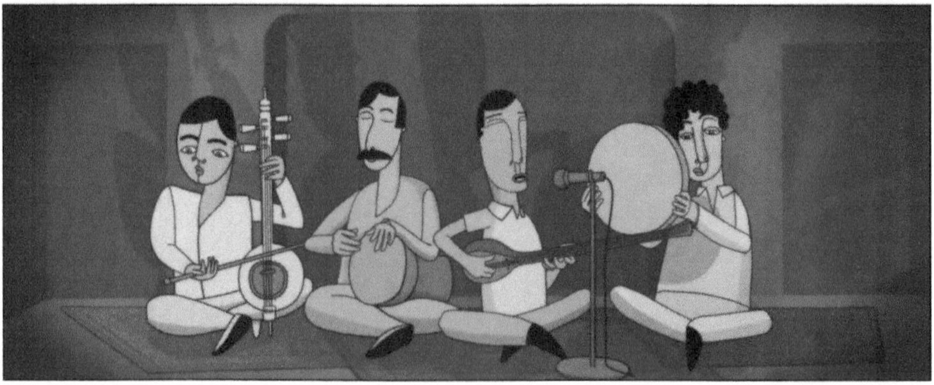

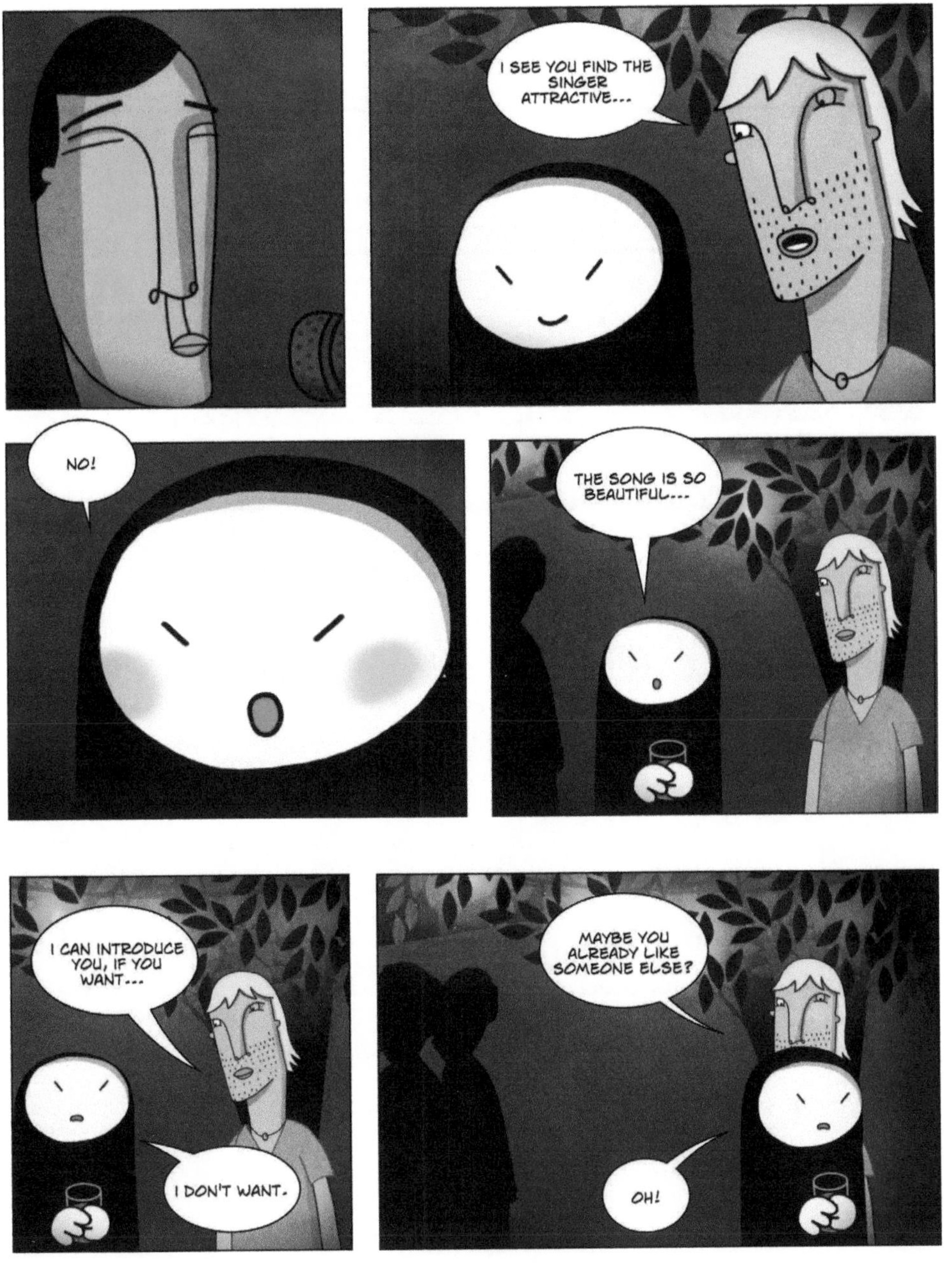
I SEE YOU FIND THE SINGER ATTRACTIVE...
NO!
THE SONG IS SO BEAUTIFUL...
I CAN INTRODUCE YOU, IF YOU WANT...
I DON'T WANT.
MAYBE YOU ALREADY LIKE SOMEONE ELSE?
OH!

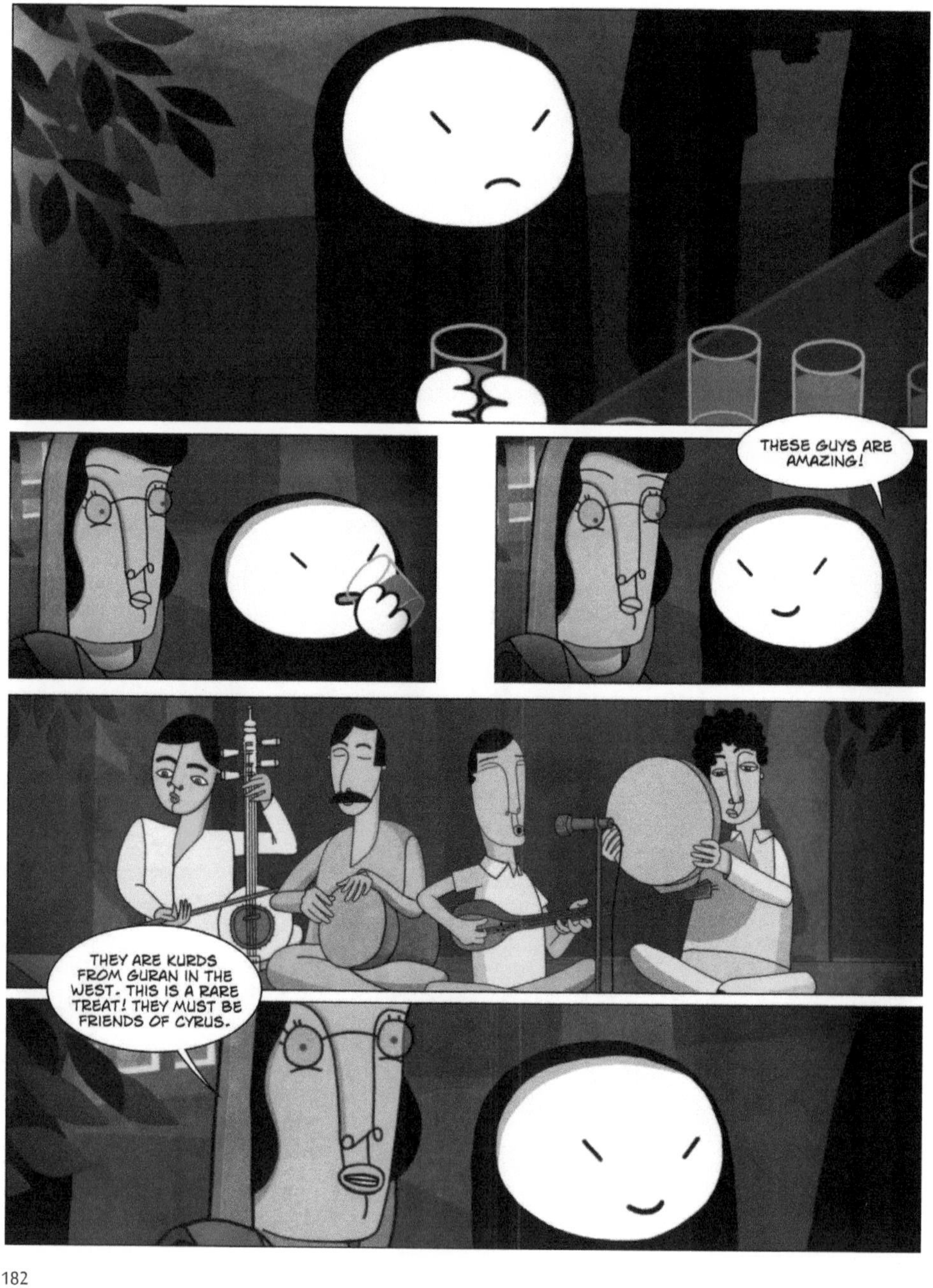
THESE GUYS ARE AMAZING!
THEY ARE KURDS FROM GURAN IN THE WEST. THIS IS A RARE TREAT! THEY MUST BE FRIENDS OF CYRUS.

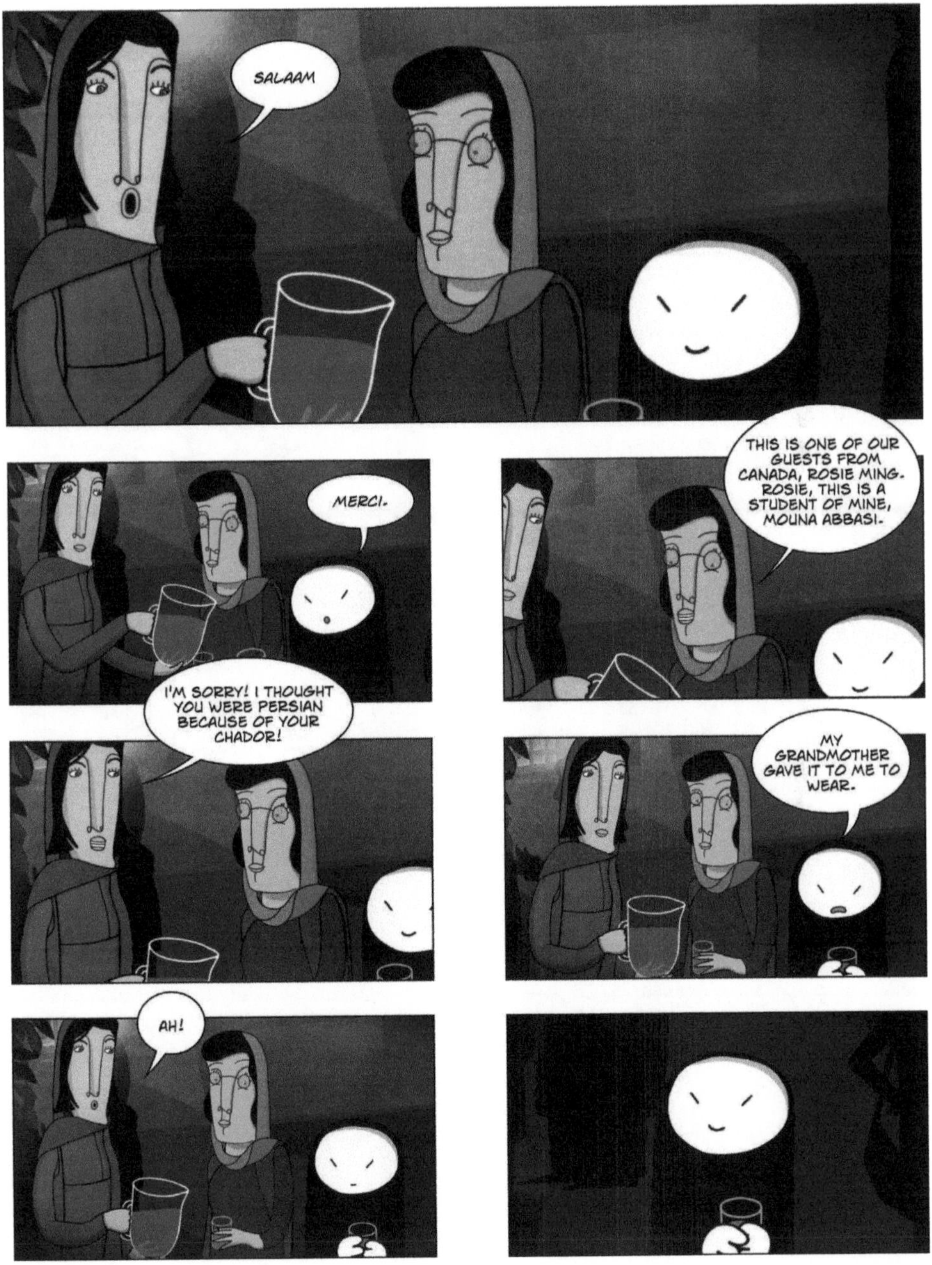
SALAAM
MERCI.
THIS IS ONE OF OUR GUESTS FROM CANADA, ROSIE MING. ROSIE, THIS IS A STUDENT OF MINE, MOUNA ABBASI.
I'M SORRY! I THOUGHT YOU WERE PERSIAN BECAUSE OF YOUR CHADOR!
MY GRANDMOTHER GAVE IT TO ME TO WEAR.
AH!

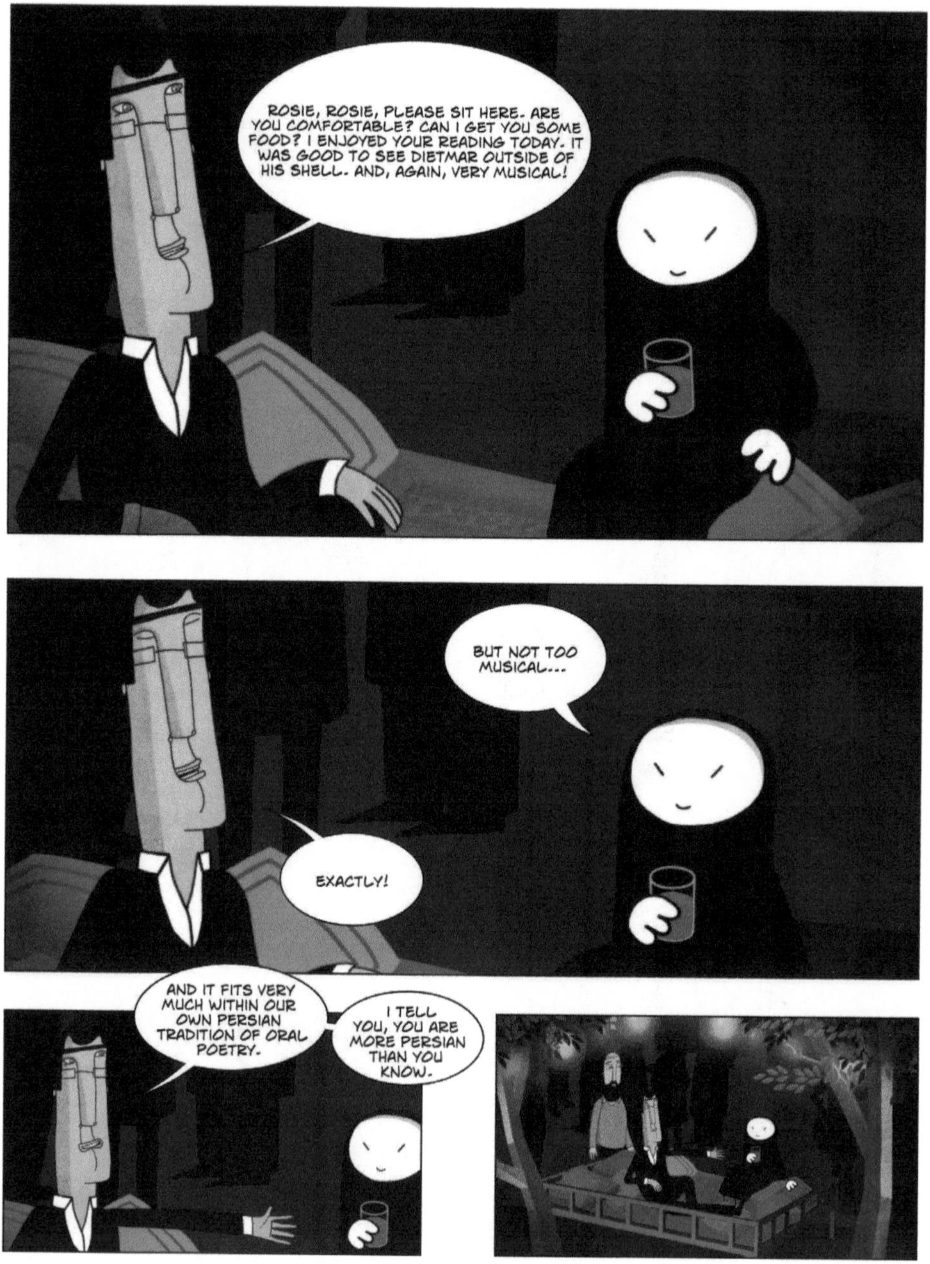
ROSIE, ROSIE, PLEASE SIT HERE. ARE YOU COMFORTABLE? CAN I GET YOU SOME FOOD? I ENJOYED YOUR READING TODAY. IT WAS GOOD TO SEE DIETMAR OUTSIDE OF HIS SHELL. AND, AGAIN, VERY MUSICAL!
BUT NOT TOO MUSICAL...
EXACTLY!
AND IT FITS VERY MUCH WITHIN OUR OWN PERSIAN TRADITION OF ORAL POETRY.
I TELL YOU, YOU ARE MORE PERSIAN THAN YOU KNOW.

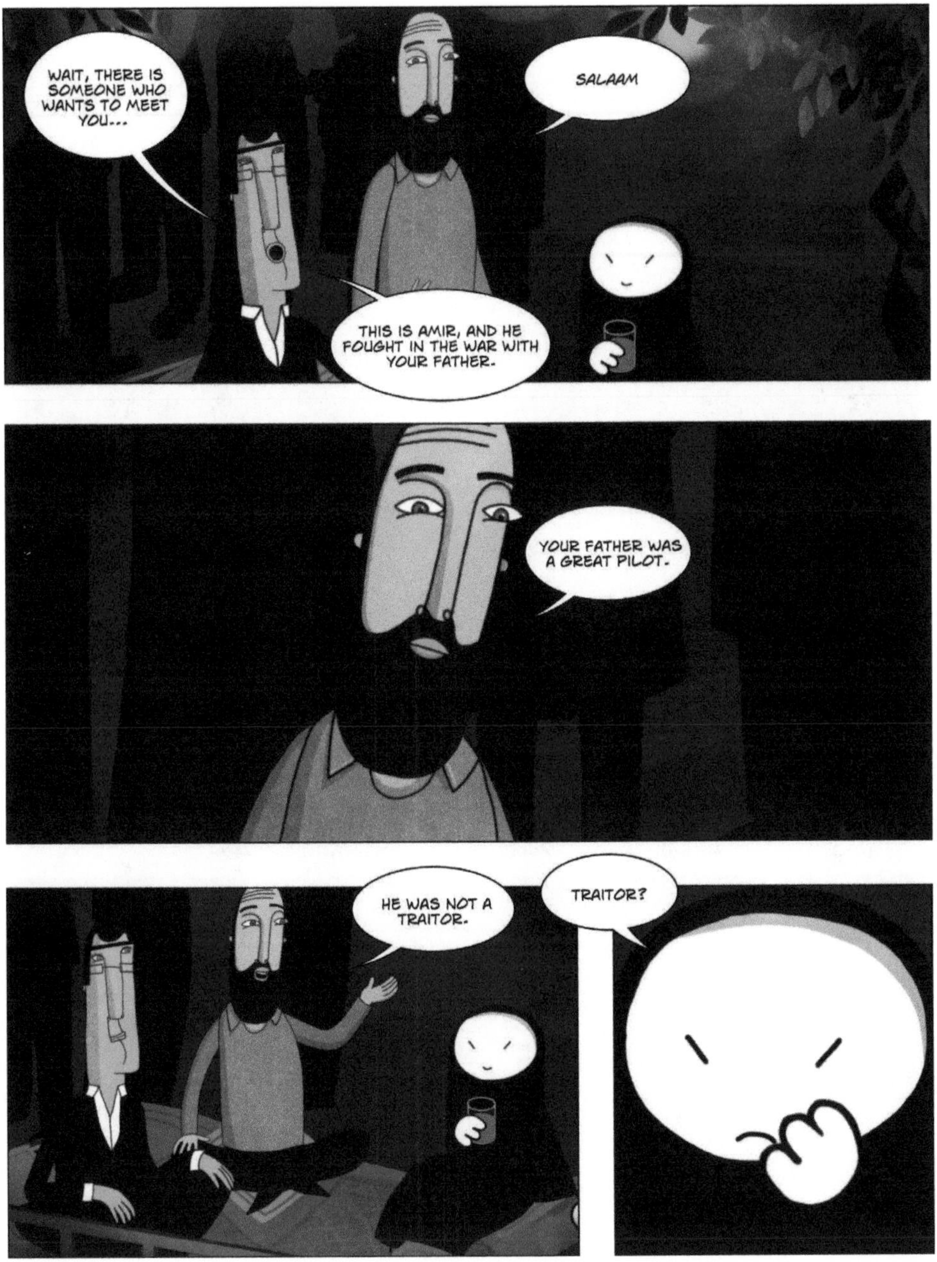
WAIT, THERE IS SOMEONE WHO WANTS TO MEET YOU...
SALAAM
THIS IS AMIR, AND HE FOUGHT IN THE WAR WITH YOUR FATHER.
YOUR FATHER WAS A GREAT PILOT.
HE WAS NOT A TRAITOR.
TRAITOR?

IN 1981, AS YOU KNOW, IRAQ ATTACKED OUR COUNTRY.
WE WERE NOT PREPARED.

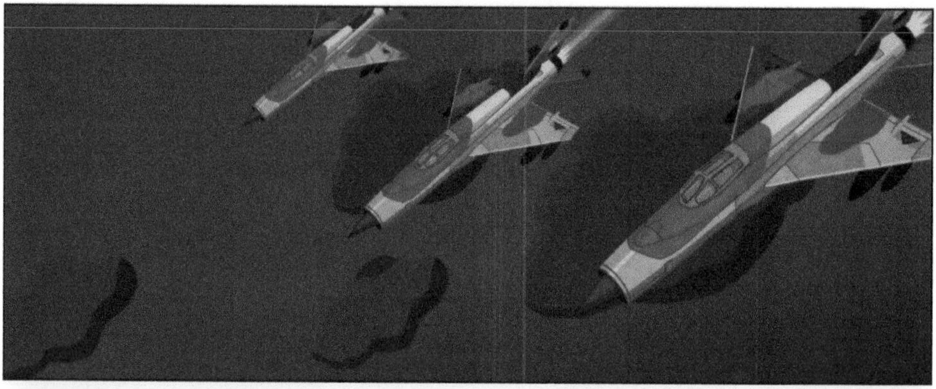

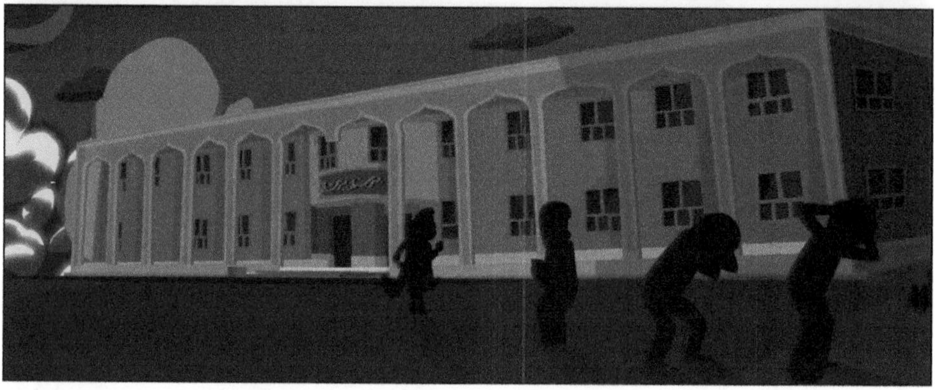

SADDAM HUSSEIN ATTACKED US, AND WE HAD NO ONE TO FIGHT.

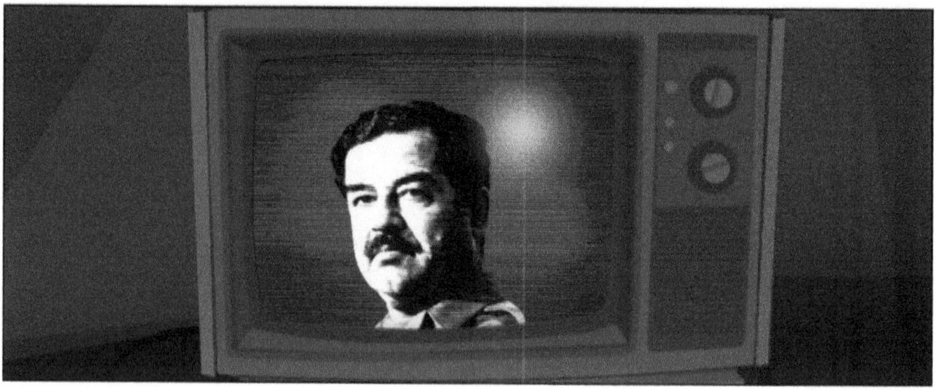

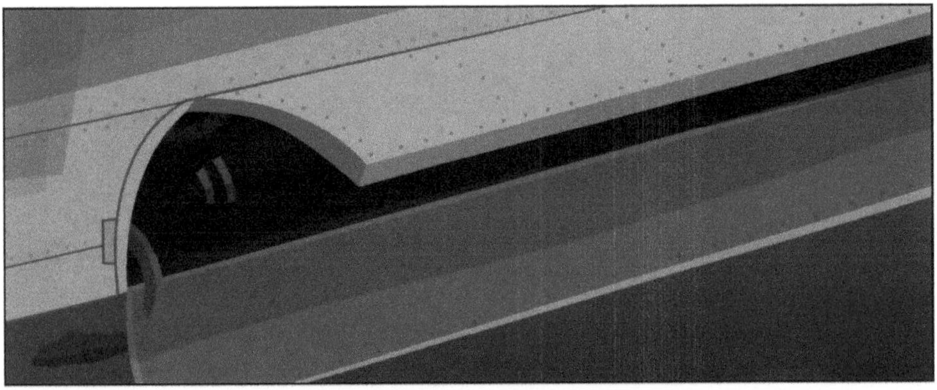

AMERICA WAS HELPING ARM THE IRAQIS...

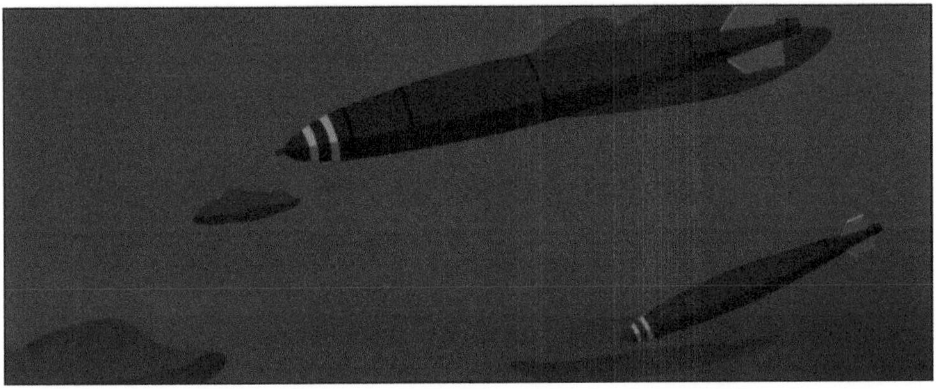

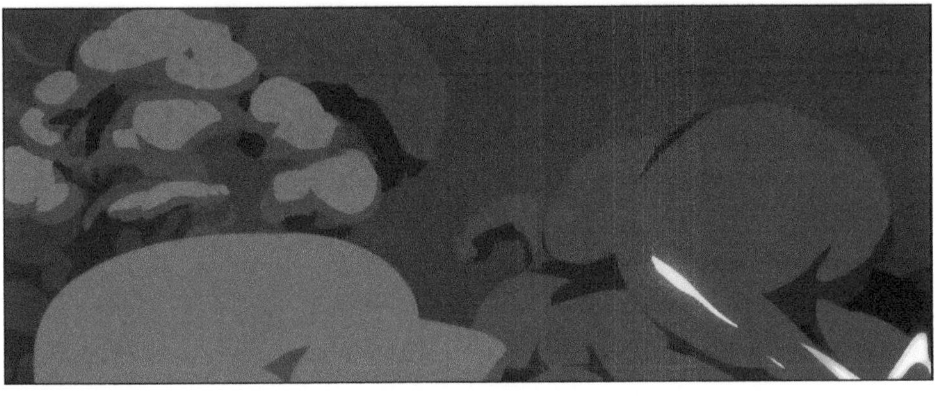

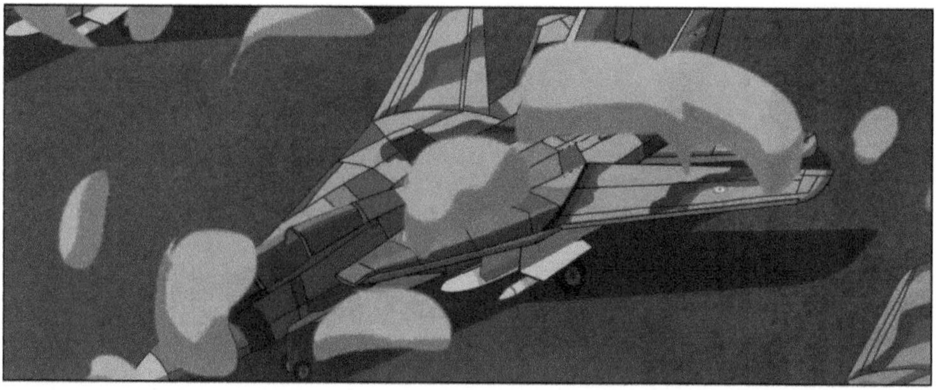

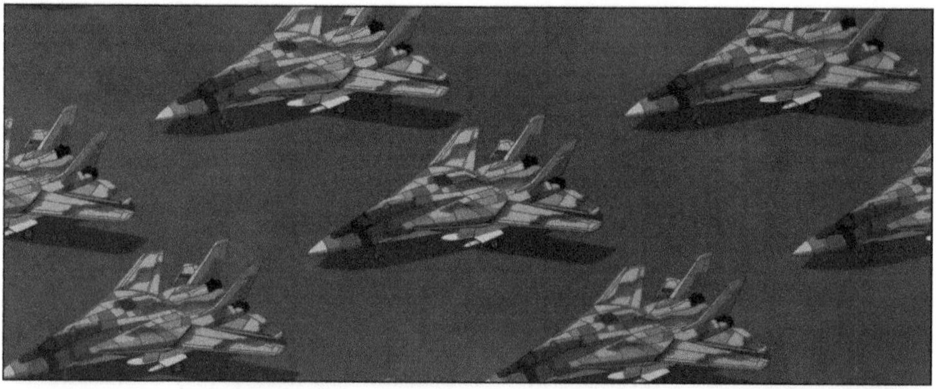

WE HAD SEVENTY-NINE FIGHTER PLANES IN OUR COUNTRY. SEVENTY-NINE. AND WE HAD NO ONE TO FLY THEM BECAUSE THE OLD MILITARY HAD ALLEGIANCES TO THE SHAH.

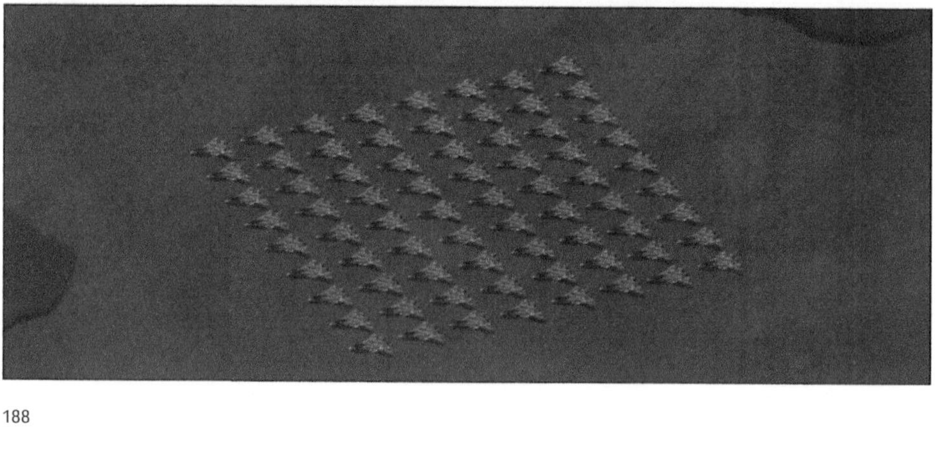

WE NEEDED EVERYBODY.

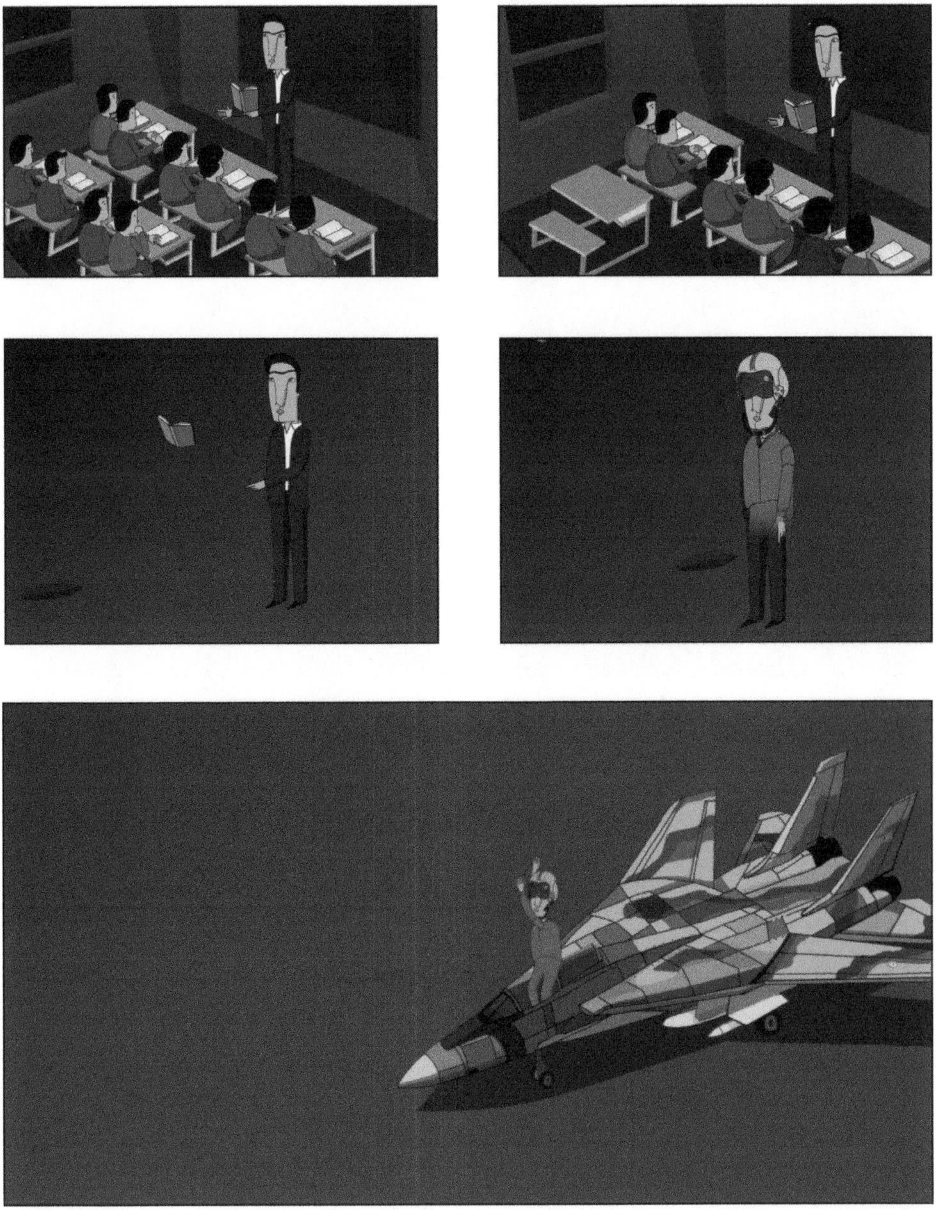

WE FOUGHT FOR TWO YEARS AGAINST IMPOSSIBLE ODDS, AND SADDAM HUSSEIN OFFERS US A CEASEFIRE, A PEACE...

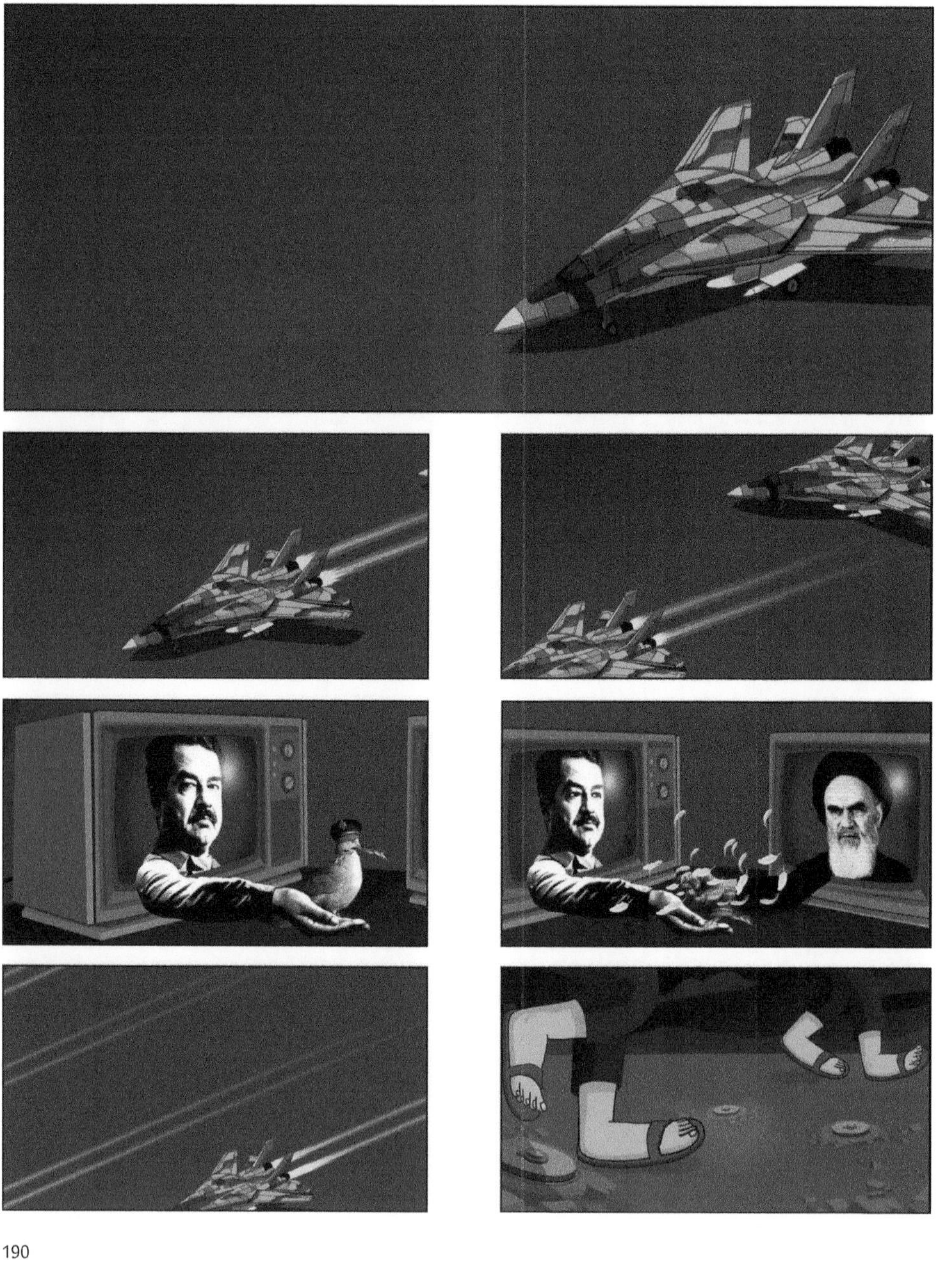

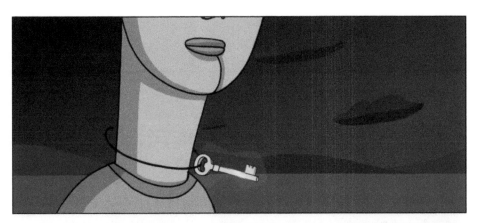

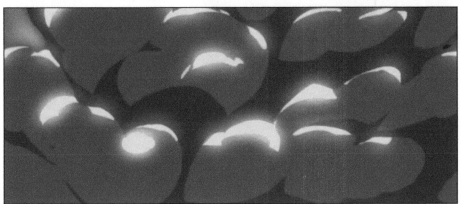

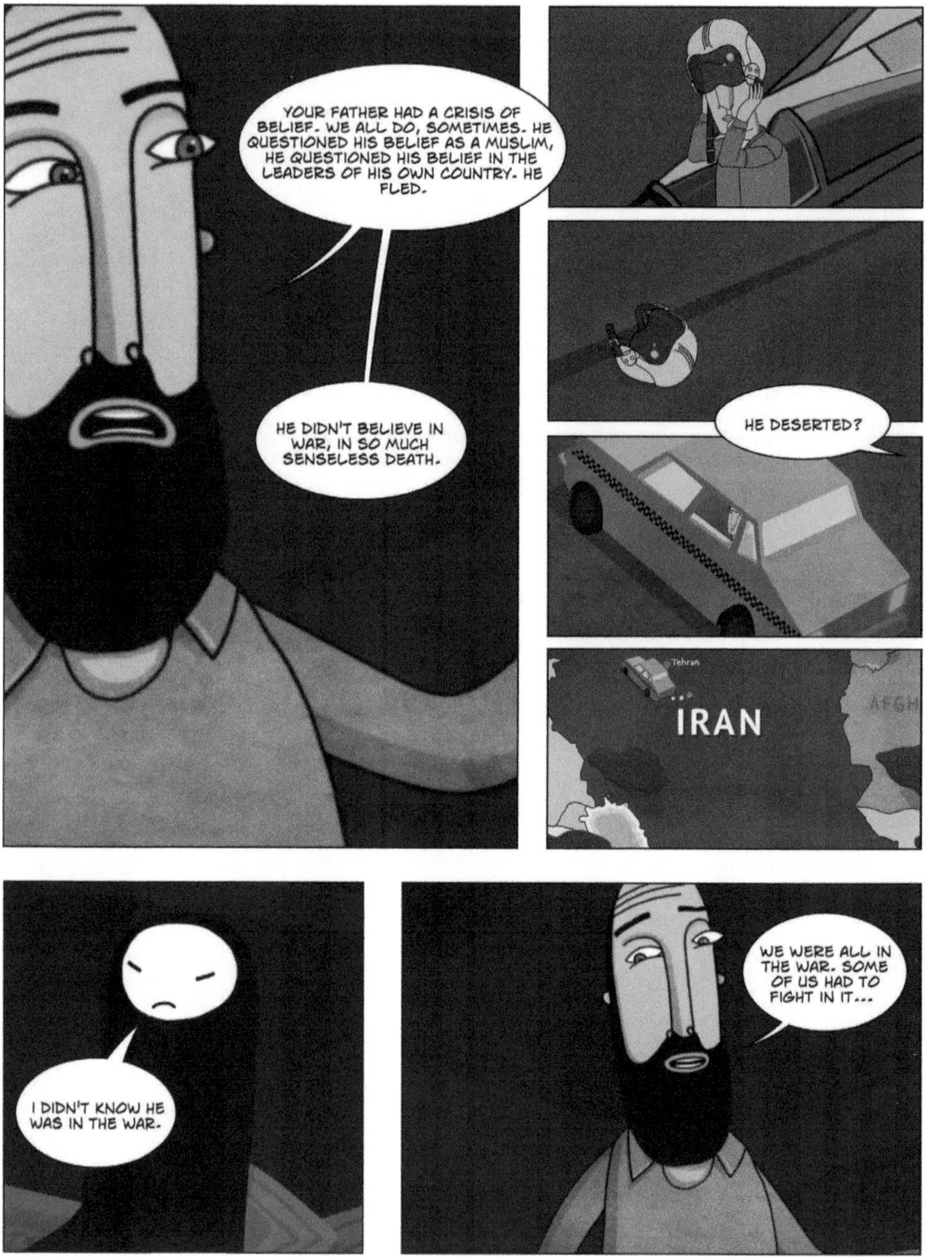
YOUR FATHER HAD A CRISIS OF BELIEF. WE ALL DO, SOMETIMES. HE QUESTIONED HIS BELIEF AS A MUSLIM, HE QUESTIONED HIS BELIEF IN THE LEADERS OF HIS OWN COUNTRY. HE FLED.
HE DIDN'T BELIEVE IN WAR, IN SO MUCH SENSELESS DEATH.
HE DESERTED?
Tehran
IRAN
I DIDN'T KNOW HE WAS IN THE WAR.
WE WERE ALL IN THE WAR. SOME OF US HAD TO FIGHT IN IT...

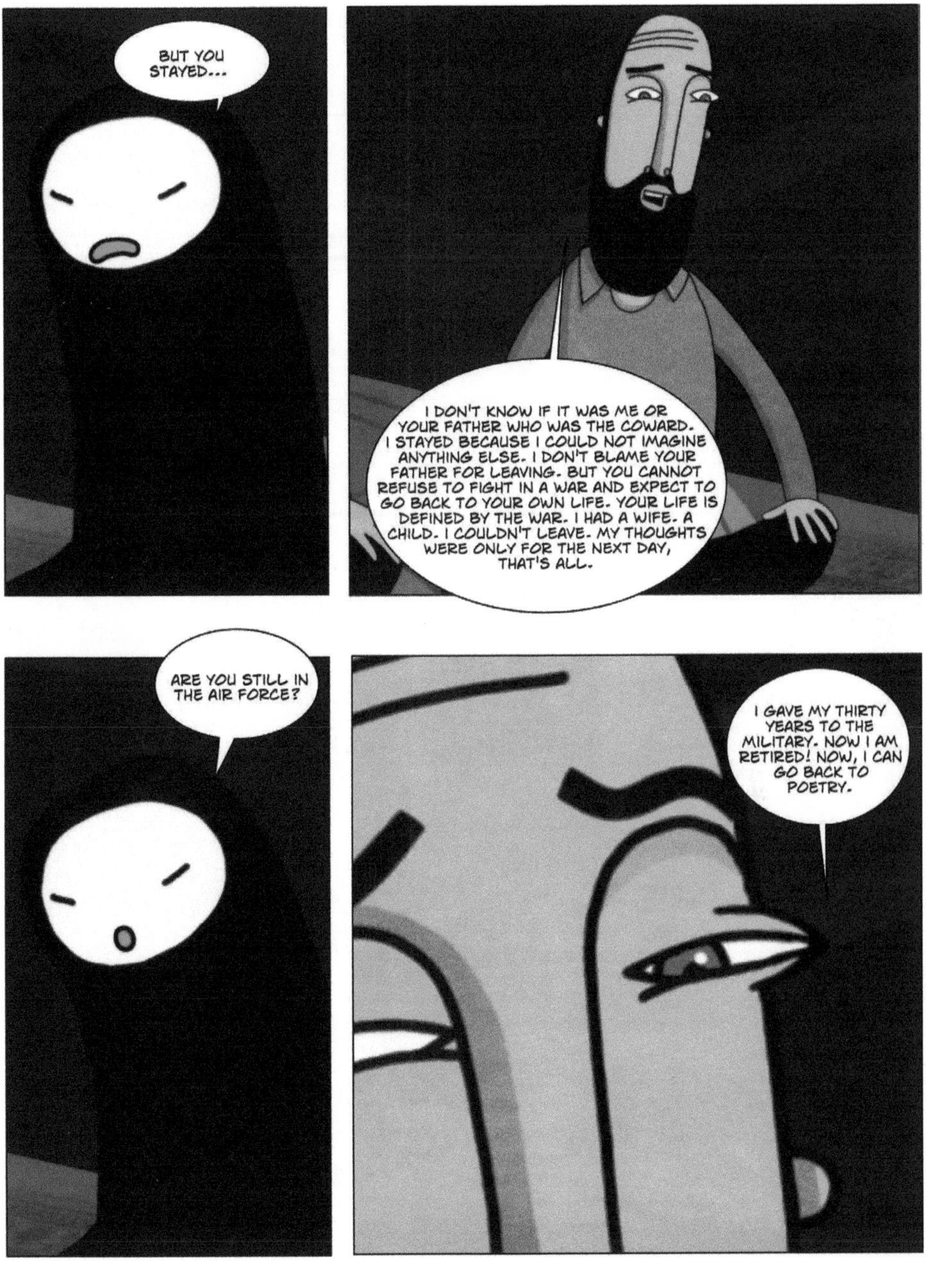

BUT YOU STAYED...
I DON'T KNOW IF IT WAS ME OR YOUR FATHER WHO WAS THE COWARD. I STAYED BECAUSE I COULD NOT IMAGINE ANYTHING ELSE. I DON'T BLAME YOUR FATHER FOR LEAVING. BUT YOU CANNOT REFUSE TO FIGHT IN A WAR AND EXPECT TO GO BACK TO YOUR OWN LIFE. YOUR LIFE IS DEFINED BY THE WAR. I HAD A WIFE. A CHILD. I COULDN'T LEAVE. MY THOUGHTS WERE ONLY FOR THE NEXT DAY, THAT'S ALL.
ARE YOU STILL IN THE AIR FORCE?
I GAVE MY THIRTY YEARS TO THE MILITARY. NOW I AM RETIRED! NOW, I CAN GO BACK TO POETRY.

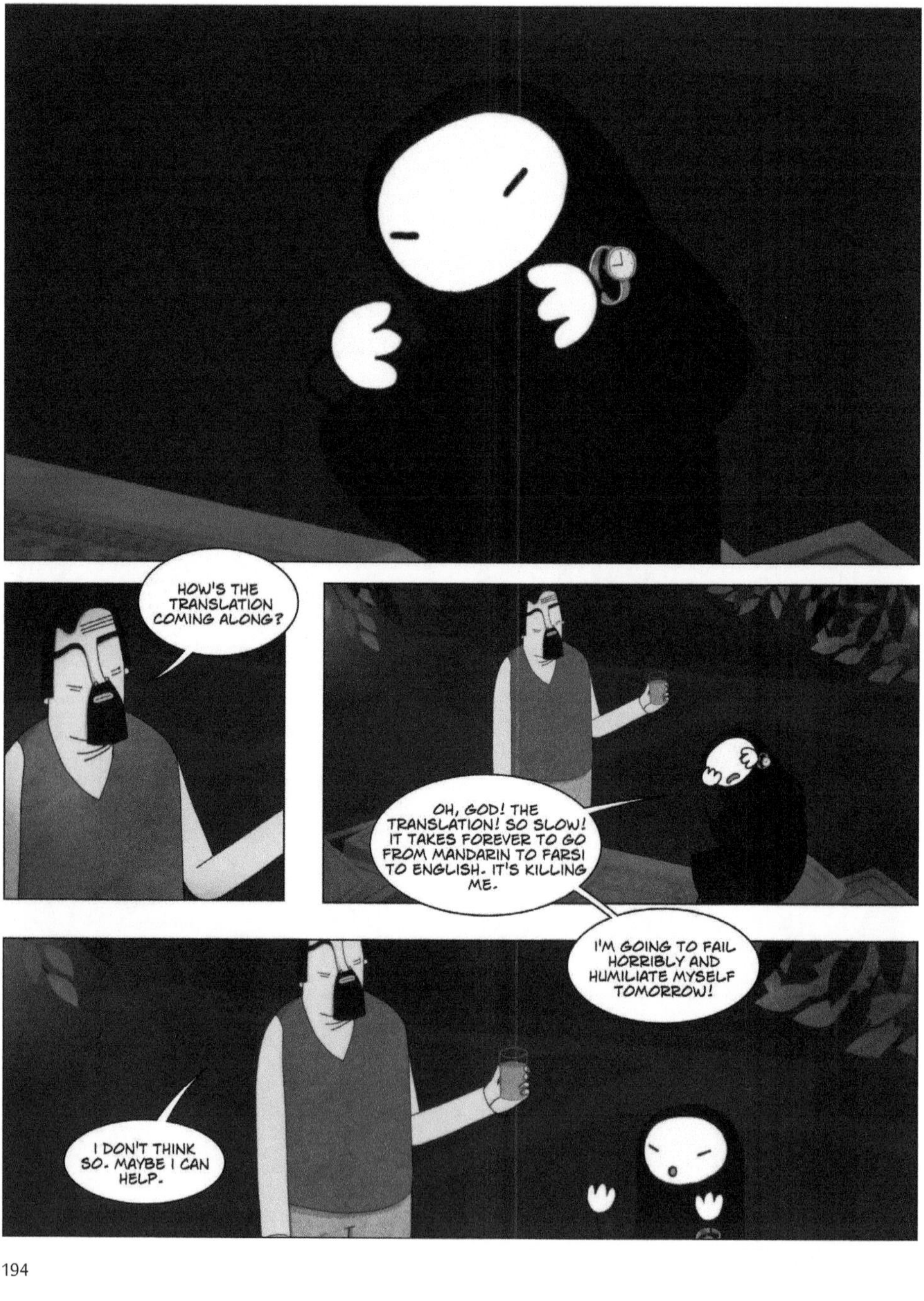
HOW'S THE TRANSLATION COMING ALONG?
OH, GOD! THE TRANSLATION! SO SLOW! IT TAKES FOREVER TO GO FROM MANDARIN TO FARSI TO ENGLISH. IT'S KILLING ME.
I'M GOING TO FAIL HORRIBLY AND HUMILIATE MYSELF TOMORROW!
I DON'T THINK SO. MAYBE I CAN HELP.

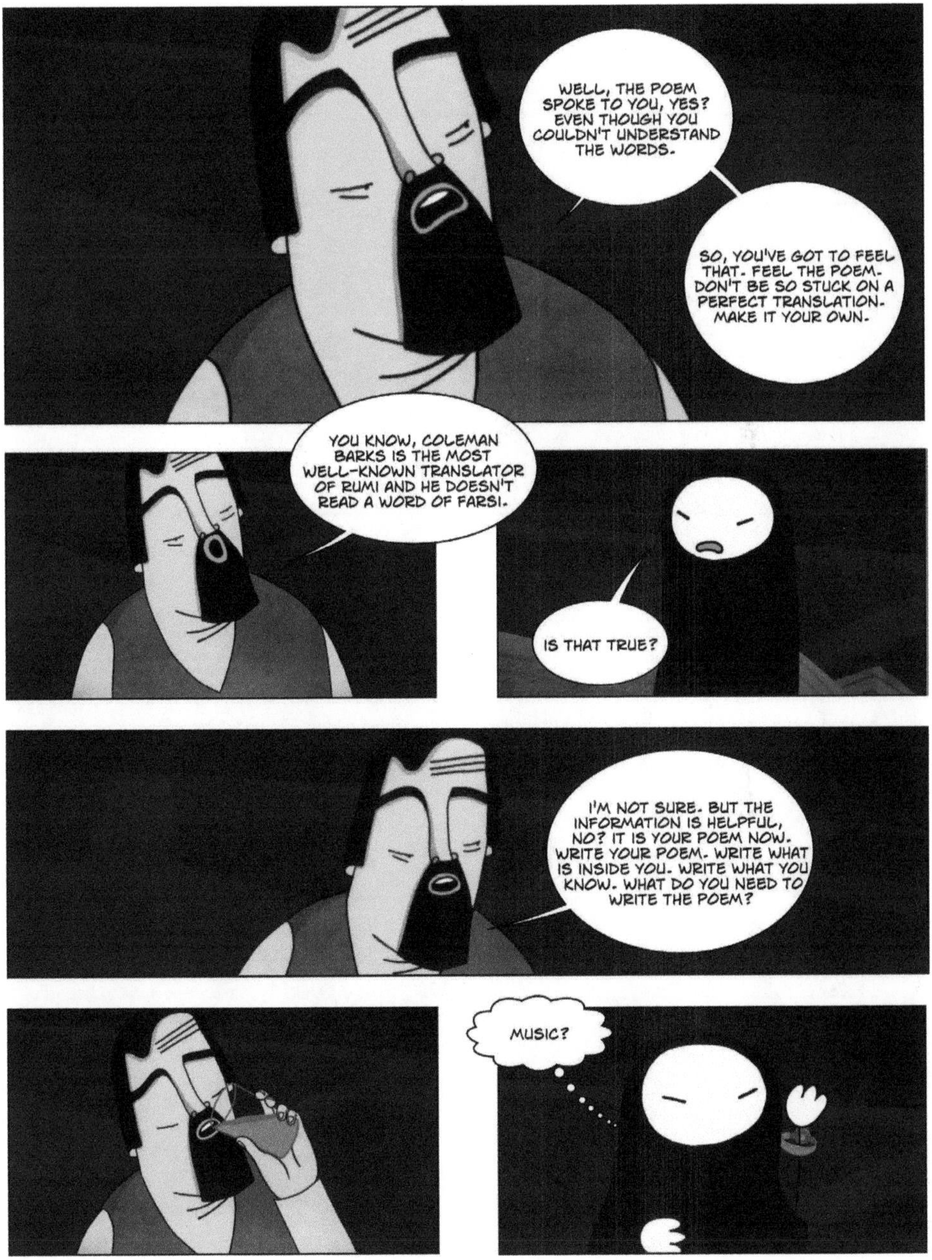
WELL, THE POEM SPOKE TO YOU, YES? EVEN THOUGH YOU COULDN'T UNDERSTAND THE WORDS.
SO, YOU'VE GOT TO FEEL THAT. FEEL THE POEM. DON'T BE SO STUCK ON A PERFECT TRANSLATION. MAKE IT YOUR OWN.
YOU KNOW, COLEMAN BARKS IS THE MOST WELL-KNOWN TRANSLATOR OF RUMI AND HE DOESN'T READ A WORD OF FARSI.
IS THAT TRUE?
I'M NOT SURE. BUT THE INFORMATION IS HELPFUL, NO? IT IS YOUR POEM NOW. WRITE YOUR POEM. WRITE WHAT IS INSIDE YOU. WRITE WHAT YOU KNOW. WHAT DO YOU NEED TO WRITE THE POEM?
MUSIC?

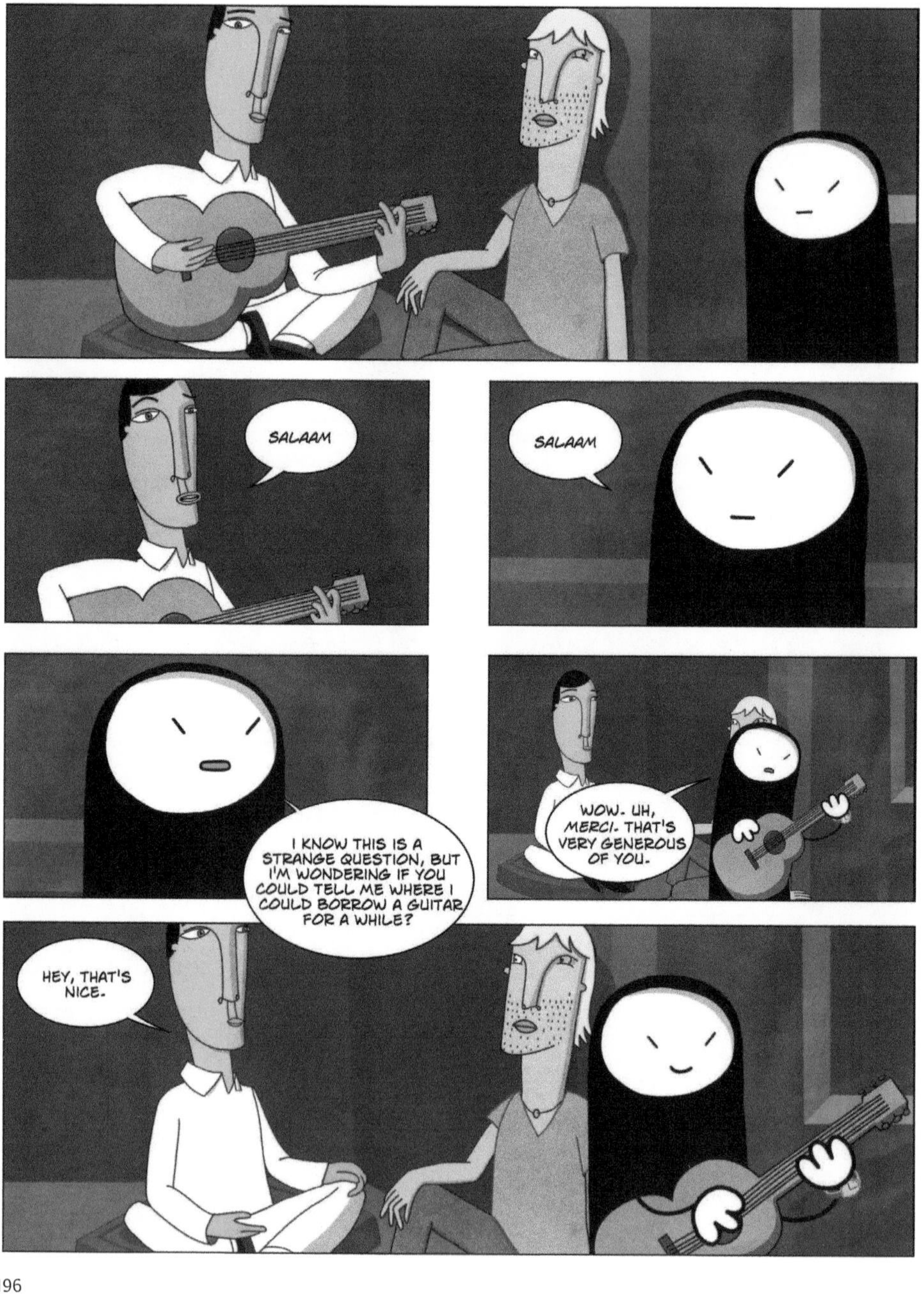
SALAAM
SALAAM
I KNOW THIS IS A STRANGE QUESTION, BUT I'M WONDERING IF YOU COULD TELL ME WHERE I COULD BORROW A GUITAR FOR A WHILE?
WOW. UH, MERCI. THAT'S VERY GENEROUS OF YOU.
HEY, THAT'S NICE.

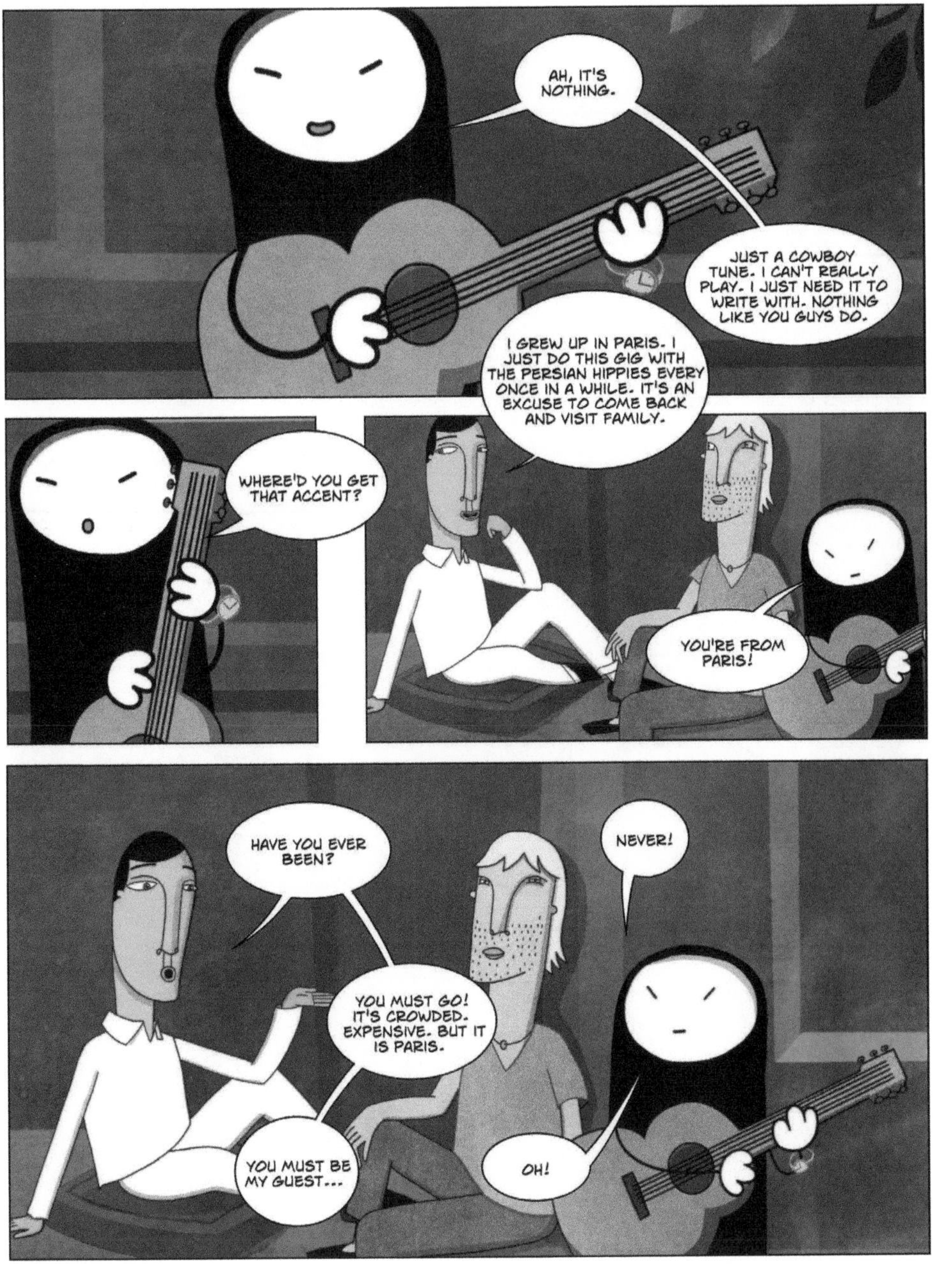
AH, IT'S NOTHING.
JUST A COWBOY TUNE. I CAN'T REALLY PLAY. I JUST NEED IT TO WRITE WITH. NOTHING LIKE YOU GUYS DO.
WHERE'D YOU GET THAT ACCENT?
I GREW UP IN PARIS. I JUST DO THIS GIG WITH THE PERSIAN HIPPIES EVERY ONCE IN A WHILE. IT'S AN EXCUSE TO COME BACK AND VISIT FAMILY.
YOU'RE FROM PARIS!
HAVE YOU EVER BEEN?
NEVER!
YOU MUST GO! IT'S CROWDED. EXPENSIVE. BUT IT IS PARIS.
YOU MUST BE MY GUEST...
OH!

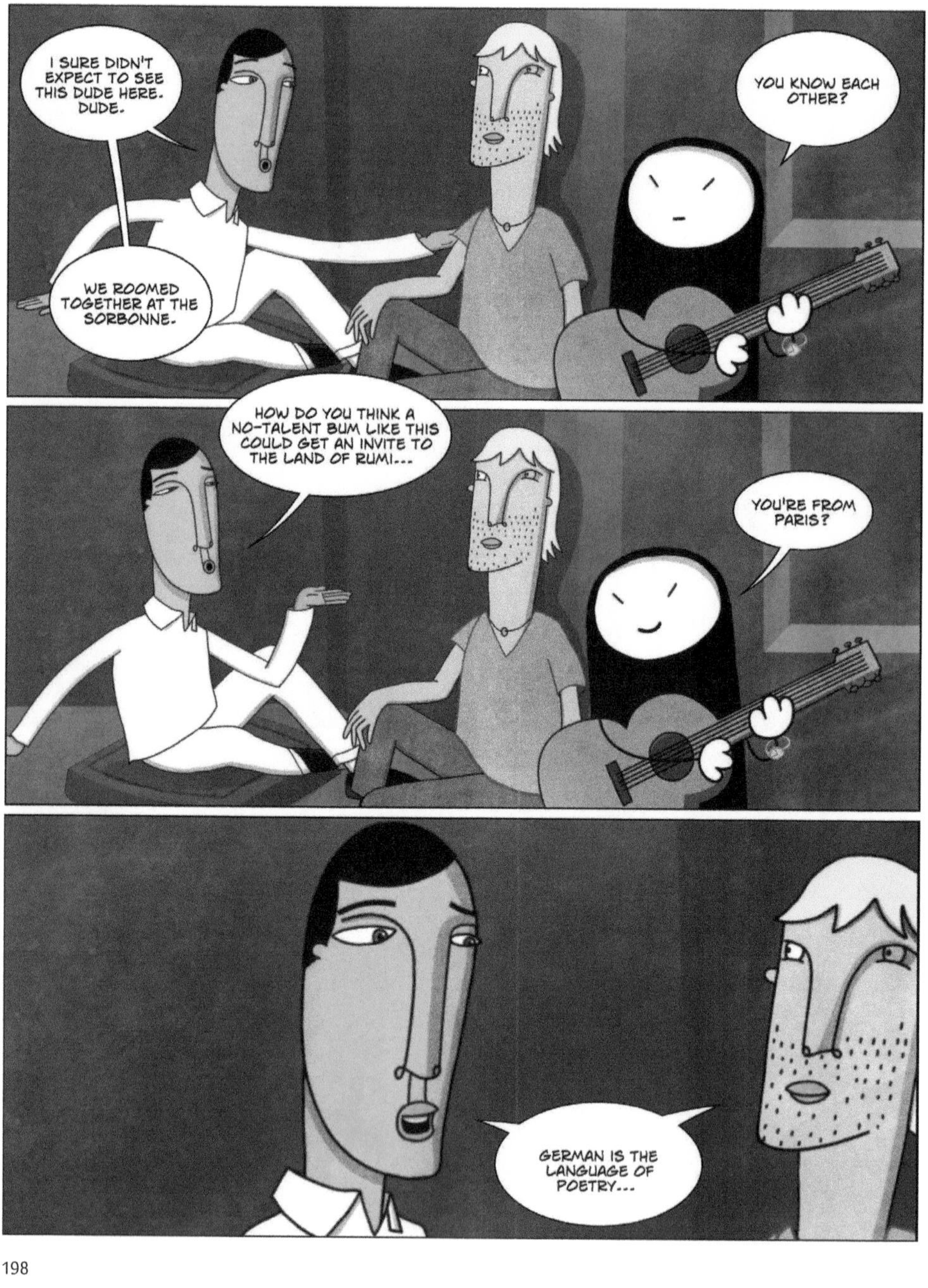
I SURE DIDN'T EXPECT TO SEE THIS DUDE HERE. DUDE.
WE ROOMED TOGETHER AT THE SORBONNE.
YOU KNOW EACH OTHER?
HOW DO YOU THINK A NO-TALENT BUM LIKE THIS COULD GET AN INVITE TO THE LAND OF RUMI...
YOU'RE FROM PARIS?
GERMAN IS THE LANGUAGE OF POETRY...

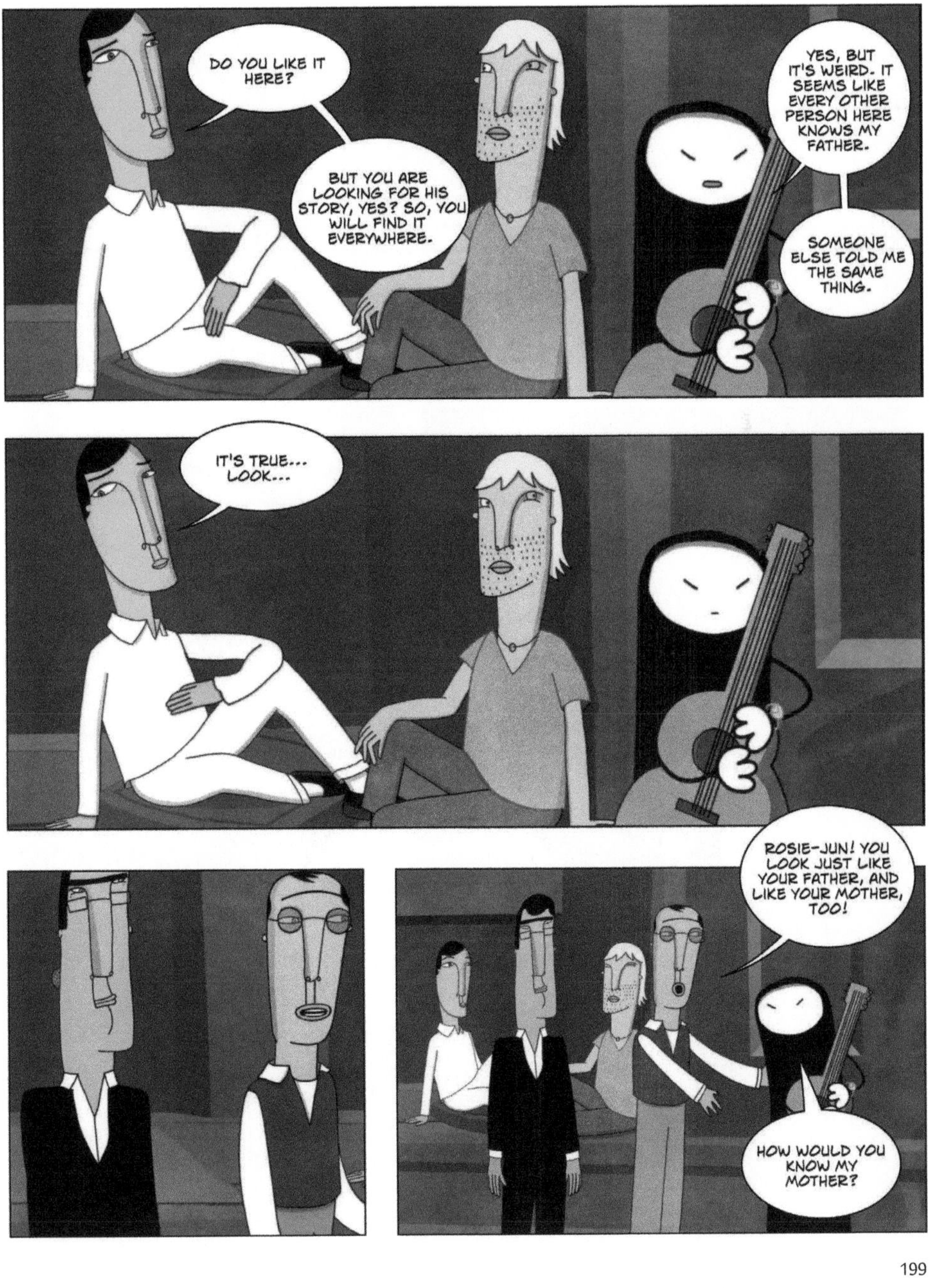
DO YOU LIKE IT HERE?
BUT YOU ARE LOOKING FOR HIS STORY, YES? SO, YOU WILL FIND IT EVERYWHERE.
YES, BUT IT'S WEIRD. IT SEEMS LIKE EVERY OTHER PERSON HERE KNOWS MY FATHER.
SOMEONE ELSE TOLD ME THE SAME THING.
IT'S TRUE... LOOK...
ROSIE-JUN! YOU LOOK JUST LIKE YOUR FATHER, AND LIKE YOUR MOTHER, TOO!
HOW WOULD YOU KNOW MY MOTHER?

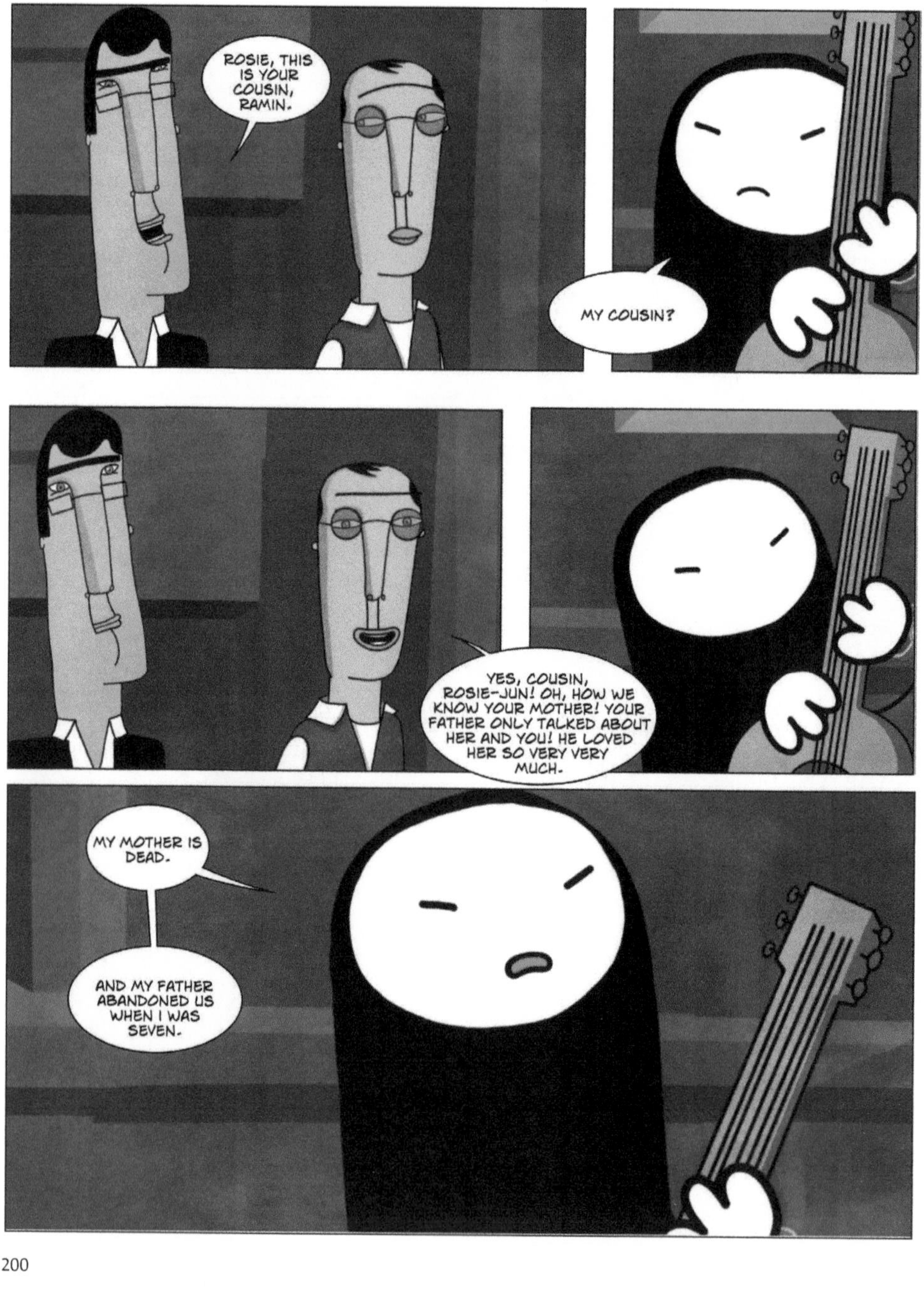
ROSIE, THIS IS YOUR COUSIN, RAMIN.
MY COUSIN?
YES, COUSIN, ROSIE-JUN! OH, HOW WE KNOW YOUR MOTHER! YOUR FATHER ONLY TALKED ABOUT HER AND YOU! HE LOVED HER SO VERY VERY MUCH.
MY MOTHER IS DEAD.
AND MY FATHER ABANDONED US WHEN I WAS SEVEN.

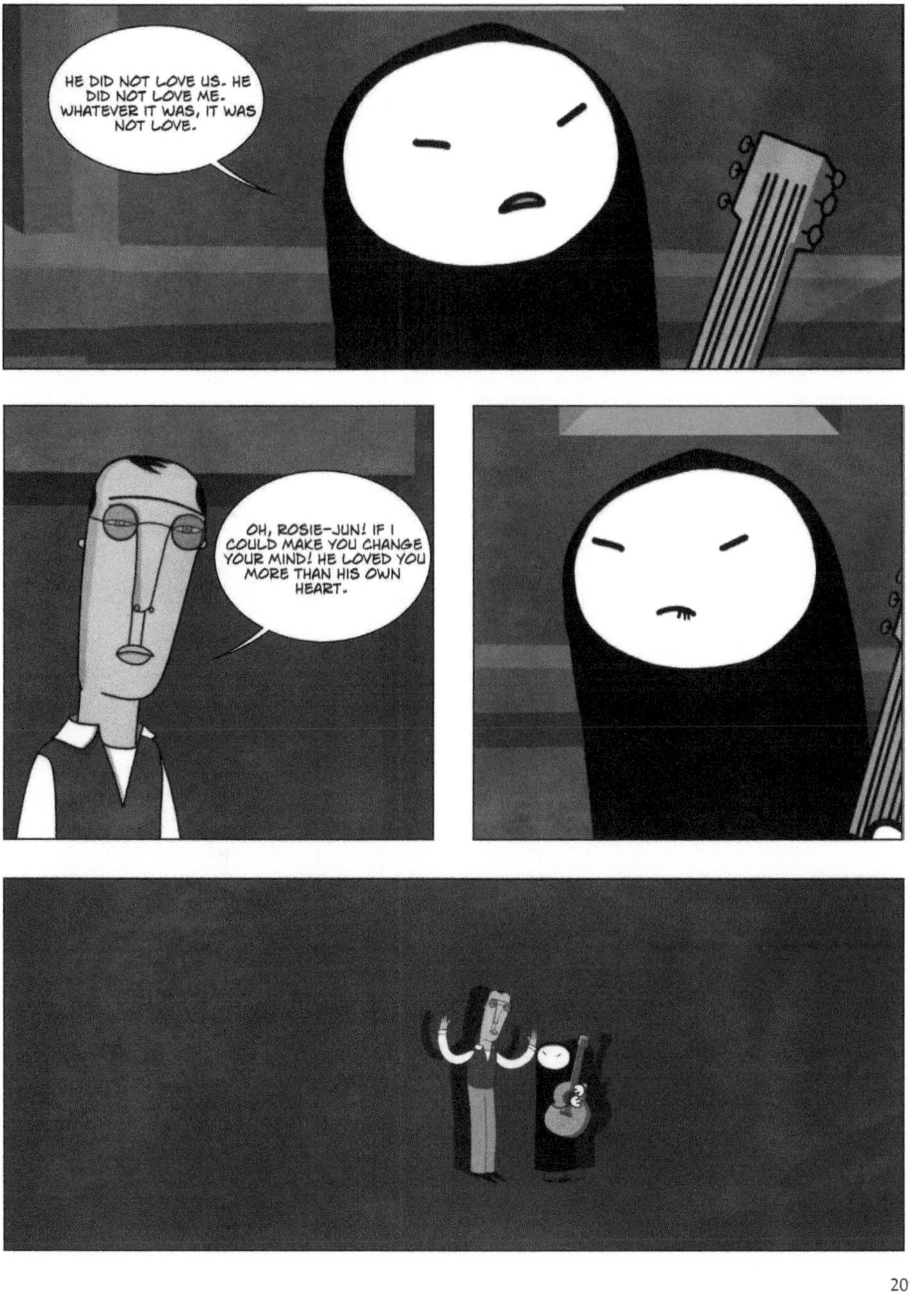
HE DID NOT LOVE US. HE DID NOT LOVE ME. WHATEVER IT WAS, IT WAS NOT LOVE.
OH, ROSIE-JUN! IF I COULD MAKE YOU CHANGE YOUR MIND! HE LOVED YOU MORE THAN HIS OWN HEART.

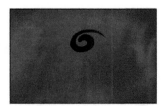

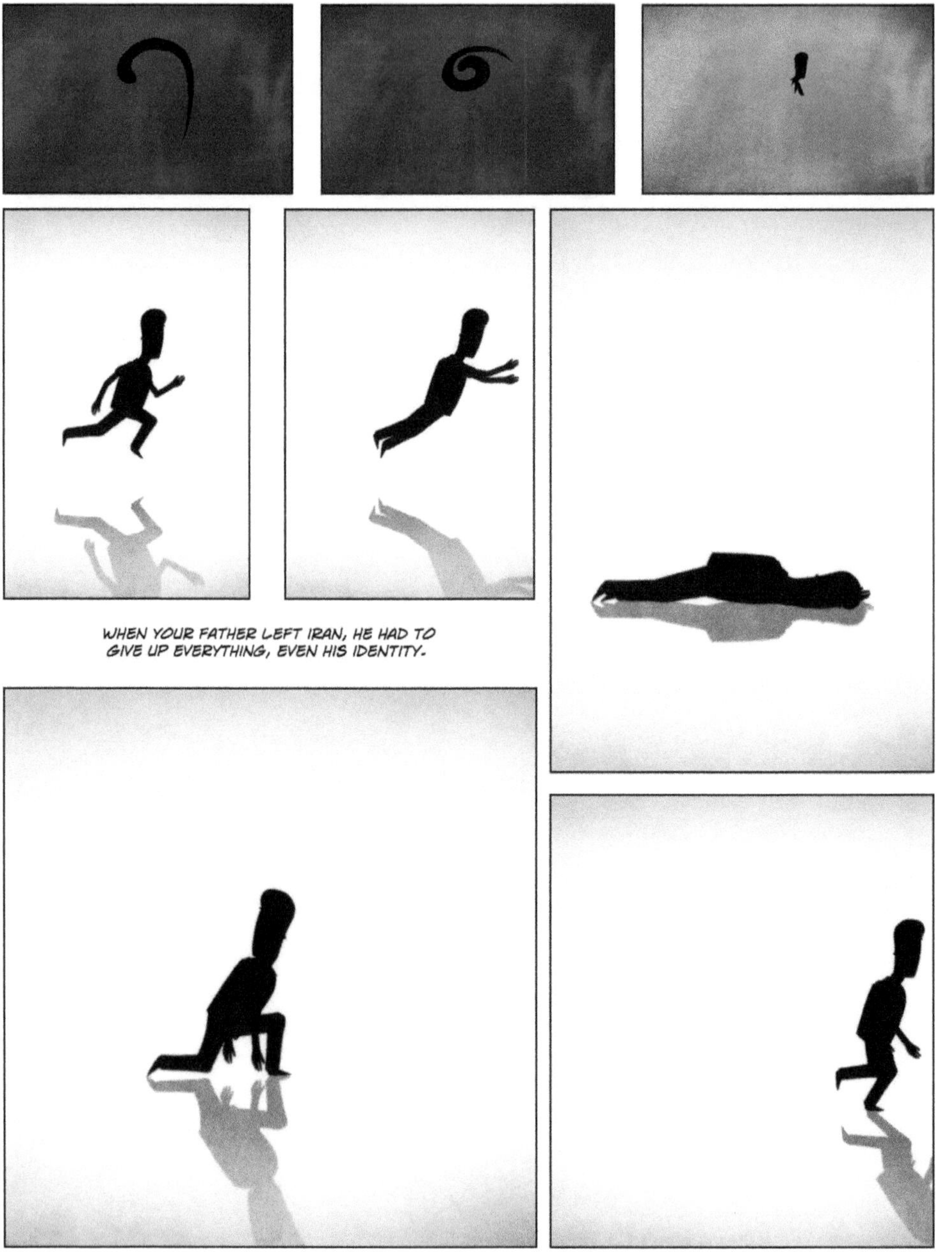
WHEN YOUR FATHER LEFT IRAN, HE HAD TO GIVE UP EVERYTHING, EVEN HIS IDENTITY.

HE ESCAPED TO TURKEY, WAITING, TRYING TO GET TO A COUNTRY WHICH WOULD ACCEPT HIM AS A REFUGEE. BUT HE COULDN'T GET PAPERS BECAUSE HE HAD NO MONEY.

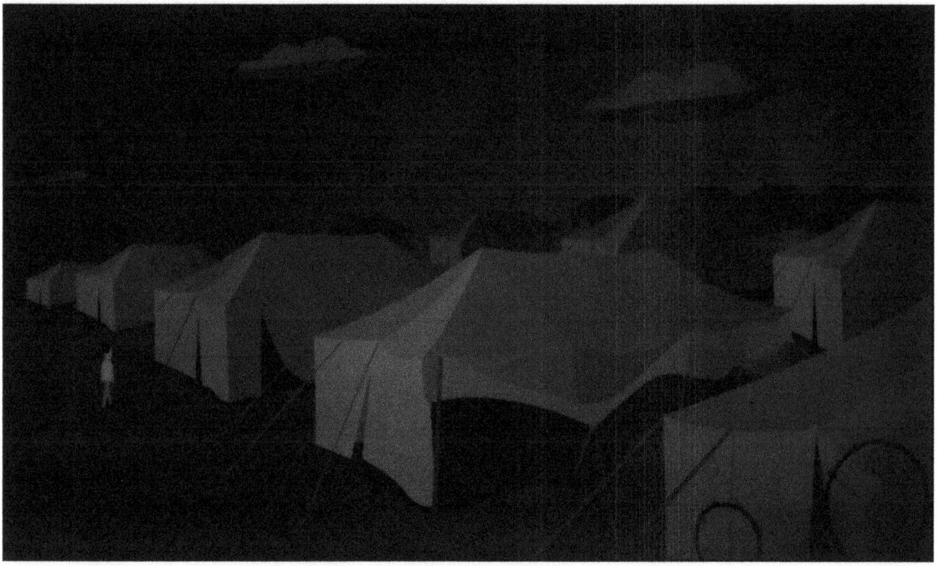

HE STAYED IN A DETAINMENT CAMP WITH OTHER MEN WHO WERE FLEEING SOMETHING. MAINLY, THEY WERE FROM AFRICA.

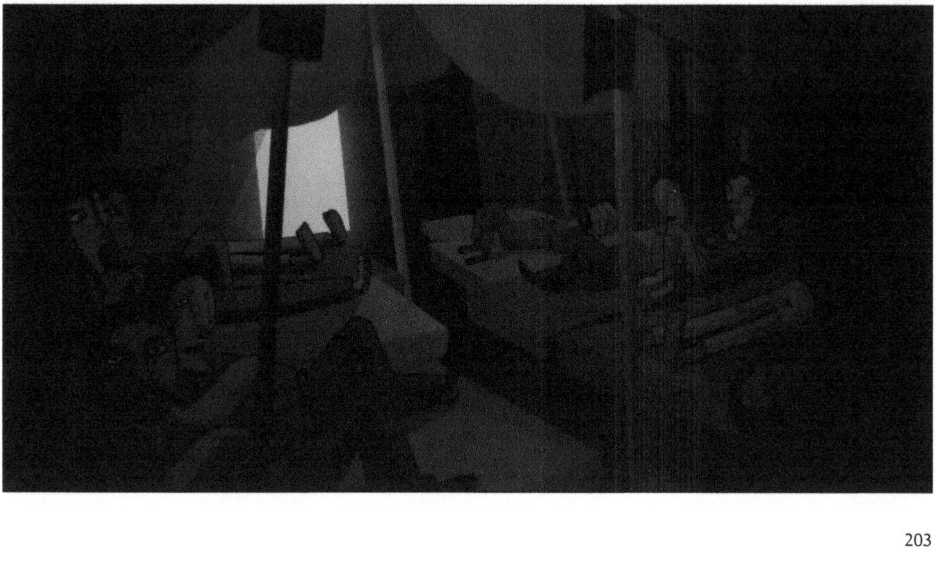

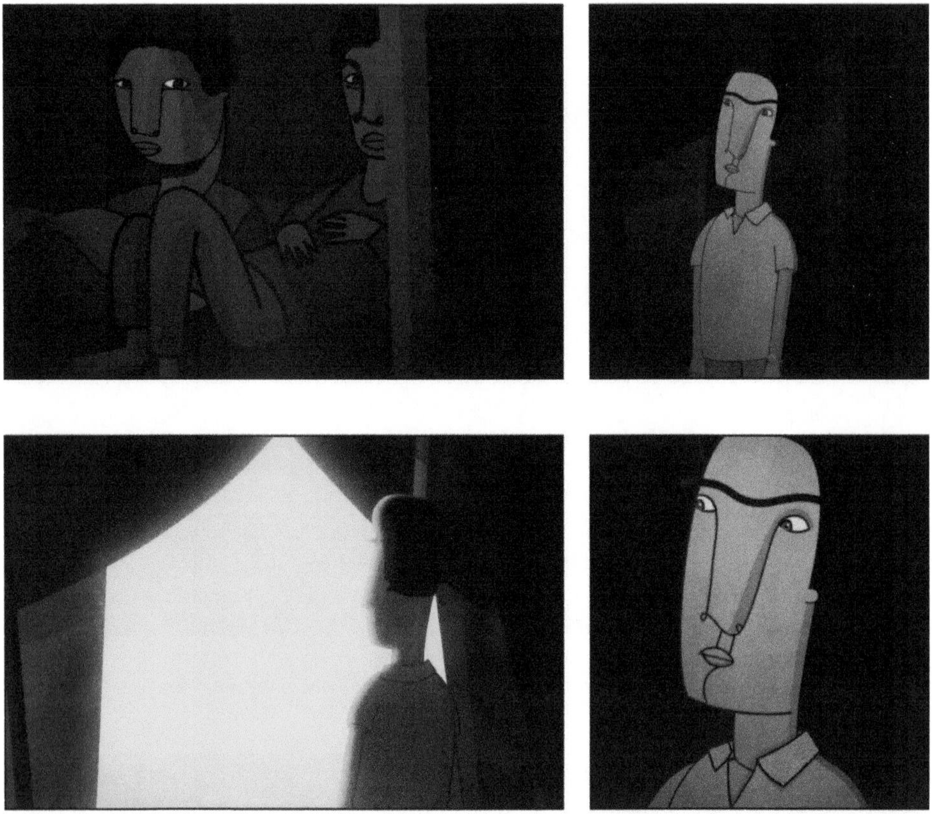

BUT THERE WERE ALL THESE BEAUTIFUL BEACHES...

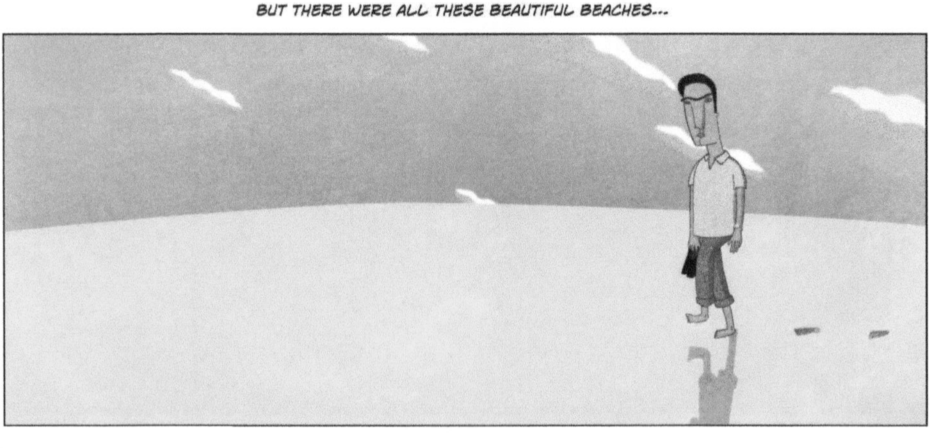

AND WANDERING ALONG THE BEACH ONE DAY, HE MEETS YOUR MOTHER, CAROLINE.

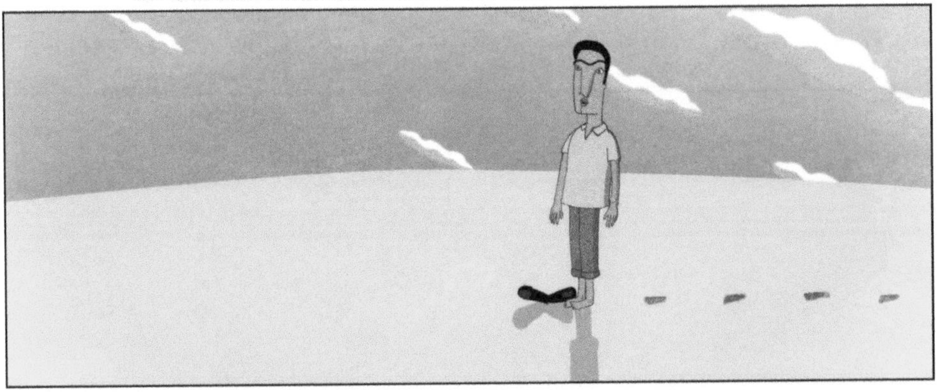

SHE IS THE MOST BEAUTIFUL WOMAN HE HAS EVER SEEN, AND HE CAN DO NOTHING BUT LOOK AT HER.

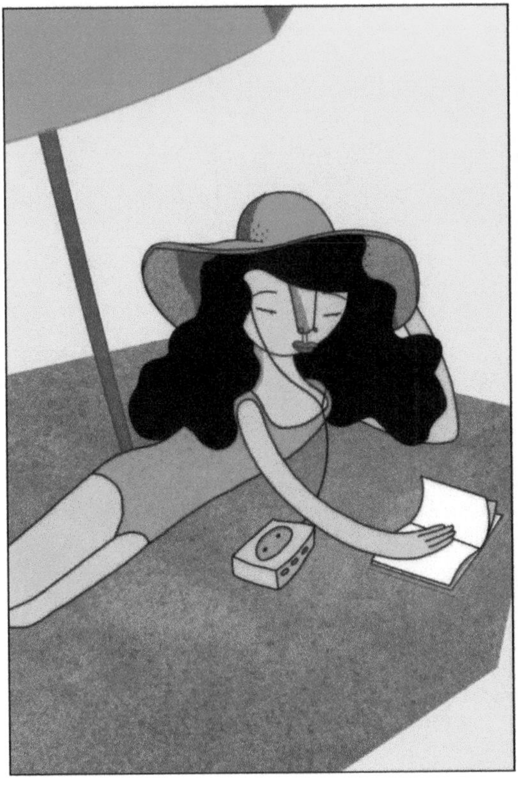

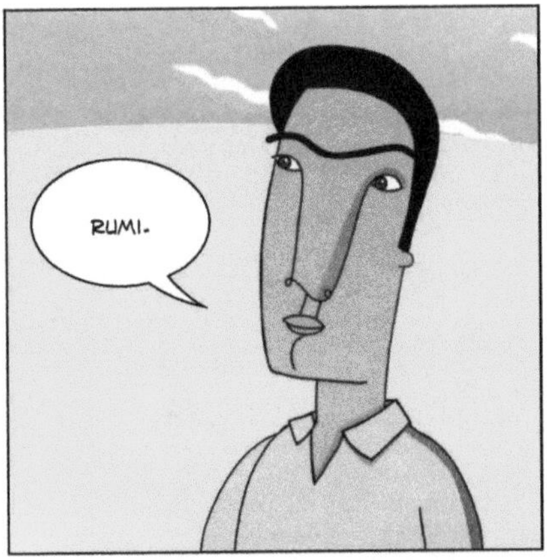
RUMI.

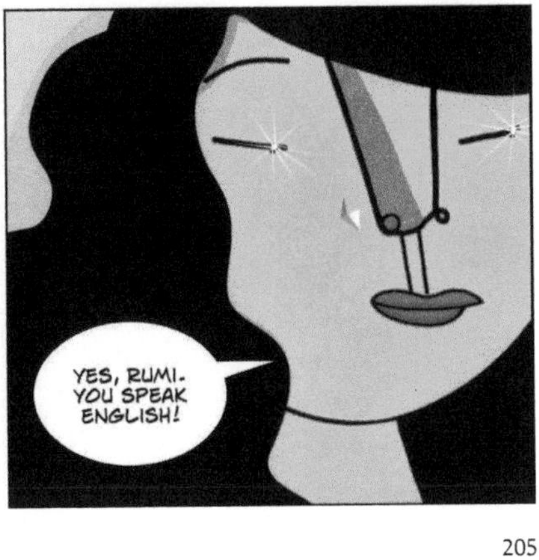
YES, RUMI. YOU SPEAK ENGLISH!

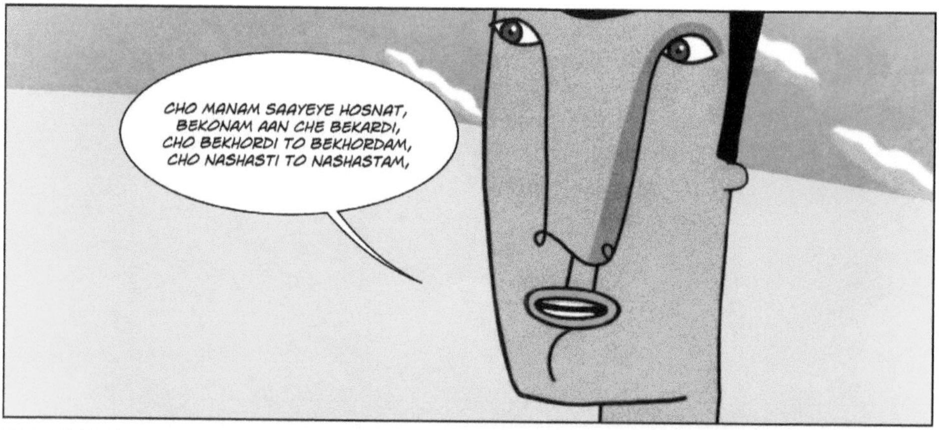
CHO MANAM SAAYEYE HOSNAT,
BEKONAM AAN CHE BEKARDI,
CHO BEKHORDI TO BEKHORDAM,
CHO NASHASTI TO NASHASTAM,

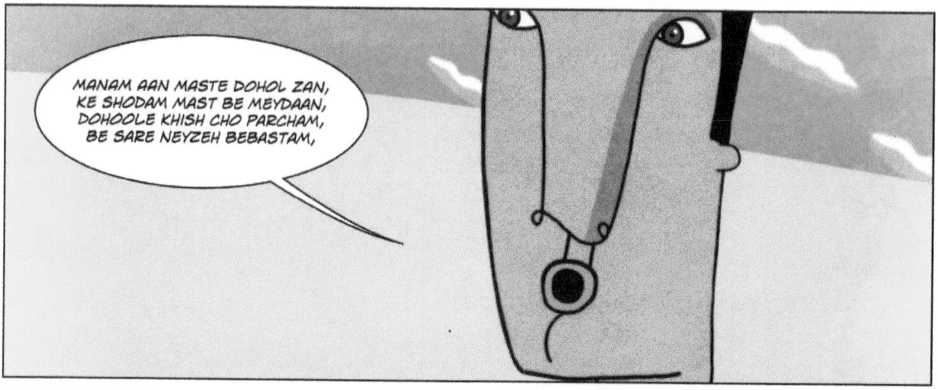
MANAM AAN MASTE DOHOL ZAN,
KE SHODAM MAST BE MEYDAAN,
DOHOOLE KHISH CHO PARCHAM,
BE SARE NEYZEH BEBASTAM,

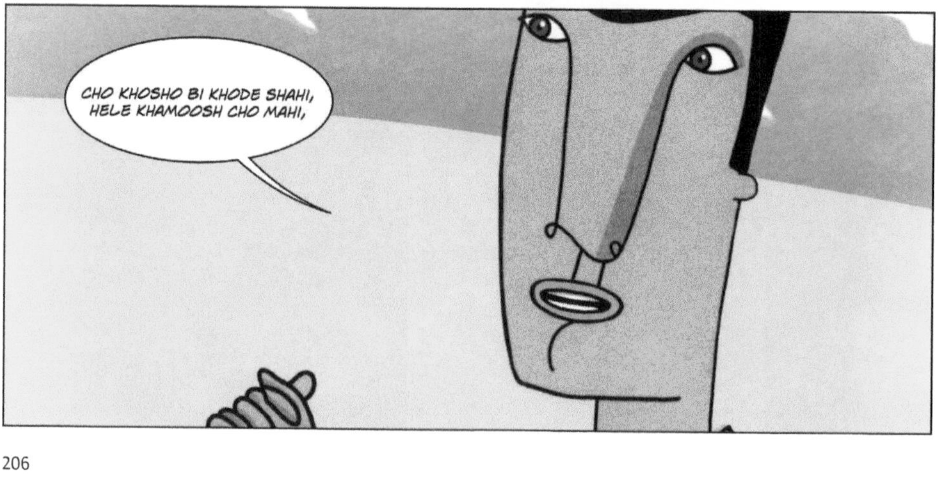
CHO KHOSHO BI KHODE SHAHI,
HELE KHAMOOSH CHO MAHI,

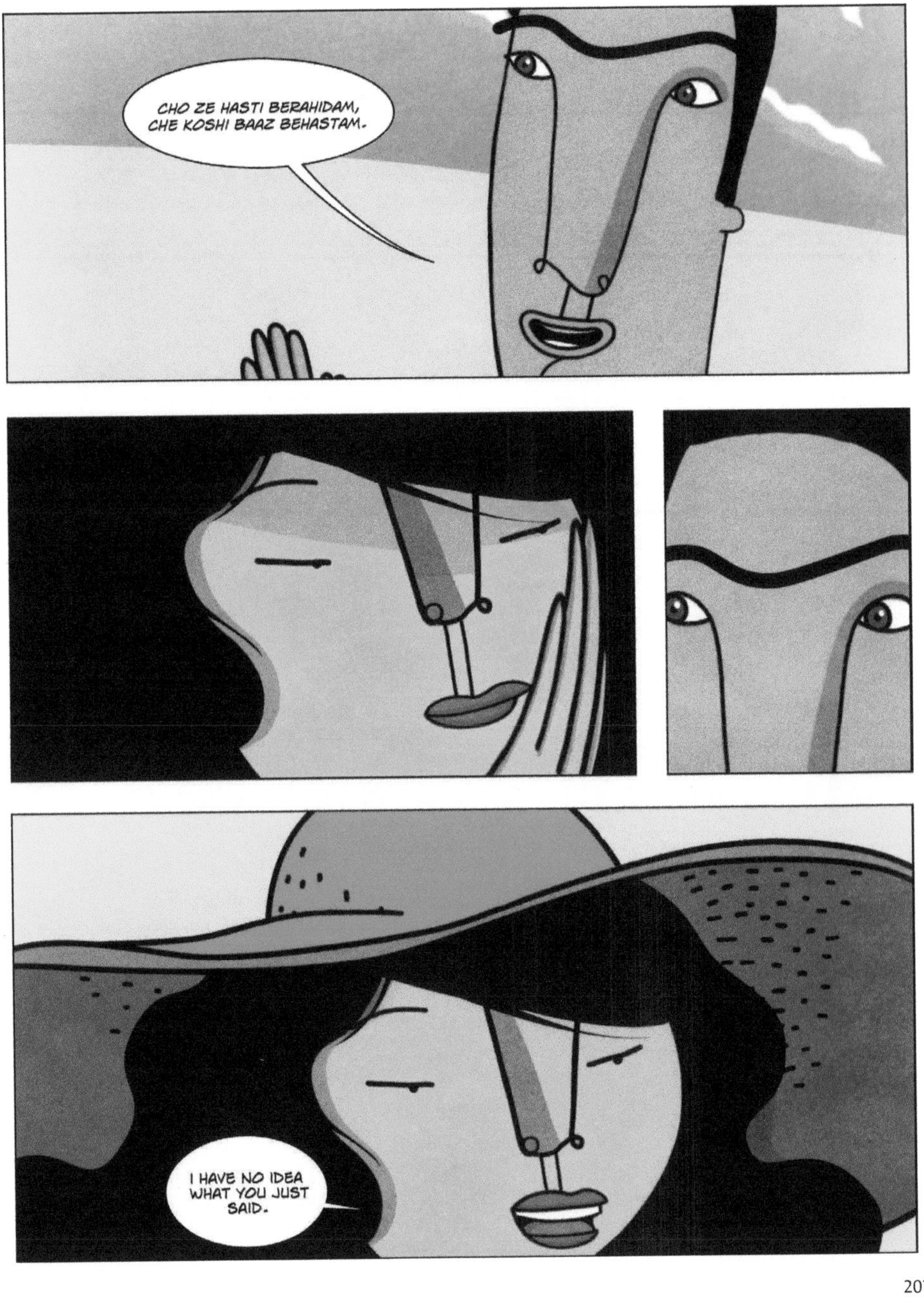
CHO ZE HASTI BERAHIDAM, CHE KOSHI BAAZ BEHASTAM.
I HAVE NO IDEA WHAT YOU JUST SAID.

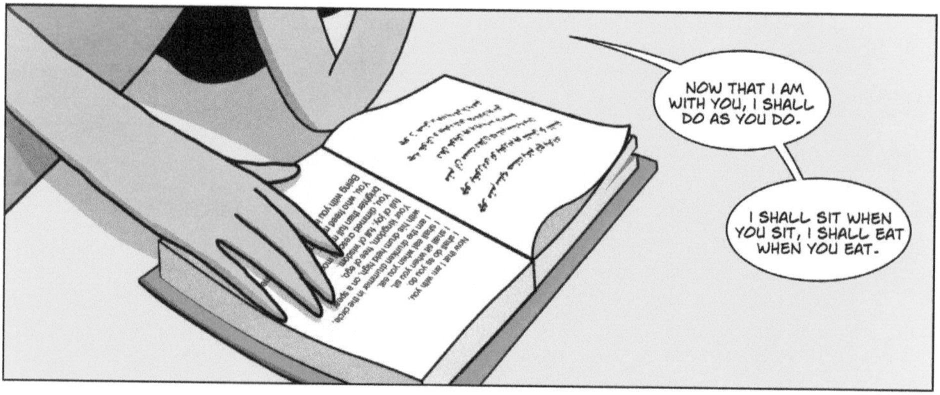
NOW THAT I AM WITH YOU, I SHALL DO AS YOU DO.
I SHALL SIT WHEN YOU SIT, I SHALL EAT WHEN YOU EAT.

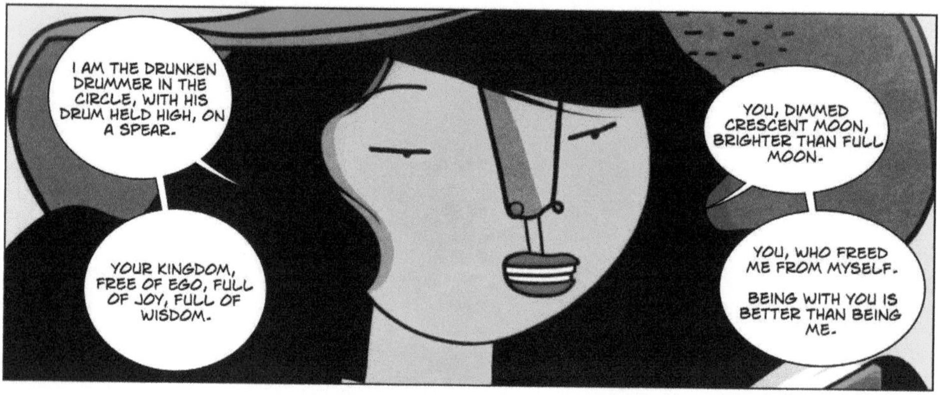
I AM THE DRUNKEN DRUMMER IN THE CIRCLE, WITH HIS DRUM HELD HIGH, ON A SPEAR.
YOUR KINGDOM, FREE OF EGO, FULL OF JOY, FULL OF WISDOM.
YOU, DIMMED CRESCENT MOON, BRIGHTER THAN FULL MOON.
YOU, WHO FREED ME FROM MYSELF.
BEING WITH YOU IS BETTER THAN BEING ME.

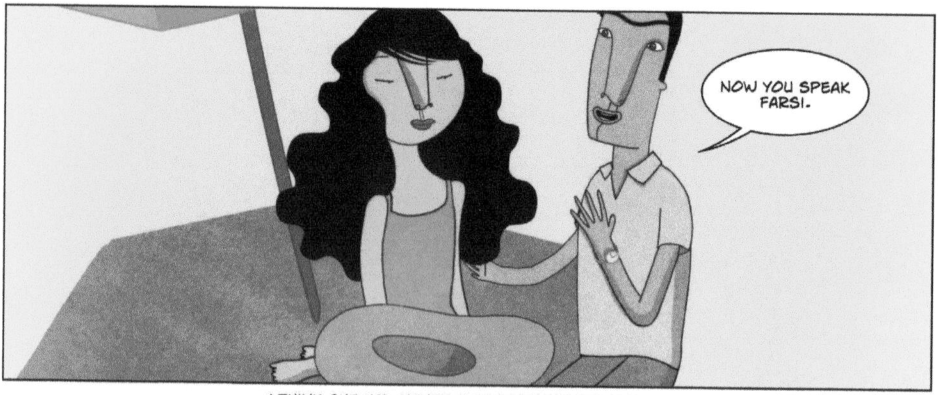
NOW YOU SPEAK FARSI.

I THINK SHE HAD NEVER MET ANYONE LIKE YOUR FATHER...

AND SHE HAD THE AIR OF SOMEONE WHO HAD NEVER BEEN IN A WAR.

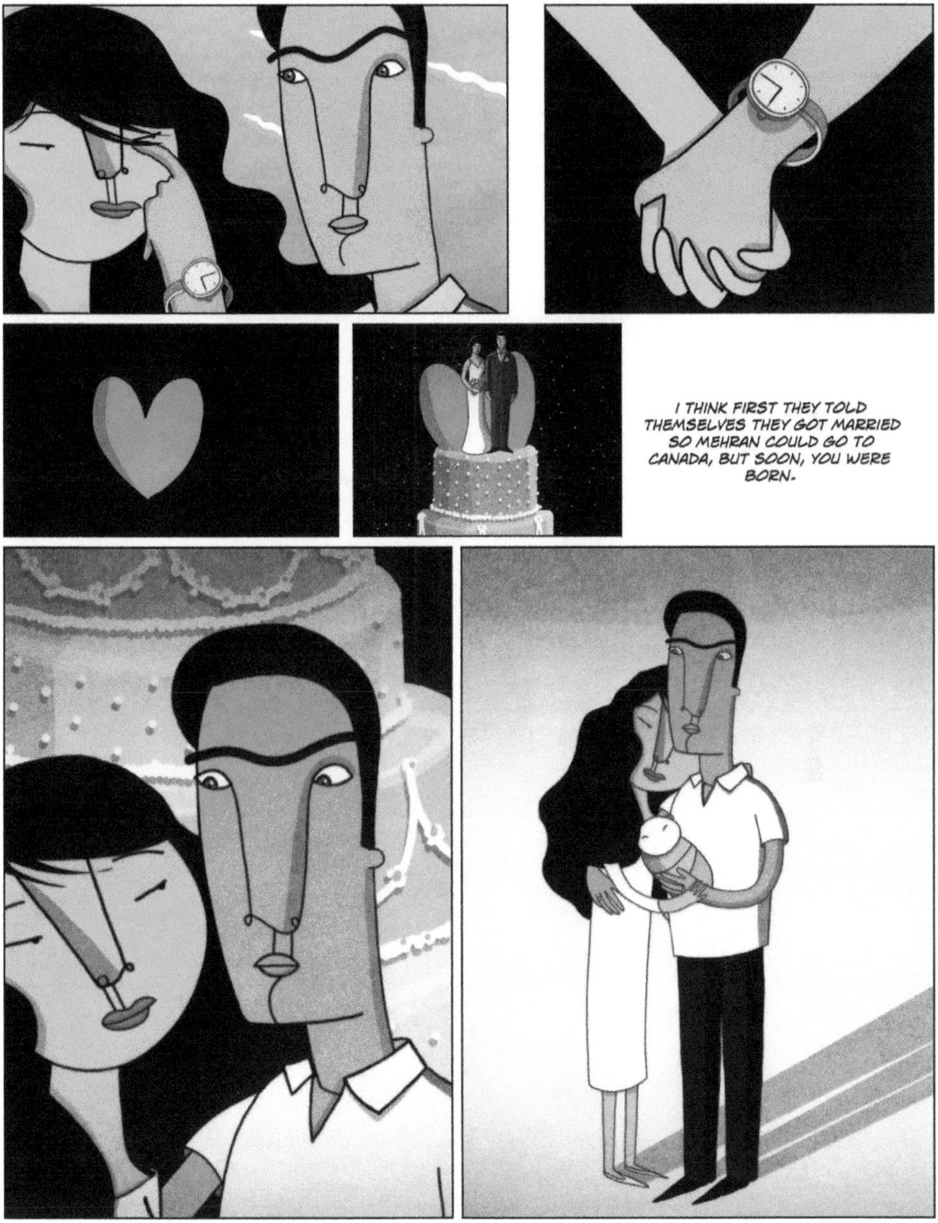
I THINK FIRST THEY TOLD THEMSELVES THEY GOT MARRIED SO MEHRAN COULD GO TO CANADA, BUT SOON, YOU WERE BORN.

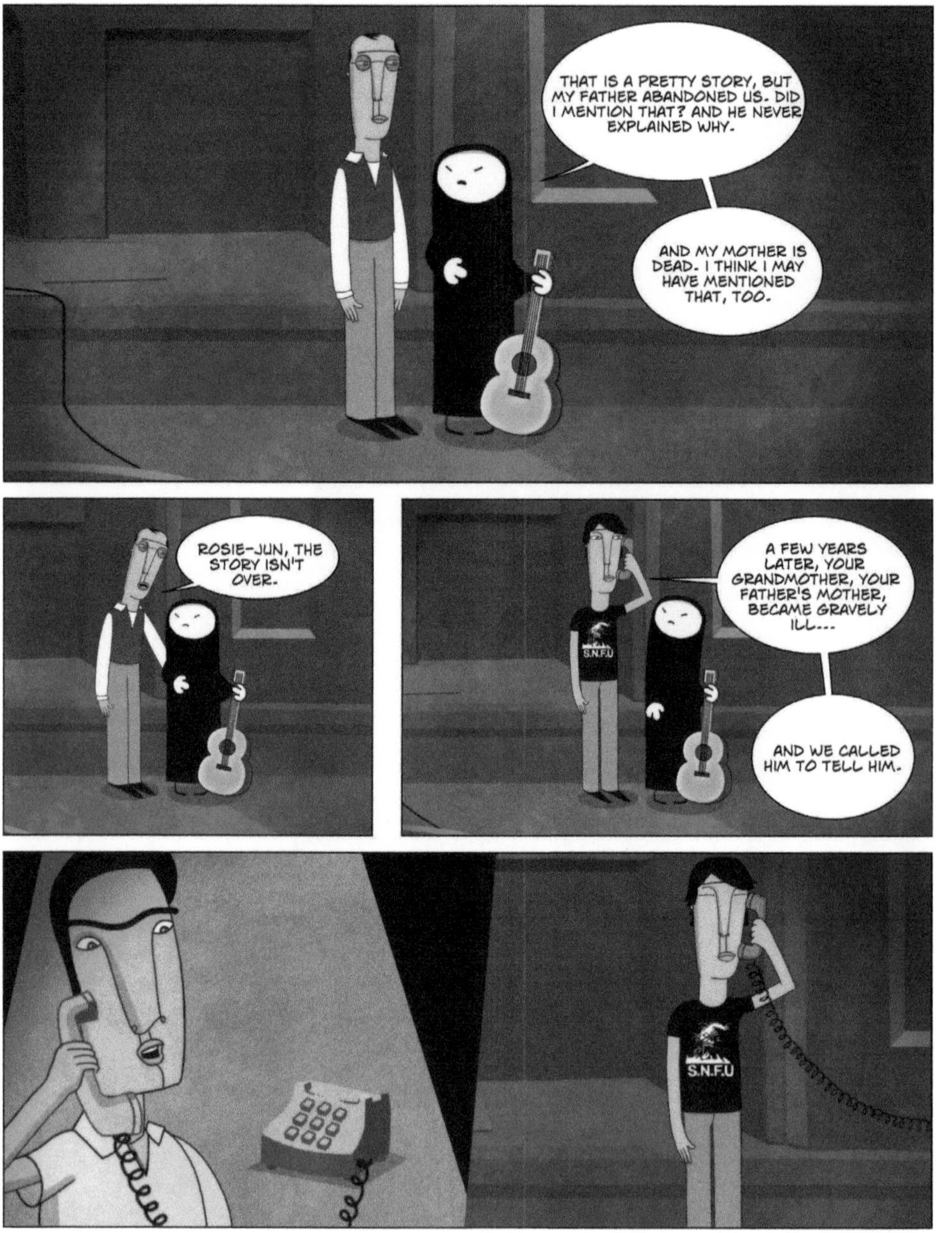
THAT IS A PRETTY STORY, BUT MY FATHER ABANDONED US. DID I MENTION THAT? AND HE NEVER EXPLAINED WHY.
AND MY MOTHER IS DEAD. I THINK I MAY HAVE MENTIONED THAT, TOO.
ROSIE-JUN, THE STORY ISN'T OVER.
S.N.F.U
A FEW YEARS LATER, YOUR GRANDMOTHER, YOUR FATHER'S MOTHER, BECAME GRAVELY ILL...
AND WE CALLED HIM TO TELL HIM.
S.N.F.U

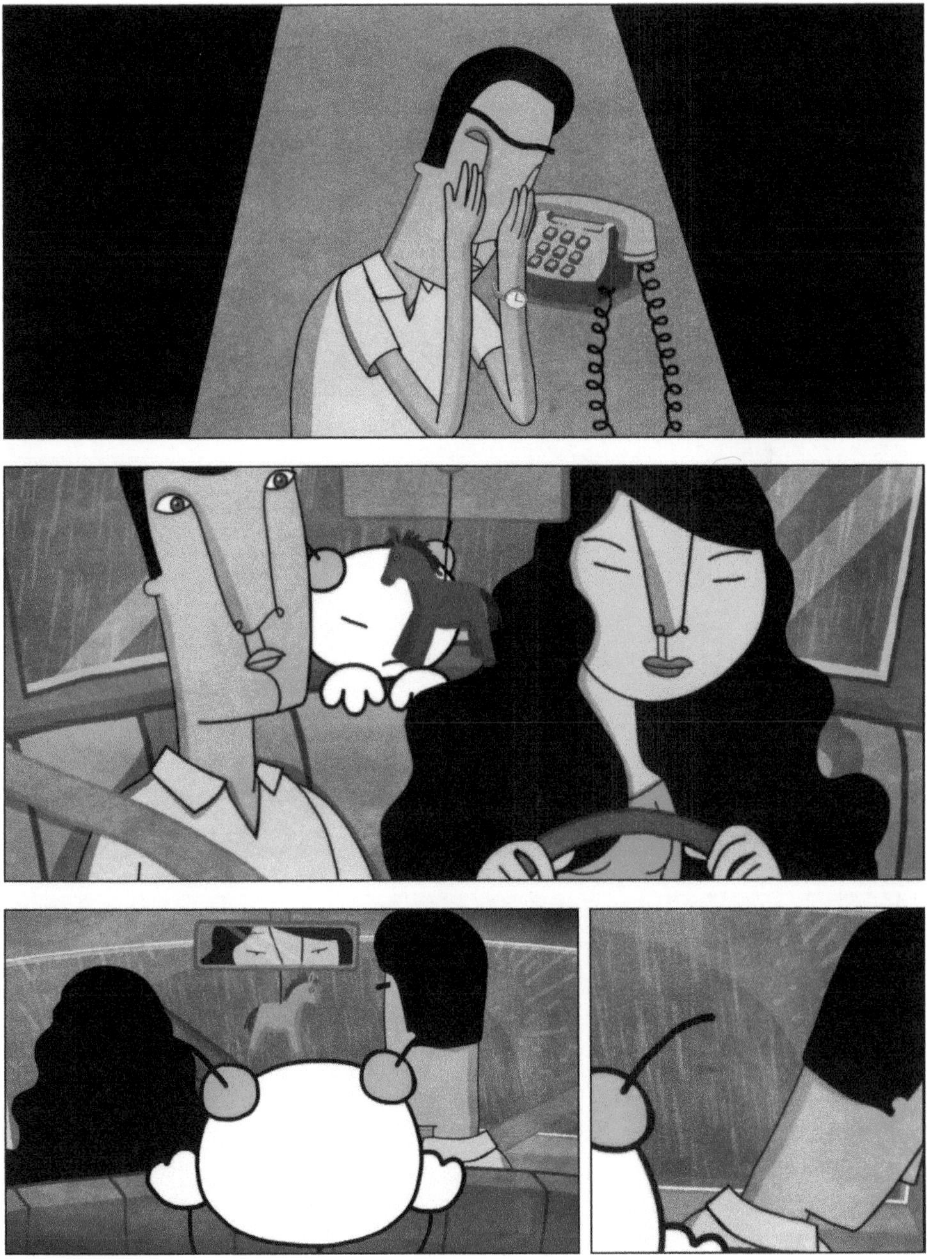

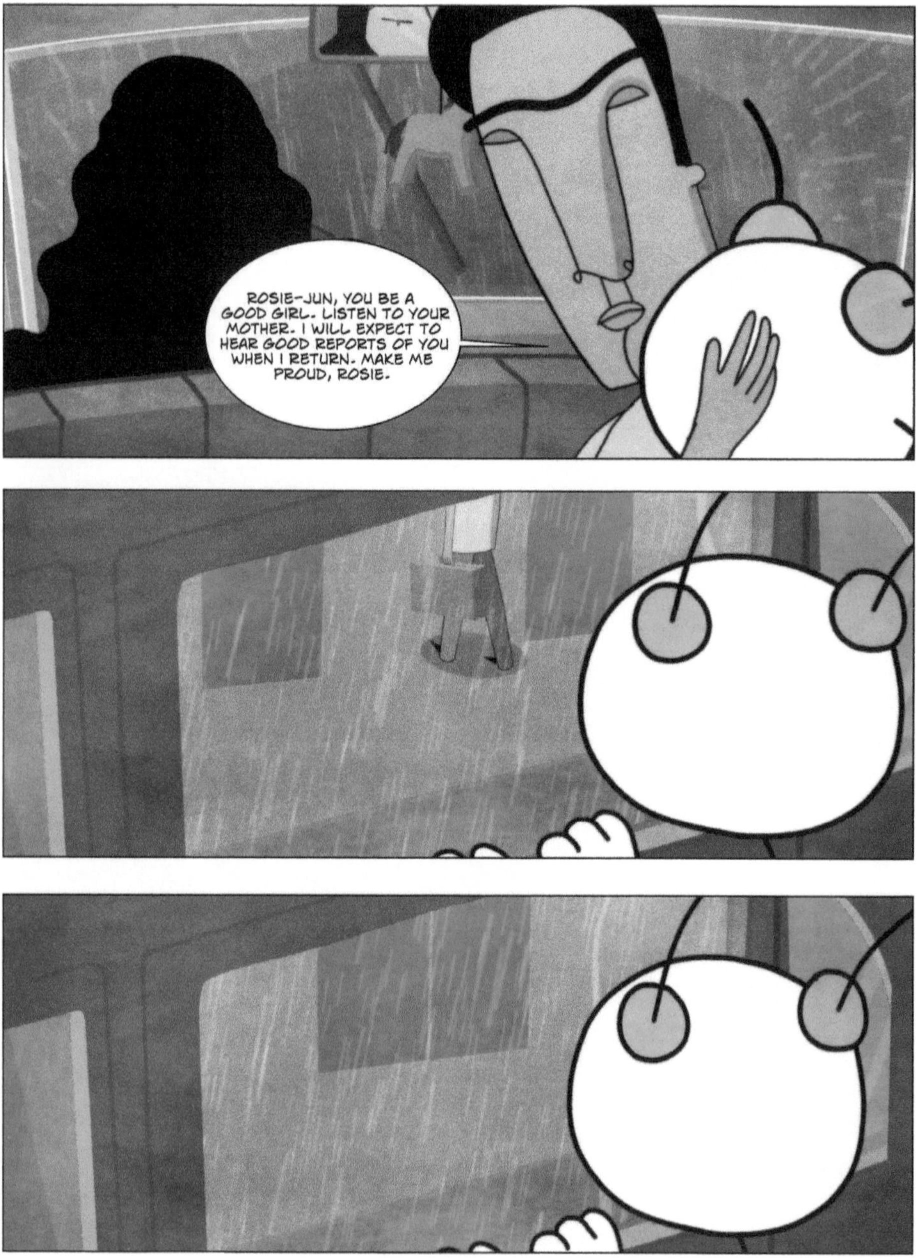
ROSIE-JUN, YOU BE A GOOD GIRL. LISTEN TO YOUR MOTHER. I WILL EXPECT TO HEAR GOOD REPORTS OF YOU WHEN I RETURN. MAKE ME PROUD, ROSIE.

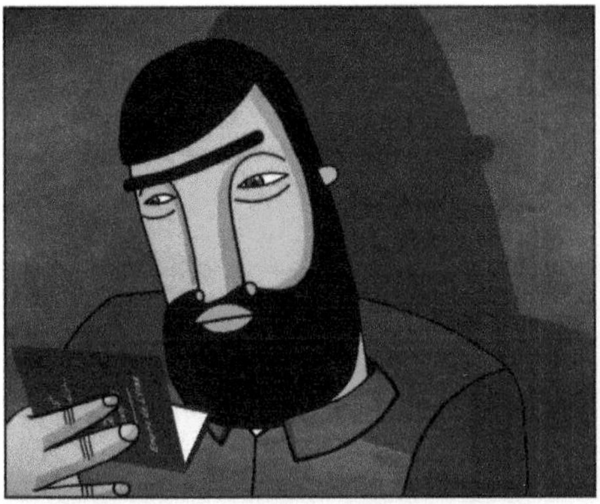

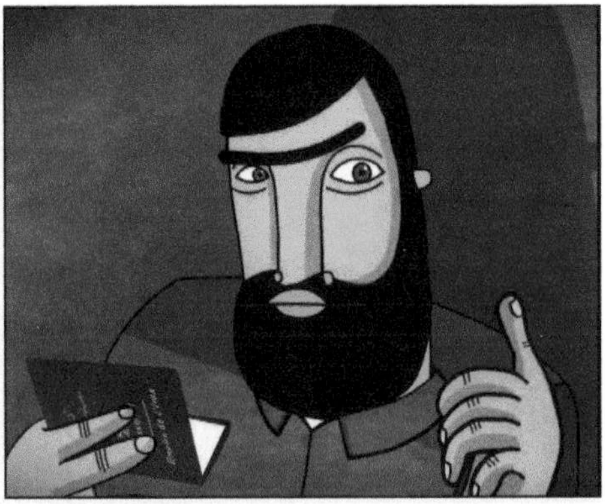

WHEN HE GETS BACK TO IRAN, THEY THROW HIM IN JAIL.

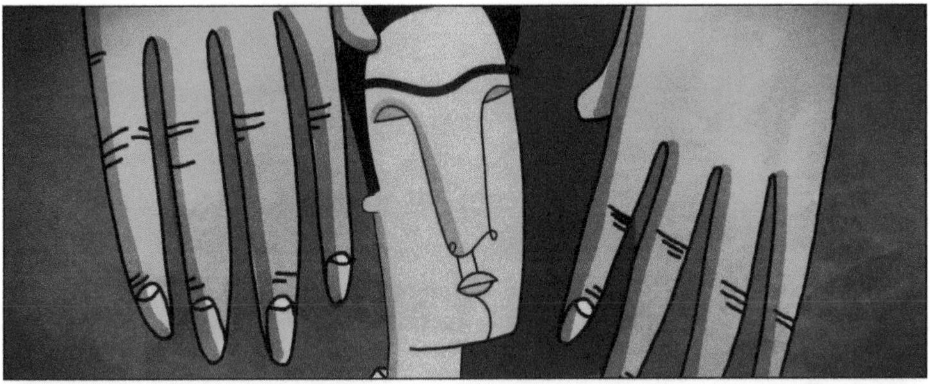

AND THEY WOULDN'T LET HIM MAKE A PHONE CALL.

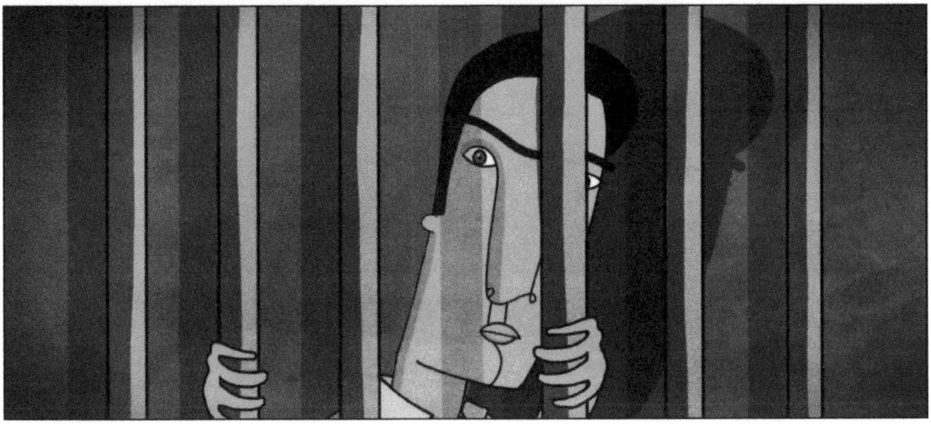

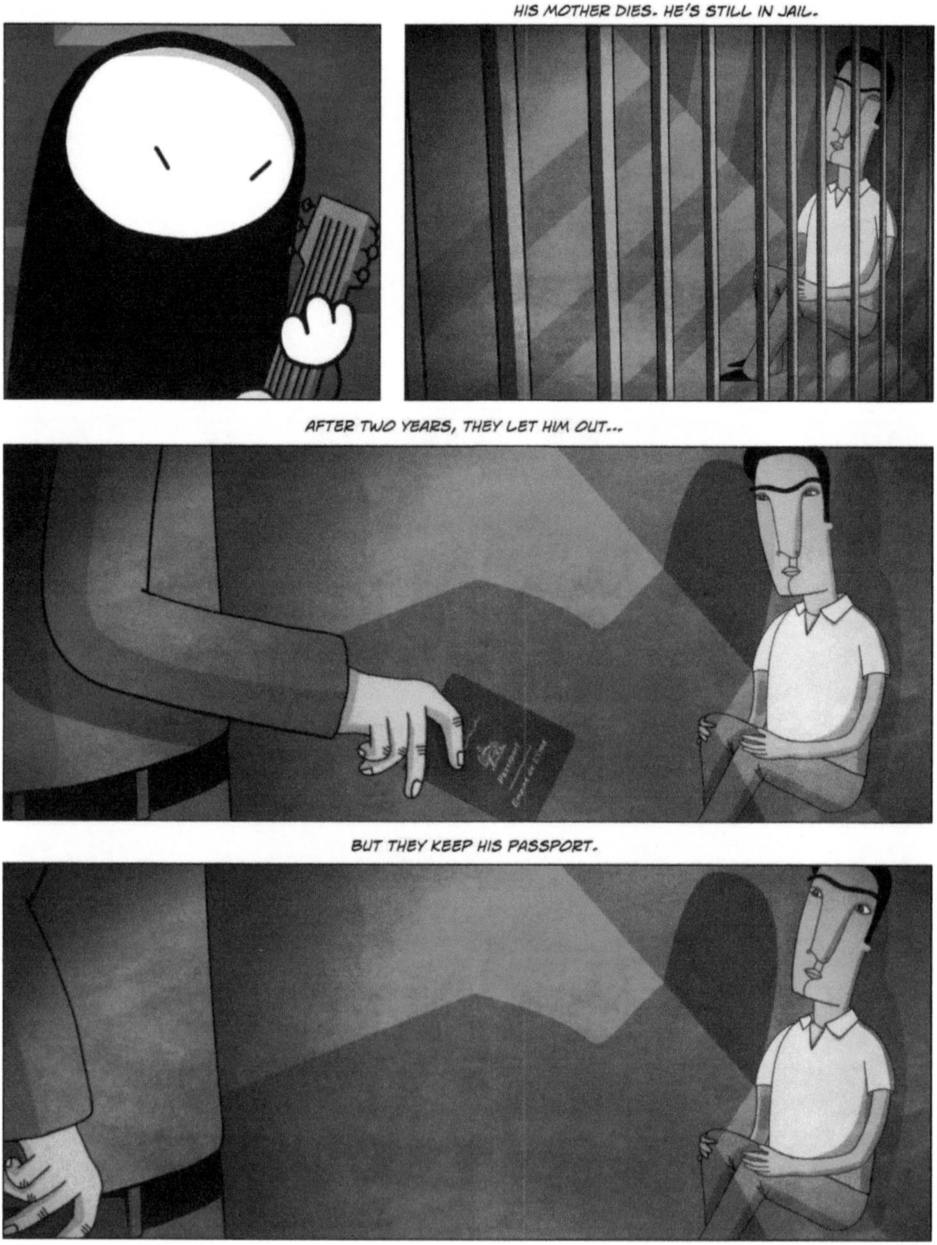
HIS MOTHER DIES. HE'S STILL IN JAIL.
AFTER TWO YEARS, THEY LET HIM OUT...
BUT THEY KEEP HIS PASSPORT.

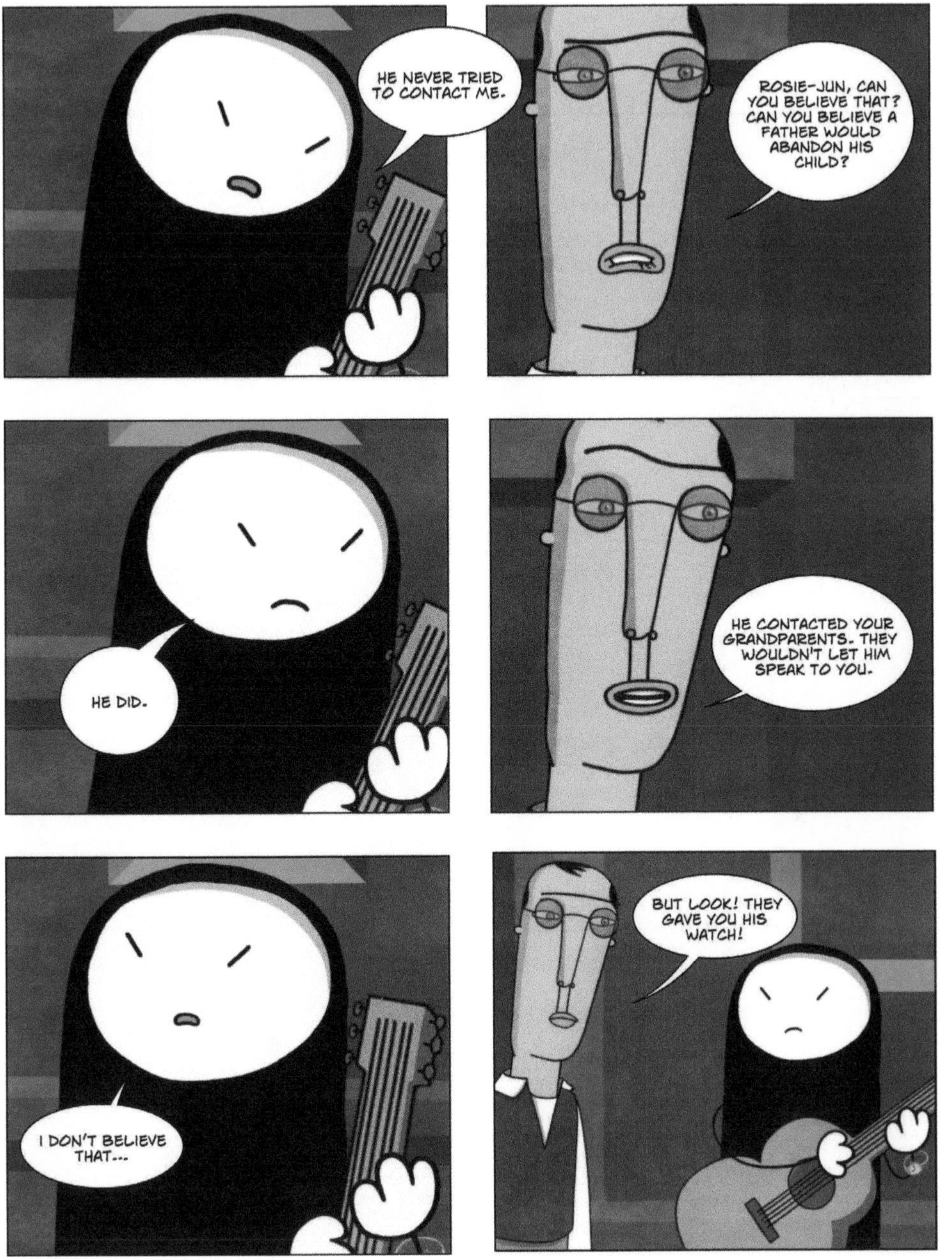

HE NEVER TRIED TO CONTACT ME.
ROSIE-JUN, CAN YOU BELIEVE THAT? CAN YOU BELIEVE A FATHER WOULD ABANDON HIS CHILD?
HE DID.
HE CONTACTED YOUR GRANDPARENTS. THEY WOULDN'T LET HIM SPEAK TO YOU.
I DON'T BELIEVE THAT...
BUT LOOK! THEY GAVE YOU HIS WATCH!

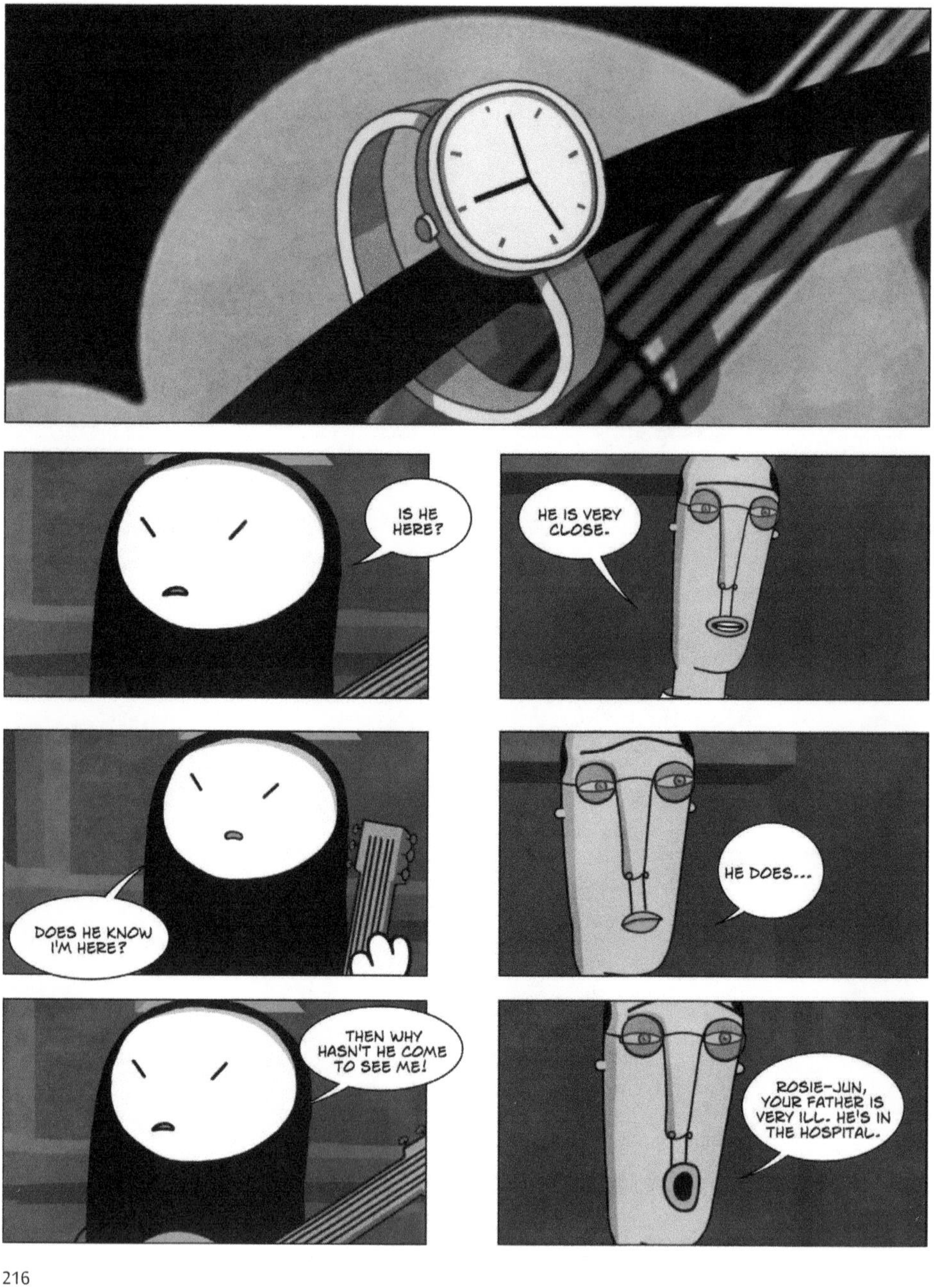
IS HE HERE?
HE IS VERY CLOSE.
DOES HE KNOW I'M HERE?
HE DOES...
THEN WHY HASN'T HE COME TO SEE ME!
ROSIE-JUN, YOUR FATHER IS VERY ILL. HE'S IN THE HOSPITAL.

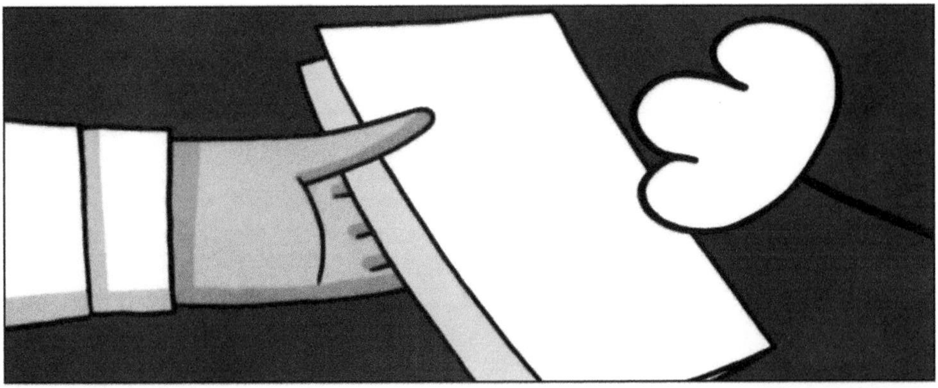

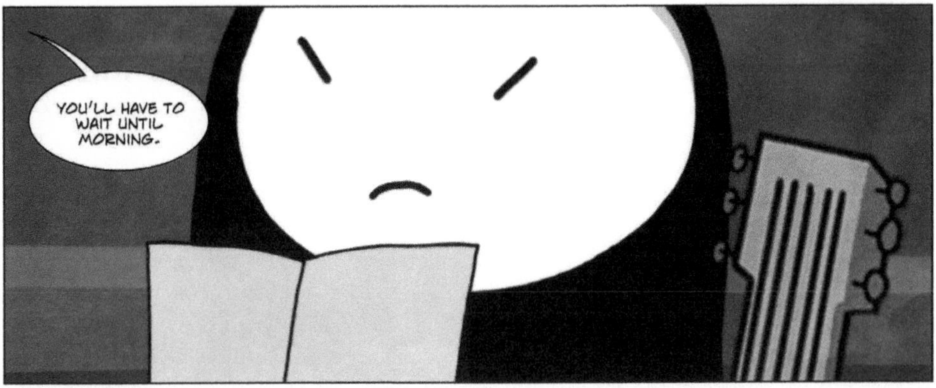
YOU'LL HAVE TO WAIT UNTIL MORNING.

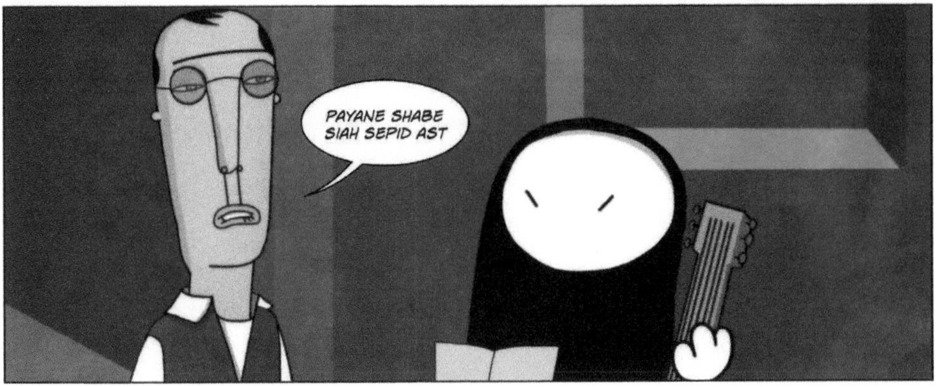
PAYANE SHABE SIAH SEPID AST

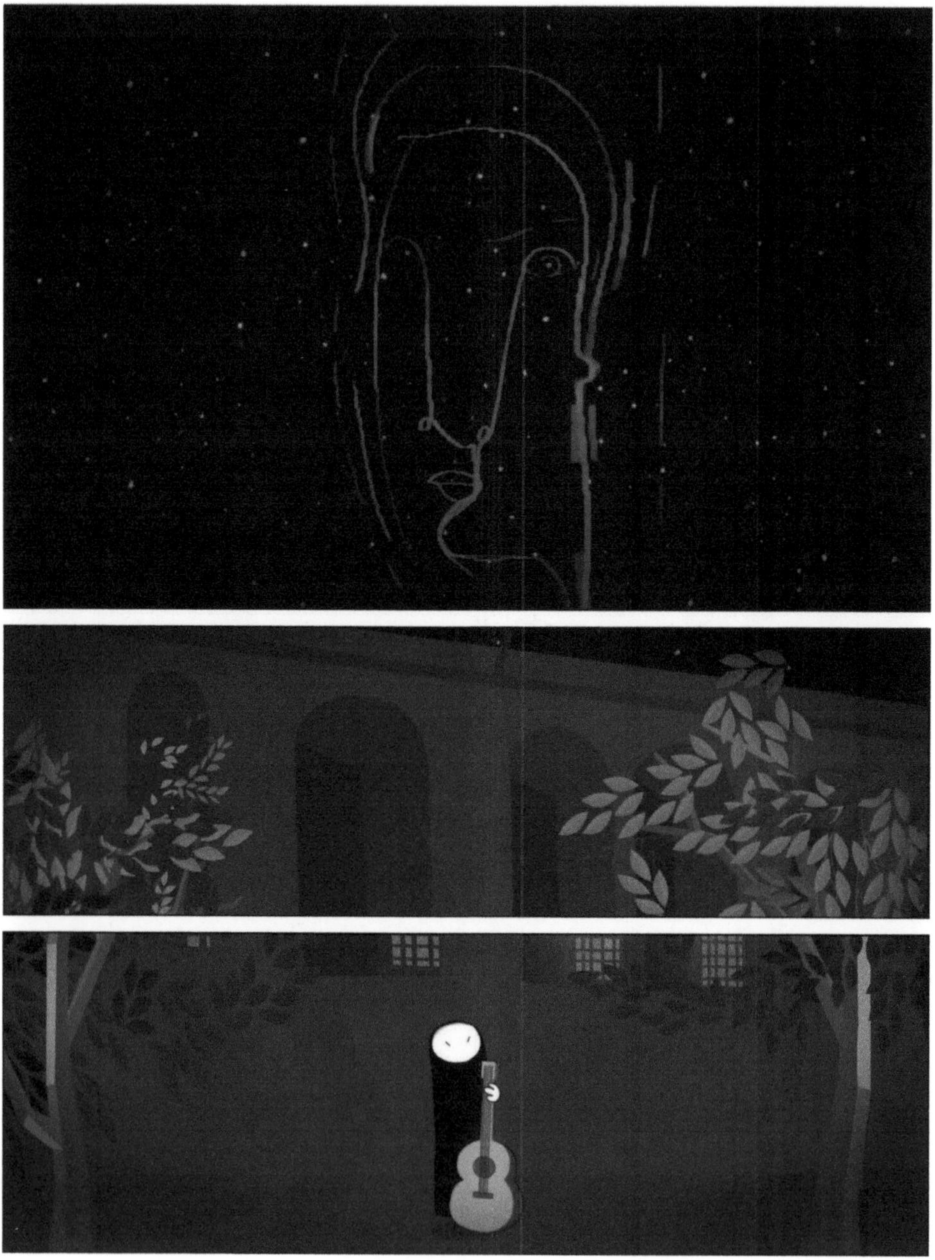

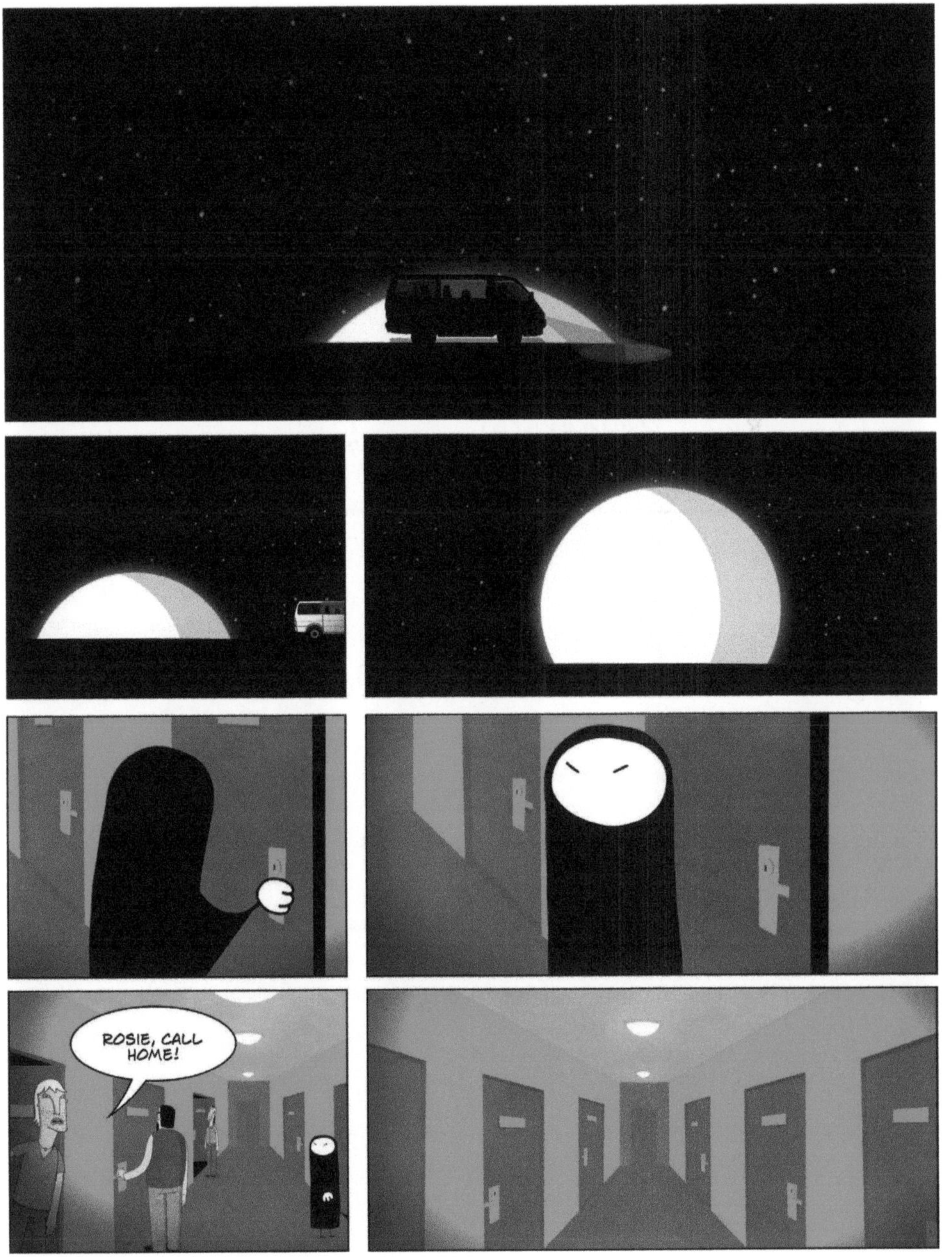
ROSIE, CALL HOME!

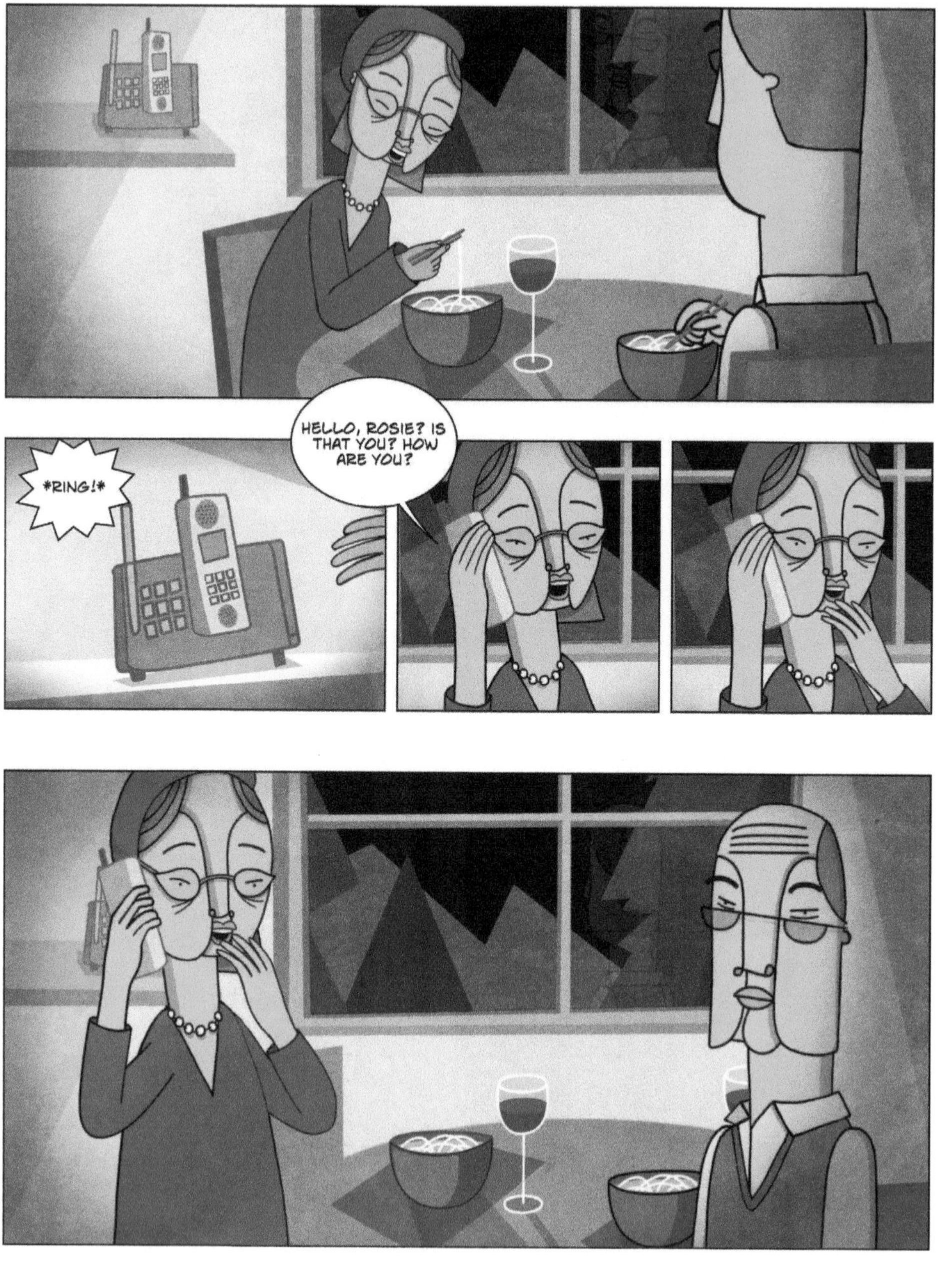
RING!
HELLO, ROSIE? IS THAT YOU? HOW ARE YOU?

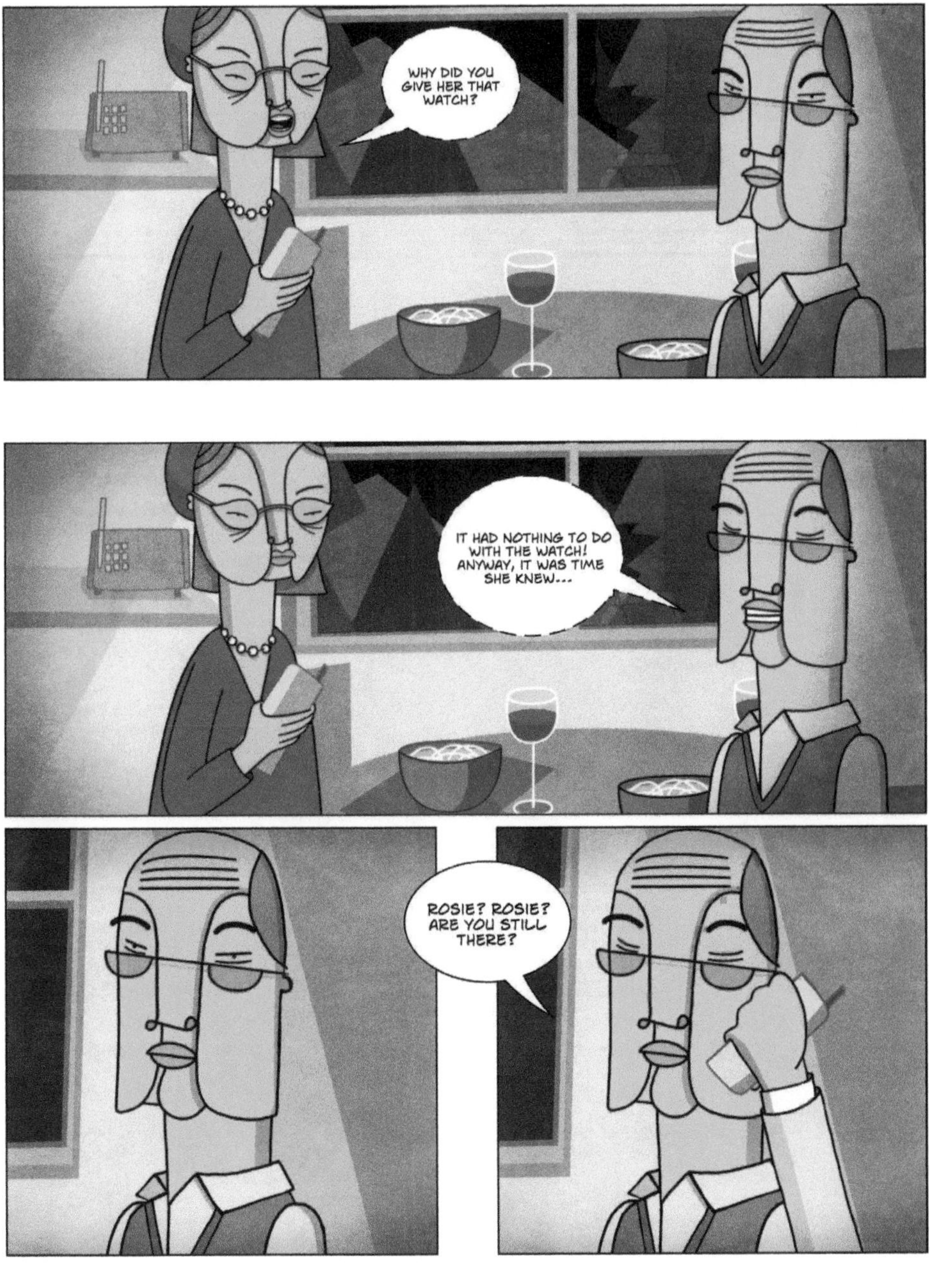
WHY DID YOU GIVE HER THAT WATCH?
IT HAD NOTHING TO DO WITH THE WATCH! ANYWAY, IT WAS TIME SHE KNEW...
ROSIE? ROSIE? ARE YOU STILL THERE?

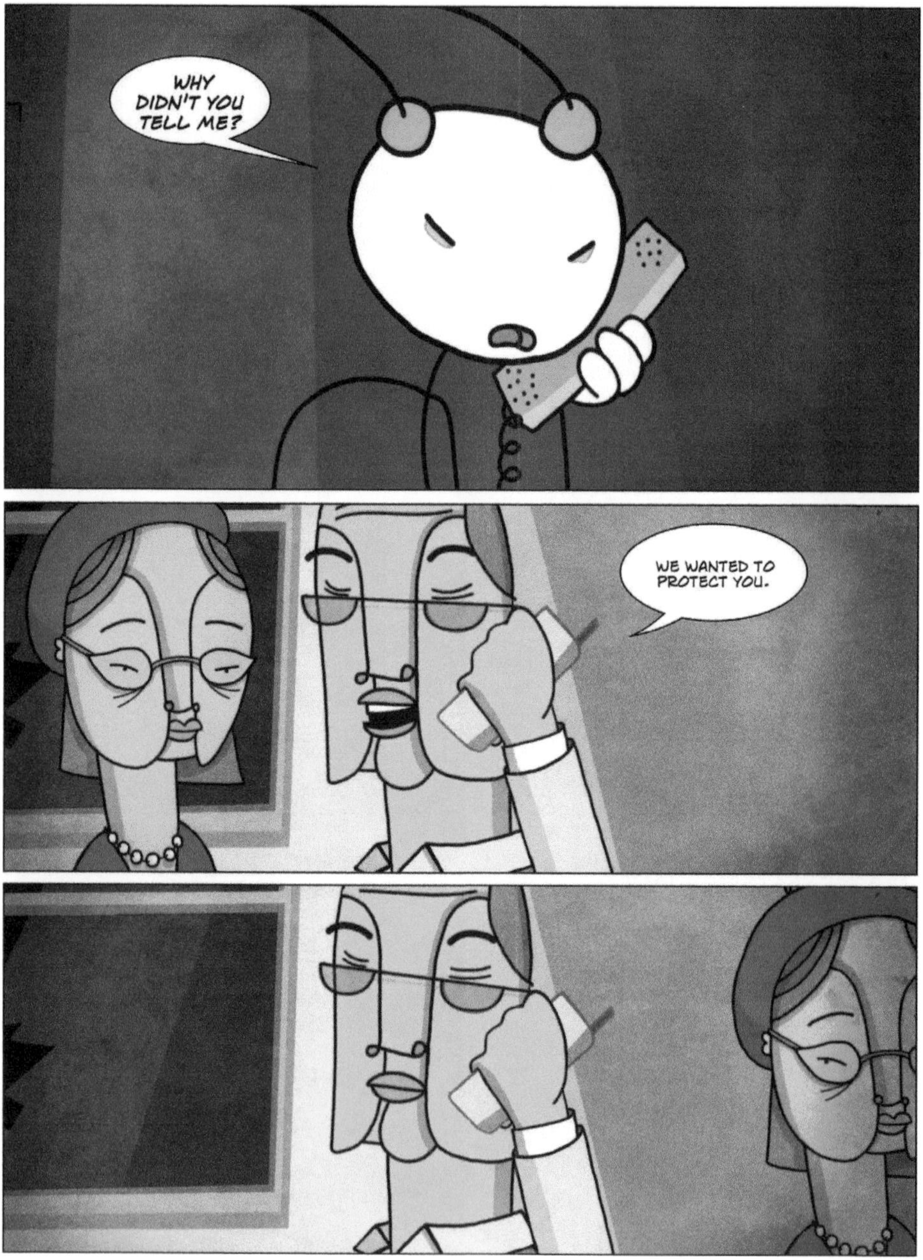
WHY DIDN'T YOU TELL ME?
WE WANTED TO PROTECT YOU.

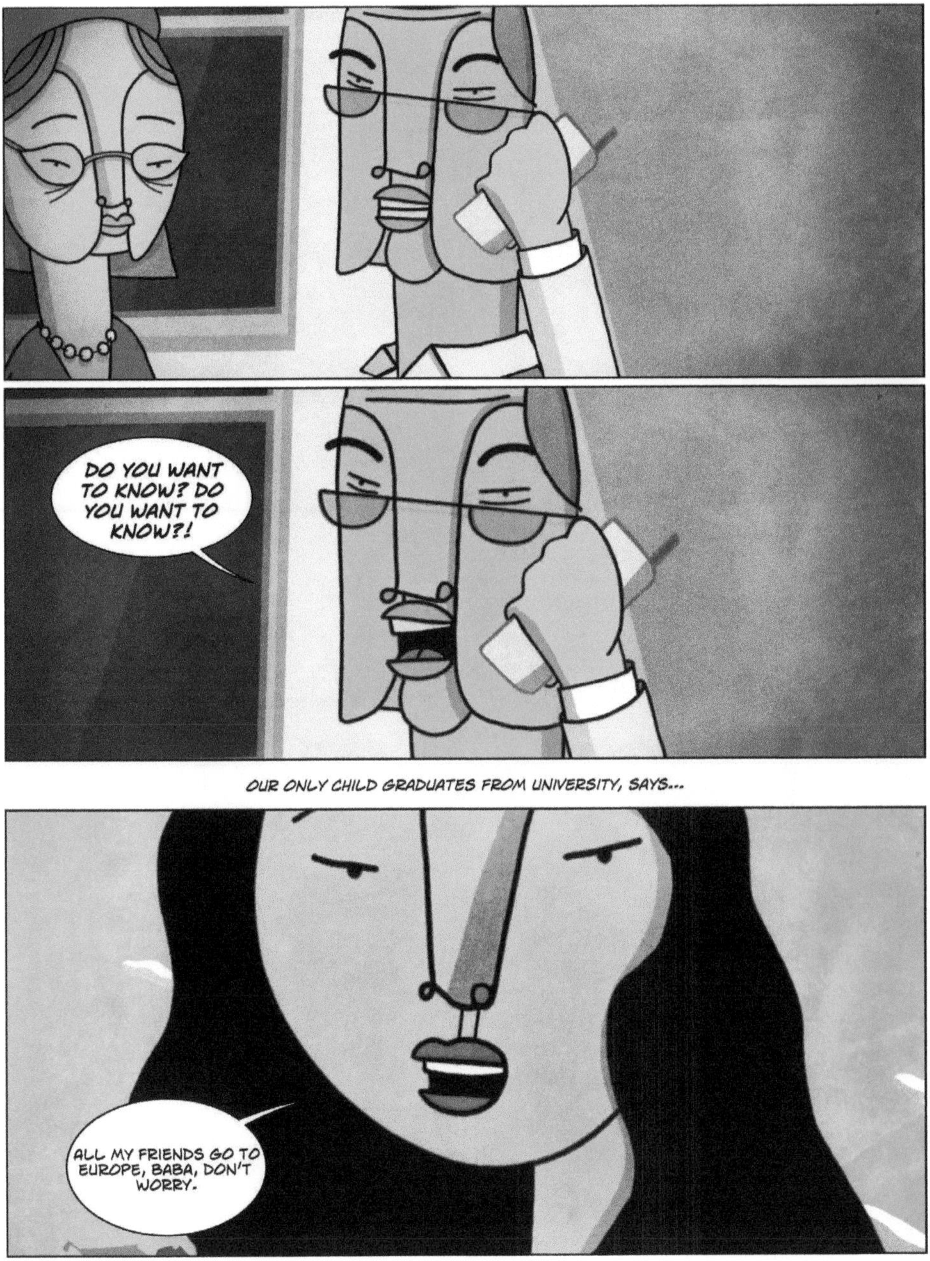
DO YOU WANT TO KNOW? DO YOU WANT TO KNOW?!
OUR ONLY CHILD GRADUATES FROM UNIVERSITY, SAYS...
ALL MY FRIENDS GO TO EUROPE, BABA, DON'T WORRY.

AND COMES BACK, PREGNANT WITH YOU...
AND MARRIED TO THIS MAN...

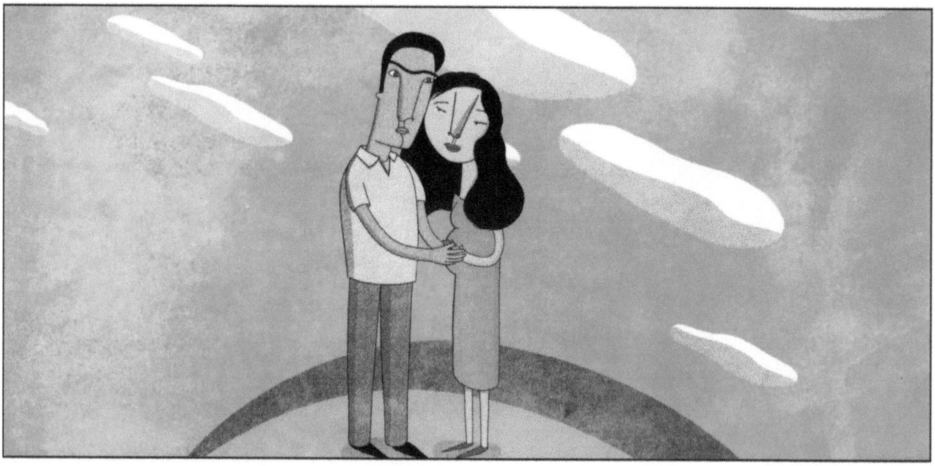

... WHO HAS THE SADDEST EYES IN THE WORLD.

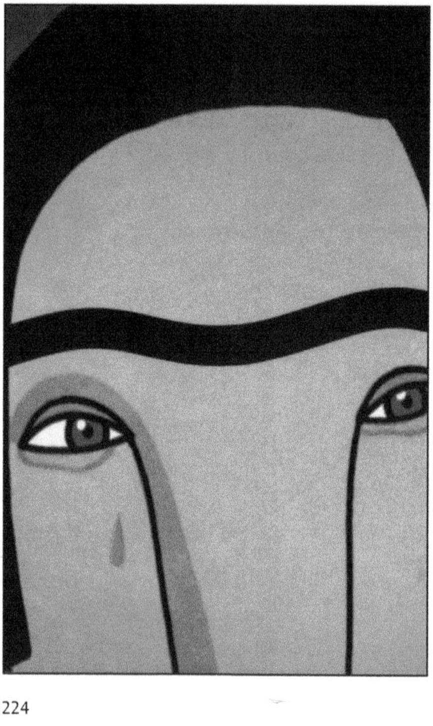

BUT THEN, YOU WERE BORN...

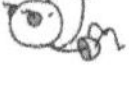

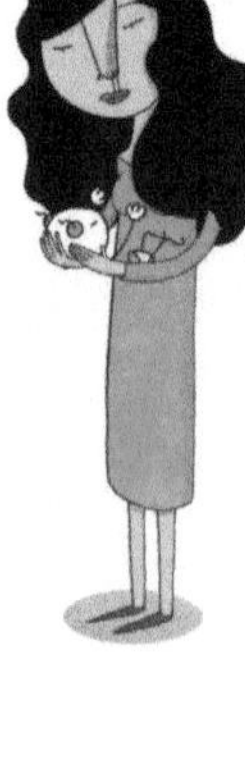

AND YOUR GRANDMOTHER AND I WERE SO HAPPY...

AND YOUR MOTHER WAS SO VERY VERY HAPPY, AND WE THOUGHT MAYBE THIS WAS OKAY.

AT FIRST, YOUR FATHER COULDN'T FIND A JOB. SO, YOU ALL LIVED WITH US FOR A WHILE...

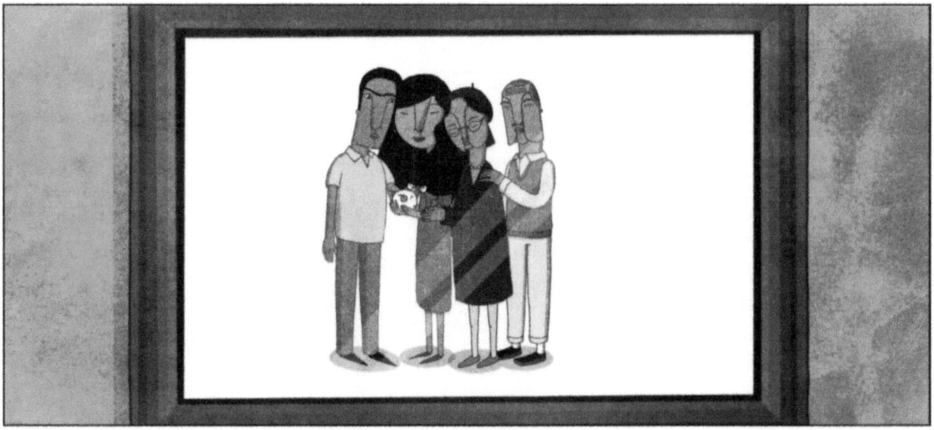

THEN HE GOT ONE, AS A DRIVER. I THINK IT WAS HARD FOR HIM.

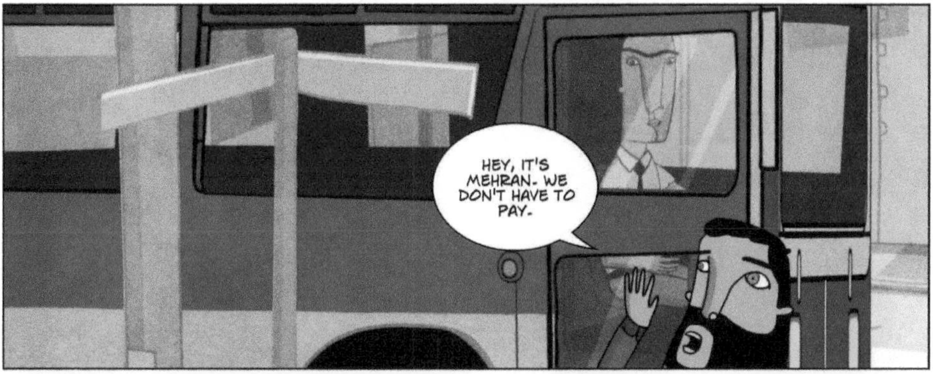
HEY, IT'S MEHRAN. WE DON'T HAVE TO PAY.

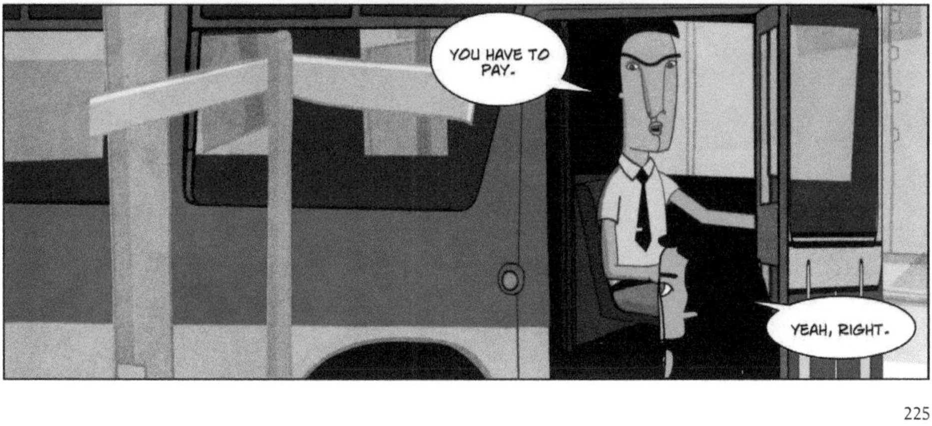
YOU HAVE TO PAY.
YEAH, RIGHT.

HE DIDN'T LIKE THE WAY OTHER PERSIANS LOOKED AT HIM.

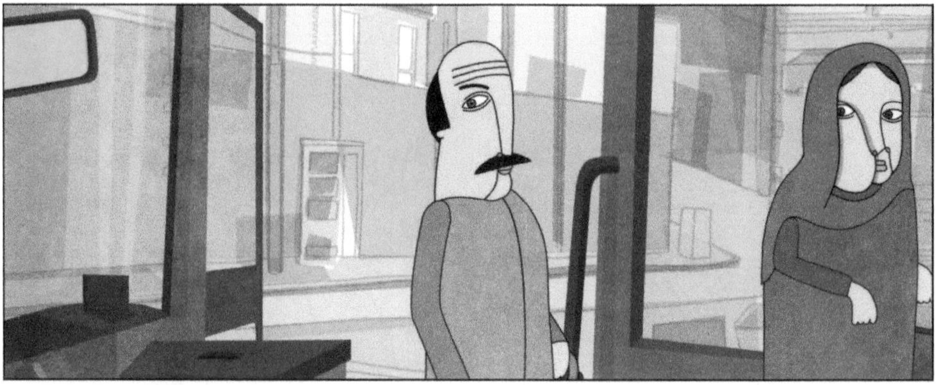

I CAN UNDERSTAND THAT. IT WAS THE SAME FOR ME WHEN I FIRST CAME TO CANADA.

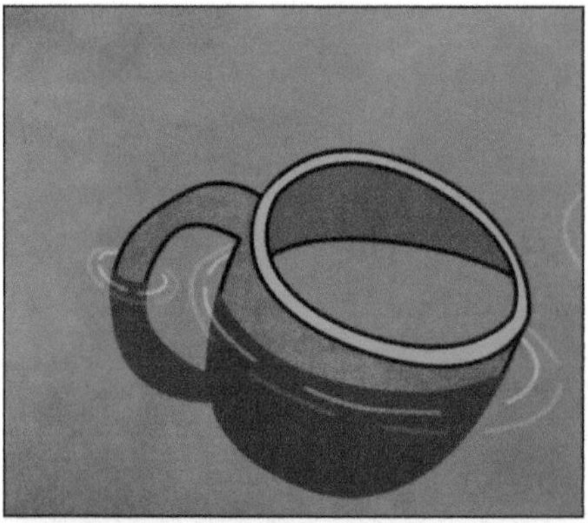

THEN, HE HEARD HIS MOTHER WAS ILL AND HE WANTED TO GO AND VISIT HER.

WE PLEADED WITH HIM NOT TO GO, WE DIDN'T KNOW WHAT WOULD HAPPEN IF HE WENT BACK TO IRAN. HOW COULD WE? WE DIDN'T KNOW WHY HE HAD LEFT IN THE FIRST PLACE. ALL WE KNEW WAS THAT HE FLED...

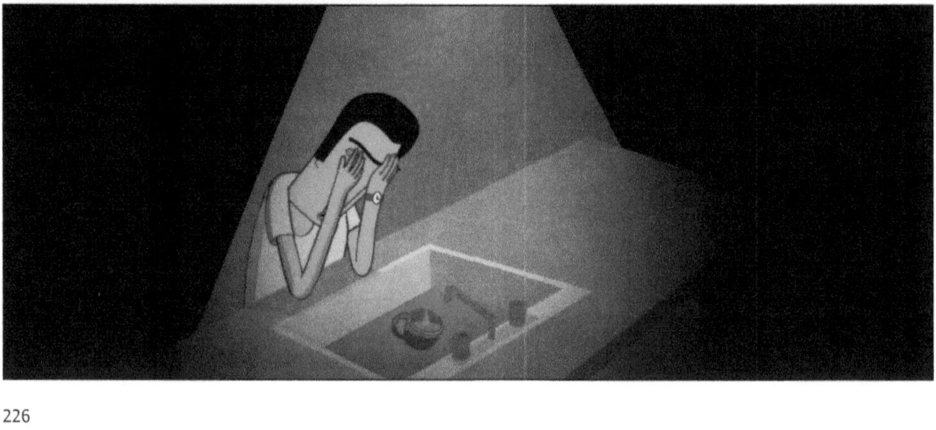

BUT HE LEFT ANYWAY. WE UNDERSTAND. IT WAS HIS MOTHER.

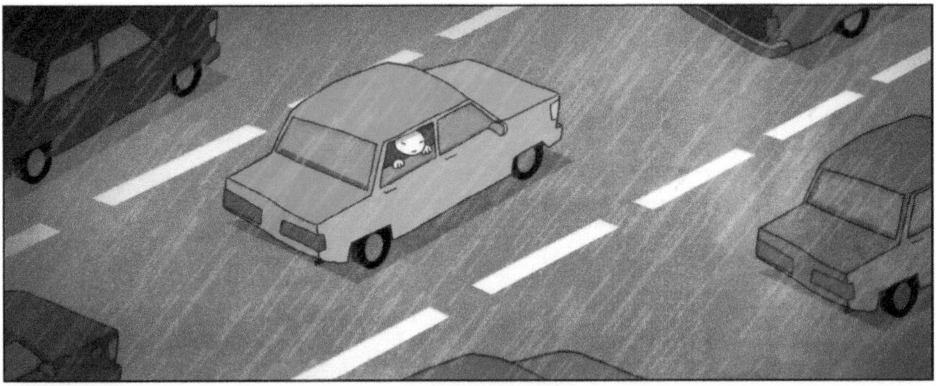

AND YOU KNOW THE REST...

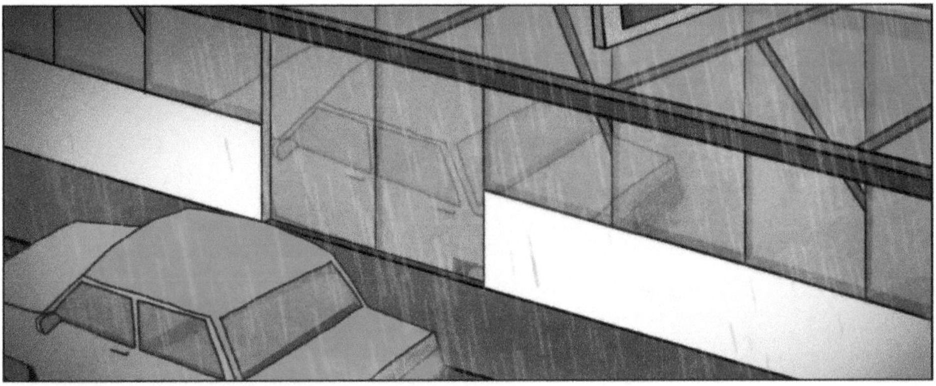

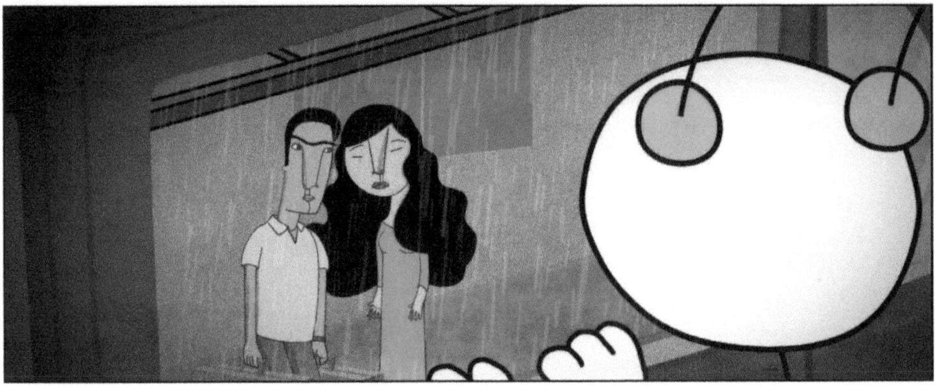

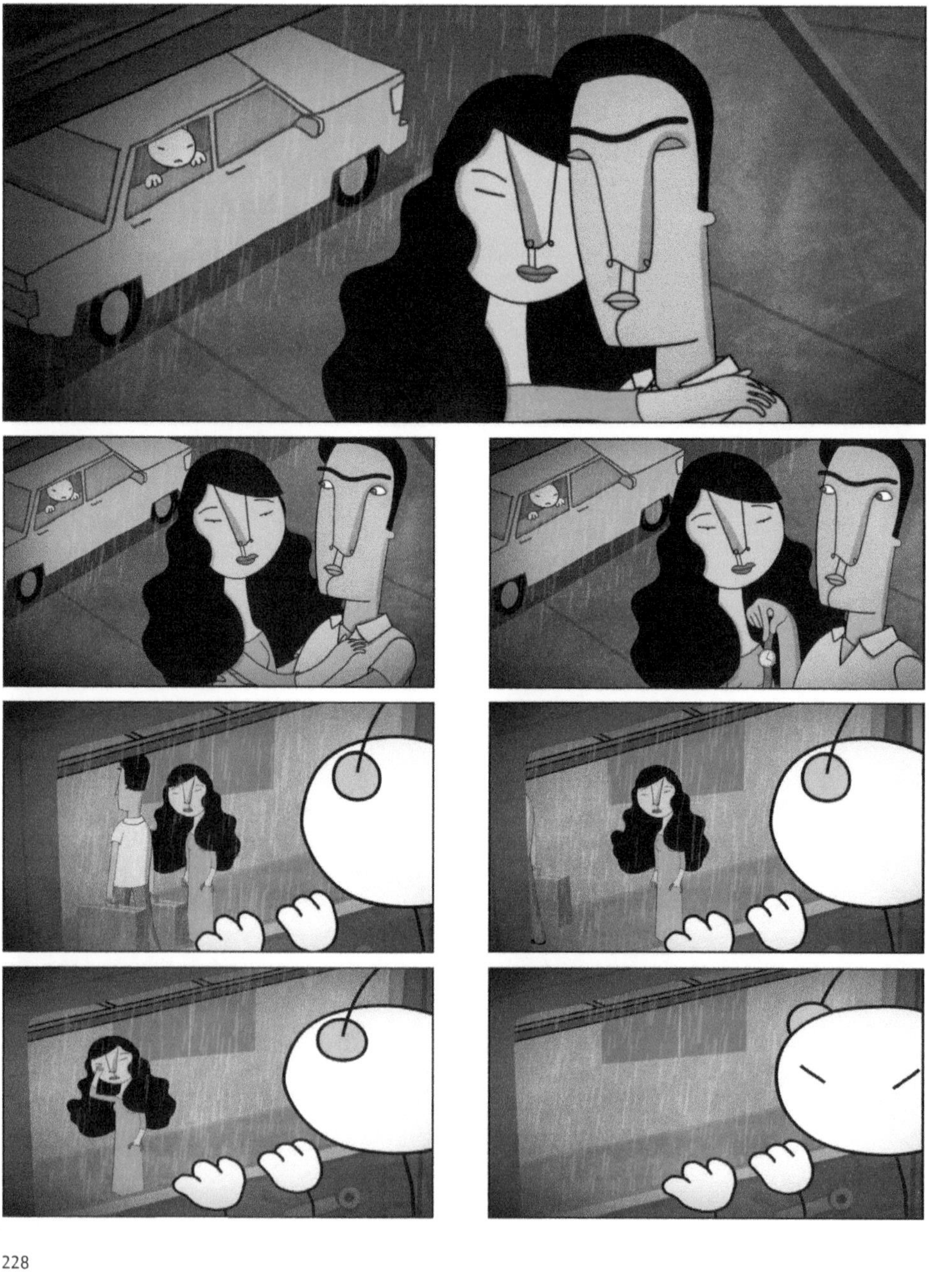

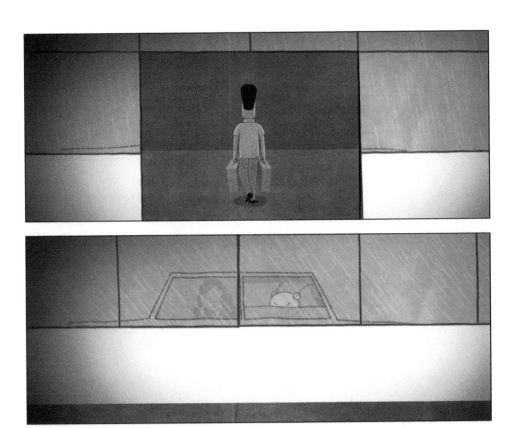

MUM?

DON'T WORRY ABOUT ME, BABY, I'LL BE OKAY...

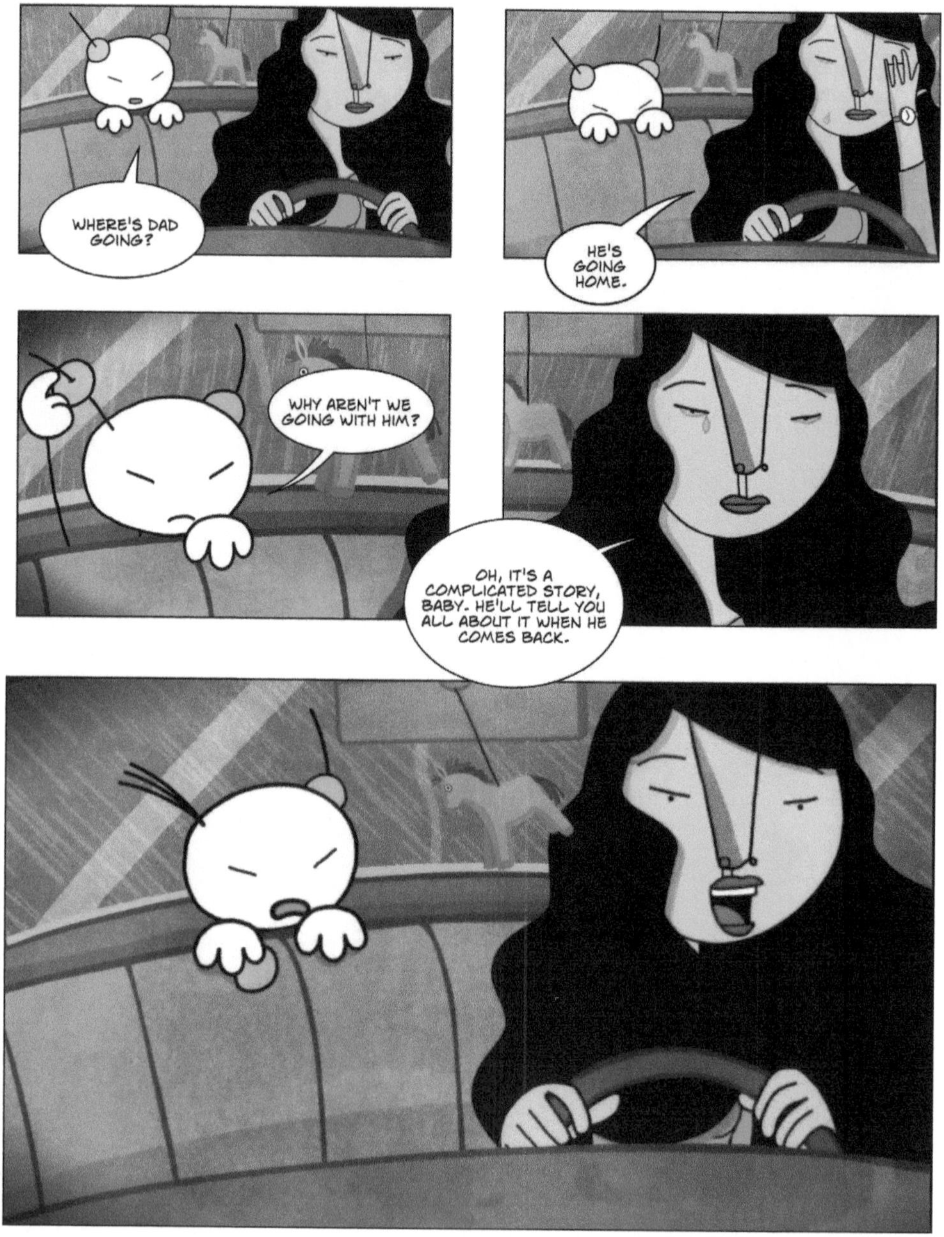
WHERE'S DAD GOING?
HE'S GOING HOME.
WHY AREN'T WE GOING WITH HIM?
OH, IT'S A COMPLICATED STORY, BABY. HE'LL TELL YOU ALL ABOUT IT WHEN HE COMES BACK.

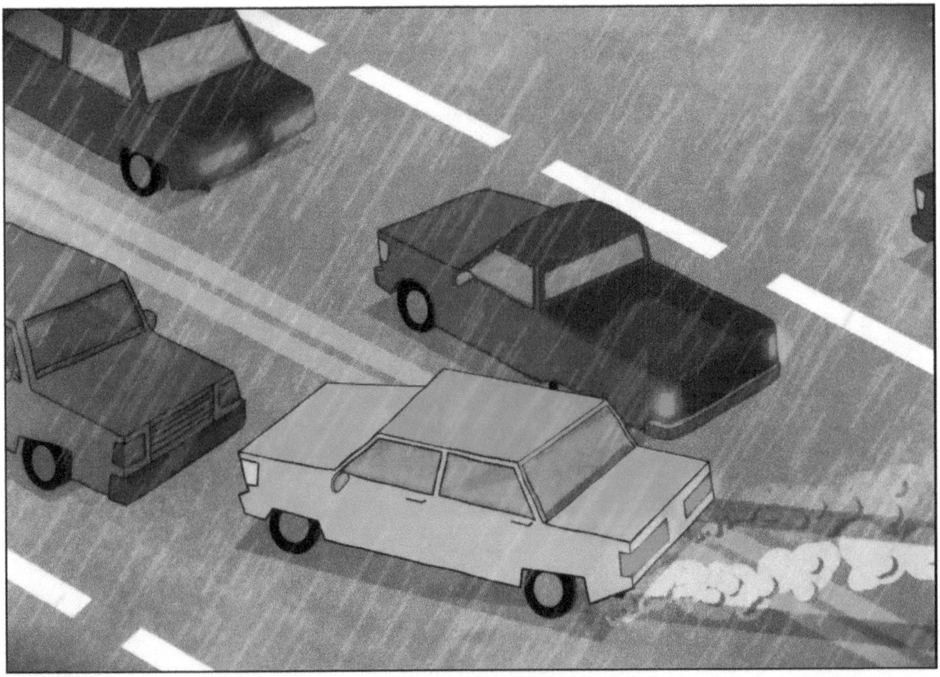

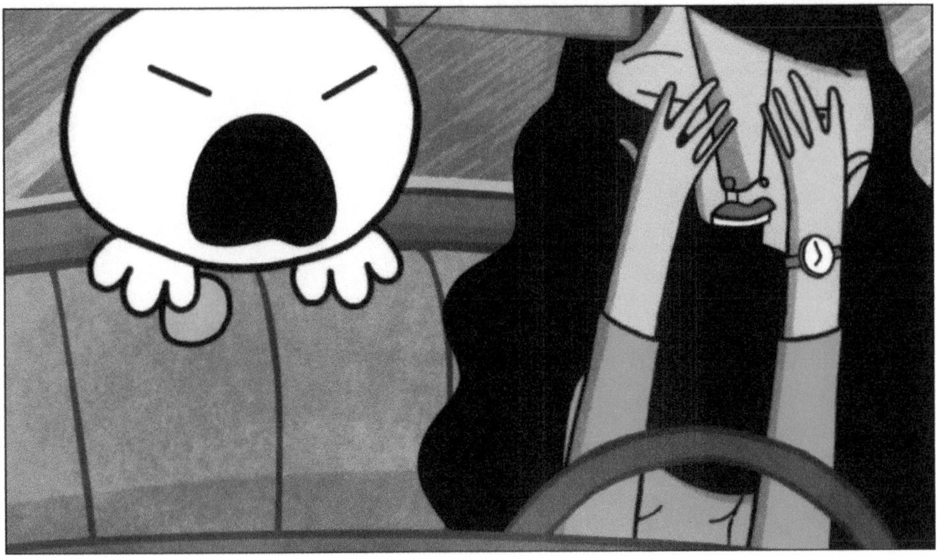

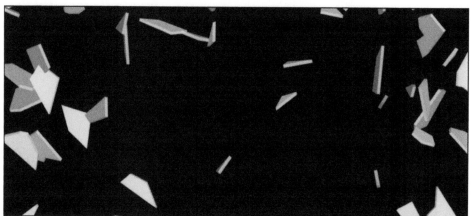

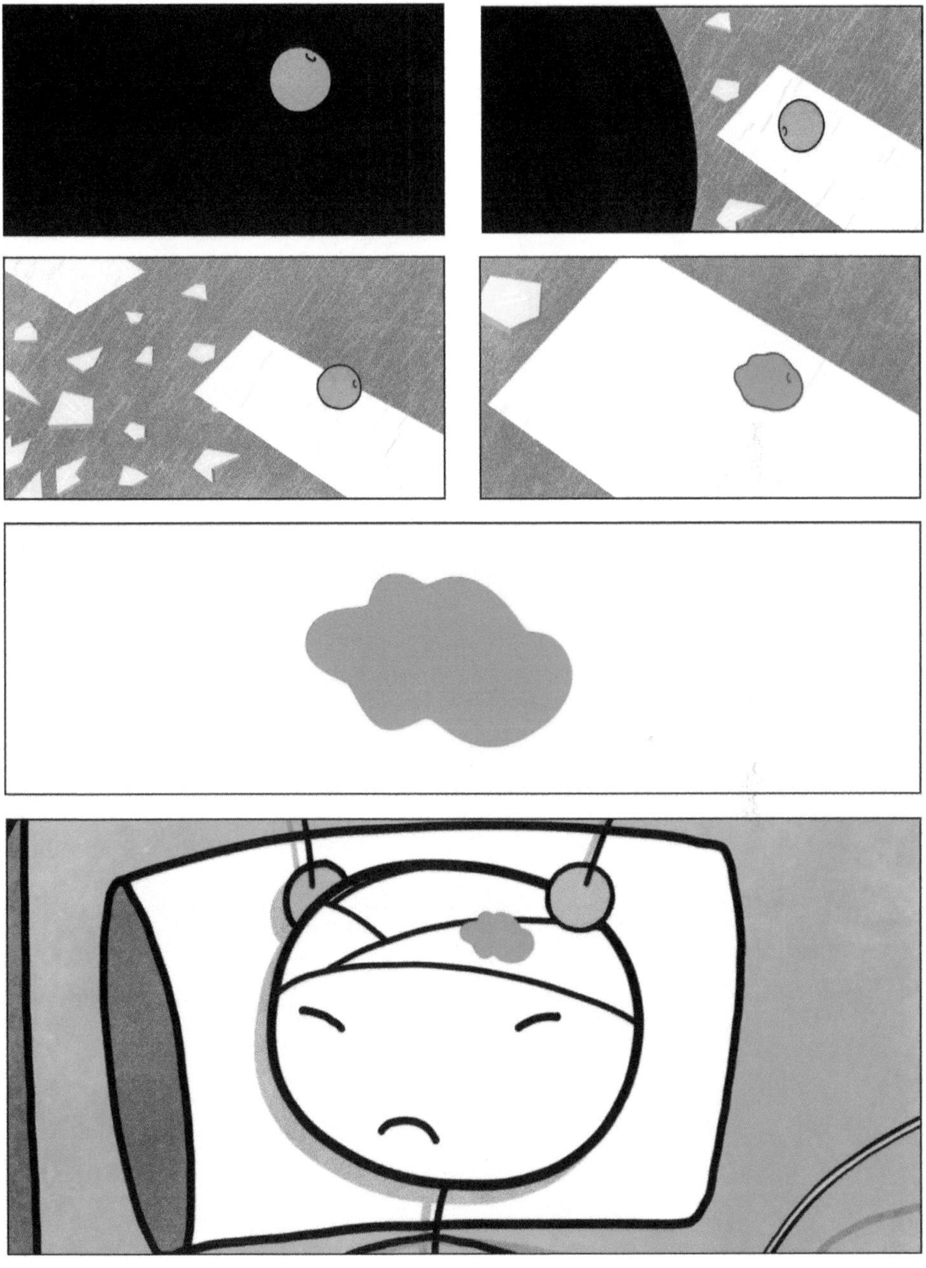

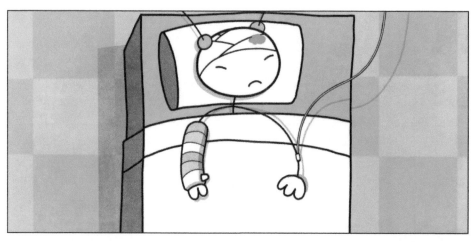

WE DIDN'T HEAR FROM YOUR FATHER FOR ALMOST A YEAR. WE HAD NO IDEA WHAT HAD HAPPENED TO HIM. IF HE WAS EVEN STILL ALIVE.

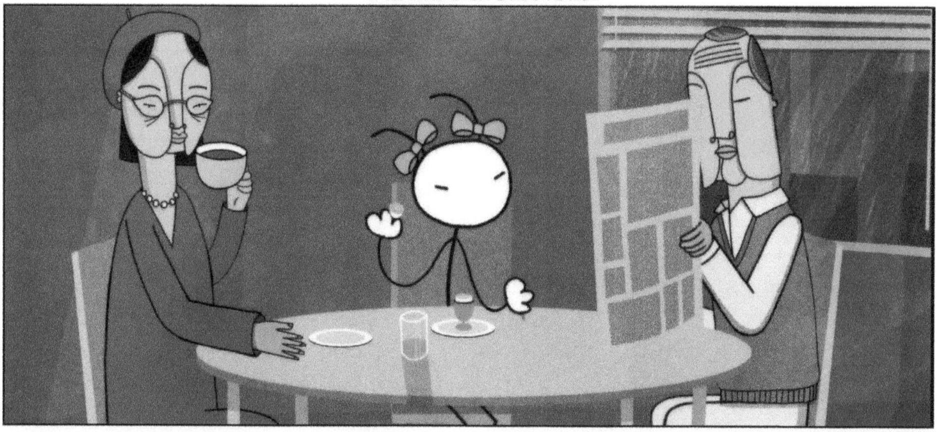

THEN, HE CALLED...

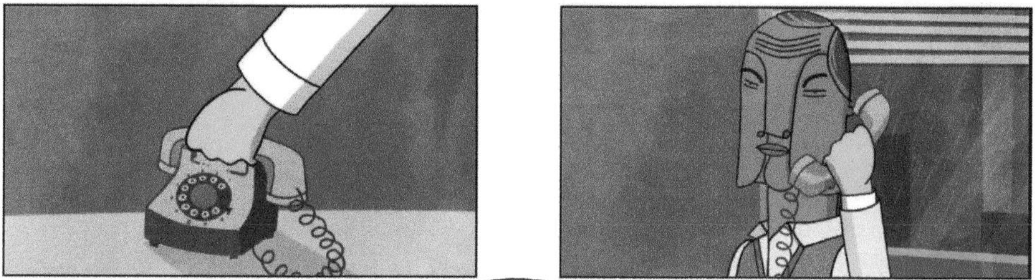

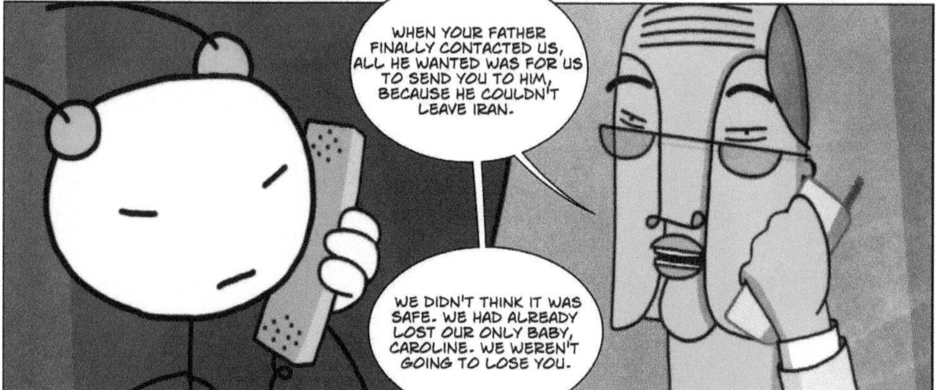
WHEN YOUR FATHER FINALLY CONTACTED US, ALL HE WANTED WAS FOR US TO SEND YOU TO HIM, BECAUSE HE COULDN'T LEAVE IRAN.
WE DIDN'T THINK IT WAS SAFE. WE HAD ALREADY LOST OUR ONLY BABY, CAROLINE. WE WEREN'T GOING TO LOSE YOU.

CAN YOU UNDERSTAND THAT, ROSIE? YOU WERE ALL WE HAD LEFT OF OUR LITTLE GIRL.

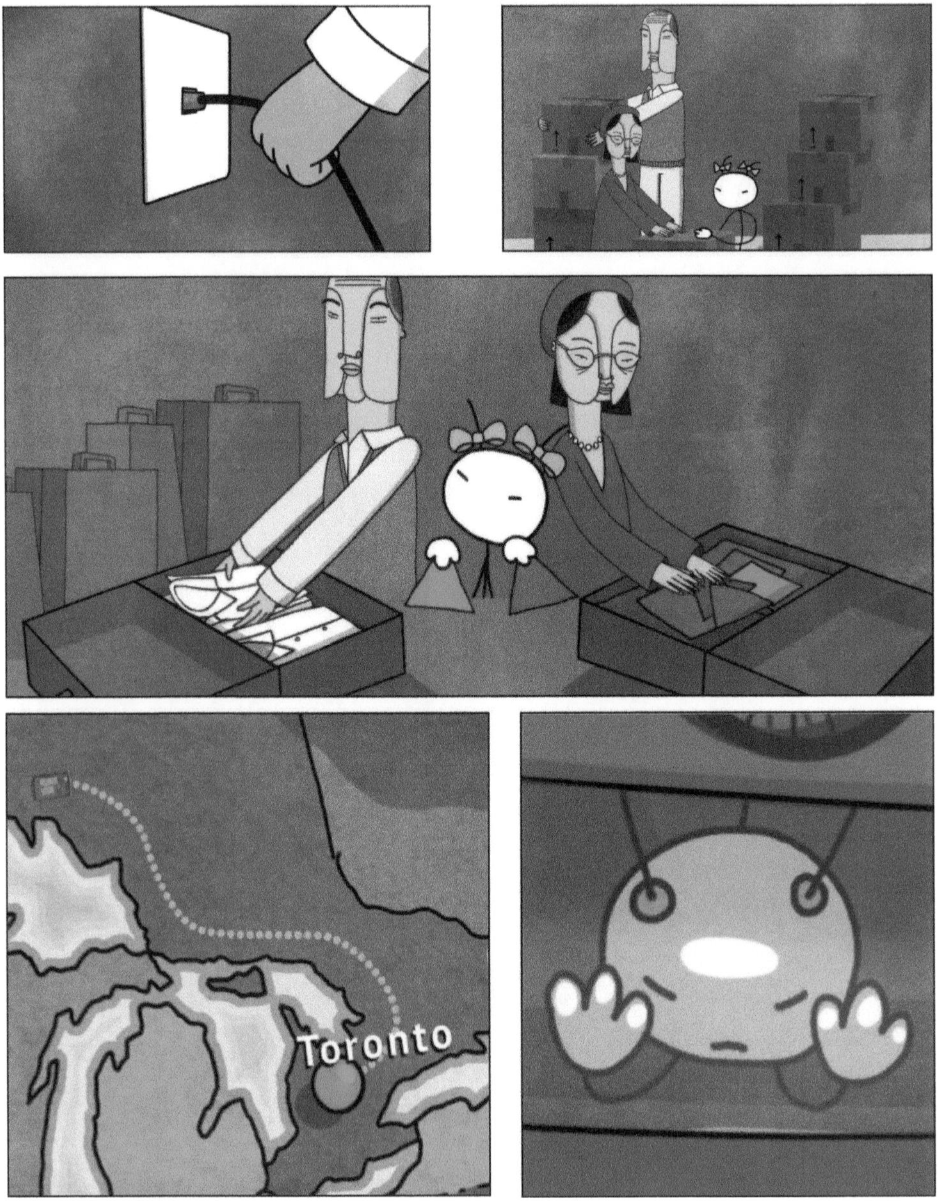
Toronto

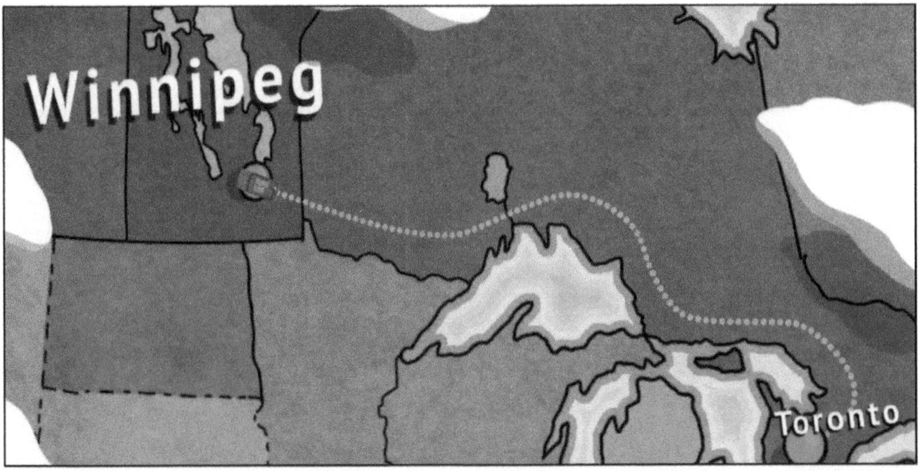
Winnipeg
Toronto

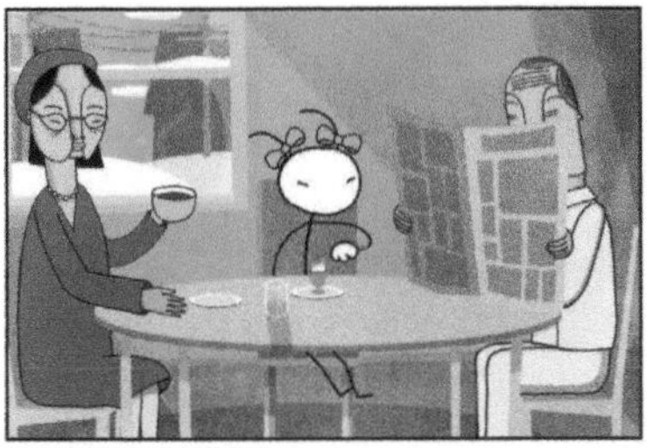

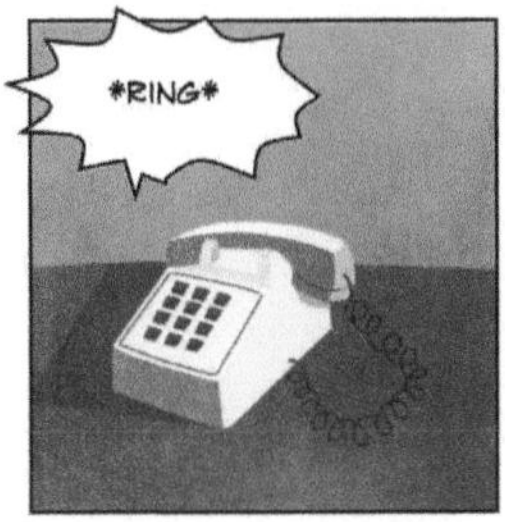
RING

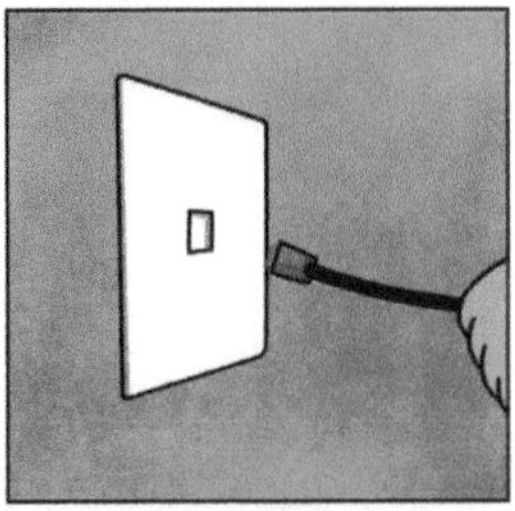

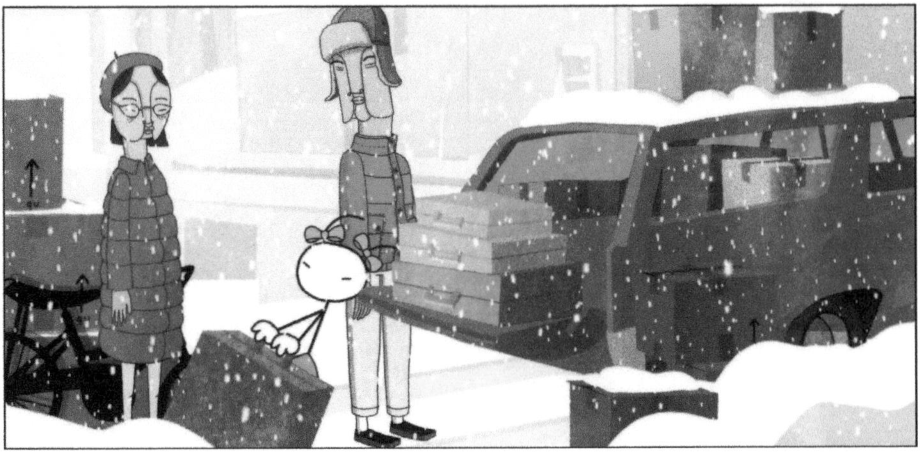

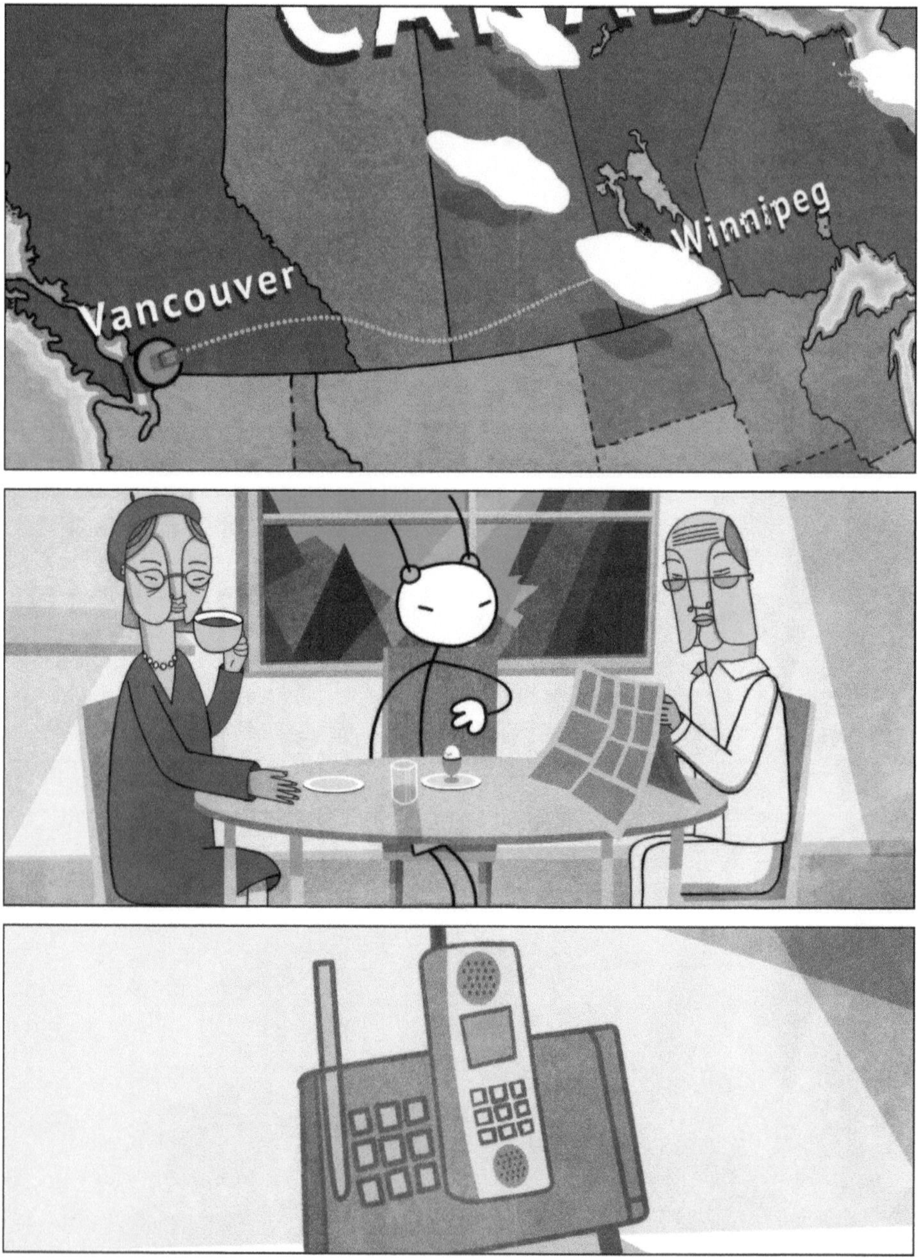
Vancouver
Winnipeg

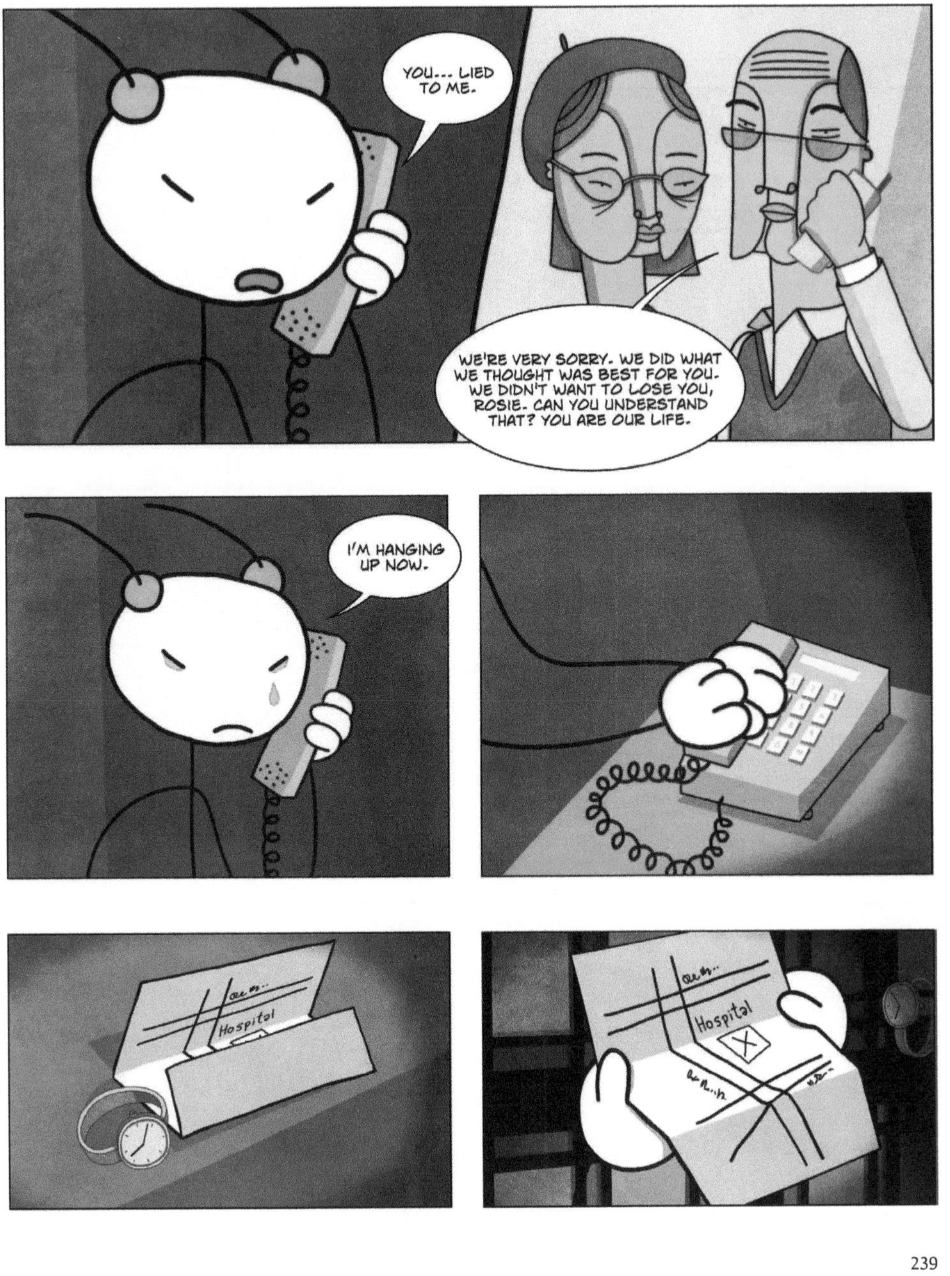
YOU... LIED TO ME.
WE'RE VERY SORRY. WE DID WHAT WE THOUGHT WAS BEST FOR YOU. WE DIDN'T WANT TO LOSE YOU, ROSIE. CAN YOU UNDERSTAND THAT? YOU ARE OUR LIFE.
I'M HANGING UP NOW.
Hospital
Hospital

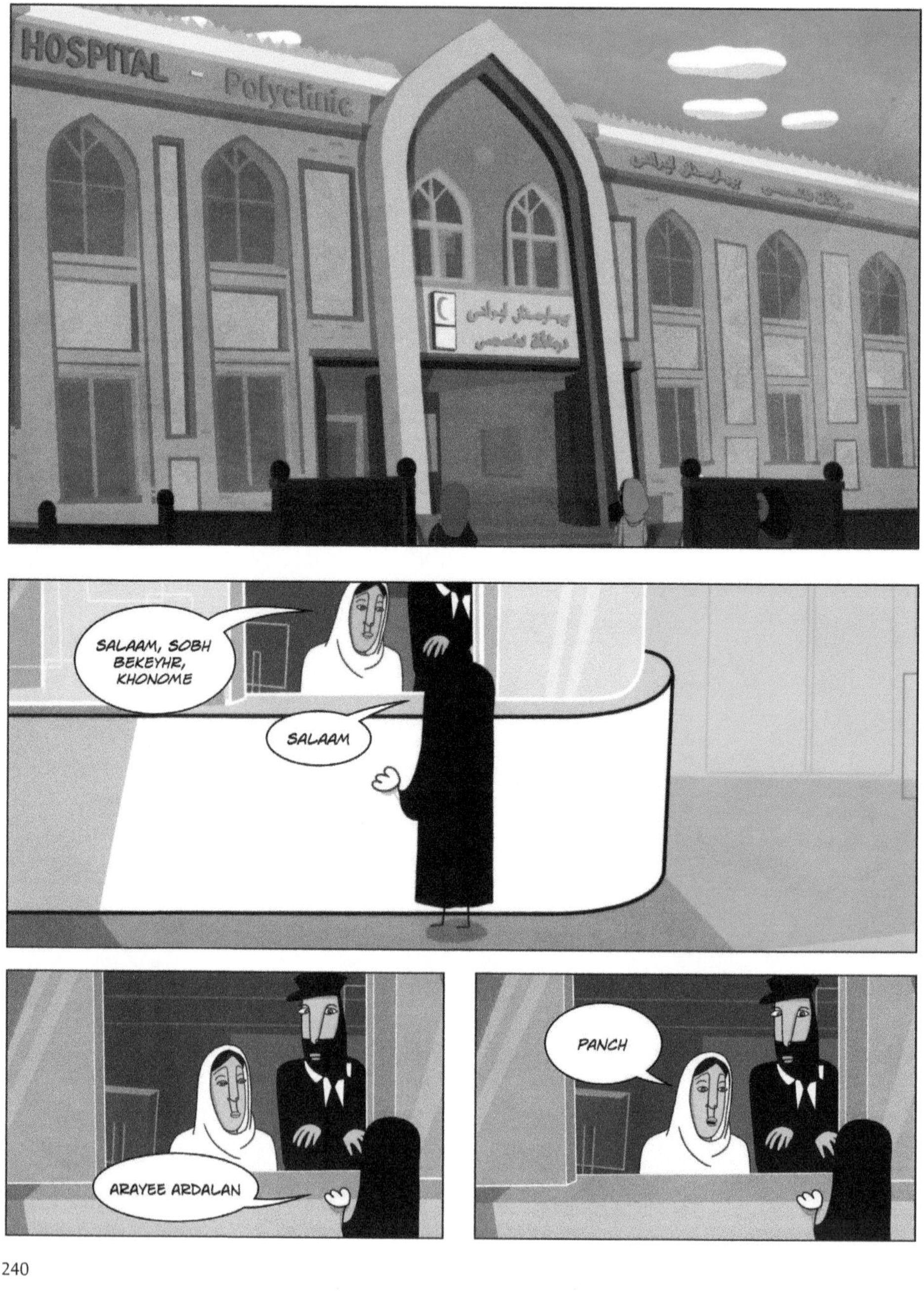
HOSPITAL
Polyclinic
SALAAM, SOBH BEKEYHR, KHONOME
SALAAM
ARAYEE ARDALAN
PANCH

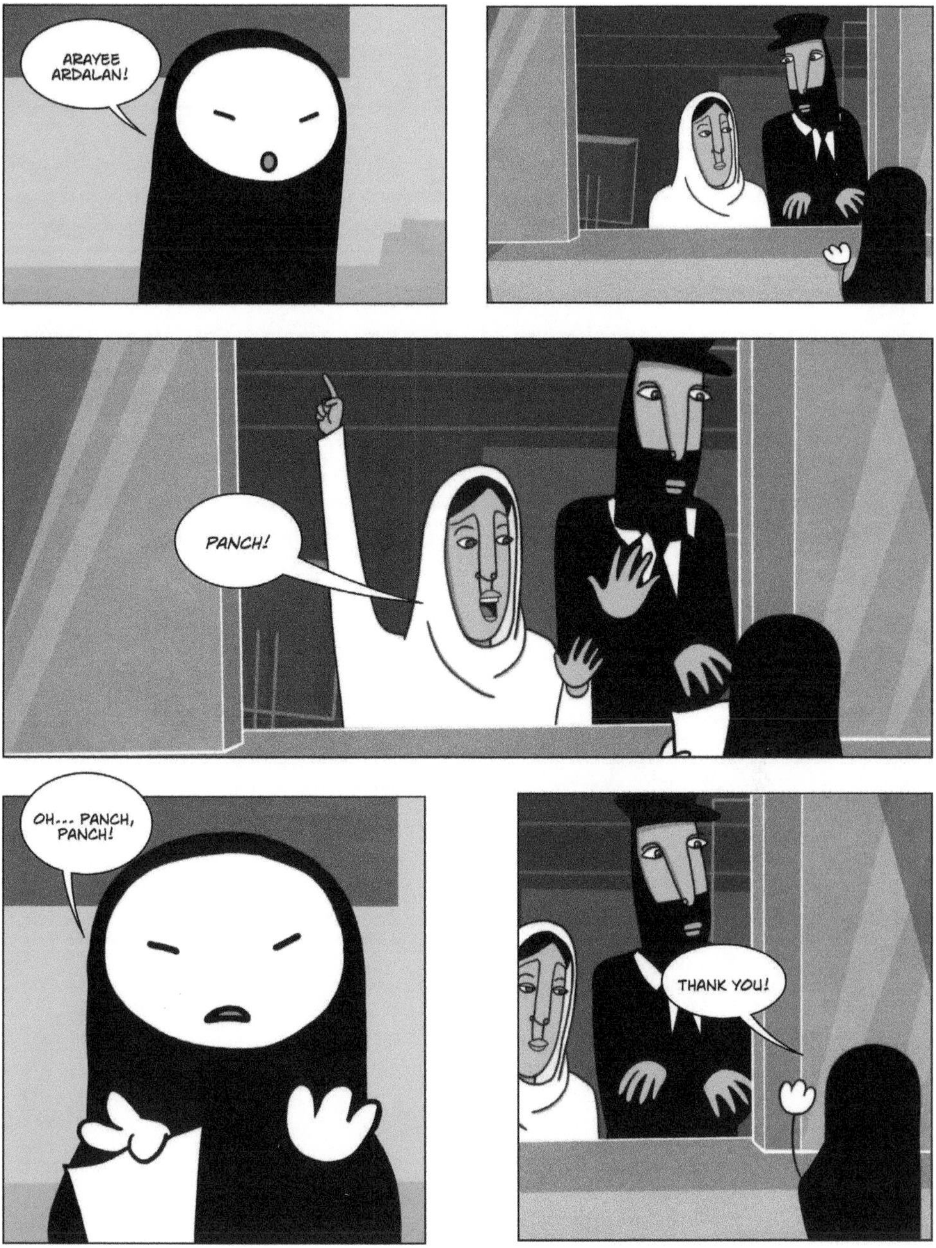
ARAYEE ARDALAN!
PANCH!
OH... PANCH, PANCH!
THANK YOU!

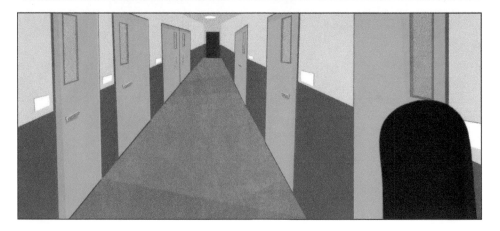

بیمارستان نمازی شیراز
اتاق ۱۰۵
بخش ۱
اتاق ۱۰۵
بخش ۱

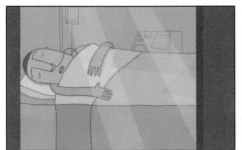

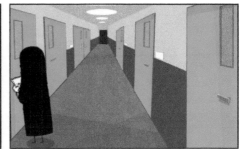

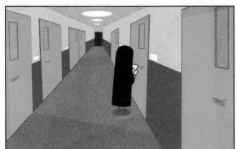

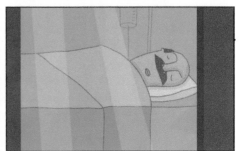

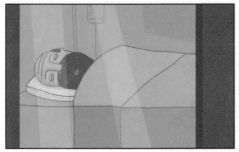

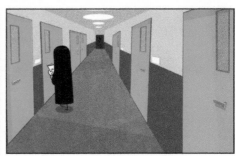

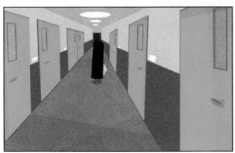

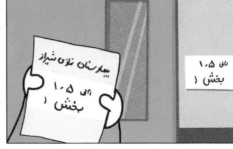

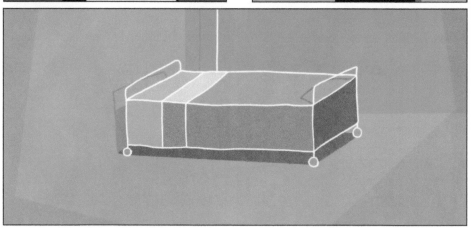

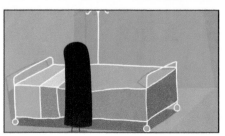

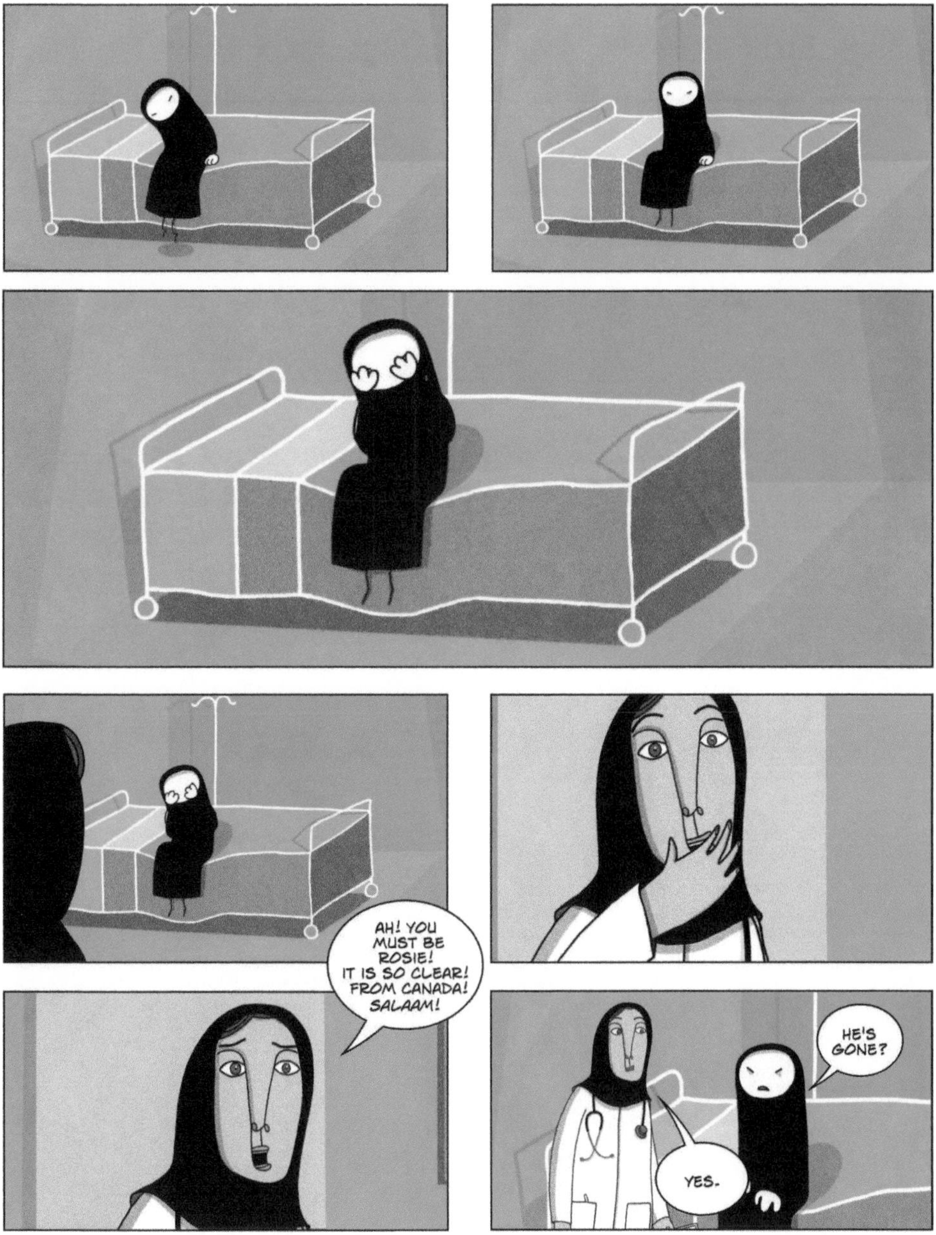
AH! YOU MUST BE ROSIE! IT IS SO CLEAR! FROM CANADA! SALAAM!
HE'S GONE?
YES.

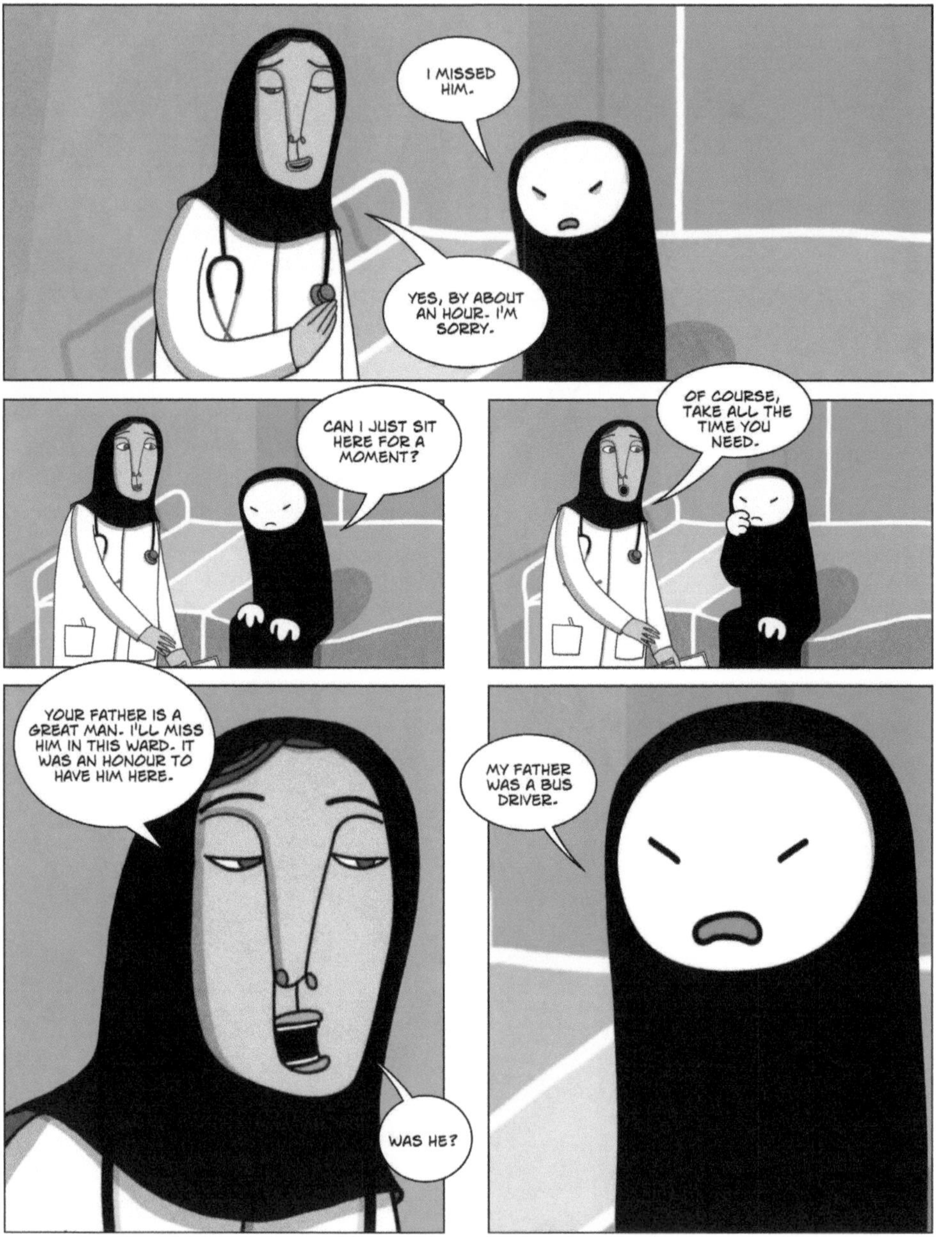
I MISSED HIM.
YES, BY ABOUT AN HOUR. I'M SORRY.
CAN I JUST SIT HERE FOR A MOMENT?
OF COURSE, TAKE ALL THE TIME YOU NEED.
YOUR FATHER IS A GREAT MAN. I'LL MISS HIM IN THIS WARD. IT WAS AN HONOUR TO HAVE HIM HERE.
MY FATHER WAS A BUS DRIVER.
WAS HE?

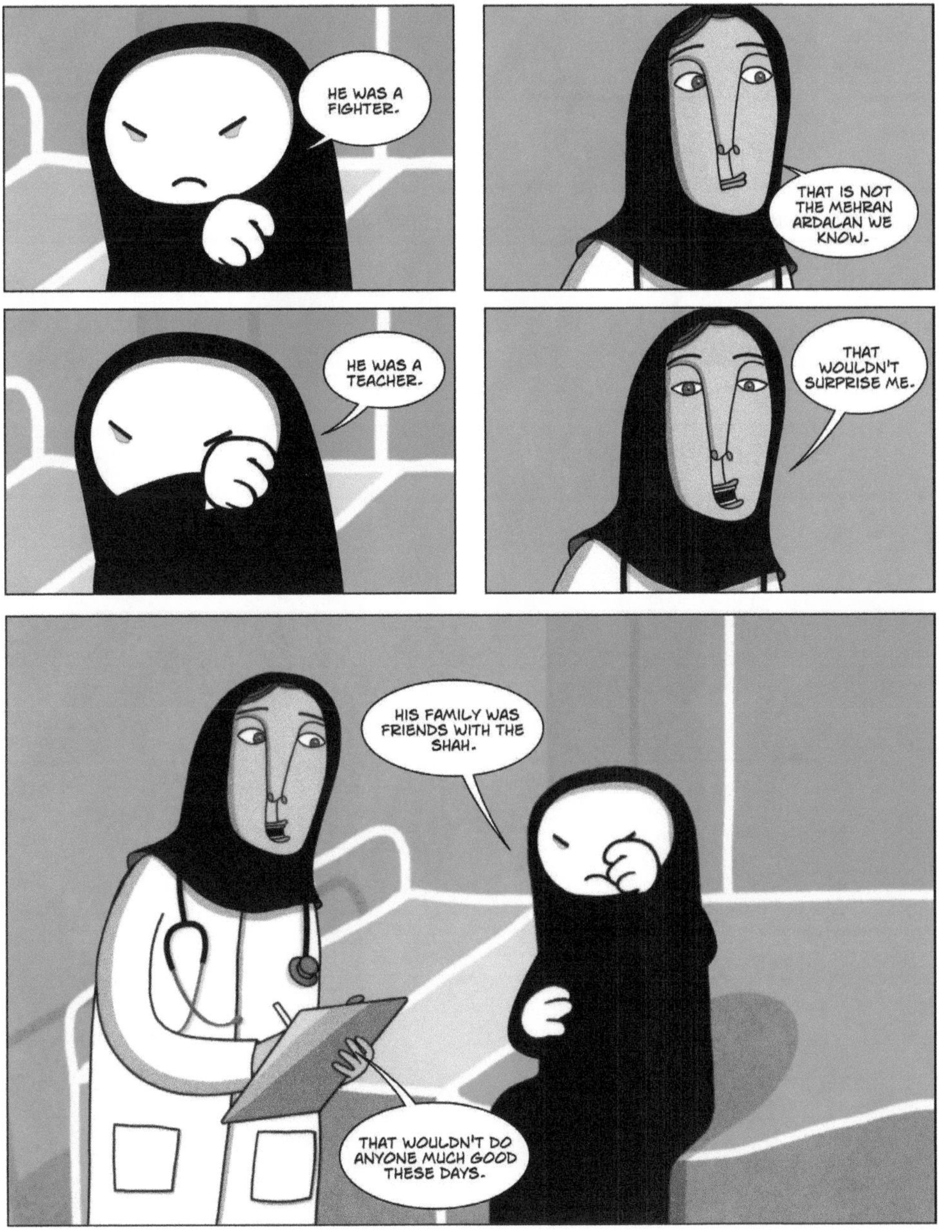
HE WAS A FIGHTER.
THAT IS NOT THE MEHRAN ARDALAN WE KNOW.
HE WAS A TEACHER.
THAT WOULDN'T SURPRISE ME.
HIS FAMILY WAS FRIENDS WITH THE SHAH.
THAT WOULDN'T DO ANYONE MUCH GOOD THESE DAYS.

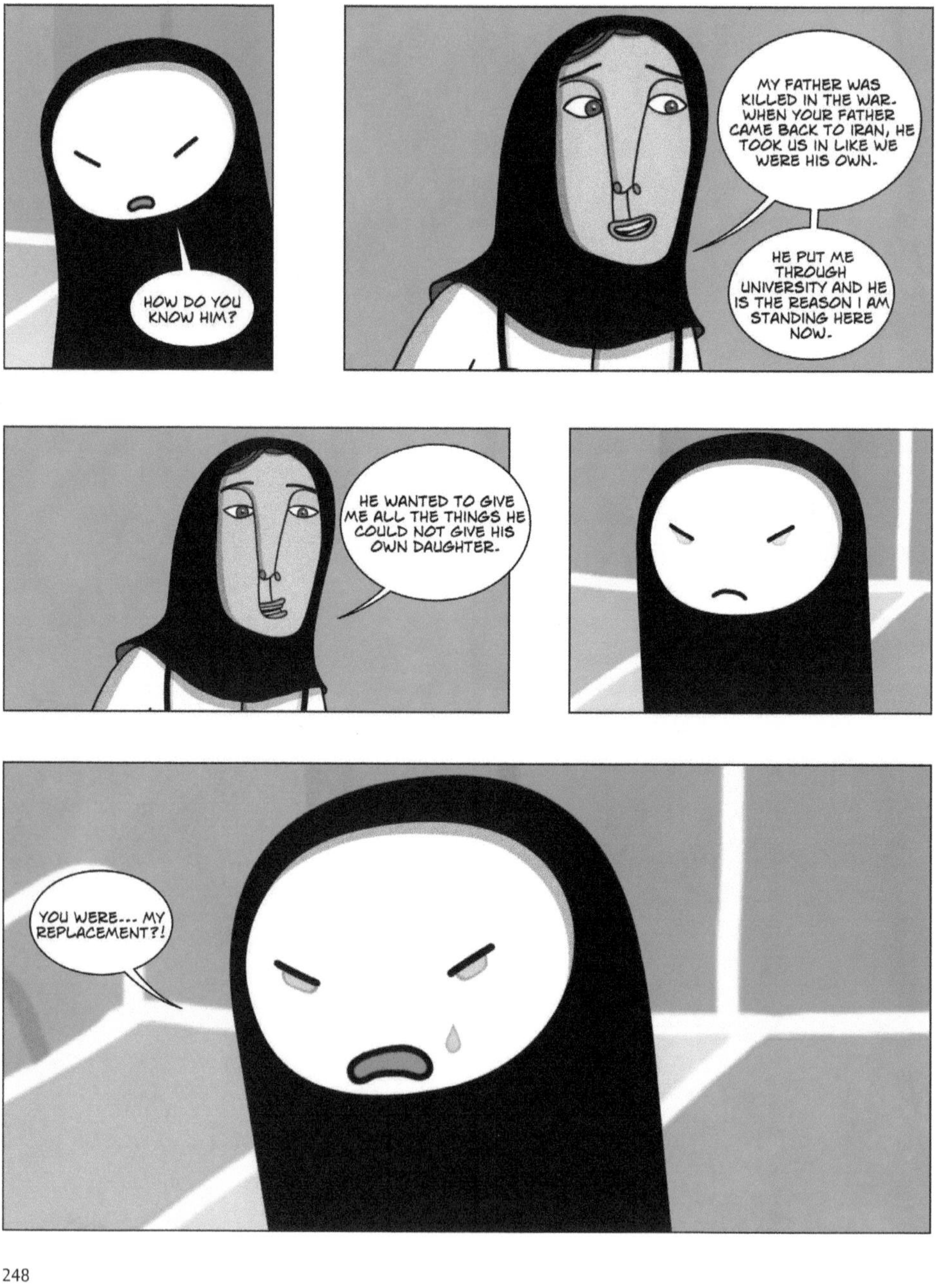
HOW DO YOU KNOW HIM?
MY FATHER WAS KILLED IN THE WAR. WHEN YOUR FATHER CAME BACK TO IRAN, HE TOOK US IN LIKE WE WERE HIS OWN.
HE PUT ME THROUGH UNIVERSITY AND HE IS THE REASON I AM STANDING HERE NOW.
HE WANTED TO GIVE ME ALL THE THINGS HE COULD NOT GIVE HIS OWN DAUGHTER.
YOU WERE... MY REPLACEMENT?!

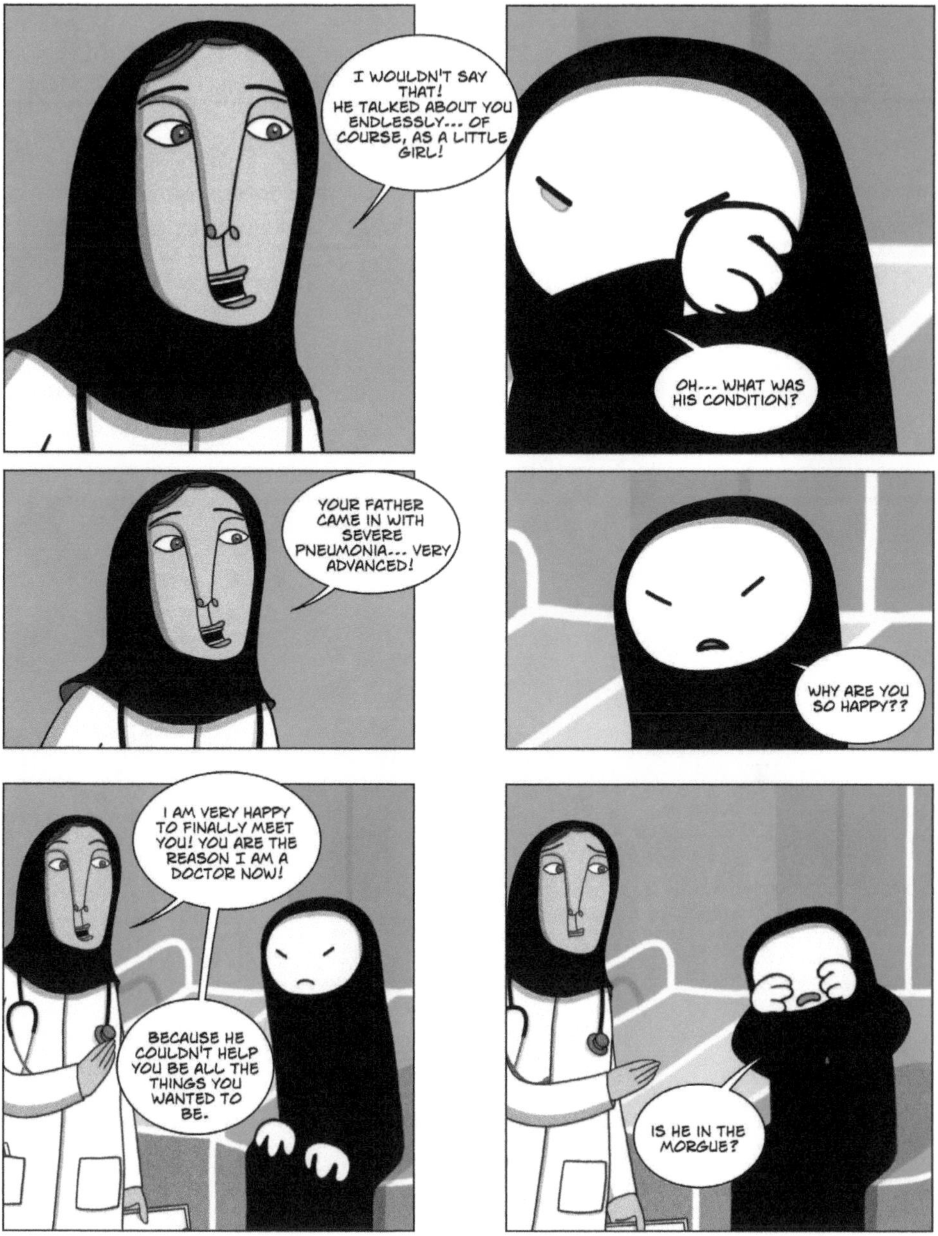
I WOULDN'T SAY THAT! HE TALKED ABOUT YOU ENDLESSLY... OF COURSE, AS A LITTLE GIRL!
OH... WHAT WAS HIS CONDITION?
YOUR FATHER CAME IN WITH SEVERE PNEUMONIA... VERY ADVANCED!
WHY ARE YOU SO HAPPY??
I AM VERY HAPPY TO FINALLY MEET YOU! YOU ARE THE REASON I AM A DOCTOR NOW!
BECAUSE HE COULDN'T HELP YOU BE ALL THE THINGS YOU WANTED TO BE.
IS HE IN THE MORGUE?

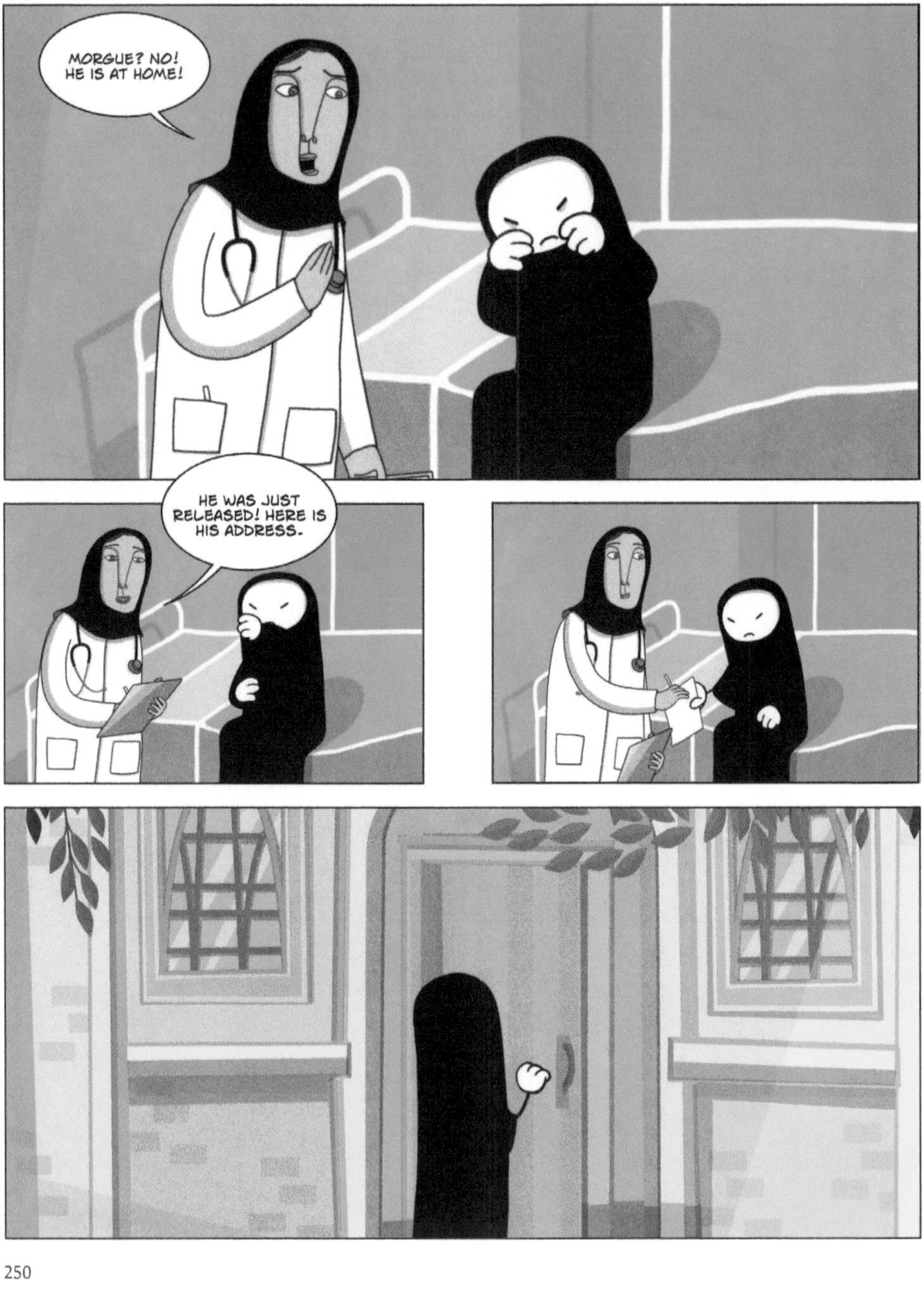
MORGUE? NO! HE IS AT HOME!
HE WAS JUST RELEASED! HERE IS HIS ADDRESS.

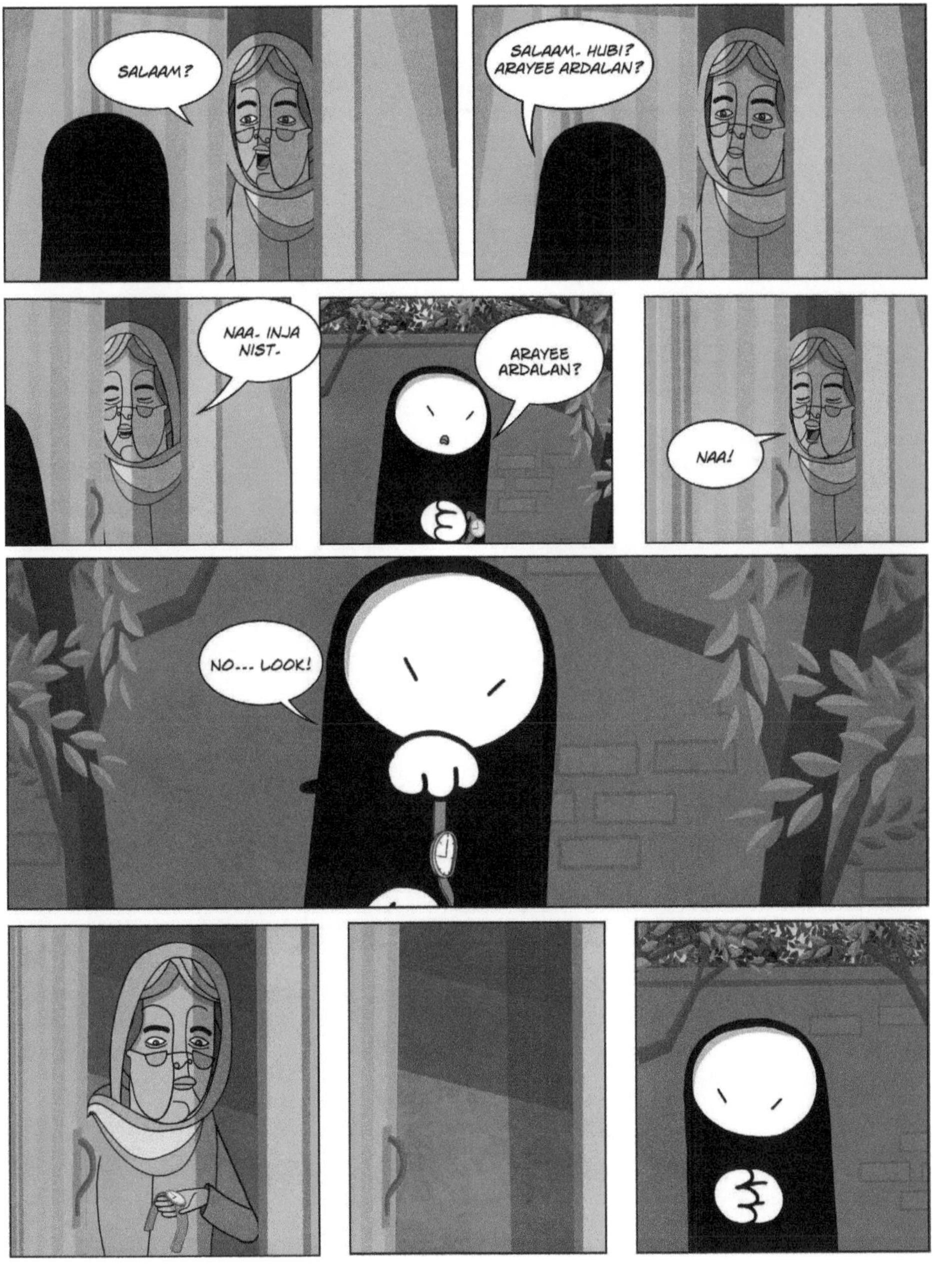
SALAAM?
SALAAM. HUBI? ARAYEE ARDALAN?
NAA. INJA NIST.
ARAYEE ARDALAN?
NAA!
NO... LOOK!

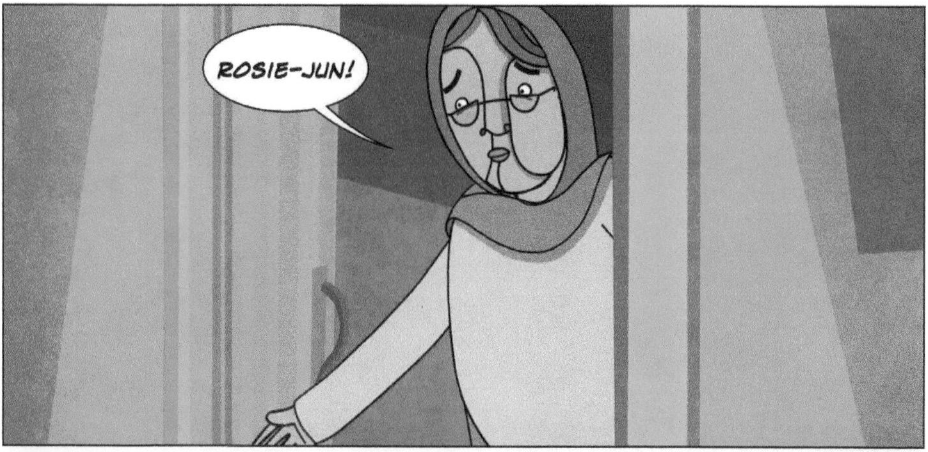
ROSIE-JUN!

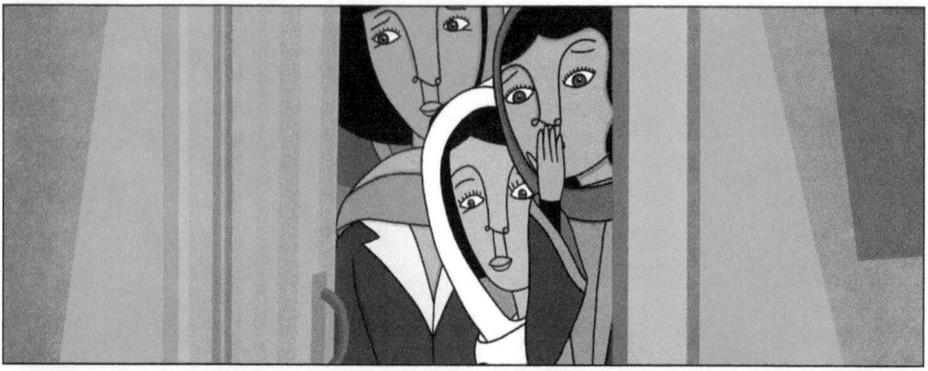

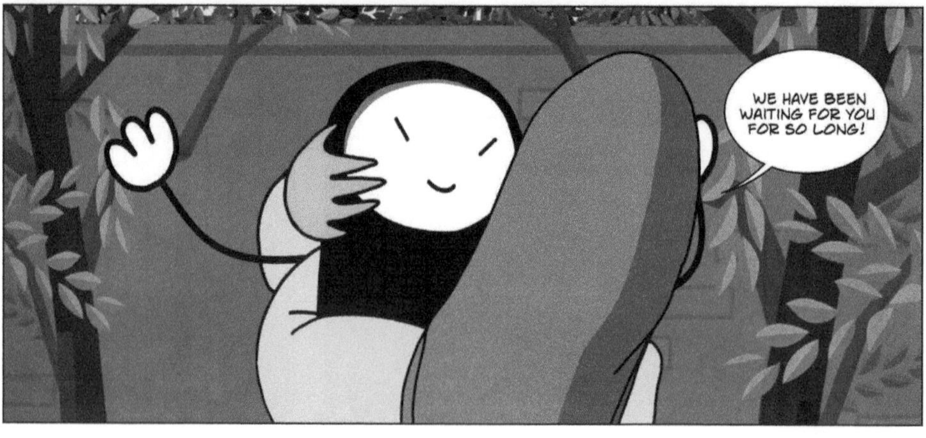
WE HAVE BEEN WAITING FOR YOU FOR SO LONG!

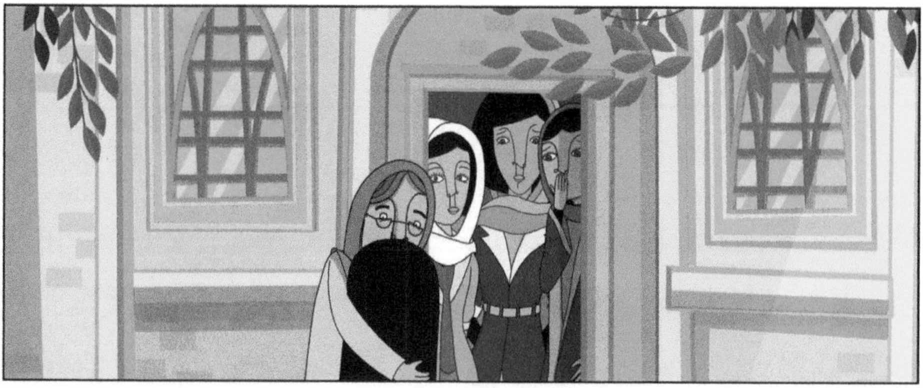

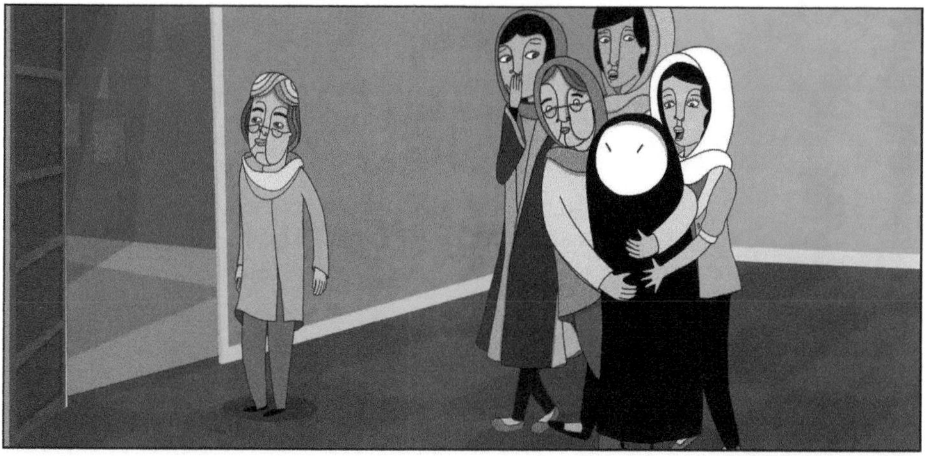

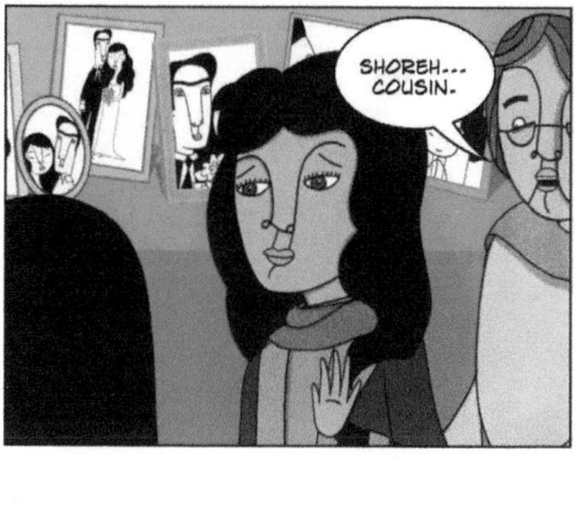
SHOREH...
COUSIN.

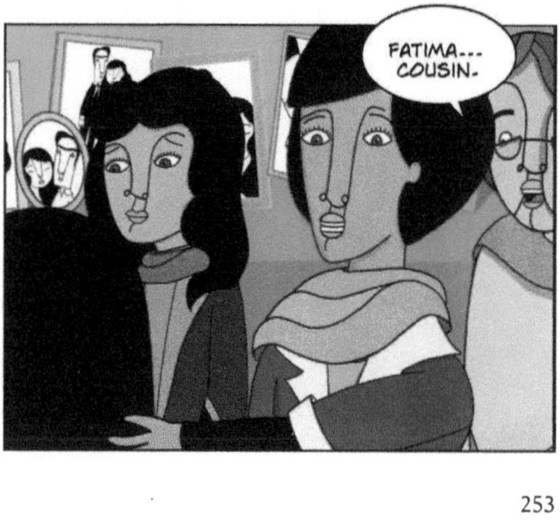
FATIMA...
COUSIN.

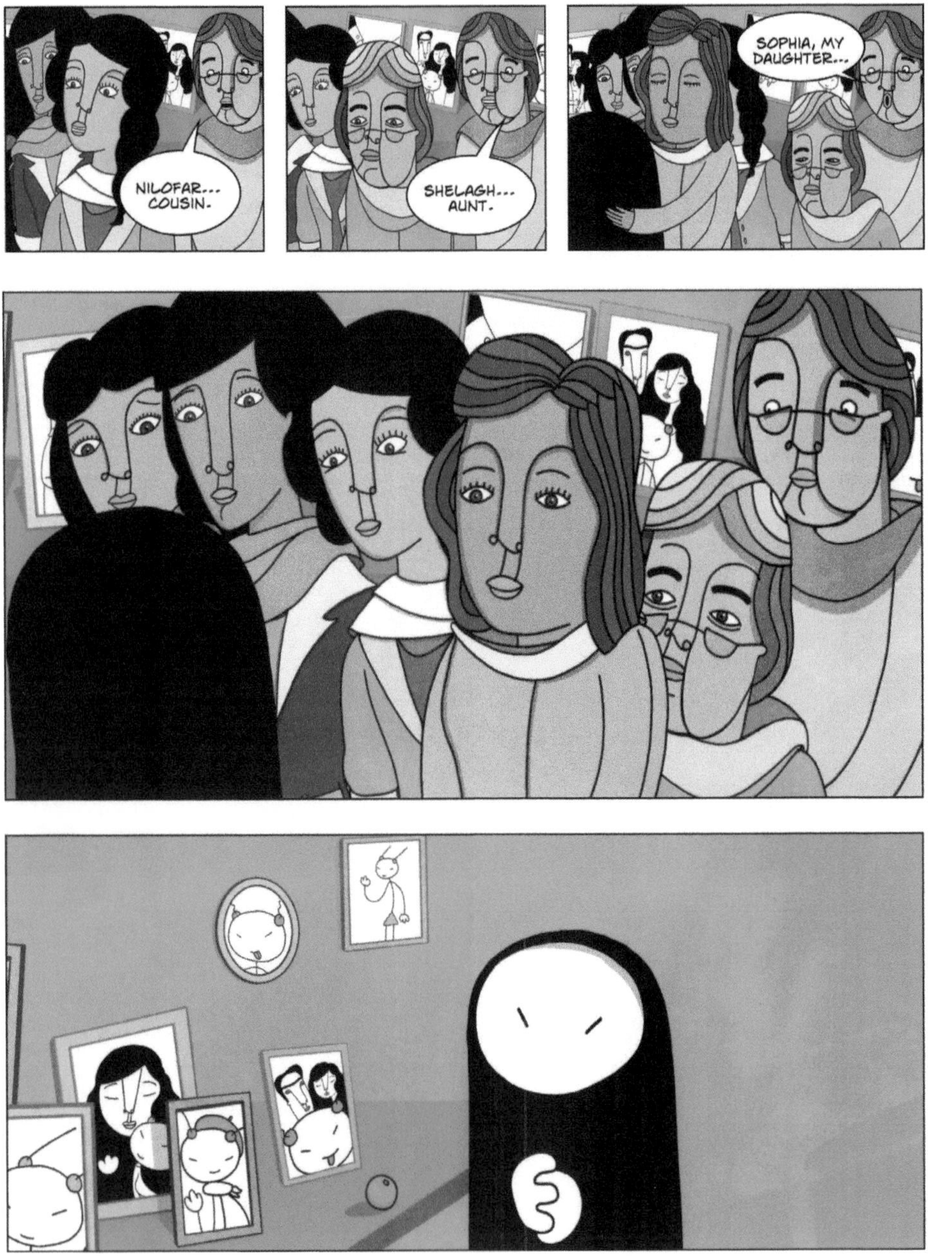
NILOFAR... COUSIN.
SHELAGH... AUNT.
SOPHIA, MY DAUGHTER...

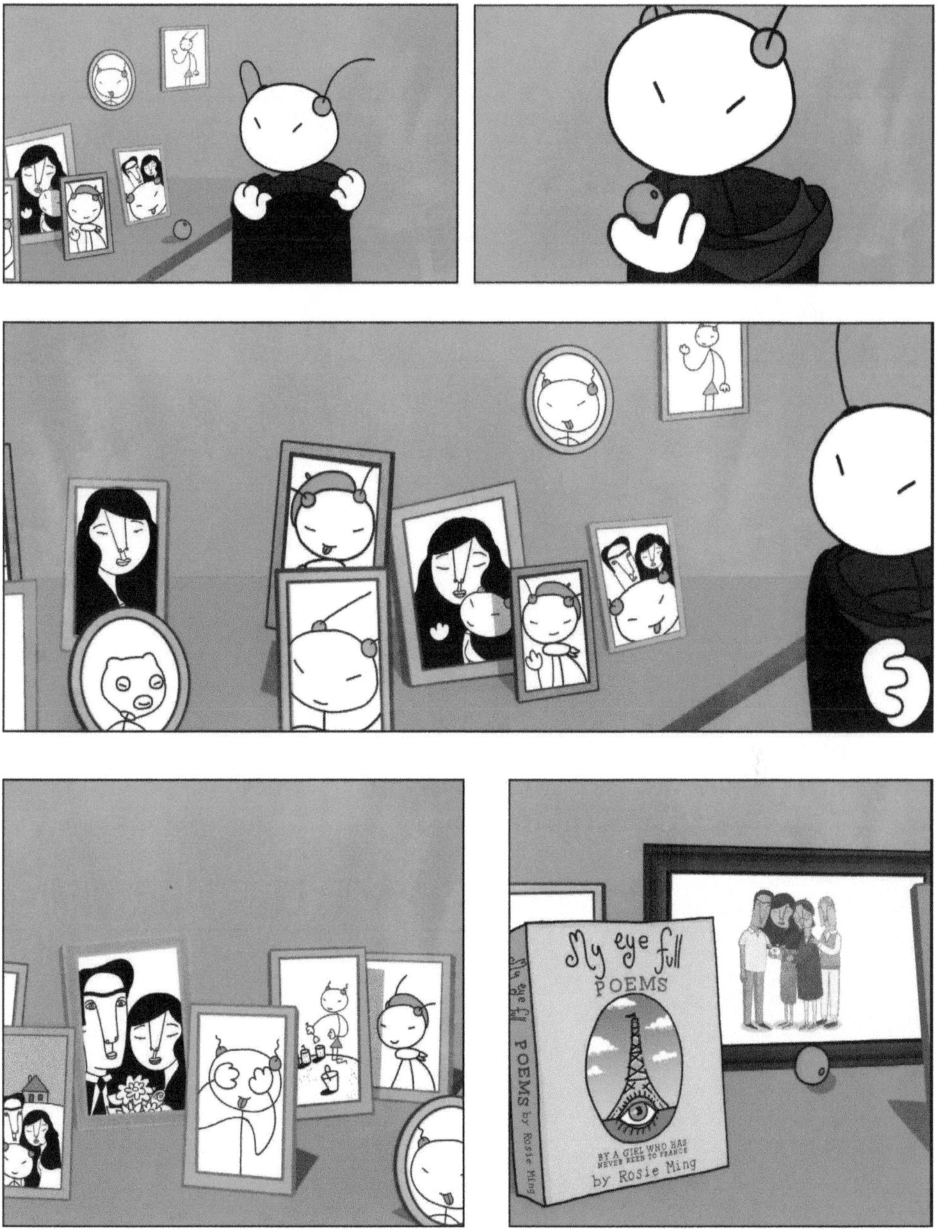
My eye full
POEMS
BY A GIRL WHO HAS NEVER BEEN TO FRANCE
by Rosie Ming
My eye full POEMS by Rosie Ming

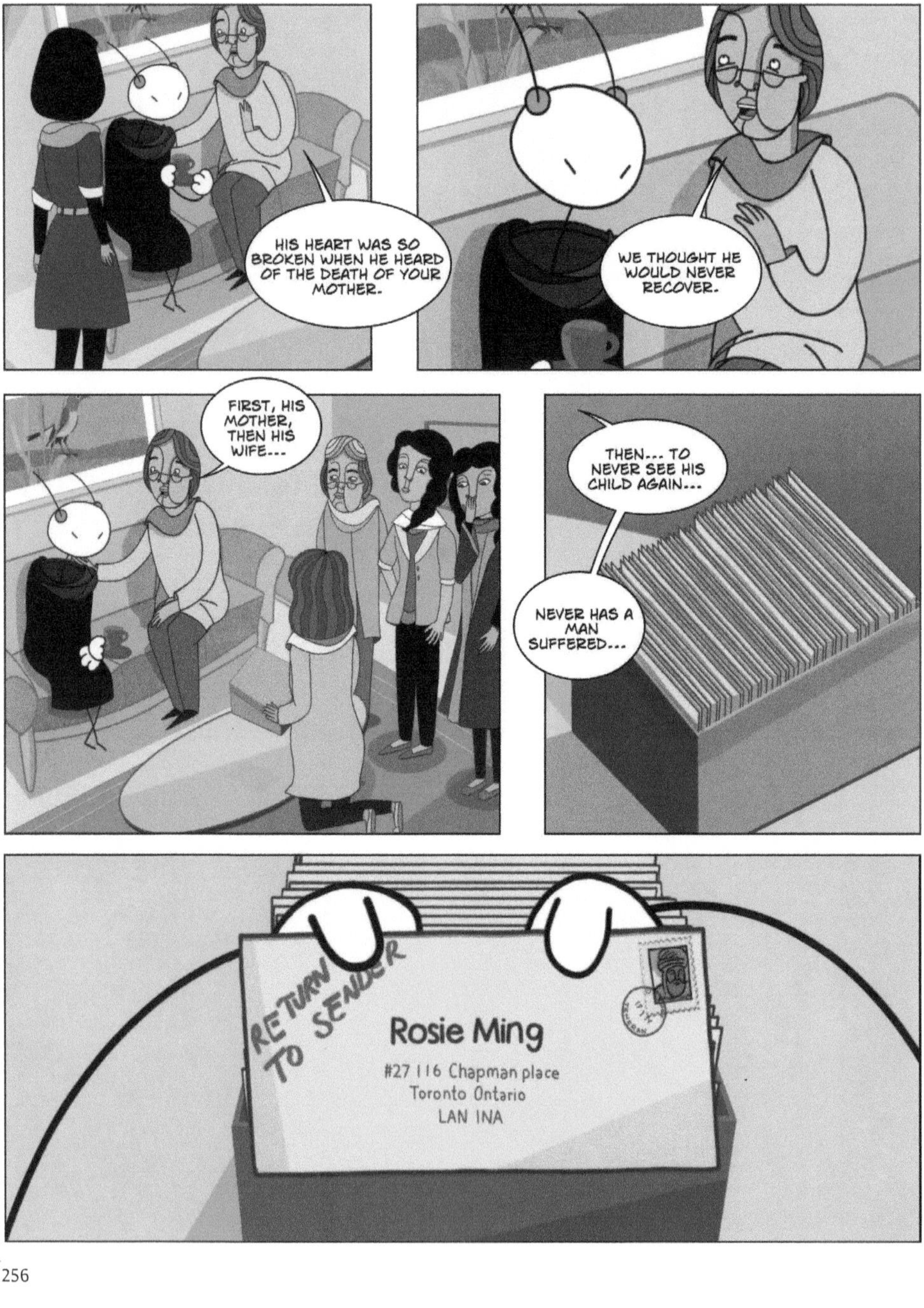
HIS HEART WAS SO BROKEN WHEN HE HEARD OF THE DEATH OF YOUR MOTHER.
WE THOUGHT HE WOULD NEVER RECOVER.
FIRST, HIS MOTHER, THEN HIS WIFE...
THEN... TO NEVER SEE HIS CHILD AGAIN...
NEVER HAS A MAN SUFFERED...
RETURN TO SENDER
Rosie Ming
#27 116 Chapman place
Toronto Ontario
LAN INA

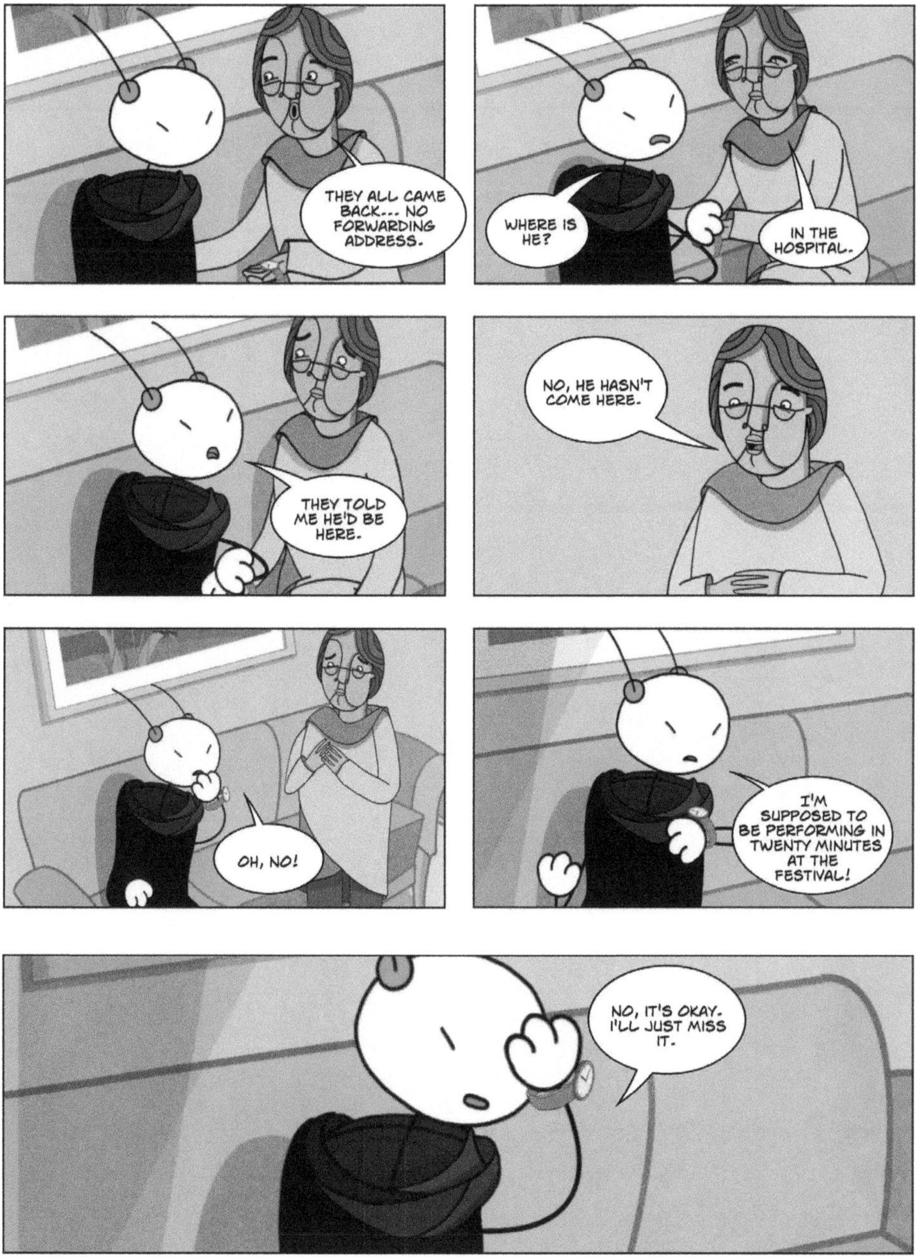
THEY ALL CAME BACK... NO FORWARDING ADDRESS.
WHERE IS HE?
IN THE HOSPITAL.
THEY TOLD ME HE'D BE HERE.
NO, HE HASN'T COME HERE.
OH, NO!
I'M SUPPOSED TO BE PERFORMING IN TWENTY MINUTES AT THE FESTIVAL!
NO, IT'S OKAY. I'LL JUST MISS IT.

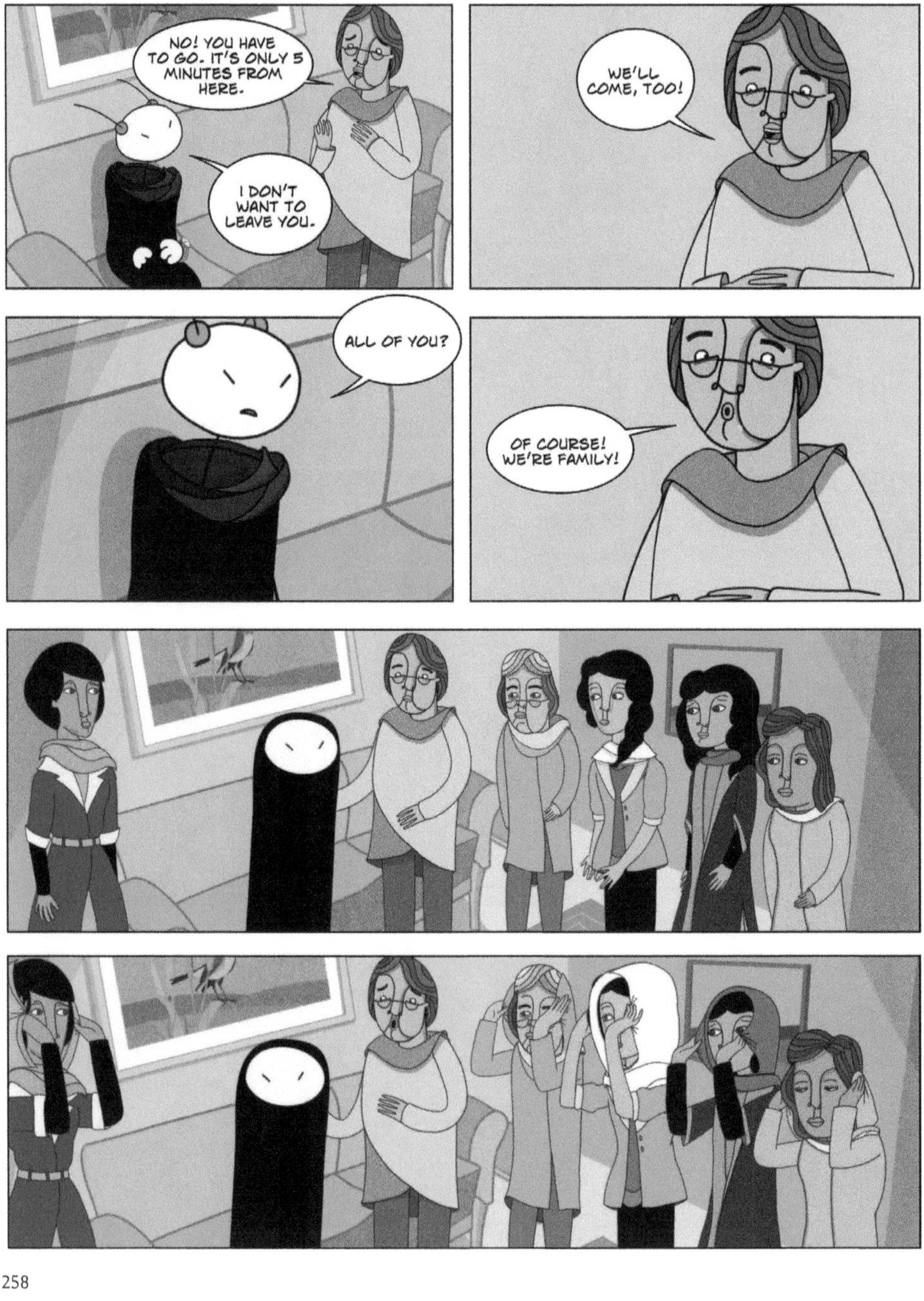
NO! YOU HAVE TO GO. IT'S ONLY 5 MINUTES FROM HERE.
I DON'T WANT TO LEAVE YOU.
WE'LL COME, TOO!
ALL OF YOU?
OF COURSE! WE'RE FAMILY!

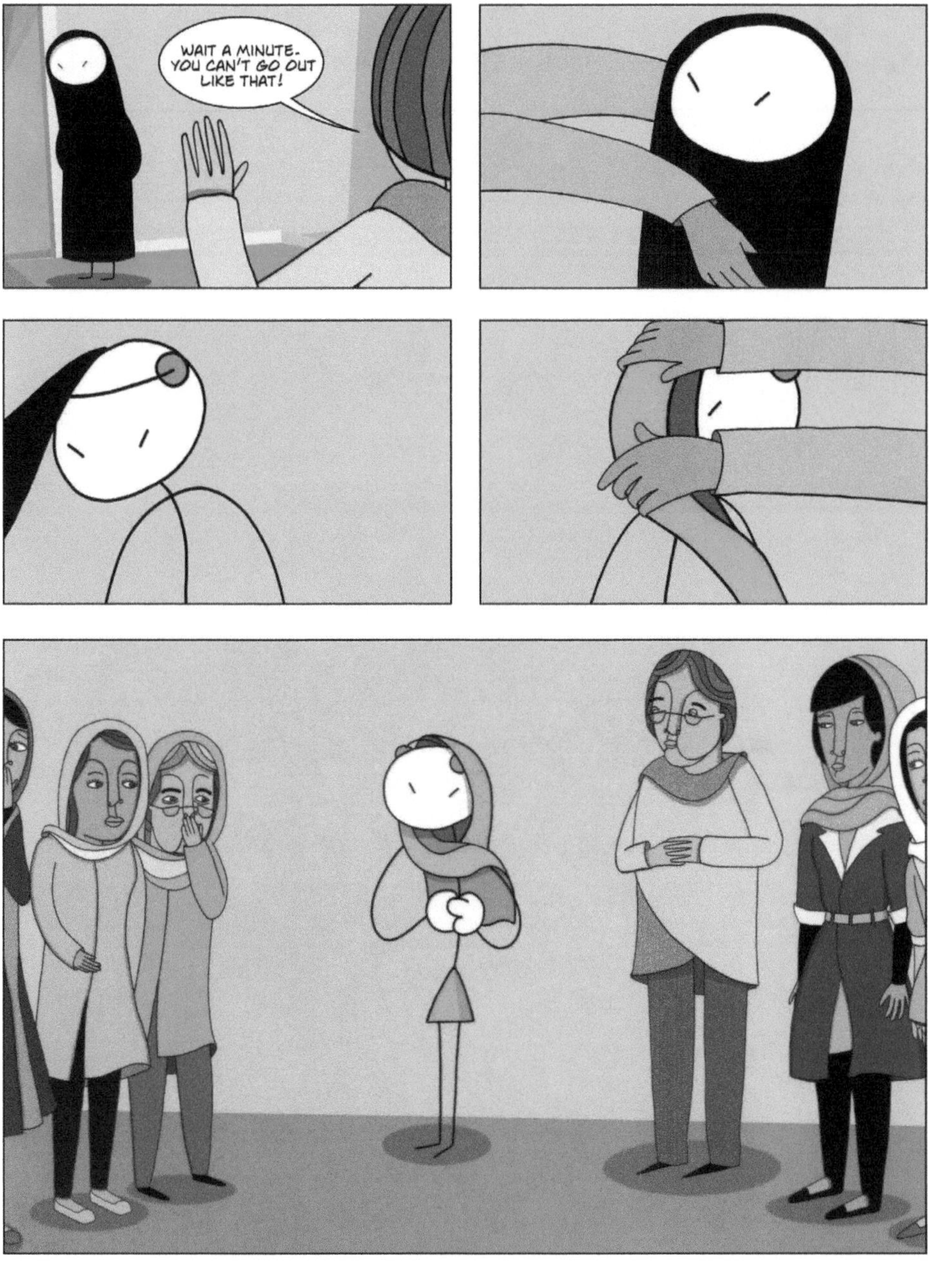
WAIT A MINUTE. YOU CAN'T GO OUT LIKE THAT!

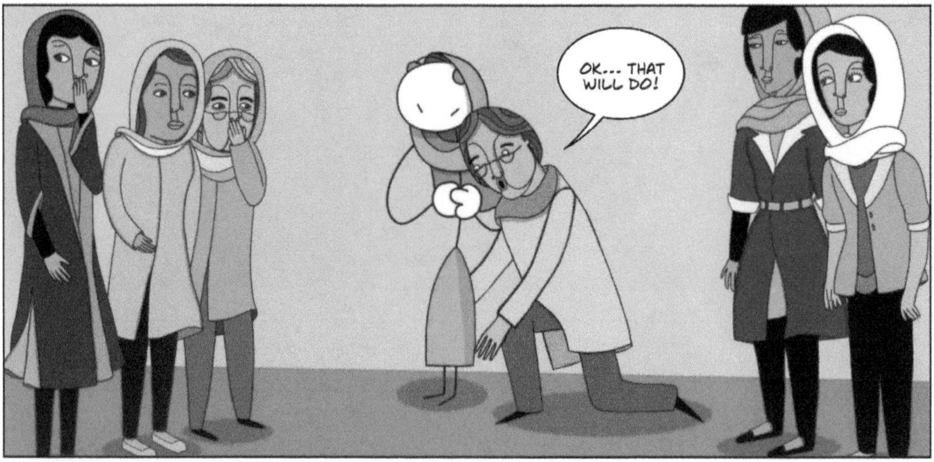
OK... THAT WILL DO!

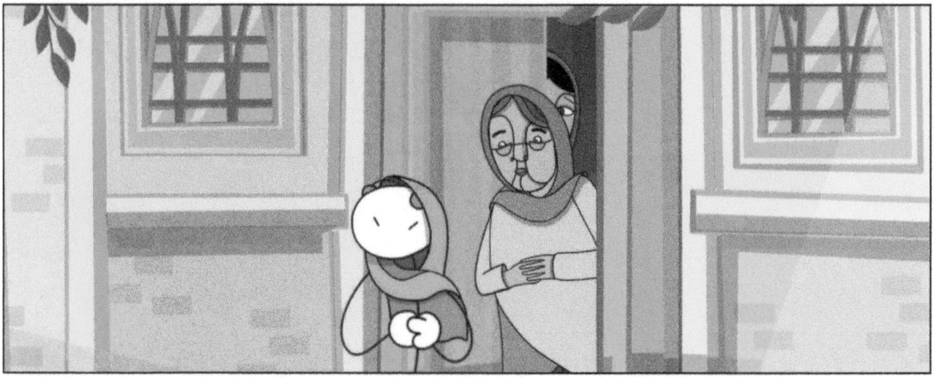

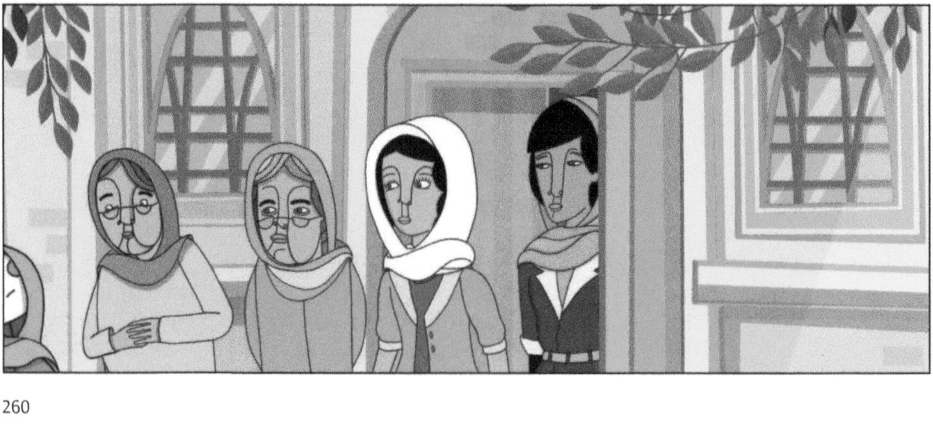

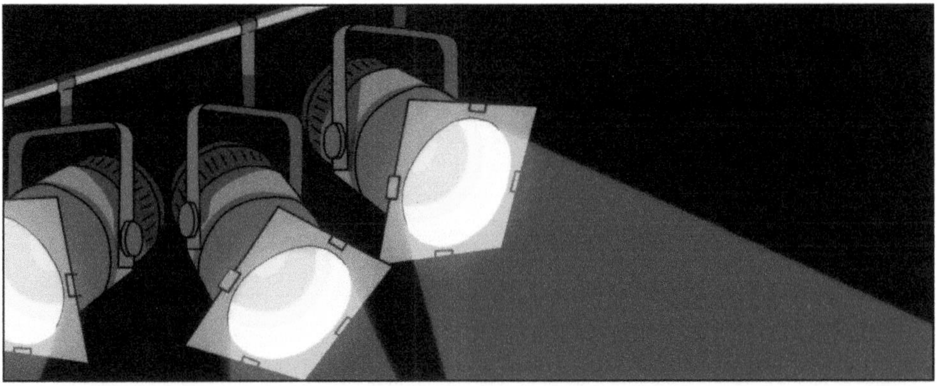

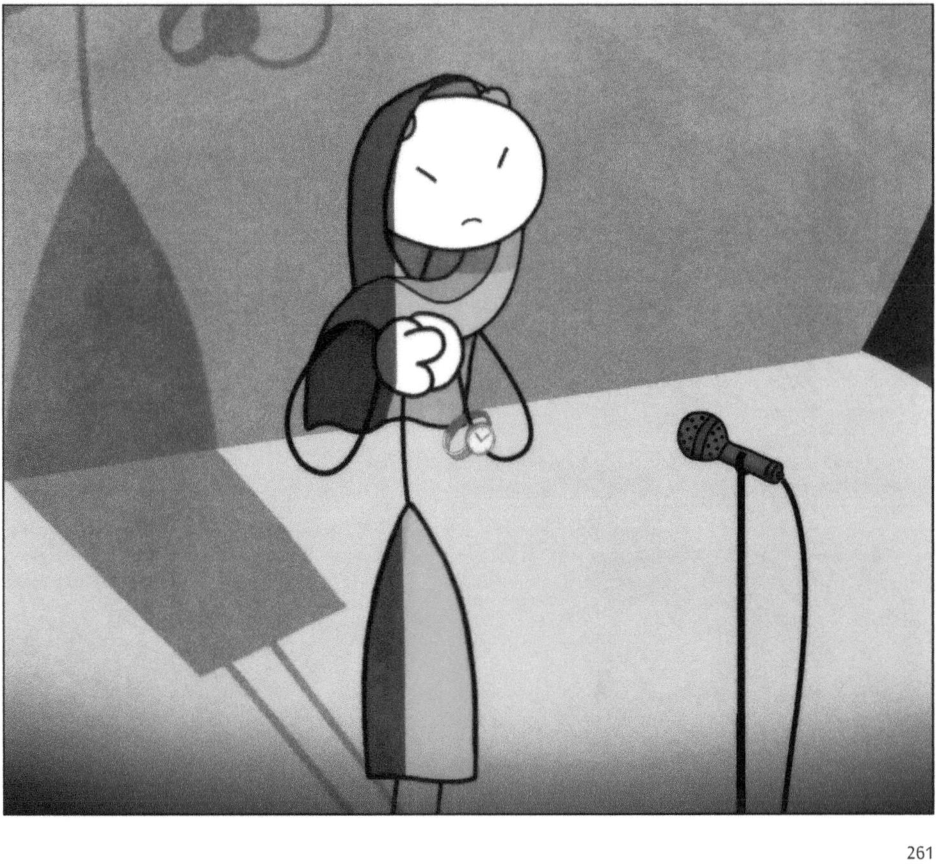

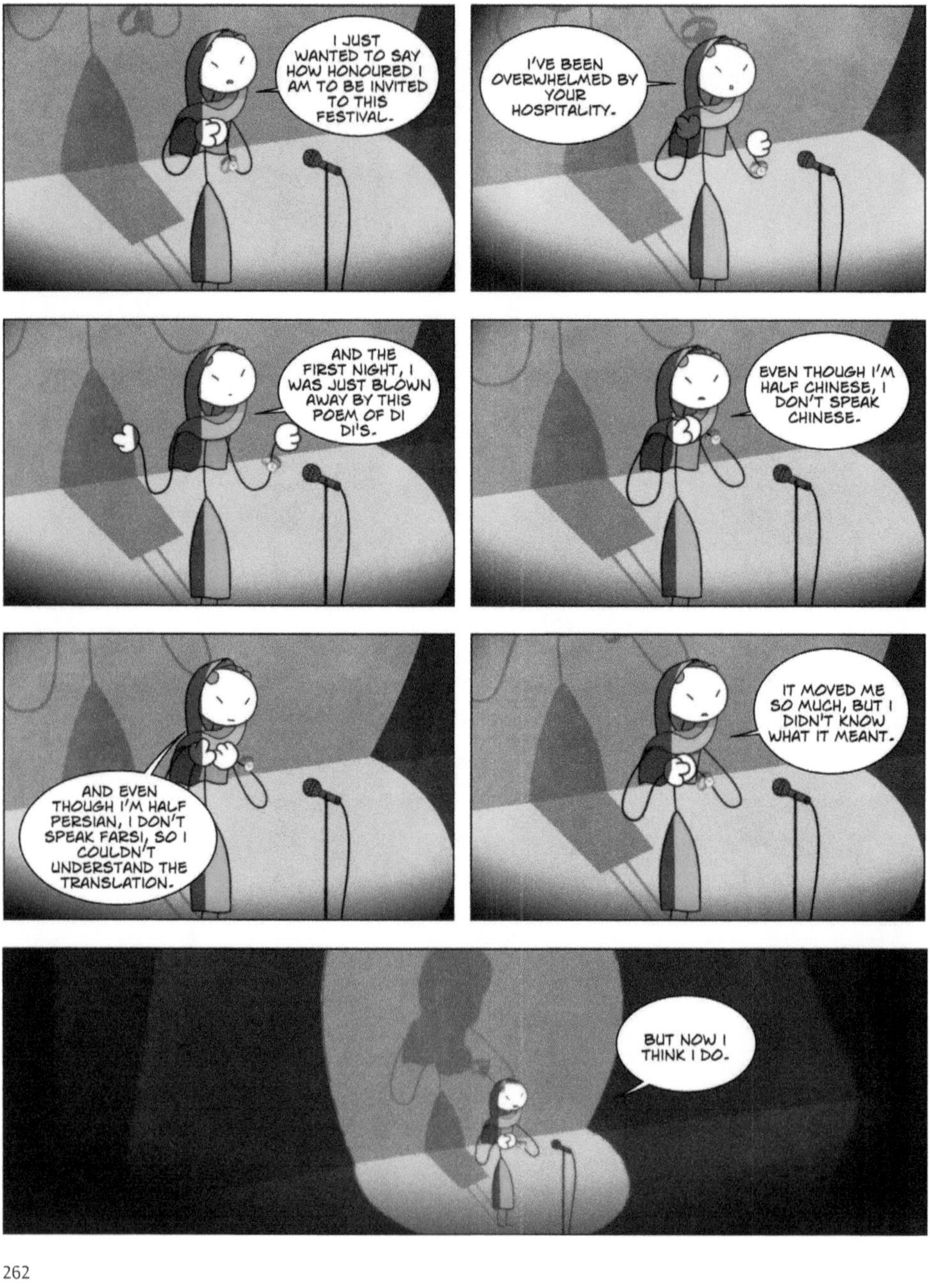
I JUST WANTED TO SAY HOW HONOURED I AM TO BE INVITED TO THIS FESTIVAL.
I'VE BEEN OVERWHELMED BY YOUR HOSPITALITY.
AND THE FIRST NIGHT, I WAS JUST BLOWN AWAY BY THIS POEM OF DI DI'S.
EVEN THOUGH I'M HALF CHINESE, I DON'T SPEAK CHINESE.
AND EVEN THOUGH I'M HALF PERSIAN, I DON'T SPEAK FARSI, SO I COULDN'T UNDERSTAND THE TRANSLATION.
IT MOVED ME SO MUCH, BUT I DIDN'T KNOW WHAT IT MEANT.
BUT NOW I THINK I DO.

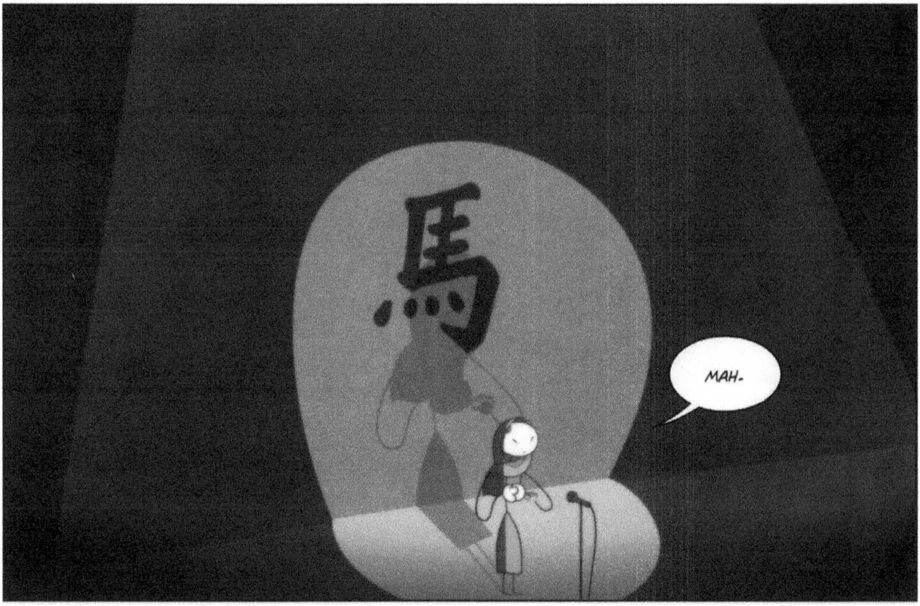
馬
MAH.

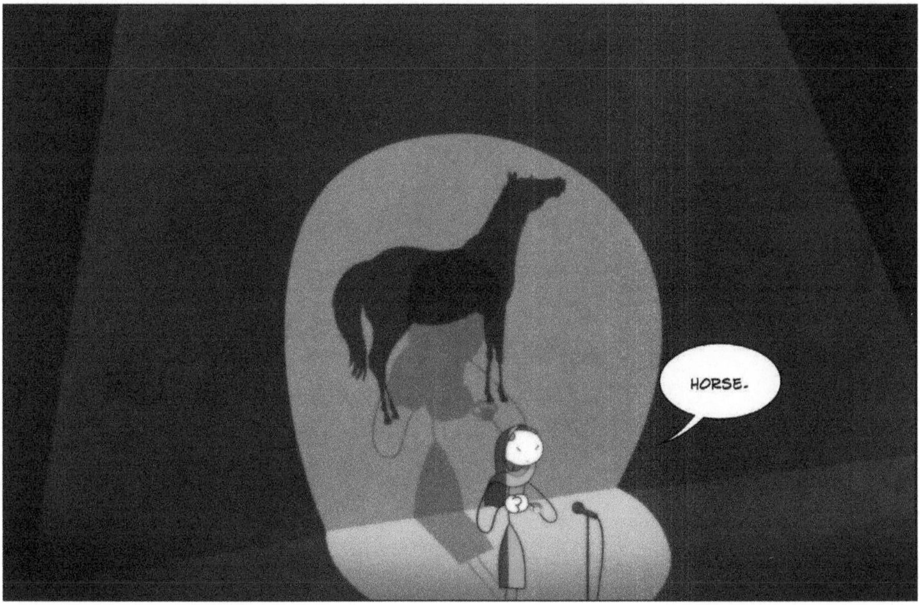
HORSE.

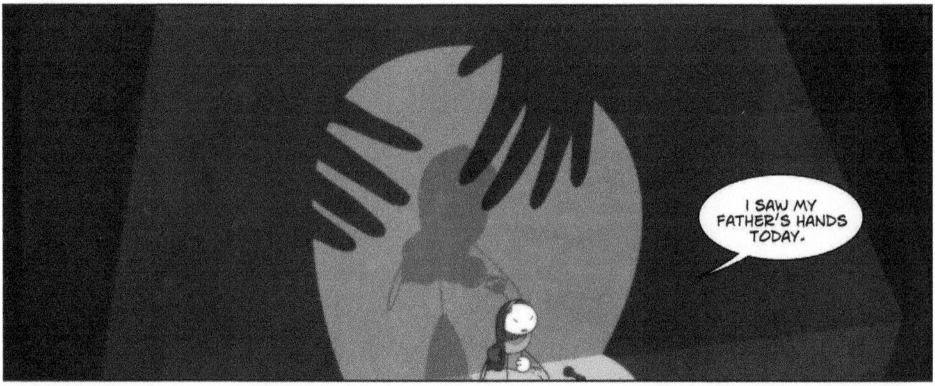
I SAW MY FATHER'S HANDS TODAY.

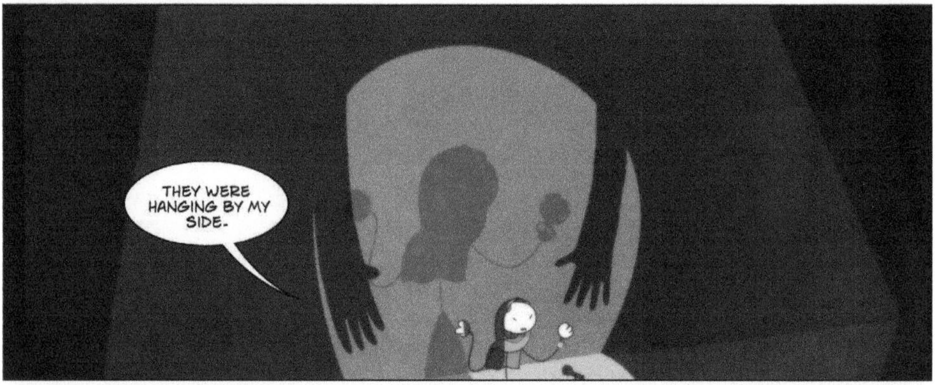
THEY WERE HANGING BY MY SIDE.

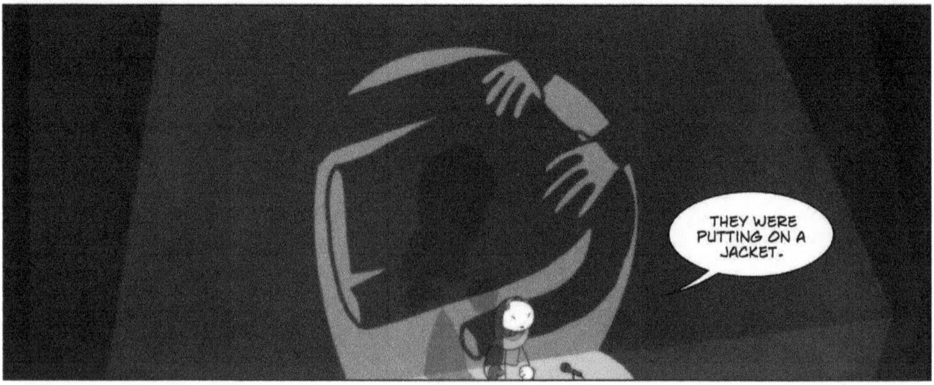
THEY WERE PUTTING ON A JACKET.

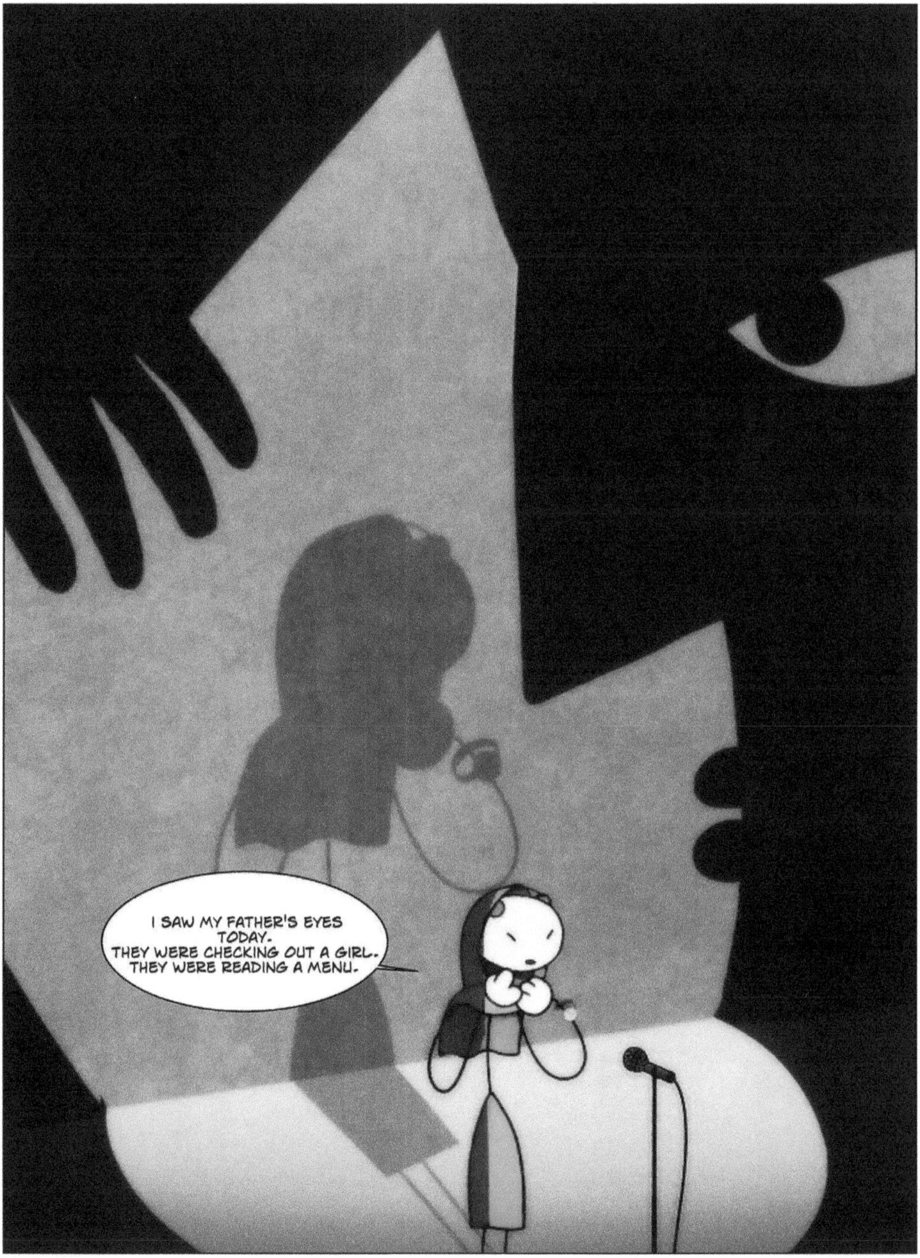
I SAW MY FATHER'S EYES TODAY. THEY WERE CHECKING OUT A GIRL. THEY WERE READING A MENU.

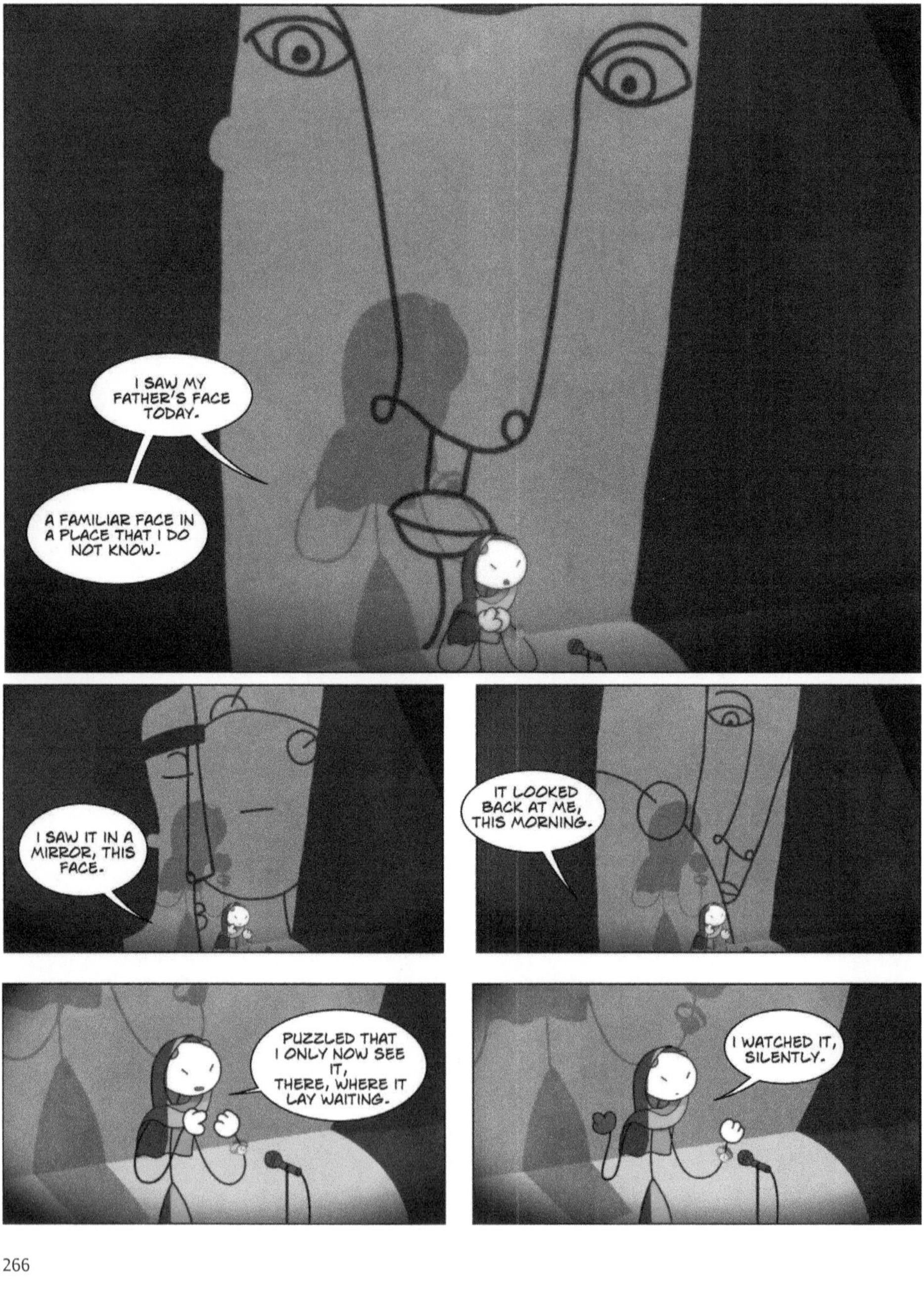
I SAW MY FATHER'S FACE TODAY.
A FAMILIAR FACE IN A PLACE THAT I DO NOT KNOW.
I SAW IT IN A MIRROR, THIS FACE.
IT LOOKED BACK AT ME, THIS MORNING.
PUZZLED THAT I ONLY NOW SEE IT, THERE, WHERE IT LAY WAITING.
I WATCHED IT, SILENTLY.

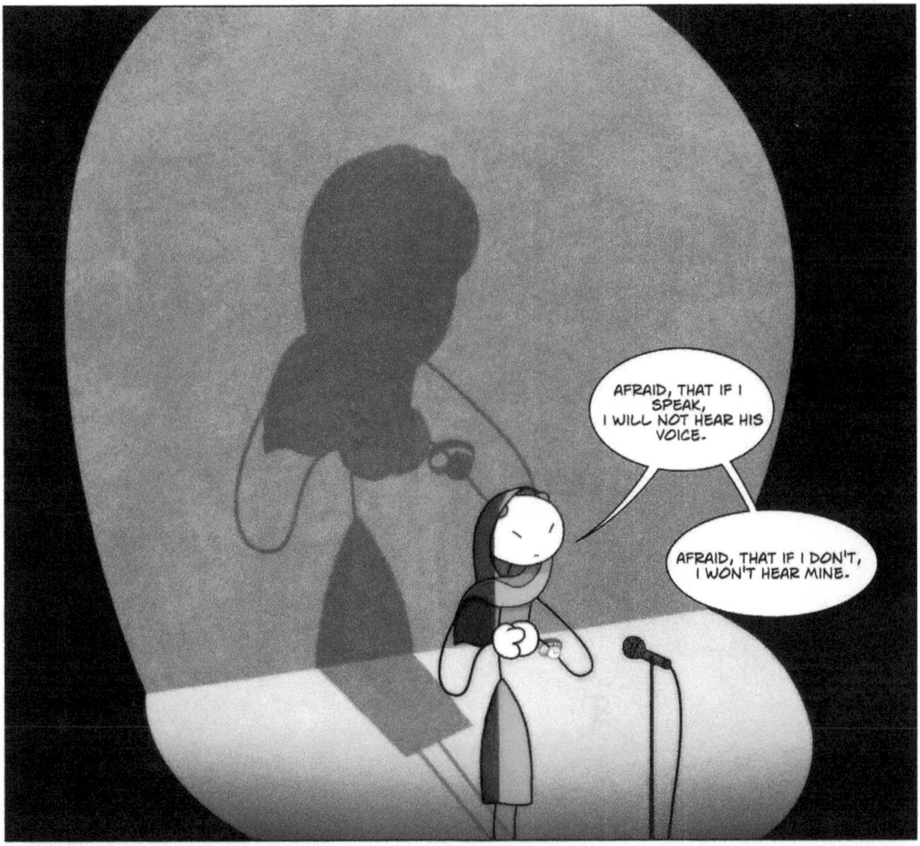
AFRAID, THAT IF I SPEAK, I WILL NOT HEAR HIS VOICE.
AFRAID, THAT IF I DON'T, I WON'T HEAR MINE.

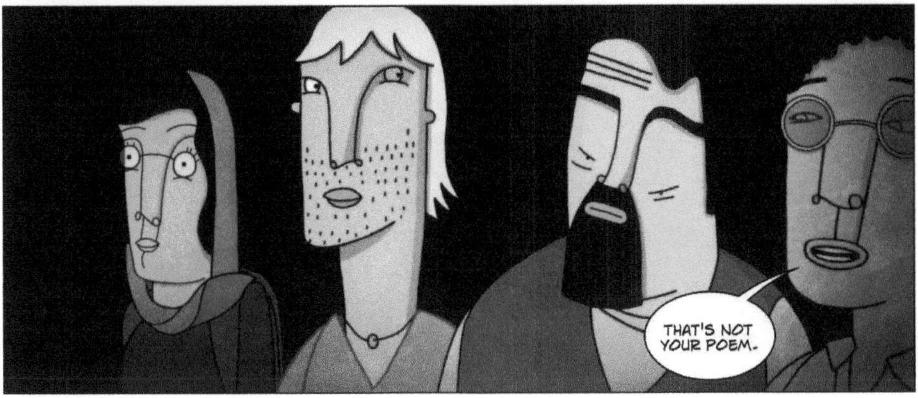
THAT'S NOT YOUR POEM.

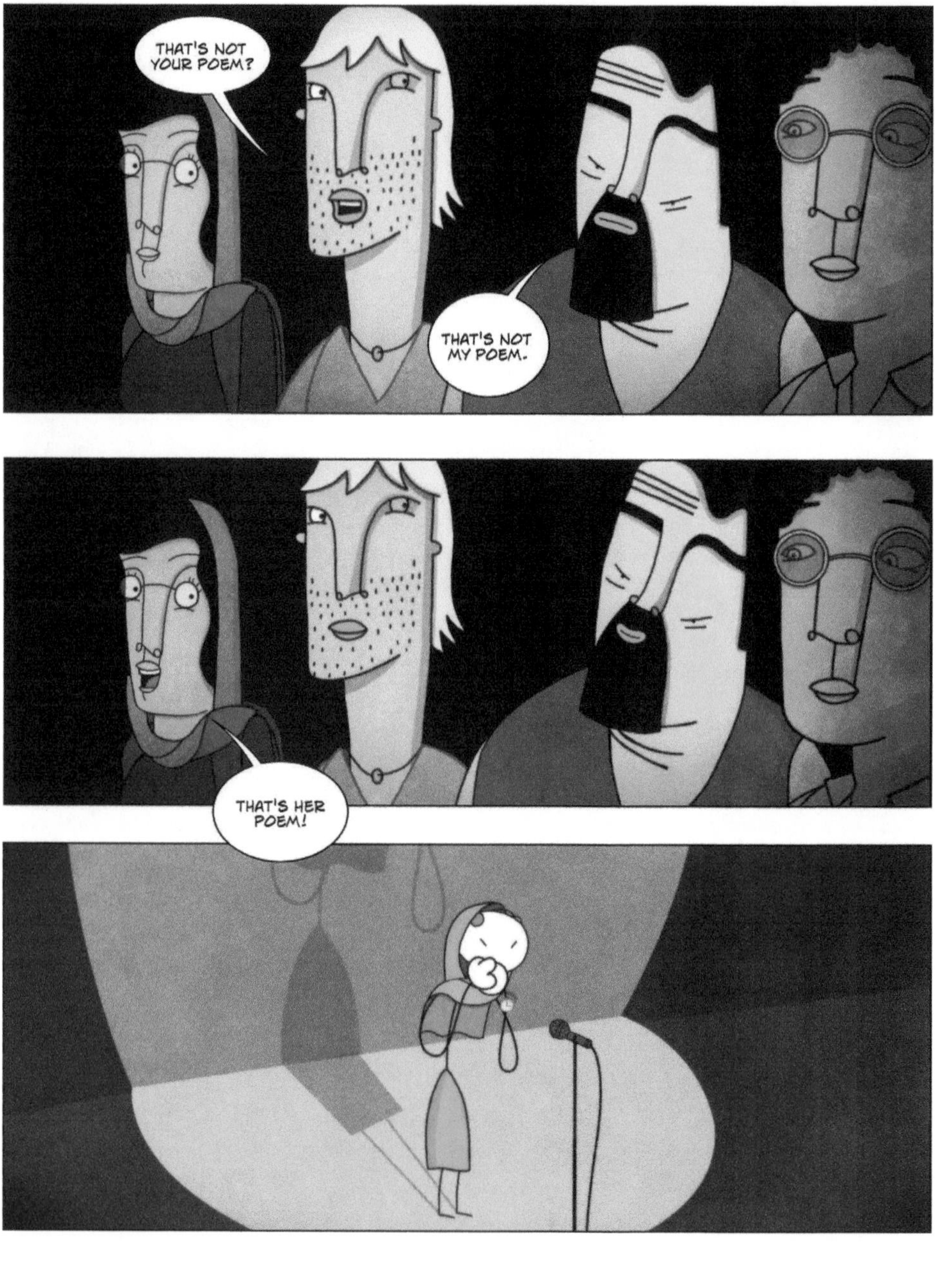
THAT'S NOT YOUR POEM?
THAT'S NOT MY POEM.
THAT'S HER POEM!

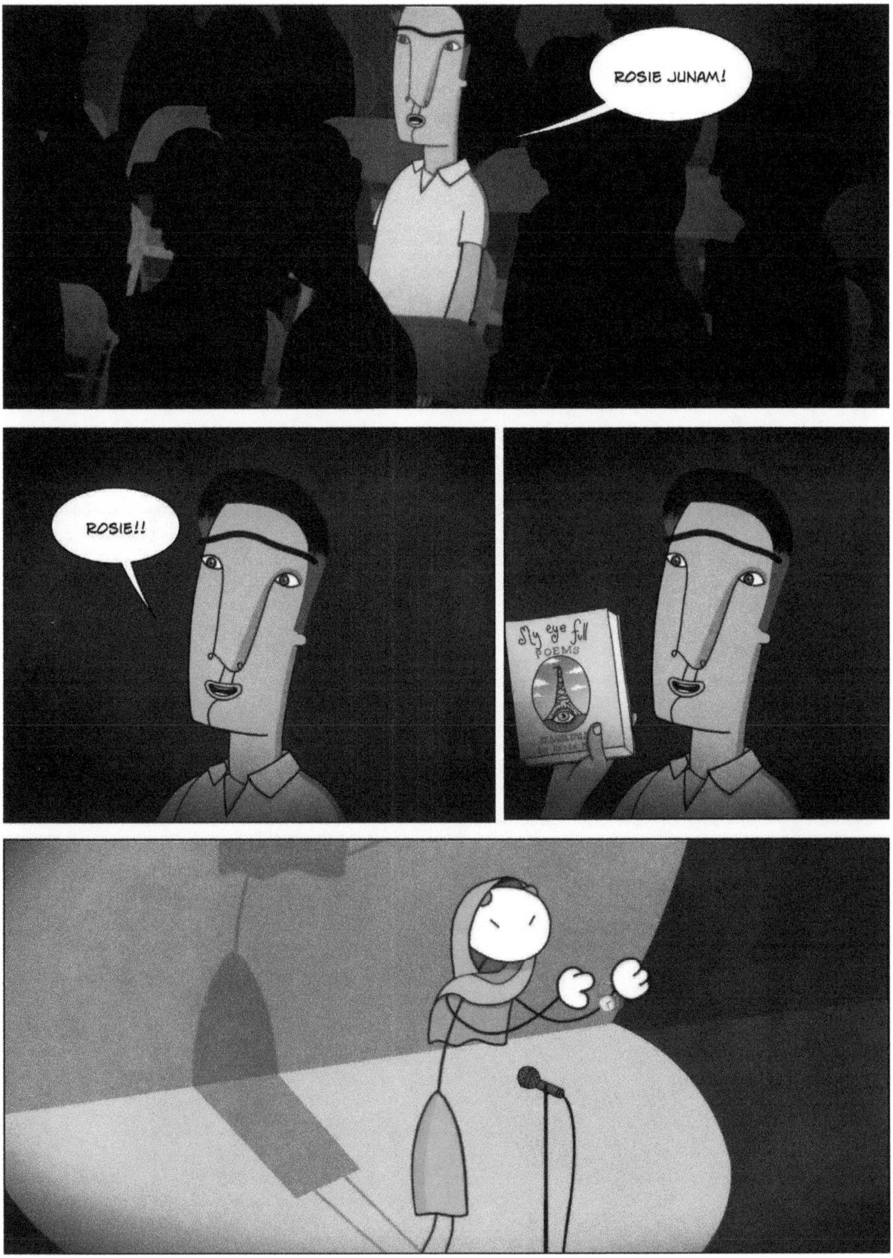
ROSIE JUNAM!
ROSIE!!
My eye full
POEMS

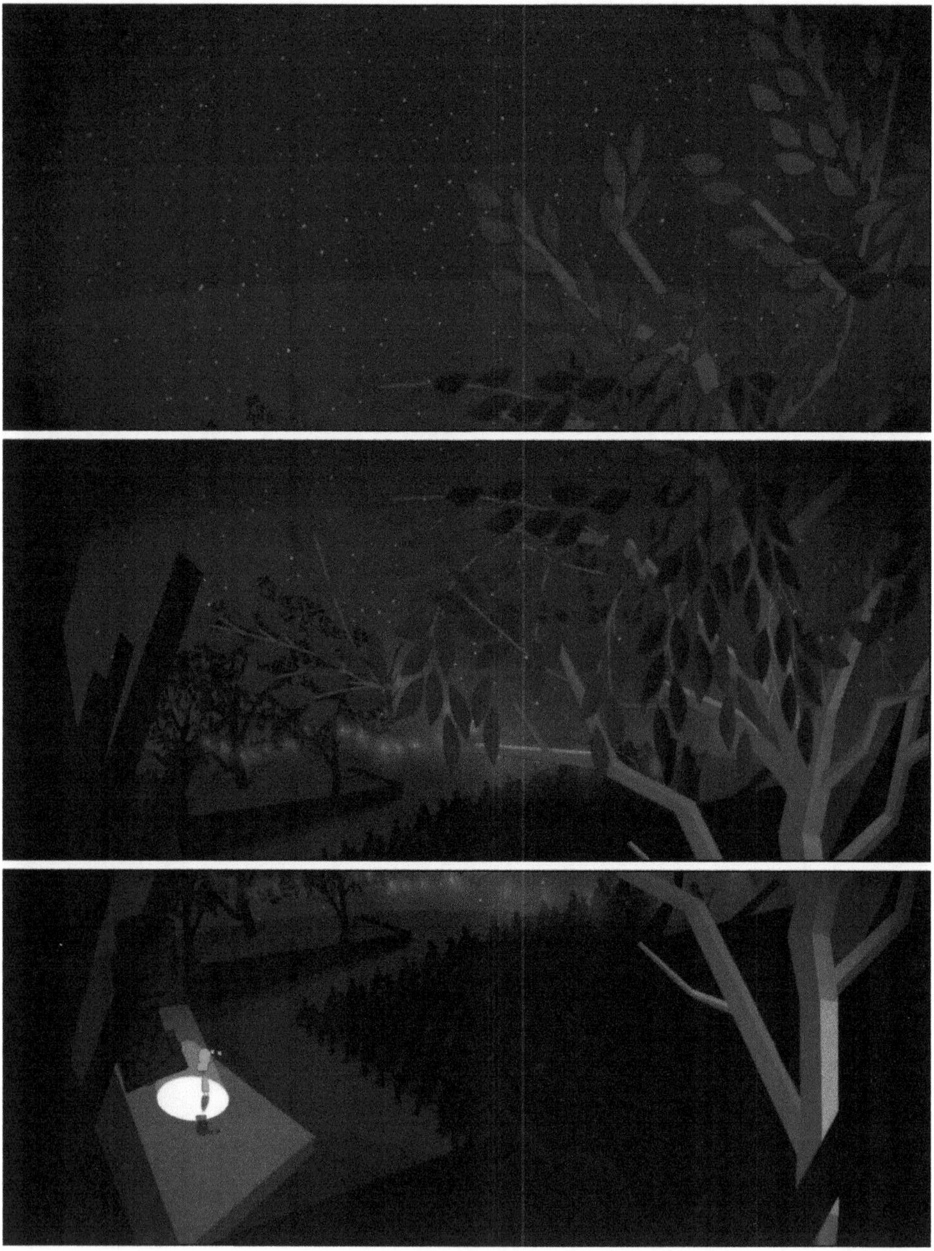

For my father

ACKNOWLEDGEMENTS

This graphic novel is also a feature-length animated film, *Window Horses: The Poetic Persian Epiphany of Rosie Ming*, written by myself and produced by Stickgirl Productions and co-produced by The National Film Board of Canada, which follows the continuing adventures of my original character, Stickgirl. Sandra Oh is the executive producer and the voice of the lead character, Rosie Ming.

The story of *Window Horses* in all its many iterations could not have been told without the help of many people, some of whom I'd like to mention here. It has been a very long odyssey and there are many people to thank.

I'd like to thank the Akademie Schloss Solitude, the BC Arts Council, Creative BC, Telefilm Canada, The National Film Board of Canada, all our Indiegogo contributors, The Canadian Film Centre and Mongrel Media for their financial support. I'd like to thank Sandra Oh for falling in love with this story and giving it wings as a film and Hope Nicholson, especially, for taking on my graphic novel and giving it flight, so to speak! Gordon Durity, Ruth Vincent and Kevin Langdale have been my constant companions along this journey. And I'd like to thank all the people whose lives and stories have inspired me, and the artists who helped bring this story to life.

IRANIAN CONSULTANTS

Maryam Najafi, Malini Mahin, Taymaz Saba, Jamal Salavati Khurdistani and especially Mehrdad Farbod (thank you for your story).

ARTISTS

Kevin Langdale is the primary illustrator and animator, with other artists contributing their own styles for the different poems and historical sections.

Kevin Langdale, Bahram Javaheri, Michael Mann, Sadaf Amini, Janet Perlman, Louise Johnson, Dominique Doktor, Shira Avni, Elisa Chee, Ian Godfrey, Nathaniel Akin, Jody Kramer, Kunal Sen, Lillian Chan, Younger Yan, Joe Chang, Christine Li, Natty Boonmasiri, Reid Blakely, Gemma Goletski, Pyrrha Powilanska-Burnell, Ceile Prowse, Mona Lisa Ali, Brad Gibson, Jesse Cote, Chloe Liu, Eben Sullivan, Patrick Dufresne, Praya Mahta, and Jacyntha Cadwell, Josue Menjivar.

POEMS

Didi's Poem - *Mah*
Written by Sean Yangzhan, 2008

Rumi's Poem - *Do You Know What This Lute Music Tells You*
From *Say Nothing: Poems of Jalal Al-Din Rumi in Persian and English*
Morning Light Press, 2009
English Adaptation by Iraj Anvar & edited by Anne Twitty
Used with permission of the authors.

Hafiz's Poem - *We Should Talk About This Problem*
From *I Heard God Laughing: Poems of Hope and Joy (reprint)*
Penguin Books, 2006
Rendering by Daniel Ladinsky
Copyright 1996 by Daniel Ladinsky and used with permission.

Taylor Mali's Poem - *The Moon, Exactly How It Is Tonight*
Written by Taylor Mali
Write Bloody Publishing, 2009
Used with permission of the author.

Rosie Ming's Poems
Written by Ann Marie Fleming

This book honestly exists to try and add a little more peace, love and understanding to our increasingly complex and conflicted world through art, poetry, history and culture.

I said it before and it is still true...
History is relatives.

- Ann Marie Fleming, 2017